Architecture Culture 1943–1968

Architecture Culture 1943–1968

A Documentary Anthology

Joan Ockman
with the collaboration of Edward Eigen

Columbia University
Graduate School of Architecture, Planning and Preservation

Columbia Books of Architecture / *Rizzoli* NEW YORK

Architecture Culture 1943–1968: A Documentary Anthology is a **Columbia Book of Architecture**. It was produced at Columbia University Graduate School of Architecture, Planning and Preservation through the office of the Dean, Bernard Tschumi, and the Director of Publications, Joan Ockman.

First published in the United States of America in 1993 by
Rizzoli International Publications, Inc.
300 Park Avenue South, New York, NY 10010

This book was supported by a grant from the Graham Foundation for Advanced Studies in the Fine Arts.

Book design by Jennifer Tobias
Printed and bound in Singapore

Library of Congress Cataloging-in-Publication Data
Architecture Culture: 1943–1968, A Documentary Anthology / edited by Joan Ockman with the collaboration of Edward Eigen.
          p.   cm.
    "A publication of Columbia University Graduate School of Architecture, Planning and Preservation."
    Includes bibliographical references and index.
    ISBN 0-8478-1511-0 (hc)
    ISBN 0-8478-1522-6 (pbk)
    1. Architecture, Modern—20th century. 2. Architectural design.
I. Ockman, Joan. II. Eigen, Edward. III. Columbia University. Graduate School of Architecture, Planning and Preservation.
NA680.A57 1993
724'.6—dc20   91-38729
                                       CIP

Contents

As flowers turn toward the sun, by dint of a secret heliotropism the past strives toward that sun which is rising in the sky of history.

—Walter Benjamin, *Theses on the Philosophy of History,* 1940

List of Documents

Foreword

Columbia's commitment to the documentation and reassessment of twentieth-century architecture, and especially its development over the last half century, goes well beyond being a desirable scholarly activity within the walls of a major university.

Throughout its long history, architecture has displayed an unusual fascination for the interplay between words and images, manifestos and actual buildings. From Vitruvius to Alberti to Le Corbusier to the present, the history of architecture is as much the history of its writings as of its buildings. Almost never can architecture be separated from the ideological context in which it was produced.

The following anthology aims to examine the relationship between historical documents and the culture in which they were first introduced. It also aims to relate these texts with an ongoing and very contemporary discourse that calls into question the boundaries between theory and practice. New interest in the idea of a theoretical practice for architects—that is, a practice grounded in theory—makes this book a very timely proposition, as many of the questions being raised today can be directed to the architecture of the recent past. Do architectural texts belong to the realm of objectivity, similar to scientific theorems whose validity can be demonstrated by actual buildings? Or do they on the contrary belong to the realm of poetic gestures and programmatic statements motivated by partisan interests? Are texts—and all theory—essentially descriptive or prescriptive?

Today, participating in an unprecedented exchange of ideas between disciplines—the arts, philosophy, literary criticism—current writings in architectural theory tend to differ significantly from the texts produced up to 1968. Paradoxically, the radical questioning that accompanied the *événements* of '68 made possible a concept of architecture as "theoretical project," as a critical project not so much aiming to be a model for future practice as meant to remain *theoretical.* In contrast, the underlying ideological stance of most written work produced by the generation active in the quarter century that followed the war more characteristically yearned toward responsible ways and means to correct the ills of society.

This is not the place to oppose generations. On the contrary, this anthology of documents and their careful *mise-en-contexte* by Joan Ockman should prove one point: that for the last half century, it has been impossible to be an architect without simultaneously acting as a critic, without thinking about the critical function of one's activity. The critical value of this publication within the overall pedagogical program of architecture thus cannot be underestimated. It is our hope that beyond serving as a key reader and companion for those concerned with issues of history and theory, it may ultimately suggest modes of articulating theory and criticism with reality, in order to achieve the transformation of that reality.

Bernard Tschumi

Acknowledgments

This book was produced through the Office of Publications at the Graduate School of Architecture, Planning and Preservation, Columbia University. Dean Bernard Tschumi was instrumental in the project's conception and facilitated it in every way during the course of development. Professor Kenneth Frampton kindly served as an advisor. The book was aided by a generous grant from the Graham Foundation. David Morton of Rizzoli International Publications provided friendly editorial encouragement.

To the many contributing authors, their family members, and agents who not only graciously permitted their writings to be published here, but in many cases provided useful background information and ideas for further research, much gratitude is owed. Special thanks to Max Bill, Alan Colquhoun, Yona Friedman, Tomás Maldonado, Colin Rowe, Denise Scott Brown, and Aldo van Eyck.

I wish to express deep appreciation to Mary McLeod, my colleague at Columbia, who read portions of the manuscript in different stages and offered all manner of intellectual assistance and friendship; and to Jean-Louis Cohen, Paris, for scholarly advice and answers to numerous questions. I am also indebted to Jos Bosman, of the Institut für Geschichte und Theorie at the ETH, Zurich; Francesco Dal Co, Venice; Jacques Gubler, Lausanne; and Fritz Neumeyer, Berlin, for generously sharing their insights with me. Among those whose memories, personal papers, or knowledge of particular subjects afforded valuable material are Richard Bullene, Anthony Eardley, Guillaume Jullian de la Fuente, Alessandra Latour, Jerzy Soltan, Thomas Hines, and Wim de Witt. Helpful suggestions or information came from Peter Eisenman, Mirjam Ijsseling, Sara Ksiazek, Robert McCarter, Tom Mellins, Andrea Monfried, Dan Naegele, Werner Seligmann, Ignasi de Solà-Morales Rubió, Robert A. M. Stern, Alison Smithson, Marc Treib, Pierre von Meiss, Michael Webb, and Val Woods.

Research was carried out in numerous libraries and collections, especially Avery Architectural and Fine Arts Library, Columbia University; the New York Public Library; and the library of the Museum of Modern Art, New York City. Appreciation goes to the librarians and staff of these institutions, in particular Kitty Chibnik of the Avery library. Marc Dessauce, M. François Ewald, Thomas Regan, and Göran Schildt kindly aided in securing specific material, as did Mary Wollever of the Art Institute of Chicago, Bonnie Goldstein of the Buckminster Fuller Institute, Evelyne Tréhin of the Fondation Le Corbusier, Oscar Munoz of the Frank Lloyd Wright Foundation, and Jonathan Kuhn, Parks Historian of the City of New York.

Almost all of the photographs in the book were taken by Peter Tolkin and Jeff Gillers. For translating assistance, my gratitude to Jörg Gleiter, Lynnette Widder, and especially Christian Hubert and Rebecca Williamson. Sincere thanks are owed to Stuart and Natalie Eigen for their support of this publication, to Madeleine Gekiere for her hospitality, and to David Hinkle for facilitating many things.

In spring 1992 I taught two seminars based on the material in this book, at Columbia University Graduate School of Architecture and at the University of Pennsylvania Graduate School of Fine Arts. For the latter opportunity I wish to thank Professor Joseph Rykwert, chairman of the doctoral program in architecture. I am deeply grateful to my students in both seminars for their receptiveness to the manuscript and their keen and insightful comments on its content.

Heartfelt appreciation to Jennifer Tobias, who designed the book with great skill and offered countless valuable suggestions in the course of its development. She brought intelligence and patience to an often unwieldy project.

Edward Eigen was my constant critical interlocutor. He fully shared the responsibilities and pleasures of bringing this project to fruition from its inception, conducting much of the research and drafting a number of the introductory articles. My lasting gratitude for his friendship and collaboration, *sine qua non*.

To Zoë Slutzky and, finally, to Bob Slutzky, who lived through it twice—first the period, then the making of this book—the present volume is dedicated. Any thank you would be an understatement.

J.O.

Introduction

1943—a year with nothing special about it, situated perhaps at the point of inflection between the sum of the errors made and the dawn of a new start.[1] *LC*

The years delimited by this book appear at once close and distant. Part of the lived experience of the generation currently dominating the senior ranks of the profession and schools, they span a period that has only recently come into critical focus. With the passage of the last quarter century, it is now possible to view with some clarity the developments that followed the "heroic" epoch of modern architecture. The present selection of writings aims to broaden this knowledge and to illuminate the role of ideology in architecture's evolution since the Second World War. It has been culled from a great variety of sources, reflecting the diversity of the field and the proliferation of published material. Limited to the literary record, it must necessarily be read in context of the contemporary buildings and projects.

"Architecture culture" underwent a significant transition during these years. In retrospect, they may be said to constitute the interregnum between modernism and what is now called postmodernism. Modernist architecture became dominant while being subjected to increasingly intense questioning. The traumatic events that marked the end of the war—the revelation of genocide on a previously unfathomable scale of organization and brutality, and the advent of atomic warfare—could only engender a *PDF line* profound crisis in rationalist thought. An ethos of progress predicated on functional determination and technical advancement offered, as many architects realized, no guarantees as far as humane values were concerned. Even as standardized building, scientific planning, and development of new technologies accelerated after the war in the context of reconstruction and rehousing, (continuing the positivist orientation,) prewar doctrine began to be revised along some of the following lines:

1. a reconciliation and integration of functionalism with more humanistic concerns: symbolic representation, organicism, aesthetic expressiveness, contextual relationships, and social, anthropological, and psychological subject matter; *began c. 1930*
2. a recovery of premodernist and antimodernist themes—above all, history, and with it, monumentality, the picturesque, popular culture, regional traditions, antirationalist tendencies, decoration, etc.—within a perspective of "evolution";
3. a replacement of functionalism by other theories like structuralism, semiology, and sociology as new bases for a "scientific" determination of form; *later*
4. neo-avant-gardism: a reassertion of the critical or radical side of modernism, but in a more ironic and dystopian context; *much later*
5. an outright rejection of modernist ideology as fatally linked to the ills of urban development and modernization, and recourse to politics or (conversely) aestheticism and autonomy. *'60s ?*

This cultural critique was bound up with the ongoing trajectory of modernization. The mobility afforded by mass availability of automobile and air transport, the globalization of information and communications, and demographic and territorial shifts produced major changes in contemporary life. Primary among these was the rapid growth of the residential suburb, especially in the United States. On the global scale, postwar geopolitical reconfigurations inflected not only ideological positions but long-range planning strategies. The war also catalyzed a second industrial revolution, bringing to the construction site a new array of synthetic materials—plastics, resins, fibers—and putting in place the infrastructure for electronic and cybernetic technology.

Crisis or continuity?

We begin in the middle of things, at the turning point of the Second World War. As historic capitals and cultural centers were being devastated in Europe and parts of Asia, pawns in a strategic and tactical game of aerial warfare, the first Liberty ships were being launched from the United States. Major victories in Italy, North Africa, Russia, and the Pacific and the decisive mobilization of American technical capability successively shifted the balance in favor of the Allied armies.

"Architecture" was hardly of primary consideration in 1943 amid a cataclysmic world picture. Yet many architects around the world, if not militarily engaged, were already employed in drawing up plans for the postwar rehabilitation of cities, towns, and villages. Those charged with the program of reconstruction had not only to address the urgent needs of rehousing and rebuilding, but also to project a vision of postwar society. On the one hand, the war had proven the potency of coordinated functional planning and industrialized production, confirming modernist ideology. In a pictorial essay entitled "Design for War," the editors of *Architectural Forum* wrote,

After many decades of functionalist preaching, this century is today producing functionally designed objects for the first time on a tremendous scale. In other words, in an extreme emergency we turn unquestioning to functional design. It is important to note that these products of ingenuity, economy, and utmost exploitation of limited materials have quite unconsciously become the most satisfying designs of our machine civilization.[2]

Yet the massive destruction of human life and the built fabric through this formidable instrumentality provided a more cautionary and ambivalent lesson.

The issue, as it now appeared to planners, was how to convert the vast war machine to the needs of peace. The *Athens Charter,* the official codification of functionalist urbanism, was published in German-occupied France in 1943, a decade after the fourth congress of the Congrès Internationaux d'Architecture Moderne (CIAM) drew it up. Appearing under the imprint of the French CIAM group, it had been edited by Le Corbusier anonymously in 1941—for fear of antagonizing the fascist caretakers in Vichy, who were to spurn his grand urban schemes a year later—and contained an introduction by the playwright and urbanist Jean Giraudoux. The latter heralded, with a trepidation unknown to those who drafted the charter in 1933, "the threshold of this new age."[3] Le Corbusier for his part reflected that the current mobilization, wresting the French economy from its previous stagnation, would be the war's major positive outcome. As he stated in *Sur les quatre routes,* also published during the war years,

In wartime the farsighted have realized immense possibilities in an alliance between the planners and industry. The war itself has bequeathed to the country a working plant. A quantity of the elements of housing can be produced in factories: dry assembly; the prefabricated house. Provision of housing will become the largest, the most urgent, the most fruitful item of the industrial program.[4]

In America the potential of transforming wartime production to meet the desperate need for housing was immediately grasped by Buckminster Fuller, among others. Before the war's end he turned his energies to persuading a Kansas aircraft manufacturer to retool its factory for the fabrication of low-cost metal houses. By 1946 his "Dymaxion" prototype was readied and exhibited to an enthusiastic public. Yet already a strong countercurrent was in motion. "Let Bucky Fuller put together the dymaxion dwellings of the people so long as we architects can design their tombs and monuments," as Philip Johnson—having in 1932 been the emissary of European modernism in America—was to put it. Johnson's remark, an ironic commentary on a statement made by Adolf Loos half a century earlier, reflected a widespread desire that emerged during the war years and became an ongoing debate of the period: for a "new monumentality."[5]

In 1943 Sigfried Giedion, José Luis Sert, and Fernand Léger, all taking refuge from the war in New York City, jointly wrote a paper entitled "Nine Points on Monumentality." In it they voiced the desire to invest modern architecture with new means of collective expression. Despite its traditional association with authoritarian regimes, they argued, monumentality was not incompatible with democracy. It was, instead, a "true expression" of the human spirit, capable of being conveyed in a language of modern forms and materials. Their statement translated (consciously or not) the esperanto of a proud and powerful nation on the eve of world triumph. Both the isolationism and the anticapitalist criticism of the late 1930s had subsided in the United States. Succeeding them was a climate of magnanimous internationalism, epitomized in Wendell Wilkie's best-selling book of 1943, *One World,* and soon to be focused on the building of the United Nations. A world rid of its recent tyrannies required, they sensed, appropriate symbolic forms.

The most potent reconciliation between an "architecture of democracy" and the modern sensibility was offered by Frank Lloyd Wright in these years. The second volume of his *Autobiography* appeared in 1943 with its credo "In the Nature of Materials." In it he continued his crusade for an "organic" architecture placing machine technology in the service of humanistic values. Also published in 1943 was Ayn Rand's novel *The Fountainhead,* in which the Wrightian protagonist was romanticized into a full-blown American symbol: the modernist genius-architect, at first thwarted by an uncomprehending society, then triumphantly vindicated for his foresight and individualism. Wright, of course, could hardly have been imagined any larger than life. The same year, he sent a petition to the United States government requesting a mandate to build his suburban dream, Broadacre City, throughout the entirety of America. The petition was signed by John Dewey, Albert Einstein, Buckminster Fuller, Walter Gropius, Henry-Russell Hitchcock, Ludwig Mies van der Rohe, Robert Moses, and fifty others.[6] In this respect, Wright and Fuller (and Moses for that matter) were alike—they believed in thinking "in the biggest way that you know how."[7]

If bravado was possible in a country that had come through the war physically unscathed, in Europe the day of inflated conceptions had passed. Pragmatism and relief tinged with hope characterized the immediate postwar period. In the war-damaged areas of the Western countries, rebuilding proceeded quickly, providing major new jobs for architects. The work was carried out with dedication, if sometimes shoddy results. In England forced austerity inspired a disciplined and on occasion distinguished design of schools, housing, and towns. Le Corbusier's Unité d'Habitation rose in Marseilles, a supreme emblem of the functionalist aesthetic. Yet on its completion, the very singularity of this great urban ship—intended prototype of a convoy that never materialized in the French landscape—lent it a tragic dimension. Its sculptural presence and surreal roofscape "spoke" with a new poetics.

CIAM, meeting in 1947 in Bridgwater, England, after a decade of inactivity, reaffirmed its earlier stance on functionalism but put new emphasis on spiritual and emotional values. Two themes were introduced: aesthetics, and how to bring modern architecture to the "man on the street." The first, passionately advanced by the young Aldo van Eyck, was, like Le Corbusier's credo of "ineffable space," a call for an infusion of poetic imagination into architecture. The second, bound up with the monumentality debate, became increasingly urgent as Stalin's social realism pervaded Eastern Europe, obliterating the culture of modernism that had thrived there prior to the war.

With heightening Western perception of Soviet repression, America appeared a beacon of freedom and opportunity. The architectural emigrés from Germany who entered this country starting in the mid-1930s—Walter Gropius, Ludwig Mies van der Rohe, Marcel Breuer, Erich Mendelsohn, and others—found an environment receptive to their ideas. Bruno Zevi, who finished his education in America during the war, went home to Italy bearing Wright's message of organicism, while the French architect Marcel Lods reported to his compatriots, after a tour in 1946, his "enthusiasm and euphoria" at witnessing the products of American civilization. Alvar Aalto, visiting the United States in 1940 at the height of Russo-Finnish hostilities, also was drawn to America during the war years. His country's pact with the Nazis halted further contacts; in 1943 he found himself obliged to head an entourage of Finnish architects to inspect German military installations, hosted by Albert Speer, Hitler's new armaments minister. But after the war he returned to teach and build Baker House at Massachusetts Institute of Technology. His infatuation was not to last, though. At first eager to establish a base here, he soon became critical of the excessive materialism of American culture.

The Americanization of modernism

With the aid sent by America under the Marshall Plan, Western Europe largely recovered from the postwar emergency by the early 1950s. It now braced for a different onslaught as the progressive modernism it had exported to the United States in the 1920s and 1930s recrossed the Atlantic in the reverse direction. Along with the material goods of the new *pax Americana* came a new set of cultural values.

The American invasion of Italy brought not only peace and national liberation, the end of destroyed cities and prostitutes, but also chewing gum, powdered milk, and Coca-Cola, and first and foremost the idea of "comfort" and the mechanization of the home. The myth of the refrigerator was born . . .[8]

If the great symbolic client of modern architecture had been the proletariat, heroic protagonist of an idealistic socialism, that of the period after was the middle class. For geared-up capitalist economies now facing the threat of overproduction, the American slogan of "better living through technology" was a manifest destiny. Focus shifted from production to consumption, marketing, and "planned obsolescence"; from "revolutionary producers" to a new class of consumers happy to leave behind the asperities of *Existenzminimum*, desirous of an ever higher standard of living and the leisure to enjoy it. The emphasis on the domestic environment gave women a central role in the marketplace even as they were denied one in the workplace (a contradiction that would have political consequences by the 1960s). From *Germany Year Zero* to *Miracle in Milan* to *La Dolce Vita:* the route led from the rigors of scarcity to an "aesthetics of plenty."[9] By the end of the decade the "economic miracles" created by the reorganization of West European production to serve technocratic and acquisitive ends had made the world ripe for full-blown consumerism. Whether the culture purveyors would play an affirmative or a critical role in this formation was not yet, however, clearly discerned.

For some, the transformation of functionalism from socialist to capitalist utopia occurred seamlessly. To Gropius there was ostensibly little disjunction in adapting the program of the Bauhaus, where he had first aspired to a partnership between art and industry, to American managerial democracy. Only a shift in rhetoric signaled the change: from "totality," an all-encompassing synthesis of art and handicraft or industrial production, to "team," a well-coordinated group of specialists. Ironically, the new corporate professionalism of the 1950s—soon decried by sociologists as engendering a society of "organization men"—was the antithesis of the cultural and social nonconformism embodied in the diverse group of personalities at the Bauhaus.

At the Hochschule für Gestaltung in Ulm, West Germany, which opened in 1955 on the Bauhaus model, the contradictions were only gradually elucidated in successive restructurings of the curriculum. An initial conception of the designer as creator of *gute Form* (Max Bill's position) gave way to that of the designer as captain—"coordinator"— of industry (Tomás Maldonado's), retreating by the mid-1960s into a critical theory of design largely confirming the Frankfurt School's critique of culture. Abraham Moles, a lecturer on information theory at Ulm, would write,

functionalist doctrine ... is essentially an ascetic doctrine and manifestation of a certain philosophy of life: that of scarcity, of rational application of existing means for clearly defined purposes. Within certain sectors of culture functionalism will retain its validity. But recently functionalism has entered a critical period due to the growth of affluent society. ... Functionalism necessarily contradicts the doctrine of affluent society which is forced to produce and to sell relentlessly. ... [The latter] creates a system of neokitsch by accumulating objects in the human environment. At this point the crisis of functionalism becomes manifest.[10]

Symptomatic was the fact that functionalism was now increasingly perceived as a stylistic manifestation linked to an earlier historical period. As such, it was doubly condemned: too abstract and elitist for the symbolic populism promulgated in the communist countries under Stalinism, it was too abstract and antiindividualistic for those in the Western countries paranoiacally professing "freedom." While the consolidation of state power in Eastern Europe left architects little leeway for opinion, in the United States for several years McCarthyism created a xenophobic climate for many of the same emigrés the country had welcomed earlier. A public housing project in Los Angeles by Richard Neutra was quashed in 1951 as "creeping socialism."[11]

Yet this was simply demagoguery on both sides, a battle of ideology fired by the intensifying Cold War. Khrushchev, seizing power shortly after Stalin's death in 1953 and more pragmatic in economic matters, reinstated functionalist building and outlawed decorative excesses. Meanwhile the cost-effectiveness implicit in a stripped aesthetic was hardly lost on capitalist builders and speculators. Big business became the second major client for postwar architecture. The new multinational corporations, surrogates for governments struggling to preserve their spheres of influence around the world, offered lucrative commissions. The leading architects were soon more preoccupied with corporate or government headquarters and single-family houses than with solutions to factories and social housing. Modernism, as now reinterpreted, largely meant a frame with repetitive components. Flexibility became interchangeability as the "modular plan" replaced the free plan and "form follow[ed] form."[12]

The ubiquitous glass curtain wall turned out to be, paradoxically, a plane as absolute as the Iron Curtain. As with the new American painting of these years, successfully proselytized by the ex-Marxist art critic Clement Greenberg, an abstract aesthetic sublimated disturbing subsurface contents.[13] In architecture, Henry-Russell Hitchcock and Philip Johnson's selective and formalistic adaptation of the modern movement, propounded two decades earlier, had a similar effect. As the received version of modernism by the 1950s, the authors' denatured concept (more nuanced in its original formulation) enabled architecture to be abstracted from specificities, making possible a truly "international style." It now penetrated all corners of the world, including the newly decolonized "Third World" countries aspiring to Western living standards, at times hybridizing local vernaculars. An exception to the mostly superficial efforts at contextualism was Le Corbusier's work in Chandigarh, a brilliant, if flawed, effort to wed Indian tradition to modernism. Closer to home, Lewis Mumford touted the "native and humane" regionalism of the San Francisco Bay area. The language of corporate hegemony was also inflected with personal inputs. Yet the subjective design approaches that now proliferated, from the eclecticism of Johnson himself or Edward Durrell Stone to the sculptural expressionism of Eero Saarinen in America, or the virtuosities of Oscar Niemeyer in Brazil and Kenzo Tange in Japan, were the other side of the glazed grids perfected by Skidmore, Owings and Merrill. "Form was king."[14]

In American design education as well, the postwar revaluation of modernism tended along formalist lines. Starting in the late 1930s, the presence of Gropius at Harvard, Laszlo Moholy-Nagy at the Institute of Design, and Mies van der Rohe at Illinois Institute of Technology grounded American pedagogy in traditions established at the Bauhaus. The didactic exposition of modernist form and materials led in many instances to refined and sophisticated results. In others, overemphasis on functional expression produced the clichés of the "decorated diagram."[15] Possibly the old Beaux-Arts orientation had been exorcised only superficially. Louis Kahn, a charismatic presence at Yale and the University of Pennsylvania during the 1950s and 1960s, arrived at his own synthesis. Meanwhile, at an educational outpost like the University of Texas at Austin, an innovative curriculum was predicated on rigorous analysis of form. The English architect-historian Colin Rowe, who was to influence two generations of American students (the later one postmodernist), linked modernism to academic tradition in his rereadings of modern architecture, calling into question the sociotechnical *Zeitgeist* that had been an article of faith for preceding historians.

A similar argument was made, though with opposite consequences, by Reyner Banham in his seminal *Theory and Design in the First Machine Age* (1961) and in Italy by Giulio Carlo Argan. For the latter writers, and for other inheritors of the "functionalist tradition," the relation between "ethics" and "aesthetics" remained a vexed one. Peter and Alison Smithson in England, initially affected by the neo-Palladianism of the Wittkowerian school, soon began challenging the modernist establishment in less academic ways, seeking a "socioplastic" basis for design. Under the banners of Team 10 and the New Brutalism they promoted an architecture of "growth and change," seeking inspiration in the spontaneity of popular culture and anthropological sources, and rejecting CIAM's mechanistic model of urbanism for more empirical "patterns of association." John Voelker, a cofounder of Team 10, articulated the new concerns:

Images:
1930. The frame building and the multilevel high-rise city, images which contained a complete urban system.
1950. Random images drawn from many sources containing single ideas which, one by one, contribute to, change, and extend the experience of space.
Program:
1930. To popularize the already established style of the modern movement—didactic.
1950. To search for a plastic system which reciprocates and intends in architectural form existing ecological patterns.
Method:
1930. To categorize the general situation and to develop it through the dialectical manipulation of the categories made.
1950. The empirical observation of particular situations and development through the architectural expression of those unique patterns observed within them.
Technique:
1930. To replace existing buildings and cities with new categorically formulated elements.
1950. The time-conscious techniques of renewal and extension derived from the recognition of the positive ecological trends to be found in every particular situation.
Results:
1930. Prototype buildings and master plans, each charged with the full "international" urban program. Irrespective of location—didactic.
1950. Building in unique situations. The elements articulate and resolve the ecological patterns, and provide instruments of research into possible development of each location.[16]

Spearheaded by Team 10's critique, the breakup of CIAM at the end of the decade was a major symbolic event. The organization had greatly broadened its base during the postwar period, drawing participants from all over the world to its ninth congress in Aix-en-Provence in 1953, and fêting the completion of Le Corbusier's Unité d'Habitation in Marseilles on this occasion. But the nocturnal celebration on the building's roof augured the end of the dream of rationalism. The "youngers," as the incipient Team 10 thought of themselves, were in an oedipal relationship with the generation of the masters, reverent but restive. Le Corbusier himself was now building Ronchamp. Three years later, absenting himself from CIAM's last official congress, held at Dubrovnik, he acknowledged the incurable rift:

It is those who are now forty years old, born around 1916 during wars and revolutions, and those then unborn, now twenty-five years old, born around 1930 during the preparation of a new war and amidst a profound economic, social, and political crisis— who thus find themselves in the heart of the present period the only ones capable of feeling actual problems, personally, profoundly, the goals to follow, the means to reach them, the pathetic urgency of the present situation. They are in the know. Their predecessors no longer are, they are out, they are no longer subject to the direct impact of the situation.[17]

By 1959 CIAM was gone. Its "museum meeting" at Henry van de Velde's Kröller-Müller in Otterlo succeeded in consigning modernism—now the "great tradition"—to history.

From metropolis to global village

If the manifesto was the generic expression of the emergent aspirations of the early-twentieth-century avant-gardes, indeed of the period of high modernism itself,[18] its moment was over by the midcentury. An architecture culture largely in retrenchment after the war, engaged in reconstructing its interrupted development or else institutionalizing itself in the professional and academic mainstream, was not disposed to such a positive form of enunciation. The missionary spirit that had once animated it deflated in a widening breach between theory and practice.

The dissolution of the unitary formation previously coalesced under the banner of CIAM further tended to produce a fragmented succession. In England, historian John Summerson wrote of British architecture in the 1950s:

. . . the old notion of a party line, a "cause" to be argued and supported by any amount of didactic talk, no longer has the slightest relevance, any more than the notion of "the international style" of the thirties has the slightest relevance. . . . We are no longer in the period of "towards an architecture." It is architecture or nothing. And if it is architecture, it is architecture continually redefined—not in words but in forms.[19]

Across the continent, in Italy, revisionism was the order of the day. The bourgeois tradition that modernism had repressed was now recuperated by means of a new emphasis on historical continuity and contextualism, lent credence by the editorial activity of Ernesto Rogers at *Casabella-Continuità*. So eclectic was the architecture emerging out of the rationalist legacy that Rogers was led to remark that the only new orthodoxy in Italian architecture was that of heterodoxy itself.[20]

Yet despite—or because of—this apparent vacuum, a "culture of criticism" began to reemerge. Indeed in Italy, where fascism and modernism had had a particularly involved relationship, an exceptionally high level of intellectual debate persisted from the earlier period. During the 1930s, *Casabella* had functioned as a rallying point for Italian rationalism under the legendary figures Edoardo Persico and Giuseppe Pagano. After the war, this tradition continued in critical battles of position, if not polemic, waged in the architectural press. Within a few years after the war, despite economic scarcity, at least a dozen significant journals concentrating on architectural subjects were publishing. In the 1950s, when Rogers renovated *Casabella* adding the suffix *Continuità*, it was the most dedicated journal "of tendency" in the world.[21]

Elsewhere the major journals were more typically geared to boosting the profession. Yet in England, notwithstanding the general lack of position-taking noted by Summerson, critical discourse was forwarded in the *Architectural Review*, where the postwar editors, once staunch modernists, now championed Swedish informality and townscape picturesque with nearly equal fervor. By 1953 the *Review* had a less sentimental interlocutor in *Architectural Design*, redesigned by the young Theo Crosby with an eye to the increasingly important student readership.

The theory-practice split was likewise ingrained in the American professional journals, which now publicized a mainstream modernism. Yet in Los Angeles *Arts and Architecture* under John Entenza positioned itself more critically relative to new work. Inaugurating its "Case Study Houses" program in 1945, it sponsored innovative designs by Californians like Charles Eames and Richard Neutra. "Little magazines," often of academic provenance, also cropped up as forums for debate, like Yale School of Architecture's *Perspecta*, founded in 1952 by George Howe, responsible for early expositions of Kahn's work and ideas.

Later in the decade, more tendentious publications appeared, aligned with specific movements. In 1958 *Le Carré bleu* was launched in Helsinki, to function largely as a vehicle for Team 10 ideas, and *Ulm* was published by the Hochschule für Gestaltung. The first number of the avant-garde *International Situationist* also appeared, advancing a "unitary urbanism." In 1959 Van Eyck became principal editor of Dutch *Forum*, making it another arena for the post-CIAM critique. The first (and only) issue of *Metabolism* came out in Japan in 1960. During the 1960s the postwar media reached a new threshold with the transformation of the architectural journal into a radical project in itself. In the paper polemics of the British Archigram, its first broadsheet published in 1961, and other groups, the "antiarchitecture" position vividly unfolded.

This diverse activity worked to break down national parochialisms and to penetrate countries isolated by geography, technological backwardness, and repressive political regimes. It preceded and followed the shifting cultural axis: from Europe to America, as well as to places outside the usual centers of ferment, where crucial architectural developments were occurring—Scandinavia, Japan, South America, Eastern Europe, India. Nor was the expanded journalistic network solely responsible for the circulation of ideas. The internationalization of firms, prestige associated with the commissioning of foreign architects, the cosmopolitanism of the schools, wider travel, and other mechanisms of dissemination contributed to the universalizing of architecture culture. At the same time, decolonization allowed voices to be heard (or images seen) from regions that a Eurocentric architecture had long ignored or relegated to exotica. The great metropolises virtually synonymous with modernism earlier in the century found themselves reduced to the scale of historical nodes in what would be described by Marshall McLuhan in 1964 as a global village.[22]

That same year the success of Bernard Rudofsky's "Architecture without Architects" exhibition at the Museum of Modern Art in New York underscored the desire of architects to look outside their discipline for new meaning and less egotistic models. The economic boom of the 1950s had slowed by the beginning of the 1960s, while the Cold War warmed into the tense confrontation of the Cuban missile crisis and an (outer) space race. The resurgence of a leftist critique of culture and steady American escalation of its misguided adventure in Vietnam now elicited a wave of anti-Americanism. Some architects attempted to regain control over a troubling reality through a return to technological solutions and scientific methodologies, while others translated their criticism into sociopolitical protest and utopian prophecy. Still others embraced popular culture or its countercultural spin-offs, learning to like Levittown or building domes in the desert.

The first tendency constituted a belated success for rationalism, now as a metalanguage. Structuralism, having originated earlier in the century, replaced the existentialist *Angst* of the 1950s as privileged intellectual current. Linguistic, semiotic, and typological approaches to design flourished on the border between science and culture, affording methods and models to the technically minded wing of the profession—architect-planners like Kevin Lynch, Christopher Alexander, Yona Friedman—as well as to new theoreticians of architectural history and form like those in Venice or at the Institute for Architecture and Urban Studies in New York City, the latter founded in 1967.

On the critical-activist side, the range of responses ran the gamut from the social reformism spurred by Jane Jacobs in America to Archigram's futurism. While Jacobs preached an urbanism continuous with the fabric of the city, Archigram projected a

a narrative, or—in the spirit of the *flâneur*—just by browsing. The introductory articles provide, in very abbreviated from, some background for the documents and are written so that the latter may be read independently. Selective bibliographic references in the articles and at the back of the book offer some points of departure for further study.

Joan Ockman
August 1992

Notes

1.   Le Corbusier, *Looking at City Planning*, trans. Eleanor Levieux (New York: Orion Press, 1971), p. 1.
2.   *Architectural Forum*, September 1943, p. 4.
3.   Le Corbusier, *The Athens Charter*, trans. Anthony Eardley (New York: Grossman Publishers, 1973), p. xix. See also Sigfried Giedion, "CIAM at Sea: The Background of the Fourth (Athens) Congress," trans. P. Morton Shand, *Architects' Yearbook* 3 (1949), pp. 36–39.
4.   *The Four Routes*, trans. Dorothy Todd (London: Dennis Dobson Limited, 1947), p. 15 (translation modified). Original French edition 1941.
5.   Philip Johnson, "Where Are We At?" in *Architectural Review*, September 1960, p. 175. See also Johnson's earlier "War Memorials: What Aesthetic Price Glory?" *Art News* 44 (September 1945), pp. 8–10, 24–25. Loos had written, "Only a very small part of architecture belongs to art: the tomb and the monument. Everything else, everything which serves a purpose, should be excluded from the realms of art" ("Architecture," 1910).
6.   Wright's decentralist vision of society was first conceived in the early 1930s and further elaborated during the postwar period in *When Democracy Builds* (1945) and *The Living City* (1958). For the document mentioned, see John Sergeant, *Frank Lloyd Wright's Usonian Houses: The Case for Organic Architecture* (New York: Whitney Library of Design, 1976), p. 201.
7.   See *Designing a New Industry: A Composite of a Series of Talks by R. Buckminster Fuller, 1945–1946* (Wichita: Fuller Research Institute, 1946), p. 9.
8.   Vittorio Gregotti, "Italian Design 1945–1971," in Emilio Ambasz, ed., *Italy: The New Domestic Landscape* (New York: Museum of Modern Art, 1972), p. 322 (translation modified).
9.   A phrase first coined by Lawrence Alloway in 1959. See Alloway's essay "The Independent Group: Postwar Britain and the Aesthetics of Plenty," in the catalogue of the same title, ed. David Robbins (Cambridge: MIT Press, 1990), pp. 49–53.
10.   "Functionalism in Crisis," *ulm 19/20* (August 1967), p. 24.
11.   See Thomas Hines, *Richard Neutra and the Search for Modern Architecture* (New York: Oxford University Press, 1982), pp. 229–30.
12.   Matthew Nowicki, "Origins and Trends in Modern Architecture" (1951) in this volume, pp. 150–56.
13.   See Serge Guilbaut, "The New Adventures of the Avant-Garde in America: Greenberg, Pollock, or from Trotskyism to the New Liberalism of the 'Vital Center,'" trans. Thomas Repensek, in Francis Frascina, ed., *Pollock and After: The Critical Debate* (New York: Harper and Row, 1986).
14.   Robert Venturi's characterization. See his preface to the second edition of *Complexity and Contradiction in Architecture* (New York: Museum of Modern Art, 1977), p. 14.
15.   For a critical assessment of the Gropius pedagogy at Harvard, see Klaus Herdeg, *The Decorated Diagram: Harvard Architecture and the Failure of the Bauhaus Legacy* (Cambridge: MIT Press, 1983). A history of postwar American architecture education remains to be written.
16.   Published in Oscar Newman, *New Frontiers in Architecture: CIAM '59 in Otterlo* (New York: Universe Books, 1961), p. 16.
17.   Letter to CIAM 10, Dubrovnik. In Newman, *New Frontiers in Architecture*, p. 16.
18.   As exemplified by Ulrich Conrads's anthology *Programs and Manifestoes on 20th-Century Architecture*, trans. Michael Bullock (Cambridge: MIT Press, 1970). Conrads's book goes up to 1963.
19.   Introduction to Trevor Dannatt, *Modern Architecture in Britain* (London: Batsford, 1959), p. 28.
20.   See Ernesto Rogers, "L'Ortodossia dell'eterodossia," *Casabella* 216 (June–July 1957), pp. 2–4. "Continuità o crisi" is the title of an editorial by Rogers in *Casabella* 215 (April–May 1957), pp. 3–4.
21.   On the relations between theory and practice in postwar Italy and France and the architect's intellectual role, see Jean-Louis Cohen's valuable *La Coupure entre architectes et intellectuels, ou les enseignements de l'italophilie* (Paris: Ecole d'Architecture Paris-Villemin, 1984).
22.   *Understanding Media: The Extensions of Man* (New York: McGraw-Hill, 1964), p. 20.
23.   *Architectural Design*, February 1970, p. 62.
24.   As cited by Jean Baudrillard in *Utopie: Revue de sociologie de l'urbain*, May 1969, p. 14.
25.   The catalogue of the exhibition is Arthur Drexler, ed., *The Architecture of the Ecole des Beaux-Arts* (New York: Museum of Modern Art, 1977). The events of 1968 figure on one page of this 500-page volume.

1943–1949

1943   Patrick Abercrombie and John Henry Forshaw, plan for Greater London
Oscar Niemeyer, church at Pampulha, Belo Horizonte, Brazil
Albert Kahn Associates, Willow Run bomber plant for Ford Motors, Ypsilanti, Michigan
Ludwig Mies van der Rohe, Metallurgical Research building, Illinois Institute of
Technology, Chicago
Gilmore D. Clark (for Metropolitan Life Insurance Company), Stuyvesant Town, New
York City (–1949)
Walter Gropius and Konrad Wachsmann, Packaged House System for General Panel
Corporation (prototype demonstration)

1944   Auguste Perret, reconstruction, Le Havre, France (–1954)
Mario Fiorentino et al., Mausoleum to Martyrs of the Ardeatine Caves, Rome (–1950)
Ely Jacques Kahn, municipal asphalt plant, New York City
Sven Backström and Leif Reinius, Gröndal residential district, Stockholm (–1945)
George Howe, Louis Kahn, and Oscar Stonorov, housing, Coatesville, Pennsylvania
Jean Prouvé, prefabricated housing units, Lorraine and Vosges France
Alfred Roth, De Mandrot house, Zurich

1945   Le Corbusier, reconstruction plan, St. Dié, France
Sven Markelius, general plan, Stockholm (–1952)
Hassan Fathy, village of New Gourna, West Luxor, Egypt (–1948)
Ludwig Mies van der Rohe, Farnsworth house, Plano, Illinois (–1950)

1946   Frederick Gibberd (Ministry of Town Planning), Harlow New Town, England (–1963)
Kenzo Tange, Peace Memorial, Hiroshima, Japan (–1956)
Lodovico Belgiojoso, Enrico Peressutti, and Ernesto Rogers, Monument to the Dead
in German Concentration Camps, Milan
Ludwig Mies van der Rohe, Illinois Institute of Technology campus, Chicago
Alvar Aalto, Baker dormitory, Massachusetts Institute of Technology, Cambridge,
Massachusetts (–1948)
Carlo Mollino, hotel and sled-lift station, Val di Susa, Italy (–1947)
William Wurster, Reynolds house, San Francisco
R. Buckminster Fuller, Dymaxion house, Wichita, Kansas (prototype)

1947   Wallace Harrison and Max Abramovitz, United Nations complex, New York City (–1952)
C. H. Aslin (Hertfordshire County Council), junior school, Croxley Green,
Hertfordshire, England (–1949)
Le Corbusier, Unité d'Habitation, Marseilles (–1952)
William Levitt, tract housing, Levittown, Long Island (–1951)
Richard Neutra, Tremaine house, Montecito, California (–1948)

1948   Ludovico Quaroni, church of Santa Maria Maggiore, Francavilla a Mare, Italy (–1957)
Pier Luigi Nervi, "Salone B" exhibition hall, Turin (–1949)
Eero Saarinen, General Motors Technical Center, Detroit (–1951)
Pietro Belluschi, Equitable Savings and Loan building, Portland, Oregon
Amancio Williams, Suspended Building for Offices (project)
Walter Gropius and the Architects Collaborative (TAC), Graduate Center, Harvard
University, Cambridge, Massachusetts (–1950)
Paul Lester Wiener and José Luis Sert, master plan for Bogotá, Colombia

1949   Alvar Aalto, town hall, Säynätsalo, Finland (–1951)
Frank Lloyd Wright, laboratory tower for Johnson Wax Company, Racine, Wisconsin
J. H. van den Broek and Jacob Bakema, Lijnbaan shopping district, Rotterdam (–1953)

Alison and Peter Smithson, Hunstanton school, Norfolk, England (–1954)
Ludovico Quaroni and Mario Ridolfi, INA-Casa housing, Via Tiburtina, Rome (–1954)
Philip Johnson, Johnson house, New Canaan, Connecticut
Charles and Ray Eames, Eames house (Case Study House), Pacific Palisades, California

1943

One of the prophetic themes to be debated in the 1940s was that of the "new monumentality." The 1937 World Exposition in Paris had been the occasion of modernism's official triumph for most of the participating countries. At the same time, though, in the confrontation that took place at the foot of the Eiffel Tower between Albert Speer's pavilion for the Third Reich, avatar of Prussian classicism, and Boris Iofan's Soviet pavilion, an embodiment of the more dynamic aspirations of social realism, the new architecture received an implicit challenge to its potency as a form of civic representation.

The accepted view was that "if it is a monument it is not modern, and if it is modern it cannot be a monument," as Lewis Mumford wrote in 1938 in *The Culture of Cities.* Earlier, Henry-Russell Hitchcock's *Modern Architecture: Romanticism and Reintegration* (1929) had helped to inculcate this idea. Yet the dichotomy between "new traditionalists" and "new pioneers" was an oversimplification. Many of those within the folds of the modern movement had realized for a long time that the new aesthetic needed to be infused with a collective and symbolic content. The dispute over Le Corbusier's League of Nations project had raised the issue in explicit terms in 1927.

On the eve of the Second World War, J. J. P. Oud, responsible for some of the most distinguished examples of international modernism during the previous decade, returned to hierarchical massing, symmetrical planning, and a cautious reintroduction of decorative elements in his Shell Building in the Hague. But the scandal provoked by Oud was only the most extreme example of the effort by architects at this time to find a synthesis between monumental expression and progressive ideology. In a catalogue introduction for an exhibition held at the Museum of Modern Art in New York in 1944 entitled *Built in U.S. A.—1932–1944,* Elizabeth Mock lauded a prize-winning design of 1939 by Eliel and Eero Saarinen and Robert F. Swanson for the Smithsonian Gallery of Art on the Mall in Washington, D.C., as a monument epitomizing "the very nature of our democracy."

Sigfried Giedion, **José Luis Sert**, and **Fernand Léger** entered the debate in 1943 with a position paper entitled "Nine Points on Monumentality." The joint pronouncement by an architectural historian, an architect-planner, and a painter—all living in New York during the war years and in close contact—was intended for publication in a volume planned by the American Abstract Artists which never appeared. A more extended discussion by each of the three from their respective outlooks was to have accompanied it. Of these, an essay by Léger appeared in 1946 in another publication by the American Abstract Artists, while Giedion's essay "The Need for a New Monumentality" came out in 1944 in a book edited by Paul Zucker entitled *New Architecture and City Planning,* a major section of which was dedicated to the monumentality question.

The approach taken in both the "Nine Points" and "The Need for a New Monumentality" was to place monumentality—"the expression of man's highest cultural needs"—within the historical evolution of modernism itself. While modern architecture had earlier been obliged to concentrate on the more immediate and mundane problems of housing and urbanism, the authors argued, its new task in the postwar period would be the reorganization of community life through the planning and design of civic centers, monumental ensembles, and public spectacles. This "third step" would involve the collaboration of architects, planners, and artists. The chief difficulty, in their view, was to invent forms of large-scale expression free of association with oppressive ideologies of the past and historicist bombast ("pseudomonumentality"). To this end, a repertory of colorful and mobile forms and lightweight, naturalistic materials was proposed. The work of contemporary artists like Picasso, Constantin Brancusi, Naum Gabo,

103–6

Alexander Calder, and Léger himself was seen as "pointing the way" for an architecture of full rather than empty rhetoric.

For Giedion this was clearly a shift from the machine *Zeitgeist* that had inspired *Space, Time and Architecture,* written in 1938–39. In an extended discussion of the League of Nations competition in that book he had commended Le Corbusier's entry specifically for its programmatic accommodation and absence of monumental rhetoric. In his article in the Zucker book—which began with the motto, "Emotional training is necessary today. For whom? First of all for those who govern and administer the people"— he stated of Le Corbusier's building, "the whole development of modern architecture towards a new monumentality would have been advanced for decades if the officials could have understood its quality." Giedion's reversal seems to have been in large part occasioned by the new impact of Frank Lloyd Wright. In an article on Wright's Johnson Wax building entitled "The Dangers and Advantages of Luxury" published at the end of 1939 in the journal *Focus,* he celebrated its overscaled columns and powerful central work hall, acknowledging that a modern administration building could "for once be based entirely on poetry."

The monumentality debate reached a point of intensity in an issue of the London journal *Architectural Review* published in September 1948 with invited contributions from Gregor Paulsson, Henry-Russell Hitchcock, William Holford, Walter Gropius, Lúcio Costa, Alfred Roth, and Giedion, and a late contribution *107–9* from Lewis Mumford in April 1949. It would surface again at CIAM's eighth *135–36* congress in Hoddesdon, England, in 1951, on the core of the city. But here, at a *125–28* moment when social realism was at its height in Eastern Europe, the theme was exorcised in the West—at least for the moment. In summing up the congress's conclusions, Giedion stated, "There is no excuse for the erection of a monumental building mass," shifting the responsibility for producing symbolic forms to "creative painters and sculptors."

Yet the impulse behind the new monumentality was not to disappear. It would be transformed, *mutatis mutandis,* in the coming decades: in the *47–54, 270–72* mythopoetic structures of Louis Kahn and the new capitols built in India and *308–13* Brazil, reemerging in the 1960s and 1970s in the historicism of the Italian *392–98, 446–49* Tendenza and the grandiloquent facades of postmodernism. Meanwhile, in *120–24, 184–88* Eastern Europe the theme would have a mirror image in the continuing struggle between social realism and functionalism.

The verse from the French song with which the "Nine Points" opens is meant to convey the preciousness of great monuments of civic architecture: "What would you give, my beauty, to see your husband again? I will give Versailles, Paris and Saint Denis, the towers of Notre Dame, and the steeple of my native countryside . . ." A partial summary of the literature on monumentality may be found in Christiane C. and George R. Collins, "Monumentality: A Critical Matter in Modern Architecture," *Harvard Architecture Review* 4 (1984).

First published in S. Giedion, Architektur und Gemeinschaft *(Hamburg: Rowohlt, 1956), pp. 40–42. English edition:* Architecture, You and Me *(Cambridge, Mass.: Harvard University Press, 1958), pp. 48–52. Copyright © 1958 by the President and Fellows of Harvard College.*

Nine Points on Monumentality
J. L. Sert , F. Léger , S. Giedion

Que donneriez vous ma belle
Pour revoir votre mari?
Je donnerai Versailles,
Paris et Saint Denis
Les tours de Notre Dame
Et le clocher de mon pays.
Auprès de ma blonde
Qu'il fait bon, fait bon, fait bon.
—From an old French song,"Auprès de ma blonde"

1. Monuments are human landmarks which men have created as symbols for their ideals, for their aims, and for their actions. They are intended to outlive the period which originated them, and constitute a heritage for future generations. As such, they form a link between the past and the future.

2. Monuments are the expression of man's highest cultural needs. They have to satisfy the eternal demand of the people for translation of their collective force into symbols. The most vital monuments are those which express the feeling and thinking of this collective force—the people.

3. Every bygone period which shaped a real cultural life had the power and the capacity to create these symbols. Monuments are, therefore, only possible in periods in which a unifying consciousness and unifying culture exists. Periods which exist for the moment have been unable to create lasting monuments.

4. The last hundred years have witnessed the devaluation of monumentality. This does not mean that there is any lack of formal monuments or architectural examples pretending to serve this purpose; but the so-called monuments of recent date have, with rare exceptions, become empty shells. They in no way represent the spirit or the collective feeling of modern times.

5. This decline and misuse of monumentality is the principal reason why modern architects have deliberately disregarded the monument and revolted against it.

Modern architecture, like modern painting and sculpture, had to start the hard way. It began by tackling the simpler problems, the more utilitarian buildings like low-rent housing, schools, office buildings, hospitals, and similar structures. Today modern architects know that buildings cannot be conceived as isolated units, that they have to be incorporated into the vaster urban schemes. There are no frontiers between architecture and town planning, just as there are no frontiers between the city and the region. Co-relation between them is necessary. Monuments should constitute the most powerful accents in these vast schemes.

6. A new step lies ahead. Postwar changes in the whole economic structure of nations may bring with them the organization of community life in the city which has been practically neglected up to date.

7. The people want the buildings that represent their social and community life to give more than functional fulfillment. They want their aspiration for monumentality, joy, pride, and excitement to be satisfied.

The fulfillment of this demand can be accomplished with the new means of expression at hand, though it is no easy task. The following conditions are essential for it: A monument being the integration of the work of the planner, architect, painter, sculptor, and landscapist demands close collaboration between all of them. This collaboration has failed in the last hundred years. Most modern architects have not been trained for this kind of integrated work. Monumental tasks have not been entrusted to them.

As a rule, those who govern and administer a people, brilliant as they may be in their special fields, represent the average man of our period in their artistic judgments. Like this average man, they experience a split between their methods of thinking and their methods of feeling. The feeling of those who govern and administer the countries is untrained and still imbued with the pseudo-ideals of the nineteenth century. This is the reason why they are not able to recognize the creative forces of our period, which alone could build the monuments or public buildings that should be integrated into new urban centers which can form a true expression for our epoch.

8. Sites for monuments must be planned. This will be possible once replanning is undertaken on a large scale which will create vast open spaces in the now decaying areas of our cities. In these open spaces, monumental architecture will find its appropriate setting which now does not exist. Monumental buildings will then be able to stand in space, for, like trees or plants, monumental buildings cannot be crowded in upon any odd lot in any district. Only when this space is achieved can the new urban centers come to life.

9. Modern materials and new techniques are at hand: light metal structures; curved, laminated wooden arches; panels of different textures, colors, and sizes; light elements like ceilings which can be suspended from big trusses covering practically unlimited spans.

Mobile elements can constantly vary the aspect of the buildings. These mobile elements, changing positions and casting different shadows when acted upon by wind or machinery, can be the source of new architectural effects.

During night hours, color and forms can be projected on vast surfaces. Such displays could be projected upon buildings for purposes of publicity or propaganda. These buildings would have large plane surfaces planned for this purpose, surfaces which are nonexistent today.

Such big animated surfaces with the use of color and movement in a new spirit would offer unexplored fields to mural painters and sculptors.

Elements of nature, such as trees, plants, and water, would complete the picture. We could group all these elements in architectural ensembles: the stones which have always been used, the new materials which belong to our times, and color in all its intensity which has long been forgotten.

Man-made landscapes would be correlated with nature's landscapes and all elements combined in terms of the new and vast facade, sometimes extending for many miles, which has been revealed to us by the air view. This could be contemplated not only during a rapid flight but also from a helicopter stopping in mid-air.

Monumental architecture will be something more than strictly functional. It will have regained its lyrical value. In such monumental layouts, architecture and city planning could attain a new freedom and develop new creative possibilities, such as those that have begun to be felt in the last decades in the fields of painting, sculpture, music, and poetry.

1943

The figure of **Frank Lloyd Wright**—Whitmanesque genius, charismatic master, prolific creator of a self-described American architecture—looms over the post-World War II period even more imposingly than the earlier part of the century. In fact, Wright, born in 1867, was continuing to proselytize, in his buildings, writings, and teaching, the very same ideas he had first articulated half a century before. As early as 1894 he had written an article exhorting architects to "bring out the nature of the materials." This theme, closely linked to his idea of organic architecture—itself derived from his "lieber Meister" Louis Sullivan—would preoccupy him for the rest of his life. In 1928 Wright wrote an eloquent series of articles for *Architectural Record* under the title "In the Cause of Architecture" focusing on the respective characteristics of different materials: stone, wood, tile and brick, glass, concrete, metal; "the logical material under the circumstances," he wrote succinctly, "is the most natural one for the purpose. It usually is the most beautiful . . ." Not surprisingly, in 1940, for the large retrospective of his work held at the Museum of Modern Art in New York he chose the same theme, "The Nature of Materials," a title that also served for the comprehensive volume by Henry-Russell Hitchcock that appeared two years later as an ex post facto catalogue. The credo that follows here, comprising a section of Wright's *Autobiography* as published in 1943, does not differ in substance from these earlier pronouncements.

On the other hand, Wright's impact at a moment when orthodox modernism was undergoing revision was enormous. His indictment of the functionalist "box"—"a white sepulture for unthinking mass-life"—reversed the equation of what he saw as an architecture dedicated to the machine with the alternative of a machine technology in the service of architecture, an architecture whose values were, above all, "humane." His major accomplishments of the middle to late 1930s—the completion of the Johnson Wax Building in Racine, Wisconsin, and of important residences like the Kaufmann house at Connellsvillle, Pennsylvania ("Falling Water"), as well as his elaboration of the Usonian house type and its suburban extension, Broadacre City—amply demonstrated the fertility of the architect's vision in his sixth decade. If earlier he could be relegated by a modern movement that did not know how to subsume him to being "the last great nineteenth-century architect," or by an Anglo-Saxon world remembering the reception of the 1910 Wasmuth edition of his work to being "Germanic," by *68–69* the 1940s he would appear prescient and fully original. For Bruno Zevi, who would return home to Italy with a transliterated concept of organic architecture after spending the war years in America, and for the stream of architects who would seek out the architectural cult at Taliesin West, Wright's thought represented a powerful antidote to the dispersed and war-damaged culture of Europe.

It may be helpful to identify the "five new resources" on which Wright's argument below is predicated, as these get somewhat buried in the idiosyncrasies of his writing style. They are *spatial*, an interior concept of room-space; *material*, the advent of glass as a "supermaterial" allowing maximum penetration of light and the disappearance of the wall; *structural*, "tenuity" or continuity of structure, especially through the use of steel and plastics; *constructional*, fidelity in building to the inherent qualities—the nature—of materials; *expressive*, integral ornament, the giving of "natural pattern" to structure.

From Frank Lloyd Wright, An Autobiography (New York: Duell, Sloan and Pearce, 1943), pp. 337–49. Copyright © 1943 by The Frank Lloyd Wright Foundation.

In the Nature of Materials: A Philosophy
Frank Lloyd Wright

Our vast resources are yet new; new only because architecture as "rebirth" (perennial Renaissance) has, after five centuries of decline, culminated in the imitation of imitations, seen in our Mrs. Plasterbuilt, Mrs. Gablemore, and Miss Flat-top American architecture. In general, and especially officially, our architecture is at long last completely significant of insignificance only. We do not longer have architecture. At least no buildings with integrity. We have only economic crimes in its name. No, our greatest buildings are not qualified as great art, my dear Mrs. Davies, although you do admire Washington.

If you will yet be patient for a little while—a scientist, Einstein, asked for three days to explain the far less pressing and practical matter of "Relativity"—we will take each of the five new resources in order, as with the five fingers of the hand. All are new integrities to be used if we will to make living easier and better today.

The first great integrity is a deeper, more intimate sense of reality in building than was ever pagan—that is to say, than was ever "Classic." More human than was any building ever realized in the Christian Middle Ages. This is true although the thought that may ennoble it now has been living in civilization for more than twenty centuries back. Later it was innate in the simplicities of Jesus as it was organic 500 years earlier in the natural philosophy, Tao (The Way) of the Chinese philosopher, Laotze. But not only is the new architecture sound philosophy. It is poetry.

Said Ong Giao Ki, Chinese sage, "Poetry is the sound of the heart."

Well, like poetry, this sense of architecture is the sound of the "within." We might call that "within," the heart.

Architecture now becomes integral, the expression of a new-old reality: the livable interior space of the room itself. In integral architecture the *room-space itself must come through.* The *room* must be seen as architecture, or we have no architecture. We have no longer an outside as outside. We have no longer an outside and an inside as two separate things. Now the outside may come inside, and the inside may and does go outside. They are of each other. Form and function thus become one in design and execution if the nature of materials and method and purpose are all in unison.

This interior-space concept, the first broad integrity, is the first great resource. It is also true basis for general significance of form. Add to this for the sake of clarity that (although the general integration is implied in the first integrity) it is in the nature of any organic building to grow from its site, come out of the ground into the light—the ground itself held always as a component basic part of the building itself. And then we have primarily the new ideal of building as organic. A building dignified as a tree in the midst of nature.

This new ideal for architecture is, as well, an adequate ideal for our general culture. In any final result there can be no separation between our architecture and our culture. Nor any separation of either from our happiness. Nor any separation from our work.

Thus in this rise of organic-integration you see the means to end the petty agglomerations miscalled civilization. By way of this old yet new and deeper sense of reality we may have a civilization. In this sense we now recognize and may declare by way of plan and building— the *natural.* Faith in the *natural* is the faith we now need to grow up on in this coming age of our culturally confused, backward twentieth century. But instead of "organic" we might well say "natural" building. Or we might say integral building.

So let us now consider the second of the five new resources: glass. This second resource is new and a "super-material" only because it holds such amazing means in modern life for awakened sensibilities. It amounts to a new qualification of life in itself. If known in ancient times glass would then and there have abolished the ancient architecture we know, and completely. This super-material *glass* as we now use it is a miracle. Air in air to keep air out or keep it in. Light itself in light, to diffuse or reflect, or refract light itself.

By means of glass, then, the first great integrity may find prime means of realization. Open reaches of the ground may enter as the building and the building interior may reach out and associate with these vistas of the ground. Ground and building will thus become more and more obvious as directly related to each other in openness and intimacy; not only as environment but also as a good pattern for the good life lived in the building. Realizing the benefits to human life of the far-reaching implications and effects of the first great integrity: let us call it the interior-space concept. This space interior realization is possible and it is desirable in all the vast variety of characteristic buildings needed by civilized life in our complex age.

By means of glass something of the freedom of our arboreal ancestors living in their trees becomes a likely precedent for freedom in twentieth century life, than the cave.

Savage animals "holing in" for protection were more characteristic of life based upon the might of feudal times or based upon the so-called "classical" in architecture which were in turn based upon the labor of the chattel slave. In a free country, were we ourselves free by way of organic thought buildings might come out into the light without more animal fear; come entirely away from the pagan ideals of form we dote upon as "Classic." Or what Freedom have we?

Perhaps more important than all beside, it is by way of glass that the sunlit space as a reality becomes the most useful servant of a higher order of the human spirit. It is first aid to the sense of cleanliness of form and idea when directly related to free living in air and sunlight. It is this that is coming in the new architecture. And with the integral character of extended vistas gained by marrying buildings with ground levels, or blending them with slopes and gardens; yes, it is in this new sense of earth as a great human *good* that we will move forward in the building of our new homes and great public buildings.

I am certain we will desire the sun, spaciousness, and integrity of means-to-ends more year by year as we become aware of the possibilities I have outlined. The more we desire the sun, the more we will desire the freedom of the good ground and the sooner we will learn to understand it. The more we value integrity, the more securely we will find and keep a worthwhile civilization to set against prevalent abuse and ruin.

Congestion will no longer encourage the "space-makers for rent." The "space-maker for rent" will himself be "for rent" or let us hope "vacant." Give him ten years.

These new space values are entering into our ideas of life. All are appropriate to the ideal that is our own, the ideal we call Democracy.

A new reality: glass

A resource to liberate this new sense of interior space as reality is this new qualification called glass: a super-material qualified to qualify us; qualify us not only to escape from the prettified cavern of our present domestic life as also from the cave of our past, but competent actually to awaken in us the desire for such far-reaching simplicities of life as we may see in the clear countenance of nature. Good building must ever be seen as in the nature of good construction, but a higher development of this "seeing" will be construction seen as nature-pattern. *That* seeing, only, is inspired architecture.

This dawning sense of the *Within* as *reality* when it is clearly seen as *Nature* will by way of glass make the garden be the building as much as the building will be the garden: the sky as treasured a feature of daily indoor life as the ground itself.

You may see that walls are vanishing. The cave for human dwelling purposes is at last disappearing.

Walls themselves because of glass will become windows and windows as we used to know them as holes in walls will be seen no more. Ceilings will often become as window-walls, too. The textile may soon be used as a beautiful overhead for space, the textile an attribute of genuine architecture instead of decoration by way of hangings and upholstery. The usual camouflage of the old order. Modern integral floor heating will follow integral lighting and standardized unitary sanitation. All this makes it reasonable and good economy to abolish building as either a hyper-boxment or a super-borough.

Haven't senseless elaboration and false mass become sufficiently insulting and oppressive to our intelligence as a people? And yet, senseless elaboration and false mass were tyrannical as "conspicuous waste" in all of our nineteenth century architecture either public or private! Wherever the American architect, as scholar, went he "succeeded" to that extent.

Another reality: continuity

But now, as third resource, the resource essential to modern architecture destined to cut down this outrageous mass-waste and mass-lying is the principle of continuity. I have called it tenuity. Steel is its prophet and master. You must come with me for a moment into "engineering" so called. This is to be an unavoidable strain upon your kind attention. Because, unfortunately, gentle reader, you cannot understand architecture as *modern* unless you do come, and—paradox—you can't come if you are too well educated as an engineer or as an architect either. So your common sense is needed more than your erudition.

However, to begin this argument for steel: classic architecture knew only the post as an upright. Call it a column. The classics knew only the beam as a *horizontal.* Call it a beam. The beam resting upon the upright, or column, was structure throughout, to them. Two things, you see, one thing set on top of another thing in various materials and put there in various ways. Ancient, and nineteenth century building science too, even building *à la mode,* consisted simply in reducing the various stresses of all materials and their uses to these two things: post and beam. Really, construction used to be just sticking up something in wood or stone and putting something else in wood or stone (maybe iron) on top of it: simple superimposition, you see? You should know that all "Classic" architecture was and still is some such form of direct superimposition. The arch is a little less so, but even that must be so "figured" by the structural engineer if you ask him to "figure" it.

Now the Greeks developed this simple act of super-imposition pretty far by way of innate tasteful refinement. The Greeks were true aestheticians. Roman builders too, when they forgot the Greeks and brought the beam over as a curve by way of the arch, did something somewhat new but with consequences still of the same sort. But observe, all architectural features made by such "Classic" agglomeration were killed for us by cold steel. And though millions of classic corpses yet encumber American ground unburied, they are ready now for burial.

Of course this primitive post-and-beam construction will always be valid, but both support and supported may now by means of inserted and welded steel strands or especially woven filaments of steel and modern concrete casting be plaited and united as one physical body: ceilings and walls made one with floors and reinforcing each other by making them continue into one another. This Continuity is made possible by the tenuity of steel.

So the new order wherever steel or plastics enter construction says: weld these two things, post and beam (wall and ceiling) together by means of steel strands buried and stressed within the mass material itself, the steel strands electric-welded where steel meets steel within the mass. In other words the upright and horizontal may now be made to work together as one. A new world of form opens inevitably.

Where the beam leaves off and the post begins is no longer important nor need it be seen at all because it no longer actually *is*. Steel in tension enables the support to slide into the supported, or the supported to grow into the support somewhat as a tree-branch glides out of its tree trunk. Therefrom arises the new series of interior physical reactions I am calling "Continuity." As natural consequence the new aesthetic or appearance we call *Plasticity* (and plasticity is peculiarly "modern") is no longer a mere appearance. Plasticity actually becomes the normal *countenance,* the *true aesthetic* of genuine structural reality. These interwoven steel strands may so lie in so many directions in any extended member that the extensions may all be economical of material and though much lighter, be safer construction than ever before. There as in the branch of the tree you may see the cantilever. The cantilever is the simplest one of the important phases of this third new structural resource now demanding new significance. It has yet had little attention in architecture. It can do remarkable things to liberate space.

But plasticity was modest new countenance in our American architecture at least thirty-five years ago in my own work, but then denied such simple means as welding and the mesh. It had already eliminated all the separate identities of post and beam in architecture. Steel in tension enters now by way of mesh and welding to arrive at actual, total plasticity if and when desired by the architect. And to prove the philosophy of organic architecture, form and function are one, it now enters architecture as the *aesthetic countenance* of *physical reality.*

To further illustrate this magic simplifier we call "plasticity" see it as flexibility similar to that of your own hand. What makes your hand expressive? Flowing continuous line and continuous surfaces seen continually mobile of the articulate articulated structure of the hand as a whole. The line is seen as "hand" line. The varying planes seen as "hand" surface. Strip the hand to the separate structural identities of joined bones (post and beam) and plasticity as an expression of the hand would disappear. We would be then getting back to the joinings, breaks, jolts, and joints of ancient, or "Classic," architecture; thing to thing; feature to feature. But plasticity is the reverse of that ancient agglomeration and is the ideal means behind these simplified free new effects of straight line and flat plane.

I have just said that plasticity in this sense for thirty-five years or more has been the recognized aesthetic ideal for such simplification as was required by the machine to do organic work. And it is true of my own work.

As significant outline and expressive surface, this new aesthetic of plasticity (physical continuity) is now a useful means to form the supreme physical-body of an organic, or integral, American Architecture.

Of course, it is just as easy to cheat by simplicity as it is to cheat with "classical" structure. So, unluckily, here again is the "modernistic" architectural picture-maker's deadly facility for imitation at ease and again too happy with fresh opportunity to "fake effects." Probably another Renaissance is here imminent.

Architecture is now integral architecture only when Plasticity is a genuine expression of actual construction just as the articulate line and surface of the hand is articulate of the structure of the hand. Arriving at steel, I first used Continuity as actual stabilizing principle in concrete slabs, and in the concrete ferro-block system I devised in Los Angeles.

In the form of the cantilever or as horizontal continuity this new economy by means of tenuity is what saved the Imperial Hotel from destruction during the great earthquake of 1922. It did not appear in the grammar of the building for various reasons, chiefly because the building was to look somewhat as though it belonged to Tokyo.

Later, in the new design for St. Mark's Tower, New York City, this new working principle economized material, labor, and liberated or liberalized space in a more developed sense. It gave to the structure the significant outlines of remarkable stability and instead of false masonry-mass significant outlines came out. The abstract pattern of the structure as a complete structural-integrity of Form and Idea may be seen fused as in any tree but with nothing imitating a tree.

Continuity invariably realized remarkable economy of labor and building materials as well as peace. Unfortunately there is yet little or no data to use as tabulation. Tests will have to be made continually for many years to make the record available to slide-rule engineers.

In the ancient order there was little thought of economy of materials. The more massive the whole structure looked, the better it looked to the ancients. But seen in the light of these new economic interior forces conserved by the tensile strength of a sheet of plastic or any interweaving of strands of steel in this machine age, the old order was as sick with weight as the Buonarotti dome. Weak . . . because there could be no co-interrelation between the two elements of support and supported to reinforce each other as a whole under stress or elemental disturbance.

So this tremendous new resource of *tenuity*—a quality of steel—this quality of *pull* in a building (you may see it ushering in a new era in John Roebling's Brooklyn Bridge) was definitely lacking in all ancient architecture because steel had not been born into building.

The tenuous strand or slab as a common means of strength had yet to come. Here today this element of continuity may cut structural substance nearly in two. It may cut the one half in two again by elimination of needless features, such elimination being entirely due to the simplification I have been calling "plasticity."

It is by utilizing mass production in the factory in this connection that some idea of the remarkable new economics possible to modern architecture may be seen approaching those realized in any well-built machine. If standardization can be humanized and made flexible in design and the economics brought to the home owner, the greatest service will be rendered to our modern way of life. It may be really born— This democracy I mean.

Involved as a matter of design in this mass production, however, are the involute, all but involuntary reactions to which I have just referred: the ipso facto building code and the fact that the building engineer as now trained knows so little about them. However, the engineer is learning to calculate by model-making in some instances— notably Professor Beggs at Princeton University.

The codes so far as I can see will have to die on the vine with the men who made them.

Materials for their own sake

As the first integrity and the two first new resources appeared out of the interior nature of the kind of building, called Architecture—so now—naturally interior to the true nature of any good building comes the fourth new resource. This is found by recognizing the nature of the materials used in construction.

Just as many fascinating different properties as there are different materials that may be used to build a building will continually and naturally qualify, modify, and utterly change all architectural form whatsoever.

A stone building will no more be nor will it look like a steel building. A pottery, or terra cotta building, will not be nor should it look like a stone building. A wood building will look like none other, for it will glorify the stick. A steel and glass building could not possibly look like anything but itself. It will glorify steel and glass. And so on all the way down the long list of available riches in materials: Stone, Wood, Concrete, Metals, Glass, Textiles, Pulp, and Plastics; riches so great to our hand today that no comparison with Ancient Architecture is at all sensible or anything but obstruction to our Modern Architecture.

In this particular, as you may see, architecture is going back to learn from the natural source of all natural things.

In order to get Organic architecture born, intelligent architects will be forced to turn their backs on antique rubbish heaps with which Classic eclecticism has encumbered our new ground. So far as architecture has gone in my own thought it is first of all a character and quality of mind that may enter also into human conduct with social implications that might, at first, confound or astound you. But the only basis for any fear of them lies in the fact that they are all sanely and thoroughly *constructive*.

Instinctively all forms of pretense fear and hate reality. *The hypocrite must always hate the radical.*

This potent fourth new resource—the Nature of Materials—gets at the common center of every material in relation to the work it is required to do. This means that the architect must again begin at the very beginning. Proceeding according to Nature now he must sensibly go through with whatever material may be in hand for his purpose according to the methods and sensibilities of a man in this age. And when I say Nature, I mean inherent *structure* seen always by the architect as a matter of complete design. It is in itself, always, *nature-pattern*. It is this profound internal sense of materials that enters in as Architecture now. It is this the fifth new resource that must captivate and hold the mind of the modern architect to creative work. The fifth will give new life to his imagination if it has not been already killed at school.

And, inevitable implication! New machine age resources require that all buildings do not resemble each other. The new ideal does not require that all buildings be of steel, concrete, or glass. Often that might be idiotic waste.

Nor do the resources even *imply* that mass is no longer a beautiful attribute of masonry materials when they are genuinely used. We are entitled to a vast variety of form in our complex age so long as the form be genuine—serves Architecture and Architecture serves life.

But in this land of ours, richest on earth of all in old and new materials, architects must exercise well-trained imagination to see in each material, either natural or compounded plastics, their own *inherent style*. All materials may be beautiful, their beauty much or entirely depending upon how well they are used by the Architect.

In our modern building we have the Stick. Stone. Steel. Pottery. Concrete. Glass. Yes, Pulp, too, as well as plastics. And since this dawning sense of the "within" is the new reality, these will all give the main *"motif"* for any real building made from them. The materials of which the building is built will go far to determine its appropriate mass, its outline, and, especially, proportion. Character is criterion in the form of any and every building or industrial product we can call Architecture in the light of this new ideal of the new order.

The new integrity

Strange! At this late date, it is modern architecture that wants life to learn to see life as life, because architecture must learn to see brick as brick, learn to see steel as steel, see glass as glass. So modern thought urges all of life to demand that a bank look like a bank (bad thought though a bank might become) and not depend upon false columns for credit. The new architecture urges all of life to demand that an office building look like an office building, even if it should resemble the cross section of a beehive. Life itself should sensibly insist in self-defense that a hotel look and conduct itself like a hotel and not like some office building. Life should declare, too, that the railroad station look like a railroad station and not try so hard to look like an ancient temple or some monarchic palazzo. And while we are on this subject, why not a place for opera that would look something like a place for opera—if we must have opera, and not look so much like a gilded, crimsoned bagnio. Life declares that a filling station should stick to its work as a filling station: look the part becomingly. Why try to look like some Colonial diminutive or remain just a pump on the street. Although "just a pump" on the street is better than the Colonial imitation. The good Life itself demands that the school be as generously spaced and a thought-built good-time place for happy children: a building no more than one story high—with some light overhead, the school building should regard the children as a garden in sun. Life itself demands of Modern Architecture that the house of a man who knows what home is should have his own home his own way if we have any man left in that connection after F.H.A. is done trying to put them, all of them it can, into the case of a man who builds a home only to sell it. Our Government forces the home-maker into the real-estate business if he wants a home at all.

Well, after all, this line of thought was all new-type common sense in architecture in Chicago only thirty years ago. It began to grow up in my own work as it is continuing to grow up more and more widely in the work of all the world. But, insulting as it may seem to say so, nor is it merely arrogant to say that the actual thinking in that connection is still a novelty, only a little less strange today than it was then, although the appearances do rapidly increase.

Integral ornament at last!

At last, is this fifth resource, so old yet now demanding fresh significance. We have arrived at integral ornament—the nature-pattern of actual construction. Here, confessed as the spiritual demand for true significance, comes this subjective element in modern architecture. An element so hard to understand that modern architects themselves seem to understand it least well of all and most of them have turned against it with such fury as is born only of impotence.

And it is true that this vast, intensely human significance is really no matter at all for any but the most imaginative mind not without some development in artistry and the *gift* of a sense of proportion. Certainly we must go higher in the realm of imagination when we presume to enter here, because we go into Poetry.

Now, very many write good prose who cannot write poetry at all. And although staccato specification is the present fashion, just as "functionalist" happens to be the present style in writing—poetic prose will never be undesirable. But who condones prosaic poetry? None. Not even those fatuously condemned to write it.

So, I say this fourth new resource and the fifth demand for new significance and integrity is ornament *integral to building as itself poetry.* Rash use of a dangerous word. The word "Poetry" *is* a dangerous word.

Heretofore, I have used the word "pattern" instead of the word ornament to avoid confusion or to escape the passing prejudice. But here now ornament is in its place. Ornament meaning not only *surface qualified by human imagination but imagination* giving *natural pattern* to structure. Perhaps this phrase says it all without further explanation. This resource—integral ornament—is new in the architecture of the world, at least insofar not only as imagination qualifying a surface—a valuable resource—but as a greater means than that: *imagination giving natural pattern to structure itself.* Here we have new significance, indeed! Long ago this significance was lost to the scholarly architect. A man of taste. He, too soon, became content with symbols.

Evidently then, this expression of structure as a pattern true to the nature of the materials out of which it was made, may be taken much further along than physical need alone would dictate? "If you have a loaf of bread break the loaf in two and give the half of it for some flowers of the Narcissus for the bread feeds the body indeed but the flowers feed the soul."

Into these higher realms of imagination associated in the popular mind as sculpture and painting, buildings may be as fully taken by modern means today as they ever were by craftsmen of the antique order.

It is by this last and poetic resource that we may give greater structural entity and greater human significance to the whole building than could ever be done otherwise. This statement is heresy at this left-wing moment, so—we ask, "taken how and when taken?" I confess you may well ask, by whom? The answer is, taken by the true *poet.* And where is this Poet today? Time will answer.

Yet again in this connection let us remember Ong's Chinese observation, "Poetry is the sound of the heart." So, in the same uncommon sense integral ornament is the developed sense of the building as a whole, or the manifest *abstract pattern of structure itself.* Interpreted. Integral ornament is simply *structure-pattern made visibly articulate* and seen in the building as it is seen articulate in the structure of the trees or a lily of the fields. It is the expression of inner rhythm of Form. Are we talking about Style? Pretty nearly. At any rate, we are talking about the qualities that make *essential architecture* as distinguished from any mere act of building whatsoever.

What I am here calling integral-ornament is founded upon the same organic simplicities as Beethoven's *Fifth Symphony,* that amazing revolution in tumult and splendor of sound built on four tones based upon a rhythm a child could play on the piano with one finger. Supreme imagination reared the four repeated tones, simple rhythms, into a great symphonic poem that is probably the noblest thought-built edifice in our world. And Architecture is like Music in this capacity for the symphony.

But concerning higher development of building to more completely express its life principle as significant and beautiful, let us say at once by way of warning: it is better to die by the wayside of left-wing Ornaphobia than it is to build any more merely ornamented buildings, as such; or to see right-wing architects die any more ignoble deaths of *Ornamentia.* All period and pseudoclassic buildings whatever, and (although their authors do not seem to know it) most protestant buildings, they call themselves

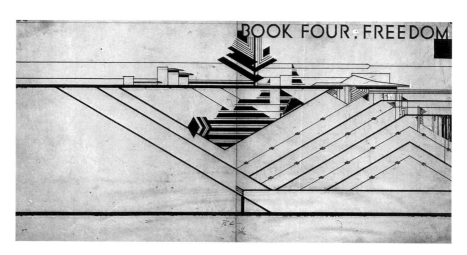

[*"Great Highway and Field of Decentralization."* Original design for title spread of *"Book Four. Freedom,"* as published in Frank Lloyd Wright, An Autobiography, *between pp. 299 and 301. Courtesy of the Frank Lloyd Wright Foundation.*]

internationalist, are really ornamental in definitely objectionable sense. A plain flat surface cut to shape for its own sake, however large or plain the shape, is, the moment it is sophisticatedly so cut, no less ornamental than egg-and-dart. All such buildings are objectionably "ornamental," because like any buildings of the old classical order both wholly ignore the *nature* of the *first* integrity. Both also ignore the four resources and both neglect the nature of machines at work on materials. Incidentally and as a matter of course both misjudge the nature of time, place, and the modern life of man.

Here in this new leftish emulation as we now have it, is only the "istic," ignoring principle merely to get the "look" of the machine or something that looks "new." The province of the "ite."

In most so-called "internationalist" or "modernistic" building therefore we have no true approach to organic architecture: we have again merely a new, superficial aesthetic trading upon that architecture because such education as most of our architects possess qualifies them for only some kind of eclecticism past, passing, or to pass.

Nevertheless I say, if we can't have buildings with integrity we would better have more imitation machines for buildings until we can have truly sentient architecture. "The machine for living in" is sterile, but therefore it is safer, I believe, than the festering mass of ancient styles.

Great power

A far greater power than slavery, even the intellectual slavery as in the school of the Greeks, is back of these five demands for machine-age significance and integrity. Stupendous and stupefying power. That power is the leverage of the machine itself. As now set up in all its powers the machine will confirm these new implicities and complicities in architecture at every point, but will destroy them soon if not checked by a new simplicity.

The proper use of these new resources demands that we use them all together with integrity for mankind if we are to realize the finer significances of life. The finer significance, prophesied if not realized by organic architecture. It is reasonable to believe that life in our country will be lived in full enjoyment of this new freedom of the extended horizontal line because the horizontal line now becomes the great architectural highway. The flat plane now becomes the regional field. And integral-pattern becomes "the sound of the Usonian heart." The cover-graph of this book, I have called it "Freedom," uses the great highway and the regional field of decentralization, uses it as a significant pattern.

I see this extended horizontal line as the true earth-line of human life, indicative of freedom. Always.

The broad expanded plane is the horizontal plane infinitely extended. In that lies such freedom for man on this earth as he may call his.

1943

In the 1940s Swedish architecture was watched closely by architects elsewhere in the world. Having remained neutral during the war, Sweden continued to build—although in reduced circumstances—at a time when architecture in most other European countries had come to a standstill. International functionalism, espoused by six of Sweden's leading architects in 1931 in their manifesto *Acceptera,* had belatedly overtaken the country in the early 1930s. By the end of the decade, however, a reaction had occurred in both domestic and public architecture against an overly rigid and formalistic interpretation of *funkis*. The new watchword was *spontanietet*, signifying a more naturalistic, informal way of working. The seminal work was Erik Gunnar Asplund's last major project before his death, Woodland Crematorium near Stockholm (1935–40). Also exemplary of the new manner were Asplund's summer house, Stennäs, in Lisön, Sorunda (1937); Sven Markelius's Swedish pavilion at the New York World's Fair (1939); and Sune Lindström's Town Hall and Hotel at Karlskoga (1940).

Nowhere did this architecture find as warm a reception as in England, where building and town planning were as tightly controlled by the welfare state as in Sweden and where a temperamental affinity was felt with the Swedes commonsensical, down-to-earth, empirical approach. In September 1943 *114–20* *Architectural Review,* having become the style's major exponent, devoted a special issue to "Swedish Peace in War," in which a selection of work appeared that had been designed and built since 1939. In their introductory note the editors declared, "Swedish housing is the most progressive in Europe in its social organization. The Cooperatives build better than anywhere else. Most buildings, especially the smaller accessory ones, are pleasant, lighthearted, almost playful, and yet strictly contemporary. A few larger public buildings have achieved a true monumentality in terms of the twentieth century. Detail is as generally sensitive as any of the eighteenth century. And even where, as sometimes occurs even in Sweden, the design of the buildings is not particularly distinguished, the way they are placed on the site and set off with rocks and conifers or silver birch—the way in fact they are landscaped—provides an object lesson for the English town planner and landscape architect." In June 1947 the *Review* coined the label "New Empiricism" to describe this style. Eric de Maré's article in the *Review* of January 1948, "The New Empiricism: The Antecedents and Origins of Sweden's Latest Style" followed. So pervasive was the influence *242–48* of Swedish architecture over the next decade that the architect James Stirling was led to comment in exasperation, "William Morris was a Swede."

Sven Backström, one of the most talented members of the younger generation of Swedish architects, was invited to contribute the following article to the "Peace in War" issue. In the 1940s and 1950s Backström and his partner Leif Reinius designed a number of important housing estates. Their Gröndal scheme in Stockholm of 1944–45 was an arrangement of star-shaped low-rise blocks, offering a honeycomb of intimate and sheltered courtyards and making economical use of the available land. The architects reused this plan type in their Örebro housing (1948–50), disposing the blocks more naturalistically in the landscape. In a subsequent article on Swedish housing entitled "Now—and After" (published in *Swedish Housing of the 'Forties,*1950), Backström noted the "complete change" in conception that had occurred since the 1930s from the indefiniteness of the open plan to spatial enclosure: "People are no longer disposed to make their bed on the balcony of a living room or to work in a study which is open to view from outside because of its wide expanse of glass."

From Architectural Review, *September 1943, p. 80. Courtesy of the author and* Architectural Review.

A Swede Looks at Sweden
Sven Backström

Although Sweden has so far managed to keep out of the war, it has, of course, affected us in various ways. Social and economic changes are taking place, and the isolation from which we suffer is very keenly felt. Imports have diminished, and a number of goods have disappeared from the market altogether. This is not least noticeable in the building trade. Iron girders, copper, asphalt, and much else are almost unobtainable. We are obliged to have recourse to home goods such as timber, bricks, cement, and iron for the reinforcement of concrete. The chief reason for their use, however, is that they do not require too much fuel for their production, since coal, being one of the items on our import list, is scarce.

The limitation of material has naturally had its effect on building. The war has also entailed limitations of another kind for building. The scarcity of material and labor has made it necessary to confine all civil building to a minimum. This means, for us, that factories and perhaps in the first place dwellings are what is chiefly built. There is much building of small unattached cottages, small flats, and to some slight extent also attached houses in rows and a few residential hotels.

Dwellings of the kind here referred to must of course be made cheap. By rationalization and standardizing we have tried to keep costs as low as possible. But the state and the municipalities have been obliged to grant loans at low interest so that flats may be let at reasonable prices. This has also made it possible to exercise a certain control. Thus, for example, the following minimum sizes of flats have of recent years become increasingly general.

Single room	18–24 square meters
One room and kitchen	33–39
Two rooms and kitchen	43–49
Three	58–65
Four	71–79
Five	87

As regards small cottages, these are as a rule made of wood on a concrete foundation. They contain two to four rooms and kitchen, in exceptional cases five rooms and kitchen. Dwellings for land workers also come under this category.

The flats are in three-story so-called "narrow houses" of brick. The depth of the house varies from 7 to 10 meters. The greater depth is from the fuel point of view more economical, so the house depth generally adopted today is 9 to 10 m. The type of flat varies from one room and kitchen to three rooms and kitchen, sometimes even four rooms and a kitchen.

Attached houses in rows are not common in this country. The Swede likes to live in his own cottage and to be able to walk all round it; and if this is not possible he generally prefers to take a flat in a big block. Of recent years, however, such prejudices have been slackening their grip, and a number of good designs have been achieved.

But apart from this development, which has been imposed on us by external factors, our architecture has a line of development to show, as it were, from within. In order to understand this rightly we must go back a matter of some ten years. It was in 1930 that Erik Gunnar Asplund created the Stockholm Exhibition at

A weekend cottage at Kalvnäs, Sorunda, by Eskil Sundahl, built of timber [1935]. Landscaping is as good as any in English eighteenth century. Note the clump and roughly circular pond in the front.

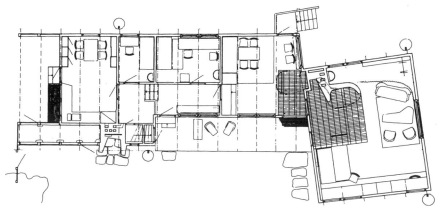

Asplund's own country house at Stennäs, built in 1937. It is of timber plastered.

Djurgardsbrunnsviken. This meant for us that the new impulses from France and Germany were in a masterly way translated and developed in the Swedish milieu and adapted to the Swedish national temperament. This was the victorious debut of functionalism in Sweden. The new ideas swept over us like an avalanche and were adopted especially by the younger generation. A clean break was made with the past. There was a determination to clear away all false romanticism and all designing in historical styles. There was a feeling that one was building for new ideal human beings, who were quite different from the older generations. The modern mode of life was considered to be completely new, and consequently the new houses were to be absolutely different from the old ones. Everything connected with tradition was suspect. Architecture was to be objective. The functionalistic principle was the guiding star and everything was to be built in the material of "our time," glass, concrete, and iron, and the building had primarily to be right from the point of view of construction. In one word, the architect was to be an engineer.

The years passed, and one "objective" house after the other stood ready for use. It was then that people gradually began to discover that the "new objectivity" was not always so objective, and the houses did not always function so well as had been expected. The big windows, for example, were all too effective as heat conductors, and people found it difficult to accustom themselves to the heat or cold behind them. They also felt the lack of many of the aesthetic values and the little contributions to coziness that we human beings are so dependent on, and that our architectural and domestic tradition had nevertheless developed. It was difficult to settle down in the new houses because the "new" human beings were not so different from the older ones. It was found that one could not with impunity break out of the natural course of development. It was realized that one had to build for human beings as they are, and not as they ought to be. And for a true understanding of our fellows both the feeling and the knowledge of the artist are essential conditions. It is not sufficient for the architect to be an engineer; he must also be an artist.

Architecture began to seek its way on new roads. Architects began to develop an ear for the shifting values and phases of actual life. Man was once more to become the point of departure and the criterion. And it was discovered that man is a highly complicated phenomenon that is not to be satisfied or understood with the help of any new epoch-making formulae. And one result of this growing insight was a reaction against the all too schematic architecture of the 1930s. Today we have reached the point where all the elusive psychological factors have again begun to engage our attention. Man and his habits, reactions, and needs are the focus of interest as never before. One tries to understand them, and to adapt the building in such a way that it really serves. And there is the desire to enrich it and beautify it in a living way, so that it may be a source of joy. The striving is for the true proportion—the neither too much nor too little. But with the delight in experiment that is part of the Swedish temperament, architecture has already tended to a much too exaggerated differentiation and division. This tendency to lose oneself in petty details of various kinds leads one to forget the whole, and simplicity. People sometimes actually need instructions before they can live in the houses!

The goal must be to reach the essential, the simple, and the objective things in architecture. We want, certainly, to retain all the positive aspects of what the 1930s gave us. A house should of course function properly and be rational in its design. But at the same time we want to reintroduce the valuable and living elements in architecture that existed before 1930, and we want to add to this our own personal contribution. To interpret such a program as a reaction and a return to something that is past and to pastiches is definitely to misunderstand the development of architecture in this country. Something that to a certain extent leads to a confusion of ideas is perhaps the forced return to building materials and methods of construction that the architecture of the thirties did not need to reckon with, and that for the younger generation of architects are perhaps unknown.

If in our democratic community architecture is allowed to progress without too great interference from without, it should be in a position to develop into a functionalism fulfilling the best and deepest requirements of the term.

1944

27–30**Louis Kahn**'s contribution to the debate on monumentality already joined by José Luis Sert, Fernand Léger, and Sigfried Giedion with their "Nine Points on Monumentality" was published in Paul Zucker's *New Architecture and City Planning* together with five other papers on the same subject, including a new essay by Giedion. It was Kahn's first extended theoretical statement. If Giedion had drawn a lesson from the war concerning the symbolic and emotional values of civic architecture, the younger architect found a different one in its "engineering achievements in concrete, steel, and wood." What impressed Kahn were the "added powers" that the new structural resources could afford architecture.

In Kahn's definition, monumentality, characteristic of the great architecture of past ages, was "a spiritual quality inherent in a structure which conveys the feeling of its eternity, that it cannot be added to or changed." At the time of this writing Kahn was associated in practice with George Howe and Oscar Stonorov. Having accepted International Style modernism in the early 1930s, he had mainly built social housing during the years of the New Deal and the war and designed little in the way of large-scale public architecture. His earlier schooling, however, had had a profound impact on him. Under the Beaux-Arts architect Paul Cret at the University of Pennsylvania, he had absorbed the lessons of rational engineering and historical form. In approaching the question of monumentality, Kahn now synthesized both inputs. A new monumentality, he concluded, could arise only by reinterpreting historical concepts of construction in light of contemporary technical possibilities.

Kahn argues that architecture's historical development led it from the compressive stone construction of Greco-Roman antiquity up to the dematerialized structural skeleton of the Gothic cathedral, a point it could not go beyond without collapsing (like Beauvais Cathedral, which he draws "after" Auguste Choisy, an important influence on his work from this date). It was the tubular steel frame, welded and capable of enormous spans, "worthy of being exposed," that now held the promise of a new expressiveness, in his view, even surpassing the monumentality of Greco-Gothic construction: "Beauvais Cathedral needed the steel we have." His sketch of a giant welded-steel arcade on axis to an idealized cultural center illustrates the point.

Although Kahn's emphasis on the potential of lightweight structures seems uncharacteristic of the more massive classicism he was to pursue later in his career, it presages the sculptural space frame of his Philadelphia City Tower project, designed in 1954 with Anne Tyng. Significantly, he rejects the implication in Giedion's argument that monumentality can be created intentionally, advancing a theory that recalls (consciously or not) Alois Riegl's *Kunstwollen*. Monuments, Kahn states, are historical manifestations of "the desires, the aspirations, the love and hate" of an epoch. In later writings he would speak of an "existence will" of architectural form, what a building "wants to be."

While acknowledging that past monuments "cannot live again with the same intensity and meaning," Kahn affirms that their greatness and didactic value remain. His structural-historicist interpretation of the monument not only 270–72looks forward to a central theme of his own work, but anticipates the reprise of the monumentality question in the 1970s in the debate over postmodernism— a debate in which his work figures as an essential point of reference.

From Paul Zucker, ed., New Architecture and City Planning *(New York: Philosophical Library, Inc., 1944), pp. 577–88. Copyright © by the Philosophical Library, a division of Allied Books.*

Monumentality
Louis I. Kahn

Gold is a beautiful material. It belongs to the sculptor.

Monumentality in architecture may be defined as a quality, a spiritual quality inherent in a structure which conveys the feeling of its eternity, that it cannot be added to or changed. We feel that quality in the Parthenon, the recognized architectural symbol of Greek civilization.

Some argue that we are living in an unbalanced state of relativity which cannot be expressed with a single intensity of purpose. It is for that reason, I feel, that many of our confrères do not believe we are psychologically constituted to convey a quality of monumentality to our buildings.

But have we yet given full architectural expression to such social monuments as the school, the community or culture center? What stimulus, what movement, what social or political phenomenon shall we yet experience? What event or philosophy shall give rise to a will to commemorate its imprint on our civilization? What effect would such forces have on our architecture?

Science has given to the architect its explorations into new combinations of materials capable of great resistance to the forces of gravity and wind.

Recent experimenters and philosophers of painting, sculpture, and architecture have instilled new courage and spirit in the work of their fellow artists.

Monumentality is enigmatic. It cannot be intentionally created. Neither the finest material nor the most advanced technology need enter a work of monumental character for the same reason that the finest ink was not required to draw up the Magna Carta.

However, our architectural monuments indicate a striving for structural perfection which has contributed in great part to their impressiveness, clarity of form, and logical scale.

Stimulated and guided by knowledge we shall go far to develop the forms indigenous to our new materials and methods. It is, therefore, the concern of this paper to touch briefly on the broader horizons which science and skill have revealed to the architect and engineer and sketch the faint outlines of possible structural concepts and expressions they suggest.

No architect can rebuild a cathedral of another epoch embodying the desires, the aspirations, the love and hate of the people whose heritage it became. Therefore the images we have before us of monumental structures of the past cannot live again with the same intensity and meaning. Their faithful duplication is unreconcilable. But we dare not discard the lessons these buildings teach for they have the common characteristics of greatness upon which the buildings of our future must, in one sense or another, rely.

In Greek architecture engineering concerned itself fundamentally with materials in compression. Each stone or part forming the structural members was made to bear with accuracy on each other to avoid tensile action stone is incapable of enduring.

The great cathedral builders regarded the members of the structural skeleton with the same love of perfection and search for clarity of purpose. Out of periods of inexperience and fear when they erected over-massive core-filled veneered walls, grew a courageous theory of stone over stone vault skeleton producing a downward and outward thrust, which forces were conducted to a column or a wall provided with the added characteristic of the buttress which together took this combination of action. The buttress allowed lighter walls between the thrust points and these curtain walls were logically developed for the use of large glass windows. This structural concept, derived from earlier and cruder theories, gave birth to magnificent variations in the attempts to attain loftier heights and greater spans creating a spiritually emotional environment unsurpassed.

The influence of the Roman vault, the dome, the arch, has etched itself in deep furrows across the pages of architectural history. Through Romanesque, Gothic, Renaissance, and today, its basic forms and structural ideas have been felt. They will continue to reappear but with added powers made possible by our technology and engineering skill.

The engineer of the latter part of the nineteenth century developed from basic principles the formulas of the handbook. Demands of enormous building quantity and speed developed the handbook engineer who used its contents, more or less forgetting basic principles. Now we hear about continuity in structures, not a new word but recently an all-important word in engineering which promises to relegate the handbook to the archives.

The I-beam is an engineering accomplishment deriving its shape from an analysis of stresses involved in its use. It is designed so that the greater proportion of the area of cross section is concentrated as far as possible from the center of gravity. The shape adapted itself to ease of rolling and under test it was found that even the fillets, an aid in the rolling process, helped convey the stresses from one section to another in continuity.

Safety factors were adopted to cover possible inconsistencies in the composition of the material of manufacture. Large-scale machinery and equipment needed in its fabrication lead to standardization.

The combination of safety factors (ignorance factor as one engineer termed it) and standardization narrowed the practice of engineering to the selection of members from handbooks recommending sections much heavier than calculations would require and further limited the field of engineering expression stifling the creation of the more graceful forms which the stress diagrams indicated. For example, the common practice of using an I-beam as a cantilever has no relation to the stress diagram which shows that the required depth of material from the supporting end outward may decrease appreciably.

Joint construction in common practice treats every joint as a hinge which makes connections to columns and other members complex and ugly.

To attain greater strength with economy, a finer expression in the structural solution of the principle of concentrating the area of cross section away from the center of gravity is the tubular form since the greater the moment of inertia the greater the strength.

A bar of a certain area of cross section rolled into a tube of the same area of cross section (consequently of a larger diameter) would possess a strength enormously greater than the bar.

The tubular member is not new, but its wide use has been retarded by technological limitations in the construction of joints. Up until very recently welding has been outlawed by the building codes. In some cases, where it was permitted, it was required to make loading tests for every joint.

Structure designs must discard the present moment coefficients and evolve new

Section Thru Beauvais
after Auguste Choisy

calculations based on the effect of continuity in structures. The structural efficiency of rigid connection, in which the shear value and the resisting moment is at least equal to the values of the supporting member, is obtained by the welding of such connections. The column becomes part of the beam and takes on added duties not usually calculated for columns.

The engineer and architect must then go back to basic principles, must keep abreast with and consult the scientist for new knowledge, redevelop his judgment of the behavior of structures and acquire a new sense of form derived from design rather than piece together parts of convenient fabrication.

Riveted I-beam plate and angle construction is complex and graceless. Welding has opened the doors to vast accomplishments in pure engineering which allows forms of greater strength and efficiency to be used. The choice of structural forms is limitless even for given problems and therefore the aesthetic philosophy of the individual can be satisfied by his particular composition of plates, angles, and tubular forms accomplishing the same answer to the challenge of the forces of gravity and wind.

The ribs, vaults, domes, buttresses come back again only to enclose space in a more generous, far simpler way and in the hands of our present masters of building in a more emotionally stirring way. From stone, the part has become smaller and cannot be seen observed and tested by the scientist through spectroscopy or by photoelastic recordings. His finding may go the architect and engineer in the more elemental form of the formula, but by that means it shall have become an instrumental part of the builder's palette to be used without prejudice or fear. That is the modern way.

Gothic architecture, relying on basically simple construction formulas derived from experience and the material available, could only go so far. Beauvais Cathedral, its builders trying to reach greater spans and height, collapsed.

The compressive stress of stone is measured in hundreds of pounds.

While not only the compressive, but also the bending and tensile stress of steel is measured in thousands of pounds.

Beauvais Cathedral needed the steel we have. It needed the knowledge we have.

Glass would have revealed the sky and become a part of the enclosed space framed by an interplay of exposed tubular ribs, plates, and columns of a stainless metal formed true and faired into a continuous flow of lines expressive of their stress patterns. Each member would have been welded to the next to create a continuous structural unity worthy of being exposed because its engineering gives no resistance to the laws of beauty having its own aesthetic life. The metal would have now been aged into a friendly material protected from deterioration by its intrinsic composition.

This generation is looking forward to its duty and benefit to build for the masses with its problems of housing and health.

It is aware of our outmoded cities.

It accepts the airship as a vital need.

Factories have adopted horizontal assembly and shifting population has required the transformation of large tracts of virgin territory at least temporarily for complete human living.

The building of a complete permanent town was attempted and almost built for the workers at Willow Run.

The nation has adopted the beginnings of social reform.

War production may become normal production on the same scale accepted as sound economics.

Still untried but pledged stand the noble principles of the Atlantic Charter.

In the days we look forward to must then the cathedral, the culture center, the legislative palace, world island—the seat of the congress of nations, the palace of labor and industry, the monuments to commemorate the achievements and aspirations of our time, be built to resemble Chartres, Crystal Palace, Palazzo Strozzi, or the Taj Mahal?

War engineering achievements in concrete, steel, and wood are showing the signs of maturity appropriate to guide the minds entrusted with the conception of buildings of such high purpose. The giant major skeleton of the structure can assert its right to be seen. It need no longer be clothed for eye appeal. Marble and woods feel at ease in its presence. New wall products of transparent, translucent, and opaque material with exciting textures and color are suspended or otherwise fastened to the more delicate forms of the minor members. Slabs of paintings articulate the circulation in the vast sheltered space. Sculpture graces its interior.

Outstanding masters of building design indicated the direction an architect may take to unravel and translate into simple terms the complexity of modern requirements. They have restated the meaning of a wall, a post, a beam, a roof, and a window and their interrelation in space. They had to be restated when we recall the conglomerations that style-copying tortured these elements into.

Efforts towards a comprehensive architecture will help to develop these elements and refine their meaning. A wall dividing interior space is not the same wall dividing the outside from the interior. Masonry shall always function as retaining and garden walls. It may be used for exterior walls for its decorative qualities, but be supplemented by interior slabs designed to meet more directly the challenge of the elements.

Structural ingenuity may eliminate the interior post, but as long as it must exist its place is reserved and its independence respected in the planning of space.

Structural problems center about the roof. The permanence and beauty of its surfaces is a major problem confronting science. The surfacing of the domes, vaults and arches appearing as part of the exterior contours of the building may be an integral part of the structural design. Stainless metal, concrete, or structural plastics, structural glass in light panes, or great reinforced glass castings may be the choice for domes and vaults, depending on the requirements, the climate, and the desired effect. The surfacing of flat roofs should be given equally serious consideration whether it is planned for use or not.

The citizens of a metropolitan area of a city and their representatives have formulated a program for a culture center endorsed by the national educational center. The citizens' committee collaborated with the architect and his staff of engineers. Costs were not discussed. Time was not "of the essence." Its progress was the concern of many.

From above we see the noble outlines of the building. Much taller buildings some distance from the site do not impress us with the same feeling of receptiveness. Its site is a prominent elevation in the outlying countryside framed by dark forests defining the interior of broad strokes in land architecture.

On the ground the first reaction comes from the gigantic sculptural forms of the skeleton frame. The backbone of the architect's central idea successfully challenges the forces which during its design challenged to destroy it. To solve the more minute complexities of the entire organism, its creator had drawn his conclusions and made his decisions from the influences of many people and things around him.

The plan does not begin nor end with the space he has enveloped, but from the adjoining delicate ground sculpture it stretches beyond to the rolling contours and vegetation of the surrounding land and continues farther out to the distant hills.

The immediate ground sculpture disciplined his mind in shaping it into stronger geometric planes and cubes to satisfy his desire for terraces and pools, steps and approaches. The landscape designer countered or accentuated these planes with again geometric and free forms interwoven with the lace leaf patterns of the deciduous tree.

The plans reveal that the vast spans shelter smaller areas designed for specific use, which are divided from the whole by panels of glass, insulated slabs, and marble. These partitions are free of the structure unrelated only to the circulation pattern. The ground plan seems continuous. The great lobby is part of the amphitheater which dips down to the stage. The light comes from above through an undulating series of prismatic glass domes.

Ahead, some distance from the entrance, is a great mural of brilliant color. As we approach it the forms clearly defined from a distance seem to divide into forms of their own, each with its own color power, clear and uncultured.

To one side is the community museum of sculpture, painting, and crafts. It exhibits the work of the younger men and women attending the vocational art academies. Here they are accepted because their talents can be judged by those who have themselves been instructed in the basic principles underlying the use of a material. The emotional adaptations are left for the exhibitor himself to evaluate by contact, comparison, and experience.

Sculpture shows the tendency to define form and construction. Marble and stone is carved as of old. Castings in new alloys and plastics are favorite methods of obtaining permanency. Solids are interwoven with sheets and tubes of metal. The subject matter exhibited has no bounds. With the new materials and tools, chemical tints, and with manufacture at the artist's disposal, his work becomes alive with ideas. Metal sprays and texture guns with fine adjustments have also become the instruments of the sculptor, painter, and craftsman. One of the younger men had cast within a large, irregular cube of transparent plastic other forms and objects of brilliant color. A sphere, planes at various angles, copper wire in free lines are seen through the plastic.

From these experiments in form the architect will eventually learn to choose appropriate embellishments for his structures. So far he has omitted them. His judgment leads him to freestanding forms in space.

Some of the younger artists are influenced by the works of an older sculptor who has developed a theory of scale in relation to space. He has argued that as the size of the structural work is increased the monolithic character of smaller work does not apply. He chose for large work a small consistent part or module of a definite shape, a cube, a prism, or a sphere which he used to construct block over block, with delicate adjustments to the effect of light and shadow, the overall form. His work seen from great distances retains a texturally vibrant quality produced by these numerous blocks and action of the sun upon them.

Before we can feel the new spirit which must envelop the days to come we must prepare ourselves to use intelligently the knowledge derived from all sources. Nostalgic yearning for the ways of the past will find but few ineffectual supporters.

Steel, the lighter metals, concrete, glass, laminated woods, asbestos, rubber, and plastics are emerging the prime building materials of today. Riveting is being replaced by welding, reinforced concrete is emerging from infancy with prestressed reinforced concrete, vibration, and controlled mixing, promising to aid in its ultimate refinement. Laminated wood is rapidly replacing lumber and is equally friendly to the eye, and plastics are so vast in their potentialities that already numerous journals and periodicals devoted solely to their many outlets are read with interest and hope. The untested characteristics of these materials are being analyzed, old formulas are being discarded. New alloys of steel, shatter-proof and thermal glass and synthetics of innumerable types, together with the material already mentioned, make up the new palette of the designer.

To what extent progress in building will be retarded by ownership patterns, dogmas, style consciousness, precedent, untested building materials, arbitrary standards, outmoded laws and regulations, untrained workmen, and artless craftsmen is speculation. But the findings of science and their application have taken large steps recently in the development of war materials which point to upset normally controlled progress and raise our hopes to the optimistic level.

Standardization, prefabrication, controlled experiments and tests, and specialization are no monsters to be avoided by the delicate sensitiveness of the artist. They are merely the modern means of controlling vast potentialities of materials for living, by chemistry, physics, engineering, production, and assembly, which lead to the necessary knowledge the artist must have to expel fear in their use, broaden his creative instinct, give him new courage and thereby lead him to the adventures of unexplored places. His work will then be part of his age and will afford delight and service for his contemporaries.

I do not wish to imply that monumentality can be attained scientifically or that the work of the architect reaches its greatest service to humanity by his peculiar genius to guide a concept toward a monumentality. I merely defend, because I admire, the architect who possesses the will to grow with the many angles of our development. For such a man finds himself far ahead of his fellow workers.

1944

In his retrospective *res gestae*, *Public Works: A Dangerous Trade* (1970), a chronicle of his tenure from 1924 to 1968 as a hard-nosed New York City bureaucrat and politician, **Robert Moses** reiterated his view that of the theorist, idealist, and realist, it is the last who "is most respected in emergencies and lasts longest." In this vein, Moses here assails the various forms of socialized land ownership and public intervention proposed by utopian and academic architects and planners. Unabashedly xenophobic, he seeks to debunk the theories of the best-known members of the emigré architectural community in the United States—Eliel Saarinen, Walter Gropius, Eric Mendelsohn— together with such "native Americans" as Frank Lloyd Wright and Lewis Mumford.

Moses himself would play the double role of archcapitalist and populist during his career. As Irving Howe wrote in *The Magazine of Art* in 1942 of Moses's accomplishments to that date, "the public services, parkways, and recreation areas of New York are an effort to superimpose a new way of life on brick, smoke, and sewage, to make the land a likeness of the people so that the people may come to be a likeness of the land." At the time of the writing that follows Moses was in the process of capitalizing on the impending electoral defeat of his long-time collaborator and adversary, New Deal mayor of New York Fiorello La Guardia. By insinuating himself into the camp of William O'Dwyer, who would emerge victorious from the mayoral race in 1945, he consolidated his prior roles as unelected head of numerous city agencies under the title of City Construction Coordinator, a previously nonexistent post. If before the war he had been content with "weaving together the loose strands and frayed edges of New York's metropolitan arterial tapestry"—as well as providing destinations for the new arteries like Jones Beach on Long Island—his postwar position empowered him to realize public works on a grand scale. With the passage of Title I of the Federal Housing Act in 1949, he had broad prerogative to condemn property in the name of "urban renewal" and a virtually blank slate for mass housing.

At the height of his operations Moses employed nearly 2,000 architects. Ironically, his housing projects ultimately derived (in compromised form) from the urbanism whose exponents he condemns in the following article. Le Corbusier's Radiant City had perhaps its fullest application anywhere under the auspices of Moses's Slum Clearance Committee. An earlier project like Stuyvesant Town (1943–48), constructed by the Metropolitan Life Insurance Company for returning veterans, had already established the precedent of building at the expense of mass evictions of the urban poor and destruction of existing communities. It was the disregard for the continuity of local culture that infuriated New York critics and planners like Jane Jacobs and Lewis Mumford. Jacobs's *The Death and Life of Great American Cities* (1961) was an attack on Moses's plans for her West Village neighborhood, while Mumford, a long-time resident of Clarence Stein's visionary Sunnyside, Queens, vented his criticism of Moses in his "Skyline" columns in the *New Yorker*. This backlash spawned the advocacy movement, a grass-roots planning effort that had its greatest effectiveness in the late 1960s.

"Mr. Moses Dissects the 'Long-Haired Planners'" was rebutted at the time of its writing by Harvard School of Design dean Joseph Hudnut. In a letter to the *New York Times* (July 23, 1944), Hudnut rose to defend the architects Moses attacked, charging him with demagoguery and attempting to safeguard the role of the professional planner from the cynical expediency of the politician.

338–40

442–45

Originally titled "Mr. Moses Dissects the 'Long-Haired Planners': The Park Commissioner Prefers Common Sense to Their Revolutionary Theories." From The New York Times Magazine, *June 25, 1944, pp. 16–18, 38–39. Copyright © 1944 by the* New York Times. *Reprinted by permission.*

Mr. Moses Dissects the "Long-Haired Planners"
Robert Moses

In municipal planning we must decide between revolution and common sense—between the subsidized llamas in their remote mountain temples and those who must work in the market place. It is a mistake to underestimate the revolutionaries. They do not reach the masses directly, but through familiar subsurface activities. They teach the teachers. They reach people in high places, who in turn influence the press, universities, societies learned and otherwise, radio networks, the stage, the screen, even churches. They make the TNT for those who throw the bombs. They have their own curious lingo and double talk, their cabalistic writings, secret passwords, and abracadabra.

First, let's have a general look at the "Beiunskis." A Beiunski is usually a refugee whose critical faculties outrun his gratitude to the country which has given him a home. He is convinced that we are a pretty backward people and doesn't mind saying that they ordered things better in the old country. "Bei uns," he says, they did it this way. The fact that we happen to like our awkward and primitive ways will not turn any genuine Beiunski from the stern task of teaching us how really cultured folks should behave. You have to be quite humorless to be a good Beiunski.

Only the other day a famous Beiunski, author of God knows how many books, sufferer for years from logorrhea and now living in a hotel overlooking one of our New York parks, wrote this gem of advice and ponderous fun to the Mayor for transmission to the city Park Commissioner:

My dear Mayor: As I know that you take small things as earnest as the so-called big things, I beg to communicate:

Daily I enjoy the skating on the small lake at the south end of Central Park. By two small improvements many occasions for falls could be avoided:

1.   The wood bridge leading from the dressing room to the ice is so overused that it should be renovated.

2.   In Europe we used to spread water on the furrowed ice at night, so that it might freeze over until the morning, and therefore form a smooth surface again.*

Hoping that you could find for me a quiet hour during the next month, I remain, dear Mr. La Guardia,

*   Yours very sincerely—*

*If there is a lack of workmen, I would be glad to do it myself every evening with a watering can and a flashlight.

Let us look now at the writings of Eliel Saarinen, who was born, educated, and practiced architecture at Helsingfors, Finland, came to the United States, and founded the Cranbrook Academy of Art in Michigan. Saarinen is one of the really great architects of our time, who forsook his profession to become a revolutionary planner. He is bitter about our faults. Saarinen believes in what he calls "organic decentralization." Here are some of the things he says about it in "The City—Its Growth—Its Decay—Its Future":

. . . concentration in the overgrown cities has caused compactness and disorder and, through these, deterioration and the spread of slums. . . . the only remedy in such circumstances is a decisive surgery which can bring openness into the compact urban

situation, and which—if executed gradually according to an organically comprehensive scheme—is the surest road . . . toward "organic decentralization." . . . It might be true, perhaps, that the most direct way of reaching this goal would be to try the decentralization principles on actual town building, so as to gather experience through practical realities rather than through theoretical generalities. However logical such a thought may sound, it must be borne in mind that in "practical realities" organic decentralization is a slow process. . . . Matters being so, it is necessary for the time being to lean upon illuminating reasoning.

This "illuminating reasoning" leads Saarinen straight into communal land ownership. Here it is in the usual jargon:

Transference of property rights is an essential part of the processes of organic decentralization. . . . This law is so much the more necessary because of the fact that transference of property rights to a considerable degree means a corresponding transference of people from one location in the city to another.

Obviously, Saarinen thinks he can apply Scandinavian experience to American conditions. This is the way they do it in Stockholm, according to John Graham Jr. in Housing in Scandinavia:

In the Inner City, property owned by the city is sold to private enterprise at prevailing market prices. The city may also sell its land in the Inner City area at a figure lower than the market value when the city is assured that the land will be put to a social use or, as expressed by the Stockholm authorities, "when the city is certain that the benefit of the low price of the land will actually redound to the good of the tenants and not the advantage of the purchaser."

If this strikes you as pretty strong stuff, have a look at another distinguished foreign figure in our midst, Walter Gropius. In his biography in Who's Who Professor Gropius describes himself as born in Berlin, founder of the Bauhaus School of Architecture, which he moved from Weimar to Dessau in Germany and thence to Harvard and Chicago universities. The Bauhaus School is known for functionalism, abstract art, and other brilliant and revolutionary ideas.

Intelligent Americans are just beginning to realize that Gropius is hurting our architecture by advocating a philosophy which doesn't belong here and fundamentally offers nothing more novel than the lally column and the two-by-four timber. Here is a quotation from The New Architecture and the Bauhaus:

It was realized that the present plight of our cities was due to an alarmingly rapid increase of the kind of functional maladies to which it is only in the natural order of things for all aging bodies to be subject; and that these disorders urgently called for drastic surgical treatment. . . . Once the evils which produce the chaotic disorganization of our towns have been accurately diagnosed, and their endemic character demonstrated, we must see that they are permanently eradicated. The most propitious environment for propagating the New Architecture is obviously where a new way of thinking corresponding with it has already penetrated. It is only among intelligent, professional, and public-spirited circles that we can hope to arouse a determination to have done

Corlears Hook Park, opposite the Brooklyn Navy Yard, reclaimed and built out into the East River Drive running through it, public housing projects on its borders—part of the East Side reclamation. Not a pipe dream, but a reality. [Courtesy of New York City Parks Photo Archive]

with the noxious anarchy of our towns.

Still another prominent modernistic architect, Eric Mendelsohn, formerly practicing in Germany and now settled in this country, in a recent lecture at the University of California contributed this little "ipse dixit" to the solution of the city traffic problem:

In the master town plan motor traffic will bypass the city area, or run as part of an independent speed network from end-stations and flying fields, underground, to the focal points of industrial, business, and residential quarters, thus clearing the city of all surface mechanical traffic.

This is certainly a cute trick if you can do it.

A few months ago there appeared in *Time* an illustrated tabloid article under the heading "Science" about an engineer-architect, described as a widely famed city planner in Britain and on the Continent before the war, now studying United States city problems on a grant from the American Philosophical Society, with the help of his wife, a physicist teaching at Queens College, and a Harvard architect of the Bauhaus School.

The studies of this group convinced them that Manhattan's basic trouble is hardening of the arteries. It may be mentioned in passing that many radical planners habitually compare municipal diseases and cures to those of the human body. This little group of earnest thinkers begins by ripping up Manhattan's midriff. A belt highway is installed eighty feet high, with six separate levels for trucks, buses, passenger cars, etc., including two levels for parking. Avenues a century old are eliminated, together with ninety per cent of the present crosstown streets. Fifteen present blocks are thrown together into each of a group of separate villages. The estimated cost of $250,000,000— about one-fifth of the correct figure.

The British revolutionary planners have had great influence here. Let us, for example, take this description in *The Architectural Forum* of November 1943 of the Uthwatt Report prepared by the Expert Committee on Compensation and Betterment and presented to the British Parliament in September 1942 by the Minister of Works and Planning:

. . . the committee proposed 1. immediate nationalization of all development rights by purchase for fair compensation in the name of the Authority; 2. all new development to be prohibited unless initiated or approved by the Authority; 3. all land to be used for new development to be acquired at fair value (less "development right") by the Authority and leased to the developer.

The *Forum* article did not exaggerate, if we judge by this direct quotation from Mr. Justice Uthwatt's committee, one of those little gems which blush unseen in the star-spangled galaxy lighting us from the midwife to the mortician:

Immediate transfer to public ownership of all land would present the logical solution, but we have no doubt that land nationalization is not practicable as an immediate measure and we reject it on that ground alone.

Stalwarts who shudder at a two-mill rise in the tax rate, who denounce postwar public works, who threaten the town with bankruptcy and ruin if municipal services are not drastically cut, demand that bureaucracy be curbed, and howl dismally if zoning standards are raised sufficiently to insure light, air, and decent living praise Uthwatt and pass the dynamite.

So intrigued were the Luce publications by the Uthwatt line of reasoning that they endorsed the entire revolutionary scheme of land expropriation and promptly developed the thesis that the revolutionaries are the true strategists while the practical planners are merely tacticians. *Fortune* in a recent number, entitled "City Planning: Battle of the Approach," said:

Another principle of modern planning, either ignored or shunned by the strictly tactical school, is that in order to be fully effective, city planning must be based on public control of the use of urban land. This means all the land without as well as within the city limits that is ever likely to become in fact a part of the urban community.

During all the popular emphasis on beautification, spectacular piecemeal attacks on specific urban problems, and half-baked public works programs, there has been growing in the minds of a handful of thinkers and planners a real grasp of fundamentals.

Vast and complicated as the whole job may appear, there is no good reason to look upon it as impossible. Strategy, to be sure, does demand a broader view of the problems of an urban community in its entirety than has been taken thus far anywhere in the world, except by the starry-eyed planners so unpopular with Commissioner Moses.

In metropolitan planning the tacticians, if that is to be our name, adapt, modify, improvise, improve, boldly but with some respect for our heritage. How often do we have the opportunity to work with the blank page, the untouched canvas, the raw land? Jones Beach and the Long Island parkway system were an exception. Why didn't the strategists seize the opportunity? Simply because it was too tough and long a fight with politics, local and big real estate opposition, legislative ignorance and stubborn nature. And, as to things nearer home, where vested interests are really entrenched, what strategists in the Harvard schools of Architecture, Regional Planning, and Economics and in editorial sanctums have been seen on the side of the angels in the sweat and mud of battle?

In a recent rather sour comment on the city's postwar program, as reflected in the exhibit recently opened to the public, a well-known New York daily newspaper made this editorial comment:

But the beauties of a program like this (unsustained as yet on any considered financial foundation) should not blind one to the fact that it does not reach to those fundamental factors of land use, land values, tax assessments, rents, and building costs which really determine the growth of a city. The program is a handsome poultice, standing ready to be slapped on the face of old New York when somebody provides the cash for the beauty treatment; it is in no sense a cure for the deeper problems which afflict her anatomy.

Let us see where this brilliant metaphor leads us. Poultices our plans may be, but is this editor really prepared to endorse the big surgical operation hinted at? Let's be sure of our diagnosis and not confuse the need of new plumbing with demands for a laparotomy. Let us remember that the surgeon is a bureaucratic government, reaching into our very vitals, and that the city might not recover from the shock of the operation. Moreover, who will pay the doctor's bill? Perhaps the patient isn't at death's door and merely needs a few vitamins. Would this paper support a program of Government ownership and control of land, drastic and arbitrary regulation of its use, complete deflation of the present real estate tax system, and adoption of the foreign revolutionary program which obviously influenced its editor? You know the answer.

Now for Frank Lloyd Wright of Wisconsin, another brilliant but erratic architect and planner. Regarded in Russia as our greatest builder, he has been enormously popular everywhere abroad. He is the author of *The Disappearing City* and founder of the Taliesin Fellowship, described as a cultural experiment in the fine arts. Here are a few samples from Frank Lloyd Wright's *Modern Architecture:*

Even the small town is too large. It will gradually merge into the general nonurban development. Ruralism as distinguished from Urbanism is American, and truly Democratic.

Last year I received from Mr. Wright a copy of his book *Taliesin* with a friendly note. The understanding was that the book would be passed around among the men upon whom I lean for advice. This reply summarizes their conclusions:

While we were generally familiar with your publications and views, my little group of earnest thinkers, or rather constructors, have read the Taliesin Pamphlet *and your more recent memorandum with considerable interest. The consensus of opinion is that we do not fully understand them. Some of the implications are most interesting, and, of course, we respect your accomplishments in the field of architecture, but it seems to us that you have taken on a little too much territory. Most of my boys feel that you would get further if you tried an experiment on a reasonable scale, frankly called it an .experiment, and refrained from announcing that it was the pattern of all future American living.*

There it is. You can't expect anything better from moles who are blind, crawl short distances under the earth, and have only the most limited objectives.

Then there is Lewis Mumford, lecturer on planning and author of *The Culture of Cities,* an outspoken revolutionary, often quoted with approval by conservatives who obviously have no notion of the implications of his philosophy. Here are Mumford's Six Stages in the Cycle of the City:

First Stage: Eopolis. Rise of the village community.
Second Stage: Polis. An association of villages or block groups having a common site that lends itself to defense against depredation.
Third Stage: Metropolis. Within the region one city emerges from the less differentiated groups of villages and country towns. . . . It becomes the . . . "mother-city."
Fourth Stage: Megalopolis. Beginning of the decline. The city under the influence of a capitalistic mythos concentrates upon bigness and power. The owners of the instruments of production and distribution subordinate every other fact in life to the achievement

of riches and the display of wealth.

Fifth Stage: Tyrannopolis. Extensions of parasitism throughout the economic and social scene: the function of spending paralyzes all the higher activities of culture and no act of culture can be justified that does not involve display and expense.

Sixth and Final Stage: Nekropolis. War and famine and disease rack both city and countryside . . . the city of the dead; flesh turned to ashes; life turned into a meaningless pillar of salt.

The progress is faintly reminiscent of the herpicide tragedy—"going, going, gone, too late for Mumford."

This brings us logically to my friend Rexford Guy Tugwell, professor, brain truster, former Under-Secretary of Agriculture and head of the Resettlement Administration, former chairman of the City Planning Commission of New York, now Governor of Puerto Rico, and author of *The Fourth Power,* a book in which he advocates the establishment of a planning authority, with members chosen for life, wholly independent of and somewhat above the executive, legislative, and judicial functions of the Government, as the last and absolute authority on all matters economic and physical.

Here is a revealing quotation from Dr. Tugwell's "The Principle of Planning and the Institution of Laissez-Faire":

The intention of eighteenth- and nineteenth-century law was to install and predict the principle of conflict; this, if we begin to plan, we shall be changing once for all, and it will require the laying of rough, unholy hands on many a sacred precedent, doubtless calling on an enlarged and nationalized police power for enforcement. We shall also have to give up a distinction of great consequence, and very dear to many a legalistic heart, but economically quite absurd, between private and public or quasipublic employments. There is no private business, if we mean by that one of no consequence to anyone but its proprietors; and so none exempt from compulsion to serve a planned public interest. Furthermore, we shall have to press sufficiently far in elementary realism to recognize that only the Federal area, and often not even that, is large enough to be coextensive with modern industry; and that consequently the States are wholly ineffective instruments for control. All three of these wholesale changes are required by even a limited acceptance of the planning idea.

This is the way the Fourth Power Planning Commission, called by Dr. Tugwell "the directive," will proceed when they get control, as described by Dr. Tugwell:

. . . evolution must necessarily be toward cooperative forms, collective customs, pragmatic morality, and technically buttressed leadership; because this is what will give us the greatest product; and also because this is the only door to the future which is available to those who regard the avoidance of force as a necessity.

In December 1940, Dr. Tugwell, as chairman of the New York City Planning Commission, proposed a new and revolutionary plan of land use. Boards of trade and real estate organizations, as well as civic groups whose tendency is to the left, fell for this green-belt plan. A handful of realists blew it up. At the public hearing before the Planning Commission, at which Dr. Tugwell presided, I made this statement:

According to the figures in the staff report, you propose to increase the area of the "green belts" by about 48,000 acres. You propose, by the adoption of this plan, to notify the owners of one-third of all the taxable land in the city shown on the land-use map as "green belts" that they are foolish to continue paying their taxes and that it's just like throwing money in the sewer, since the land has no "economic future" for residence, business, or industry. Just what do you expect this to do to property owners and to the city's financial structure?

No one in this city has greater enthusiasm for the expansion of park and recreation areas than I have, and this applies with equal force to the city's State officials who for years have labored to develop and coordinate the city, suburban, and state park and arterial program in New York. This group, as the result of long practical experience, has developed a healthy contempt for the kind of watercolor planning which consists of splashing green paint at a map and labeling the resulting blobs as "open areas," "green belts," "breathing spaces," etc. Actual accomplishments in New York City since 1934, and in the state and suburbs since 1924, were brought about by people who labored day and night for limited objectives in the face of great difficulties. These accomplishments were not brought about by itinerant carpetbag experts splashing at a ten-league canvas with brushes of comet's hair. I recommend that you file the "Master Plan of Land Use" and forget it.

That was the end of the green-belt scheme, and nothing has been heard of it since.

Adolf Berle, Dr. Tugwell's predecessor as chairman of the City Planning Commission, on the eve of his resignation to become Assistant Secretary of State, lunched with me to talk over some details he was mopping up. As he struggled with his overcoat he left with me this farewell, which I hereby contributed to the growing collection of Berliana: "It's all very well for you, Bob, to spend your time on local street openings, but I'm off to Washington to solve the Chinese problem." You can't ask a global planner to waste his time on the sidewalks of New York.

There are too many people who not only lack the ability to work with others toward realizable objectives but who do not like the community and therefore want to tear it up by the roots, toss the pieces in the air, and start afresh in the open country. The man who loves his city will recognize its faults and shortcomings, but will never damn it entirely out of hand and dismiss it as a monstrosity. It takes time to plan a city, as Vachel Lindsay said in his famous poem, "On the Building of Springfield":

Record it for the grandson of your son—
A city is not builded in a day.
Our little town cannot complete her soul
Till countless generations pass away.

The man who does not love his country and his own town can do nothing for them. It does not matter whether it be the land or place of his birth or of his adoption—so long as he becomes part and parcel of it. Carl Schurz did as much for the United States as any native son of no matter how deep and distinguished roots. The patriotic conservative will find plenty of faults at home. He should be eager to remedy them, but he must be loyal to the institutions and to the local scene in which his lot is cast. To revolutionary planning sophisticates this will seem simple to the point of imbecility, but truths, like ballads, are always simple.

1945

Espace indicible: **Le Corbusier**'s credo attesting to the transcendent power of painting, sculpture, and architecture opens his 1948 book *New World of Space.* It was conceived three years earlier when, as the architect describes in a note in *Modulor 2,* he was inspired by the almost mystical experience of staring at one of his paintings on a wall of his house until the wall seemed to dissolve under the intensity of his reverie. Le Corbusier originally published it in 1946 in a special issue of *L'Architecture d'Aujourd'hui* entitled "Art," and he republished it in both *The Modulor* (1950) and *Modulor 2* (1955). He also left fragmentary notes for a book of the same title which he contemplated writing as late as 1959.

The idea of art as an access to a metaphorical "fourth dimension," an all-encompassing release from real time and space, had been foreseen by the poet Apollinaire with respect to cubism in 1910. But Le Corbusier's fervent reaffirmation of this notion in the context of not only painting and sculpture but architecture came at a crucial point in his career, after a moment of "enforced silence." His experience of the war years was deeply disillusioning. The German occupation of Paris in 1940 caused him to abandon his studio for the small town of Ozon in the Pyrenees, in the demilitarized zone of the country controlled by the pro-German Vichy regime. There Le Corbusier spent eighteen months painting, writing, and making trips to the wartime capital in central France, trying to persuade the puppet administration of Marshal Pétain to grant him a major role in planning the reconstruction of postwar France. This ambivalent episode in his career was in large part an effort to obtain a go-ahead to proceed with his grand schemes of the 1930s, in particular his project for Algiers. It was also, however, the culmination of his increasing attraction to the elitist and authoritarian politics of French syndicalism at a time when, disenchanted with the premises of liberal democracy on the American model, he came to believe that technocratic planning was the best route to sweeping social transformation and the implementation of a new architectural order. The Algiers plan was unanimously rejected by the Vichy government in 1942 after a hostile campaign waged in the local press. Although Le Corbusier never expressed regrets about his would-be affiliation with Vichy, his rebuff there was decisive in returning him to a more moderate—if more cynical—view of power and his own political role: "in the end you find that you are not capable of understanding everything and that it is better to do than not to do, to do than to say."

Despite his frustration and curtailment of professional activity in these years—or because of it—however, his editorial and theoretical production was nothing short of astonishing. Between 1941 and 1944 he was responsible for six books. Returning to Paris in 1943 he established and chaired the Assemblée de Constructeurs pour une Rénovation Architecturale (ASCORAL), a French section of CIAM, which issued the volume *Manière de penser l'urbanisme;* and he anonymously edited the *Charte d'Athènes,* published under the ASCORAL emblem the same year with a portentous introduction by Jean Giraudoux. He also began developing his "tool of universality," the Modulor, a measurement scale keyed to the proportions of the human body and based on the golden section.

Yet it was the "ineffable" vision of Le Corbusier's more private persona, that of the painter and artist, that provided a necessary reconciliation for the thwarted reformism of the public man during these years. He thus came to see the domination and control of space within the work itself as the highest possible manifestation of the architect's will. The dialectic that had always existed in his thought between the creative intuition of art—of "pure plastic emotion"—and the geometric rationalism governing architecture now found a synthesis within architecture and the poetry latent in the right angle. The latter became the subject of an "autobiographical" visual-verbal poem written between 1948 and 1952. Geometry, based on "hidden laws" of harmony, could become an instrument of enormous power when, and only when, it was imbued with the most acute plastic sensibility.

The concomitant accent in Le Corbusier's writing at this date on the more extroverted theme of a synthesis of the "major arts"—painting, sculpture, architecture—also reflects the shift in his thinking from a sociopolitical to a more aesthetic and symbolic vision of architecture. The idea, which had perhaps always been implicit in Le Corbusier's thought, was first broached directly at CIAM's Athens congress in 1933 by Fernand Léger, for whom it was later to *27–30* become associated with the idea of a modern monumentality. Le Corbusier himself explicitly spoke of a synthesis of the arts in an article two years later. But it was after the war that it would become a characteristic theme, taking on an emancipatory charge in an appeal that he published in December 1944, five months after the liberation of Paris, in the journal *Volontés*, an organ of the French Resistance to which he was now a contributor: "C'est une épopée plastique qui commence." The special 1946 issue of *L'Architecture d'Aujourd'hui*, containing the original of the text that follows, consisted of sections on architecture, painting, sculpture, and tapestry illustrating work by Le Corbusier, Brancusi, Picasso, Giacometti, Savina, Léger, Miro, and Jean Lurçat, among others, and addressing the question of artistic collaboration. A year later, *100–2* the theme would be adopted by CIAM at its Bridgwater congress, and in 1950 by the Groupe Espace—an international association of artists and architects formed in Paris—as a founding program. Meanwhile, it took architectural form in 1950 in Le Corbusier's two "Porte Maillot" projects for temporary and permanent exhibition pavilions.

But above all the revelation of *espace indicible* opened the path that would lead Le Corbusier over the next two decades from the inspired rationalism of his early and middle career to the poetic transcendence of his late realizations: from the Unité d'Habitation in Marseilles (1946–52) to the church of Ronchamp (1950–54), the monastery of La Tourette (1957–60), and the Indian capital complex at Chandigarh (1952–65).

For more on the transformation of Le Corbusier's politics from the 1930s through the war years, see the forthcoming book by Mary McLeod, *Urbanism and Utopia: Le Corbusier from Regional Syndicalism to Vichy.*

Published as "L'Espace Indicible" in L'Architecture d'Aujourd'hui, *out of series number "Art," January 1946, pp. 9–10. English translation in Le Corbusier,* New World of Space *(New York: Reynal & Hitchcock, 1948), pp. 7–9. Courtesy of Fondation Le Corbusier.*

Ineffable Space
Le Corbusier

Taking possession of space is the first gesture of living things, of men and of animals, of plants and of clouds, a fundamental manifestation of equilibrium and of duration. The occupation of space is the first proof of existence.

The flower, the plant, the tree, the mountain stand forth, existing in a setting. If they one day command attention because of their satisfying and independent forms, it is because they are seen to be isolated from their context and extending influences all around them. We pause, struck by such interrelation in nature, and we gaze, moved by this harmonious orchestration of space, and we realize that we are looking at the reflection of light.

Architecture, sculpture, and painting are specifically dependent on space, bound to the necessity of controlling space, each by its own appropriate means. The essential thing that will be said here is that the release of aesthetic emotion is a special function of space.

Action of the work (architecture, statue, or painting) on its surroundings: vibrations, cries or shouts (such as originate from the Parthenon on the Acropolis in Athens), arrows darting away like rays, as if springing from an explosion; the near or distant site is shaken by them, touched, wounded, dominated, or caressed. *Reaction of the setting:* the walls of the room, its dimensions, the public square with the various weights of its facades, the expanses or the slopes of the landscape even to the bare horizons of the plain or the sharp outlines of the mountains—the whole environment brings its weight to bear on the place where there is a work of art, the sign of man's will, and imposes on it its deep spaces or projections, its hard or soft densities, its violences or its softnesses. A phenomenon of concordance takes place, as exact as mathematics, a true manifestation of plastic acoustics; thus one may speak of one of the most subtle of all orders of phenomena, sound, as a conveyor of joy (music) or of oppression (racket).

Without making undue claims, I may say something about the "magnification" of space that some of the artists of my generation attempted around 1910, during the wonderfully creative flights of cubism. They spoke of the *fourth dimension* with intuition and clairvoyance. A life devoted to art, and especially to a search after harmony, has enabled me, in my turn, to observe the same phenomenon through the practice of three arts: architecture, sculpture, and painting.

The fourth dimension is the moment of limitless escape evoked by an exceptionally just consonance of the plastic means employed.

It is not the effect of the subject chosen; it is a victory of proportion in everything—the anatomy of the work as well as the carrying out of the artist's intentions whether consciously controlled or not. Achieved or unachieved, these intentions are always existent and rooted in intuition, that miraculous catalyst of acquired, assimilated, even forgotten wisdom. In a complete and successful work there are hidden masses of implications, a veritable world which reveals itself to those whom it may concern, which means: to those who deserve it.

Then a boundless depth opens up, effaces the walls, drives away contingent presences, *accomplishes the miracle of ineffable space.*

I am not conscious of the miracle of faith, but I often live that of ineffable space, the consummation of plastic emotion.

Here I have been allowed to speak as a man of the laboratory, dealing with his personal experiments carried out in the major arts which have been so unfortunately dissociated or separated for a century. Architecture, sculpture, painting: the movement of time and of events now unquestionably leads them toward a synthesis.

[The figure] necessitates the horizon of the ground or architectural walls. Infinite horizon into which the radiant waves are going to sink, architectural walls poised to echo, to bring to life this acoustic time-space phenomenon evoked at the beginning of these notes. [Untitled, but one of the "Ozon" series, oil on wood, 1929/1944. From L'Architecture d'Aujourd'hui, *January 1946, pp. 16–17. Copyright © 1992 ARS, N.Y./SPADEM, Paris.]*

1945

With his book *Verso un'architettura organica* (published in 1945, in English in 1950), Bruno Zevi launched a new debate within Italian architectural discourse. The concept of "organic architecture" was derived from the architecture and

31–41

writings of Frank Lloyd Wright, by which Zevi had been strongly affected while finishing his architecture education in the United States during the war. Zevi soon

249–52

broadened it to embrace the architecture of Alvar Aalto and much else that he deemed to be "humanistic" and "democratic." The rhetoric of democracy had a potent, if still artificial, ring in a country recently liberated from authoritarianism and trying to grasp the complexities of transforming a fascist bureaucracy into the liberal administrative structures of modern planning. Organic architecture was intended as to have an emancipatory effect in sociopolitical terms as well as to provide a spatial critique of the rigidity and academicism Zevi considered implicit in "rationalism." "The organic in architecture is defined in opposition to the theoretical, the geometric, the artificial standards, the white boxes and cylinders so much part of the first period of modern architecture," he wrote.

While this was hardly a sufficient description on which to inaugurate a new design practice—especially given the inherent difficulty of translating the Wright model to Italian soil—and still less a social movement, Zevi's founding in the same year of the review *Metron,* under the editorial direction of Luigi Piccinato and Mario Ridolfi, and of the Association for Organic Architecture (**APAO**) afforded his cause two instruments of some moment. Groups of young architects in search of a rallying point gathered in Rome, Palermo, Turin, and elsewhere around the slogan of organicism. The Italian scene became engaged in these years in the debate between Zevi's "battle for an integrated culture, an integrated architecture" and proposals for an evolutionary development within the historical perspective of prewar Italian rationalism, the latter position

77–79

promoted by a group formed in Milan at the same time—Movimento Studi d'Architettura (MSA).

APAO's attempts to function as a political pressure group—calling for socialization of industrial, financial, and agrarian holdings, analysis of existing cultural institutions, and greater emphasis on regional-scale planning, and even presenting a slate of candidates in the Roman municipal elections in 1946—were largely ineffective, especially as its program was unspecific and was in any case diffused by the vagueness of the basic concept as a critical category. Nor was the attempt very persuasive to identify as "organic" various projects designed over the next five years by architects like Carlo Scarpa, Marcello D'Olivo, and Giuseppe Samonà. Yet Zevi's critique had the important consequence of throwing open a historical discussion on the modern movement heritage and establishing an operative context for postwar criticism.

For an idea of the polemical tenor surrounding the debate over organicism, see Zevi's report to the first national APAO congress in *Metron* 23–24 (1947), "L'architettura organica di fronte di suoi critici."

Published as "La Costituzione dell'Associazione per l'Architettura Organica a Roma" in Metron *2 (September 1945), pp. 75–76. Courtesy of Bruno Zevi.*

Constitution of the Association for Organic Architecture in Rome
APAO

1. The origin of modern architecture is essentially in functionalism. Whether or not there is an evolution of functional architecture today into organic architecture, we are convinced that functionalism is the root of modern architecture, and not the trends toward neoclassical stylization, nor the provincialism of the minor styles.

2. Organic architecture is at once a social, technical, and artistic activity, directed toward creating the climate for a new democratic civilization. Organic architecture means architecture for man, modeled according to the human scale, according to the spiritual, psychological, and material necessities associated with man. Organic architecture is thus the antithesis of the monumental architecture that serves myths of state. It opposes the major and minor axes of contemporary neoclassicism—the vulgar neoclassicism of arches and columns, and the false neoclassicism that is born from the pseudomodern forms of contemporary monumental architecture.

3. We believe in urban planning and in architectural freedom. No matter what direction each of us intends to follow, we shall always refuse to use antidemocratic means to gain power. Indeed, we believe in the right to architectural freedom, in the limits of urban planning.

Inseparable from our belief in architecture is our belief in some general principles of a political and social order. The following principles for us constitute the ideal premise for organic architecture:

1. Political liberty and social justice are inalienable elements in the construction of a democratic society. All the fascisms and all the institutions that have favored it and that might be capable of making it rise again are therefore to be condemned.

2. A constitution is necessary that guarantees to its citizens freedom of speech, of press, of association, of worship; equality of race, religion, and sex before the law; full exercise of political sovereignty through institutions founded on universal suffrage. No reason justifies suppression of democratic liberties.

3. Alongside democratic and individual liberties, the constitution must guarantee social liberties to the whole of its citizenry. We therefore believe in socialization of the industrial, financial, and agrarian complexes whose monopolies are contrary to the interests of the collectivity. We believe in the liberation of the labor forces and in the end of the exploitation of labor for selfish ends.

We must move toward international cooperation of peoples, opposing all those forms of myths and nationalistic and autarchic biases that have been causes and characteristics of fascism. To ask for freedom and justice for one's own country is justified to the extent to which this freedom and this justice are identified with liberty and justice for all countries.

1945

Joseph Hudnut served as acting dean and then dean of Columbia University School of Architecture for two years before becoming dean of Harvard's Graduate School of Design in 1935, a position he held for eighteen years. He was among the first of the leading American architects schooled in traditional architecture to recognize the importance of the modern movement. As a progressive educator, he facilitated the introduction of modern architecture into American schools still dominated by Beaux-Arts tradition. The most

pp. 176–80 consequential decision of his tenure at Harvard was to bring Walter Gropius to the school as senior professor (he had earlier hoped to bring him to Columbia). He was also responsible for bringing Gropius's compatriots Marcel Breuer and Martin Wagner to the Harvard faculty.

A practicing architect with training in engineering and a teacher of architectural history, Hudnut wrote on architecture "with a witty and felicitous pen," as Lewis Mumford put it. Over the years his humanist outlook made him increasingly critical of functionalist dogmatism. The following essay, also published in Italian in 1945 in Bruno Zevi's journal *Metron*, represents the first use in an architectural context of a term that was to have a much-vexed development. The "post-modern owner" whom Hudnut here envisions as ideal client for a house he will design will be unsentimental and inured to the "collective-industrial scheme of life," but will "claim for himself some inner experiences, free from outward control, unprofaned by the collective conscience."

First published in Architectural Record *97 (May 1945), pp. 70–75. Republished in revised form in Joseph Hudnut,* Architecture and the Spirit of Man *(Cambridge: Harvard University Press, 1949), pp. 108–19. Also in Lewis Mumford,* Roots of Contemporary Architecture *(New York: Reinhold, 1952), pp. 306–16. Copyright © 1949 by the President and Fellows of Harvard University.*

The Post-Modern House
Joseph Hudnut

I have been thinking about those factory-built houses, pure products of technological research and manufacture, which are promised us as soon as a few remaining details of finance and distribution are worked out: houses pressed by giant machines out of plastics or chromium steel, pouring out of assembly lines by the tens of thousands, delivered anywhere in response to a telephone call, and upon delivery made ready for occupancy by the simple process of tightening a screw. I have been trying to capture one of these houses in my mind's eye; to construct there, not its form and features only but the life within it; to give it, if my readers will pardon me, a local habitation and a name.

I was assisted in this effort recently during an airplane trip to New York. As we left Boston we flew over a parking lot beside a baseball stadium and half an hour later, as we approached New York, over that immense parking area which lies back of Jones Beach. In each of these thousands of automobiles were ranged in herringbone patterns, all of them so far as we could see from the sky exactly alike—their forms, except for varying fancies in streamlining and nickel plate, being the perfect harvest of the technological mind unadulterated by art. It seemed to me that, parked in this way, these thousands of automobiles foreshadowed those future suburbs in which every family will have each its standardized mass-produced and movable shell, indistinguishable from those of its thousand neighbors except by a choice of paint and the (relative) ambitions of their owners to be housed in the latest model.

Now I am aware that uniformity in house design is for the greater part of mankind a condition which is often necessary and not always regrettable—a circumstance clearly illustrated by that cloudburst of Cape Cod cottages which is even now saturating our New England landscapes and which, it may be, is as distinct a forerunner of future standardizations in our houses as is the parked automobile. Just the same there is an important difference between these millions of wooden cottages and the more rigorous shapes of factory-built houses, a difference only obliquely related to materials and processes of manufacture. The factory-built house, as I imagine it, fails to furnish my mind with that totality of impression with which the word house (meaning a building occupied by a family) has always filled it: it leaves unexhibited that idea of home about which there cling so many nuances of thought and sentiment. My readers may count me a romanticist if they wish—and perhaps they can conceive of a home without romance?—but I do not discover in any one of the types of house prefigured in the published essays of technologists that *promise of happiness* which, in houses, is the important quality of all appearances.

My impression is obviously shared by a wide public—a circumstance which explains in part the persistence with which people, however enamored of science, cling to the familiar patterns of their houses. Among the soldiers who write letters to me there is, for example, one in Tokyo who describes at some length, and not without eloquence, the many labor-saving devices, the new ideas in planning, the new materials, insulatings, and air-conditionings which are to beautify his new house. He ends his letter with the confident hope that these will not in any way change the design of the house which he expects me to build for him. He has in mind, if I have understood him correctly, a Cape Cod cottage which, upon being opened, will be seen to be a refrigerator-to-live-in; and I am by no means sure which of these requirements, assuming them to be inconsistent, is the more prescriptive. Having learned that I am an architect tinged with modernism, my soldier fears that I may be tempted to suspend his house from a tree or pivot it on a mast around which it can be made to revolve or perhaps give it the outward shape of an aluminum bean, and I take it that he is unwilling that my enthusiasm for a technological absolutism should carry me that far. He would like all the newest gadgets but would like these seasoned with that picture, sentiment, and symbol which, to one writing from Tokyo, seem to be of equal importance. He would have mechanization but would not, in the phrase of a distinguished historian of art, allow mechanization to take command. I shouldn't be surprised to learn that his requirements reflect accurately those of the Army, the Navy, the Air Force, the WAC, and the WAVES.

Our soldiers are already sufficiently spoiled by compliments and yet I must admit that here is still another instance in which their prescience overleaps the judgments of science. Beneath the surface naiveté of my friend's letter there is expressed an idea which is of critical importance to architecture: a very ancient idea to be sure, but one which seems sometimes to be forgotten by architects. The total form and ordinance of our houses are not implied in the evolution of building techniques or concepts of planning. They do not proceed from these merely; they cannot be imagined wholly from these premises. In the hearts of the people at least they are relevant to something very far beyond science and the uses of science.

I wish to be understood in this matter. I am not excessively fond of Cape Cod cottages. In their native habitat these are quaint in form and charming in their forthrightness, and yet I find the type somewhat tedious now that it has been repeated four or five million times. I do wish that those contractors who spread their white nebulae of houses around our great cities might now and then tempt their market with some new form of sweetmeat. To speak frankly these represent a species of exploitation not more excusable than any other. Nevertheless it is a fact, patent to the most superficial observer, that millions of people find in the commutations of architecture compensations for an experience of which most of them are ignorant. They are the pale but necessary substitutes for the experience of an architecture in which emotional values are fused into technological values. Until we achieve that fusion Cape Cod cottages will take command.

Our architects are too often seduced by the novel enchantments of their techniques. I have known architects whose attitudes and ideals are not different from those of engineers; who find sufficient reward for their work in the intellectual satisfactions afforded by their inventions; who are quite indifferent to the formal consequences of their constructions—beauty being a flower which will spring unbidden from beneath their earnest feet. There are others who discover with such an excess of fervor the dramatic possibilities of concrete cantilevers and iron *piloti* that they forget to ask if these are in any way appropriate to the idea to be expressed. There are still others whose logic is so absolute that they will allow no felicity of form to go unexplained by economic necessity or technical virtuosity, nor will they permit any beauty to be enjoyed until justified as a consequence of the slide rule, and frequently her presence in their calculate halls will be acknowledged only after an argument.

Like a ministering angel the machine enters our house to give a new perspective and economy, a new range and efficiency, to the processes of daily living; to lengthen the hours of freedom; to dispel a thousand tyrannies of custom and prejudice, to lift mountains of drudgery from our shoulders. Like a herald from a young king newly crowned the machine announces a new dynasty and welcomes us to its liberating authority. Like a first breath of April the machine purifies and invigorates. Architects are right to love the machine; they could not otherwise build a modern house.

We are right to love the machine but we must not permit it to extinguish the fire on our hearth. The shapes and relationships, the qualities and arrangements of color, light, textures, and the thousand other elements of building through which the human spirit makes itself known: these are the essential substance of a house, in no way incidental to patterns of economy or physical well-being. Through these our walls are made to reach out beyond utility to enclose the ethereal things without which a house is, in any real sense, a useless object. Through these they speak to us of security and peace, of intimate loyalties, love and the tender affection of children, of the romance for which our soldiers hunger, of an adventure relived a thousand times and forever new; nor is that too much to expect of a house.

There is a way of working, sometimes called art, which gives to things made by man qualities of form beyond those demanded by economic, social, or ethical expediency; a way of working which brings into harmony with ourselves some part of our environment created by us; which makes that environment, through education, a universal experience; which transforms the science of building into architecture.

If a dinner is to be served it is art which dresses the meat, determines the order of serving, prepares and arranges the table, establishes and directs the conventions of costume and conversation, and seasons the whole with that ceremony which, long before Lady Macbeth explained it to us, was the best of all possible sauces. If a story is to be told it is art which gives the events proportion and climax, fortifies them with contrast, tension, and the salient word, colors them with metaphor and allusion, and so makes them cognate and kindling to the heart. If a prayer is made, it is art which sets it to music, surrounds it with ancient observances, guards it under the solemn canopies of great cathedrals.

The shapes of all things made by man are determined by their functions, by the laws of materials and the laws of energies, by marketability (sometimes) and the terms of manufacture; but these shapes may also be determined by the need, more ancient and more imperious than your present techniques, for some assurance of importance and worth in those things which encompass humanity. That is true also of all forms of doing, of all patterns of work and conduct and pageantry. It is true of the house and of all that takes place in the house; for here among all the things made is that which presses most immediately upon the spirit—the symbol, the armor, and the hearth of a family. The temple itself grew from this root; and the House of God, which architecture celebrates with her most glorious gifts, is only the simulacrum and crowning affirmation of the spiritual knowledge which illumined first the life of the family and only afterward the lives of men living in communities.

Here is that *shelter* which man shaped in the earth one hundred thousand years ago, the pit which became the wattle hut, the cave, the mound dwelling, the Sioux lodge, and the thousand other constructions with which our restless invention has since covered the earth; the *shelter* which in a million forms has accompanied man's long upward journey, his companion and shield and outer garment. Here is that *home* which first shaped and disciplined our emotions and over centuries formed and confirmed the habits and valuations upon which human society rests. Here is that *space* which man learned to refashion into patterns conformable to his spirit: the space which he made into architecture.

This theme, so lyrical in its essential nature, can be parodied by science. An excess of physiological realism, for example, can dissemble and disfigure the spirit quite as ingeniously as that excess of sugar which eclecticism in its popular aspect pours over the suburban house. A "fearless affirmation" of the functions of nutrition, dormation, education, procreation, and garbage disposal is quite as false a premise for design as that clutter of rambling roofs, huge chimneys, quaint dormers, that prim symmetry of shuttered window and overdoor fanlight, which form the more decorous disguise of Bronxville and Wellesley Hills; nor have I a firmer faith in the quaint language and high intentions of those sociologists who arrive at architecture through "an analytical study of environmental factors favorable to the living requirements of families considered as instruments of social continuity." I am even less persuaded by biologists: especially those who have created a vegetable humanity to be preserved or cooled or propagated in boxes created for those purposes. I mean those persons who make diagrams and action photographs showing the impact upon space made by a lady arranging a bouquet or a gentleman dressing for dinner or 3.81 children playing at kiss-in-the-ring and who then invite architects to fit their rooms around these "basic determinants." My requirements are somewhat more subtle than those of a ripe tomato or a caged hippopotamus, whatever may be the opinion of the Pierce Foundation.

We have developed in our day a new language of structural form. That language is capable of deep eloquence; and yet we use it too infrequently for the purposes of a language. Just as the historical styles of architecture are detached from modern technologies and by that detachment lose that vitality and vividness which might come from a direct reference to our times, so our new motives are detached from the idéa to be expressed. They have their origin not in the idea but in problems of construction and in principles of planning. We have not yet learned to give them meanings sufficiently persuasive. They have often interesting aesthetic qualities, they arrest us by their novelty and their drama, but too often they have very little to say to us.

The architects of the Georgian tradition were as solicitous as we are of progress in the science of building. They designed their houses with the same care for practical use that they spent, for example, upon their coaches and their sailing ships; and yet their first consideration was for their way of life. When I visit the streets of Salem I am not so confident as are some of my colleagues that her architects suffered from a limited range of materials and structural methods. Standing in the midst of a culture alien to their quaint formalisms, these houses yet make known to me the idea they were meant to capture. I understand them as I might understand a song sung in a foreign tongue. We are too ready to mistake novelty for progress and progress for art. I tell my students that there were noble buildings before the invention of plywood. They listen indulgently but they do not believe me.

I sometimes think that we have to defend our houses against the new processes of construction and against the aesthetic forms which these engender. We must remind ourselves that techniques have a strictly limited value as elements of expression. Their competence lies in the way we use them. However they may intrigue us, they have no place in the design of a house unless they do indeed serve the purpose of the home and are congenial to its temper. When, as often happens, their only virtue is their show, their adventitious nature is soon realized; they are then as great an impediment to our melody as an excess of ornamentation. The mighty cantilever which projects my house over a kitchen yard or a waterfall; that flexible wall and stressed skin; these fanaticisms of glass brick; these strange hoverings of my house over the firm earth—these strike my eyes but not my heart. A master may at his peril use them; but for human nature's daily use we have still proportion, homely ordinance, quiet wall surfaces, good manners, common sense, and love. These also are excellent building materials.

The world will not ask architects to tell it that this is an age of invention, of new excitements and experiences and powers. The airplane, the radio, the V-bomb, and the giant works of engineering will give that assurance somewhat more persuasively than the most enormous of our contraptions. Beside the big top of industry our bearded lady will not long astonish the mob.

It should be understood that I do not despise the gifts of our new sciences; and certainly the architects of the 1920s made convincing demonstrations of the utility of these in an art of expression. They used structural inventions not for their own sake nor yet for the sake of economy and convenience merely, but as elements in a language. Functionalism was a secondary characteristic of their expressive art which had as its basic conception, so far as this is related to the home, a search for a form which should exhibit a contemporary phase of an ancient aspect of life. To this end new materials were used, old ones discarded; but the true reliance was not upon these but upon new and significant relationships among architectural elements—among which enclosed space was the prime medium, walls and roof being used as a means of establishing spatial compositions. To compose in prisms rather than in mass, to abolish the facade and deal in total form, to avoid the sense of enclosure, to admit to a precise and scrupulous structure no technique not consonant with the true culture of our day: these were the important methods of an architecture never meant to be definite or "international"—which offered rather a base from which a new progress might be possible, a principle which should have its peculiar countenance in every nation and in every clime. I should not venture here to restate a creed already so often stated had not a torrent of recent criticism distorted this architecture into a "cold and uncompromising functionalism," had it not been made the excuse for an arid materialism wholly alien to its intention.

We must rely not upon the wonder and drama of our inventions but upon the qualities, beyond wonder and beyond utility, which we can give them. Take, for example, *space*. Of all the inventions of modern architecture the new space is, it seems to me, the most likely to attain a deep eloquence. I mean by this not only that we have attained a new command of space but also a new quality of space. Our new structure and our new freedom in planning—a freedom made possible in part at least by the flat roof—has set us free to model space, to define it, to direct its flow and relationships; and at the same time these have given space an ethereal elegance unknown to the historic architectures. Our new structure permits almost every shape and relationship in this space. You may give it what proportion you please. With every change in height and width, in relation to the spaces which open from it, in the direction of the planes which enclose it, you give it a new expression. Modern space can be bent or curved; it can move or be static, rise or press downward, flow through glass walls to join the space of patio or garden, break into fragments around alcoves and galleries, filter through curtains or end abruptly against a stone wall. You may also give it balance and symmetrical rhythms.

If then we wish to express in this new architecture the idea of *home*, if we wish to say in this persuasive language that this idea accompanies, persistent and eloquent, the forward march of industry and the changing nature of society, we have in the different aspects of space alone a wide vocabulary for that purpose.

I have of course introduced this little dissertation on space in order to illustrate this resourcefulness. I did not intend a treatise. I might with equal relevance have mentioned light, which is certainly as felicitous a medium of modern design, or the new materials which offer so diversified a palette of texture and color, or the forms and energies of our new types of construction, or the relationships to site and to nature made possible by new principles of planning. There are also the arts of painting and sculpture, of furniture-making, of textiles, metalware, and ceramics—all of which are, or ought to be, harmonious accessories to architecture.

I have heard architects explain with formulas, calculations, diagram, and all manner of auricular language, the advantages of the glass wall—of wide areas of plate glass opening on a garden—when all that was necessary was to say that here is one of the loveliest ideas ever entertained by an architect. People who *feel* walls do not need to compute them; and people who are deaf to the rhythms of great squares of glass relieved by quiet areas of light-absorbing wall may as well resign the enjoyment of architecture. Because they are free of those "holes punched in a wall," of that balance and stiff formalism in window openings which proclaim the Georgian mode, because we can admit light where we please, we have in effect invented a new kind of light. We can direct light, control its intensity and its colorations; diffuse it over space, throw it in bright splashes against a wall, dissolve it and gather it up in quiet pools; and from those scientists who are at work on new fashions in artificial light we ought to expect not new efficiencies merely or new economies merely, but new radiances in living.

Space, structure, texture, light—these are less the elements of a technology than the elements of an art. They are the colors of the painter, the tones of the musician, the images out of which poets build their invisible architectures. Like color, tone, and image they are most serviceable when they are so used as to make known the grace and dignity of the spirit of man.

Of course I know that modern architecture must adjust its processes to the evolving pattern of industry, that building methods must attain an essential unity with all the other processes by which in this mechanized world materials are assembled and shaped for us. No doubt the wholesale nature of our constructions imposes upon us a monotony and banality beyond that achieved by past architectures—a condition not likely to be remedied by prefabrication—and no doubt our houses, as they conform more closely to our ever advancing technologies, will escape still further the control of art. Still more inimical to architecture will be those standardizations of thought and idea already widely established in our country; that assembly-line society which stamps men by the millions with mass attitudes and mass ecstasies. Our standards of judgment will be progressively formed by advertisement and the operations convenient to industry.

I shall not imagine for my future house a romantic owner, nor shall I defend my client's preferences as those foibles and aberrations usually referred to as "human nature." No, he shall be a modern owner, a post-modern owner, if such a thing is conceivable. Free from all sentimentality or fantasy or caprice, his vision, his tastes, his habits of thought shall be those most necessary to a collective-industrial scheme of life; the world shall, if it pleases him, appear as a system of casual sequences transformed each day by the cumulative miracles of conscience. Even so he will claim for himself some inner experiences, free from outward control, unprofaned by the collective conscience. That opportunity, when the universe is socialized, mechanized, and standardized, will yet be discoverable in the home. Though his house is the most precise product of modern processes there will be entrenched within it this ancient loyalty invulnerable against the siege of our machines. It will be the architect's task, as it is today, to comprehend that loyalty—to comprehend it more firmly than anyone else—and, undefeated by all the armaments of industry, to bring it out in its true and beautiful character.

1946

Ernesto Nathan Rogers was one of the most active figures on the Italian architectural scene during the postwar years. A member of the firm of Banfi, Belgiojoso, Peressuti and Rogers (BBPR), formed in 1932 by four classmates at the Milan Politecnic, he was, with his partners, a protagonist in the evolution of rationalism, and as the most journalistically inclined of the four, increasingly engaged in publishing work. After an initial infatuation with fascism on the part of many modernist architects ended in the late 1930s, and with the promulgation of racial laws, the BBPR became involved in antifascist activities. This led to Banfi and Belgiojoso's deportation to a concentration camp, where Banfi died in 1945; Rogers, a Jew, took refuge in Switzerland. Upon Italy's liberation, the three surviving members of the firm reunited, and Peressuti designed the BBPR's monument to the war deportees, a steel cage of lyrical minimalism. They also participated, with Franco Albini, Ignazio Gardella, Pietro Lingeri, and eighteen other architects, in the Movimento di Studi per l'Architettura (MSA), constituted in Milan in spring 1946. An outgrowth of a collaboration by the same architects on a master plan for the Milan region, MSA was dedicated to studying "the various problems of architecture principally in relation to the most urgent necessities of

100–2 the reorganization of social life." Advocating continuity with CIAM's prewar research, the rationalist Milan group entered into direct debate with Bruno Zevi's

68–69 Association for Organic Architecture, formed at the same time in Rome.

Rogers also took over the editorial direction of the magazine *Domus* at this

260–65 date. Founded in 1928 by the architect and designer Gio Ponti, *Domus* had from its inception been an important vehicle for a range of progressive cultural tendencies. Rogers, however, had a more programmatic agenda in mind for the magazine, to which he now added the subtitle "Casa dell'uomo," echoing the title of a book published by Le Corbusier and François de Pierrefeu in 1942. In his opening editorial of January 1946, which follows here, he explicitly announced his intention: to address the most basic needs of material existence while also concerning himself with cultural questions. "It is a matter of forming a style, a technique, a morality as terms of a single function."

This synthesis had a particular meaning in postwar Italian culture. The most pressing concern of reconstruction in Italy, as elsewhere, was housing. The year before, Rogers had published an article in Elio Vittorini's new journal *Politecnico* entitled "A House for Everyone." But for socially inclined architects the question of rehousing a displaced populace went beyond pragmatic concerns. In a postwar climate imbued with the pathos of the recent partisan struggle, it encompassed emotional as well as material exigencies. The populist attitude that pervades the Italian neorealist cinema of these years also informs Rogers's *Domus,* as it does a book like the *Manuale dell'architetto* edited by the Roman architect Mario Ridolfi and published in 1946 by the U.S. Information Service. Ridolfi qualified the quantitative criteria of the typical professional handbook with local know-how, celebrating the traditions of manual labor and craftsmanship.

By December 1947 Rogers's program proved too challenging for *Domus.* He was fired, and the editorship returned to Ponti. In an editorial entitled "Saluto" (Farewell), he expressed his frustration at having failed to reach more than an elite readership through the pages of an expensive magazine that was still acting primarily as an arbiter of taste. It would be six years later, when he would take

200–4, 300–7 over the direction of *Casabella,* that he would succeed in realizing his program of transforming a journal of architecture into an efficacious cultural instrument.

Published as "Programma: Domus, la casa dell'uomo" in Domus, *January 1946. Republished in Ernesto N. Rogers,* Esperienza dell'Architettura *(Turin: Giulio Einaudi, 1958), pp. 115–18. Courtesy of Studio BBPR and Julia Banfi.*

Program: Domus, the House of Man
Ernesto Nathan Rogers

On every side the house of man is cracked (if it were a boat we would say it leaks).

On every side the voices of the wind enter and the laments of women and children go out.

We should hurry to it with some bricks, or beams, or panes of glass, and instead here we are with a magazine. We give no bread to the hungry, no raft to the shipwrecked, only words.

If the sense of solidarity has not deserted us and we are still conscious of our acts, this offering of ours of words, as much as it may seem inopportune, must also have in its intentions a concrete meaning that justifies its existence.

Traveling through Italy, along the Aurelian or Emilian Way or into Puglia or Sicily, one sees a huge decay: ruins upon ruins. Surely things are the same in Provence or in Britain. Things are the same all over Europe.

Confronted with so many disasters, our impulse would be to translate moral feeling into the precision of an economic fact: how many families are without a house? how much material is necessary? how much time?

One thinks that winter is coming now and they will be cold.

One cannot think about anything else.

What value does beauty have for these people?

Poetry, music, painting, proportion threaten to become empty ambitions of our egotism as intellectuals: objects of luxury, instruments of sin.

The other day while listening at a friend's house to a concert, surrounded by the full cadences of a seventeenth-century composer, I suddenly felt my face burn with a deep shame (just like that which ignited the terrible conscience of Saint Augustine) and doubts came over me, which became a thick throng of menacing ghosts. "What are you lingering here for?"

But when the soloist took his bow from the viola and the last hovering note merged with the applause, I could not help clapping my hands with the rest of the public (and these were, I assure you, respectable people who do not dedicate their lives to self-indulgences).

The contrast between art and morals becomes noticeable precisely at times when the problems of existence have to be confronted on a plane of greater seriousness than customary, so that in most religious epochs or in those most anxious to affirm the immanent values of society, many believe—even if they are moving in opposite directions—they should turn their back on art.

These are, on one hand, the ascetic; on the other, the moralist. And both, when they do not simply become iconoclasts, end up by reducing art to a mere means to reach the end of their philosophizing : a *strumentum regni,* help, support, sustenance for that realm that for the first is negation of matter and for the second of spirit. On the other hand, there is he who, with greater conceit than the religious and less altruism than the humanitarian, focusing only on himself, repelled from any other communion or community, amuses himself with art as if it were opium to gratify his hedonistic world. Such is the aesthete, a gambler without innocence.

Far from the ascetic, and also from the materialist and the aesthete, and yet recognizing that each of these tendencies contains a portion of the truth, our ideal places itself in the middle, in the triangle's center of gravity.

The truth is in the proportional relationship; the words that we offer are then there, in that relationship: do we want to define ourselves as functionalists?

We want to be among those who urgently seek to reunite the threads into a synthetic knot whose every part is equally necessary to the consistency of the whole.

Why renounce men? why renounce gods? why renounce beauty, which often takes the place of virtue in connecting them?

No problem is solved if it does not at once respond to utility, morals, and aesthetics.

A house is no house if it is not warm in winter, cool in summer, serene in every season, receiving the family in harmonious spaces. A house is no house if it does not contain a corner for reading poetry, an alcove, a bathtub, a kitchen. This is the house of man. And a man is no man if he does not possess such a house. Does this house exist? Did it ever exist?

I am told that originally the Greek word *domos,* from which the Latin *domus* derives, signified the most elementary human habitation: enclosure, shelter.

But *domus* is a learned elocution taken by the Romans from the acceptation already in use to designate the complex of elements comprising the masters' houses in town.

Domus was not the house of man, but of a socially privileged family; all the other Latin terms indicate instead definite buildings rather than that typical one, better suiting the concept—apparently abstract, but in fact much more vital—of the human dwelling.

But think of the English: *home* (I should like to demonstrate, despite the philologists' opinions, that *home* and *homo* have the same origin); and think, why not, also of the German: *Heim;* the two beautiful adjectives *homely* and *heimlich,* which we so poorly translate with *casalinga* or *domestico,* express the material and spiritual needs of every man in his house.

Even fuller of meaning is the French saying *chez moi, chez toi, chez soi;* it actually seems that the constructive elements take on the outlook of the owner.

I want to have a house that may look like me (in better aspects): a house that may look like my humanity.

Taken to extremes our argument can lead to utopia or to the commonplace, since, if we ask too much, we aim for the unattainable, and if, however, we only look at what surrounds us we risk contenting ourselves with too little.

The house is a problem of limits (like, for that matter, almost every other problem of existence). But the definition of these limits is a problem of culture, and this is precisely what the house is in the end (like, indeed, the other problems of existence).

If so, words too are building material. And a magazine too can aspire to be that.

It is a matter of finding in one's mind the old nature (and here Rousseau may be right), but by following the fruitful road of experience (which is the generous reward for our lost virginity).

There are many useless things that appeal to bourgeois vanities, but also many marvelous ones, which most people cannot yet enjoy.

A magazine can be an instrument, a filter for establishing the criterion of choice.

From what we have said, one can infer what our aims are, as well as the hopes that we place in objectives unattainable by our forces alone.

It is a matter of forming a style, a technique, a morality as terms of a single function. It is a matter of building a society.

There is no time to waste in illustrating trifles.

Let us all help each other to find the harmony between human measure and divine proportion.

1946

From the start of his career in the early 1920s French architect **Marcel Lods** had been interested in the rationalized production of architecture. He experimented with advanced prefabrication techniques together with Eugène Beaudoin in commissions like his high-rise workers housing estate at Drancy near Paris (1934), as well as in smaller projects like the Roland Garros Aeroclub at Buc (1938), where he and Beaudoin collaborated with Jean Prouvé in a novel use of lightweight metallic construction methods based on aircraft engineering.

At the end of the war, Lods worked with Le Corbusier on a plan for the industrialized region around Saint-Gaudens in the Pyrenees. Then, in 1946, he made a first trip to the United States. His "euphoric" reaction was not altogether surprising given his own predilections, yet it dramatizes the impact of American technology on European architects at this date. Le Corbusier too visited the United States in 1946, as French delegate to the United Nations Headquarters Commission. A decade earlier, his souvenirs of his first trip to America, recorded in *When the Cathedrals Were White,* had been highly ambivalent (a "fairy catastrophe"). On his second encounter, despite the frustrations of a ten-month hunt for a site for the building (and his subsequent disappointment in being denied the commission), he would write, "In this world of 1946, the U.S.A. is the country of wealth and equipment; the entire world comes to its shores."

For Lods, the experience was unreservedly positive. American images of power and plenitude—the acrobatic system of roadways crisscrossing "space-time"; the pure poetry of energy evoked by the Tennessee Valley Authority dam works; the Ford plant at River Rouge, Detroit, which seemed to him almost a movie set; and on a smaller scale, the lightweight, technical architecture of Viennese emigré Richard Neutra, open to the California landscape—heralded a new civilization, at times violent and jarring, but vital and optimistic. In the postwar European climate of acute material and labor problems, Lods looked forward to a day when France would be able to shift its sights from uncertainties of production to matters of distribution and quality on the American model.

The immediate difficulties of rebuilding in France were compounded by a serious prewar housing shortage and a stagnant building industry. In 1948 reconstruction efforts intensified with the replacement of Roland Dautry by Eugène Claudius-Petit—a long-time supporter of Le Corbusier's urbanism and, like Lods, an enthusiastic proponent of American technology—as Minister of Reconstruction and Urbanism. Claudius-Petit called for the construction of 20,000 new dwellings a month as a "question of life or death" for France, and stressed standardization and mechanized construction technologies. The two most important building programs carried out during these years—Auguste Perret's reconstruction of Le Havre (1947–54), a dry monumental exercise in modular rationalism, and Le Corbusier's Unité d'Habitation in Marseilles (1946–52), which would galvanize functionalist planning for a more than a decade—epitomized in different ways the French postwar imperatives of rationalized construction. Lods too was actively involved in the reconstruction efforts, designing a master plan for Sotteville-les-Rouen (1946–55), where he built slab housing for workers. He had less success with his urban plan for the Rhine city of Mainz, drawn up with Gérald Hanning in 1946–48. Here Lods's radical imposition of Corbusian principles of urbanism in a contested border zone imbued with nationalistic sentiments met strong antagonism from the populace. After the German mayor solicited a counterproject from Stuttgart architect Paul Schmitthenner, Lods's scheme was scrapped for a conservative one.

Published as "Retour d'Amérique" in L'Architecture Française, *no. 54 (January 1946), pp. 23–28. Courtesy of Martine Lods.*

Return from America
Marcel Lods

My friend Roux-Spitz has asked me to summarize and comment for the readers of *L'Architecture Française* on the memories that I evoked at the Salle Pleyel under the title "Images of America."

The very lively impressions I received over there gave my trip a true "tonic" character.

Tonic like all voyages, of course, particularly those that the French take abroad to "recharge their battery" . . . But far from being the most tonic among them.

How precious is this possibility of renewing oneself, of refreshing oneself.

Having for a long time argued and struggled to admit certain points of view, the French now feel themselves a little "flat."

They now feel exhausted by eternal negations, perpetual saying of "it's impossible," or "that's not done," or "that's never done," finishing with the inevitable "that's not done *in France.*"

Quickly, then, to the trip. Quickly to the contact with the points of the universe where "that's done here."

Before the war it was easy: Germany (before 1930), Czechoslovakia, England, Switzerland, Belgium, Holland—one had nothing but choice. It became more difficult . . . after having been impossible during five mortal years.

Yet I was able to see England in 1944.

The lessons were different, but not inferior to those of America. In 1945 I saw, finally, the United States, and just afterward, Switzerland.

In the course of the trip to the U.S.A., I experienced such a feeling of enthusiasm and euphoria that I promised myself to share it with my compatriots upon my return.

Encounters are violent, rapid, sometimes brutal . . . but what power, what plenitude! It is this plenitude that I wanted to bring back to my country, this satisfaction that all the world cannot fail to experience in the face of the realizations, the technical and human successes of the U.S.A.

Our country needs "faith." The peevish habits of surrender acquired in all domains since 1918 make this "faith," this enthusiasm necessary.

It is thoroughly filled with this ardor that I have attempted to evoke my very general study of the great American achievements.

If I have spoken of plans for extension and urbanism of American cities, it is to try to make people here understand the efficacity of this effort, which, not content to consecrate an enormous budget to the establishment of these great plans (thirty million dollars for Chicago), still consents—and this is done in important cities like Kansas City (as large as Marseilles)—to a supplementary expenditure in order to publish them in the most pleasant and remarkable fashion, and thus to put them at the disposition of the city's inhabitants.

If I have spoken of beaches, certain of which over there can accommodate up to 50,000 bathers, and which offer them all the pleasures, all the comforts, all the installations possible, not forgetting transportation, it is to make us understand all of the immense wealth that lies latent along our admirable coasts, today devastated in part, but called to life again in conditions that must be made much superior to what we have known in the most successful French beach resorts.

If I have spoken of "highways," of "parkways," magical networks of circulation routes on the periphery of cities, which extend out to their broad outskirts and do not

The Tennessee dam in the Tennessee Valley gives an idea of the scale of numerous works undertaken. [Tennessee Valley Authority and Bureau of Reclamation, storage dam and powerhouse, Norris, Tennessee, 1936.]

The Bronx-Whitestone Bridge, one of the gigantic bridges which tomorrow will be too small. [O. H. Ammann, chief engineer; Allston Dana, engineer of design; Aymar Embury II, architect; Bronx-Whitestone Bridge, Eastern Boulevard at 177th Street, New York City, 1939. Photograph by Rodney McCay Morgan.]

cease to grow, it is so that my country might allow itself to try these admirable solutions, which reduce by a considerable measure all the accidents, all the risks, all the delays of which our drivers never cease to complain.

If I have spoken of bridges—of their beauty, their grandeur—it is to try to convey to us the scale of the great works of tomorrow, which, in spite of human efforts and daring, risk not being grand enough.

I have also spoken of prefabrication. I have said much about it; it is a subject that is familiar to me and to which I have brought since 1929 (date of our first "prefabricated" construction) a certain interest and a large part of my efforts.

I believed, all of us were able to believe after this devastating war, that the "prefabrication" of houses, or rather the "fabrication of houses with the aid of modern industrial processes," was going to rally to its cause the great majority of votes.

Everything led us there: the volume of destruction, which only added deplorably to a national housing situation in France already obsolete and crumbling, the scarcity of labor that was making itself felt in all regions, each having too few hands to meet its own repairs and the normal and logical development of its land.

Yet one begins again to argue . . . Can we hope today to resolve this?

I believe that the whole of the current debate on this question can be summed up in a few sentences.

Everything, or almost, comes back to knowing if it is correct that a certain number of elements of life have been profoundly modified by changes that all, without exception, stem from the introduction into our civilization of mechanical force (hardly three centuries old).

Undoubtedly one had, before the generalization of this force, found plenty of machines capable of transforming, managing, making more usable the different *animal* forces; undoubtedly one also learned to employ certain *natural* forces with the aid of more or less sophisticated machines.

The wheel of the mill that turns thanks to the river current and the sail that uses the action of the wind to make the boat go forward are such machines.

But before steam there was no true *production* of energy useable in the present manner. . .

There existed one exception, and not to mankind's credit: firearms. These in effect utilized, for the launching of projectiles, an energy truly "issuing" from a chemical combination invented by man.

It was, in fact, the cannon of Crécy that first permitted "fabrication of energy" by the combustion of gunpowder. The misfortune is that over the centuries this magnificent invention was used only for destruction.

Fundamentally nothing has changed, and today as in the distant past we consent more to considerations, efforts, and works for war than for peace . . . and, if one day we see atomic energy used to peaceful ends, it will nonetheless remain the case that it was for purposes of war that this thing came into the world.

But let us return to our subject. Here it is then, one fine day, man endowed with this marvel: energy available in ever greater quantity. Whatever seemed fixed forever is no longer so. The wealth of the world, which had remained stable over centuries, finds itself, from the moment when energy is obtainable without limitation, indefinably increased. Abundance replaces scarcity. One is preoccupied much more with distributing products than insuring their fabrication; production is no longer insufficient; respite appears. The revolution achieves all.

From the sewing needle to the transatlantic liner, including clothing, medicine, vegetable preserves, and meat products, everything evolves . . . And at what a pace! Everything? no . . . not exactly everything. There remains the building trade, which refuses to evolve.

Let us not pretend that it does not move a little . . . But it only evolves with many reservations and rather bad will. It "allows" evolution to impose itself, which is a deplorable system.

It is necessary to *conduct* the evolutions, not *submit* to them.

It is necessary to be *in front* in order to direct and not *behind* in order to follow.

It is more fatiguing, it involves more risks—that's clear—but all things considered, it involves fewer of them than waiting until things take care of themselves.

Whereupon we can draw a solid lesson from our American friends. They have truly, among themselves, confronted the problem objectively. With respect to what I have called the "evolution of the traditional" (there is much of it), they have pushed mechanization and the equipment of the building site as far as possible. Human labor is truly reduced to a minimum. For all operations, from the smallest to the largest, they utilize mechanical energy to the maximum; screwing, riveting, boring are done with the aid of mechanical equipment of small or medium size; fabrication, transport of cement, its pouring on site, its mixing, digging, movements of earth are done with the aid of pieces of apparatus, some of which (recall the gigantic excavator described by Kérisel in a recent lecture) are of extraordinary dimensions.

In the total manufacture the human hand intervenes less and less. One day it will no longer intervene except to direct the machine, while waiting for the next day (it has already commenced) when manufacturing will conduct itself all alone.

That is what one sees in America.

Admittedly for one who believes in it, who defends it aided only by a small number of apostles as convinced as he is, there is reason for enthusiasm!

It is somewhat regrettable that we still may still wonder whether such a thing is possible . . . that it is a matter of grand plans, new highway systems, modification of agricultural methods, design of new towns, or prefabrication applied to construction, that we still pose problems with the conceit of a professor having covered the question, long since resolved.

But we do not travel. We have not seen without leaving home . . . There may be some disturbing surprises in store for us. Our country needs to act, needs to have faith.

A rather curious confirmation of this state of things has occurred since the date of my lecture: look at the cry of alarm raised by the press over the departure of the elites!

Today there are numerous worthy people, young and old, who believe that the "precious French sense of proportion" with which we have justified for twenty years all our timidities, mediocrities, and surrenders comes in our century of upheaval with unfortunate inopportuneness.—

Those who are not able to rouse their enthusiasm for half-measures, those who burn with desire to dedicate themselves body and soul to an action that is not abortive, those who leave us . . . or want to leave us, which amounts to the same thing.

We risk that on the day when events will have definitively settled this debate (the entire universe not appearing to be dependent on the volition of France) we will have nothing to attack and resolve the problems that we have finally agreed to recognize but the collaboration of those who have done everything to slow down the machine and to justify surrender.

1946

Buckminster Fuller posed his famous question, "Madam, do you know how much your house weighs?" at the end of the Second World War when the inefficiency of production in the housing industry begged comparison with the unprecedented mobilization of industrial technology for military production. Looking to aircraft manufacture as a model, Fuller concluded that the key to optimized performance was weight. He set out to design a house based on the principle of maximum performance per pound.

The formative moment in Fuller's thinking had occurred during the previous world war, when, stationed on a Navy battleship as a mechanical engineer, he realized that it was impossible to win a war with outdated equipment. At the same period his infant daughter, living with his wife in poor-quality wartime housing, became ill. Fuller would attribute her later death to the "messy world of ignorance and superficiality in houses." He began projecting his technical solution in 1927, a domical metal dwelling called the Dymaxion (dynamic plus maximum efficiency). In 1944 he succeeded in building a prototype of it when he persuaded Beech Aircraft of Wichita, experiencing a labor shortage because of the war's expected end, of the potential of converting from war production to housing. "There is no basic difference between the fabricating of aluminum parts for the Dymaxion house and for the fuselages of B29s," Fuller asserted.

In a speech of January 1946—excerpted below—to engineers from twelve leading aircraft companies recruited to join him in the prototype's production at Beech, Fuller elaborated the ideas behind the 6,000-pound, 1,075-square-foot house. With unbounded optimism, he saw his design as the basis for a full-scale airframe dwelling industry that could redress postwar housing shortages in the most efficient way in terms of technology, cost, and ecology. "We will set up a new industry," he told his audience, "that promises to go on to rehouse the whole world and employ the whole world in the continuous wealth-making of improving living advantages." This sweeping vision came from his conviction that only by thinking "in the biggest way you know how" could problems of the scale now facing "man-world-universe" be solved. In 1946 the Beech plant fabricated the components for two prototypes. One of these was assembled and exhibited to enthusiastic reviews: 30,000 people expressed interest in owning a Dymaxion house (estimated to sell for $6,500, including installation). However, when Fuller continued to fret over design details and failed to raise the ten million dollars needed for the initial tool-up, the house was never put into mass production.

Had it been built, Fuller's "dome home" would have been a far more drastic *machine à habiter* than Le Corbusier had ever imagined. Ultimately, his radical disregard for aesthetic issues limited the impact of his ideas on architecture. But if schemes like the Dymaxion and later his geodesics failed to mushroom in the profusion he predicted, being reserved largely for pavilions, radar and weather housings, and small shelters, the ever more visionary message of this "comprehensive designer" to a new space-age culture had a critical impact. A tireless proselytizer on behalf of the future of the planet, Fuller was to inspire both the most pragmatic and most utopian of the new generation—from the scientific research at Ulm to the science fiction of Archigram, from the survival-kit shelters of an American dropout culture to the plug-in dreams of both the Japanese megastructurists and Reyner Banham.

288–99, 365–69
319–34
370–78

From Designing a New Industry: A Composite of a Series of Talks by R. Buckminster Fuller, 1945–1946 *(Wichita: Fuller Research Institute, 1946), pp. 38–42. Republished in James Meller, ed.,* The Buckminster Fuller Reader *(London: Jonathan Cape, 1970), pp. 212–21. Copyright © the Estate of Buckminster Fuller. Courtesy of the Buckminster Fuller Institute, Los Angeles.*

Designing a New Industry
R. Buckminster Fuller

[. . .] We have now actually met the original theoretical requirements of the physical problem. We have gotten down to the proper weight. We are down, not including the bathroom and the partitions, to 5,400 pounds. The copper bathroom now in the house weighs 430 pounds—but in aluminum with plastic finish, as we are going to manufacture it, the bathroom will weigh around 250 pounds. The partitions, two bathrooms, kitchen, laundry, and energy unit will probably come to not more than 2,000 pounds. We will be right on our curve of the size of things man can mass produce in 1946. In other words, due to the development of the airplane industry, the house has become an extremely practical and now very real affair.

Overnight [there was] the necessity of democracy for a great number of planes to accommodate the increasing mobility of man brought about by war, because man had not provided ways of developing that air technology expansion through peaceful means. This was because man was not living in a preventive pathology, as I pointed out earlier, but in a curative pathology, which has to have war to bring about the inevitable and major economic changes. *Industry* as preoccupied with the airplane overnight became *four times* as large as *industry* preoccupied with the automobile. People do not seem to realize it, but that is what happened.

You must now realize this evolution was simply the *principle* which we have defined earlier this evening as constituting *industry* itself being comprehensively tuned up through its inherent self-improving advantages, which had been accumulating increment for a generation, to demonstrate dramatically a new range and degree of ability. Therefore the *airplane* industry should not be thought of as a species of industry apart, for instance, from the *automobile* industry or the *hat* industry. It should be thought of as the phenomenon industry itself, simply mobilized to its best ability or to its most recent record high in *standards of performance.*

In *industry,* as preoccupied with aircraft manufacture and maintenance during World War II, the standards and tolerances of precision that could be maintained, the size of units, the relative strength, the degree of complexity control all represent a sum total of somewhere around a ten-to-one magnitude increase in technical advantages over *industry* as we know it before this war idling along on 1917 standards.

For us now as composite proprietors, workers, and consumers, to give up the standards of industry as recently preoccupied with the technical necessities of world-wide flight of man in order to assist him to establish ultimate world-wide democracy, and to go back instead to the phase of industry as we knew it in its earlier preoccupation with exploitation of man's innate tendency to *mobilize for security,* by tentative adaptation of the automobile to his paralyzed domiciling, would be to actually deflate our whole economic ability by 90%. To deflate our economic ability 90% is to decrease our potential ability 90%, which, as viewed from old-fashioned static economics simply means a 900% inflation of prices, relative to wage-hour dollars. It is an unthinkable thing. I don't think it is going to happen.

I think our house is going to have an important part in helping us to keep on upward instead of downward in historical degree of technical advantage that was developed during World War II. I don't have to talk to you much about that. You have heard about the possibility of using the aircraft plants. Last year the president of your company delivered an excellent address to the National Convention of the International

Association of Machinists: printed copies are available, I commend it to you. It covers the subject of the aircraft industry's inclusion of the manufacture of *airframe dwellings,* the name we have given to that portion of dwelling machines to be manufactured by the airframe industry. Wright Field calls our dwelling machines "stationary airplanes." The power plant and electrical manufacturing and many other areas of the older industry's component parts manufacturers will provide the organic apparatus of our dwelling service.

The big fact that confronts us is that you of the aircraft industry have suddenly developed a whole new world which has recently been operating four times as much technology as was ever operated before—which happened to represent precisely the level of technology for which I had been waiting to get my house realized. We had suddenly broken through into a world where young architects who didn't have building design jobs and who couldn't find building design jobs because building technology had stalemated suddenly found the aircraft world a very good place to go. In this welcoming world of aircraft they matriculated rapidly into the performance-per-pound language. They now think that way irrevocably. Everybody, throughout the whole aircraft industry thinks that way. It is no longer a *hard mental* job for us to sit down and talk, as we have talked tonight, *about how much housing weighs, too.*

Here is one more thing on the economics side I would like you to think about. Housing, as you have known it up to now, used the wood or stone or clay which was at hand. These component materials were not understood scientifically to any important degree. Wood might be considered *pretty* as oak, or pretty as maple. One was a little harder or softer to work and suited a man better than another. But it was little understood what a tree was. Despite academic study, man's understanding of trees was popularly vague. Then trees began to be used industrially by the chemical industry. It began to develop wood pulps and other by-products of wood. To some extent this began to affect the "scarcity" or "quantity" of wood relative to its availability for house building. These new industries, particularly newsprint pulp, exhausted a lot of it. Builders had to take greener and greener lumber as stock piling dwindled.

During World War II one of the most extraordinary things that happened, in its broad effects on technology and on economics, is what the Germans were forced to accomplish in wood chemistry in order to plan on how to survive during this extraordinary industrial warfare, which they introduced and in which energy played such an important role. The Germans had to plan in advance on being bombed out of their oil fields. It was obvious that they could plan to use oil to a certain extent but that eventually their most vulnerable position was their oil supply. This was an "oil warfare" in a big way. Therefore the Germans set about finding other important sources of energy. They went to wood technology. The chemistry of wood developed in many directions in Germany. They suddenly discovered that here was Nature's most important trick in impounding sun energy—and in a most useful way, for therefrom you could release energy in many useful directions. They immediately brought it to the one great "Grand Central Station" of energy, in its most storable form, which was *alcohol.* From alcohol of various kinds you could make foods—first for cattle, then for people. You could make high-octane gas or synthetic rubber or plastics. The chemistry of wood began playing such an important part that the scientists in Washington were talking about it constantly and there was a book published called *The NIgger in the Woodpile,* which was what Germany had.

Wood technology has advanced the basic economic case for wood to such an important position in the advancing technical world that we no longer can afford to use wood in the careless way we have in the past—to put it in houses for termites to eat up, or a possible fire to consume. Even if we could, world-wide technology forces our technical hand as it never has before; the rest of the world is now industrializing and is starting at the most advanced World War II levels of technology and not at our 1861 or 1890 or 1917 level. Industrial technology is born of latent knowledge and is not an inventory of obsolete machinery, so wood is in a very new historical position. How does that affect the historical wood house picture?

As children of the pioneers also came along to build a house—or their grandchildren wanted to—there was no longer much wood on the farm. They had to go increasing distances for it. Finally they went out of the state for it. Today they have to send 1,000 to 5,000 miles for most of their building wood.

They were using it simply by habit because it was originally handy and suddenly they had exhausted that supply. Long ago wood boxes disappeared from our cellars. In the war's great motion, packing cases went all over the world. That broke the wood supply equilibrium altogether. World increased paper needs and the new chemistry of wood-energy conversion makes it unthinkable that wood will ever again be available in any large way for building it into houses, even into prefabs which average 70% wood. Wood is suddenly going from "for free" as it sat stacked on the farm because it had to be cleared away, to a rapidly inflating price structure—owing not so much to its scarcity, as to its newly recognized inherent wealth.

On the other hand, there are now the many *by-products of the soil* and *by-products of the wood* which chemistry is developing, whether it is cellulose as plastics, or the metals developed from the clay, etc., which were just kicking around unrecognized on the early farm. These by-products, however, were very expensive to extract in the beginning and called for a large energy expenditure and fancy and complicated mammoth plants with giant stills and ovens such as required millions of dollars to install and develop. Few industries could afford to buy the original specialty by-products of high performance characteristic.

However in developing the aircraft industry, we had to have *high performance per pound,* so for a military plane the federal government could afford to pay for special alloys of aluminum and steel. Then we suddenly called for an enormous wartime application of industry to produce those same materials and they were brought into relatively low cost brackets. They could be extremely low for they came from sands, clay, coal, air, water, etc. Producers however held up their prices during the war because of the enormous amount of inspection necessary. In order to amplify industry to the ability to mass produce planes, which meant withstanding terrific stresses with minimum of weight and bulk, it was necessary to be supercareful of the quality of the materials. So the cost of inspection, pyramided upon inspection all along the line, was reflected in the high price structure of those materials, despite quantity production.

We now have enough 24ST aluminum in war surplus and scrap to make it worthwhile to segregate 24ST scrap so that the aluminum company will say, "We will give you 24ST—because we can now recirculate the scrap, and it is better scrap, actually having a little higher alloy content and preferable qualities—at a much lower price than you have been paying." Just within a couple of postwar months I am beginning to see price structure of aircraft metals and other high performance materials on the way down. As you study the basic economics of the plastics or aluminum industry, you find the price structure has got to go down as we employ their mass production by our less stringent standards and large mass outlet. Why?—Because we have alternate materials for every part's design.

In the materials we are dealing with in our new airframe houses, we are in a deflating price structure, while wood of the conventional house is in a very rapidly inflating price structure.

Those are some of the really outstanding trend data for you. If you would like to have in mind before you go away some of the absolutes in the old building world, so you can see where you are situated as you enter our endeavor with us, I will read these figures. I gave you the all-time high in housing which was in 1925, when 827,000 dwelling units were built, of which 572,000 were single-family dwellings, of which 270,000 had some interior plumbing. The top wartime total of dwelling units in one year was 575,000. That was 300,000 less than 1925, despite very much larger population and despite very much increased technology in all other directions. That was 1943 and was in all classes of dwellings.

We find that during the war a lot of other kinds of dwellings or shelters were developed, in which Quonsets were among those with which to reckon. In case authorities determine that "Our standard of living will have to go down during the 1946–47–48 housing emergency, and two million G.I.s who have made the mistake of getting married and are looking for someplace to live will have to live in Quonsets and prefabs," what would be the projected production of Quonset huts and other prefabs? Sixty thousand Quonsets in one year is that industry's reported top capacity. The prefabricated house industry indicated in a recent government survey that it hoped to double its production from the best prediction year during the war to a new total of 142,950 units. That is the capacity they dreamed about. Their best war capacity rate, which was never sustained, amounted to a potential 71,475 houses per year. That doesn't come anywhere near your need this coming year just for two million homeless G.I.s and their brides, paying no attention at all to the rest of the housing shortage, which is somewhere about twelve million in the United States. Those are important figures for you to have in mind to know whether you are on the right track in joining up with us here in the airframe dwelling machine industry.

I must caution you that you will be confronted constantly by the statement that mass production of houses eliminates the aspect of individuality which is so cherished by humans and without which they are afraid they will lose the identity of their personality; therefore, mass production of houses will never gain popular acceptance.

My answer to that is that reproduction or regeneration of form is a fundamental of nature and that it is neither good nor bad in itself. However, reproduction of originally inadequate or awkward forms, or poor mechanics or wasteful structures, either by the hand of man or by the regeneration of the biological species, tends to amplify the original characteristic. If the original is annoying, reproductions become increasingly annoying; if the original is highly adequate to its designed purpose, reproductions become increasingly pleasing in that confirmation of adequacy. In the latter light, we continuously admire a fine species of cultivated rose or nature's wildflowers—the more frequently repeated, the more beautiful. Conversely, the more frequently we see a maimed soldier, the more disheartening becomes the repetition. There would be even less virtue of the so-called individuality in discovery of soldiers' sons born with half a face blown away, or with three legs.

Individuality goes far deeper than these surface manifestations with which people have sought to deceive one another as to the relative importance of their status in the bitter struggle to validate one's right to live. Those who were powerful but ugly and lazy paid for fine clothes and fine surface architecture, and a superstition has persisted that people who could afford to pay must be superior individuals. The powerful have whipped the weak for centuries on end to instill that superstition. As long as *might excelled over right* that superstition had to continue. Now that we propose housing to be produced by an industry in which *right makes might* at less than a pound per horsepower the superstition is obsolete.

There is no individuality in conventional houses. They are all four-square boxes with varying lengths of rotting wood Greek column nailed onto the front, every house so similar that without signboards the stranger cannot tell the difference between one American town and another, let alone detect individuality in the separate and pathetic homes.

On the other hand, it has been discovered that the more uniform and simple the surfaces with which the individual is graced, the more does the individuality, which is the abstract life, come through. Trained nurses in uniform working in a hospital are notoriously more attractive as individuals than the same girls in their street clothes when off duty.

To somebody who says, "what are your houses going to cost?" we are not yet able to say very accurately, but the indications are the cost will be relatively low. "That," we say, "is very unimportant." My argument—and I hope yours—is going to be that costs are entirely relative. Your wage structure is going up fairly fast. If your wage structure is different, your price will be different. Houses that cost $5,000 before the war are now costing $8,000. Houses reflect relative prices. Suppose we are somewhere around or below the $5,000 mark—I think that is pretty good.

What is more important, however, I think is for us all to realize the actual picture of production potential of our houses in terms of the capacity of the metals produced for the aircraft industry during this war. Not going outside of the aircraft capacity—not infringing at all on the old building world, leaving it to build as best it can, we can get set up in the aircraft plants and be producing two million houses a year just as fast as we can get ready. Just as fast as you boys can get out good production drawings and complete your calculations and get this house tooled up, we can produce two million houses a year.

That is talking entirely new figures and we can amplify the aluminum capacity and amplify the aircraft capacity and get up to five million houses and approach the automobile figures. That is perfectly reasonable. There is nothing fantastic about that number of units. We are talking about something we know is really practical.

As it is practical and we really need two million houses right now for G.I.s, and need twelve million for people in substandard and crowded houses in the United States, and need thirty million houses for 100% bombed-out families in the war-torn countries, I say the cost of *not* having our houses is not only enormous, it is history's tragedy. It leads rapidly into lawlessness and ill health, to an enormous cost to society. I would ask a senatorial committee or a congressional committee asking me what houses cost, *"How much is it going to cost not to have our houses?"* That is what is important and I really look at the accumulating national debt as the accumulation of the cost of maintaining curative pathology instead of investing a few billions in establishing a preventive pathology through a scientific worldwide housing service industry. We have already come a long way downhill from the industrial peak in the face of an enormous ability to create wealth and put our environment under control. The initial cost is very important. If we can get the thing rolling, we can make houses available to everyone who wants houses, and very rapidly obsolete all old standards of living. We will set up a new industry that promises to go on to rehouse the whole world and employ the whole world in the continuous wealth-making of improving living advantages.

That is clear enough as a simple picture to the building trades. Some of the building trades people I talk to understand this, and it is very clear to mechanics that we are talking about starting up a new industry and not a new house. They are not going to be so concerned about whether the building trades are employed in erecting those houses. The building trades men tell me they have participated in the building of less than 4% of single-family dwellings. It is not a very important item to them. When you talk to them about giving them a new industry, the new industry, like the telephone, would cause a great deal of bricklaying of the individual plants, the power stations, etc. Therefore, you want to say, all of you, that you are designing an additional industry which is going to get everybody busy. Your labor man doesn't mind the idea of short man-hours, or better working conditions or steady year-round work.

Beech figures show way less than 100 man-hours per house to manufacture. Our indications are that in the field we will start with 100 man-hours and before we get through with developing the boom jig upon which we are going to hang the house as we assemble it and feed the parts off the tailboard to give a very fast assembly, we will be down to relatively few man-hours—40 man-hours or something like that—in the field. (That of course is not what we are going to do out here in the early days.)

I will prophesy however than within two years we will be down to somewhere under 100 man-hours from raw material as delivered to the aircraft industry (that is, as sheet aluminum in rolls, steel in rods and tubes, etc.) to finished house—under 100 man-hours. So your living cost is going to be low and your standards high and rapidly rising.

Obviously, boys, the thing is now reasonably good enough to dare to put it out on the world, and the world will be reasonably tolerant enough with it to "take" all the bugs that are still in it. It is full of them. But we have harnessed out there now in our prototypes the right principles within the right weight and the right dimensions, so that's where you boys have to take over.

Thank you very much.

1946

The young Hungarian constructivist painter, photographer, and filmmaker who proclaimed himself against "emotionalism" in art and who, on Walter Gropius's invitation and together with Josef Albers, took over responsibility for the foundation course at the Weimar Bauhaus in 1923 appears all technician in the classic photographs of the time. In his five years at the Bauhaus, **Laszlo Moholy-Nagy** was instrumental in reconstituting the *Vorkurs,* turning it from the metaphysical and intuitive approach of his predecessor, the "mystic" Johannes Itten, to a disciplined curriculum based on design fundamentals. Yet by 1928, when he resigned from the school—now located in Dessau under the directorship of the radical technocrat Hannes Meyer—Moholy-Nagy had arrived at a "biological" approach to design education. This conception was based on an integration of objective technical expertise with the individual's comprehensive experiential and emotional development. In his letter of resignation, he registered his protest against the Meyer regime: "We are now in danger of becoming what we as revolutionaries opposed: a vocational training school which evaluates only the final achievement and overlooks the development of the whole man."

It was this philosophy, first set out in his book *Von Material zu Architektur* (1929; translated as *The New Vision,* 1930, 1938), that Moholy-Nagy brought from Europe to America. He came to the United States in 1937 by way of

176–80
England, again on the recommendation of Gropius (who was now at Harvard), to direct the New Bauhaus in Chicago. Modeling the school on the pedagogy honed at Dessau, Moholy-Nagy sought to combine practical experience of materials and design techniques with study of the humanities and natural sciences, the latter taught by University of Chicago faculty who shared his educational ideas. When financial backing failed in 1938, Moholy-Nagy raised the funds to open the School of Design a year later. This institution received college status in 1944 and was renamed the Institute of Design, with a major increase in enrollment. At these successive institutions, Moholy-Nagy passionately pursued "the conscientious training of a new generation of producers, consumers, and designers" according to the approach he outlines in the following statement.

Unlike at the original Bauhaus, where there was no formal instruction in architecture until the Meyer years, architecture was central at Chicago from the start, the department being headed by native Chicagoan George Fred Keck. In 1946 after Moholy-Nagy died of leukemia, the architect Serge Chermayeff became director of the school. Later the Institute of Design was absorbed into Illinois Institute of Technology and in 1955 its architecture program consolidated under Mies van der Rohe. A comprehensive history of the Moholy-Nagy years in Chicago is contained in *Moholy-Nagy—Experiment in Totality* (1950) by his wife, Sibyl Moholy-Nagy. Hans Wingler's *The Bauhaus: Weimar, Dessau, Berlin, Chicago* (1969) includes documentation on the later history of the school.

The New Vision was completely revised and supplemented with an autobiographical essay in 1946, while a final statement of Moholy-Nagy's educational and aesthetic ideas, *Vision in Motion,* was published posthumously the following year. These two books, along with *Language of Vision* (1944) by Gyorgy Kepes, a close associate and member of Moholy-Nagy's faculty, are justly deemed classics of their time. With its calibrated asymmetrical layout, vivid imagery drawn from twentieth-century art, architecture, industrial design, and nature, and powerful use of photography as medium—both means and spirit—of the new technology, *Vision in Motion* infuses the exposition of Moholy-Nagy's didactics with the full power of the space-time imagination.

From L. Moholy-Nagy, Vision in Motion *(Chicago: Paul Theobald, 1947), pp. 63–68, 96. Courtesy of Hattula Moholy-Nagy.*

New Education—Organic Approach
Laszlo Moholy-Nagy

The Background—the Bauhaus

The Institute of Design, Chicago, is a laboratory for a new education. Founded for the training of artists, industrial designers, architects, photographers, and teachers, it embodies the principles and educational methods of the Bauhaus modified in accordance with the circumstances and demands of this country.

The old Bauhaus, an art university, established the principle that mass production of goods and modern architecture needed not only engineers but also artists with fresh mentality and exact information about old and new materials. The Bauhaus held that this information has to be coupled with a thorough knowledge of the means of expression as well as with the principles and practices of industry; that machines can be legitimate "tools" of the artist and designer. These were basic premises which had to be understood in order to give an industrial product a maximum of function and efficiency.

At the time the Bauhaus was founded the term "industrial designer" did not exist and the profession had not yet crystallized. The profession gained its status through the work of the Bauhaus. But beyond the newly won designation, function, and scope of the designer-specialist, others goals were developed. It became evident that not the specialist, but the man *in toto,* in all his vitality and potentiality, must become the measure of all educational approaches.

The Institute of Design, Chicago, building on these foundations, tries to stimulate the student's energies in their totality. The curriculum relies strongly on creative potentiality. The main intention is to produce an adequate rhythm between the biological capacities of the student and the contemporary scene. The goal is no longer to recreate the classical craftsman, artist, and artisan, with the aim of fitting him into the industrial age. By now technology has become as much a part of life as metabolism. The task therefore is to educate the contemporary man as an *integrator,* the new *designer* able to reevaluate human needs warped by machine civilization. The healthy function of a man's body, his social performance and welfare, his nutrition, clothing, and housing needs, his intellectual pursuits and emotional requirements, his recreation and leisure, should be the center of endeavors. An education which is responsible for such a totality must be indivisible, integrating elements of art, science, and technology. Such an indivisible education may then produce the genius for the social and biological mastery of our age.

Although the vocational goal is kept in mind in its technological training, the Institute of Design emphasizes the growth of the individual within the group. Hence art, natural and social sciences, "Intellectual Integration," are fixtures in its curriculum. Such an integrated training aims at more than the education of "free" artists in the old sense. The students must learn—besides the aesthetic means of expression—the technology of materials, and they must experience the organic, evolutionary use of the material. They are trained to articulate all media after they have been given the knowledge of relationships out of which the substance of expression takes shape. They have to face practical design problems too, to satisfy given needs with given means in order to earn a living. If, through stimulation by all of the practical and spiritual material offered during their training, some of them choose the career of a "free artist," the choice is their own prerogative and responsibility though certainly the Institute's delight.

The foundation (basic) course

The first year Basic Course is the backbone of the educational program. It radiates its principles far into the curriculum of the later specialized vocational fields, design and architecture. The Basic Course consists of three great chapters of information and experimental work in constant correlation:

1. *Technology*
   Basic elements of workshop training
   a.   The use of hand tools and machines
   b.   Materials. An understanding of the physical properties of structural materials, such as wood, clay, plastics, metal, paper, and glass
   c.   Study of shapes, surfaces, and textures
   d.   Study of volume, space, and motion. A training in the fundamental elements of design

2. *Art*
   Basic elements of plastic representation
   a.   Life drawing
   b.   Color work
   c.   Photography
   d.   Mechanical drawing
   e.   Lettering
   f.   Modeling
   g.   Literature (Group Poetry)

3. *Science*
   To provide the necessary basis for the Institute's courses, enough mathematics, physics, and social sciences, as well as liberal arts, are taught.

Through these integrated studies the student is given assistance in developing latent aptitudes, so that his eventual decision and choice of specialization is based upon his own education experience. "Specialization" means here the choice of a workshop, not a vocational goal. Since the industrial designer must be versatile, he must be trained in the most diverse fields. This, however, without the mastery of—at least—one field, easily could encourage dilettantism.

Policy

The policy is, first, not to dominate the student; second, to provide him with the opportunity to become conscious of the world and himself through exercises which simultaneously train the intellectual and emotional spheres. The exercises are generally of such nature that he cannot look for solutions in books or in museums. Because these exercises have no direct counterpart in tradition but are built around his potentialities and tools and materials, they direct his vision to new and unexplored channels. The student must use his imagination and wit, he must debate and contemplate, he must make independent findings. Since he is not allowed to imitate past solutions, he soon finds the power to face new situations fearlessly, to develop new habits of imagination. This relieves him of the necessity of identifying or even comparing his work with past performances. This policy is a powerful incentive for the teacher too, as it lessens the danger of clinging to traditional fixations or to academic certitudes.

Occasionally the contemporary artist's intuitive research can be applied, in a simplified version, to educational exercises in order to build up in the student a new concept of living and working through analogous experimentation. The tactile (touch) exercises in the Institute are, for example, derived from cubism and futurism, teaching that rich emotional values can be released on a sensory level otherwise neglected, namely, touch. Cubist and Schwitters collages have been the godfathers of the texture exercises in drawing, color work, and photography; the constructivists opened up a large experimental area for mobile sculpture, for *virtual* volume, and for fundamental tasks in light and space articulation. The principles of Mondrian, Malevich, and others could be adapted for camouflage; the stone carvings and plaster casts of Arp, Moore, and Hepworth for the free-shaped hand sculpture; Bruguiere's paper photos for light modulators. Naturally, the student cannot be transformed into an "artist" with such "exercises," but they can open for him the doors of expression and condition him to a new vision. Such exercises are especially useful in the first year courses where the student step by step comes to understand the methodology of creative approach. At the same time, skills are acquired automatically, for in these exercises the ideal of "skills" is taken as a matter of course. The attitude of the school encourages experimentation. The student works with different techniques and "learns" skills. He never has the feeling of forced learning since skills are needed as a matter of course for the solution of the tasks for which his interest has been awakened. Stimulated by the unusual or unknown, he is anxious to perform adequately. He looks for the best possible solution. He collects the necessary data and material; he reasons about the components of his "design"; he investigates different techniques—past and present— for its realization. Since it can be executed only with "skills," he turns his energies toward their mastery. Without being made conscious of the fact that his efforts at execution are an integral part of the learning process, he "learns" to handle tools and machines, materials and their technology.

The educational technique
There are a number of points which deserve consideration.

Among the exercises, one of the most important is the reexamination of tools and materials so that a given work can be executed in terms of their basic qualities and characteristics. One could call this approach an artless, unprejudiced search which, first on a modest but later on a growing scale, conditions one to creative thinking and acting, to inventiveness and intuitive assurance of judgment. This idea has an affinity with the kindergarten play technique as well as with the apprentice education of the old craftsman. There is, however, a great difference in orientation. The "play" of the grown-up, while it offers opportunity for relaxed explorations and collection of data, has implicitly a constructive direction. Through the collaboration of teachers who have the power of discrimination, the significant points are quickly recognized in the experiments and through subtle leadership the "play" is brought to purposeful results. An education in the crafts develops responsibility toward the product as a whole and through this it teaches the student discipline. But the crafts are not emphasized in opposition to machine work. The machine is understood as a very efficient "tool" which—if properly used—will serve the creative intention as well as the traditional hand tool.

A second principle is to break down complex tasks into fundamental components so that they can be digested one after the other and then brought into functional relationship. The requirement is, however, that even such elementary exercises, though they may combine only a few elements, must achieve entity, "form," must produce a coherent whole.

In all exercises a certain rhythm is introduced through an alternating pattern of freedom and restriction. First, expression is encouraged with the greatest range of emotional interpretation without any censorship. For example, a tactile chart, an illuminating, enriching exercise for the fingers, can be composed solely with the power of intuition. But after that, a photographically precise rendering of the chart, its facsimile, has to be made. This requires minute observation, a coordination of the eye and hand. With this combination of approaches swift emotional decisions are brought into an organic relationship with the relatively slower process of the critical mind.

Practicing correlations

A number of exercises which confront the student are aimed toward self-discovery; that is, the awakening of his own creative abilities. The exercises are mostly built upon sensory experience through work with various materials, with their technology, the skill of the fingers, the hands, the eye and the ear, and their coordination. This is accomplished through tactile charts composed of textures and hand-sculptures carved out of wood, which are to be handled and felt; through machine woodcuts which make lumber as elastic as rubber; through folding, rolling, cutting, and other manipulations of flat paper sheets which lead to the understanding of basic three-dimensional structures; through plane, volume, and space division and their further articulation. In addition there is work with sheet metal and wire, glass, mirrors, plastics, drawing and color, mechanical drawing, photography, group poetry, and music—a full range of potentialities.

These subjects, organized in the first year curriculum, become correlated through a method of simultaneous handling of the same problem in the various workshops. classrooms, and studios, emphasizing the mutual influence of technique and materials. For example, when a sculpture is made in the modeling workshop, the same sculpture is used in the photo studio to serve as a study for light and shape definition. Again the same sculpture is utilized as a departure for volume and space analysis in mechanical drafting, as a theme in drawing and color exercises, and the same object will also be analyzed in the science and technology classes. Since in such an approach many different angles must be considered, the student gains a comprehensive understanding of the single object. He learns that this method can be utilized for various subject matters, giving him the courage to attack other problems without inhibition and fear and with a sharpened sense of logical and emotional interpretation.

Summing it up: the training is directed toward imagination, fantasy, and inventiveness, a basic conditioning to the ever changing industrial scene, to the technology-in-flux. This works "forward" as well as "backward": that is, concerning future developments or old-fashioned tasks.

The last step in this technique is the emphasis on integration through a conscious search for relationships—artistic, scientific, technical, as well as social. The intuitive working mechanics of the genius gives a clue to this process. The unique ability of the genius can be approximated by everyone if only its essential feature be apprehended: the flashlike act of connecting elements not obviously belonging together. Their constructive relationships, unnoticed before, produce the new result.

If the same methodology were used generally in all fields we would have *the* key to our age—*seeing everything in relationship.* [. . .]

Fig. 76. O Henry Kann, 1941
Experiments for plywood legs for furniture

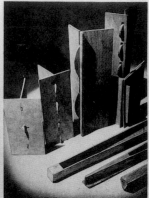

Fig. 77. O Design class, Institute of Design, 1941
Experimental plywood joints

Fig. 78. O Elic Nekimkin
Elastic wall
This structure originated through experiments with new plywood joints. The construction of the single elements can be seen in closeup in the illustration at the right

Fig. 74. O T. Torre Bueno, 1940
Papercut

Fig. 75. O Georgianna Green, 1941
Shock-absorbing wiremesh pillow

Fig. 79. O Millie Goldsholl, 1943-1944
Welding with plastic
One of the most interesting discoveries of the Institute during the war was friction welding. Mrs. Goldsholl says about her experiments, "It started out with a curiosity about how two plastic dowels would stick together when drilled into each other. The surprise came when the visual outlines of the injected dowel disintegrated where the two were joined. Apparently the intense heat caused by friction and then pressure had melted the contacting surfaces into a single transparent unit"

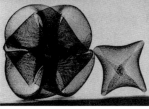

[Vision in Motion, *p. 83.*]

The architecture department

Architectural education is in a state of flux. Though there is a "notion" that the developments of the industrial age require some attention, the fixations of the "beaux arts" have so far held fast against a thorough change in terms of the new requirements. But the pressure of contemporary art and technology mounts. People have begun to appreciate the new industrial materials—steel, aluminum, plate glass, cement—the basis for a new structural thinking and the idea of "prefabrication for mass production." They have also become increasingly aware of the inevitable social requirements which will mold future architecture. Under these influences there exists a certain readiness to apply new methods of approach to architectural education.

In order to work efficiently and intelligently, artists, industrial designers, architects, have to master the fundamentals of plane, volume, space, and motion (space-time). The fundamentals of drawing, color, modeling, mechanical drafting, photography, mathematics, physics, chemistry, and the humanities are the same in both architecture and industrial design. Thus the coordination of the education of the artist, designer, and architect is one of the most important aspects of training in the Institute of Design.

Knowing the essentials of architecture, the product designer will be able to cope with its demands. This is important because most of his work will in one way or another be incorporated into architecture. On the other hand, the architect will more capably judge the objects and products needed in his work; and his knowledge of industrial processes will be his guide for a long-awaited experimentation with mass-scale housing.

In the Institute for Design, the education of the architect and designer is united. Every design student, from the third semester on, is not only a member of a special workshop but automatically also of the Architectural Department. After the eighth semester the degree of Bachelor of Design can be received, after the twelfth, the Master of Arts. [. . .]

1947

The International Congresses for Modern Architecture (**CIAM**) were founded in 1928 at La Sarraz, Switzerland, by a group of the leading modern architects. The most important document to emerge from their series of pre-World War II meetings was the *Athens Charter*, a set of principles of urbanism organizing planning into four key functions—dwelling, work, recreation (both mental and physical), and circulation. The result of CIAM's fourth conference in 1933, it was published in France in 1943 under German occupation. The charter became the principal point of reference for the organization's subsequent activity.

A fifth CIAM congress took place in Paris in 1937, while a sixth scheduled for 1939 in Liège was canceled because of the war. For the next eight years, CIAM's international operation was curtailed, although local initiatives continued in countries around the world. One of these was the Chapter for Relief and Postwar Planning founded in New York in 1944 as a CIAM section in the Western Hemisphere, including Richard Neutra, José Luis Sert, Knud Lönberg-Holm, Paul Nelson, and Harwell Hamilton Harris as officers, and counting among its members Sigfried Giedion, Walter Gropius, Oscar Stonorov, William Wurster, Mies van der Rohe, Wallace Harrison, Joseph Hudnut, Vernon DeMars, Lawrence Kocher, Pierre Chareau, and Ernest Weissmann. (On this group, which undertook studies on the new United Nations, and in general on CIAM from 1939 to 1947, see the forthcoming documentation by Jos Bosman, to be published by the ETH-Zurich.)

226–36 It was not until September 1947 that CIAM held its next international meeting. This took place in Bridgwater, England, and was hosted by the MARS Group, the English wing of CIAM. The purpose, as reflected in the following statement, was to reestablish communication among the members and to determine CIAM's role in the new period. Sert, whose *Can Our Cities Survive?*— an application of the principles formulated at Athens—had been published in 1942, was chosen to succeed Cornelis van Eesteren as president. Consensus was strong that CIAM should not be a group of isolated personalities as it had tended to be prior to the war, but rather a task-oriented working congress carrying out defined activities. The organization's statutes were redrafted to open membership to all architects who accepted its principles and agreed to participate in the work teams that were to be formed, without limitation, in the various countries—a step that would contribute to the large increase in CIAM's membership by the time of its ninth meeting in Aix-en-Provence in 1953.

181–83, 347–60 More significantly, the reunion of the "masters" at Bridgwater also saw the emergence of an internal critique by a new generation of architects who had come to maturity in the intervening years. Among those who would shortly play a crucial role in CIAM's future were the Dutch architects Jacob Bakema and Aldo van Eyck. Van Eyck made a plea for CIAM to move beyond a rationalistic and mechanistic conception of progress to a more creative understanding of the human environment: "Imagination remains the only common denominator of man and nature, the only faculty capable of registering spiritual transformation . . ." The theme of imagination had also been evoked in two questionnaires prepared for the meeting, one by J. M. Richards for the MARS Group, the other by Giedion and the artist Hans Arp, raising, for the first time within CIAM, questions of aesthetics and of architecture's relationship to the other arts. The introduction of 64–67 these themes—the latter having been of special concern to Le Corbusier since the war's end—presented a rallying point for the reconvening congress. "Finally," Le Corbusier declared, "imagination comes to CIAM."

From Sigfried Giedion, CIAM: A Decade of Contemporary Architecture *(Zurich: Girsberger, 1954), p. 24. Courtesy of CIAM-Archiv, Institut für Geschichte und Theorie der Architektur, ETH Zurich.*

Reaffirmation of the Aims of CIAM
CIAM 6, Bridgwater

1.   Preamble We, the CIAM architects from many countries, in Europe, America, Asia, and Africa, have met at Bridgwater after an interval of ten years.

These have been years of struggle and separation during which, as a consequence of the threat of Fascist domination, political, economic, and social questions have taken on a new significance for everyone. At the same time technical progress has been accelerated by intensive scientific research and the needs of war production. The technique of planning has also moved forward as a result of the experience some countries have gained in social organization.

These factors are together responsible for a new conception of integrated planning which is now emerging. Allied with this is a new contemporary consciousness that finds its definitive expression in the arts.

We are faced with an enormous task in rebuilding the territories devastated by the war as well as in raising the standard of life in undeveloped countries where great changes are now taking place. We therefore feel that this, our sixth congress, is an occasion when we must review our past activities, examine our present situation, and determine our policy for the future.

2.   Background Our earlier declarations—that of La Sarraz in 1928 and the Athens Charter of 1933—reflected the architect's growing sense of his responsibilities toward society. They were drawn up with reference to a particular time and particular situation, but we consider many of the statements made in them to be fundamental and we now reaffirm the following points from these declarations.

"We emphasize that to build is a primal activity in man, intimately associated with the evolution and development of human life . . ."

"Our intention . . . is to reestablish the place of architecture in its proper social and economic sphere . . ."

"We affirm today the necessity for a new conception of architecture satisfying the spiritual, intellectual, and material needs of present-day life. Conscious of the effects on social structure, brought about by industrialization, we recognize the necessity of a corresponding transformation of architecture itself . . ."

"Planning is the organization of the functional conditions of community life: it applies equally to town and country, and operates within the divisions: a. dwelling; b. places of work and c. of recreation; d. circulation, connecting these three . . ."

"The aims of CIAM are: a. to formulate the architectural problem of today; b. to represent the idea of a contemporary architecture; c. to instill this idea into technical, economic and social thought; d. to watch over the contemporary development of architecture."

The Declaration of La Sarraz was primarily an attempt to express some of the realities of the contemporary situation and to recognize the inevitable emergence of new forms from the application of new means to meeting human needs.

Many of the ideas for which we were then working are now widely accepted, and the subsequent Athens Charter has laid a similar foundation in the field of physical and social planning. Among the achievements of recent years are:

A general acceptance of the idea of social planning and, in many countries, the adoption of planning legislation—including legislation for land reform—which will assist the realization of this idea.

A growing recognition of the important part played by scientific method in the development of architecture, which has resulted in the advance of building technique.

A trend toward the reintegration of the plastic arts—architecture, sculpture, and painting—and thereby toward a clearer understanding of contemporary forms of artistic expression.

3. The aims of CIAM The progress that has been made in the last ten years and the confidence in the ideals of CIAM expressed by the younger generation convince us that the continuation of the CIAM congresses is fully justified. The sixth congress redefines the aims of CIAM as follows:

"To work for the creation of a physical environment that will satisfy man's emotional and material needs and stimulate his spiritual growth."

To achieve an environment of this quality, we must combine social idealism, scientific planning, and the fullest use of available building techniques. In so doing we must enlarge and enrich the aesthetic language of architecture in order to provide a contemporary means whereby people's emotional needs can find expression in the design of their environment. We believe that thus a more balanced life can be produced for the individual and for the community.

4. The tasks ahead Having members in so many countries, CIAM is in a strong position to put the experience gained in one part of the world at the disposal of another. The social concepts and legislative experiments of countries that have made progress in these fields can give direction to the technical development of highly industrialized countries, and technical experience from elsewhere can be brought to the assistance of countries that are still in process of industrialization.

An urgent task for CIAM is to ensure that the highest human and technical standards are attained in community planning of whatever scale, from the region to the single dwelling. CIAM also feels called upon to examine the implications of the process of industrialization that is now being applied to building, in order to ensure that such necessary technical developments are controlled by a sense of human values.

5. Future policy With the purpose of fulfilling the aims outlined above, CIAM intends to pursue a policy that will:

Popularize its principles as widely as possible, by means of books, periodicals, exhibitions, films, the radio, and other means of addressing the people of all countries.

Formulate the principles that should govern the education of architects and take all possible measures for the reform of existing educational methods.

Support in every way the activities of the local and national groups of CIAM, especially by establishing contacts with official authorities, national and international, and by promoting beneficial legislation and other effective measures.

Encourage CIAM groups to keep in touch with public needs and observe the progress of the public's understanding of CIAM principles, with the object of assisting modern architecture to develop in sympathy with the aspirations of the people it serves.

1947

Construction of the Shell office building in the Hague, designed by the Dutch architect **J. J. P. Oud**, was completed in 1942 during the German occupation of Holland. Oud's workers housing estates of the 1920s—from Spangen and Oud-Mathenesse to Hoek van Holland and Kiefhoek—ranked among the foremost achievements of functionalist design in Europe. The Shell building thus shocked many with its apparent regression to a monumental and ornamented classicism. The effect of the imposing front elevation with its vertical window articulation and use of decorative patterning was hardly mitigated by glass stair towers and a circular dining volume. To those outside Holland who first saw photographs of the building after the war, the "solemn and aggressive" facade treatment suggested earlier polemics by the Hamburg architect Fritz Höger, whose Sprinkenhof of 1926–28 Oud's building (consciously or not) recalled.

27–30   Yet Oud's turn to monumentality was not as unlikely as it seemed. Certainly it was in keeping with a trend presaged at the World Exposition in Paris in 1937, the year Oud began designing the building. It was also related, closer to home, to a Dutch movement of the mid-1930s led by Arthur Staal and Sybold van Ravensteyn. These architects, calling themselves "Group 32," rejected the strict functionalism of the Amsterdam CIAM group "De 8 en Opbouw" in favor of more artistic expression, drawing a distinction between honorific civic structures and pragmatic buildings like low-cost housing and factories. The debate between the two factions was waged in a series of projects for city halls, culminating in the Amsterdam city hall competition of 1939. But Oud himself had anticipated this argument much earlier. In an essay entitled "The Monumental Townscape" published in 1917 in the first issue of *De Stijl,* while professing the rationalist line of Berlage over the "decadent" ornamentalism of the Amsterdam school, he advocated an urban monumentality achieved by "building in blocks or large groupings," emphatic volumetric rhythms, and collaboration between the different arts. Later, at the height of his functionalist period, his Volkuniversiteit in Rotterdam (1924–25) was an exercise in pure representationalism.

In December 1946, *Architectural Record*—with editorial input from Philip Johnson, who in 1932, with Henry-Russell Hitchcock, had cited Oud as one of
137–48   the four masters of the new modern architecture—published a highly critical article on the Shell building entitled "Mr. Oud Embroiders a Theme." Juxtaposed with an article vaunting the purism of Mies van der Rohe's Crown Hall, the article stated, "The plan of the Shell Building is hard to distinguish from straight academic. Its major forms seem to be not enascent from the problem but are recognizable as repertory out of the architect's notebook. The very insistent, heavy, separate, imposed pattern of 'decoration' seems visually related not to a keen process of expanding apperception but rather to the pleasant reminiscences of peasant art. [. . .] What did Oud find lacking in his earlier approaches? In this instance was he unconsciously slipping back into an easily popular answer or was he seeking something else?" Oud wrote back in English with the following reply, which the editors found to be worded "so expressively, even in a foreign tongue" that they printed it unedited.

Despite his stated conviction of the building's success, however, Oud did not persist in this direction after the 1940s. In late years, in works like the Utrecht Building in Rotterdam (1954–61) and his Miesian convention center in the Hague (1957–63), he would return to his earlier rationalism. Ironically, Johnson's own
189–92   work was to retread the path of Oud's excursion into monumentality. For background on the monumentality debate in Holland, see the forthcoming essay by Wim de Wit, "For Art's Sake: Modernist Debates in Holland in the 1930s."

From Architectural Record *(March 1947), p. 18. Courtesy of* Architectural Record.

Mr. Oud Replies
J. J .P. Oud

My dear Editors,

The wish to challenge sharply what I am doing is a wish I can understand.

Meaning that when someone is fixed to a style of development which seems clear enough, it must be a disappointment to see him escape the rules once based upon this belief. Yes, I comprehend very well your wish to go at me!

But let me defend myself and allow me to state that this is not my mistake. I have always tried to keep myself far away from all "rules." Seeing something "new" the world is immediately willing to give it a label and to place it in a partition.

I know definitely that I myself never succumbed to this labeling.

Since I attempted to go my own way in architecture I always had only one device— a device which has guided me up to now!—"seeking clear forms for clearly expressed needs." This proved to me not to be a matter of static, it was a thing of dynamic order. The rules it brought were not of a formal nature but very informal ones. It became evident that they were changing, within distinct limits, with the development of the idea.

In the beginning I was working on laborer-dwellings and my aim was to find a good and agreeable form for them; a form—so to speak—as exact and as clear as the form of a good car, a good steamer, a good electrical tool. In other words, I was searching for a good "common" form. And we have attained much in this respect.

The world, however, does not exist only out of cars, steamers, tools, neither out of houses, factories, etc. There are grades in the usual things of our existence and in my opinion there are for that reason also grades in our architecture. Even in good democracy there will be order of precedence in the family: the father has—or should have—another function from that of the son. Analogous with this, domestic building in our society has another function from that of an office building, a town hall, or a church.

Little by little, I discovered that the form of a laborer-dwelling or a factory cannot be the end of all architectural wisdom. It is an error to imply that this is true and that we have already reached "new architecture" by this means. It seems to me at present quite all right that the new domestic architecture is the base of new architecture; that it should be already new architecture itself, I deny emphatically.

Architecture itself—old or new—can and must give: emotion. It has to transport the aesthetic vision of one man (the architect) to another man (the onlooker). And why should it not? Are we in our modern times so condemned that we dare not set our own stages? Are we really so dried up that we don't allow ourselves to play a bit now and then? It is a very important fact which is too often forgotten in the case of new architecture!

We know now how to make "new building" by the application in a clear manner of concrete, plate glass, steel, etc. We did this, as previously mentioned, with success. But we never dare forget that the aesthetic emotion emanating from simple works like the work in question is an aesthetic emotion on a very low level. Building like this—and the majority of building is of this kind—is a wonderful start toward new architecture but new architecture itself has still to be found. One could say with some exaggeration: it is the bass to the music but not its essence. In some cases: the lyric, not the epic side of architecture.

Now: new architecture is what I strived at in my "Shell Building." It may be that it has more traditional ballast in it than former work of mine. I don't know. But it would not

MR. OUD EMBROIDERS A THEME

Shell "I.B.M." Building, the Hague

J–J. P. Oud, Architect

THE RECORD publishes this building with the question, what does it mean in the design cycle?

Some twenty-five years ago, the young J-J. P. Oud of Holland was one among a small number of great leaders who shared a fresh insight. They found architecture too cluttered with fairy tales, Latin, and obscure reference, to make coherent sense. So they swept the boards clear of all embroidery and determined to tell the story of their own day, and tell it in terms only of clear, factual, direct, and current speech. It is scarcely necessary to recount what subsequently happened. They largely won the day. In common with all great art, the best works these men produced held up the mirror to life, gave the community what only great art gives — a deeper self-recognition.

Small artists always had difficulty with this more austere form of expression. In unimaginative hands the "plain facts" were dull, meager, ugly, and insuf-

ficient. And sometimes that was the nature of the program, not remediable by any straightforward handling.

Here, now, is Oud himself resorting to embroidery. The plan of the Shell Building is hard to distinguish from straight academic. Its major forms seem to be not enascent from the problem but are recognizable as repertory out of the architect's notebook. The very insistent, heavy, separate, imposed pattern of "decoration" seems visually related not to a keen process of expanding apperception but rather to the pleasant reminiscences of peasant art.

There is no doubt that large sectors of the public will find this a "pretty" building. But for an architect of Oud's stature such an aim would not have been high enough. What did Oud find lacking in his earlier approaches? In this instance was he unconsciously slipping back into an easily popular answer or was he seeking something new?

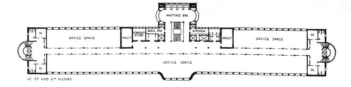

[From Architectural Record, December 1946, p. 80.]

be the first time in my efforts that I went back a bit to make myself fit for going further on the way I seek to explore: in this case a more difficult way to tread than the way of the laborer-dwellings!

Should you have time and opportunity to study the "Shell building" in reality I make bold that you shall have to establish the fact that I succeeded in finding new solutions. I agree with one of the critics you quoted that my ornament is not at all traditional. That it is developing after new directions and that it functionally is well placed into the composition.

And by the way: do you know that the "Shell Building" up to now already has been used for 5 years—sometimes by 600, sometimes by 1,000 employees—and that I never heard one complaint about the practical functioning of the building? What do you think could "functionalism" do more in this respect? And why should it be forbidden to give functional doing a spiritual form? Functioning alone as a leading principle—my experience taught me this—results in aesthetical arbitrariness. Don't forget this.

Yes, I am sure the "Shell Building" is an effort to arrange new practical needs in a well-considered and aesthetically well-shaped form. I must confess here that I have no belief in the application of the form of laborer-dwelling and factories to office buildings, town halls, and churches!

The whole world in laborer-dwelling-style must be unorganic and dull!

To resume: I tried to bring all that what we gained up to now in the field of new architecture to a cultural higher level. You think I went back on my way. I am not so sure of it. Look for instance one day at the building itself and see what I reached in the light and bright tone of the building as a whole: not like with plastering in a semipermanent manner but by the use of fine and durable material. Well, trials of the same kind you will find in the whole shape as well as in the form of the details of the building. Trials to come to a new architecture on a more spiritual base.

Did I succeed? Other people may judge this. I can only say for myself that I hope to be able to try it again and again to make further progress in this direction. To have the opportunity to help new building rise to new architecture. And this, my dear editors, still in the base of my old device: "seeking clear forms for clearly expressed needs."

With my very best wishes, etc.

J. J. P. Oud

1947

With this article for his Skyline column in the *New Yorker* magazine, **Lewis Mumford** touched off a debate that in some respects paralleled that

114–20 surrounding the "New Empiricism" in England. Against the abstract functionalism of the machine aesthetic, Mumford here champions a "native and humane form of modernism which one might call the Bay Region style." The latter was exemplified by a West Coast tradition that originated at the turn of the century with Bernard Maybeck and John Galen Howard, and continued in the work of an architect like William Wurster. Mumford found in this work "a free yet unobtrusive expression of the terrain, the climate, and the way of life on the Coast." In contrast to the English reception of Swedish architecture, however, Mumford's regionalism was not primarily aesthetic. His idea of the region, which emerged as early as 1924 in his book *Sticks and Stones*, had to do with understanding and managing the natural environment. He saw this approach not only as a potential form of resistance to the "relentless spread of venal and mechanical civilization," but as an index of the advancement of modern culture.

Mumford's prime target in his *New Yorker* article was the International Style

137–48 as codified by Henry-Russell Hitchcock and Philip Johnson in their 1932 exhibition at the Museum of Modern Art in New York (to which catalogue Mumford had himself contributed an article on housing), and now practiced by "academic American" epigones of the European masters. But he also took the opportunity to chide critics like Henry-Russell Hitchcock and Sigfried Giedion for recently switching stripes—Hitchcock to the "personalism" of Frank Lloyd Wright,

27–30 Giedion to monumentality, which in Mumford's view only amounted to new formalisms. Not surprisingly his attack provoked a heated conference at the same museum in February 1948, entitled "What Is Happening to Modern Architecture?" Among the participants were Hitchcock, Johnson, Gropius, Alfred Barr, Marcel Breuer, Talbot Hamlin, George Nelson, and Serge Chermayeff. Mumford, accused of chauvinism and sentimentality, attempted to clarify his position in a letter directed to Barr shortly afterward, writing, "I am utterly bewildered at the general extent and depth of misunderstanding of what I thought I had very plainly expressed in *The New Yorker*. For the point about the Bay Region style, in which it definitely departs from your restricted definition of an International architecture, is that it cannot be characterized by any single mode of building; and it certainly cannot be reduced to redwood cottage architecture, as you almost said in so many words. It is precisely the variety and range and universality of it that I was stressing . . ."

Further development of the argument came from Mumford in 1949, on the occasion of an exhibition at the San Francisco Museum of Art entitled "Domestic Architecture of the San Francisco Bay Region." In his statement for that catalogue Mumford again affirmed that "the main problem of architecture today is to reconcile the universal and the regional, the mechanical and the human, the cosmopolitan and the indigenous." Repercussions of the Bay Region argument would be heard over the next decade, with some of Mumford's original antagonists, if not converted, at least searching for their own compromises. See, for example, "The New Regionalism" (*Architectural Record*, January 1954) by Giedion, where the latter recasts the issue as a matter of building under specific

176–80 geographic conditions; and Gropius's "Eight Steps toward a Solid Architecture" in the present volume. The issue would remain an abiding theme of Mumford's social vision of architecture to the end of his career.

From The New Yorker, *11 October 1947, pp. 106, 109. Courtesy of the Gina Maccoby Literary Agency. Copyright © 1947 by Lewis Mumford; renewed 1975 by Lewis Mumford.*

The Skyline [Bay Region Style]
Lewis Mumford

[. . .] new winds are beginning to blow, and presently they may hit even backward old New York. The very critics, such as Mr. Henry-Russell Hitchcock, who twenty years ago were identifying the "modern" in architecture with Cubism in painting and with a general glorification of the mechanical and the impersonal and the aesthetically puritanic have become advocates of the personalism of Frank Lloyd Wright. Certainly Le Corbusier's dictum of the twenties—that the modern house is a machine for living in—has become old hat; the modern accent is on living, not on the machine. (This change must hit hardest those academic American modernists who imitated Le Corbusier and Mies van der Rohe and Gropius, as their fathers imitated the reigning lights of the Ecole des Beaux-Arts.) Mr. Sigfried Giedion, once a leader of the mechanical rigorists, has come out for the monumental and the symbolic, and among the younger people an inclination to play with the "feeling" elements in design—with color, texture, even painting and sculpture—has become insuppressible. "Functionalism," writes a rather pained critic in a recent issue of the *Architectural Review* of London, "the only real aesthetic faith to which the modern architect could lay claim in the interwar years, is now, if not repudiated, certainly called into question . . . by those who were formerly its most illustrious supporters."

We are bound to hear more of this development during the next decade, but I am not alarmed by the prospect. What was called functionalism was a one-sided interpretation of function, and it was an interpretation that Louis Sullivan, who popularized the slogan "form follows function," never subscribed to. The rigorists placed the mechanical functions of a building above its human functions; they neglected the feelings, the sentiments, and the interests of the person who was to occupy it. Instead of regarding engineering as a foundation for form, they treated it as an end. This kind of architectural one-sidedness was not confined to the more arid practitioners. Frank Lloyd Wright, it is said, once turned upon a client—let's call him John Smith—who had added a few pleasant rugs and comfortable Aalto chairs to Mr. Wright's furnishings, and exclaimed, "You have ruined this place completely, and you have disgraced me. This is no longer a Frank Lloyd Wright house. It is a John Smith house now."

Well, it was time that some of our architects remembered the nonmechanical and nonformal elements in architecture, that they remembered what a building says as well as what it does. A house, as the Uruguayan architect Julio Vilamajó has put it, should be as personal as one's clothes and should fit the family life just as well. This is not a new doctrine in the United States. People like Bernard Maybeck and William Wilson Wurster, in California, always practiced it, and they took good care that their houses did not resemble factories or museums. So I don't propose to join the solemn gentlemen who, aware of this natural reaction against a sterile and abstract modernism, are predicting a return to the graceful stereotypes of the eighteenth century. Rather, I look for the continued spread, to every part of our country, of that native and humane form of modernism which one might call the Bay Region style, a free yet unobtrusive expression of the terrain, the climate, and the way of life on the Coast. That style took root about fifty years ago in Berkeley, California, in the early work of John Galen Howard and Maybeck, and by now, on the Coast, it is simply taken for granted; no one out there is foolish enough to imagine that there is any other proper way of building in our time.

The style is actually a product of the meeting of Oriental and Occidental architectural traditions, and it is far more truly a universal style than the so-called international style of the 1930s, since it permits regional adaptations and modifications. Some of the best examples of this at once native and universal tradition are being built in New England. The change that is now going on in both Europe and America means only that modern architecture is past its adolescent period, with its quixotic purities, its awkward self-consciousness, its assertive dogmatism. The good young architects today are familiar enough with the machine and its products and processes to take them for granted, and so they are ready to relax and enjoy themselves a little. That will be better for all of us.

1948

Gaston Bachelard's seminal *La Poétique de l'espace* (The Poetics of Space) appeared in 1958. His early career had been devoted to the philosophy of science. By the late 1930s, however, influenced by psychoanalysis and surrealism, he turned his attention to the phenomenology of the poetic image. A year after finishing *L'Expérience de l'espace dans la physique contemporaine* (1937), the unorthodox thinker published *La Psychanalyse du feu* (1938), the first of a suite of books on the four cosmic elements—earth, air, fire, water— conceived as the foundation of what he would call the "material imagination."

The intellectual crisis that led Bachelard to turn from reason and science to poetry, and from time to space, coincides with what appears to be a more *419–28* widespread "epistemological break" in mid-twentieth-century thought. (Bachelard himself had earlier coined this concept with respect to the Einsteinian revolution *172–75* in physics.) A plaque made by an artist of the Cobra group, an avant-garde movement founded in the late 1940s, consists of a signpost with an arrow next to the name "Malraux" pointing one way and one next to "Bachelard" pointing the other. Le Corbusier had come to a similar crossroads at this date, relinquishing *64–67* his earlier politics of engagement for the postwar poetics of ineffable space.

In the excerpt that follows, from a chapter titled "The Childhood House and the Oneiric House" in *La Terre et les rêveries du repos* (The Earth and the Reveries of Rest, 1948), Bachelard first introduces the theme of the oneiric axis of the house, an image to which he will return in *The Poetics of Space*. For the philosopher of the spatial imagination, the house "bears the essence of the notion of home." A refuge, a retreat, a center, a place of everyday life, it harbors the psychic polarity of attic and cellar, essential sources for a richly experienced "dreaming life" of dwelling and "a tool for analysis of the human soul." For this reason, Bachelard writes, "inhabited space transcends geometrical space."

One can hardly overlook the parallel (but independent) development of *129–34* Bachelard's thought and that of Martin Heidegger, whose essays "Building, Dwelling, Thinking" and ". . . Poetically Man Dwells . . ." date from 1951. Interestingly, underlying their common shift from philosophy to poetry and the affinities between Bachelard's elemental cosmos and Heidegger's "fourfold" is a similar rootedness in provincial life and an inherent resistance to technology and urbanization. To Heidegger's image of the Black Forest farm one may compare Bachelard's nostalgia for the house rooted in the earth of his native French countryside. The sentiment, evident in the following excerpt, finds still stronger expression in *The Poetics of Space,* where Bachelard writes: "In Paris there are no houses, and the inhabitants of the big city live in superimposed boxes. . . . They have no roots and, what is quite unthinkable for a dweller of houses, skyscrapers have no cellars. From the street to the roof, the rooms pile up one on top of the other, while the tent of a horizonless sky encloses the entire city. But the height of city buildings is a purely exterior one. Elevators do away with the heroism of stair climbing so that there is no longer any virtue in living up near the sky. *Home* has become mere horizontality. The different rooms that compose living quarters jammed into one floor all lack one of the fundamental principles for distinguishing and classifying the values of intimacy. But in addition to the intimate nature of verticality, a house in a big city lacks cosmicity. For here, where houses are no longer set in natural surroundings, the relationship between house and space becomes an artificial one. Everything about it is mechanical and, on every side, intimate living flees."

From Gaston Bachelard, La Terre et les rêveries du repos (Paris: José Corti, 1948), pp. 106–12. Translated by permission of the Dallas Institute of Humanities and Culture, 2719 Ruth Street, Dallas. Texas 75201.

The Oneiric House
Gaston Bachelard

[. . .] The child is there by his mother, living in the middle part. Will he go with the same courage to the cellar and to the attic? The worlds are so different from each other. In one darkness, in the other light; in one muted sounds, in the other clear ones. The phantoms above and the phantoms below have neither the same voices nor the same shadows. The time spent in each does not have the same tonality of anguish. And it is quite rare to find a child who has courage enough for both. Cellar and attic can be detectors of imagined miseries, of those miseries which often, for all of life, leave their mark on the unconscious.

But let's not live only the images of a tranquillized life, in a house carefully exorcised by good parents.

Let's descend to the cellar, as in older times, candle in hand. The trap-door is a black hole in the floor; the night and its freshness are under the house. How many times in dreams will one make again this descent into a sort of walled night? The walls too are black under the gray hangings of the spider. Oh, why are they *slippery*? Why is there a stain on the dress? A woman must not descend into the cellar. It is the business of the man to go fetch the new wine. As Maupassant said (*Mont-Oriol,* vol. 3): "For only males go to the cellar." How steep and worn the staircase is, how the steps shine! All those generations when the stone steps were not washed. Above, the house is so clean, so bright, so well ventilated!

And then here is the earth, the black and humid earth, the earth under the house, the *earth of the house.* Some stones to wedge the wine barrels. And under the stone, a dirty creature, the wood louse, who finds a way—like so many parasites—to be fat at the same time as he is flat! How many dreams, how many thoughts come in the time it takes to fill a liter from the barrel!

Once one has understood the oneiric necessity to have lived in a house that comes forth from the earth, that lives rooted in its black earth, one reads with infinite dreams that curious page where Pierre Guéguen describes the "Treading of the New House" (*Bretagne,* p. 44): "Once the new house was finished, one forced the earth to become a solid and flat base under one's boots. For this one mixed sand and slag together, plus a magical binder made of sawdust and sap, and one invited the young people of the town to come stamp on this mud." And an entire page tells us of the unanimous will of the dancers who, under the pretext of making the soil solid and firm, set themselves to bury the evil spirits.[1] Do they not in this way fight against the repressed fears, against the fears that will transmit themselves from generation to generation, in this refuge constructed upon trampled earth? Kafka too lived for an entire winter in a dwelling on the ground. It was a little house in Prague on Alchymistengasse. He writes (as Max Brod cites, *Franz Kafka,* p. 184): "It is a very particular feeling to have one's own house, to be able to close the door—not of one's room, not of one's apartment, but that of one's whole house—on the world; to tread on the snow that covers the silent street directly upon leaving one's lodging . . ."

In the attic are lived the hours of long solitude, hours that range from sullenness to contemplation. It is in the attic that one sulks in absolute abandon, sulks unwitnessed. The child hidden in the attic basks in his mother's anguish: where is he, that sulker?

It is also in the attic that one does interminable reading, far from those who pick up books because they have already read too much. In the attic one dresses up in the costumes of one's grandparents, with shawl and ribbons.[2] What better museum for reveries than a crowded attic! There old things attach themselves for life to the soul of a child. A reverie brings back to life a family's past, the youth of one's ancestors. In four lines a poet sets into movement the shades of the attic: *In some corners / of the attic / I found / living ghosts / stirring* (Pierre Reverdy, *Plupart du temps*, p. 88).

Then too the attic is the domain of the dry life, of a life that is preserved through drying.[3] Here is the withering linden flower, crumbling in one's hand, and here are the raisins hanging in the hoop of a wine barrel, marvelously lustrous like the clusters of grapes with their clear lights . . . For all fruits the attic is a world of autumn, a world of October, the most suspended of all the months . . .

If one has the chance to ascend to the family attic by a narrow stair, or by a stair without bannister, squeezed a little between the walls, one can be certain that a beautiful diagram will inscribe itself for life in the dreamer's soul. Through the attic the house takes on a singular height; it participates in the aerial life of nests. In the attic the house is in the wind (cf. Giono, *Que ma joie demeure*, p. 31). The attic is truly "the lightweight house," like that in the dream of d'Annunzio, living in a chalet in Landes: "The house on the branch, light, sonorous, quick" (*Contemplation de la mort*, p. 62).

Moreover, the attic is a changing universe. The attic in evening has great terrors. Alain-Fournier's sister has noted its dread (*Images d'Alain Fournier*, p. 21): "But all that is the garret by day. That of the night—how will Henri be able to stand it? How will he be able to put up with it? How will he be stand to be alone in this other universe into which one enters above, without forms or limits, open under the dead nocturnal clarities to a thousand presences, a thousand rustlings, a thousand whispering transactions?" And by the half-open door Alain-Fournier in *Le Grand Meaulnes* sees again the attic (chap. 7): "And all night we feel around us, penetrating into our bedroom, the silence of the three attics."

Thus there is no true oneiric house that is not organized vertically. With its cellar well in the earth, its ground floor for daily life, the floor where one sleeps, and the attic next to the roof, such a house has all that is necessary for symbolizing deep fears, the platitudes of daily life almost touching the ground, and sublimations. Clearly a complete oneiric topology would demand detailed studies; it would also require one to consider refuges that are sometimes very particular: a cupboard, the undercroft of a stairway, an old fireplace can offer suggestive outlines for the psychology of the enclosed life. This life must, moreover, be studied in the two opposite senses of prison and refuge. But in totally adhering to the intimate life of the house that we are characterizing in these pages, we leave to one side the rages and fears nourished in a child's prison. We speak only of positive dreams, of dreams that will return all through life, impelling innumerable images. Thus one can state as a general law the fact that every child who is enclosed desires an imaginary life; and dreams, it seems, are the grander the smaller the refuge in which the dreamer feels himself to be. As Yanette Delétang-Tardif says (*Edmond Jaloux*, p. 34): "The most enclosed being is a *generator of waves*." Loti renders to perfection this dialectic of the dreamer huddled in his solitude and these waves of reveries in quest of immensity: "When I was a small child I had here some little nooks which represented Brazil to me, where I truly succeeded in giving myself the impressions and fears of the virgin forest" (*Fleurs d'ennui. Suleima*, p. 355). One gives the child a profound life by according him a place of solitude, a corner. A Ruskin, in the great dining room of his parents, passed long hours confined in his "corner."[4] He speaks of it at length in his memories of childhood. At base, the closed-in and the extroverted life are both psychic necessities. But so as not to become abstract formulas, it is necessary that they be psychological realities with a setting, a decor. For these two lives, the house and the fields are both necessary.

Can one sense now the difference in oneiric richness between the country house constructed truly on the earth, in an enclosure, in its own universe, and the edifice in which a few compartments serve for our lodging and which is constructed only on the asphalt of cities? Is this paved room where more trunks than wine barrels are piled up a cellar?

Thus a philosopher of the imaginary encounters—he too—the problem of the "return to earth." One must excuse his incompetence, given that he is treating this social problem only at the level of a study of the dreaming psyche; he would be satisfied if only he could engage the poets to construct for us, with their dreams, "oneiric houses" with cellar and attic. They would help us to shelter our memories, to shelter them in the unconscious of the house, in accord with the symbols of intimacy to which real life has not always the possibility of giving root.

Notes

1.	In an article in *Journal Asiatique* ("La Maison védique"), October 1939, Louis Renou indicates a rite, prior to the building of the Vedic house, of "appeasement of the ground."

2.	Cf. Rainer Maria Rilke, *The Notebooks of Malte Laurids Brigge* (New York: W. W. Norton, 1949), pp. 92–93.

3.	Anyone who would like to live, with Mary Webb, in the attic of Sarn, will know these impressions of the *economized life.*

4.	Cf. J.-K.Huysmans, *Against the Grain* (Harmondsworth: Penguin Books, 1971), p. 26. Des Esseintes installs in his living room "a series of niches."

1949

The late 1940s saw the revival in England of the eighteenth-century philosophy of the picturesque. This singularly British combination of modern architecture and national sentimentality went under the name of "Townscape." It involved "the art of giving visual coherence and organization to the jumble of buildings, streets, and spaces that make up the urban environment." Spurred by an ongoing series in the *Architectural Review*, a journal edited by previously staunch modernists like Nikolaus Pevsner (author of *Pioneers of the Modern Movement*, 1936) and J. M. Richards (*Introduction to Modern Architecture*, 1940), Townscape was founded on the relational principle of "significant differentiation," an urban contextualism looking to find either character or art in the heterogeneous composite "out there."

42–46 The *Review*'s polemical rediscovery of the virtues of the national vernacular coincided with its campaign for Swedish informality—the "New Empiricism." Both these humanistic enthusiasms must be seen against the background of English postwar reconstruction. Of paramount import were the housing developments, schools, and new towns being built under the auspices of the new British welfare state in those economically strapped years. They were optimistic projects, many by talented and progressive architects working in the county councils' architecture offices, the only source of work at this date. Architects attempted to

231–41 make the best of a difficult situation, mixing pared-down functional planning with "people's detailing" and other accommodations to an English sense of coziness. The English modern movement, which had never sat entirely comfortably with continental doctrinalism, now drew sustenance from its own Garden City and Arts and Crafts traditions. Though the *Review*'s position was satirized at the time—the editors received gifts of cobblestones and drain covers—the Townscape concept provided theoretical justification for a nonconformist English modernism and ascribed aesthetic value to the idiosyncrasies of everyday life.

The following writing is excerpted from a long article entitled "Townscape: A Plea for an English Visual Philosophy Founded on the True Rock of Sir Uvedale Price." Bylined "I[vor] de Wolfe," *nom de plume* of **Hugh de Cronin Hastings**, another of the *Review*'s editors, it is followed by a "casebook of out there," a set of images and sketches assembled by Gordon Cullen, didactically catalogued under the rubrics "vista," "incident," "pattern," "roofscape," "wallscape," and so on. Cullen, art editor of the *Review* at this date, continued to expand the Townscape imagery in similar casebooks within the journal's pages for more than a decade. Uvedale Price, the honorific father figure invoked in the title, was an English landscape theorist who published a three-volume *Essay on the Picturesque* in 1794. The term *sharawaggi* supposedly derives from a Chinese word that entered English parlance in the seventeenth century to describe landscaping principles based on asymmetry, informality, and variety— in the *Review*'s tendentious interpretation, a premodern concept of free planning.

A string of art historical articles by Pevsner and others, culminating in Pevsner's 1955 radio talks published as *The Englishness of English Art*, did not fail to produce specious comparisons between eighteenth- and twentieth-century

341–46 design. A succinct critique is contained in a letter by Alan Colquhoun to the *Review*, July 1954. For further background on the *Architectural Review* of the 1940s and after, see Reyner Banham, "Revenge of the Picturesque: English Architectural Polemics, 1945–1965," in John Summerson, ed., *Essays on Architectural Writing Presented to Nikolaus Pevsner* (1968), and Joseph Rykwert, "Review of a Review," in *Zodiac* 2 (1959); for an Italian perspective, see Matilde Baffa, "L'architettura al vaglio di una rivista inglese," *Casabella* 220 (July 1958).

From Architectural Review, *December 1949, pp. 360–62. Courtesy of the Estate of H. de C. Hastings.*

Townscape: A Plea for an English Visual Philosophy
I. de Wolfe [Hugh de Cronin Hastings]

[. . .] Nine people out of ten are surrounded in the home by household gods whose arrangement is as capricious as their origin is various: a Biedermeier escritoire, *The Lion Slayer,* a Buhl cabinet, an act of Parliament clock by Tribe of Petworth, Daniel prints of Abyssinia, a dead collection, a horsehair chair covered·in chintz, an Aalto table, or a less arty assortment from Great Aunts, the Near East, and Oxford Street. Looked at from the point of view of those Parisian flats in which ageing couples live in a flawless Louis milieu, the bric-à-brac of the average home is anarchist, appalling. True. And again the children's golf clubs and overcoats may upset the ensemble. Yet the taste can be extremely high that quite ordinary tasteless philistines show in the disposition and relationship of their bits and pieces even when those pieces are intrinsically worthless. There are thousands of homes of families-in-the-street which can offer satisfying arrangements of objects simply because their owners pursue quite unselfconsciously the Picturesque philosophy of giving every object the best possible chance to be itself.

This natural understanding (Uvedale Price's phrase), this sensibility to the relations between differences, this superrealism, is the quality which cries out to be transferred from the interior to the exterior of the cave. There are exceptions (like Bath), even in England, but in general an easy anarchy, pleasant or unpleasant as luck dictates, reigns in the streets as in our homes. Missing in the streets, however, is the controlling hand found inside the home—which makes exactly all the difference between conscious purpose, veiled though it may be even to the party executing it, and chaos that may or may not be amusing, but is inexorably accident (or the Unconscious at work) and thus not in our power to control. Step to the front door, and take a look at the market square outside.

It is a country town and the principal building, or anyway the one that takes the eye, is the solicitor's house, a large square lichened early eighteenth-century stone building with buff window architraves, thick white glazing bars, and a monumental wisteria draped over the dummy window. Backed up as it is by several other Georgian buildings, the eighteenth century provides the keynote for the square.

But what do we have next door? None other than a Venetian Gothic chemist built originally of white brick but now overpainted a mixture of mid-purple brown and golden brown, windows and woodwork white, advertising antacid powders in an ornamental Grecian. Are we to tear this down and put up a Queen Anne Chemist with buff architraves and white glazing bars, antacid powders advertised in Tragan and of course wisteria?—the answer isn't an outright yea or nay, nor is it "let's compromise and put up a Tudor chemist with blackletter legends"; it is, *for the town planner as opposed to the architect*, rather a question. What do the Venetian Gothic chemist and the Georgian solicitor's houses do to each other, the lichen, the buff, the mid-purple brown? There is a possibility that they may do something nice. As a matter of fact, in the case I am thinking of, they do. Are we then going to accept Spec. Builders' Venetian? As *architects*, no; as *town planners,* yes. Yes, we are. Whatever the elements out of which the scene is built, it is on purely visual and not on professional architectural grounds that we as radical planners shall admit or spurn them, and when Venetian Gothic does a useful visual job, let it be given a run for its money.

How does one decide? How does one decide on the bric-à-brac in one's room or

material directly from the forms of the past but we should have a greater respect for the spirit of the past. [The U.S.S.R. does not impose the culture of Mother Russia on the rest of the country, but it encourages the culture of each region, always rejecting what is not fitting to the time. This is the difference between the U.S.S.R. and the Hitlerian "Herrenvolk" mentality, which even tried to destroy important archaeological sites in Poland in order to erase all trace of the rooted culture. The Polish CIAMs fight against formalism, but also against the academic professors who employ eclectic forms.]

The new Warsaw will conserve its link with the past—that is to say, it will preserve all that is good in the lines of roads, open places, the connections with the Vistula, and with all remaining evidences of its ancient culture. In defending and preserving our national culture we defend and preserve international culture.

We of CIAM must revise our attitude. The Bauhaus is as far behind us as Scamozzi. [It is time to pass from the Athens Charter to reality.]

1950–1959

1950   Le Corbusier, chapel of Notre-Dame-du-Haut, Ronchamp, France (–1954)
Matthew Nowicki with William Henley Deitrick, arena, Raleigh, North Carolina
Max Bill, Hochschule für Gestaltung, Ulm, Germany (–1955)
Lodovico Belgiojoso, Enrico Peressuti, Ernesto Rogers (BBPR), Velasca tower, Milan (–1958)
Ludwig Mies van der Rohe, 860 Lake Shore Drive apartments, Chicago (–1952)
Luigi Moretti, "Il Girasole" apartment house, Rome
Adalberto Libera, Tuscolano residential district, Rome (–1954)
Mario Ridolfi, INA housing, Viale Etiopia, Rome (–1954)
Giuseppe Samonà, Luigi Piccinato et al., INA-Casa housing, Mestre, Italy (–1956)
Affonso Eduardo Reidy, Pedregulho housing, Rio de Janeiro (–1952)
Erich Mendelsohn, Russell house, Pacific Heights, San Francisco (–1951)
Raphael Soriano, Curtis house (Case Study House), Los Angeles
Frederick Kiesler, Endless House (second project)

1951   Le Corbusier, master plan and government buildings, Chandigarh, India (–1965)
Sir Hugh Casson (director of architecture), Festival of Britain, London
J. J. P. Oud, Utrecht Life Insurance Building, Rotterdam (–1954)
Skidmore, Owings & Merrill (Gordon Bunshaft), Lever House, New York City
Egon Eiermann, linen mill, Blumberg, Germany
Eduardo Torroja, Institute of Construction and Cement, Madrid
Ludovico Quaroni, Federico Gorio et al., Martella village, near Matera, Italy (–1954)
Vladimir Bodiansky, Georges Candilis, Shadrach Woods, ATBAT housing, Morocco (–1956)
Minoru Yamasaki, Pruitt-Igoe housing, St. Louis (–1956)
Bruce Goff, Bavinger house, Norman, Oklahoma

1952   Sven Markelius, Sven Backström, Leif Reinius et al., satellite town of Vällingby, near Stockholm (–1956)
Kenzo Tange, City Hall, Tokyo (–1957)
Le Corbusier, monastery of La Tourette, Evreux-sur-l'Abresle, France (–1956)
Luigi Figini and Gino Pollini, church of the Madonna dei Poveri, Milan (–1954)
Ludwig Mies van der Rohe, Crown Hall, Illinois Institute of Technology, Chicago (–1956)
Félix Candela, Cosmic Ray Laboratory, University of Mexico, Mexico City
Skidmore, Owings & Merrill (Gordon Bunshaft), H. J. Heinz Company plant and warehouse, Pittsburgh
Hermann Henselmann, housing on Strausberger Platz, Stalinallee, Berlin (–1954)
José Antonio Coderch de Sentmenat, Paseo Nacional housing, Barcelona (–1954)
Peter and Alison Smithson, Golden Lane housing, London (project)

1953   Frank Lloyd Wright, Price Tower, Bartlesville, Oklahoma
Rudolf Schwarz, St. Michael's church, Frankfurt-am-Main
Jane Drew and Maxwell Fry, Ibadan University campus, Nigeria (–1959)
Wallace K. Harrison and Max Abramovitz, Alcoa building, Pittsburgh
Walter Gropius (TAC) and Pietro Belluschi, Pan American building, New York City (–1958)
Marcel Breuer, De Bijendorf department store, Rotterdam (–1957)
London County Council Architects Department (J. Leslie Martin et al.), Alton East housing, Roehampton, London (–1956)

1954   Louis Kahn, Jewish community center and bathhouse, Trenton, New Jersey (–1959)
Edward Durrell Stone, United States embassy, New Delhi
R. Buckminster Fuller, geodesic dome for Ford Motor Company, Detroit
Gio Ponti et al. (with Pier Luigi Nervi), Pirelli tower, Milan (–1959)
Ludwig Mies van der Rohe, Seagram building, New York City (–1958)
Victor Gruen and Associates, Northland shopping center, outside Detroit

Roberto Gabetti and Aimaro Isola, Bottega d'Erasmo, Turin
SCIC (Société Centrale Immobilière de la Caisse des Depots), Grand Ensemble of
Sarcelles, outside Paris (–1974)
Hans Scharoun, Romeo and Juliet apartments, Stuttgart (–1959)
Ignazio Gardella, apartment house on the Zattere, Venice (–1958)
Le Corbusier, Jaoul houses, Neuilly-sur-Seine, France (–1956)
Jean Prouvé and André Sive, experimental houses, Meudon, France

1955 Arne Jacobsen, town hall, Rødovre, Denmark
Aldo van Eyck, Children's Home, Amsterdam (–1960)
Emile Aillaud, Les Courtillières housing, Pantin, outside Paris (–1960)

1956 Frank Lloyd Wright, Guggenheim museum, New York City (–1959)
Alvar Aalto, church of Vuoksenniska, Imatra, Finland (–1959)
Hans Scharoun, Philharmonic Hall, Berlin (–1963)
Eero Saarinen, TWA Terminal, Queens, New York (–1962)
I. M. Pei, Mile High Center, Denver

1957 Jacob Bakema and J. H. van den Broek, plan for North Kennemerland, Holland (–1959)
Jørn Utzon, opera house, Sydney, Australia (–1966)
Hugh Stubbins, congress hall, Berlin
Pier Luigi Nervi, Palazetto dello Sport, Rome (–1959)
Luis Barragán and Mathias Goeritz, satellite towers, Mexico City
Paul Rudolph, Arts and Architecture building, Yale University, New Haven (–1963)
Louis Kahn, Richards Research Laboratories, Philadelphia (–1965)
Vittoriano Viganò, Marchiondi Institute, Baggio, outside Milan
Werner Moser, Max Haefeli, Rudolph Steiger, Zur Palme office block, Zurich (–1964)
Franco Albini with Franca Helg, Rinascente department store, Rome (–1961)
Alvar Aalto, Hansaviertel apartments, Berlin
Kunio Maekawa, Harumi apartments, Tokyo

1958 Kiyonori Kikutake, Marine City, Tokyo (project)
Yona Friedman, Spatial City (–1961; project)
Viljo Revell, city hall, Toronto
Carlo Scarpa, Castelvecchio Museum restoration, Verona (–1964)
Le Corbusier, Philips pavilion, World's Fair, Brussels
Bernard Zehrfuss et al. (with Jean Prouvé), National Center for Industries and
Technology exhibition hall, Paris
Luis Barragan, "Red Wall" at Las Arboledas residential district, Mexico City
Dimitris Pikionis, landscaping, Philopappus Hill, Athens

1959 Oscar Niemeyer, Chapel and Palace of the Dawn, Brasilia
Louis Kahn, Salk Institute of Biological Studies, La Jolla, California (–1965)
James Stirling and James Gowan, Engineering Laboratories, Leicester University,
Leicester, England (–1964)
Josep Martorell, Oriol Bohigas, David Mackay (MBM), housing on Avenida
Meridiana, Barcelona (–1964)
Atelier 5, Halen housing, Bern (–1961)
Paolo Soleri, Earth House, Scottsdale, Arizona

1950

In spring of 1950 a delegation from the East German Ministry of Building made a "study trip" to the Soviet Union. The result was the promulgation, on July 27, of the following directive concerning urban planning in the **German Democratic Republic**. Of prime concern was the rebuilding of historic cities like Berlin, Dresden, and Rostock that had suffered extensive damage during the war. Also paramount was a realignment with Soviet revisionism concerning the role and function of cities within the national life of the new communist state.

Official East German policy thus presented itself at the start of the 1950s.in direct opposition not only to contemporaneous reconstruction initiatives being undertaken in the capitalist West, but also to the progressive urbanism and architecture developed in Germany in the 1920s. Against the abstract functionalism of CIAM and the formalism of the Bauhaus, now seen as symptoms of the spiritual crisis of a dying capitalist system, the new conception stressed realism—popularly apprehensible artistic forms—and called for the cultural and historical determination of the existing city. Germany's architectural heritage, which was portrayed as ravaged not only by "Anglo-American bombs" but by a dehumanizing machine aesthetic, was to be restored through the return to a national equivalent of the Moscow palace style. This meant, at least in Berlin, Schinkelian classicism. Any contradictions raised by uncomfortable associations between neoclassicism and the official architecture of the recent fascist regime were played down. The ideologues depicted a Nazi *Kasernenstil* that had more affinities with 1920s *Zweckrationalität* than with the tradition that had produced Schinkel, Gilly, and the revolutionary culture of the French Enlightenment.

135–36 The following document, focusing on the core of the city, coincides in both date and subject matter with CIAM's eighth congress in Hoddesdon. It is instructive to compare them. The form of the new East German city was now to be determined by its plazas, honorific axial streets (as opposed to functional traffic arteries), monumental buildings including skyscrapers, and multistory housing blocks. In an implicit critique of the four urban functions of CIAM, the category of circulation or transportation was replaced by "culture" (point 2). High-speed traffic was to be rerouted to the city's perimeter and urban growth carefully controlled, thus creating the "compact city" as a unitary structure efficiently integrating all urban functions and respecting the city's historical dimensions. The atomization of the center implicit in both *Zeilenbau* and Garden City planning was rejected (point 12), while new emphasis was laid on provision of urban parks and recreation areas. As far as housing was concerned, functional planning principles were upheld, but the idea of the minimal dwelling, considered as degraded to the point where it could afford little more than higher profit margins to builders and real estate speculators, was replaced by the intention to provide as many communal amenities as present economic conditions would allow.

The major outcome of these ideas was the ambitious five-year plan that East Germany adopted in 1952 as a national building program. Its most celebrated component was the building of Stalinallee in Berlin, touted as "the first socialist street in Berlin." The architect Hermann Henselmann, previously associated with the *Neues Bauen*, lined either side of the entry to the avenue with symmetrical housing blocks notable for both their up-to-date functional accommodation and their classicizing facades symbolizing a tower and gate. In popular terms, the avenue, built very largely through public contributions of money, materials, and labor, was a major success, drawing thousands of tourists from both East and West after its opening (borders had not yet been closed) and knitting an entire urban district to the honorific centerpiece.

392–98 A decade later the Italian architect Aldo Rossi would praise Stalinallee as "the last great street of Europe." In fact, despite the overtly propagandistic and rigidifying effects of East German urban policy in these years, the effort to rethink the city in symbolic and historical terms and to overcome the division between architecture and urbanism did produce a serious alternative to Western

184–88 planning—at least for a few years. In December 1954 Nikita Khrushchev changed the course of architecture in Eastern Europe once again with his rehabilitation of functionalism in the interests of cheaper building. Henselmann returned in 1957–60 to the same street, now renamed Karl-Marx-Allee in a period of de-Stalinization, and erected slab housing in the new stripped-down style.

Meanwhile, West Germany's response to the imposition of Stalinallee was to reassert its solidarity with the West. Preparations began in 1953 for a

249–52 permanent international housing exhibition in the Hansaviertel section of West Berlin. A few years later the city sponsored a competition called "Hauptstadt Berlin," in which Western architects, in an overt provocation to the East, were invited to submit proposals for the restructuring of 24,000 acres in the eighteenth-century center of Berlin, much of it in the Russian sector at the heart of the capital of the German Democratic Republic. In both instances the Western-style urbanism of "democracy and modernity," represented by its most prominent practitioners, demonstrated, among other things, its inherent potential for disjunction and scalelessness.

On East German urbanism in these years, see, in addition to the early issues of the periodical *Deutsche Architektur (D.A.)*, two articles by Christian Borngräber, "Das nationale Aufbauprogramm der DDR," *Arch +* 56 (April 1981), and "Die sozialistische Metropole: Planung und Aufbau der Stalinallee und des Zentrums in Ost-Berlin 1949–1961," in Jochen Boberg et al., eds., *Die Metropole: Industriekultur in Berlin im 20. Jahrhundert* (1986).

From Planen und Bauen *9 (1950), pp. 288–93. Republished in Lothar Bolz,* Von deutschen Bauen: Reden und Aufsätze *(Berlin: Verlag der Nation, 1951), pp. 32–52; and in Deutsche Bauakademie,* Handbuch für Architekten *(Berlin: Verlag Technik Berlin, 1954), pp. 101–3. Translated by Lynnette Widder.*

Sixteen Principles for the Restructuring of Cities
German Democratic Republic

The urban planning and architectural form of our cities must express the social order of the German Democratic Republic, the progressive traditions of our German people, and the large-scale aims bound to the growth of all of Germany. The following principles serve these ends:

1. The city as a form for inhabitation did not develop by coincidence. The city is the most economical and culturally rich form in which the communal life of human beings can be accommodated, as proved by centuries of experience. The city is, in its structure and architectural form, the expression of the political life and the national consciousness of the people.

2. The aim of urban planning is the harmonious satisfaction of the human demand for work, inhabitation, culture, and recreation.

The fundamentals and methods of urban planning rest on naturally given conditions, on the social and economic basis of the state, on the highest accomplishments of science, technology, and art, on the demands of economic expediency, and on the use of the most developed elements of the people's cultural heritage.

3. Cities in and of themselves neither "come into existence" nor "exist" as such. Cities are built at a specific scale by industry for industry. The growth of the city, its population, and its area are determined by industry, administrative organs, and cultural institutions.

In the capital city, the significance of industry as a determinant of urban form retreats behind that of administrative and cultural institutions.

The determination and affirmation of urbanistic factors is exclusively the prerogative of the government.

4. The growth of the city must be subjugated to the fundamental principle of usefulness, and must consequently remain within predetermined limits. Excessive growth of the city, its population, and its area leads to incorrigible deformations in the organization of cultural life and the daily infrastructural servicing of its population, as well as in the productivity and development of industry.

5. Urban planning must be founded on the principle of the organic and on the conservation of the historical structure of the city while alleviating its inadequacies.

6. The center constitutes the city's appointed core [*Kern*]. The city's center is the political midpoint of the life of the populace.

At the city's center lie the most important political, administrative, and cultural spaces. On the city center's plazas, political demonstrations, parades, and popular celebrations take place.

The city center comprises the most important and monumental buildings. It dictates the architectural composition of the city's plan and architectural silhouette.

7. In cities built along rivers, the river with its quais is one of the major arteries and architectural axes.

8. Traffic should serve the city and its populace, not divide and encumber it.

Transit traffic should be removed from the center and from central areas, and diverted to outlying areas or to a ring road.

Freight traffic via train or water should also be removed from the central areas.

The determination of major traffic arteries must respect the closed, quiet nature of residential areas.

In determining the width of major traffic arteries, it is to be noted that width is less significant than the appropriate solution of crossings.

9. The city's appearance, its individual artistic form, is determined by plazas, major streets, and significant buildings in its center (in large cities, by skyscrapers). Plazas are the structural foundation of city planning and the city's overall architectural composition.

10. Residential districts are made up of residential neighborhoods whose hearts are the neighborhood centers. In these centers are all the necessary cultural, commodity, and community facilities for the life of the populace within these neighborhoods.

The second component in the structure of the residential districts is the residential complex. The complexes are formed by a group of residential quarters unified by gardens, schools, kindergartens, child-care centers, and service facilities necessary to the populace's daily life. Urban traffic may not be permitted to penetrate these residential complexes. Nonetheless, neither the complexes nor the larger residential areas may become internally oriented, isolated elements. Their structure and planning is dependent upon the structure and demands of the city as a whole.

As the third component in the structure, the residential quarters have primarily the significance of the complexes in terms of planning and the determination of form.

11. Density and orientation are not the only factors determining healthy and restful living conditions and access to light and air. The routing of traffic is as significant.

12. It is impossible to transform the city into a garden. It is unquestionably necessary to provide sufficient greenery, but fundamentally it is undeniable that in the city, life is urban. In the suburbs or in the country, life is more pastoral.

13. The multistory building is more economical than the one- or two-story building. In its character, too, it is appropriate to the large city.

14. Urban planning is the foundation of architectural form-giving. The central responsibility of urban planning and the architectural formation of the city is the creation of an individual, unique appearance for that city. The architecture must be in content democratic and in form national. To that end, architecture makes use of the experience of the people as concretized in the developed traditions of the past.

15. There is no abstract scheme for urban planning or for determining architectural form. The embracing of the essential factors and demands of life is decisive here.

16. The planning and realization of parts of the city like plazas and major streets, with their adjacent housing quarters, are to be carried out simultaneously with work on the city plan and in harmony with it.

1951

The second "Darmstadt Conversation" took place at the Mathildenhöhe artists colony in Darmstadt. Designed by Joseph Olbrich, Peter Behrens, and five other architects on commission from the grand duke of Hesse as a showcase of Jugendstil modernism, it was billed on its inauguration in 1901 as "the first document of German art." In 1951 the city of Darmstadt marked the colony's fiftieth anniversary with an architecture exhibition and colloquium entitled "Man and Space." Among the keynote speakers was the philosopher Martin Heidegger, who delivered one of his fundamental essays of the postwar period, "Building, Dwelling, Thinking." Also featured were the philosopher José Ortega y Gasset, who spoke on "The Myth of Man behind Technology," and the architects Otto Ernst Schweizer and **Rudolf Schwarz**. The latter's lecture is excerpted below. Other members of the prewar generation taking part included Otto Bartning, Paul Bonatz, Wilhelm Kreis, Richard Riemerschmid, and Ernst Neufert.

The conservative tenor at Darmstadt had already been established the previous year with a colloquium entitled "The Image of Man in Our Time." A clash occurred between abstract and representational artists, resulting in a kind of tribunal—joined by the art historian Hans Sedlmayr, whose book *Loss of Center* (1948) had been influential in architectural and artistic circles—against the "dehumanizing" and "spiritless" legacy of modernist abstraction. Not unrelated to

125–28 the revisionism taking place at this time in East Germany, the Darmstadt conversations were an effort to salvage a less materialistic, "authentically" German cultural tradition out of the Nazi debacle. They coalesced a dissenting position within a postwar Germany largely desirous of solidarity with the West.

Schwarz, a student of Hans Poelzig, had been active in the 1920s in a Catholic youth movement led by the philosopher of religion Romano Guardini. Among Schwarz's writings of this period was a seminal essay, *Orientation by*

163–66 *Technique,* which had had a powerful impact on Mies van der Rohe among others. Here Schwarz—anticipating Heidegger—affirmed technology's exhilarating potential as an "archproduction," but warned of the need to control it. As in the following paper, he condemned the rise of rationalist instrumentality as spiritually endangering, calling for a religio-philosophical "mastery."

Schwarz's architectural work includes a series of modern church buildings executed between 1928 and 1961. During the Nazi period he constructed farms in the annexed French territory of the Lorraine; his rationalized interpretation of regional tradition was among the examples of *Neues Bauen* tolerated within the eclectic program of the regime. He also worked out a Germanization plan for the same region combining functional zoning with a network of symbolic centers oriented around the type of collective gathering places evoked in the following lecture. After the war he served as director for the reconstruction of Cologne. In January 1953, two years after the Darmstadt paper, he published a polemical article in *Baukunst und Werkform* entitled "Bilde, Künstler, rede nicht" (Create, artist, do not talk) criticizing the Bauhaus as a proselytizing academy of style. The year-long debate that ensued in the journal engaged, among others, Walter Gropius. Clearly the desire for a modern expression of collective order, ties to the soil, and symbolic "German" form did not suddenly disappear with the nation's defeat. Rather it could be sustained through a dissociation of culture and politics in the name of "spirituality." For Schwarz's writings, see the selection edited by Maria Schwarz and Ulrich Conrads, *Rudolf Schwarz. Wegweisung der Technik und andere Schriften zum Neuen Bauen 1926–1961* (1979).

From Otto Bartning, ed., Darmstädter Gespräch: Mensch und Raum *(Darmstadt: Neue Darmstädter Verlaganstalt, 1951), pp. 62–67. Courtesy of Klaus Holzapfel for NDV Neue Darmstädter Verlaganstalt.*

Concerning the Building Art
Rudolf Schwarz

[. . .] The human spirit has a sort of secret capacity to erect abstract systems in which it shackles and imprisons itself. The nineteenth century—with enormous constructive acuity—devised such systems, beginning with the concept of science, which was a "container," precisely a "concept," a system with which to grasp, to seize things from the outside, but which was entirely indifferent to the content of this same concept. The only purpose of this large container of the scientific knowledge of that time was to make the world comprehensible, to make it possible to obtain a grip on the world. Its purpose was to assure that something produced an effect. The question of truth was not posed. It was perhaps the most grandiose prison construction that the human spirit ever designed for itself. But too late did timid protests try to oppose it. I need only recall Scheler, who wanted to bring the science of government in line with cultural and religious knowledge, or with still other types of knowledge more concerned with method that tried to show that the concept never produces truth because it only realizes the gripping, clutching hand itself; that one only becomes conscious of things when feeling comes to the hand's clutching grasp, or, for others, when the eye comes, and astonished and wondering, perceives how the world everywhere exists in forms, each of which signifies truth in an irreplaceable way only revealed to vision. When another—Kaiser—comes and says that the ear too participates in the cognition of the world, the ear which has the capacity to register the sound of the world; and when, finally and in sum, it is said that the concept in no case suffices for the perception and understanding of the world, but rather that the whole man is required, with all his senses and capacities lovingly lavished on the world to be perceived, then it becomes apparent how fearful this prison, this jail in which the century had placed itself, really was. One could pursue the example of the fence, by looking at industry for instance, where working mankind is imprisoned and fenced into an entirely abstract economic system that disregards him and the quality of his goods, a system concerned only with attaining something measurable, namely the fiction of accumulating fictitious money. It matters little what happens to man, who as an economic being is nothing but a number in this money-accounting; and it also matters little what the value of man's work actually is—it is a fiction that does not pose the question concerning the quality of his goods, the quality of production, but only the money value.

Thus we see in industry again this strange abstract container constructed by the human spirit, this system of coordinates into which real life is forced. The same goes for technology, originally a high and nobly intended form of the world, arising out of the fitting continuation of the Gothic, out of the otherworldly souls of lonely seekers of God whose sole purpose was to lighten the material burden of the world—for these men of the late Middle Ages found it nobler for an image to arise from little rather than from much matter. Having arisen out of such noble desires and speculations, technology was originally a genuine and great form of a public and possible world. But the nineteenth century realized that one could subjugate the world with this universal form and could get it in one's grip and grasp. It made out of technology a claw and a tool with which to grasp the world, to pull it to pieces, to work it to death.

This idea of the abstract system, this gridwork into which the human spirit projects itself and pens itself up, is perhaps the most revealing image through which one may understand the situation of that time. And this effective, though unfortunate, world-will

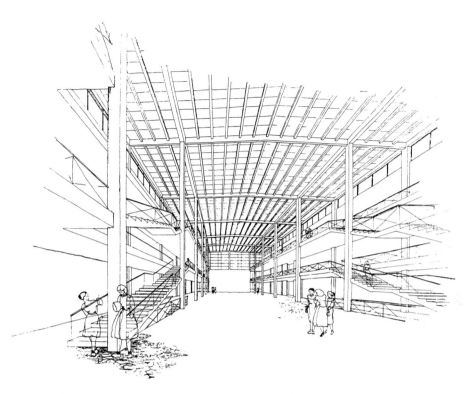

[Rudolf Schwarz, girls' school between city church and city chapel.] Above: Recess hall. Below: Overall view from southwest. [From Darmstädter Gespräch: Mensch und Raum, pp. 156–57.]

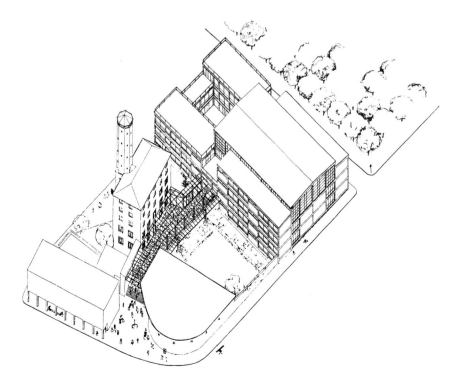

also turned its attention to the architect, and what else could it order than precisely this container and this fence, the great prison of mankind; and architects delivered it punctually. What is the mass city of the end of the nineteenth century—or, let us say, of the 1880s and 1890s—other than the fully adequate expression of this fence and prison, with its system of controllable corridors, its streets where one can control crowds and keep them in check, and its all-around fenced-in rectangular and corner blocks of houses and "rental barracks" where mankind was stuffed into boxes without regard for whether this was healthy or humane or spiritual or in any way necessary? Nothing but silos and warehouses for men, in which they were permitted to be not men but laborers or "hands," as the English say. This was demanded of architects, ordered, delivered, and paid for. But whenever architecture really felt itself called to higher things, one also gave it those higher tasks, ordering, delivering, and paying also for them. It was charged with decorating atrocities, with removing the exalted emblems of the past and pasting them as pediments on banks, as Gothic tracery on post office buildings—a ransacking done by the period to holy things; for the pediment was once the place of the gods on the front of the temple, and the cathedral once bore the tracery.

In effect this was how it was arranged. The masters whose memory we celebrate here believed in an inwardly shining, inwardly fructifying world celebrating its own beauty, and they found no approval for it and no relenting, for what was ordered was the great world prison, the great abstract gridwork of the world's coordinates in which it was desired to pen up life. Surely had they been great fighters and not just great artists, perhaps they might have won this fight. But what can a handful of artists—great artists and good artists—do against such a world view? Other forces would have had to intervene for this will to allow architecture to come in for a modest share in the great human revolt.

Certainly one experienced at that time a rebirth or, much more, an astonishing awakening of aesthetic teachings. It is the time of the great aestheticians, the great art historians, who made artistic things into an object of knowledge. Indeed, this knowledge was something of an oasis, a small light in the darkness. For this new aesthetics the art form was not a form made to order, but form-becoming spirit; and it understood how to preserve art in its own sphere of influence. For this our thanks are due to it. Questionable remains the striking lack of content of its presumed scientific concepts. Aesthetic categories—like Wölfflin's—allow for the most diverse contents. One fails to recognize that it is a matter of things here, things which are part of life, which are not just living a life of false aesthetic appearance, which are—is this not so?—even full-blooded and potent things of life. Here it is apparent how pale and impotent this aesthetics is. The word of the aesthete already has something wan and dry about it. Aesthetics has unfortunately benefited architecture very little. Certainly it taught us to notice many beautiful things. The great tide of art historical books, which to this day flows through Europe, has led many a man to beauty. We do not want to say anything against them. They are splendidly photographed and splendidly printed and cleverly written, but here is evident a small symptom which perhaps all too often escapes our notice: All these books, whether they revolve about large or small, known or unknown buildings, or about whole periods of art history—all these books have many illustrations, and these illustrations are photographed. It is necessary to remind ourselves, however, that earlier, decades ago, there were no photographs in our textbooks, only measured drawings, and that only recently, with the photographic apparatus, is there an instrument that avails itself so readily to the lonely, isolated aesthete, namely the man who alone confronts a great work and even—for all I know—makes observations about it, but from opposite it, not inside it. The camera is a machine that is set up on a certain spot and stares at a large space through a single eye. Perhaps we have not made it sufficiently clear how inadequate and fundamentally unworthy this method is for approaching great works of architecture. I might mention a book, just because it is a good book of its kind: Hürlimann's *The Cathedrals of England*, recently published. Yes, good God, these grandiose works have from all standpoints been peered up at and out from, and intersections and remarkable corners have been discovered; and the whole is a fearsomely banal business, exactly that of a photographer. But our architecture is more than this. What musician would not be shocked if he were offered a record rather than a well-written score? But precisely this—and more—is what is being done to us. Architecture has developed its own language, or better, its own method, to compose its score, and this is: plan, elevation, section. To this belongs measure, and with it the task is carried out. Thus speaks architecture. What sort of experience the individual may have, should have, or fails to have through this plan is completely indifferent with regard to this language. For the plan shows a form to which the individual only very modestly contributes. The individual has contributed to this form along with hundreds and thousands of others. They have collectively brought forth this circle, which, perhaps, is nothing like a simple circle. Naturally the individual can look closely at this circle if he finds the time in an intermission from ritual activities. But it is not this individual who has brought forth this plan—which is absolutely objective and capable of being written down like a mathematical formula—he has not brought it forth but society: as an achievement that is only possible on its own level. The taking of photographs and all that goes with it overlooks the real achievement of architecture: namely the fact that many individuals have contributed something to it. Many individuals sacrifice themselves, give themselves to a collective undertaking, and then suddenly a form blossoms forth for them, which would have been completely closed to the individual, who might well view it like a traveler with a travel guide, but who could never bring it forth himself.

This matter is a little difficult. I will now try to explain it.

You all know that there are two great basic forms that occidental building art has come up with over thousands of years, centralized form and longitudinal form, centralized building and longitudinal building: centralized building as the deepest reflection of a people condensed in a single work; longitudinal building as the enclosure in built form of the path on which a people is proceeding. Both forms, which are entirely simple—in any old art history book one can examine the plans, they are the utmost in simplicity that there is—both forms are unattainable by the single individual. Round form is something that remains fully closed off to the individual since he is not circular by nature. The human being is directional; he has a certain space; in front of and behind him there is nothing more. Round form is unattainable by the individual. But it offers itself up immediately when there are several people who reach out hands to each other, whether sitting around a meal table or doing a dance. When all of them enter into a secret together, all at once they create a round form among themselves. With longitudinal form it is the same. Certainly the individual is involved along the way; man is a creature who is fated to be on the way. But the individual's way opens before him, and he must pursue it; behind remains only a trace. A longitudinal building does not arise from this. A longitudinal building originates when a people line up in rows, next to one another, behind one another. Then suddenly the longitudinal building is there. This great and basic architectural form is then, for the first time, given, when many overcome themselves, put themselves into the work, when they sacrifice themselves unconditionally, giving themselves to the commonality. Through their sacrifice they become a part of a wholly other world-form, a wholly new way of Being, which will also again be given back to people as individuals; for they still retain their individuality. The earlier example of the overvaluation of the egocentrical central-point perspective of the photograph, in contrast to the plan, to the well-conceived plan that comes out of the architecture school, may indeed show you how very much the architectural work is mistaken in its essential achievement. The production of plans, elevations, and sections, of measures—this is the prodigious achievement of architects. It is an achievement that can be attained only through the sacrifice of many people in a collectivity. Then, however, this sacrifice will be rewarded through the bestowing and unlocking of a whole world of forms, which the individual himself could never have delivered up, could never have brought forth. Moreover, what is thereby brought forth is as valid as a figure of geometry or a law that a people makes for itself. It is thoroughly clear, absolutely unembellished in its fundamental conception: for the most part, the simpler the forms, the greater and more the building is of genius. These are laws of life, which, however, are not mandated in the form of containers, but are laws laid down by a people themselves.

Certainly not to obey the "order of the day"—architecture has nothing to do with that. The term "modern architecture" is an absurdity in itself. There is no modern architecture, because architecture is never of the day or of the year, but only reckons with the space of time. It is in conformity with architecture's own nature that it does not reckon on the individual, nor on the hour and its so-called command, but that it is rooted in the great community of those now living, and also in the other great community in which the age is rooted. It is historical in the sense that it projects its great conceptions forward, just as it did at the time the first great cathedral was built for future centuries to live in.

Therein stands the achievement of architecture, in my opinion; that it, in consequence of a devotion, an unconditional submission of the individual to the community, creates new forms. But these forms are gradated hierarchically. Raised up in its new forms, this community becomes capable of being raised up anew in a still greater and still further advanced form. One could call this the program of a city plan. Naturally I cannot give a full account of these things here. It is of the essence of architecture, which continuously rises up from the greater form into a still greater one, to which it now unites several such small forms—whether village or countryside or city or surface of the earth (or whatever it is called at that moment)—again and again in a new process of sacrifice, of submission. [. . .]

1951

CIAM 8 took place in 1951 in the town of Hoddesdon in Somerset, England, under the auspices of the MARS Group, the London-based wing of CIAM. The reason for a second meeting in England so soon after the Bridgwater congress was that it was the year of the Festival of Britain, a great popularizing exhibition in London that was intended to bring modern architecture to the British public.

100–2

At a deliberate remove from this activity, in a "lonely Victorian mansion . . . not far from London though without rail connection to it," as Sigfried Giedion described the meeting's setting, CIAM focused on the core of the city. This theme represented a conscious expansion of the four basic urban functions that had been elaborated in the *Athens Charter*—dwelling, work, recreation, and circulation. As such, it brought to a head many of the crucial issues that had been shaping the postwar debate: monumentality and symbolic representation, the question of collective values, the relationship of modern architecture to historic places and artifacts. In more material terms, the recent experience of reconstructing city centers destroyed by wartime bombardment and the need to respond to the disintegration of urban life caused by accelerating suburbanization called for new attention. In his opening statement CIAM president José Luis Sert called for a reversal of the trend toward unplanned decentralization and a new process of recentralization. The participants offered original applications of CIAM principles to civic centers at every scale of human gathering and within a very broad geographic purview: these ranged from proposed centers for rural villages in Holland and Norway, to neighborhoods in urban and suburban locales in the United States and Europe, to new towns like Stevenage in England and St. Dié in France, to interventions and reconstructions in major cities like Coventry, Hiroshima, Bogotá, and Chandigarh.

Although some of the conclusions reached by the congress amounted to more emphatic restatements of principles that had already been established in the *Athens Charter* (points 2, 3, and 4), the consensus that the city center should be a compact and singular formation represented a new postulation. Likewise, the preoccupations with controlling commercial signage and exploiting the animating effects of variable or mobile elements were concerns stemming from the city's more recent development. Significant, however, with respect to the resurgence of social realism in Eastern Europe at this date was the congress's reversal on the issue of monumentality. Giedion declared in his summary of the proceedings that the problem was "not one of designing stonily magnificent civic centers," and that therefore "there is no excuse for the erection of a monumental building mass." In the earlier "Nine Points on Monumentality," he, Sert, and Fernand Léger had envisaged large free-standing architectural ensembles dominating "vast open spaces," juxtaposing the lightweight materials and naturalistic elements of modern architecture with "the stones which have always been used." Clearly even this image—however rooted in modernist thinking— had become too dangerous by 1951, and the rhetoric of human scale and spontaneity, together with recourse to the Corbusian theme of a synthesis of the arts, appeared safer ground for contemporary civic expression. "The essence of the city is that it is a rendez-vous," the congress affirmed.

125–28

27–30

64–67

On CIAM 8 at Hoddesdon, see *The Heart of the City*, cited below.

From The Heart of the City: Towards the Humanisation of Urban Life, *ed. J. Tyrwhitt, J. L. Sert, and E. N. Rogers (New York: Pelligrini and Cudahy, 1952), p. 164. Illustration, p. 158. Courtesy of CIAM-Archiv, Institut für Geschichte und Theorie der Architektur, ETH Zurich.*

Summary of Needs at the Core
CIAM 8, Hoddesdon

1. That there should be only one main Core in each city.

2. That the Core is an artifact—a man-made thing.

3. That the Core should be a place secure from traffic—where the pedestrian can move about freely.

4. That cars should arrive and park on the periphery of the Core, but not cross it.

5. That uncontrolled commercial advertising—such as appears in the Cores of many cities today—should be organized and controlled.

6. That varying (mobile) elements can make an important contribution to animation at the Core, and that the architectural setting should be planned to allow for the inclusion of such elements.

7. That in planning the Core the architect should employ contemporary means of expression and—whenever possible—should work in cooperation with painters and sculptors.

Confusion at the Core.

1951

Henry-Russell Hitchcock here reconsiders, from a vantage point of two decades, the seminal book and exhibition on which he and Philip Johnson collaborated in 1931–32. *The International Style: Architecture since 1922* brought together a set of related tendencies that had already reached maturity in Europe but were little known as yet in the United States. Focusing on the work of "the four leaders of modern architecture"—Walter Gropius, Le Corbusier, J. J. P. Oud, and Ludwig Mies van der Rohe—it advanced the thesis that the work of these young Europeans (some of it executed, but much of it still in the form of projects) collectively represented "a drastic and unified architectural revolution."

The companion exhibition, held at the Museum of Modern Art in New York in early 1932, further defined the new movement in terms of a set of aesthetic and stylistic principles. Along with the four European masters it included five Americans—Frank Lloyd Wright, Raymond Hood, the firm of Howe and Lescaze, Richard Neutra, and the (afterward obscure) Bowman brothers. Intended as a counter to the work then being shown at the Architectural League's annual exhibitions, the show was the museum's first venture into the exhibition of architecture.

Hitchcock's retrospective article amounts to a qualified retraction of the earlier argument. Although he cites passages from the book to show that he and Johnson did not intend to be so dogmatic in their stylistic prescriptions as interpretation subsequently would have it, he acknowledges the arbitrariness of many of their inclusions and exclusions and the undesirable consequences of *a priori* stylistic rules. It was precisely the latter, he admits in hindsight, that led a third generation of modern architects to a form of sterile and inhibiting academicism. "The idea of modern should remain . . . somewhat loose rather than too closely defined," he affirms.

Hitchcock particularly seeks in the present article to redress the definition of modern architecture in favor of Wright. His relative neglect in 1932, he suggests, was partly due to the fact that in the late 1920s Wright was more active in writing magazine articles than in building. Hitchcock had become convinced *31–41* of Wright's preeminence in the course of preparing a major catalogue on his work, *In the Nature of Materials: The Buildings of Frank Lloyd Wright—1887–1941*, in conjunction with MoMA's large retrospective on the architect in 1940. Hitchcock also acknowledges in the following article the seminal contributions of some other "early moderns"—Auguste Perret, Victor Horta, and Louis Sullivan—as well as of Alvar Aalto. Viewing the time at which he is writing as a transitional one, "between a 'high' and a 'late' period," he predicts that architecture will *189–92* become increasingly "diverse" over the next twenty-five years. At this moment, Philip Johnson, having been a devotee of Mies van der Rohe for many years, was also pursuing a revision of the earlier formulation and of the lessons of the Masters. Hitchcock notes of his coauthor, who had recently completed a glass house for himself in New Canaan, Connecticut (1949), together with a brick guest house on the same site, "Mr. Johnson has given the most effective evidence of his own broad interpretation of the International Style in the buildings he has designed . . . "

The following article takes the form of commentary interspersed with a series of quotations from the 1932 book. The passages in italics are from the latter.

From Architectural Record, *August 1951, pp. 89–97. Courtesy of Mosette Broderick.*

The International Style Twenty Years After
Henry-Russell Hitchcock

The International Style was prefaced by a statement by Alfred Barr, the Director of the Museum of Modern Art. In his first paragraph he made a claim which the authors themselves might well have considered immodest:

. . . They have proven beyond any reasonable doubt, I believe, that there exists today a modern style as original, as consistent, as logical, and as widely distributed as any in the past. The authors have called it the International Style.
    To many this assertion of a new style will seem arbitrary and dogmatic . . .

And how! A quarter century after Gropius's Bauhaus at Dessau and Le Corbusier's Pavillon de l'Esprit Nouveau at the Paris Exposition of Decorative Arts of 1925 first made evident that something like a concerted program for a new architecture existed, it is still by no means necessary to conclude that the "International Style" (which they and other European architects were then maturing) should be considered the only proper pattern or program for modern architecture.

The work of many architects of distinction such as Frank Lloyd Wright, who make no bones about their opposition to the supposed tenets of an International Style, certainly belongs to modern architecture as much as does the work of Gropius and Le Corbusier. Yet the particular concepts of a new modern style which date from the Twenties do conveniently define that crystallization—that convergence of long imminent ideas—which then took place in France and Germany and Holland, and which a quarter century later has spread throughout the civilized world. (Only, I believe, in Russia are the forms of the International Style unpopular—to put outright official proscription rather mildly!)

In general, it has been the concept of "style" itself, as implying restraint or discipline according to *a priori* rules of one sort or another, which has been hardest for architects, as distinguished from critics and writers, to accept. The introduction of the 1932 book was therefore devoted to defending "The Idea of Style" and this defense is still relevant—even if its validity is also still debatable—today:

The chaos of eclecticism served to give the very idea of style a bad name in the estimation of the first modern architects of the end of the nineteenth and the beginning of the twentieth century.

The most distinguished older modern architects, notably Wright and Gropius, are still perhaps the most perturbed by the idea that anything that can properly be called a style, in the historic sense of that word, can have any worthwhile part to play in the architecture of the twentieth century. Yet Wright himself obviously has a highly individualistic style—several, for that matter—and it is also obvious that that personal style (or those styles) of his could be utilized as a framework of architectural advance, if his precepts for "Organic Architecture" were widely accepted and conscientiously followed.

Gropius is proud of the fact that it is difficult to tell the work of one of his pupils from that of another—a difficulty that he in fact rather exaggerates. (For the work of Paul Rudolph, for example, differs a great deal from that of the members of what might be called the Boston Suburban School.) But what is this anonymity that the Chairman of the Harvard Department of Architecture admires in his pupils' work but a common style? It is not the "Gropius" or the "Bauhaus" style, moreover, but merely an important part of the broader International Style, as that is practiced by the third generation of modern architects in the Northeastern United States.

The individualistic revolt of the first modern architects destroyed the prestige of the (historic) "styles," but it did not remove the implication that there was a possibility of choice between one aesthetic conception of design and another.

To refuse a comparable liberty of choice today, merely because twenty-five years ago the development of modern architecture began to be notably convergent, is certainly a form of academicism. This is already only too evident in just the places one would expect to find it, that is, in prominent architectural schools and in large highly institutionalized offices. Modern architecture in the 1950s should have room again for a range of effects as diverse, if not as divergent, as Victor Horta's Maison du Peuple in Brussels of 1897, an early modern building largely of metal and glass that is too often forgotten now, and Wright's River Forest Golf Club (as first built in 1898), of ordinary wooden-frame construction, in which most of the concepts of his now "classic" prairie houses of the next decade were already almost fully mature.

The individualists decried submission to fixed aesthetic principles as the imposition of a dead hand upon the living material of architecture, holding the failure of the (stylistic) revivals (of the nineteenth century) as a proof that the very idea of style was an unhealthy delusion.

Much of what Dean Wurster has called "Drugstore Modern" suggests that the "individualists" were less completely in the wrong than we admitted twenty years ago. Certainly too rigid a concept of what is stylistically "permissible" is always stultifying. But throughout most of the intervening period our contention that:

The idea of style, which began to degenerate when the revivals destroyed the disciplines of the Baroque, has become real and fertile again

has been supported by what has occurred.

The idea of modern style should remain, as it presently is in fact, somewhat loose rather than too closely defined. There will, however, always be some sort of style in the arts of self-conscious periods, whether it is so recognized, and so called, or not. Since it is impossible to return, under the circumstances of advanced civilization, to the unselfconscious production of supposedly styleless "folk arts," it is well to be aware that there is a problem of style. To attempt to dismiss style altogether is culturally ingenuous; it is also Utopian, or more accurately, millennial (in one sense at least, there were no "styles" in the Garden of Eden!).

The unconscious and halting architectural developments of the nineteenth century, the confused and contradictory experimentation of the beginning of the twentieth, have been succeeded by a directed evolution. There is now a single body of discipline, fixed enough to integrate contemporary style as a reality and yet elastic enough to permit individual interpretation and to encourage general growth.

Today that "fixing" is resented, just because it has been so successful. Yet the establishment of a fixed body of discipline in architecture is probably the major achievement of the twentieth century, not any technical developments in building production that have yet become universally accepted; modern technical developments have recurrently disappointed the optimists and they have failed, perhaps even more conspicuously, to live up to the bolder prophecies of nineteenth-century critics.

After twenty-five years, it is the "elasticity" and the possibility of "general growth" within the International Style which should be emphasized. That was already beginning to be evident to Philip Johnson and myself twenty years ago. Few of our readers, alas, seem to have given us credit for what were then readily dismissed as mere "escape-clauses."

The idea of style as the frame of potential growth, rather than as a fixed and crushing mould, has developed with the recognition of underlying principles such as archaeologists discern in the great styles of the past. The principles are few and broad.

Too few and too narrow, I would say in 1951 of the principles that were enunciated so firmly in 1932:

There is, first, a new conception of architecture as volume rather than as mass. Secondly, regularity rather than axial symmetry serves as the chief means of ordering design. These two principles, with a third proscribing arbitrary applied decoration, mark the productions of the international style.

Today I should certainly add articulation of structure, probably making it the third principle; and I would also omit the reference to ornament, which is a matter of taste rather than of principle. The concept of regularity is obviously too negative to explain very much about the best contemporary design; but I can still find no phrase that explains in an all-inclusive way the more positive qualities of modern design.

In opposition to those who claim that a new style of architecture is impossible or undesirable, it is necessary to stress the coherence of the results obtained within the range of possibilities thus far explored. For the international style already exists in the present; it is not merely something the future holds in store. Architecture is always a set of actual monuments, not a vague corpus of theory.

After twenty years there are many, many more "architectural monuments" in existence; the results are still coherent, but the "corpus of theory" is both firmer and broader, if also harder to define. The mistake made by many readers of the *International Style* was—and if anyone reads the book now, instead of depending on his memory or on secondhand reports of its contents, I fear, still is—to assume that what the authors offered as a diagnosis and a prognosis was intended to be used as an academic rule-book.

It is an old story now, on the other hand, that Wright came very close indeed to the International Style in certain projects of the late 1920s, or such as that for an apartment house for Elizabeth Noble in Los Angeles, and that many of his most famous later works, such as Falling Water, seem to include definitely "international" ideas. The architects of the San Francisco Bay Region, whom some critics have wished to build up as the

Wright's Johnson Wax Building . . . architect's feats as an innovator . . . [Frank Lloyd Wright, Johnson Wax Building, Racine, Wisconsin, 1936.]

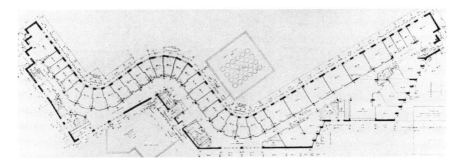

. . . Striking illustration of the increased use of curved and oblique forms. [Alvar Aalto, Senior House at M.I.T., 1947–51. Ground floor plan. Plan varies slightly from the one published originally.]

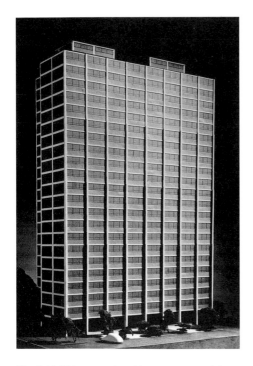

Mies in his Chicago apartment houses . . . moved closer and closer to Sullivan . . . [Ludwig Mies van der Rohe, Promonotory Apartments, Chicago, 1949. Model. View varies slightly from the original.]

protagonists of a more humanistic school opposed to the International Style, have also frequently followed its principles almost to the point of parody—although admittedly not in their best and most characteristic country-house work. Between these extremes of loose interpretation by one of the original definers of the International Style and of partial, or even at times complete, acceptance of its tenets by those theoretically most opposed to it, lies the great bulk of current architectural production.

Following the section devoted to "The Idea of Style" in the 1932 book came one on the "History" of modern architecture. We said then (rather condescendingly) of the architects active from 1890 to 1920:

Today it seems more accurate to describe the work of the older generation as half-modern.

In 1951 there seems no reason at all not to claim that the work of the older generation of modern architects was "early modern," not "half-modern." The achievements of the earlier men seem much greater today in retrospect, moreover, than they did twenty years ago. Without Wright's work of the last twenty years, it is hard to believe now that the full scope of his greatness could have been appreciated as it certainly had been in 1932 by many architects and critics for almost a generation. Yet it still seems a true enough historical statement to say that:

There was no real stylistic integration until after the war (of 1914–18).

The crystallization of what will perhaps in historical terms some day be called the "high" phase of modern architecture came in the 1920s. Now I suspect we are entering the "late" phase. Leaving that prognosis aside, much of what we wrote twenty years ago about the "early modern" architects still seems true.

Wright was the first to conceive of architectural design in terms of planes existing freely in three dimensions rather than in terms of enclosed blocks. Wagner, Behrens, and Perret lightened the solid massiveness of traditional architecture, Wright dynamited it.

Such things as the interior of Otto Wagner's Postal Savings Bank in Vienna, of about 1910, or Behrens's German General Electric turbine factory in Berlin, of 1912, appear today more extraordinary, in relation to what had preceded them in the previous century, than they did then.

Wright from the beginning was radical in his aesthetic experimentation.

Wright's Yahara Boat Club, of 1902, in Madison, Wisconsin, prefigured, a decade before Cubism reached maturity, most of the plastic innovations that contact with abstract painting and sculpture were to suggest, some fifteen years later, to the young European architects who initiated the International Style. The plan Wright prepared for a house to be built for himself in 1903, incorporating all the living areas except the kitchen in one articulated flow, is obviously an early prototype of the one-room houses that are frequently supposed to be a postwar development of the last five years.

Perret was, perhaps, a more important innovation in construction.

Perret's church at LeRaincy outside Paris, of 1933, remains more striking than much of the shell-concrete construction of the last decade. But Perret's later work has seemed less bold, both structurally and aesthetically, and he belongs in the main to the early twentieth century. Wright's Johnson Wax Building in Racine, of 1938, particularly with the addition of the new laboratory tower completed last year, reveals on the other hand that the American architect's feats as an innovator in construction had not even reached their peak in 1932. If such buildings as Notre Dame du Raincy and the Racine structures are not prime examples of modern architecture, the word "modern" has no meaning. On the other hand, they certainly do not fit conveniently into the frame of the International Style as it was envisaged between 1922 and 1932.

With regard to the moment of stylistic crystallization in the 1920s I think it is still true to say, as we wrote in 1931:

. . . the man who first made the world aware that a new style was being born was Le Corbusier.

Furthermore, no one has done more than Le Corbusier ever since to extend and loosen the sanctions of the International Style. That was already apparent in 1932 in his house for Mme. de Mandrot at Le Pradet, of 1931, and in his Errazuriz house of the same date in Chile. It is in some respects perhaps less evident today, at least in New York, since the UN office building (in whose design he played some part) may be considered "early" Le Corbusier—like his Paris projects of the twenties—rather than postwar Le Corbusier, at least in the form in which it has been executed.

In (Le Corbusier's) Citrohan house model of (1919–)1921 . . . the enormous window area and the terraces made possible by the use of ferro-concrete, together with the asymmetry of the composition, undoubtedly produced a design more thoroughly infused with new spirit, more completely freed from the conventions of the past, than any thus far projected.

It is interesting to compare the Citrohan house with Wright's Millard house in Pasadena, designed a year later. Note the similarity of the volume-concept of the interior, with the two-story living-area in front opening on a balcony, and the bedrooms and services on two levels behind. In 1931 it was hard to appreciate the originality in concept and in structure of the Millard house, because the patterned surface produced with the concrete blocks was so different from the smooth rendered surfaces which were still the sign-manual of the International Style, particularly as illustrated in the work of Le Corbusier before 1930. Now I think it is evident that such surface-patterning is a perfectly legitimate expression of the casting process by which Wright's blocks were made. Above all, thirty years have proved that patterned concrete surfaces, like Wright's of the 1920s, generally weather rather agreeably. The rendered surfaces of the early "International" buildings of the same period too often cracked and grew stained, thus losing all that quality of platonic abstraction which made them so striking.

(Le Corbusier) was not the only innovator nor was the style as it came generally into being after 1922 peculiarly his own. He crystallized; he dramatized; but he was not alone in creating.

Le Corbusier was certainly a good deal responsible for there being a recognizable international style. Yet Gropius's work and the work of his pupils is doubtless more typical of the style; and he has always been an equally effective proponent, even if he does continue to disown the idea of style at every opportunity.

It was in Mies's projects of 1922 that his true significance as an aesthetic innovator first appeared. In a design for a country house he broke with the conception of the wall as a continuous plane surrounding the plan and built up his composition of intersecting planes. Thus he achieved, still with the use of supporting walls, a greater openness even than Le Corbusier with his ferro-concrete skeleton construction.

Mies's country-house project of 1922, with its bearing walls of brick and its Van Doesburg-like plan, seems even more significant today than it did twenty years ago. It very evidently does not fit either the principle of enclosed volume or the principle of regularity. (This serious critical dilemma seems hardly to have been noted in 1931.)

The next section of the book was concerned with "Functionalism." For in 1932 *The International Style* was conceived as a counterblast to Functionalism, at least as we then understood that term.

Some modern critics and groups of architects both in Europe and in America deny that the aesthetic element in architecture is important, or even that it exists. All aesthetic principles of style are to them meaningless and unreal.

There are still those who insist that architecture ought to be entirely a matter of technics and that architects should therefore hand over the whole field of building to engineers. But the glorification of engineering is a less popular critical gambit than it was earlier. (Then it will perhaps be recalled there was even a "Great Engineer" in the White House!) Yet, looking back over the building production of the last two generations, it is evident that the really great engineers have frequently built edifices which were more monumental and in many ways more visually effective than what most architects were able to achieve. The grain elevators of the Great Lakes ports stimulated Le Corbusier's ideas of what the new architecture might be like quite as much as did the "Tubism" of his friend the painter Léger. The engineer Freyssinet's hangar at Orly, of 1925, is still something that architects have been unable to rival for grandeur and clarity of form. The Goodyear Airship Dock at Akron is almost as impressive. What this really means is that some engineers are very good architects!

. . . (It is) nearly impossible to organize and execute a complicated building without making some choices not wholly determined by technics and economics. . . . Consciously or unconsciously the designer must make free choices before his design is completed.

Some sort of architectural style inevitably arises from the characteristic ways in which those free choices are made. Thus functionalism, even in the drastic terms of the twenties, could have turned into a style, and to some Europeans it seems to have become one—the International Style, in fact! It is not necessary, of course, that engineers, or those architects who prefer to think of themselves as "pure" functionalists, should be able to explain in words their principles of design. (Some engineers at least, such as Arup and Samuely in England, can do so, however, and often very ably.)

. . . Critics should be articulate about problems of design; but architects, whose training is more technical than intellectual, can afford to be unconscious of the effects they produce. So, it may be assumed, were many of the great builders of the past.

As I have already noted, Mr. Johnson has given the most effective evidence of his own broad interpretation of the International Style in the buildings he has designed, rather than in writing. My own writing of the last twenty years, and perhaps particularly the book on Frank Lloyd Wright, *In the Nature of Materials* (1942), indicates—sometimes implicitly, sometimes explicitly—how my own ideas have been modified. It is worthwhile, nonetheless, to consider here a particular principle of the International Style as we saw it in 1932, notably the one concerning "Architecture as Volume." That was at best an ambiguous phrase, since volume is properly "contained space," while we were then chiefly concerned with the avoidance of effects of mass in the treatment of the exteriors of buildings.

Contemporary methods of construction provide a cage or skeleton of supports. Now the walls are merely subordinate elements fitted like screens between the supports or carried like a shell outside them.

The particular relationship of skeleton and shell which we then considered most characteristic of the International Style can best be illustrated, paradoxically, by the plan of a building that has never been accepted as representative of the style, Perret's church at LeRaincy, of 1923.

It is true that supporting wall sections are still sometimes used in combination with skeleton structure.

An early example of this, by one of the recognized leaders of the International Style, is illustrated in the plan of Le Corbusier's de Mandrot house of 1931. We considered that rather an exception. But today a very large number of modern American houses include (often quite arbitrarily it would seem) sections of supporting masonry, sometimes of brick, sometimes of rustic stonework, and very frequently of cinder or other concrete blocks introduced for effects of contrast and also because of their suitability in certain functional and structural situations. The idea may be abused but it can no longer be considered exceptional or reactionary.

The effect of mass, of static solidity, hitherto the prime quality of architecture, has all but disappeared; in its place there is an effect of volume, or more accurately, of surface planes bounding a volume. The prime architectural symbol is no longer the dense brick but the open box.

Certainly this statement is even truer, in a general way, than it was twenty years ago. Yet my fellow author, Mr. Johnson, not only used a towerlike cylinder inside his house of glass in New Canaan, but contrasted the ultimate openness of the main house with a guest house of brick, almost as solid in appearance as if it had no interior whatsoever!

The most dramatic illustrations of the various methods of expressing interior skeletons still remain the American skyscrapers; but there are now rather more of them than there were in 1932, so that the character of their construction is better understood by the general public.

The McGraw-Hill Building comes nearest to achieving aesthetically the expression of the enclosed steel cage, but it is still partially distorted into the old silhouette of a massive tower. ... Yet the architect, Raymond Hood, in the Daily News Building which is in other ways less pure in expression, handled the setbacks so that they did not suggest steps and brought his building to a clean stop without decorative or terminal features.

It has too often been forgotten—and apparently was by us when writing in 1931—that long before Raymond Hood's day the Bayard or Conduit Building, of 1897, in New York, by Louis Sullivan, or better still his Gage Building, of the next year, at 18 South Michigan Avenue in Chicago, illustrated more clearly than Hood's skyscrapers, then newly completed, the proper architectural expression of steel-skeleton construction in the external cladding of a tall edifice. The later New York skyscrapers (and particularly those since the war that seem most literally to follow the precepts of the International Style in their design) are certainly not more expressive than these 50-year-old buildings. It is also interesting to note that Mies van der Rohe, in his Chicago apartment houses of the last few years, has moved closer and closer to Sullivan in the exterior treatment, whether the skeleton inside be of ferro-concrete or of steel. Even 20 years ago it was very difficult, apparently, to seen the grandeur of the Sullivanian forest through the lush foliage of the ornament.

Style is character, style is expression; but even character must be displayed, and expression may be conscious and clear or muddled and deceptive. The architect who builds in the international style seeks to display the true character of his construction and to express clearly his provision for function. He prefers such an organization of his general composition, such a use of available surface materials, and such a handling of detail as will increase rather than contradict the prime effect of surface of volume.

The articulation of visible supports should also have been mentioned, whether isolated (as for example in the Johnson glass house or Mies's Farnsworth house on the Des Plaines river near Chicago) or actual sections of bearing wall (as in Le Corbusier's Le Pradet house or his house in Chile). A very striking example of vigorous articulation, in a quite sculptural way, of interior supports was in fact illustrated in the book, Aalto's Turun Sanomat Building at Abo in Finland, of 1930.

The flat roof was almost the sign-manual of the International Style in the early days. A loophole which proved very prophetic was left (fortunately) in the text on this subject:

Roofs with a single slant, however, have occasionally been used with success. Flat roofs are so much more useful that slanting or rounded roofs are only exceptionally justified.

The last sentence certainly represented a puristic and also a pseudofunctional position. But roofs are certainly of great importance in determining the character of the architecture of any period, particularly as regards small structures such as houses. Many architects have now swung so far from the belief that roofs must be flat that there is a tendency to overexploit elaboration of the sky-plane.

Since the roof was expected 20 years ago to be invisible, a great deal of space was given to the surfacing of exterior walls in the 1932 book.

The spirit of the principle of[continuous] surface covers many exceptions to its letter. The type of construction represented by Mies van der Rohe's Barcelona pavilion, as well as that represented in Le Corbusier's house at Le Pradet, leads to a treatment of surfaces sensibly different from that which has been primarily stressed here.

Obviously these exceptions should have been a warning that the aesthetic "necessity" for the treatment of exterior walls as continuous surface was being much exaggerated. Curiously enough, California architects, working mostly with wood, have of late years been more faithful to the principle of continuity of surface than the European architects who were originally the most devoted to rendered and painted surfaces of cement.

The general statement with which this section concluded had its sound points:

The principle of surface of volume intelligently understood will always lead to special applications where the construction is not the typical cage or skeleton of supports surrounded by a protecting screen. The apparent exception may not prove the validity of the general principle, but it undoubtedly indicates its elasticity. Rigid rules of design are easily broken once and for all; elastic principles of architecture grow and flourish.

Rather than proceed with so detailed a commentary, it may be well to lead into a conclusion to this article by quoting a few of the more general remarks of twenty years ago which seem to remain valid still.

The second principle of contemporary style in architecture has to do with regularity. The supports in skeleton construction are normally and typically spaced at equal distances. Thus most buildings have an underlying regular rhythm which is clearly seen before the outside surfaces are applied. Moreover, economic considerations tend to favor the use of standardized parts throughout. Good modern architecture expresses in its design this characteristic orderliness of structure and this similarity of parts by an aesthetic ordering which emphasizes the underlying regularity. Bad modern design contradicts this regularity. Regularity is, however, relative and not absolute in architecture.

. . . the nearer approaches to absolute regularity are also approaches to monotony. . . . The principle of regularity refers to a means of organization, a way of giving definite form to an architectural design, rather than to an end which is sought for itself.

. . . The avoidance of symmetry should not be arbitrary or distorted. . . . The mark of the bad modern architect is the positive cultivation of asymmetry for decorative reasons. For that can only be done in the majority of cases at the expense of common consistency and common sense. The mark of the good modern architect, on the other hand, is that the regularity of his designs approaches bilateral symmetry.

Exceptions to general rectangularity are only occasionally demanded by function and they may introduce complications in the regular skeleton of the structure. Non-rectangular shapes, particularly if they occur infrequently, introduce an aesthetic element of the highest positive interest. . . . They need seldom occur in ordinary building, but in monuments where the architect feels justified in seeking for a strongly personal expression, curves will be among the elements which give most surely extreme positive or negative aesthetic value. Curved and oblique forms seldom find a place in the cheapest solution of a given problem. But, if they can be afforded, they succeed, as they fail, on aesthetic grounds alone.

Aalto's Senior House at the Massachusetts Institute of Technology, of 1948, is obviously the most striking illustration of the increased use of curved and oblique forms. Whether most people approve of this prominent building or not, they tend to assume that Aalto was here consciously breaking with the rigidities of the International Style. Actually, as the paragraph above makes evident, even this notable postwar structure, though it may be at the extreme limit of the International Style as we understood it twenty years ago, is still in actual opposition to its sanctions only in the expressive irregularity of the plan and a few rather minor details, such as the willful roughness of the brickwork and the excessive clumsiness of some of the membering. Aalto was really reacting here, not against the International Style, but against that vulgar parodying of its more obvious aspects—the "Drugstore Modern"—which had become ubiquitous in the previous decade.

It was naturally to be expected, as the International Style became more widely accepted, that more and more weak and imitative architects would attempt to exploit its characteristic features. In 1932 we were amazingly optimistic and full of faith. We wrote:

Anyone who follows the rules, who accepts the implications of an architecture that is not mass but volume, and who conforms to the principle of regularity can produce buildings which are at least aesthetically sound. If these principles seem more negative than positive, it is because architecture has suffered chiefly in the last century and a half from the extension of the sanctions of genius to all who have called themselves architects.

But it has not, of course, worked out that way. Many docile architects, and even builders outside the profession, have followed the rules dutifully enough, but their buildings can hardly be considered aesthetically sound. Doubtless the principles educed twenty years ago were too negative, and now we are ready, probably too ready, to extend the sanctions of genius very widely once more. If my tentative prognosis be correct, that we stand now at another change of phase in modern architecture between a "high" and a "late" period, we must expect many vagaries in reaction against the too literal interpretation of the International Style. We may also expect—and indeed already have with us—an academic current which is encouraging the repetition of established formulas without creative modulation. If the next twenty-five years are less disturbed by depressions and wars than the last have been, I suspect that our architecture will grow more diverse in kind. But I doubt if we will, for the next generation or more, lose contact altogether with the International Style, if that be interpreted as broadly as it was meant to be in 1932.

The International Style was not presented, in the 1932 book which first gave currency to the phrase, as a closed system; nor was it intended to be the whole of modern architecture, past, present, and future. Perhaps it has become convenient now to use the phrase chiefly to condemn the literal and unimaginative application of the design clichés of twenty-five years ago; if that is really the case, the term had better be forgotten. The "traditional architecture," which still bulked so large in 1932, is all but dead by now. The living architecture of the twentieth century may well be called merely "modern."

1951

Matthew Nowicki's untimely death in 1950 at age forty cut short a very promising career. The accident occurred during the architect's flight home from planning the new capital of Chandigarh in India. The commission, which Nowicki had undertaken for the American firm of Mayer and Whittlesey, subsequently fell to Le Corbusier and British architects Maxwell Fry and Jane Drew, who retained elements of his master plan, although not very faithfully. But despite the brevity of a professional life spanning barely a decade and a half, Nowicki embodied—in the view of a critic like Lewis *107–9* Mumford—a twentieth-century ideal of the humanist architect.

Born in Siberia of Polish parents and widely traveled, Nowicki was trained in architecture and engineering at the Warsaw Polytechnic in the mid-1930s, years when the modern movement was breathing new life into Beaux-Arts curriculums. Le Corbusier's work deeply affected Nowicki at this time. During the occupation of Poland he participated in the resistance, emerging after as chief of planning for central Warsaw. In this capacity he took advantage of an opportunity to come to America to enlist support in rebuilding his devastated city. This led to his appointment as Polish delegate on the United Nations planning commission in New York, then engaged in choosing a building site. As its youngest member, Nowicki came into direct contact with Le Corbusier and other leading modernists idealistically projecting the institution that was to bring about "one world."

In 1947–48, when Communist takeover of Poland precluded his return, he applied for American citizenship. At the same time he was invited to join the faculty of the School of Design at North Carolina State College in Raleigh, then under the enlightened deanship of Henry Kamphoefner. In his two years at Raleigh, Nowicki developed an original pedagogical philosophy based on the integration of architecture, landscape architecture, city planning, and other design arts into a "single frame." To the regular design curriculum he added humanities, stressing architectural history, regional studies, and human sciences at a time when most architecture schools were neglecting these disciplines. He also designed, with William Henley Deitrick, his major built work, the arena at the North Carolina State Fair. This was an audacious engineering construction, compared at the time to Eugène Freyssinet's hangars at Orly: two giant parabolic arches meeting close to the ground to carry the double convex roof and frame the grandstands. Mumford wrote that it sang of "an architecture of democracy: a new architecture such as Whitman had foretold."

The following essay, published posthumously, is an acute analysis by Nowicki of the evolution of modern design up to his own day. It advances the thesis that the functionalist architecture developed in the nineteenth century was sidetracked by early twentieth-century aesthetics, which replaced problems of structure and materials with those of form. The adage "form follows function" was inverted to a stylistic formula. Function began to follow form, and technical elements were used to play a compositional rather than structurally necessary role. In a successive development functionalism, earlier understood as accommodating exact physical requirements, became a matter of providing its opposite, anonymous flexibility: "the free plan is replaced by the modular plan." Nowicki ends by calling for a further evolution of the idea of function from physical exactitude to the greater humanism of "the minute exigencies of life."

For Mumford's appreciation of Nowicki, see his four-part article, "The Life, the Teaching and the Architecture of Matthew Nowicki," in *Architectural Record*, June–September 1954.

From The Magazine of Art, *November 1951, pp. 273–79. Republished with slight variations as "Function and Form" in Lewis Mumford,* Roots of Contemporary Architecture *(New York: Reinhold, 1952), pp. 411–18. Courtesy of Stanislaw Nowicki.*

Origins and Trends in Modern Architecture
Matthew Nowicki

I suspect that I shall no longer provoke you as much as I should by opening with a statement that sometime ago, our design became a style. No matter how ingeniously we dodge the unpleasant issue, it comes at us with full force in thousands of creations of the contemporary designer. A style, with all the restrictions, disciplines, limitations, and blessings that we usually associate with the term. A style in the similarities between designs which differ basically in the purpose of their use and destination, subordinating to its demands a refrigerator or a motor car, a factory or a museum. A style which perhaps follows sales, quoting Edgar Kaufmann, just as form followed function, in the words of Greenough, and as Renaissance architecture followed antique models in the work of Palladio. A style as pronounced, as defined, more limited perhaps, and as legitimate for our times as the style of the Renaissance was in its day.

In the growing maturity and self-consciousness of our century, we cannot escape recognition of this fact, and we have to realize what it implies. We can no longer avoid this term "style" simply because it brings to our minds unpleasant memories. We cannot keep on pretending that we are able to solve our problems without a precedent in form.

We have to realize that in the overwhelming majority of modern design, form follows *form* and not *function*. And even when a form results from a functional analysis, this analysis follows a pattern that leads to a discovery of the same function, whether in a factory or a museum. Approached in a certain way, the answer to every architectural problem is a flexible space, with no reason why one flexible space should be different from another, and many practical reasons why they should be alike.

In saying all this, I am not advocating diversity in design for its own sake. Such a diversity is just a confirmation of the rule of regimentation that always is the result of a style. The more one attempts to escape one's period, the more one becomes part of it. The constructive diversity that provides strength to an expanding and virile civilization is the result of creative sensitivity to the eternally changing circumstances where "every opportunity stands alone."

This sensitivity is the main source of something for which I have no better word than freshness. Freshness is a physical part of youth, and youth disappears with time. This is the law of life, equally true in the case of an individual or a civilization. Freshness can be preserved if its source depends not on the physical state of being young, but on the consciousness of its origin. Some individuals preserve this creative freshness in their maturity. Those are the great artists. Some civilizations preserve this freshness for ages and then become great cultures. For although maturity aims at perfection, and the stride toward perfection must end with an unchanging standard of classical excellence, consciousness of the source of freshness can provide a magnified scope to this stride. The magnitude of this scope is the measure of ambitions and strength of a civilization, and the prophecy of its future achievements.

Thinking in terms of the contemporary, or should I say modern, period of design, we realize that it has passed its early youth. The experiments with form, with the new space concept, the playfulness with the machine to live in, the machine to look at or to touch, in architecture, painting, and sculpture are more remote than the time-span alone would indicate. There was a freshness in those youthful days of the aesthetic revolution, a physical freshness of a beginning. There was a diversity in those days of forms that grew without any direct precedent in form.

I speak of architecture because it incorporates the full field of design. In its changes we can discover those that affected interior design, industrial design, problems of organized landscape, and others, with or without a separate name. And it is these changes of the architectural concept that I propose to analyze with the aim of establishing our present position in their chain. From this analysis of changes I will not develop any law or analogy, nor will I make predictions on what the coming change will be. I propose to define our present position because this is our strategic point of departure for the investigation of the full field of opportunity that lies within our period. In order to define our present stage, I shall try to trace it to its origins.

It seems to me that the beginning of modern architecture has its roots in the domestic structure of the late Renaissance. It was then that the problem of human comfort was rediscovered. Functionalism in terms of the importance of good living was introduced, along with a number of technical gadgets of which the stove in Fountainebleau was probably a vanguard. Architecture descended from its pedestal of heroism and rapidly started to grow human and even bourgeois. In France, after the death of Louis XIV, the despotic *Roi soleil,* the private residence "building boom" produced a plan wherein areas of different use were defined and located with regard to one another. This new type of plan differed from its predecessor, in which a sequence of rectangular, round, oval, or otherwise-shaped interiors had a changing use, and one ate, slept, or entertained in any one of them, according to a passing or a more permanent fancy. This change was not the beginning of functionalism—since architecture always had to satisfy a function—but was rather the beginning of its modern interpretation.

Renouncing heroism, architecture diminished its scale, becoming cut to the size of an ordinary man. A comparison between the Palace of Versailles and the Petit Trianon would provide a good illustration of this change. In this alteration of the predominant scale and the introduction of problems of comfort, we can find the beginning of our architecture. These changes, essential as they were, however, could not alone produce the new form. Other factors were finally to complete the picture. One of them was expressed by the German architect Karl Friedrich Schinkel in 1825 after his visit to the industrialized Manchester in his famous question, "Why not a new style?" The eternal desire for change was responsible for violent shifts of the attitude toward form throughout the nineteenth century. To illustrate this violence and its extremes, I would like to quote two striking and not very well known examples. In the early years of the century, a French archaeologist proposed a system for destroying the Gothic cathedrals, considered in the days of the Empire as edifices of barbarism. His suggestion was to cut a groove at the base of the limestone columns, to surround them with piles of wood, and then to set fire to them. The archaeologist was convinced that under this treatment, each unsavory structure would crumble "in less than ten minutes," relieving civilization of its shameful presence.

A few decades later Ruskin, paving the way for the Pre-Raphaelite movement, wrote in his *Modern Painters* that no public funds should be spent to purchase paintings later then Raphael, as the spirit of art was confined to the medieval period and had been replaced by the superficial technology of a craft.

Out of these shifts of sympathies came the consciousness that some basic change in the eclectic sequence is indispensable. This was the psychological background to what we call the "modern" form. And although we shudder at the word *style,* Schinkel's search for its new expression contributed perhaps as much as any other factor to the birth of modern architecture. But no new form of architecture could have been created without a new structure, and psychological receptiveness had to wait its fulfillment until the structural possibilities ripened.

The middle of the last century with Paxton's Crystal Palace—its modular reerection on a new site, its space concept of openness—created a new era. The ensuing use of cast iron, then of ferro-concrete and steel, created the spine of the new frame structure, which from then on was dominant in modern building. Independence of the partitioning wall from the frame created the free plan, and thus all elements of the new architecture were present at the beginning of our century.

What would have been the characteristics of modern architecture had it followed the direction of those early days? Its form, influenced strongly by the expression of the structure, would have been intricate and detailed. The logical development of the skeleton would have accentuated the delicate ribs dividing areas of the building into supporting and supported members. The resulting form would perhaps acquire the lightness and openness of lacework filled with translucent or opaque screen. In its final state, the screen would probably be replaced with a secondary skeleton filling the lacework with still more lacework.

This was the way the Gothic skeleton had developed, with its stained-glass windows, and this was the road explored by Paxton, Labrouste, Eiffel, and their contemporaries. Modern architecture instead chose a road different in every respect from these expectations. To understand this change of destiny we must make a digression.

Architecture with its social, economic, and technical complexities never took the lead in aesthetic changes. As a rule it followed other media of art. The changes of taste in the nineteenth century, already mentioned, affected architecture very profoundly, but they resulted from factors remote to the problems of building design.

The great change introduced by the Renaissance can be quoted here as a striking example of the same problem. At the rebirth of the classical idiom, the medieval Gothic structure reached the climax of its growth. Its further life and growth were interrupted by an aesthetic wave unrelated to the techniques of architecture. No structural competition to the Gothic building was offered by the new style; the building methods of the Renaissance were crude in comparison to the advanced standards of the medieval mason. The change in architecture followed the changing aesthetic of the period, and the responsibility and credit for this change should rest with its men of letters. Thus Petrarch and Dante fathered the architecture of the Renaissance.

A somewhat similar thing happened in the case of modern architecture. This time the change in taste was inspired by painters rather than by men of letters. The broad and open manner of Cézanne, the architectonic painting of Synthetic Cubism, introduced a new taste for purity and simplicity of form. The development of the structural skeleton mentioned above could not be molded into the new aesthetic. Problems of structure and materials became secondary in a period preoccupied with the aesthetics of form. One has the impression that for an architect of the early twenties, construction was a necessary evil. Architecture became "idealized" and "dematerialized." Colorful planes meeting at the corners of the cube emphasized the lack of material thickness. Structural detail was eliminated in conformity with the demands of purity, and the idealized structure reacted badly to time and weather. A column in this architecture became simply a cylinder surrounded by planes, a vertical

Above: Discipline of today's modular plan. Saarinen, Saarinen and Associates, Engineering Staff Office Building, General Motors Technical Center, near Detroit, 1951. Each glass unit is based on a modular pattern in which the mullions serve not only to divide the windows, but also as columns forming an integral part of the structure. Below: Le Corbusier, Modulor. Scale for harmonic measurement of space based on the human figure. The two series of numbers take their respective bases from the height of a standing man (left) and from the height of a man with arm upraised (right).

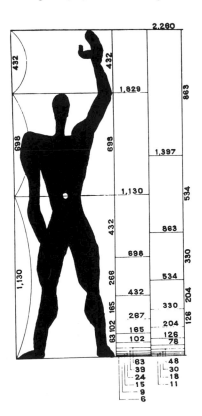

among horizontals. The contrast of this juxtaposition had to be achieved in a manner that would satisfy the intellect, so that no shape was created without a function which it should both express and serve. But in order to create the shape, a function was created or conveniently overemphasized. Here my thoughts wander to those two massive cylinders dividing the steps of Le Corbusier's Salvation Army building in Paris. Emphasized more than any other structural element in the building, they functioned as ventilation shafts. Maybe if by now they have already become technically obsolete, they have lost their functional meaning while preserving their compositional importance. This architecture of the International Style, romantically disposed to the overimpressive technology, developed a notion which I shall call that of *functional exactitude*. Truth in architecture was considered as the exact expression of every function. When a building became technically obsolete, thus no longer ideally serving those changing functions, it was to be removed and replaced by a more efficient one.

The concept of functional exactitude found a source of decorative qualities in the inventive interpretation of human life and movement. One might say that this architecture became the decoration of function. The period of functional exactitude looked for its inspiration toward the physical function; psychological aspects were not considered in its philosophy. The concept of controlled environment resulted; the main purpose of architecture became the control of *physical* environment to the *physical* satisfaction of the user.

The recent changes in modern architecture are perhaps as radical as those separating the 1920s from their predecessors. True, we share our vocabulary with this period of yesterday, but the same words now have a different and often a basically opposite meaning. We still speak of functionalism, but while then it meant exactitude, now it means flexibility. Those are two opposite concepts. In our thoughts we often give priority to the psychological rather than to the physical function of humans. The concept of a short-lived structure to be removed with the rapid change of technology has been replaced by a notion of architecture that will be our contribution to the life of future generations. Le Corbusier has introduced a measure on which this contribution can be composed: the "Modulor," with its mystique of the golden section. This measure of good proportion is most significant for the change of values—no longer the measure of functional space nor the measure of time, but a measure of beauty. Whatever the validity of such a measure may be, it is interesting to notice that in the sequence of "time, space, and architecture," the emphasis is shifting toward the last word in terms of the mystery of its art.

The free plan is replaced by the modular plan. Again these are two opposite notions. A module is the most rigid discipline to which a plan can be subjected. A modular plan in reality is the opposite of a free plan. We are no longer preoccupied with the proximities of related functions but with the nature of space that leads from one function to another. It is no longer "how quickly to get there" but "how to get there" that matters most in our plans. It seems that from a quantitative period we have jumped into a qualitative one.

These changes are not always conscious nor pronounced to the degree here indicated. It is an irresistible temptation to express such changes in the most striking manner possible, but in order to be objective one must realize that a dividing line between periods can never be geometrically defined. Such a division can better be compared to a wide ribbon which simultaneously separates and joins, like a gray belt

Functional flexibility expressed through decoration of structure. Matthew Nowicki and William Henley Deitrick, model for additions to State Fair Grounds, Raleigh, North Carolina [1949–50]. Above: Livestock Judging Pavilion. Below: View showing Livestock Judging Pavilion, under construction, on left; Grandstand and Exhibit Building on right.

1949), "Only a quality product that is also satisfactory in its form is capable of procuring for Swiss industry all the necessary prestige in the international field." The linkage between industry, the world market, and formal perfection had been established in the European Werkbund debates earlier in the century—where the problem had been the same, namely how to make European goods competitive with American ones—as well as in the Bauhaus. Bill updated the concept, further developing it in a book of 1952, *FORM: A Balance Sheet of Mid-Twentieth-Century Form*. Education, he stressed, was the key to the institutionalization of good modern taste: through education, consumers would learn to appreciate the value of goods that combined functionality and modern materials with harmonious design, and creative artists would learn how to produce them. This approach became basic to his conception of the program at Ulm.

Bill was also directly involved in pedagogical activities at this date. He had turned down the directorship of the Institute of Design, offered to him just prior to Moholy-Nagy's death, preferring to stay in Europe, but played a role in revamping the *Kunstgewerbeschule* in Zurich. He also took part after the war, together with members of the BBPR and other Milan architects, in preliminary efforts to set up a Bauhaus-derived school in a former factory building in the north of Italy. With this background, when asked to participate in planning the new school at Ulm, he seized the opportunity, persuading the founders to modify their idea of the institution to one geared to educating creative designers.

After five years of preparation, the HfG officially opened in spring 1955 with Bill as its director. The school offered departments of product design, architecture, city planning, information, and visual communication in addition to a first-year basic design course, initially taught by Albers as visiting professor. The fine arts were to have been incorporated later in the curriculum. The intention was to establish a latter-day Bauhaus, reoriented to the needs of the new mass-industrial society. Bill retained the older school's basic philosophy, rejecting the concept of specialization insofar as it precluded the possibility of the artist's integration within industrial production. Intrinsic to his conception was the design of the campus. The central workshop, classroom, and communal areas were to have been linked to a string of dormitory buildings freely disposed along a spine joining working and living (in the event only one dormitory was built), while the spartan detailing of the whole in concrete, adhering to a proportional module, not only was a matter of economic necessity but befitted a school dedicated to a rigorous aesthetic.

It was Bill's insistence on the primacy of the creative artist that led to a fatal *288–99* conflict with his successor, the Argentine Tomás Maldonado, whose scientific and antiart orientation had, if anything, more affinity with Hannes Meyer's regime at the Bauhaus than Gropius's. The conflict occasioned Bill's resignation from the school in 1957. Nor, ironically, was Bill's theory of good form immune from precisely the opposite charge: that of turning the free experimentalism of the original Bauhaus into a dogmatic method and a style furthering a materialistic consumer society. The latter accusation was leveled against the Ulm school by the avant-garde artist Asger Jorn. Jorn, whom Bill had initially considered inviting *172–75* to teach at the school, criticized the HfG from the podium of his "International Movement for an Imaginist Bauhaus."

From Max Bill, FORM: Eine Bilanz über die Formentwicklung um die Mitte des XX. Jahrhunderts, *trans. P. Morton Shand (Basel: Karl Werner A.G., 1952), pp. 162–67. Courtesy of the author.*

Education and Design
Max Bill

Although every human being with normal sensibility can recognize good and pleasing forms at first glance there is overwhelming evidence that the bulk of the population seldom buys things which answer this description. Most articles of new and good design are dearer than those of the same type which the average customer has been accustomed to purchase and good older designs are no longer made. But the main reason is that he instinctively fights shy of buying anything which does not reflect an undefined, and indeed indefinable, "popular demand," even if he likes it and finds it no more expensive.

Hence the myth of public taste, or rather the conventional belief in its existence, is one of the chief obstacles to the diffusion of good design. The persistent cultivation of this myth is the happy hunting ground of unscrupulous manufacturers and middlemen who employ all the resources of publicity to persuade the consumer (which in such cases means everybody) that the myth is a reality. Now it has often been noticed that the consumer is, at bottom, far more responsive to good and pleasing forms than might be supposed from his marked reluctance to accept them, the reluctance being due to his own uncertainty or ignorance, and the adroit commercial manner in which both are continually exploited. Thus what is sold is what is advertised, and what is advertised is what the consumer "ought" to buy. Every newspaper or other periodical's advertising columns are full of preposterously exaggerated claims which the reader has no possible means of testing. The object of all these high-flown advertisements is to keep on setting new fashions from season to season: fashions which hop about like performing fleas from traditional to streamlined forms, and thence back again either to sham-rustic or more highly ornate classical styles as the case may be. This insane game of musical chairs presents an apparently insuperable barrier to any effective public demand for good design. But the barrier is really advertising, and the only way to counter such propaganda is by education.

I want to make it quite plain that by "education" I mean the original sense of the word: development of a pupil's natural capacities, not the usual attempt to force them into some predetermined mold. We all know that the whole of our educational system is crying out for radical reform. But although a consideration of its defects and remedies is no part of my present purpose, the influence exercised by the more restricted field of education concerned with design has a very direct bearing on the subject matter of this book.

There has been no lack of educative attempts to enlist the aid of beauty in civilizing mankind, though most of them came to grief when confronted with the realities of modern life. That physical surroundings have a profound formative influence, in an aesthetic sense, on spiritual and moral development has long been recognized. Ruskin and Morris, who regarded industrialization as the greatest enemy of human happiness, believed that a cultural renascence could be brought about by the revival of handicrafts. It was thanks to them that England led the way in preaching appreciation of good design and quality in workmanship, but by the beginning of the present century the lead had passed to Germany.

A famous modern designer, Henry van de Velde, was at that time acting as artistic adviser to the industries and traditional crafts of the Grand Duchy of Sachsen-Weimar. In 1902 he opened his "Kunstgewerbe-Seminar" (Technical College for Artisans) at

[Ludwig Mies van der Rohe, master plan, Illinois Institute of Technology, Chicago, 1940–41. Photomontage.]

[Max Bill, Hochschule für Gestaltung, Ulm, 1950–54. Design sketch.]

Weimar, and in 1906 a "Kunstgewerbeschule" (School of Arts and Crafts) in the same town, both of which he directed in person. These two institutions undertook to provide conscientious designers with a proper technical training and to advise industrialists and manual craftsmen on all questions of design. Two years later a nucleus of the most progressive German designers and manufacturers founded the "Deutscher Werkbund" with the object of promoting better understanding of the need for good design among the general public. Papers read at its earlier meetings by Van de Velde, Muthesius, and Naumann, and the gist of its annual reports, set forth standpoints which have lost none of their actuality in the present day. Similar and closely allied bodies were formed in Austria, Switzerland, and Sweden, and the encouraging measure of success their efforts achieved in those countries is now universally acknowledged.

On Van de Velde's recommendation Walter Gropius was chosen to succeed him at the end of the First World War in what had by then become a republicanized Weimar. It was here that, after publishing his well-known "Manifesto," Gropius in 1919 merged the "Kunstgewerbe-Seminar" with the "Kunstgewerbe-Schule" as a single state institution renamed the "Bauhaus." In 1925 local conditions necessitated the transference of the Bauhaus to Dessau, where Gropius was able to erect those epoch-making buildings he designed to house its expanded activities. Hannes Meyer became the director on Gropius's retirement in 1928, and it was under his successor, Ludwig Mies van der Rohe, that the Bauhaus was forcibly closed down by the Nazis in 1933. The life of the Weimar Republic was short, but while it lasted no school of design enjoyed higher prestige or had such far-reaching influence. This was because the Bauhaus concentrated its efforts on meeting the practical requirements of the present and the immediate future and those who worked there on prototypes for things in daily use were, as the world subsequently realized, among the most outstanding designers of their generation.

Whereas the training given at the Bauhaus laid the fullest emphasis on the designer's creative responsibility to society, a very different principle was adopted at Taliesin in the U.S.A., where Frank Lloyd Wright always encouraged his pupils to become individualists, and still sets them to work on the sort of problems which are a direct echo of his own decidedly one-sided philosophy of design. This deliberate fostering of individualism has no place, however, in the curriculum of either the Institute of Design or the School of Architecture attached to the Illinois Institute of Technology in Chicago; the first conforms in the main to the Bauhaus model, while the second naturally enough reflects the conception of architecture held by its present director, Ludwig Mies van der Rohe.

Several fairly successful attempts have been made during recent years to establish schools of the Bauhaus type or to transform existing ones along the same lines. The "Hochschule für Gestaltung" (High School for Design) which the "Geschwister Scholl Stiftung" planned to build on the upper slopes of the Kuhberg at Ulm, in memory of Frau Inge Aicher-Scholl's brother and sister who were murdered by the Nazis, is one that gave every promise of being an enlightened further development of Bauhaus traditions. Thanks to the keen interest in this ambitious project shown by the former American High Commissioner in Germany, Mr. John J. McCloy, and his staff, and the active help of both in authorizing contributions to the building fund, its early realization has now become possible.

The prospectus of the Ulm "Hochschule für Gestaltung" opens as follows:

This school is a continuation of the Bauhaus but it includes some new departments of design which twenty to thirty years ago had not then assumed the importance they have since acquired. Its underlying principle is the combination of a broad but thorough technical training with a sound general education on rational modern lines. By this means the enterprise and constructive spirit of youth can be infused with a proper sense of social responsibilities and taught that cooperative work on important problems of contemporary design is a major contribution to the most urgent task of the present age: the humanizing of our increasingly mechanistic civilization.

Instruction and research, individual experiments and teamwork, will be made complementary to one another, the maintenance of a just balance between theoretic knowledge and its practical application being the basis of training throughout the course. At every stage of it the students will be called upon to explain and justify their individual work in order to accustom them to logical thinking and encourage self-reliance. Living in the closest contact with their teachers, and working together with them in groups, will ensure that each student receives a comprehensive education in design and a thorough grounding in other subjects.

The internal layout of the school is a free arrangement of intercommunicating workshops, laboratories, and studios, with adjoining hostels for the students and teaching staff. Since the students cooperate actively in the organization of their work, and they, like their teachers, live within the school precincts, there is every guarantee that they will become a purposeful international community.

[1953]

"My main work has been the planning of buildings. I have never written or spoken much," stated **Ludwig Mies van der Rohe** in a letter written in the early 1960s. Glibness did not come readily to this practitioner of one of the most exacting and succinct architectures of the century. "Anyway the most important things cannot be discussed," he noted elsewhere. It was instead his habit to condense his thoughts into terse notes or, when public occasion demanded, aphoristic enunciations. These frequently contained fragmentary citations or echoes of the ideas of thinkers who had had a seminal influence on his intellectual development. The following note cards from a lecture given in Chicago in the early 1950s—years when he was completing his Lakeshore Drive apartments and working on the design of Crown Hall at Illinois Institute of Technology—are typical in this regard.

By the time Mies left Europe in 1938 to become director of architecture at Armour Institute of Technology in Chicago, his philosophy of architecture—which he chose to call *Baukunst,* building art—was fully mature. Building art, in his view, was a consequence of neither technical functionality nor aesthetic formalism, but rather, as he had put it in 1928, "the spatial expression of spiritual decisions." This view of the relationship between "technology and the soul," the preoccupying theme of his subsequent writings, was derived largely from three sources. One was Friedrich Dessauer's *Philosophie der Technik* (1927), a book he read assiduously which placed technology in the domain of a "science of values." More important was the thought of the Berlin Catholic theologian Romano Guardini, especially his book *Briefe vom Comer See* (Letters from Lake Como, 1928). In Guardini Mies, whose only academic education consisted of three boyhood years at the cathedral school of Aachen, discovered a philosophy that combined a life-affirming view of modern civilization with faith in the existence of an objective order underlying reality. Directly mediating between these ideas and architecture were the writing and work of the Catholic architect Rudolf Schwarz, who was closely associated with Guardini. Schwarz's essay *Wegweisung der Technik* (Orientation by Technology,1929) was, in Mies's words, "a way station in my development." Later Mies would write an introduction to one of Schwarz's books and, two years after Schwarz's death, a statement memorializing this "thinking building master."

129–34

It is important to stress this intellectual background in Mies's thought, not only because it provides an illuminating context in which to read his writings, but also because it shows the distance that this primary exponent of modern architecture sought to take from the latter's positivism and stylistic formations. For an examination of these ideas in relation to Mies's built work, Fritz Neumeyer's recent book is invaluable (see source note below). It is noteworthy that the following undated lecture, originally written and delivered in German, not only contains the title of Schwarz's polemic of 1953, "Create, artist, do not talk," in its crossed-out last line—an exhortation originally made by Goethe and later repeated by H. P. Berlage, another architect of great significance to Mies—but it also contains (note card 15) a direct echo of a point Schwarz makes in that same article concerning the "nearness" of history. On this internal evidence the document has been placed in the present sequence.

From an undated and untitled manuscript in the Library of Congress bearing the notation "Manuscript of one important address Mies gave here in German." First published in Fritz Neumeyer, Mies van der Rohe—das kunstlose Wort: Gedanken zur Baukunst *(Berlin, Siedler Verlag, 1986). English edition:* The Artless Word: Mies van der Rohe on the Building Art, *trans. Mark Jarzombek (Cambridge, Mass.: MIT Press, 1991), pp. 325–26. Translation courtesy of MIT Press.*

[With Infinite Slowness Arises the Great Form]
Ludwig Mies van der Rohe

[*card 1*]

Ladies and Gentlemen:

The attempt to revitalize the building art from the direction of form has failed. A century's worth of effort has been wasted and leads into the void. That heroic revolution of extremely talented men at the turn of the century had the time span of a fashion. The invention of forms is obviously not the task of the building art. Building art is more and different. Its excellent name already makes it clear that building is its natural content and art its completion.

[*card 2*]

Building, where it became great, was almost always indebted to construction, and construction was almost always the conveyor of its spatial form. Romantic and Gothic demonstrate that in brilliant clarity. Here as there structure expresses the meaning, expresses it down to the last remnant of spiritual value. But if that is so, then it must follow that the revitalization of the building art can only come from construction and not by means of arbitrarily assembled motifs.

[*card 3*]

But construction, that loyal safekeeper of an epoch's spirit, had rejected all that was arbitrary and created an objective basis for new developments. And so it has happened here also. The few authentic structures of our period exhibit construction as a component of building. Building and meaning are one. The manner of building is decisive and of testimonial significance.

[*card 4*]

Construction not only determines form but is form itself. Where authentic construction encounters authentic contents, authentic works result: works genuine and intrinsic. And they are necessary. Necessary in themselves and also as members of a genuine order. One can only order what is already ordered in itself. Order is more than organization. Organization is the determination of function.

[*card 5*]

Order, however, imparts meaning. If we would give to each thing what intrinsically belongs to it, then all things would easily fall into their proper place; only there they could really be what they are and there they would fully realize themselves. The chaos in which we live would give way to order and the world would again become meaningful and beautiful.

[*card 6*]

But that means to let go of the self-will and do the necessary. To articulate and realize the timely and not prevent what wants to and must become.

[*card 7*]

In other words: serve rather than rule. Only those who know how hard it is to do even simple things properly can respect the immensity of the task. It means to persevere humbly, renounce effects, and do what is necessary and right with loyalty.

[*card 8*]
Only yesterday one spoke of the eternal forms of art, today one speaks of its dynamic change. Neither is right. Building art is beholden neither to the day nor to eternity, but to the epoch. Only a historical movement offers it space for living and allows it to fulfill itself. Building art is the expression of what historically transpires. Authentic expression of an inner movement.

[*card 9*]
Fulfillment and expression of something immanent. This may also be the reason why the nineteenth century failed. Unsuspected and deep beneath all the confused attempts of that time ran the quiet current of change, fed by forces of a world that was intrinsically already different, and a jungle of new forms broke out. Unusual and of wild power. The world of technical forms; large and forceful.

[*card 10*]
Genuine forms of a genuine world. Everything else that occurred looked, next to that, pale and marginal. Technology promises both power and grandeur, a dangerous promise for man who has been created for neither one nor the other. Those who are truly responsible feel depressed and respond to this promise by searching for the dignity and value of technology.

[*card 11*]
Is the world as it presents itself bearable for man?
More: is it worthy of man or too lowly?
Does it offer room for the highest form of human dignity?
Can it be shaped so as to be worthwhile to live in?

[*card 12*]
And finally: is the world noble enough to respond to man's duty to erect a high and magnanimous order? These are questions of immense weight. One can quickly affirm them and quickly negate them, and one has done that.

[*card 13*]
To the careful, however, beyond all prejudices and misjudgments, technology appears as a world which is what it is, specific and narrow, dependent on the panorama of its own time just as any other building art, and precluding a host of possibilities.

[*card 14*]
There is no reason to overestimate this form. But it is, like all other authentic forms, both deep and high. Called to the one, attempting the other. A real world.— If that is true, then technology, too, must change into building art to complete itself. It would be a building art that inherits the Gothic legacy. It is our greatest hope.

[*card 15*]
But none of this comes about by itself. History does not come about by itself. [*addition in the original manuscript:* History must be done.] And historical measurements are

shorter than many realize. Only thirty life spans separate us from the Acropolis. And the breathing span of the Middle Ages was too short for it to complete its cathedrals. [*addition to the original manuscript:* We have all reason to be wide awake and not sleep away our time.]

[*card 16*]
Furthermore, the technological age is not as young as it may appear. Whitehead transferred the hour of its birth into the seventeenth century. That may be. The ultimate reasons for what occurs today may be found in the discussion of lonely monks behind quiet Romanesque monastery walls.

[*card 17*]
With infinite slowness arises the great form the birth of which is the meaning of the epoch. [*crossed out:* But a reconciliatory forgiving kindness of history permits great things to die in their greatness and spares them from old age.] Not everything that happens takes place in full view. The decisive battles of the spirit are waged on invisible battlefields.

[*card 18*]
The visible is only the final step of a historical form. Its fulfillment. Its true fulfillment. Then it breaks off. And a new world arises.

[*card 19*]
What I have said is the ground on which I stand; that which I believe and the justification of my deeds. Convictions are necessary, but in the realm of one's work they have only limited significance. In the final analysis it is the performance that matters [*crossed-out addition in original manuscript:* That is what Goethe meant when he said: Create, artist, do not talk.]

1953

By the late 1920s the "heroic" period of the avant-garde had ended with a return to order in most countries. The war and its aftermath had had a further chilling effect on radical aesthetics. In this climate the International Situationist movement was something of an exception. Founded in Italy in 1957 by Guy Debord, Asger Jorn, Giuseppe Pinot-Gallizio, and five others, it was collaged out of a handful of experimental groups alive in the late 1940s and 1950s, notably the Lettrist

172–75   International and the International Movement for an Imaginist Bauhaus. For a little more than a decade, in the course of internal transformations, the small cadre of artists and intellectuals who made up the group succeeded in producing a prophetic critique of art and society couched in terms of the city, the mass

314–18   media, and the relations of everyday life. They augured the resurgence of an oppositional culture that would come to fruition in the student strikes of 1968.

The following writing by **Ivan Chtcheglov** represents the original expression of the idea of unitary urbanism, a concept central to the Situationist movement in the late 1950s. It was published in the first issue of the *International situationniste* bulletin in June 1958 under Chtcheglov's pseudonym, Gilles Ivain, with the following note: "The International Lettrist had adopted this report on urbanism by Gilles Ivain in October 1953; it constitutes a decisive element of the new orientation then taken by the experimental avant-garde." A fantasy evoking the oneiric flâneurism of Louis Aragon's *Paysan de Paris* and reminiscent of the "transrational" architectural poetics of Velimir Khlebnikov, Chtcheglov-Ivain's text focuses programmatically on the city as a field of social and artistic action. He envisions the urban milieu as a site for the construction of ludic and performative situation-spaces or events. The "first experimental city" would contain rooms "more conducive to dreams than any drug" and a Disneyland of districts where every fantasy could be enacted through "controlled tourism." Through play "the baroque stage of urbanism" could become "a means of knowledge."

The inaugural issue of the *Internationale situationniste* also included the following definitions of concepts central to the Situationist program:

Constructed situation: a moment of life concretely and deliberately constructed by the collective organization of a unitary ambiance and a game of events;

Psychogeography: the study of specific effects of the geographical environment, consciously organized or not, on individuals' emotions and behavior;

Dérive: a mode of experimental behavior linked to the conditions of urban society: a technique of transient passage through varied ambiances. Also used to designate a specific period of continuous deriving;

Unitary urbanism: the theory of the combined use of arts and techniques for the integral construction of a milieu in dynamic relation with experiments in behavior.

Chtcheglov himself remains an obscure figure. A nineteen-year-old Czech emigré at the time of this writing, he was destined to become a Situationist "from afar," having in 1954 been "demitted" from the Lettrist movement for "mythomania, delirium of interpretation, and lack of revolutionary consciousness." Plans conceived with a roommate that year to blow up the Eiffel Tower landed him first in jail, and then, after subsequent bad behavior, in a mental institution, where he remained in Situationist martyrdom.

Published as "Formulaire pour un urbanisme nouveau" in Internationale situationniste 1 (June 1958), p. 15. In English in Ken Knabb, ed. and trans., Situationist International Anthology (Berkeley: Bureau of Public Secrets, 1981), p. 19. The International situationniste bears this notice: "All the texts published in the Internationale situationniste may be freely reproduced, translated, or adapted, even without indication of source." Translation courtesy of Ken Knabb.

Formulary for a New Urbanism
Gilles Ivain [Ivan Chtcheglov]

> *Sire, I am from another country.*

We are bored in the city, there is no longer any temple of the sun. Between the legs of the women walking by, the dadaists imagined a monkey wrench and the surrealists a crystal cup. That's lost. We know how to read every promise in faces—the latest stage of morphology. The poetry of the billboards lasted twenty years. We are bored in the city, we really have to strain still to discover mysteries on the sidewalk billboards, the latest state of humor and poetry:

Shower-Bath of the Patriarchs
Meat Cutting Machines
Notre-Dame Zoo
Sports Pharmacy
Martyrs Provisions
Translucent Concrete
Golden Touch Sawmill
Center for Functional Recuperation
Saint Anne Ambulance
Cafe Fifth Avenue
Prolonged Volunteers Street
Family Boarding House in the Garden
Hotel of Strangers
Wild Street

And the swimming pool on the Street of Little Girls. And the police station on Rendezvous Street. The medical-surgical clinic and the free placement center on the Quai des Orfévres. The artificial flowers on Sun Street. The Castle Cellars Hotel, the Ocean Bar, and the Coming and Going Cafe. The Hotel of the Epoch.

And the strange statue of Dr. Philippe Pinel, benefactor of the insane, in the last evenings of summer. To explore Paris.

And you, forgotten, your memories ravaged by the consternations of two hemispheres, stranded in the Red Cellars of Pali-Kao, without music and without geography, no longer setting out for the hacienda *where the roots think of the child and where the wine is finished off with fables from an old almanac.* Now that's finished. You'll never see the hacienda. It doesn't exist.

The hacienda must be built.

All cities are geological; you cannot take three steps without encountering ghosts bearing all the prestige of their legends. We move within a *closed* landscape whose landmarks constantly draw us toward the past. Certain *shifting angles,* certain *receding* perspectives, allow us to glimpse original conceptions of space, but this vision remains fragmentary. It must be sought in the magical locales of fairy tales and surrealist writings: castles, endless walls, little forgotten bars, mammoth caverns, casino mirrors.

These dated images retain a small catalyzing power, but it is almost impossible to use them in a *symbolic urbanism* without rejuvenating them by giving them a new meaning. Our imaginations, haunted by old archetypes, have remained far behind the sophistication of the machines. The various attempts to integrate modern science into new myths remain inadequate. Meanwhile abstraction has invaded all the arts, contemporary architecture in particular. Pure plasticity, inanimate, storyless, soothes the eye. Elsewhere other fragmentary beauties can be found—while the promised land of syntheses continually recedes into the distance. Everyone wavers between the emotionally still-alive past and the already dead future.

We will not work to prolong the mechanical civilizations and frigid architecture that ultimately lead to boring leisure.

We propose to invent new, changeable decors.(. . .)

Darkness and obscurity are banished by artificial lighting, and the seasons by air conditioning; night and summer are losing their charm and dawn is disappearing. The man of the cities thinks he has escaped from cosmic reality, but there is no corresponding expansion of his dream life. The reason is clear: dreams spring from reality and are realized in it.

The latest technological developments would make possible the individual's unbroken contact with cosmic reality while eliminating its disagreeable aspects. Stars and rain can be seen through glass ceilings. The mobile house turns with the sun. Its sliding walls enable vegetation to invade life. Mounted on tracks, it can go down to the sea in the morning and return to the forest in the evening.

Architecture is the simplest means of *articulating* time and space, of *modulating* reality, of engendering dreams. It is a matter not only of plastic articulation and modulation expressing an ephemeral beauty, but of a modulation producing influences in accordance with the eternal spectrum of human desires and the progress in realizing them.

The architecture of tomorrow will be a means of modifying present conceptions of time and space. It will be a means of *knowledge* and a *means of action.*

The architectural complex will be modifiable. Its aspect will change totally or partially in accordance with the will of its inhabitants.(. . .)

Past collectives offered the masses an absolute truth and incontrovertible mythical exemplars. The appearance of the notion of *relativity* in the modern mind allows one to surmise the *experimental* aspect of the next civilization (although I'm not satisfied with that word; say, more supple, more "fun"). On the bases of this mobile civilization, architecture will, at least initially, be a means of experimenting with a thousand ways of modifying life, with a view to a mythic synthesis.

A mental disease has swept the planet: banalization. Everyone is hypnotized by production and conveniences—sewage system, elevator, bathroom, washing machine.

This state of affairs, arising out of a struggle against poverty, has overshot its ultimate goal—the liberation of man from material cares—and become an obsessive image hanging over the present. Presented with the alternative of love or a garbage disposal unit, young people of all countries have chosen the garbage disposal unit. It has become essential to bring about a complete spiritual transformation by bringing to light forgotten desires and by creating entirely new ones. And by carrying out an *intensive propaganda* in favor of these desires.

We have already pointed out the need of constructing situations as being one of the fundamental desires on which the next civilization will be founded. This need for absolute creation has always been intimately associated with the need to play with architecture, time, and space. (. . .)

Chirico remains one of the most remarkable architectural precursors. He was grappling with the problems of absences and presences in time and space.

We know that an object that is not consciously noticed at the time of a first visit can, by its absence during subsequent visits, provoke an indefinable impression: as a result of this sighting backward in time, *the absence of the object becomes a presence one can feel.* More precisely: although the quality of the impression generally remains indefinite, it nevertheless varies with the nature of the removed object and importance accorded it by the visitor, ranging from serene joy to terror. (It is of no particular significance that in this specific case memory is the vehicle of these feelings. I only selected this example for its convenience.)

In Chirico's paintings (during his Arcade period) an *empty space* creates a *full-filled time.* It is easy to imagine the fantastic future possibilities of such architecture and its influence on the masses. Today we can have nothing but contempt for a century that relegates such *blueprints* to its so-called museums.

This new vision of time and space, which will be the theoretical basis of future constructions, is still imprecise and will remain so until experimentation with patterns of behavior has taken place in cities specifically established for this purpose, cities assembling—in addition to the facilities necessary for a minimum of comfort and security—buildings charged with evocative power, symbolic edifices representing desires, forces, events past, present, and to come. A rational extension of the old religious systems, of old tales, and above all of psychoanalysis, into architectural expression becomes more and more urgent as all the reasons for becoming impassioned disappear.

Everyone will live in his own personal "cathedral," so to speak. There will be rooms more conducive to dreams than any drug, and houses where one cannot help but love. Others will be irresistibly alluring to travelers . . .

This project could be compared with the Chinese and Japanese gardens in *trompe l'oeil*—with the difference that those gardens are not designed to be lived in at all times—or with the ridiculous labyrinth in the Jardin des Plantes, at the entry to which is written (height of absurdity, Ariadne unemployed): *Games are forbidden in the labyrinth.*

This city could be envisaged in the form of an arbitrary assemblage of castles, grottos, lakes, etc. It would be the baroque stage of urbanism considered as a means of knowledge. But this theoretical phase is already outdated. We know that a modern building could be constructed which would have no resemblance to a medieval castle but which would preserve and enhance the *Castle* poetic power (by the conservation of a strict minimum of lines, the transposition of certain others, the positioning of openings, the topographical location, etc.).

The districts of this city could correspond to the whole spectrum of diverse feelings that one encounters *by chance* in everyday life.

Bizarre Quarter—Happy Quarter (specially reserved for habitation)—Noble and Tragic Quarter (for good children)—Historical Quarter (museums, schools)—Useful Quarter (hospital, tool shops)—Sinister Quarter, etc. And an *Astrolaire* which would group plant species in accordance with the relations they manifest with the stellar rhythm, a planetary garden comparable to that which the astronomer Thomas wants to establish at Laaer Berg in Vienna. Indispensable for giving the inhabitants a consciousness of the cosmic. Perhaps also a Death Quarter, not for dying in but so as to have somewhere to live in peace, and I think here of Mexico and of a principle of cruelty in innocence that appeals more to me every day.

The Sinister Quarter, for example, would be a good replacement for those hell holes that many people once possessed in their capitals: they symbolized all the evil forces of life. The Sinister Quarter would have no need to harbor real dangers, such as traps, dungeons, or mines. It would be difficult to get into, with a hideous decor (piercing whistles, alarm bells, sirens wailing intermittently, grotesque sculptures, power-driven mobiles, called *Auto-Mobiles*), and as poorly lit at night as it is blindingly lit during the day by an intensive use of reflection. At the center, the "Square of the Appalling Mobile." Saturation of the market with a product causes the product's market value to fall: thus, as they explored the Sinister Quarter, the child and the adult would learn not to fear the anguishing occasions of life, but to be amused by them.

The principal activity of the inhabitants will be the *Continuous Dérive.* The changing of landscapes from one hour to the next will result in complete disorientation. (. . .)

Later, as the gestures inevitably grow stale, this dérive will partially leave the realm of direct experience for that of representation. (. . .)

The economic obstacles are only apparent. We know that the more a place is *set apart for free play,* the more it influences people's behavior and the greater is its force of attraction. This is demonstrated by the immense prestige of Monaco and Las Vegas—and Reno, that caricature of free love—although they are mere gambling places. Our first experimental city would live largely off tolerated and controlled tourism. Future avant-garde activities and productions would naturally tend to gravitate there. In a few years it would become the intellectual capital of the world and would be universally recognized as such.

1954

Though peripheral to any mainstream history of architecture, the polemical role played by the Danish artist **Asger Jorn** is of interest as it represents not only an effort to sustain an avant-garde position in these years, but also an aesthetic critique of architecture. Jorn had worked in Le Corbusier's office in 1937–38, executing mural decoration for the Pavillon des Temps Nouveaux. He also worked for a time in Fernand Léger's atelier, but soon gravitated to the more spontaneous aesthetic of the surrealist circles in Paris. Returning to Copenhagen when the war broke out, he served as principal theoretician of a group of young "abstractionist-surrealists" that included artists, architects, and poets. As a student of aesthetics, sociology, and political economy and a member of the Danish communist party, Jorn wrote during these years on subjects ranging from appreciations of kitsch in art to denunciations of functionalism in architecture. After the war, he returned south and in 1948, together with the Dutch painter Constant Nieuwenhuys and the Belgian poet and critic Christian Dotremont, founded the group "Cobra" (an acronym for Copenhagen/Brussels/Amsterdam).

After Cobra's demise in 1951 and his recuperation from an illness, Jorn launched a new campaign: the International Movement for an Imaginist Bauhaus. Founded in Switzerland in 1953, it was intended as "the answer to the question *where and how* to find a justified place for artists in the machine age." As its
157–62   polemical antagonist it took Max Bill's newly founded Hochschule für Gestaltung in Ulm. Jorn attacked Bill for academicizing the Bauhaus's program, which he saw as revolutionary in its day but now turned reactionary by virtue of Bill's institutional orientation and fetishizing of "good form." A skirmish took place at the Milan Triennale in 1954, where Jorn replied contentiously to a paper in which Bill had stated, "The function of the artist is not to express himself, but to create harmonious objects serving man." Jorn responded, "Is it possible to safeguard freedom and the desire for experimentation under the new historical conditions?"

In 1955 a meeting between Jorn and the Italian painter Giuseppe Pinot-Gallizio led to the establishment in the Piedmontese city of Alba of an "experimental laboratory" that became the base of the Imaginist Bauhaus. There, a small group of "free experimental artists" worked with ceramics and unconventional materials in an antiacademic setting , exploring radical theories of decoration and urbanism. The group included at one time or another fellow Cobra founder
314–18   Constant, who arrived in 1956 and stayed to develop the new theory of unitary
167–71   urbanism; the Chilean sculptor Matta, who had also worked in Le Corbusier's office in the 1930s; and the Italian architect-designer Ettore Sottsass, Jr. Close contacts with other avant-garde groups led to collaboration with the International Lettrists, led by Guy Debord in Paris. In 1957, at a meeting in Alba, Jorn, Pinot-Gallizio, Debord, and several others founded the International Situationist movement, merging their activities into a program of "psychogeographic" action.

In the following essay Jorn approvingly cites an argument made by Rudolf
129–34   Schwarz, who had also mounted an attack on the Bauhaus. This is clearly a case of strange bedfellows, although it demonstrates just how broad-based the critique of functionalism had become. At the same time, the diametric opposition
288–99   between Jorn's critique of Bill's program and that of Tomás Maldonado reveals the wide breach between the cultures of aesthetics and science.

First published as "Argomenti a proposito del Movimento Internazionale Per Un Bauhaus Immaginista contro un bauhaus immaginario e sua ragione attuale" in Asger Jorn, Immagine e forma *1 (Milan: Editoriale Periodici Italiani, 1954), unpaged [8–10]. Republished in French with slight modifications in Asger Jorn,* Pour la Forme—Ebauche d'une méthodologie des arts *(Paris: Internationale situationniste, 1958), pp. 15–16. Translated from the Italian. Courtesy of the Asger Jorn Heirs.*

Arguments apropos of the International Movement for an Imaginist Bauhaus, against an Imaginary Bauhaus, and Its Purpose Today
Asger Jorn

The Bauhaus has become a fixed conception for all who participate in the creation of architectural forms and of applied art and utilitarian forms. Its force field extends across many lands and continents. Its spiritual atmosphere, intense and fresh, continues to act. Never will its impact be spent, for the guarantee of its permanence lies in the spirituality and enthusiasm, the magic and the innate seriousness of its creators. There will always be young people who will follow in a new manner the path indicated by the Bauhaus.
—Peter Röhl, *Baukunst und Werkform,* 1 February 1954

Here I stand in front of my twenty-four students. One of them, who comes from a university in the south of Germany, says to me, "This debate about the past, the Bauhaus, and all these explanations are pretty interesting, but we young people can only relate to them as disinterested spectators who have no part in them. Ultimately, all of this does not concern us at all. What interest do architectural theories petrified in 1930 have for us?" I confess that this kind of talk has given me much cause for thought.
—Peter Gundwin, *Baukunst und Werkform,* 1 February 1954

Bauhaus is the name of an artistic inspiration.
—Asger Jorn, in a letter to the director of the New Bauhaus at Ulm, the architect Max Bill, 16 January 1954

Bauhaus is not the name of an artistic inspiration, but the meaning of a movement that represents a well-defined doctrine.
—Max Bill, in a letter to Asger Jorn, 23 January 1954

If Bauhaus is not the name of an artistic inspiration, it is the name of a doctrine without inspiration—that is to say, dead.
—Asger Jorn, in a letter to Max Bill, 12 February 1954

All new cultural developments, even the most practical and utilitarian ones, must begin as spiritual ideas and artistic inspirations.

It is a historical given that the formal language of functionalism finds its origin in cubist painting. This path is natural. It is evidently easier to draw than to construct; one must imagine before one can create. Architecture is always the ultimate realization of a mental and artistic evolution; it is the materialization of an economic stage. Architecture is the last point of realization of all artistic effort because to create a work of architecture means to construct an ambience and to establish a way of life. The conditions of life have changed profoundly since the last war. This fact manifests itself especially in the creative arts. We move today to a mental and artistic revolution that violently confronts the dead language of cubism and constructivism. Certain architects thus find themselves obliged to defend an already anemic position, one that increasingly approaches total anemia. Max Bill writes, in a letter to Asger Jorn (14 January 1954): "We do not intend by 'art' some kind of 'self-expression,' but rather a true art. We do not agree with the work of the Cobra group, nor with that of similar groups." This viewpoint logically corresponds to that expressed by Bill in an earlier writing (1 December 1953): "For us at Ulm, the art in question is considered in a different manner than it was in the old Bauhaus, where self-expression passed for an integral part of the form."

Gropius writes on the other hand: "The creative artist makes choices according to his own feelings among a range of possible solutions on the same economic level. For this reason, art carries the imprint of its creator." This point of view explains the interest and sympathy in the relations between the old Bauhaus and expressionist artists like Kokoschka and Marc Chagall. Today the situation is entirely changed. The new Bauhaus, fallen into a doctrinaire and conservative formalism, shows itself hostile to all effort at self-expression, and its purpose is only to bring order to already existing elements. This is a real fault because precisely today we have need of a new, living Bauhaus, intense and fresh, which can reunite and fertilize the experiences of all the creative arts. It is above all a fault since precisely in questions of personal expression, new and important conceptions appear at this moment and reveal unlimited creative possibilities.

Originality	—	*Subjectivity*	—	*Order*
Experiment	—	*Expression*	—	*Form*
Aesthetics	—	*Ethics*	—	*Logic*
Idea	—	*Art*	—	*Science*

What is the importance of personal expression in form? Gropius claims to understand its importance, but does not define it. Does he then only accept its importance out of convention? Isn't personal expression absolutely useless in form? He writes, "It is an error to consider it necessary to emphasize individualism at any price," and moreover, "in the art of modern construction one clearly recognizes a tendency toward objectivization of personal and national interests. Architecture is always national, and always individual also. But of these three concentric circles—*individual, nation, humanity*—it is the last, the greatest, that encompasses the others."

"Gropius did not know what it means to think," observes Rudolf Schwarz in a heretical critique of the old Bauhaus, and the preceding quotation would seem to bear this out; the most dangerous aspect of all this is that Gropius's confusion is common to all modern architects. The three concentric circles he names have nothing to do with objectivization; on the contrary, objectivization signifies exclusion, isolation, abstraction— that is, the opposite of the all-encompassing. Furthermore, the three circles do not represent circles of objectivities, but circles of interest, of mutually inseparable subjectivities. Humanity exists thanks to individuals, and the interest of the individual goes beyond his own personal existence. The interests common to humanity represent a collective subjectivity. We have arrived at a new conception of subjectivity today. It revolutionizes the entire theoretical and ideological basis of future art and technique. We have linked these phenomena, and they have entered into an organic and living synthesis; we have created a dynamic conception of art and technique; and the ultimate end of all the arts and all the techniques is to create common values, to serve human interests. But no art or technique has previously begun in this way because it is impossible: every undertaking begins as useless play within a closed circle of interests, perhaps only as personal gratification. But individual gratification and its personal expression are not without interest for other individuals inasmuch as they suggest new possibilities or experiments. This is the case even when the interest manifests itself only in the form of passive admiration. In personal expression there is a synthesis of two phenomena: a human interest and an original or new solution—that is to say, subjectivity and individualism are two independent and distinct elements. A "self-expression" can be absolutely conventional and insignificant if it expresses a limited being; at the same time, a new and original thing can have no interest if it satisfies no human desire. This is why the conception of art current among theoreticians of modern art like *Herbert Read* is false and reactionary. For them art is composed of two elements: self-expression and order. The constructivists, with the abolition of personality, reduce art to a pure question of order. We, on the contrary, add to the two preceding elements a "third variable" which is that of experimentation, of innovation. What is the importance of experiment in art? It is at once essential and indefinable; experiment in art and technique is like yeast in bread; far from adding something to the work itself, it inspires it and expands it to a dramatic scale. We have discovered along with modern science that evolution does not occur on the basis of a doctrine but on the basis of several doctrines in contradiction, through their complementary action. Functionalist activity between the two wars is closely linked to the complementary artistic tendencies of the epoch (dada, expressionism). We are neither dadaists nor expressionists. Surrealism intervened in the meantime and it would be stupid to ignore it.

1954

Walter Gropius's career spans from 1911, when, at twenty-eight years old, he designed the steel and glass Fagus Factory in collaboration with Adolf Meyer, to the 1950s and 1960s, when, as one of the ranking modern masters, he served as head of The Architects Collaborative (TAC), a large Boston-based design firm that he founded in 1945 in equal partnership with some of his students. His sustained productivity over half a century encompassed all facets of architecture, extending to urban planning, theater design, and prefabrication technologies (like the Packaged House System that he designed with Konrad Wachsmann in the 1940s). His two major contributions to architecture education—the directorship of the Weimar and Dessau Bauhaus in the 1920s, and the chairmanship of the school of design at Harvard from 1937–52—give evidence of the distance traveled. From a role once vanguard and institutionally marginal, he succeeded during his tenure at Harvard in positioning himself in the very mainstream of academic and professional practice, decisively overturning the Beaux-Arts bases of American architectural education in favor of modernism. No single idea indicates Gropius's sea-change so well as the transformation of his earlier concept of "totality" into "teamwork," one of the major preoccupations of his postwar thinking. Through the managerial ethos of teamwork—voluntaristic collaboration among creative specialists leading to cultural integration and consensus—Gropius sought to provide not only a counter to the myth of the individual architectural genius, but a democratic and inclusivist reinterpretation of the "scope of total architecture."

Teamwork and an acknowledgment of the architect's new professional role as that of both leader and servant were, in Gropius's view, not only ethical obligations, but antidotes to a weakening world culture beset by overspecialization, conformism, and commercialism. His evangelical message of social responsibility, propounded during the latter half of his career at every opportunity—from America to Japan, in his capacity as vice-president of CIAM, in published articles and books spanning from *Scope of Total Architecture: A New Way of Life* (1955) to *Apollo in the Democracy: The Cultural Obligation of the Architect* (1968)—was reverentially received as a basis for contemporary practice by many leading architects, especially in postwar Europe. Among the latter were Nikolaus Pevsner in England and Ernesto Rogers and Giulio Carlo Argan in Italy. In his book *Walter Gropius e la Bauhaus* (1951), Argan portrayed Gropius as a noble figure optimistically advancing the cause of a technical civilization while attempting to safeguard freedom and individualism from totalitarian encroachment. Yet ironically the social thrust of his message was to be little reflected in the corporate milieu in which his most successful students in America practiced—architects like Philip Johnson, Paul Rudolph, Ulrich Franzen, John Johansen, I. M. Pei, and Edward Larabee Barnes. Nor was Gropius better served by the schemes built by his own firm TAC. While TAC maintained a level of quality in buildings like the Graduate Center for Harvard University (1948–50), others like the ill-conceived Pan American Building in New York City (1958, with Pietro Belluschi) and the John F. Kennedy Federal Building in Boston (1961–66), a brutal exercise in formalism, seriously undermined the master's credibility.

The following essay is an efficient summary of Gropius's major ideas during this period. Its eight points are directed as advice to the "young men" of the profession, whom he urges to "earn . . . the right to captain the team."

From Architectural Forum, *February 1954, pp. 156–57, 178, 182. Revised as "Architect—Servant or Leader?" in Walter Gropius,* Scope of Total Architecture *(New York: Harper & Brothers, 1955), pp. 91–98. Courtesy of Beate Forberg Johansen.*

266–69

77–79
253–59

189–92

Eight Steps toward a Solid Architecture
Walter Gropius

1. *Forget the battle of the styles and get to work on the development of architecture for better living*

Modern architecture is not a few branches of an old tree—it is new growth coming right from the roots. This does not mean, however, that we are witness to the sudden advent of a "new style." What we see and experience is a movement in flux which has created a fundamentally different outlook on architecture. Its underlying philosophy knits well with the big trends in today's science and art, steadying it against those forces which try to block its advance and retard the growing power of its ideas.

The irrepressible urge of critics to classify contemporary movements which are still in flux by putting them neatly in a coffin with a style label on it has increased the widespread confusion in understanding the dynamic forces of the new movement in architecture and planning. A style is a successive repetition of an expression which has become settled already as a common denominator for a whole period. But the attempt to classify and interpret living art and architecture while it is still in the formative stage as a "style" or "ism" is more likely to still than to stimulate creative activity. We live in a period of reshuffling our entire life; the old society went to pieces under the impact of the machine; the new one is still in the making. The flow of continuous growth, the change of expression in accordance with the changes of our life, is what matters in our design work, not the characteristics of a potential style.

And how deceiving a precipitate terminology can be. Let us analyze, for instance, that most unfortunate designation, "The International Style." It is not a style because it is still in flux, nor is it international because its tendency is the opposite, namely, to find regional, indigenous expression derived from the environment, the climate, the landscape, the habits of the people.

Styles, in my opinion, should be named and outlined by the historian only for past periods. In the present we lack the dispassionate attitude necessary for impersonal judgment of what is going on. As humans we are vain and jealous and that distorts objective vision. Why not leave it, then, to future historians to settle the history of today's growth in architecture and go to work and let it grow?

Let us also leave to historians the question of one architect's influence on another. In a period when the leading spirits of mankind try to see the human problems on earth as interdependent as one world, any chauvinistic national prejudice regarding the shares claimed in the development of modern architecture must result in narrowing limitation. Why split hairs about who influenced whom when all that really matters is whether the results achieved improved our life? I daresay that we all are much more influenced today by each other than architects of former centuries because of the rapid development of interchange and intercommunication. This should be welcome as it enriches us and promotes a common denominator of understanding so badly needed. (I tried to encourage my students to let themselves be influenced by ideas of others, as long as they felt able to absorb and digest them and to give them new life in a context that represented their own approach to design.)

2. *Design buildings to accommodate the flexible, dynamic features of modern life— not to serve as monuments to the designer's genius*

If we look back to see what has been achieved during the last thirty to forty years, we find that we have almost done away with that artistic gentleman architect who turned out charming Tudor mansions with all modern conveniences. This type of applied archaeology is melting in the fire of our convictions: 1) that the architect should conceive buildings not as monuments but as receptacles for the flow of life which they have to serve, and 2) that his conception should be flexible enough to create a background fit to absorb the dynamic features of our modern life.

We know that a period piece of architecture could never satisfy such a demand, but we sometimes forget that it is just as easy to create a modern straitjacket as a Tudor one particularly if the architect approaches his task solely with the intention of creating a memorial to his own genius. This arrogant misapprehension of what a good architect should be often prevailed, even after the revolution against eclecticism had already set in. Designers who were searching for new expression in design would even outdo the eclecticist by striving to be "different," to seek the unique, the unheard of, the stunt.

This cult of the ego has delayed the general acceptance of the sound trends in modern architecture. Remnants of this mentality must be eliminated before the true spirit of the architectural revolution can take root among the people everywhere and produce a common form expression of our time after almost half a century of trial and error. This will presuppose a determined attitude of the new architect to direct his efforts toward finding the best common denominator instead of toward the provocative stunt. Preconceived ideas of form, whether the outcome of personal whims or fashionable styles, tend to force the stream of life in a building into rigid channels and to hamper the natural activities of the people for whom the buildings were built.

3. *Diagnose the client's real needs and give him a consistent building*
The pioneers of the new movement in architecture developed methodically a new approach to the whole problem of "design for living." Interested in relating their work to the life of the people, they tried to see the individual unit as part of a greater whole. This social idea contrasts strongly with the work of the egocentric prima-donna architect who forces his personal fancy on an intimidated client, creating solitary monuments of individual aesthetic significance.

I do not mean that we architects should docilely accept the client's views. We have to lead him into a conception which we must form to fit his needs. If he calls on us to fulfill some whims and fancies of his which do not make sense, we have to find out what real need may be behind these vague dreams of his and try to lead him in a consistent, overall approach. We must spare no effort on our part to convince him conclusively and without conceit. We have to make the diagnosis of what the client needs on the strength of our competence.

4. *Gain competence in all fields of building to earn the client's confidence and the right to captain the team*
When a man is ill he certainly wouldn't tell his physician how to treat him. Architects are rarely treated with such respect. If we have not been competent enough to deserve being trusted, we had better make sure that we are in the future—in design, in construction and in economy, as well as in the social conception, which embraces the three other components of our work. If we do not make ourselves highly competent in all these fields, or if we shun responsibility in leading the way, we resign ourselves to the level of minor technicians.

Architecture needs leadership and conviction, if necessary, even in defiance of the client. It cannot be decided upon by clients, or by Gallup polls, which would most often reveal only a wish to continue what everybody knows best.

5. *Make better use of science and the machine to serve human life*

There is an argument going on which distorts the aim of modern architecture and therefore needs clarification. We hear: "The modern accent is on living, not on the machine." And Le Corbusier's slogan, "The house is a machine for living," is old hat. With it goes a portrait of the early pioneers in the modern movement as men of rigid, mechanistic conceptions, addicted to the glorification of the machine and quite indifferent to intimate human values. Being one of these monsters myself, I wonder how we managed to survive on such meager fare. The truth is that the problem of how to humanize the machine was in the foreground of our early discussions and that a new way of living was the focus of our thoughts.

To devise new means to serve human ends, the Bauhaus, for instance, made an intense attempt to live what it preached and to find the balance in the struggle for utilitarian, aesthetic, and psychological demands. The machine and the new potentialities of science were of greatest interest to us, but the emphasis was not so much on the machine itself as on better use of the machine and science in the service of human life. Looking back, I find that our period has dealt too little with the machine, not too much.

6. *Seek genuine regional expression—but not by relying on old emblems and local fancies*

Another confusing factor in the development of modern architecture is the appearance now and then of deserters from our cause who fall back on nineteenth-century eclecticism for lack of strength to go consistently through with a rejuvenation from the roots up. Designers turn back to features and fancies of the past to be mixed into the modern design, fondly believing this will create greater popularity for modern architecture. They are too impatient to reach their goal by legitimate means and so they only conjure up a new "ism" instead of a new genuine regional expression. True regional character cannot be found through sentimental or imitative approach by incorporating either old emblems or the newest local fashions which disappear as fast as they appear. But if you take the basic difference imposed on architectural design by the climatic conditions of California, say, as against Massachusetts, you will realize what diversity of expression can result from this fact alone if the architect will use the utterly contrasting indoor-outdoor relations of these two regions as the focus for his design conception.

7. *Extend architectural education into the field to obtain a better balance between knowledge and experience*

One problem that all architectural schools have in common is this: as long as our teaching centers around the platonic drafting board, we are perpetually in danger of raising the "precocious designer." For it is almost unavoidable that the lack of practical experience in the field, in the crafts and industrial processes of building, leads at least some students to an all-too-ready acceptance of current style ideas, fads, and clichés. This is the consequence for an all-too-academic training. Therefore, any opportunity to go into the field and to take part in all or any phases of the building process should be readily grasped by the young designer as a most essential discipline to establish balance between knowledge and experience.

8. *Add community activity to office activity to become a leader as well as a servant*

Should an architect be a servant or a leader? The answer, already implicit in what I have said, is simple: put an "and" in place of the "or." Serving and leading seem to be interdependent. The good architect must serve the people and simultaneously show real leadership built up upon a real conviction: leadership to guide his client as well as the working team entrusted with the job. Leadership does not depend on innate talent only, but very much also on one's intensity of conviction and willingness to serve. How can he reach this status? I have often been asked by students what I could advise them to do to become independent architects after leaving school and how they could avoid selling out their conviction to a society still pretty ignorant of the new ideas in architecture and planning. My answer is this:

Making a living cannot be the only aim of a young man who would want above all to realize his ideas. Your problem is, therefore, how to keep the integrity of your conviction intact, how to live what you preach, and still find your pay. You may not succeed in finding a position with an architect who shares your approach in design and who could give you further guidance. Then I would suggest you take a paying job wherever you can sell your skill, but keep your interests alive by a consistent effort carried on in leisure hours. Try to build up a working team with one or two friends in your neighborhood, choose a vital topic within your community, and try to solve it, step by step, in group work. Put ceaseless effort into it, then some day you will be able to offer the public, together with your group, a well-substantiated solution for this problem for which you have become an expert. Meanwhile, publish it, exhibit it, and you may succeed in becoming an adviser to your community authorities. Create strategic centers where people are confronted with a new reality and then try to weather the inevitable stage of violent criticism until people have learned to redevelop their atrophied physical and mental capacities to make the proper use of the proffered new setup. We have to discern between the vital needs of the people and the pattern of inertia and habit that is so often advanced as "the will of the people."

The stark and frightening realities of our world will not be softened by dressing them up with the "new look," and it will be equally futile to try to humanize our mechanized civilization by adding sentimental fripperies to our homes. But if the human factor is becoming more and more dominant in our work, architecture will reveal the emotional qualities of the designer in the very bones of the buildings, not in the trimmings only; it will be the result of both good service and good leadership.

1954

CIAM's ninth congress was held in Aix-en-Provence in the summer of 1953. Organized by the French group ASCORAL, it was the largest congress to date, with 500 members making the trip to the south of France from all over the world. It culminated in a nocturnal fête on the rooftop of Le Corbusier's recently completed Unité d'Habitation in Marseilles, "lit up like a beacon," as *L'Architecture d'Aujourd'hui* put it, "to show to the young of CIAM the way to a true modern architecture."

The task of the congress was the preparation of a charter of habitation, envisaged as a sequel to the charter of urbanism written in Athens in 1933. Participating as members of the MARS Group in their first CIAM congress, the young English architects Alison and Peter Smithson contributed a "study grille"— the form of standardized presentation required by CIAM following its seventh meeting in Bergamo—entitled "Urban Reidentification," prepared in conjunction with William and Gillian Howell and John Voelker. It was intended "in direct opposition to the arbitrary isolation of the so-called communities of the Unité." Organizing their scheme according to a "hierarchy of human association" instead of the four-function hierarchy promulgated at Athens—dwelling, work, recreation, circulation—and proposing a reciprocal relationship between height and population density, the Smithsons put forward four new categories: house, street, district, and city. At the scale of the large city, they offered a scheme for a multilevel residential complex, Golden Lane, which they had recently designed as a competition project for a bombed site in London. It featured above-grade pedestrian "street decks" and flexible connections to the ground and to places of work. The motivating idea was the creation of a vital sense of communal life. Especially effective in the Smithsons' grille was the use of Nigel Henderson's photographs of children playing happily in the streets of London's East End slums. The nitty-gritty of "reality" was meant to counteract the diagrammatic and static purism of *Athens Charter* urbanism: "hygienic, correctly spaced, with excellent wide roads. What was missing was man," as Peter Smithson later said.

At the congress the Smithsons formed alliances with a number of like-minded colleagues among the younger members of CIAM. These included Aldo van Eyck and Jacob Bakema from Holland, whose concerns were closely akin to their own. All were strongly impressed by the work of the Moroccan group ATBAT—a team composed of Vladimir Bodiansky, Georges Candilis, and Shadrach Woods—which had been designing Muslim housing in Casablanca. With its "golden suns on wands," their grille conveyed a "new language of architecture generated by patterns of inhabitation." Jointly concluding that "life falls through the net of the four functions," the younger generation of architects meeting in the coffee klatches at Aix agreed that the "primary contact" occurs "at the doorstep between man and men."

This shared philosophy led to a meeting in late January of the following year in Doorn, Holland, attended by Peter **Smithson** and John **Voelker** from England, Jacob **Bakema**, Aldo **van Eyck**, and H. P. Daniel **van Ginkel** from Holland, and—reflecting the current interest in sociology and ecology—Hans **Hovens-Greve**, a social economist working in the municipal planning office in Rotterdam (who ceased to be involved with the group after this date). Bakema showed his recently completed Lijnbaan shopping center for Rotterdam. Out of the discussions came the "Doorn Manifesto," calling once again for a subordination of the four functions to what the participants considered more fundamental questions relating to the specific scale and type of human collectivity. Peter Smithson inserted a simplified diagram showing the "valley plan of civilization" into the manifesto; it was taken from an article of 1925 by Sir Patrick Geddes, a figure who had recently aroused interest in CIAM circles.

100–2

The meeting at Doorn initiated a more lasting association among the members of the CIAM "phoenix group," self-consciously constituted along generational lines and shortly to be joined by Candilis and Woods as well as Rolf Gutmann of Switzerland. Their aggressive challenge to the older organization was directed at an establishment not only clinging nostalgically to the program of La Sarraz and Athens even as it strove to make it more humanistic, but by now more or less enervated from earlier battles. To the "youngers" thus fell the charge to prepare the brief for the congress's tenth meeting. With this task in view they designated themselves "Team 10."

17   CIAM 10 was ultimately held in Dubrovnik, and the theme, as prepared by Team 10, was "problems of the human habitat." At the congress an exacerbation of the generational schism (which Le Corbusier anticipated in choosing not to attend) together with a series of arguments over administrative issues (the congress's unwieldy size, for one) brought to a head the crisis of confidence in CIAM's viability. Largely through the Smithsons' uncompromising stance, the outcome was the organization's dissolution. The actual disbanding dragged out over the next couple years. A "reunion" meeting in 1959, held in Henry van de Velde's Kröller-Müller Museum in Otterlo, Holland, was sponsored by Team 10. Forty invited participants whose average age was "about forty" attended,

270–72   including special guest Louis Kahn, an *eminence grise* at fifty-eight. At the end of the sessions a resolution was passed in which the participants agreed to drop the name CIAM from their activities. This was the congress's final gathering.

The members of Team 10 continued to collaborate as a self-styled "family," publishing a couple versions of the *Team 10 Primer* in the 1960s—a compilation of their individual and joint writings and projects—and meeting periodically. Their extended ranks included Polish emigré Jerzy Soltan, José Coderch de

335–37   Sentmenat of Spain, Giancarlo de Carlo of Italy, and Ralph Erskine of Sweden. For documentation and some subjective commentary on the history of Team 10 by one of its protagonists, see, besides the *Primer,* two other books edited by Alison Smithson: *The Emergence of Team 10 out of C.I.A.M.* (1982) and *Team 10 Meetings: 1953–1984* (1991). See also Aldo van Eyck's summary of CIAM's

347–60   history and ideas in a special issue of the Dutch journal *Forum* (1959), entitled "The Story of an *Other* Idea," prepared for the Otterlo meeting.

Facsimile of manuscript published in Alison Smithson, ed., The Emergence of Team 10 out of C.I.A.M. *(London: Architectural Association, 1982), pp. 33–34. Also published in "The Story of an* Other *Idea," Forum 7 (1959), p. 231. Courtesy of Alison and Peter Smithson.*

Doorn Manifesto—CIAM Meeting 29–30–31 January 1954, Doorn
Bakema, van Eyck, van Ginkel, Hovens-Greve, Smithson, Voelker

Statement on Habitat

1. La Charte d'Athènes proposed a technique which would counteract the chaos of the 19th century and restore principles of order within our cities.

2. Through this technique the overwhelming variety of city activities was classified into four distinct functions which were believed to be fundamental.

3. Each function was realized as a totality within itself. Urbanists could comprehend more clearly the potential of the 20th century.

4. Our statement tries to provide a method which will liberate still further this potential.

As a direct result of the 9th Congress at Aix, we have come to the conclusion that if we are to create a Charte de l'Habitat, we must redefine the aims of urbanism, and at the same time create a new tool to make this aim possible.

Urbanism considered and developed in the terms of the Charte d'Athènes tends to produce "towns" in which vital human associations are inadequately expressed.

To comprehend these human associations we must consider every community as a particular *total* complex.

In order to make this *comprehension* possible, we propose to study urbanism as communities of varying degrees of complexity.

These can be shown on a Scale of Association as shown below:

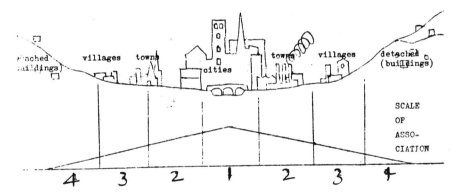

We suggest that the working parties [crossed out: "commissions"] operate each in a *field* (not a point) on the Scale of Association, for example: isolated buildings, villages, towns, cities. This will enable us to study particular functions in their appropriate ecological field.

Thus a housing sector or satellite of a city will be considered at the top of the scale (under City, 1), and can in this way be compared with development in other cities, or contrasted with numerically similar developments in different fields of the Scale of Association.

This method of work will induce a study of human association *as a first principle,* and of the four functions as *aspects* of each total problem.

1954

Postwar reconstruction efforts in the Soviet Union and elsewhere in the Eastern bloc had sought to redress the severe housing shortages and the problems of urban rebuilding by stringently controlling and standardizing building production. In 1948 the Soviet Academy of Architecture was asked to draw up plans for various building types, taking into account regional differences in climate, ways of life, and technical resources for five areas of the country. Fifty plans for dwellings and 200 for public buildings were subsequently approved and adopted by the Committee on Architectural Affairs. These standardized models prescribed not only technical specifications but also stylistic ones in line *125–28* with the sweeping program of social realism in the arts instituted two years earlier by Stalin's "controller of culture," Andrei Zhdanov. In the interests of realizing an architecture conveying the message of "responsibility to the people," major attention was now focused on formal matters like the incorporation of traditional details and the use of appropriate decorative motifs.

Stalin's death in March 1953 and the accession of **Nikita Khrushchev** as first secretary of the Communist party occasioned an about-face in this approach. Khrushchev's general belt-tightening and decentralizing measures in building production were extended to architecture in the policy speech excerpted below, presented at the All-Union Conference of Builders and Architects. "Architects, like all builders, must make a sharp turn toward problems of construction economy," he stated. ". . . An architect, if he is to keep abreast of life, must know and be able to use not only architectural forms, ornaments, and decorative elements; he must know the new progressive materials, reinforced-concrete sections and parts, and, most of all, must have an excellent understanding of construction economy."

Ironically, this led to a qualified rehabilitation of Russian constructivist architecture, now appreciated for its functional and technical orientation over the pastry-cook facades and formalistic planning of Stalin's reconstruction program. In November 1955 stylistic superfluities in planning and building were officially eliminated. By 1958 seventy percent of the architectural building components in the Soviet Union were prefabricated, as opposed to twenty-five percent in 1950. However, Soviet officials continued to promulgate prototype plans for multistory housing blocks, schools, hospitals, commercial establishments, restaurants and theaters, hotels, and other building types. Thus, as the work shown the same year in the Soviet section at the international exhibition in Brussels demonstrated, the change in direction hardly meant a recovery of the experimental building and planning carried out during the revolutionary period of the 1920s. The projects displayed in Brussels reflected a stripped-down facade treatment and fewer obligatory symmetries, but in rigidity of conception remained very similar to the work carried out under Stalin.

Published in Pravda *and* Izvestia, *28 December 1954, p. 1. In English in* The Current Digest of the Soviet Press, *vol. 6, no. 52, pp. 7–9. Translation courtesy of* The Current Digest of the Soviet Press.

Remove Shortcomings in Design, Improve Work of Architects
Nikita Khrushchev

Comrades! Successful industrialization, improvement in the quality and reduction in the cost of building depend to a considerable extent on design organizations, on the work of architects and designers.

The interests of industrializing construction dictate the need to reorganize the work of design organizations and to make standardized designing and application of existing standardized designs the chief thing in their work.

Widespread use of reinforced-concrete parts, sections, large blocks and new and effective materials is a new element in building techniques which imperatively requires us to give up obsolete design methods. (Applause)

Nevertheless, many workers in design organizations underestimate the importance of standardized designs.

This is shown by the following. Of the 1,100 construction and design organizations in the country only 152 even partially engage in standardized designing. From 1951 to 1953 inclusive, not more than one percent of the allocations for design work was used on standardized designing. In 1953 only twelve percent of the total volume of industrial building was carried out according to standardized designs. And matters have not improved very much in 1954.

I have had occasion to talk to many engineers and architects about design. They are all agreed that standardized designs considerably simplify and improve construction work. In practice, however, many architects, designers in industrial buildings, and sometimes even technicians follow only their own plans.

Why does this happen? One apparent cause is that we have tolerated shortcomings in training architects. Many young architects who have scarcely crossed the threshold of the institute and have not yet got properly on their feet follow the example of masters of architecture and wish to design only buildings of an individual character, are in a hurry to build monuments to themselves. While Pushkin created for himself a monument unwrought by human hands, many architects want to create for themselves monuments "wrought by human hands" in the form of buildings built according to individualized designs. (Laughter, applause)

It must be realized that if we were to build all industrial constructions, housing, and other buildings according to separate designs the rate of building would be considerably slower and its cost would increase tremendously.

Many planners, architects, and designers do work creatively and produce much that is new and useful, but there are also major shortcomings in this matter. Certain planners do not take into account the new sections, parts, and materials being manufactured by plants of the building industry but continue to base their work on backward building methods.

Take housing construction. Why not choose the best designs for housing and repeat them many times in construction work? Let architects submit their designs for such buildings in competition!

It is now essential to select the best designs for large-block residential buildings. Design organizations of the Moscow Soviet drafted design solutions for residential buildings with walls of large panels or blocks. The solution proposed by I. V. Zholtovsky, member of the U.S.S.R. Academy of Architecture, was recognized at that time as one of the best. Since then blueprints could have been drawn from this plan, adopted as standard, and used for building large-block residential construction for several years. Yet this has not been done.

Why are there 38 standardized designs for schools in use at the present time? Is this expedient? Apparently it has come about because many officials have a spendthrift attitude toward building. We must select a limited number of standardized designs for apartment houses, schools, hospitals, building for kindergartens and nurseries, stores, and other buildings and installations and carry out mass building only according to these designs for, let us say, five years. At that time let us have a discussion and if there are no better designs, let us extend the use of these for another five years. What is wrong with that, comrades?

What are the advantages of building according to standardized designs? They are very great once one decides to build, there is already a plan in existence, and it is known how large the site must be, what parts and materials will be needed, and how many workers will be required. Everything is clear. Such conditions will help us to accelerate construction work and to reduce its cost considerably.

Or take questions of designing industrial buildings and installations. Designs for industrial buildings, like standardized designs for apartment houses, call for many identical sections and identical spans. Columns and girders and other elements in each span remain unchanged. Standardized designs for industrial building should be drawn up with a view to the possibility of placing production and auxiliary shops of different branches of industry in these buildings. Buildings for different purposes can be built from the same units. To achieve this it is essential to draw up standardized designs for industrial buildings, making use of uniform arrangements of columns, uniform heights and loads, uniform stairwells, uniform apertures for windows and doors, and the like.

The use of such standardized designs will make it possible to organize the factory manufacture of structural parts and sections and abandon conventional construction for the assembling of buildings, carrying out this work in short periods of time. We must achieve this, comrades.

To introduce standardized designs we must be determined and persistent, for we may meet resistance in this matter. Evidently there are some people who need a good explanation of the necessity for standardized designs.

The use of standardized designs in building will have a tremendous effect on economizing, speeding up, and improving construction work. Of this there is no doubt. (Stormy applause)

[. . .] Comrades! We have no disagreement with the architects on basic matters— on the need to build comfortable homes and dwelling units. And these are important matters, a question of people's living comforts. The number of large and small apartments, their floor space, ceiling heights—on such questions, as a rule, there is no divergence of opinion. But differences always arise as soon as we come to the problem of the architectural design of building facades. The question of the artistic-architectural treatment of a building has proved most complex.

Certain architects have been carried away with putting spires on buildings, with the result that such buildings resemble churches. Do you like the silhouette of a church? I do not wish to argue about tastes, but in apartment houses, such an appearance is not necessary. The modern apartment house must not be transformed by architectural design into a replica of a church or a museum. This affords the residents no comfort, and only complicates the utilization of the building and raises its cost. Yet certain architects do not take this into consideration.

Architect Zakharov, for example, submitted plans for constructions on Bolshaya Tula Street in Moscow of apartment houses which differ little in their outlines from churches. He was asked to explain this and answered: "We have brought our plans into harmony with the tall buildings; the silhouette of the buildings must be clear." These, it would seem, are the sort of problems which occupy Comrade Zakharov most of all. He needs beautiful silhouettes, but the people need apartments. They do not want to admire silhouettes but a place to live! [Applause] In the blueprints for the apartment-house project of Lyusinov Street, the architect had decided to place pieces of sculpture at the building corners, from the eighth floor up. On the highest floor, it was planned to cut off the corners; in these sliced-off corners windows were to be built and it was proposed to place pieces of sculpture on the window sills along the outer wall. A pentagonal room with a window in the corner is awkward, not to mention the fact that the people in this room would have to look at the back of a piece of sculpture for their entire life. It is understandable that life in such a room would not be especially pleasant. It is well that these houses were not built, and that Comrade Zakharov was restrained from such artistry.

And all this is called architectural-artistic decoration of the building! No, comrades, these are distortions in architecture, these spoil materials and cause unnecessary expenditure. Moscow organizations took a correct stand when they dismissed Comrade Zakharov from management of the architectural studio. But it should have been done sooner for the good of the work.

Two large factories making reinforced-concrete parts opened at the beginning of this year in Moscow are producing, but we have as yet only one approved design for a girder-and-panel structure. Who is guilty of holding back the designing? Many architects are to blame and particularly Comrade Vlasov, Chief Architect of the city of Moscow. He is a good architect, but sometimes he lacks the necessary persistence.

It is necessary in every way to support and encourage good work in designing, and especially in standardized designing. It is necessary to consider and perhaps revise the accepted system of payment for work of the designers. We should establish a system of payment which will better stimulate their work. (Applause)

The serious shortcomings in the work of design organizations and of individual architects can in many ways be explained by improperly based principles emanating from the Academy of Architecture and a number of chief architects. [. . .]

Leading architects constantly stress the artistic aspect, and say little about the cost and comfort of housing and other buildings. It is understandable that we must struggle against any such divorce of architecture from the vital tasks of construction.

Some architects try to justify their incorrect stand on waste in designs by referring to the need to combat constructivism. But they waste state funds under the guise of fighting constructivism.

What is constructivism? Here is how the *Large Soviet Encyclopedia,* for instance, defines this tendency: "Constructivism . . . substitutes barren technical aspects 'born of the construction design' (hence the name constructivism) for artistic design. Demanding functional 'logic,' 'rationalism,' in construction the constructivists actually reached aesthetic admiration of form unrelated to content. . . . The consequence of this is the antiartistic, dull 'box style' characteristic of modern bourgeois architecture. . . . Constructivism was sharply criticized in many Party directives and decrees . . ." (*Large Soviet Encyclopedia,* 1953, vol. 22, p. 437)

This definition of constructivism is, of course, not exhaustive. But the description of constructivism I have cited showed the groundlessness of some architects disguising themselves in phrases about fighting constructivism while actually sacrificing convenience of internal design and use of the building for the sake of facades, that is, for form's şake, and thereby showing a disregard for the essential needs of people.

Some architects, declaiming about the need to combat constructivism, go to the opposite extreme—they decorate building facades excessively and often unnecessarily, thus wasting state funds.

Buildings which lack towers, superstructures, and porticos with columns, or have facades which are not adorned with sham detail, are called boxes and condemned as relapses into constructivism. Such architects should probably be called constructivists in reverse, since they themselves are lapsing into "aesthetic admiration of form divorced from content."

It is impossible to resign oneself any longer to the fact that many architects hide behind phrases about the struggle against constructivism and about socialist realism in architecture while spending the people's funds extravagantly.

Constructivism must be combated by sensible means. One must not be carried away with architectural decorations and aesthetic adornment; one must not build absolutely unjustified towers or place pieces of sculpture on them. We are not against beauty but against superfluities. Building facades should be beautiful and attractive because of the good proportions of the entire building, the good proportions of the window and door openings, the skillful arrangement of balconies, the correct utilization of the texture and color in the facing materials, and honest delineation of the parts and sections of the walls in large-block and large-panel construction. [. . .]

1955

Philip Johnson made these remarks in an informal talk to students at Harvard University's School of Architectural Design. His tone is typically iconoclastic, all the more so as the talk was given at a school predicated on the pedagogy of Walter Gropius, who had retired shortly before and under whom Johnson had himself been a student at Harvard in the early 1940s.

The mid-1950s marked a transitional juncture in Johnson's career, a period of work the architect was later to call "functional-eclectic." He had completed his glass house for himself in New Canaan, Connecticut, in 1949. Though ostensibly a supremely purist statement, it was in fact full of heresies with respect to the lessons of his master, Mies van der Rohe, whose contemporaneous Farnsworth house Johnson's building acknowledged mostly in the breach. A study of the developmental drawings for the glass house reveals a succession of stylistic experiments ranging from a scheme commenting on Wright's Usonian houses of the 1940s to a solid wall scheme punctuated by "Syrian" arches.

In these years Johnson was in the process of trying to disembarrass himself of the rules of International Style modernism that he, together with Henry-Russell Hitchcock, had been instrumental in formulating in 1932. Although the crutches against which he admonishes in the following essay—history, seductive drawing, utility, comfort, economy, serving the client, structure—represent an attack not only on the functionalist ethos but on ideological rationalizations for form-making in general, his oedipal relationship to his modernist formation is overt: "We have very fortunately the work of our spiritual fathers to build on. We hate them, of course, as all spiritual sons hate all spiritual fathers, but we can't ignore them, nor can we deny their greatness." It is highly ironic that an architect-critic with such an innate predisposition to traditional aesthetics should have been one of the primary messengers of American modernism. Johnson's ideological cynicism vis-à-vis the social program of modern architecture is matched only by his affinity for Schinkel, Soane, and nineteenth-century romantic classicism. This partly explains the ambivalent role of the earlier book in promoting modernism while at the same time transforming it from a cultural movement into an aesthetic style. Two decades later it only remained for Johnson to liberate architectural form from his own prescriptive imagery to complete the reduction of modernism to connoisseurship.

Johnson's contemporaries were likewise pushing the latter-day International Style in increasingly formalistic directions in the 1950s—whether by manipulating a still modernist formal language, as in the case of Eero Saarinen, Paul Rudolph, I. M. Pei, Craig Ellwood, and Pietro Belluschi; or an increasingly historicist one, as for Minoru Yamasaki and Edward Durrell Stone. Yet no architect had a more privileged role in both the corporate and intellectual establishments of America. In his stylistic changes as well as his flagrantly provocational pronouncements, Johnson's maverick challenges to the modernist orthodoxy that he had helped to establish did more than any other architect of his generation to usher in the stylistic eclecticism that would mark the first phase of American postmodernism.

Given as a talk at Harvard University School of Architectural Design on December 7, 1954. Published in Perspecta 3 *(1955), pp. 40–44. Republished in* Philip Johnson, Philip Johnson Writings *(New York: Oxford University Press, 1979), pp. 137–40. Courtesy of the author.*

137–48

The Seven Crutches of Modern Architecture
Philip Johnson

Art has nothing to do with intellectual pursuit—it shouldn't be in a university at all. Art should be practiced in gutters—pardon me, in attics.

You can't learn architecture any more than you can learn a sense of music or of painting. You shouldn't talk about art, you should do it.

If I seem to go into words it's because there's no other way to communicate. We have to descend to the world around us if we are to battle it. We have to use words to put the "word" people back where they belong.

So I'm going to attack the seven crutches of architecture. Some of us rejoice in the crutches and pretend that we're walking and that poor other people with two feet are slightly handicapped. But we all use them at times, and especially in the schools where you have to use language. It's only natural to use language when you're teaching, because how are teachers to mark you? "Bad entrance" or "Bathrooms not backed up" or "Stairway too narrow" or "Where's head room?" "Chimney won't draw," "Kitchen too far from dining room." It is so much easier for the faculty to set up a set of rules that you can be marked against. They can't say, "That's ugly." For you can answer that for you it is good-looking, and *de gustibus non est disputandum.* Schools therefore are especially prone to using these crutches. I would certainly use them if I were teaching, because I couldn't criticize extra-aesthetic props any better than any other teacher.

The most important crutch in recent times is not valid now: the *Crutch of History.* In the old days you could always rely on books. You could say, "What do you mean you don't like my tower? There it is in Wren." Or, "They did that on the Subtreasury Building —why can't I do it?" History doesn't bother us very much now.

But the next one is still with us today although, here again, the *Crutch of Pretty Drawing* is pretty well gone. There are those of us—I am one—who have made a sort of cult of the pretty plan. It's a wonderful crutch because you can give yourself the illusion that you are creating architecture while you're making pretty drawings. Fundamentally, architecture is something you build and put together, and people walk in and they like it. But that's too hard. Pretty pictures are easier.

The next one, the third one, is the *Crutch of Utility,* of usefulness. This is where I was brought up, and I've used it myself; it was an old Harvard habit.

They say a building is good architecture if it works. This building works perfectly— if I talk loud enough. The Parthenon probably worked perfectly well for the ceremonies they used it for. In other words, merely that a building works is not sufficient. You expect that it works. You expect a kitchen hot-water faucet to run hot water these days. You expect any architect, a graduate of Harvard or not, to be able to put the kitchen in the right place. But when it's used as a crutch it impedes. It lulls you into thinking that that is architecture. The rules that we've all been brought up on—"The coat closet should be near the front door in a house," "Cross-ventilation is a necessity"—these rules are not very important for architecture. That we should have a front door to come in and a back door to carry the garbage out—pretty good, but in my house I noticed to my horror the other day that I carried the garbage out the front door. If the business of getting the house to run well takes precedence over your artistic invention the result won't be architecture at all; merely an assemblage of useful parts. You will recognize it next time you're doing a building; you'll be so satisfied when you get the banks of elevators to come out at the right floor you'll think your skyscraper is finished. I know. I'm just working on one.

That's not as bad, though, as the next one: the *Crutch of Comfort*. That's a habit that we come by, the same as utility. We are all descended from John Stuart Mill in our thinking. After all, what is architecture for but the comforts of the people that live there? But when that is made into a crutch for doing architecture, environmental control starts to replace architecture. Pretty soon you'll be doing controlled environmental houses which aren't hard to do except that you may have a window on the west and you can't control the sun. There isn't an overhang in the world, there isn't a sun chart in Harvard University that will help. Because, of course, the sun is absolutely everywhere. You know what they mean by controlled environment—it is the study of "microclimatology," which is the science that tells you how to recreate a climate so that you will be comfortable. But are you? The fireplace, for example, is out of place in the controlled environment of a house. It heats up and throws off thermostats. But I like the beauty of a fireplace so I keep my thermostat way down to sixty, and then I light a big roaring fire so I can move back and forth. Now that's not controlled environment. I control the environment. It's a lot more fun.

Some people say that chairs are good-looking that are comfortable. Are they? I think that comfort is a function of whether you think the chair is good-looking or not. Just test it yourself. (Except I know you won't be honest with me.) I have had Mies van der Rohe chairs now for twenty-five years in my home wherever I go. They're not very comfortable chairs, but, if people like the looks of them they say, "Aren't these beautiful chairs," which indeed they are. Then they'll sit in them and say, "My, aren't they comfortable." If, however, they're the kind of people who think curving steel legs are an ugly way to hold up a chair they'll say, "My, what uncomfortable chairs."

The *Crutch of Cheapness*. That is one that you haven't run into as students because no one's told you to cut $10,000 off the budget, because you haven't built anything. But that'll be your first lesson. The cheapness boys will say, "Anybody can build an expensive house. Ah, but see, my house only cost $25,000." Anybody that can build a $25,000 house has indeed reason to be proud, but is he talking about architecture or his economic ability? Is it the crutch you're talking about, or is it architecture? That economic motive, for instance, goes in New York so far that the real-estate-minded people consider it un-American to build a Lever House with no rentals on the ground floor. They find that it's an architectural sin not to fill the envelope.

Then there's another very bad crutch that you will get much later in our career. Please, please watch out for this one: the *Crutch of Serving the Client*. You can escape all criticism if you can say, "Well, the client wanted it that way." Mr. Hood, one of our really great architects, talked exactly that way. He would put a Gothic door on a skyscraper and say, "Why shouldn't I? The client wanted a Gothic door on the modern skyscraper, and I put it on. Because what is my business? Am I not here to please my client?" As one of the boys asked me during the dinner before the lecture, where do you draw the line? When do the client's demands permit you to shoot him and when do you give in gracefully? It's got to be clear, back in your own mind, that serving the client is one thing and the art of architecture another.

Perhaps the most trouble of all is the *Crutch of Structure*. That gets awfully near home because, of course, I use it all the time myself. I'm going to go on using it. You have to use something. Like Bucky Fuller, who's going around from school to school —it's like a hurricane, you can't miss it if it's coming: he talks, you know, for five or six hours, and he ends up that all architecture is nonsense, and you have to build something like discontinuous domes. The arguments are beautiful. I have nothing against discontinuous domes, but for goodness sake, let's not call it architecture. Have you ever seen Bucky trying to put a door into one of his domed buildings? He's never succeeded, and wisely, when he does them, he doesn't put any covering on them, so they are magnificent pieces of pure sculpture. Sculpture also cannot result in architecture because architecture has problems that Bucky Fuller has not faced, like how do you get in and out. Structure is a very dangerous thing to cling to. You can be led to believe that clear structure clearly expressed will end up being architecture by itself. You say, "I don't have to design any more. All I have to do is make a clean structural order." I have believed this off and on myself. It's a very nice crutch, you see, because, after all, you can't mess up a building too badly if the bays are all equal and all the windows the same size.

Now why should we at this stage be that crutch-conscious? Why should we not step right up to it and face it: the act of creation. The act of creation, like birth and death, you have to face yourself. There aren't any rules; there is no one to tell you whether your one choice out of, say, six billion for the proportion of a window is going to be right. No one can go with you into that room where you make the final decision. You can't escape it anyhow; why fight it? Why not realize that architecture is the sum of inescapable artistic decisions that you have to make. If you're strong you can make them.

I like the thought that what we are to do on this earth is to embellish it for its greater beauty, so that oncoming generations can look back to the shapes we leave here and get the same thrill that I get in looking back at theirs—at the Parthenon, at Chartres Cathedral. That is the duty—I doubt if I get around to it in my generation—the difficulties are too many, but you can. You can if you're strong enough not to bother with the crutches, and face the fact that to create something is a direct experience.

I like Corbusier's definition of architecture. He expressed it the way I wish I could have: "L'architecture, c'est le jeu savant, correct et magnifique des formes sous la lumière"—"Architecture is the play of forms under the light, the play of forms correct, wise, and magnificent." The play of forms under the light. And, my friends, that's all it is. You can embellish architecture by putting toilets in. But there was great architecture long before the toilet was invented. I like Nietzsche's definition—that much-misunderstood European—he said, "In architectural works, man's pride, man's triumph over gravitation, man's will to power assume visible form. Architecture is a veritable oratory of power made by form."

Now my position in all this is obviously not as solipsistic, not as directly intuitional as all that sounds. To get back to earth, what do we do next if we don't hang on to any of these crutches? I'm a traditionalist. I believe in history. I mean by tradition the carrying out, in freedom, the development of a certain basic approach to architecture which we find upon beginning our work here. I do not believe in perpetual revolution in architecture. I do not strive for originality. As Mies once told me, "Philip, it is much better to be good than to be original." I believe that. We have very fortunately the work of our spiritual fathers to build on. We hate them, of course, as all spiritual sons hate all spiritual fathers, but we can't ignore them, nor can we deny their greatness. The men, of course, that I refer to: Walter Gropius, Le Corbusier, and Mies van der Rohe. Frank Lloyd Wright I should include— the greatest architect of the nineteenth century. Isn't it wonderful to have behind us the tradition, the work that those men have done? Can you imagine being alive at a more wonderful time? Never in history was the tradition so clearly demarked, never were the great men so great, never could we learn so much from them and go our own way, without feeling constricted by any style, and knowing that what we do is going to be the architecture of the future, and not be afraid that we wander into some little bypath, like today's romanticists where nothing can possibly evolve. In that sense I am a traditionalist.

1955

The most important new landscape to take root in the twenty-five years after the war was suburbia. Ever since the late nineteenth century reformers like Ebenezer Howard had called for decentralization as a remedy for the congested and unhealthful conditions of large cities. With the advent of the automobile, enclave communities like Clarence Stein and Henry Wright's Radburn, built in suburban New Jersey just before the Depression, and the Greenbelt Cities created in the 1930s by Franklin Delano Roosevelt's Resettlement Administration were attempts to reconcile Garden City principles with planning for the car. More all-encompassing was Frank Lloyd Wright's Broadacre City, put forward in 1935,

40–41   based on a posturban society democratically dispersed throughout "Usonia" (Wright's Emersonian name for the United States) over an infinitely extensible grid of roads. But before the Second World War these were still visionary ideas. In England as late as 1945 only one car was projected for every ten houses.

By the midcentury, however, decentralization was a fact of life, especially in America. A retooled war machine was producing vast tracts of suburban housing, like the Levittowns built on Long Island and outside Philadelphia in the late 1940s, for a new generation of "baby-boomers." By the late 1950s there were sixty million cars on American roads. In 1960 the figure for automobile ownership in England jumped to one car per house. In between the new suburban settlements and the cities there began to emerge a vernacular roadscape identifiable precisely by its amorphousness. Almost universally

446–49   condemned—at least until Robert Venturi and Denise Scott Brown's populist intuition in the 1960s that it was "almost all right"—the suburban strip was an irrepressible accumulation of unplanned accidents and ad hoc services providing residual accommodation to expanding bedroom communities.

114–19   Commentators in journals like the *Architectural Review* in England catalogued the aesthetic outrages of "motopia" in foreboding (coyly mixed with an eye to the

135–36   picturesque incident), while CIAM members sought to reverse the flow by revitalizing the urban cores that were increasingly being abandoned.

In America, it was more than clear that suburbia would have to be taken on its own terms. Among the first to give serious consideration to ameliorating the new life style was the American architect **Victor Gruen**, a Viennese emigrant who had studied under Peter Behrens. "Millions of others have been there first and taken the parking place," as he sized up the burgeoning problems of an already receding American dream. If the idea of the suburban shopping center as a consumerist utopia, a place to shop for goods with "joy and gusto" and to recenter a sprawling community of "rugged individualists," has its naiveté now, in the mid-1950s it presented itself in the hues of healthy capitalist development joining forces with progressive modernism. Integrated planning and clustering of like services were seen as key to controlling the anarchic tendencies of the marketplace. From the early 1950s on Gruen's offices, employing up to 250 architects in Los Angeles, Detroit, New York, San Francisco, Minneapolis, and Miami, produced a series of successful shopping centers. Complexes like Northland near Detroit were distinguished by their exemplary ability to translate economic and demographic factors into architectural amenities: careful siting, serious attention to landscaping, well-detailed signage and illumination. Fed by a well-engineered system of access roads, the magnetized field of commerce— the mall—effectively transformed the Crystal Palace prototype into a multilevel hangar of Miesian modularity set afloat in an ocean of car parking.

Originally presented as a lecture at the International Conference of Design in Aspen, Colorado. Published in Arts and Architecture, *September 1955, pp. 18– 19, 36–37. Courtesy of Gruen Associates and* Arts and Architecture.

Cityscape and Landscape
Victor Gruen

We are swamped with an avalanche of new inventions, discoveries, machines, and gadgets. Our outlook is blurred by daily papers, television, magazines. We are exposed to philosophy, art criticism, analytical psychology, nuclear fission, spiritualism. We are confronted with abstractivism, nonobjectivism, new realism, surrealism until we all feel as if we are swimming in the middle of a big pot of "genuine, kosher, Hungarian goulash, dixie style."

If we don't want to get trapped, doubtful, and actionless at the co-merging of the clover leaves, we have to stop looking and listening around and get on the road. Proceeding in accordance with such decision in the field of architecture, one soon finds oneself in the stream of creative action, challenged by limitations, restraining discipline, and many other problems.

Architecture's most urgent mission today is to convert chaos into order, change mechanization from a tyrant to a slave, and thus make place for beauty where there is vulgarity and ugliness. Architecture today cannot concern itself only with that one particular set of structures which happen to stand upright and be hollow "buildings" in the conventional sense. It must concern itself with all man-made elements which form our environments, with road and highways, with signs and posters, with outdoor spaces as created by structures, with cityscape and landscape.

In talking about cityscape and landscape, I would like to define the terms as I use them:

Cityscape obviously is a setting in which man-made structures are predominant.

Landscape is an environment in which nature is predominant.

Just as there are many kinds of landscapes—mountainous areas, tropical settings, desert lands—there are many types of cityscape. Usually we connect with the term in our minds an orderly pattern of substantial buildings, avenues, boulevards, filled with hustling people.

The vast majority of cityscape looks completely different. Let me categorize the various species:

There is *technoscape*—an environment shaped nearly exclusively by the apparatus of technology in its respectable and less reputable forms. It is a cityscape dotted with oil wells, refineries, high voltage lines, derricks, chimneys, conveyors, dump heaps, auto cemeteries.

There is *transportationscape*—featuring the tinny surfaces of miles of cars on the concrete deserts of highways, freeways, expressways, parking lots, clover leaves, tastefully trimmed with traffic signs, garlands of power lines, and other dangling wire. Transportationscape also includes vast arid lands of airplane runways and railroad yards.

There is *suburbscape*—in all its manifestations from plush settlements of more or less historic mansions to the parade grounds of the anonymous mass housing industry where dingbats are lined up for inspection. Suburbia with phony respectability and genuine boredom effectively isolated from the world by traffic jams.

And there is *subcityscape*—a category covering probably more acreage than all the others combined, a collection of the worst elements of cityscape, technoscape, and transportationscape—the "red and green light district" of our major cities—the degrading facade of suburbia, the shameful introduction to our cities, the scourge of the metropolis.

Subcityscape consists of elements which cling like leeches to all our roads, accompanying them far out to where there was, once upon a time, something called *landscape; subcityscape*—consisting of gas stations, shacks, shanties, car lots, posters, billboards, dump heaps, roadside stands, rubbish, dirt, and trash.

Subcityscape fills up the areas between cities and suburbs, between cities and towns, between cities and other cities. Subcityscapes spread their tentacles in all directions, overgrow regions, states, and country.

Subcityscape is the reason why city planning, before it has even had a chance to become effective in our times, is already obsolete and why it has to be replaced by regional planning.

And now let's consider the term *landscape* a little more. There is a difference between it and *nature* as such. Landscape is nature with which man has made intimate contact—nature with human habitations. Landscape is the rolling hills in Pennsylvania with farmhouses. Landscape is the mountain valleys in Tyrol with toy villages strewn about. Landscape is a New England rural area with the slim finger of the church tower pointing up, a rocky coast with a fishing village, an Italian lake with colorful houses clinging to a steep shore.

Landscape is the successful marriage of nature and human endeavor, a surrounding in which man-made and nature-made elements cooperate to effect highest enjoyment.

The technological age is not favorable for the creation of landscape and, for the time being, I am afraid we have to regard it as a historic relic to be preserved and protected wherever possible.

Once upon a time the world was full of wonderful landscape and beautiful stretches of nature. At that time people complained because it was so hard to get to those places and one had to be satisfied with reading accounts of the courageous adventurers who traveled on foot and on horse and on sailboat.

Today we are nations on wheels. Today we can fly on the "installment plane" anywhere in the world. Improved working conditions allow millions to buy cars. Forty-hour weeks have created the "weekend." Paid vacations seem, to many, like the fulfillment of their longing for the enjoyment of landscape and nature. But the millions are betrayed and swindled out of their hard-gained advantages.

Hours of their free time are stolen by traffic jams. Their nerves are frayed by traffic risks, and when they finally reach the target of their dreams, the piece of landscape or nature, millions of others have been there first and taken the parking place and, even if one is finally found, the dream looks tainted with beer cans and trash, studded with the elements of subcityscape.

We have become a nature all "dressed up" with no place to go. What is to be done? A long, hard, and stubborn fight is ahead.

The blitzkrieg of technology has taken us by surprise. It has dented our spiritual and physical defenses. There may still be a chance to win if we fight with conviction and perseverance and humility. There may be a chance ' the creative people of this age crawl out of their miscellaneous ivory towers and wage battle on the level on which it counts, on the battleground of reality.

We architects experience that the individual structures which we erect cannot obtain their full measure of effectiveness because their settings are unsympathetic. Only in the rarest cases are we lucky enough to find a setting which is in congruity with the structure.

Disturbing, distasteful noises and ugly surroundings are the rule rather than the exception. Smog, poisonous fumes, traffic difficulties add to the discord. Our efforts to create tiny islands of order in the wild sea of anarchy are condemned to failure. Consider a moment the pathetically small number of planned cityscapes created in this country in the twentieth century.

Rockefeller Center, a few colleges, maybe half a dozen residential projects, a few shopping centers—everything else which was built, good, bad, or middling, is threatened with failure, not because of its own inadequacy, but because of the inadequacy of its surroundings.

Before the technological blitzkrieg, cityscape and landscape were neatly and clearly separated. In the Middle Ages it was most effectively done with fortified walls and moats.

Cityscape has spilled over the walls, has spread out in the form of subcityscape and, in the midst of the dirty mire, float suburbia and the landscape waiting to be rescued. Our task today is to bring order on a steadily widening scale. We have to unscramble the melée of flesh and machines, pedestrians and automobiles, junkyards and homes. This is a Herculean task. That it is not quite hopeless I would like to illustrate by the experience of my personal battle against the suburban commercial slum.

Until a few years ago the only form of shopping facilities known in suburbia consisted of long rows of one-story structures along the arterials connecting suburbs with the city core. These strip developments still exist, and unfortunately, due to unwise zoning practice, they still grow. The story of their growth sounds like a recipe for building successfully commercial slums.

Their original purpose—to serve suburban customers and to produce profit—is not fulfilled in the long run. Their customers must hunt for parking spaces, cross busy highways repeatedly, walk in dismal surroundings for long stretches. They offer poor shopping conditions and a depressing shopping atmosphere. They do, however, succeed beautifully in the step-by-step deterioration of the surrounding residential areas by their appearance, their noise, their smells, their traffic congestion. Owners and tenants of surrounding residential areas move out, slums develop, and having driven its good customers away, the shopping strip slowly deteriorates, the stores move away, another mile out into the suburb, where they start planfully and effectively to ruin a new environment. Their vacated buildings are taken over by second-hand stores, marginal operators, used-car dealers, and saloons, and the commercial slum is completed.

In these suburban store strips architectural elements, if such ever have existed, are solidly covered by the ugly rash of blatant signs, blinking cascades of neon, paper streamers. The suburban store strip shows commercialism at its worst.

Against this sorry backdrop, there appeared a few years ago a new building type—the planned, integrated shopping center. The importance of this event for twentieth-century architecture can, in my opinion, hardly be exaggerated. It is the first large-scale, conscious planning effort made by the forces usually considered as upholders of rugged individualism. The planned shopping center furnishes the proof of the possibilities and of the effectiveness of self-imposed restraint and discipline. How far this self-discipline has been exercised has been illustrated by one little detail of the largest of these planned shopping centers, Northland near Detroit. The huge branch department store of this center has, as its only identifying sign, two-and-a-half inch lettering near the entrance doors.

I would like to discuss with you in detail the main principles of shopping center design because I feel that they have significance for other elements of our cityscape including our city cores. Here are the five important ones:

1. Creation of effectively separated spheres of activity:
   The sphere of access;
   The sphere of car storage;
   The sphere of service activities;
   The sphere of selling;
   The sphere of walking and relaxation.
2. Creation of opportunities for social, cultural, civic, and recreational activities.
3. Overall architectural planning as related to function, structure, and aesthetics.
4. Encouragement of individualistic expression of commercial elements but subordinating these expressions to overall discipline by means of architectural coordination, sign control, and a code of behavior concerning matters like show window stickers, opening hours, show window lighting, etc.
5. Integration with the surrounding environment in matters of traffic, usage, protection, and aesthetics.

These principles have been more or less consciously and, with different degrees of success, applied to about a dozen existing regional shopping centers in the nation. They are also used as the basis of about forty large shopping centers now in the construction or advanced planning stage. The effect of this new phenomenon on the American suburban scene is extremely interesting and gratifying.

Northland near Detroit, which has now been operating for more than a year, has, in the words of many residents, "changed our lives." It has filled that great unanswered need of sprawling suburbia for a crystallization point.

Visited by fifty million people in the first year of its existence, it has already become Detroit's "festival place" where all the important civic events for which there is no place elsewhere, like Army Day, Fourth of July, Christmas and Easter, and many others are celebrated. On such days, there is in the landscaped courts and malls the atmosphere of a gay fiesta. But all through the year, weekdays and holidays, thousands promenade, amble, gossip, sit around on garden benches, study outdoor exhibits which at different times feature giant bombers, fashion shows, garden furniture, new car models, and art. They participate in the events in the two auditoriums, in the community center, and in Kiddyland; they lunch or dine in one of the dozen eating places; they have made it their club, their public park, the center of their social activities.

The residents of surrounding areas are well satisfied too. Instead of the feared deterioration usually connected with the appearance of commercial facilities, they experience a pleasant surprise. None of the traffic spilled into the residential streets, there are no evil sights, no evil noises, no evil smells. Neither did they mind that, because of the vicinity of so many desirable facilities, the demand for residential sites in the neighborhood grew and the value and their property rose considerably.

The fifty million people who came to Northland did one other thing also. They shopped—they did it with so much joy, intensity, and gusto that the sales figures per one square foot of store area reached amounts unprecedented in suburban shopping facilities to date.

The basic principles of Northland area are applied to a number of other shopping centers but also, and maybe this is more significant, to other types of projects.

In two suburban areas we are planning at present the construction of recreational health centers. Their concept is to combine, in one indigenous environment, related facilities like hospitals, clinics, laboratories, medical and dental offices, nurses' homes, hotel accommodations for visitors, and the related commercial services like restaurants, lunchrooms, cafeterias, pharmacists' medical supply stores. Following the shopping center pattern, we create on the one hand separation between various usages and, on the other hand, combine the functions of all buildings of the same denomination, thus creating a common access road system, common parking areas, common heating and air conditioning services and common loading, deliveries, repair and maintenance areas. In the midst of the various buildings there will be, reserved for pedestrians, outdoor spaces richly landscaped, offering restfulness and creating another segment of twentieth-century cityscape.

For two other cities we are planning suburban regional office centers. We are employing for them the same principles as for the shopping and health centers.

We are working on the extension of this principle of creating integrated nuclei for other clearly defined usages. We are planning home buildings and furnishing centers, research and laboratory centers, light industry centers.

And, as we proceed with these various plans for many cities of the nation, it seems to us that here might be a weapon for a successful counterattack in the technological blitzkrieg. If we use the weapon and if we can create large numbers of these clusterlike centers, we will be able to raze the tenantless strips of shanty towns along our roads and when the rubble is cleared away, we will plant trees and shrubs and grass and flowers where the suburban slums stood. We will gain space to widen strangled thoroughfares, space for picnic grounds, playgrounds, parks; we will get rid of wide stretches of subcityscape.

And we are trying another move. We are trying to apply this process of making order by departmentalization and integrated planning to our existing city cores. We are working on a number of replanning projects for downtown areas of smaller cities and on one project for the rehabilitation of a city of 600,000.

The mainspring of our design intention is the wish to create undisturbed and beautiful areas in which one can walk. The size of these areas is determined by human scale, by manageable walking distances; each such walking area, with its building, forms one superblock. They serve various purposes, sometimes more than one. There will be a block for shopping, a block for offices and shopping, a block for civic activities, a block for hotels and offices. The blocks are interconnected by a spinelike promenade which, besides pleasant walkways, features some auxiliary means of motion such as moving sidewalks and small exhibition-type electric buses.

The blocks are surrounded by a car storage area which, depending on varying conditions, will take the form of garages, multiple-deck parking, underground parking, or surface parking. All service traffic moves on underground roads. The car storage areas are looped by traffic access and circulatory roads from which branch off feeder roads toward the spine promenade between the individual blocks. Some of these feeder roads interconnect by dipping under the promenade.

The traffic access and circulatory road system is integrated and connected with the roads of the outlying city portions and with the existing and projected expressway system.

The measures for curing the ills of the business area would not be complete and effective without the rehabilitation of downtown residential areas. They have to be made desirable again for the millions of Americans who today are involuntary suburbanites, for all those people who hate gardening and commuting, for all those people who would like to be near their offices and near the theaters and museums and libraries, but who cannot do so because living near downtown has become synonymous with living in slums.

Slum clearance is not good enough if it results in the replacement of old slums by brand-new ones with better plumbing. We have to create new urban neighborhoods offering a variety of living unit types for all tastes and pocketbooks from low-cost housing to luxury apartments.

Once the slums which choke the heart of our cities are removed and replaced with highly desirable living environments, new life blood will flow into the rebuilt city core, and with freeways and rapid transit transportation interconnecting the rejuvenated downtown area with healthy satellite towns, a new age of enjoyment of urban life may be born.

You realize, of course, that these are big and costly plans, but there is in this country today an atmosphere extremely favorable to their implementation. These plans are practical because they are firmly founded on our existing economic system. The suburban centers—shopping centers, health centers, office building centers, etc.— are profitable ventures and downtown rehabilitation is profitable too in the sense of saving tremendous real estate values from deterioration, in the sense of being the only means of staving off accelerated downfall and disaster.

I am encouraged by the fact that during the last years architects and planners in many cities have actually received commissions for downtown master planning projects. I am encouraged by the fact that rehabilitation has moved into the public limelight. I am encouraged by my personal experience in the work with my friends and associates, Yamasaki and Stonorov, in connection with the downtown rehabilitation project in Detroit. Here, a citizens' committee composed of bankers, merchants, automobile industry executives, union leaders, minority representatives, have not only put an amazing amount of work and energy but also a large amount of dollars into the venture of taking measures to save downtown.

For success on a grand scale, we will need more than plans and energy and even money. We will need the legal weapons to fight the battle, we need more effective legislation for condemnation proceedings, we need new zoning laws, and we may need federal funds at least as guarantee for loans for urban and suburban rehabilitation. We need educational programs for our architectural schools in which integrated planning is stressed, and we need the active help and cooperation of artists, designers, and creative men in all fields in order to win in the blitzkrieg of technology.

1955

77–79 Six years after leaving *Domus*, **Ernesto Nathan Rogers** assumed the editorship of *Casabella*, adding the subtitle *Continuità*. Under the direction of Edoardo Persico and Giuseppe Pagano in the 1930s, *Casabella* had been the premier organ of Italian rationalism. It had not appeared since 1943, however, except for three reconstruction issues in 1946 edited by Franco Albini and Giancarlo Palanti. During his tenure from 1953 to 1964, Rogers would again make the review a preeminent journal of tendency, in not only Italy but the world.

In his opening editorial for the new series (January 1954) Rogers explained his theme of "continuity." Continuity meant elaboration and expansion of the tradition interrupted by the war. The crucial point was that modernism was to be placed within the overall trajectory of architectural history, and history was to be interpreted in a progressive sense. "The concept of historicity"—as defined by the philosopher Enzo Paci and cited by Rogers—"is closely linked to dynamic development and process." In the following article written a year later, Rogers introduced a related concept of equal import. This concerned *preesistenze ambientali*—existing conditions. Here again the crux lay in considering "context" not nostalgically but as evidence of the traditions, tastes, needs, and environmental factors specific to a location and the culture of its inhabitants. From this Rogers derived a new program for architecture: "to insert the needs of life into culture and—conversely—to insert culture into everyday life."

To put Rogers's own position into context it is necessary to recall the historical circumstances under which the modern movement emerged in Italy.

253–59 Despite the early appearance of futurism, Italian modernism contained deep contradictions from the outset. These included initial ties between architects and the political regime, a belated modernization process, and the especially strong presence of the past in Italy's historic cities. In the late 1930s rationalist architects were already courting "postrationalist" solutions. These culminated in the rhetorical "betrayals" at the E '42 exhibition in Rome of 1941–42—among them a grandiose Palazzo delle Poste e dei Telegrafi designed by Rogers's own firm, the BBPR. After the war unorthodox tendencies continued to proliferate, drawing now on the humbler populist images inspiriting a climate permeated

68–69 with partisan sentiments or else embracing "organic" alternatives. By the 1950s the gamut had become much wider, leading Rogers in 1957 to speak of heterodoxy itself as the only current orthodoxy. Most notorious of the deviations from modernist precepts was the Bottega d'Erasmo in Turin (1954), a studied evocation of late-nineteenth-century taste and building tradition by Roberto Gabetti and Aimaro Isola, who pronounced the failure of the modern movement in a letter to *Casabella* in 1957. A heresy of similar magnitude was Ignazio Gardella's finely detailed house on the Zattere in Venice (1954–58), described by Giulio Carlo Argan as the "Ca' d'Oro of modern architecture." The third major exemplar was the BBPR's own Velasca tower in Milan (1950–57). While Rogers rationalized the building's medieval image in terms of a historical analysis of the

300–7 urban context, the subsequent eruption of full-scale polemics over the style that came to be known as Neoliberty reveals the fine line between Rogers's pursuit of a progressive historicism and what appeared to some as uncritical eclecticism.

399–401 On the prophetic theme of existing conditions, see also Rogers's subsequent article "Il problema del costruire nelle preesistenze ambientali" (1957), published in his *Esperienza dell'architettura*, pp. 311–16.

"Le preesistenze ambientali e i temi practici contemporanei" from Casabella-Continuità 204 (February–March 1955), pp. 3–6. Republished in Ernesto N. Rogers, Esperienza dell'architettura (Turin: Giulio Einaudi, 1958), pp. 304–10. Courtesy of Studio BBPR and Julia Banfi.

Preexisting Conditions and Issues of Contemporary Building Practice
Ernesto Nathan Rogers

There are at least two steps forward that contemporary architecture can take consistent with its own theoretical premises. One regards the more precise affirmation of its own practical means within the framework of perfecting the techniques aimed at establishing its own figurative language in physical reality. The other regards the further deepening of this language in the sense of being ever more comprehensive of the cultural values in which new forms historically insert themselves.

I have already stated some presuppositions that appear to me necessary in order that the judgment concerning a specific architectural work not be schematically abstract, but identify itself with the contextual conditions (and thus also the historical ones) in which the work is manifested.

For example, I said that one might accuse of formalism a critique that, in evaluating *a posteriori* the significance of a Brazilian building, does not take into account the fact that the latter arises precisely in Brazil; conversely, one might accuse of formalism an architect who does not absorb *a priori* into his work the particular and characteristic contents suggested by the context.

Immediately there arises here a more general problem whose terms can be posed as follows: since every work of architecture tends to be, by definition, a work of art, and every work of art is, by definition, an original act, what is the limit that an artist must not exceed in order for his creation not to depart—so to speak—from the margins of the real and enter organically into the given spatial-temporal situation? The struggle between conservators and innovators is always about the practical evaluation of this theoretical dilemma. The confusion in the discussions is owed, beyond the specific sympathies of each, to the fact that neither one nor the other understands the true meaning of the terms of the controversy.

Many of those considered innovators share with the so-called conservators the common flaw that they start from formal prejudices, maintaining that the new and the old are opposed rather than represent the dialectical continuity of the historical process; both are limited, in fact, to the idolatry of certain styles frozen into a few images, and they are incapable of penetrating the essences that are pregnant with inexhaustible energies. To pretend to build in a preconceived "modern style" is as absurd as to demand respect for the taboo of past styles.

One who today confronts a creative problem must insert his own thought into objective reality, which each time presents itself in terms of its own interpretation; one will not design a building in Milan that is the same as one elaborated for Brazil and, in fact, in every street of Milan will seek to construct an edifice appropriate to its circumstantial conditions.

Precisely because the method of approaching the problems is the same, it follows that the solution to every problem is different.

And the problem involves not only examining the pertinent data from the standpoint of practical function, but also specifying and localizing the other data with exactitude and responsibility.

A building in Milan will be different if it is to be used for offices rather than for dwelling—this is natural—but also if it is on one terrain rather than another, next to certain preexisting buildings rather than others. The synthetic characterization of the different technical elements unmistakably expresses an artist's style, nor can these elements fail to acknowledge in the very act of creation all those forces that are at play in the field of their own actions.

The context is the place of these preexistences and anything that did not feel their influence would be vague and indeterminate.

The first architectural manifestations of the modern movement were limited to isolating phenomena and aimed at an objectivity of expression that could represent any artistic product in itself, in the autonomous limits of its individual existence. Even F. L. Wright and Le Corbusier, though sensitive to the suggestions of the "natural environment" (the one seeking to merge with it according to a romantic taste, the other opposing it according to a classical conception), did not have, for a long time, either occasion or desire or, therefore, consciousness of the possible links with a "cultural context."

The same urbanistic designs, though extending the spatial measure of the zone of influence, resulted in autochthonous, indifferent, or , indeed, drastically antagonistic visions with respect to the preceding historical reality.

Speaking very schematically—as we have been doing—one can say that the problem of historical continuity (and therefore of the knowledgeable historicization of modern phenomena with respect to those that are of the past yet permanent parts of our life) is a fairly recent acquisition of architectural thought: symptomatic of the evolution of the masters cited are, for example, the Casa Masieri in Venice by the first and the architectural ensemble in the Punjab by the second, where both have tried to reconcile the specific cultural tradition to the respective fields of their new artistic operations. Whoever appeals today to national culture—when it is not a nationalistic reactionary or a demagogue prompted by the recall of folklore or, on the other hand, of scholastic styles—intends that architecture be rooted in the profound strata of tradition, suck up its nourishment and be qualified by it; it is a necessary integration of contemporary reality, complex and varied, with the immense patrimony of inherited experience.

If one admits, with sufficient modesty, that we are still operating within the orbit of the methodological process initiated by Gropius, one can easily recognize that a vast evolution is possible by following along the path undertaken, not only without falling into any contradiction with its original postulates, but increasingly by carrying those same principles to their utmost consequences: this same method allows us to enlarge the horizons of research and to include in them new, coherent results.

The functional relationship between utility and beauty, while at first limited to expressing the world circumscribed from within—and almost tautological—and the entity of a determinate architectural organism, now radiates out and expands, influencing vaster zones where the cultural exchange becomes more intense, more sensitive, more dramatic: substantially more human.

The notion of the "maison de l'homme" develops beyond the abstract and undiscriminating schema of ideal man: it deepens, acquiring the sense of human history in its dramatic past vicissitudes, and enlarges to recognize the distinct individuality of modern society (and therefore also of the popular classes) which only now finds the force to flourish again. The inclusion of these new contents cannot fail to have an effect on appearances, since forms are modeled on them, unmediated, in terms of physical representation.

One can lament that some weak artists have remained uncomfortable in reconfiguring the feelings that they propose to express and have borrowed the language of old discourses (of vernacular or cultivated architecture), but it is also undeniable that the better ones have tried to find means fit to communicate, in an original way, poetic intentions.

It is as difficult to specify a detailed method of adjudicating problems and prospective solutions as, conversely, it is to confine reasoning to anodyne generalization: it will thus be appropriate to pause only for a brief examination of some questions of method to try to frame our initial query concerning the relationship between invention and contextualization.

One can object that every invention already contains implicitly in itself its own particular interpretation of the context (negative or positive), but only if one wants to deny that it is possible to distinguish different moments, different emphases, in the creative process; it is thus that one can underline different attitudes resulting from a deepening consciousness of the specific problem.

To consider the context means to consider history. Since the greater penetration of the meaning of the context is one of the most characteristic arguments of present-day philosophical thought, architectural thought, even if slowly, cannot remain uninfluenced: by considering the past and the present in terms of the internal motivation of their characteristic contents, one increasingly affirms and strengthens two notions that, even if they seem contradictory on first view, are perfectly linked.

The first is that the events of the past find their reason in the coherent consistency of the original acts that have determined them; the second is that the present is, in its turn, an original creation. That which, however, disintegrates history unifies it in a sense of continuity whereby the past is projected into present occurrences and the latter are joined together in finding their roots in anterior facts.

To be modern means simply to sense contemporary history within the order of all of history and thus to feel the responsibility of one's own acts not from within the closed barricade of an egotistic manifestation, but as a collaboration that, through one's contribution, augments and enriches the perennial contemporaneity of the possible formal combinations of universal relationship.

To construct a building in a context already characterized by works of other artists imposes the obligation to respect these presences in the sense of bringing in one's own energy as new nourishment for the perpetuation of their vitality.

That cannot be achieved except by a creative act. But this act cannot be gratuitous; since the first masters of the modern movement considered each thing as if it were primordial (did they not refuse even to put an antique piece of furniture within their walls?), we now know how to discount long genealogies of precursors, and we feel the step that we are taking to be like that of a mountain climber on a rope. If we build in a natural landscape we seek to interpret its character and practical exigencies; in an urban landscape we will be inspired by the same principle, such that in every case our intuitive act will not find thorough fulfillment if it is not the personal interpretation of objective givens. The copying of traditional forms will obviously be impossible, but so will the design of an architecture only abstractly satisfying our taste and the conditions of contemporary technology, insufficiently corresponding to new feelings.

Forms must convincingly document the subtlest ethical claims of collective and individual man, continuing the ancient discourse.

It is necessary that our language be capable of responding to the questions of the present time without reticence—explicitly. To insert the needs of life into culture and—conversely—to insert culture into everyday life: this is the task of the architect; to build a single reality through synthesis, recognizing too that the observance of technical requisites is indispensable to its formation.

The influence of the objective givens in the process of architectonic synthesis is thus relevant in that, instead of isolating the components of a practical order by reducing observation to a mere statement of those data (that which reduces a phenomenon to a naturalistic vision as if it were a simple biological manifestation), one can achieve an analysis where those factors are elucidated. Here is the second step to be taken.

It is undeniable that the polemical operation of the first masters of the modern movement, not sufficiently conscious of the cultural influences that were historically immanent in their doctrine, thus used technology more often as a symbol than as a necessary means—which it truly is—for clarification (and materialization) of the expressive language. Except, perhaps, Auguste Perret, who posed as an aim the practical problem of building correctly, very few considered this fundamental quality; nor did an architecture result which, even when its poetic motives were founded on rational grounds, was capable of resolving these premises into their ultimate physical instances.

For many years we have had an antipathy for eaves and cornices, and it appeared that only the flat roof could satisfy our designs; the vertical window appeared to us inadequate to express ourselves. All this, if it was justified within the limits of a courageous updating of the figurative language—as far as one can justify the idiosyncrasy concerning antique furniture—finished by making the weakest fall into formalistic aestheticism.

Such historical reasons, from the polemical birth of modern architecture, remain as an inevitable heredity governing the actions of contemporary architects, and even many of the youngest do not succeed in liberating themselves from it entirely.

One reacts to the cultural and practical conditions of the predecessors in a one-sided manner; either one is inspired by the forms of the past—national, regional, ethnic—on an imitative plane of taste alone; or, on the other hand, one is preoccupied by technical insufficiencies as explained by technocrats: both approaches are deluded about resolving the problem through a dissociated consideration of the two terms.

Nonetheless criticism is right to consider with interest the one and the other, if history is not only the mirror of exemplary and well-balanced actions, but also the chronicle of honest attempts. It is intended that the two steps forward that we have indicated separately, out of convenience of examination, not be dissociated in judging the architectural phenomenon, which fulfills its complete process only when one arrives at their synthesis.

Achieving this synthesis and in particular evaluating the historical context, without having to subject it to practical solutions dictated by the novelty of the subject matter, is something so arduous that it ought to be considered a sublime and most rare miracle. But only when this is realized will the work that manifests it merit the name of architecture, which is neither sculpture nor machine.

1956

The following essay, sequel to another of the same title and date, was written in winter of 1955–56 at the University of Texas in Austin, where the authors met while teaching a design studio. **Colin Rowe**, trained as an architect in Liverpool and afterward in art history under Rudolf Wittkower at the Warburg Institute, had left a teaching post at Liverpool to study town planning with Christopher Tunnard at Yale on a Fulbright fellowship. Subsequently he accepted an invitation to teach in Texas from the school's new chairman, Harwell Hamilton Harris. **Robert Slutzky**, a painter, also came to Texas from Yale on Harris's invitation, having just graduated from Yale's fine arts school, where, as a student of Josef Albers, he had found himself reacting critically to Bauhaus orthodoxy and influenced by Gestalt studies in visual perception. In Austin Rowe and Slutzky formed part of a group of "Texas Rangers," architects and artists from the East Coast and Europe—including John Hejduk and the Swiss Bernhard Hoesli—who imported to an American backwater an original methodology of teaching architectural design based on configurational principles of form.

Rowe and Slutzky also shared a strong admiration for the work of Le Corbusier, whose reputation in the United States at this time was still eclipsed by that of Mies van der Rohe and Gropius. In 1947, two years before Wittkower's *Architectural Principles in the Age of Humanism* appeared in book form, Rowe had published a seminal essay, "The Mathematics of the Ideal Villa," in which he made an original comparison between the geometric principles underlying the villas of Le Corbusier and Palladio. This essay, together with Wittkower's book and Le Corbusier's *Modulor* (1950), gave impetus to a new preoccupation with geometry and proportional studies among English architects. Wittkower closed his book with the remark that "[the theory of proportion] is again very much alive in the minds of young architects today, and they may well evolve new and unexpected solutions to this ancient problem." Dubbed the "New Palladianism," and more broadly the "New Formalism," the tendency was given further credence by another Rowe essay, "Mannerism and Modern Architecture" (1950). Drawing an unorthodox parallel to a period then being revived by historians like Pevsner, Rowe discerned mannerist tendencies in modernist buildings by Mies van der Rohe, Adolf Loos, and the Bauhaus architects, as well as Le Corbusier, on the basis of their cultivated "visual ambiguity" and "inverted spatial effects."

Meanwhile, in America at this date, it was the formalist art criticism of Clement Greenberg that held sway in aesthetic-intellectual circles, and Rowe and Slutzky's "most undeviating regard for formal structure . . . most remorseless and sophisticated visual logic" (as they characterize their own approach to architecture in the following essay) must also be seen within this context. The two "Transparency" essays were originally submitted to *Architectural Review*, which rejected them, presumably for their anti-Gropius bias. The first "Transparency" was ultimately published in *Perspecta* 8 seven years later, and became a basic text serving to dispel the positivist aura still clinging to "space-time" modernism and widely establishing the authors' distinction between literal and phenomenal transparency. The sequel, which deals primarily with surface configuration, was not published for another eight years, by which date the dominance of formalism was already under attack; this may explain its lesser reputation. Yet in its emphasis on facade manipulation and its "indiscreet" juxtaposition of modern and premodern examples, it directly anticipates the postmodernism of the 1970s and 1980s—a development in which Rowe, through his book *Collage City* (1978) and his teaching at Cornell University, was to play a major role.

From Perspecta *13/14 (1971), pp. 286–301. Diagrams of San Lorenzo by Daniel Libeskind. Courtesy of the authors and* Perspecta: The Yale Architectural Journal.

Transparency: Literal and Phenomenal (Part 2)
Colin Rowe and Robert Slutzky

Can there be in visual space a simultaneous perception of two objects one behind the other? When I look through a transparent object do I really see a complete, unbroken surface? Or is this the case: I see only parts of the nearer object, and, through gaps in its surface, parts of the other object and from these fractional sections I mentally construct the two surfaces? Further: are we able to see two complementary colors as one behind the other even though both are stimulating the same retinal area? It is easy from common experience with transparent glass or gelatine to confuse the issue here. We are not referring to the "real space" in which, of course, one object is closer to the observer than the other. Our problem deals rather with phenomenal, visual space.[1]

In a previous article we elaborated through a discussion of several Cubist and post-Cubist paintings certain meanings which have attached themselves to the word *transparency*. With the Bauhaus, Garches, and Le Corbusier's project for the Palace of the League of Nations serving as primary points of architectural reference, two kinds of transparency were distinguished, *literal* and *phenomenal*. Literal transparency, it was stipulated, could be experienced in the presence of a glazed opening or a wire mesh; but no definite conclusions as to the prerequisites of phenomenal transparency were presented. However, the examples of Garches and the League of Nations at least suggested circumstances which might be the cause of this manifestation; and thus it was implied that phenomenal transparency might be perceived when one plane is seen at no great distance behind another and lying in the same visual direction as the first. Consequently, it was further implied that among the causes (or, if one prefers it, the by-products) of phenomenal transparency there might be found a preference for shallow space, or where such space was not possible, for a stratification of deep space, so that the phenomenal as opposed to the real space could be experienced as shallow. But some of these suppositions are of so tendentious and so arguable a nature that in this present article it is proposed to consign them to temporary oblivion, and to concentrate attention, not upon the three-dimensional or spatial aspects of phenomenal transparency, but as far as possible upon its two-dimensional manifestations—upon phenomenal transparency as pattern.

Substituting the United Nations building for the Bauhaus, and Le Corbusier's Algiers skyscraper project for his villa at Garches, we might arrive at a parallel between the two former roughly approximate to the parallel which was maintained between the two latter. Thus the Secretariat of the United Nations may stand as a monumental example of literal transparency; and the Algiers skyscraper may represent almost a textbook example of that other transparency which Gyorgy Kepes defines as the capacity of figures to interpenetrate without optical destruction of each other.[2]

The published drawings of the Algiers block (*figure 1*) show a tower whose organization may be apprehended in a variety of ways:
1. The eye may be engaged by the three horizontal bands which divide the structure into four definite areas.
2. If these are overlooked or become recessive the eye may become absorbed with the cellular pattern of the *brise-soleil* and this pattern will gradually be felt to extend itself behind the horizontal bands.
3. As the disruption of the *brise-soleil* pattern to the left of the facade becomes

apparent, the observer will construct a further figure which, in mediating the two *brise-soleil* grids, appears as a kind of channel cutting open the facade and connecting the *pilotis* of the lower floors with the incidents upon the roof.

4. When this new figure is discovered to be interwoven with the three central floors of the building, the eye (or the mind) is compelled to provide further explanation and the observer comes to see the composition as a kind of E-shaped overlay imposed upon the "neutral" background provided by the *brise-soleil*.

These four variations are presented, not necessarily in the order in which they might be experienced, nor as excluding further interpretations to which they give rise, but simply with the object of establishing the basic figures whose presence a quite naive individual might detect.[3]

With the United Nations building and the Algiers skyscraper as almost classic exemplars of literal and phenomenal transparency, it would surely be possible to sustain a classification of modern architecture according to the absence or presence of these qualities, but to do so would involve unnecessarily tedious analysis. The two interpretations which have been laid upon the word *transparency* become apparent from the comparison of these two buildings, and only in order to reinforce this distinction of meaning does it seem necessary to include a further parallel—one between Pietro Belluschi's Equitable Life Insurance building in Portland, Oregon (*figure 2*), and I. M. Pei's Mile High Center in Denver, Colorado (*figure 3*).

The former is evidently an instance of literal transparency. Direct, matter of fact, a kind of lucid academic critique of the Chicago architecture of the 1880s, it shows few of those characteristics which Kepes lists as those of (phenomenal) transparency. It barely exhibits either overlapping or interpenetrating figures, perhaps little contradiction of spatial dimensions; nor does it offer the observer a means of "simultaneous perception of different spatial dimensions";[4] and, except for its surface flatness, it is without equivocal meaning.

On the other hand, the Denver building, which displays a comparable regard for the structural frame and which is equally transparent in the literal sense, exhibits all of the foregoing ambiguities. Confronted with the Mile High Center the observer perceives:

1. the vertical and horizontal gridding of a black structural frame;

2. a further system of gridding provided by a blue subframe which is constituted by the window mullions and the horizontal transoms or sill members;

3. that each of these frames provides a visual reinforcement of the other and that their overlapping leaves some doubt as to where the floor levels of the building are to be found.

Further discrimination leads to the awareness that the black structural frame lies entirely in one vertical plane and thus to the color black a specific spatial depth is attributed. Concurrently, an attempt is made to attribute a similar specific spatial depth to the color blue—only to reveal that the horizontal members of the blue subframe pass behind the black frame, while its vertical members pass in front. Hence, an equivocal contradiction of spatial dimensions results from this interweaving or overlapping of two figures which are simultaneously apprehended; and in order to explain this situation, first the black frame and then the blue will become dominant for the observer. At one time he will accept the existence of the blue frame in the two distinct spatial layers which it occupies, but at another he will seek to interpret its color according to the logic of color displayed in the black frame. Thus he will come to suppress the modeling of the blue frame and attempt to see it as entirely flat, but in doing so he will be obliged to see either

1

2

3

the horizontal or vertical members of the black frame as pressed forward, or pressed back, or warped by the tension which has been introduced.

This building is presumably an exceptionally succinct statement of a phenomenal transparency, but to certain types of mind the elegant post-Miesian achievement which it represents will suggest not only Chicago but also Italy. It is undoubtedly indiscreet to pluck such a building as the Farnese villa at Caprarola (*figure 4*) from out of its cultural background and to propose that it may be examined face to face with this recent office building from Denver. The functions of the two buildings are not similar; their structural systems could scarcely be more unlike; the social context, the technology, the economy, the content which each implies can scarcely be related. But for the present we are concerned neither with function nor structure (as generally understood), nor with the social context, technology, economics, or content; but simply with the manifestations which reveal themselves to the eye.

Presented with one of the two identical garden facades of Caprarola, the observer recognizes a building organized in terms of two major stories and he is quite shortly aware of:

1. the primary articulation of the wall which the orders and their respective entablature establish;

2. a further articulation of the wall which is effected by means of a sort of lattice of flat stone strips.

This stone latticework which forms a visual insulation between the pilasters and the plastic activity of the windows functions in two primary manners—as a subsidiary pilaster which serves the "real" pilasters and confirms the vertical punctuation of the facade, and as a frame which serves the bay, indicating a system of paneling and providing the facade with a number of horizontal emphases of an importance almost equal to that of the lower entablature.

Thus the imposition of pilasters upon lattice leads (as at Denver) to an uncertainty as to the floor level and to an ambiguity as to the basic unit of the facade. By implication of the pilasters there are two major horizontal divisions; by implication of the projecting window heads below and window sills above, both of which may be read as lattice, a tripartite division of the facade is deduced. The overlapping and interlacing of these two systems and the fluctuations of significance to which each gives rise can pass without comment, for at Caprarola, as at Denver, it is apparent that the observer finds himself in the presence of an architectural tapestry whose warp and woof are immediately apparent to the eye, but whose invisible threads his organizing instinct mentally reconstructs.

Now if Caprarola as well as Denver shows phenomenal transparency, we are obliged to conclude that, after all, it is neither a new, nor even a post-Cubist manifestation; and perhaps if we were to trace back the evolution of literal transparency down the long route leading from the United Nations building via such conspicuous monuments as the Bauhaus and the Crystal Palace, to the great glass and stone cages of the later Middle Ages, we might also discover in these buildings some evidence of phenomenal transparency in the nave of St. Denis (*figure 5*), for instance, where the triforium rather than appearing as an independent unit will seem to be an intersection of the clerestory and the nave arcade, sometimes being subsumed within the first, and on other occasions presenting itself as a projection of the second.

Thus almost any medieval or Quattrocento Venetian palace will reveal similar attributes to a greater or lesser degree, and the organization, although not the asymmetry, of the Ca d'Oro (*figure 6*) may be considered representative of the type. In the Ca d'Oro a basically bipartite facade is presented, where one center is determined by the loggias to the left, and the other by the cutting of three square windows through the plane of the wall surface to the right. Each of these two centers is invested with the control of sharply contrasted, clearly defined, and apparently symmetrical areas, which are isolated from each other by a thin, almost embroidered pilaster providing visual support for a heraldic trophy displayed on the second floor. But almost immediately after one recognizes this trophy, one proceeds to question it. It coordinates the space around itself and compels a symmetrical interpretation of the two windows between which it is placed, so that these windows are read together, and hence by means of this reading, the pilaster becomes, not the frontier between two opposed units, but the spine of an element straddling these units and demanding a revision of one's initial assumption as to the nature of each.

Once perceived, the uncertain valency of this pilaster quite undermines the primary response to the Ca d'Oro facade; and, as the element which it has now produced receives further attention, this becomes even more problematical. Since it is symmetrical on the second floor, one is predisposed to believe this element to be symmetrical on the first; and when discovered not to be the case, when the two windows flanking the pilasters on this floor are discovered to be unequal, then further figural variations are automatically sponsored. Now an attribution of symmetry to any one unit of the facade is discovered to be unwarranted, and each of the two major units acquires the ability to enlarge itself by absorbing this third; so that while the right-hand and left-hand sections of the facade are constantly augmented and diminished, infinitely more subtle relationships are now constructed, and, activating these, one might notice the schema provided by the rhythm of the projecting balconies and also the elaborating frilling of the cornice which, as a kind of arpeggio to the facade, provides a system of notation serving to intensify the polyvalent activity of the wall below. By these and other means, horizontal and vertical, and L- and T-shaped configurations are finally precipitated within the intricate formal meshwork, so that first one element and then another comes to function as a kind of gear, the apprehension of which sets in motion whole systems of reversible mechanics.

The permutations inherent in a structure of this kind are identical with those which issue from less eccentric Venetian facades, and of these the sixteenth-century Palazzo Mocenigo (*figure 7*) might be considered reasonably characteristic. Here, in a facade vertically divided into three, each division in itself is symmetrical, and the symmetry of each is reinforced in the center by triply repeated arches and on the sides by the elaborately mounted heraldic displays which are compressed between the windows of the *piano nobile*.[5] However, under sustained observation these apparently clear divisions of the facade begin to change. First, it is noticed that the central division enjoys the capacity to extend itself at the expense of the other two; and secondly, that the sides show a certain tendency to infiltrate, to slide in behind the outer bays of the central motif; while, following these initial realizations, the constituents of the facade enter into a successive series of relationships. At one stage the outer windows become isolated slots emphasizing the extremities of the wall; at another this same quality of slot is transferred to the central arched windows; and, presently, the heraldic trophies assume essential significance as the bonding element between these peripheric and central developments. At this stage the facade is dominated by a system of double H's; but, as its underlying structure becomes elucidated, this composition is displaced by

4

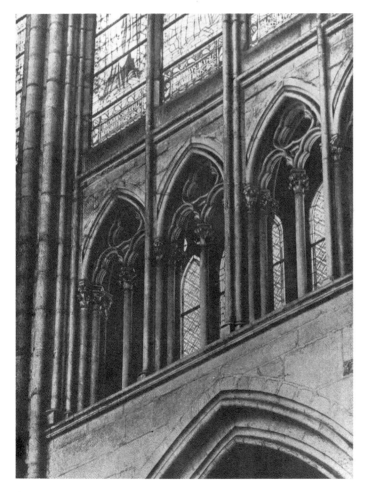

5

a cruciform element which is implied by the plastic development of the principal floor and the association of the superimposed central arches. But the process of subtraction and addition continues, and as the upper and lower stages of the palace are now noticed to show a paneling of the wall, and as the *piano nobile* does not sustain the paneling, by the discontinuity of elements, another figure is raised into significance. Just as formerly the heraldic trophies effected a bridge between the center and extremities of the facade, now the central windows of the principal floor become the bridging element which integrates these two areas.

These different readings abstracted from the Palazzo Mocenigo by no means exhaust the possibility of still further ones; but they are in themselves a sufficient exposition of the functional multiplicity with which each and every part of the design is endowed. Substantially the building is of Venetian origin; but the presence of certain features obliges one to presume the possibility of other influences also; and thus, on the top floor, because some Michelangelesque origin might be suspected for the profiles of the window pediments, one might also believe that something of the explicit nature of the overlapping and interlocking of figures derives from the same source.

Certainly in both the drawings and model of Michelangelo's proposed facade for San Lorenzo (*figures 8, 9, 9a*) everything that the traditional Venetian nuances of the Palazzo Mocenigo might obscure becomes clarified and exposed; and for this reason San Lorenzo requires little introductory comment. A wall surface modeling in low relief is articulated by means of a skeletal organization of columns and pilasters, by suites of moldings, string courses, architraves, and a pediment.

So much is obvious; but it now becomes necessary to note the transpositions to which this skeletal organization proceeds to lend itself. Thus, to allow the eye to travel sideways across the design, four vertical elements—the coupled pilasters and columns—might be seen as contributing to the existence of a grid and as defining three larger spatial intervals (*figure 10a*). But almost immediately this information is then subjected to "correction." These three spatial intervals, while they can appear identical in width, are, in reality, far from being so. The central is distinctly narrower than the flanking ones; and as a result, and in collaboration with the central pediment, a subversion of the initial reading is instigated. The inner sets of pilasters and columns now disengage themselves from the outer. They cease to participate in the apparent and "neutral" grid. Instead they begin to appear as subservient to a hierarchical and centralized situation; and thus, in place of the quadripartite interpretation of the facade, there develops a tripartite division (*figure 10b*).

Likewise, if the eye travels up and down this surface there is something comparable which happens. Here to be noted is an elementary contrast between a low and a high relief. Columns below turn into pilasters above, and, thereby, a basic horizontal division becomes enforced (*figure 10c*). But this, again, becomes an interpretation which cannot be sustained. The areas of emphatically high and emphatically low relief are separated by a contested territory (is it the attic to the one or the pedestal to the other?) which progressively insists upon its autonomy and which, accordingly, compels yet further revision (*figure 10d*).

But so intimate and manifold are the interrelationships of figure which inhere within this organization that seriously to insist upon any initial or dominant interpretation is to be quite arbitrary; and therefore, rather than try to impose a private version of the continuous oscillations of appearance which San Lorenzo provides, it might be more expedient simply to allude to some of the more notable figures which it displays.

6

7

These include:

1. a fluctuating series of H-shaped figures which are promoted by the intersection of the narrow bays and the "attic-pedestal" (*figure 10e*);

2. a rotated H-shaped figure provided by the lateral banding of niches, plaques, and central aedicule—"window"—in the upper wall, and by the equivalent banding and gapping of doors and panels in the lower wall (*figure 10f*);

3. an expanding series of cruciform figures which are derived from the intersection of the "attic-pedestal" and the central bay (*figure 10g*);

4. a checkerboard reading which is created by three segmental pediments of the outer doors and of the upper "window" (*figure 10h*);

5. an inverted checkerboard which overlaps the preceding one and which is derived from the two circular plaques with their connected niches (*figure 10i*);

6. an inverted T-shaped figure generated by the impact of the pediment above and the high relief development below which comprises some kind of reflection of the volume of the building lying behind, and is presumably a residue of earlier studies (*figure 10j*).

A quite random observation of San Lorenzo discloses the immanence of at least such configurations as these; but a more discriminating examination can discover more concealed and subtle modulations. The segmental pediments of the upper "window" and outer doors may again be noticed. These establish a triangle of interest; and, since the visual elements comprising this triangle are almost alike, there is a tendency to attribute to them a corresponding size. However, since one of these elements is smaller than the other two, there is a further tendency to assume it to be located at a greater distance from the eye; and thus, when seen in conjunction with the two doors below, the remarkable underscaling of the central "window" (together with the understructure of its immediate vicinity) introduces a curious tension between the readings of the horizontals and verticals in the wall plane. Providing an implication of depth, this underscaling suggests that beyond this vertical plane and visible through it there lies a perspective recession or an inclined surface to which each of these three elements is attached (*figure 10k*).

With this last and almost Cubist transparency which Michelangelo has introduced, specific analysis of San Lorenzo need not be carried further. It should be apparent that these phenomena which we have examined are of an order closely comparable to those which we might find in many modern paintings—for instance, in the later paintings of Mondrian; and although to erect a parallel between a Michelangelo facade and a Mondrian painting may at first appear as frivolous as a comparison between Caprarola and the Mile High Center, almost any representative of Mondrian's *Boogie Woogie* series might justify such a parallel. Thus, whoever chooses to examine with any care the incomplete *Victory Boogie Woogie* of 1943–44 (*figure 11*) will be obliged to extract from it a series of transparencies—of triangles, cross shapes, T's, and U's which the composition may be said to spill over in a manner similar to San Lorenzo.[6]

Obviously dissimilar as regards their content and their more overt formal manifestations, both *Victory Boogie Woogie* and San Lorenzo are at least alike in defying any accurate description of what they are. In San Lorenzo a lucidly symmetrical, monochromatic composition is saturated with alternative readings. In *Victory Boogie Woogie* an asymmetrical composition derives qualities of excitement from color, congestion, and the symmetrical nature of its individual parts. The readings of San Lorenzo are for the most part explicit; those of *Victory Boogie Woogie* are less expressed.

8

9

9a

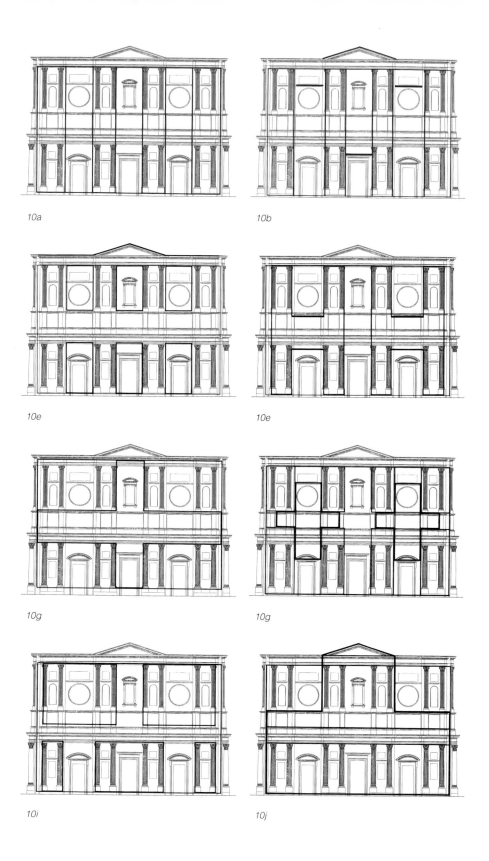

10a

10b

10e

10e

10g

10g

10i

10j

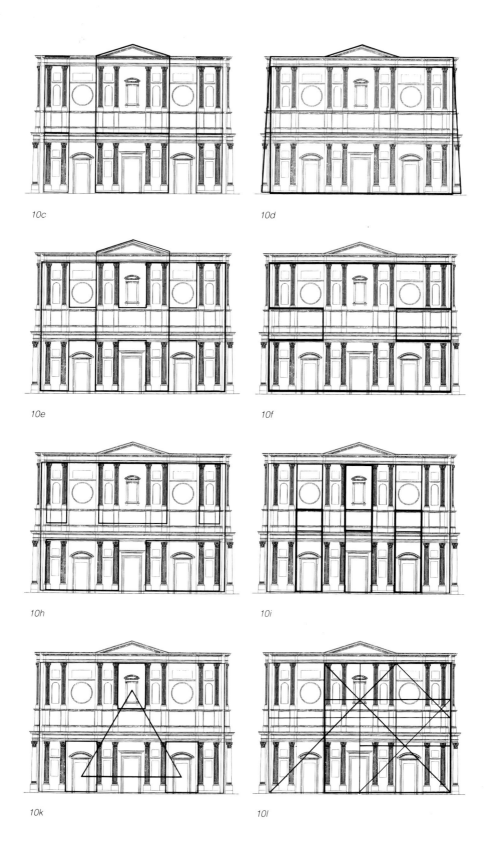

10c

10d

10e

10f

10h

10i

10k

10l

The fluctuations of Michelangelo's facade are sudden; those of Mondrian's painting are less violent. In *Victory Boogie Woogie* the different areas of white gradually congeal to provide the central cruciform figure; and this figure slowly dissolves before a further interpretation in which the vertical axis provides a dominant element. But in both painting and facade there might be noticed a tendency of the different elements to build, to coordinate themselves, to amalgamate by means of proximity or common contour into larger configurations. Thus in *Victory Boogie Woogie,* while areas of red and areas of blue distributed throughout the canvas offer two alternative constellations, adjacent reds and blues show a tendency to withdraw from these systems and to unite into a series of larger wholes. In San Lorenzo these same propensities may be noticed. There, where a constellation of rectangular areas and columns and a rival constellation of circular and quasicircular elements are to be found, coalitions are constantly formed between the contiguous representatives of each system.

Again the facade and painting both show a disposition of frontally aligned objects which are arranged within a highly compressed space; both show these objects functioning as a series of relief layers for the further articulation of this space; and both show a framework syncopated by a staccato punctuation—in the one case of conventional architectural elements, in the other of small colored squares. In Michelangelo's design the wall plane which provides the mount, i.e., the "negative" background upon which these individual elements are displayed, has the ability to assume an opposite role, i.e., to become in itself a "positive" element or a series of "positive" elements; and in Mondrian's picture one is conscious of the white areas behaving in the same manner. Thus in any primary interpretation of *Victory Boogie Woogie* the white rectangles will appear to designate a basic ground, a rear surface which supports the yellows, reds, blues, and grays; but, unlike Michelangelo's wall, Mondrian's white plane can cease to be recessive and, by exerting a pressure on the figures which initially it appeared to subsume, it can become as highly charged an element or series of elements as they.

By not permitting the eye to penetrate any far removed space, this rear plane prohibits a resolution of *either* composition in depth, and thus in each case its presence may be said to disturb the possibilities of central focus. In each case by investing the space of canvas and facade with a lateral structure, this plane functions as a generator of peripheral emphasis and replaces any one focal point by a series of differentiated episodes. By these means it acquires an overall surface tension, becoming a kind of tightly stretched membrane which acts upon the different elements it supports and in turn is reacted upon by them. Imbued by these elements with tautness, it presses them further forward; and thus, by reason of the spatial constriction which it creates, this rear plane serves both as the catalyst and as the neutralizer of the successive figures which the observer experiences.

Comparisons, parallels, and analyses such as these could be prolonged almost indefinitely, but possibly enough has been said to indicate the constancy of the manifestation which in contemporary works Moholy and Kepes have recognized as transparency.[7] In all instances their transparency—our phenomenal transparency—has taken place within a highly abstracted and intellectualized work of art; and in every case it has been the product of the most undeviating regard for formal structure, of the most remorseless and sophisticated visual logic. So much for the general context in which phenomenal transparency seems to appear; but for Moholy the transparency of meanings to which he responds in the writings of James Joyce is a method of building

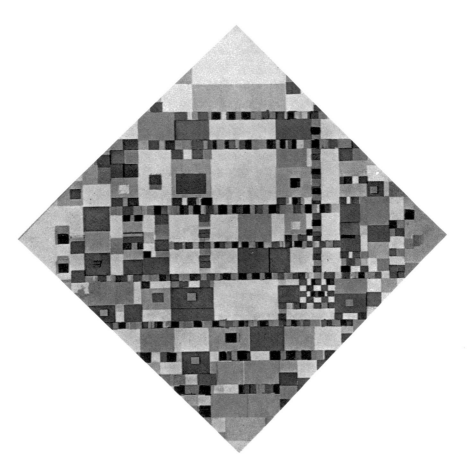

11

up a rich and manifold completeness. It is the literary analogue of the transparency revealed by Cubism—and this transparency, whether literal or phenomenal, is conceived by him to be a kind of symbol of space-time, which is mystically validated by the discoveries of science, and which, as a unique means of achieving cultural integration, is assumed to be inherent to the whole ethos of the twentieth century. But, if there is any substance to the preceding investigations, then transparency is not the exclusively post-Cubist development which he supposed; it is independent of either modern physics or Minkowski; it is not characteristic of the twentieth century alone; and it has no necessary correlation with any impending integration of culture. In fact, almost the reverse could be claimed; and San Lorenzo, the Palazzo Mocenigo, and Caprarola, at least, could be presented as the evidences of a Mannerist malaise, as the illustrations of "a self-conscious dissenting, frustrating style," as the indices to "a period of tormenting doubt and rigorous enforcement of no longer self-understood dogma," as the external effects of mental disquiet, disequilibrium, schism.[8]

Now, that these two widely separated interpretations of closely related phenomena—the one insisting on the virtues, the other on the dubieties, of phenomenal transparency—should exist side by side without any public embarrassment need not be hard to understand. In the first case, the mental block of so many modern architects against history is notorious; and, in the second, the unwillingness of so many art historians to enter into serious criticism of contemporary achievement is one of the more patent limitations of that species. But if we can allow that in all the instances discussed, the method of raising fluctuating figures into ambiguous prominence is a common denominator which all share, then it becomes a matter of some urgency to know how, in the face of two such radically different evaluations of this common denominator, any justice can possibly be done to it.

One may of course propose that a common method of organization does not necessarily predicate an identity of psychic content; that the pursuit of phenomenal transparency may be sane, creative, and responsible (a received idea of modern architecture); or that it may be deranged, capricious, and delinquent (a received idea of Mannerism); but, if this proposition is unacceptable, then we are faced with a serious critical dilemma.

The temptation is to escape it; and several attractive routes of escape do suggest themselves. Thus, we might, for instance:

1. choose to deny the existence of phenomenal transparency as a visual manifestation;

2. stigmatize the perception of phenomenal transparency as a product of hyperaesthetic sensitivity, or assert that its pursuit is no more than a formalistic side track of contemporary painting and architecture;

3. attribute a protomodernity to Michelangelo, Vignola, and the rest, or suggest that the contemporary architect who uses phenomenal transparency is Mannerist in spite of himself.

Escape route 1 is a congested road. Escape route 2 is a kind of spiritual *Autobahn* which permits its travelers the pleasing illusion that in some sequestered *cul de sac* Picasso, Braque, Gris, Léger, Mondrian, and Le Corbusier are all involved together in some esoterically purposeless rite. Escape route 3 drags us on a sinuous detour through a linguistically picturesque terrain. The use of the first we might condemn as irresponsible and myopic; the use of the second we might dismiss as philistine; while of the third we might say it is of no use. It is a kind of conquest of the problem by definition, that is, no conquest at all, for if we are at the liberty to attribute a protomodernity—or a deutero-Mannerism—to all and sundry, then we make nonsense of the notion of modernity and whimsically subvert the categories of history. With all these escape routes ultimately closed, the problem therefore remains unilluminated, unsolved—at least in its wider implications. However, in its narrowest implications the mere *existence of the problem* at least suggests that phenomenal transparency does have a basis in common vision, and does imply, on our part, some kind of archetypal response toward it.

In considering phenomenal transparency in this way, entirely at a perceptual level, it has not been possible to overlook gestalt psychology, since the gestalt psychologists, in their analysis of perception, seem to have been preoccupied with just those questions which are central to any examination of the problem. "Configuration," "figure-ground," "field," "common contour," "proximity," "constellation"—sometimes inadvertently and sometimes consciously our vocabulary has been saturated with the gestalt phraseology, precisely because of the adequacy of its terms. Quite briefly, the Algiers skyscraper, the Denver building, Caprarola, the nave of St. Denis, the Ca d'Oro, the Palazzo Mocenigo, San Lorenzo, *Victory Boogie Woogie* look like some elaborate orchestrations of the rather curious little diagrams which are to be found so profusely scattered through any treatise on gestalt;[9] and if in the presence of these diagrams we can overcome our primary amusement at what seems to be a discrepancy between a highly intellectual psychology of perception and its highly ingenuous visual examples, we might recognize these as exhibiting, in the most primitive form, the crucial circumstances which permit the development of the more complicated structures we have examined.

Thus, if we are not deterred by the combination of Art Nouveau and believe-it-or-not characteristics displayed by *figure 12,* it might be accepted as a representation of a basic figural ambiguity which has been consistently encountered. "Normally one sees a plain vase; it is only after a period of fixation that the profiles of two figures spring forth. What was once ground becomes figure and vice versa."[10] Similarly in *figure 13* identical conditions are induced. One sees a black Maltese cross imposed upon a white octagon; but, by reason of the spatial quality of the eight constituent triangles, one's experience of this diagram inevitably reverses itself.

The possibilities of such "transfiguration" are illustrated with rather more subtlety and perhaps with rather more direct architectural relevance in *figure 14.* In figure 14 a group of rectangles is presented, but "the figure may also be seen as two H's with certain intervening lines." These H's exist, but it is an effort to see them; and figure 14 in fact was set up by the gestaltists to prove precisely this—that in spite of the existence of the H's, "despite our extensive past experience of the letter H, it is nevertheless the articulation of the presented object (i.e., the rectangles) which determines what we shall see."[11]

But with certain minor modifications of figure 14 the coexistence of the H's and the rectangles can become quite explicit, so that in *figure 14a,* we are conscious of both. In figure 14a, by stripping off the top and bottom closures of the rectangles, the H-figures become completely exposed, but the rectangles themselves survive as unavoidable inferences which the observer constructs by reason of identical length, proximity, and similarity of their ingredient elements. Preoccupation with the rectangles in figure 14a leads to a fixation upon the four lines which constitute their horizontal axis; and, because of their identity of direction, ultimately these are seen as the visible parts of one continuous line which is presumed to pass behind a solid matter whose area concurs with that of the three rectangles. Thus, by reason of the breaking of this line, not only is an implication of depth introduced into a two-dimensional surface, but also the presumption as to the existence of the rectangles receives confirmation.

In *figure 14b,* a further modification of the same figure, all these activities become rather more manifest. In this diagram the behavior of the horizontal lines becomes much clearer. The observer is either disposed to see four horizontal lines each of which functions as the cross bar of an H and is therefore led to complete two further H-figures; or, alternatively, he is led to see one interrupted horizontal line which appears as a split running through the middle of a background plane; but, in each case, through an automatic interpretation of the presented object, he is led to provide it with a ground or to frame it within a field. Inside this field H's simultaneously function as the disengaging elements between dominant rectangles and also as the dominant figures themselves; while, as the observer's sensitiveness to the organization increases, it becomes apparent that the minor rectangles must also be built up and that further H-shaped figures with double vertical members must be accepted (*figure 14c*).

It is not necessary to say more in order to demonstrate the applicability of this last diagram to the facade of San Lorenzo or to that of the Algiers skyscraper; it is equally evident that the kind of perceptual activity which this diagram involves is of the same order as that which is exercised at a much higher level, with longer periods of fixation, in a painting by Léger or Mondrian; and in all these cases the figure-ground phenomenon which is exemplified may be said to be the essential prerequisite of transparency.

According to gestalt theory, while figure is generally seen as figure by reason of its greater closure, compactness, density, and internal articulation, and while ground is generally seen as ground by reason of its lack of these qualities, in the figure-ground relationship the ground, although it may at first appear anonymous, is neither subservient nor passive. As an environment imposing a common relationship on all that happens, it is also an enclosure containing figures which it lifts into prominence; and these, by reason of the prominence with which they become endowed, react upon the ground and provide it in turn with a figural significance. There is thus in figure-ground a double function inherent to each of the components. Each can be itself and its opposite; so that any specific instance of figure-ground is a condition of being of which the components are at once the product and the cause, a structure which becomes significant by reason of reciprocal action between the whole and its parts, and—one might say—an area of reference, qualified by and at the same time qualifying the objects which are referred to it.

In complicated examples of figure-ground such as those we have examined, the ground obviously contains several figures, and these in themselves also function as subsidiary grounds supporting further configurations. Gestalt theory maintains that the observer organizes these discrete visual stimuli according to certain laws, which are stated as factors of proximity, similarity, direction, closure, experience, "good curve," "good gestalt," "common fate," "objective set," and the untranslatable *Prägnanz*.[12] "Gestalt theory," it is stated, "does not hold that the senses carry amorphous material on which order is imposed by a receiving mind," but attributes powers of discrimination to the senses, refusing "to reserve the capacity of synthesis to the higher faculties of the human mind," and emphasizing instead "the formative powers . . . ," "the intelligence of the peripheral sensory processes."[13] In other words gestalt theory conceives the act of perception not as a simple stimulus-response reaction but as a process which might

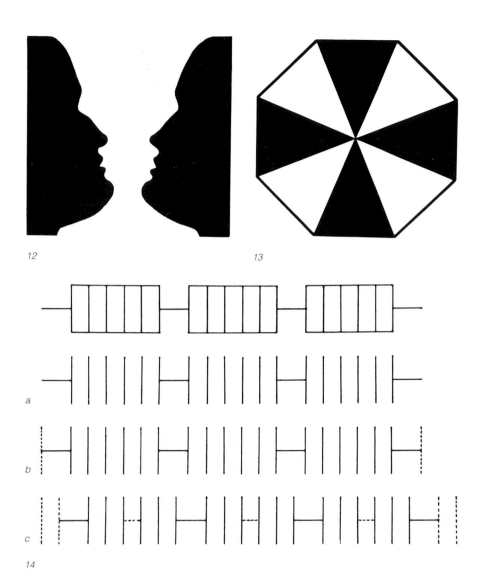

12

13

a

b

c

14

be characterized as follows: "constellation of stimuli—organization—reaction to results of organization."[14] Further, gestalt supposes that mental activity and organic behavior are subject to the same laws, "that 'good shape' is a quality of nature in general, inorganic as well as organic," so that "the processes of organization active in perception somehow do justice to the organization outside in the physical world."[15]

But supposing the senses are endowed with "intelligence," with powers of discrimination, with organizing capacity; and supposing physical and psychical processes to be governed by the same rule. In themselves these hypotheses really seem to have very little to do with what appears to be the inordinate gestalt interest in phenomenal transparency, which it recognizes under a variety of names as "phenomenal identity," "double representation," "duo- formation."[16] One is apt at first to consider this interest to be no more than a reflection of an intellectual style which has characterized the first half of the twentieth century, to regard it for instance as parallel to the critical literary interest in ambiguity disclosed by such studies as William Empson's *Seven Types of Ambiguity,* to the art-historical interest suggested by the reinterpretation of the sixteenth century, to the artistic interest implied by Analytical Cubism and so much of modern architecture. But although the preliminary gestalt researches into figural ambiguities do date from the years during which Analytical Cubism made of phenomenal transparency a principal method of composition, it must be recognized that something of the gestalt "taste" for figural ambiguities is related to the emphasis upon field.

For gestalt theory the existence of a field is a prerequisite of all perceptual experience. Consciousness of field, it is assumed, must precede consciousness of figure; and figure in itself is inconceivable in isolation. In this article attention has been directed toward visual fields alone, and gestalt theory does seem to have favored visual illustration of field; but obviously field as such must vary with the nature of the objects and/or perceptions involved. For instance, in the case of our apprehension of a tree the field may be provided by a mountain, or a lake, or the wall of a house, or any number of things; in the case of our apprehension of a poetic metaphor—in itself a field—the larger field may become a sonnet; in history a given epoch may endow with "field properties" the idiosyncrasies of the various figures which it supports. But in all these cases the field is assumed to be more than the sum total of the elements which it embraces. Genetically it is prior to them. It is the condition of their quality and the reason for their behavior.

It may now become possible to see that the gestalt interest in ambiguity is not merely arbitrary. The unstable, equivocal figure-ground phenomenon, whose fluctuations may be either sluggish or volatile, brings the supporting matrix, the field, into high prominence. Figure-ground is figure-field keyed up to a pitch of maximum contrast. It is field revealed as positive; and thus for gestalt it is the ultimate summary, the classic condensation of the field idea.

Notes

1.   Wilhelm Fuchs, *On Transparency,* in W. D. Ellis, *A Source Book of Gestalt Psychology* (London, 1938), p. 89.

2.   Gyorgy Kepes, *Language of Vision* (Chicago, 1944), p. 77.

3.   "Intervention of the plastic sensibilities. All seemed to be implacably controlled by the succession of rational requirements. . . . The plan was rigorously symmetric. But by a further tracing of the Golden mean the posture of the facade has become asymmetric. The form seems to swell to the left then shift to the right. It is responding to the double call of the site. The cliff, the sea." From Le Corbusier and François de Pierrefeu, *The Home of Man* (London, 1948), p. 129. It is in these terms that Le Corbusier describes the fluctuating figures which the Algiers skyscraper provides.

4.   Kepes, p. 77.

5.   It is interesting to notice that the facade of the Palazzo Mocenigo (a refacing of an older medieval structure), although symmetrical in all its parts, is not in itself symmetrical.

6.   The diamond is a result of a rotated square whose diagonals, formerly tending to be read as vectors inducing recessional perspective, now become an ideal right-angle armature stiffening that plane and investing the points, rather than the edges, with the capacity to act as terminals to the scanning eye. In this performance, a "gravity-free," buoyant, and thoroughly frontalized plane is established, exerting pressure from behind to any chromatic figuration placed upon it.

7.   Laszlo Moholy-Nagy, *Vision in Motion* (Chicago, 1947), p. 350. Kepes, p. 77.

8.   For these quotations see Nikolaus Pevsner, "The Architecture of Mannerism," in *The Mint* (1946), pp. 132, 136. They may be regarded as reasonably representative of a received idea.

9.   Kurt Koffka, *Principles of Gestalt Psychology* (New York, 1935); Wolfgang Kohler, *Gestalt Psychology* (New York, 1929); L. Hartmann, *Gestalt Psychology* (New York, 1935); Ellis, *A Source Book of Gestalt Psychology*.

10.   Hartmann, p. 25.

11.   Ellis, *A Source Book of Gestalt Psychology*, p. 58.

12.   See Max Wertheimer, "Laws of Organization in Perceptual Forms," in Ellis, p. 71.

13.   Rudolf Arnheim, "Gestalt and Art," in *Journal of Aesthetics and Art Criticism,* no. 8 (1943), p. 71.

14.   Hartmann, p. 100.

15.   Arnheim, p. 73.

16.   Phenomenal identity: Ellis, p. 147; double representation and duo formation: Koffka, p. 178.

1957

In an address to the Royal Institute of British Architects upon being awarded its annual Gold Medal, Sir **John Summerson** offered a compact theoretical formulation of modern architecture. What distinguished modern architecture from all its predecessors, according to Summerson, was its reliance on the *program* as a source of unity, whereas the preceding periods of architecture had taken formal imitation as their basis. Summerson defined program as "a description of the spatial dimensions, spatial relationships, and other physical conditions required for the convenient performance of specific conditions."

As Summerson himself was to note upon republishing the paper more than thirty years later, his argument represented a kind of last gasp of prewar English modernism. The latter was a period dominated by the MARS (Modern Architectural Research) Group, the English wing of CIAM founded in 1933 by the Canadian emigré architect and engineer Wells Coates. The group included Maxwell Fry, J. M. Richards, F. R. S. Yorke, Berthold Lubetkin (briefly), Denys Lasdun, Leslie Martin, the three principals of the firm of Connell, Ward and Lucas, the historian-critic P. Morton Shand, and other left-oriented London practitioners. They succeeded in bringing the continental modern movement to an eclectic and anemic English architectural scene, advancing a rational approach to aesthetics and construction and promoting the use of materials close to the industrial process. Although outside of several innovative houses and schools they realized only a small volume of built work in the 1930s, they effectively transformed the outlook of a generation of young British architects to the ethical ideal of (in Fry's words) "a comprehensive architecture for the use of a highly technical and reasonably integrated society."

During the war years a linear plan for London was published by a German emigré member of the MARS Group, Arthur Korn. Visionary in scope, it was decisively rejected in 1943 in favor of a traditional radiocentric plan by Patrick Abercrombie and John Henry Forshaw. After the war ended the group continued to exert a strong influence in the architecture offices of the county councils where towns, schools, and housing for the new welfare state were then being designed. At the same time, the objective aesthetic which Yorke had celebrated in *The Modern House in England* in 1937 began to look increasingly sterile. Richards, a founding member of the group, advocated a return to a quainter form of architecture in his book *Castles on the Ground* (1946) and together with his fellow editors in the pages of the *Architectural Review*. The Festival of Britain,

114–20

which was staged in 1951 on the centenary of the Crystal Palace and coincided with the MARS Group's hosting of CIAM's eighth meeting in Hoddesdon, further

135–36

relaxed the prewar rigorism. It remained for a new generation of architects to

181–83

deal the death blow. Peter and Alison Smithson, who joined the MARS Group in 1951 and presented their work under its name at CIAM 9 in Aix-en-Provence, finished by disbanding the group five years later.

The late 1950s were "the moment," as Summerson would write in hindsight, "when the thought of my generation—the MARS Group generation—lost touch with the real world." As such, a theory giving credence to architecture's ability to carry out social aims through rational means "was not the conclusion which history required." Despite its opacity to the ferments in English architecture by this date, though, Summerson's theory remains a register of the aspirations of a generation of architects and an insightful analysis of the vicissitudes of rationalism in the history of architectural ideas from Perrault through Le Corbusier.

From R.I.B.A. Journal, *June 1957, pp. 307–10. Republished in John Summerson,* The Unromantic Castle and Other Essays *(London: Thames and Hudson, 1990), pp. 257–66. Courtesy of the author.*

The Case for a Theory of Modern Architecture
John Summerson

Ever since the modern movement got onto its feet, questions have been asked about what it stands on. An association of some kind between what is vaguely called "theory" and what is vaguely called "modern architecture" continues, I believe, to be a topic frequently debated, and I am told that teachers in some of the schools feel a practical need for some sort of theoretical formula as a means of introducing students to the principles of modern design. Hence this paper, which offers nothing new but is simply an investigation—an attempt to discover whether there does exist any basis of principle applicable to modern architecture, different from the bases applicable to any other architecture, or alternatively whether such a basis can be abstracted out of prevailing practice and ideas.

I should like to take this alternative first because it offers an obvious *prima facie* case. I think it is a bad case but it is necessary to put it up in order to put it down. Modern architecture exists to the extent that there are plenty of buildings which everyone in this room would immediately classify as products of the modern movement on the basis of certain recurrent formal arrangements and relationships. Embarrassed as we are by the use of such expressions as "the modern style," "manner," or "idiom" there is positively no denying the consensus of characterization. Modern architecture is there all right. Furthermore, closely associated with this architecture are a number of ideas—ideas expressing modernity in one sense or another, nearly always either by analogy with the past or by analogy with some other activity than architecture. The architects who design the buildings tend to quote and promote these ideas and it would be very difficult to show that this complex of architecture and ideas is anything short of valid in relation to present-day conditions. There is indeed no other complex of forms and ideas which seriously rivals it. Now, in a situation like this, it may be argued, it should be possible to put together a theory of architecture without very much difficulty. It is simply a question of two rather prolonged exercises in analysis and synthesis. First, of assembling the ideas, examining their common trends of meaning, and reaching a series of general concepts. Second, of abstracting formal characteristics from a select repertory of modern buildings, eliminating merely modish elements, and providing a grammar of form. It would then only remain to illustrate how the forms embody the ideas. The whole exercise would, it may be supposed, add up to something like a Palladio of modern architecture, a pedagogical reference book not in any way restricting further development but consolidating the achievements of modern architecture, clarifying them and providing a departure platform for new experiments.

Such is the *prima facie* case for a specific theory of modern architecture. I have tried to make it sound plausible but of course it is hopelessly gimcrack. Only imagine for a moment the task of isolating characteristically modern forms from whole buildings. Only imagine the horror of stirring around in the rag-bag of aphorisms, platitudes, and fancy jargon and trying to determine their common trend and resultant meaning. The imagination boggles, and when it does that is a sure sign that something stupid is being attempted. So let us leave this whole enterprise and look for firmer ground on which to start our inquiry.

We had better consider first what is in our minds when we think about a "theory" of architecture. The elementary meaning is a conspectus of knowledge in any particular field. A theory of architecture may be, like many of the treatises of the eighteenth century, purely encyclopedic, without any explicit philosophical orientation at all. It may be, like Julien Guadet's famous work,[1] a series of discursive studies of types and elements, in lecture form, within a closed tradition whose validity is taken for granted. Or it may be of that curious kind represented by John Belcher's well-known book[2] of half a century ago in which a list of interesting words is compiled (scale, vitality, restraint, refinement, etc.), each providing the title for a short essay which gives it a glow of meaning, without ever reaching down to fundamental concepts at all.

But I suspect that what is in our minds when we talk about architectural theory now is something both less extensive and more profound than these—a statement of related ideas resting on a philosophical conception of the nature of architecture—in short, *principia*. Since Alberti wrote his *De Re Aedificatoria* in the middle of the fifteenth century there have been a certain number of statements of this kind, though not (when all derivatives are written off) quite as many as you might think and few, mercifully, as difficult to understand as Alberti. They are usually to be found lodged in some section of an encyclopedic work (e.g., Alberti, lib. ix) or forming introductions to a course of lectures (e.g., Durand) or, more rarely, as independent polemical essays (e.g., Laugier). It is worth emphasizing that to state the principles of architecture does not at any time take very many words. It is the demonstration by historical instance and the exposition of grammar which fill up the tomes. This evening my quest is for statements of root principle.

If we review the statements of principle which have attracted attention in the course of the last five hundred years we may be struck by the fact that they are much more easily related to each other than they are to the architecture prevailing at the time they are written; which suggests that just as architectural style has evolved from generation to generation, each changing the favored accentuation of the last, so architectural thought has developed phase by phase with its own dialectic. There has been, in fact, an evolving process in theory just as there has been in style, and the two processes have not made anything like the same pattern. Each has been and is in fact autonomous, to the extent that it would be possible to write a history or architectural theory without reference to a single actual building and even a history of architectural style without a single reference to architectural theory—though I am not suggesting that anybody should try.

The actual relationship of architectural theory to architectural production at any given time is problematic. It is perfectly possible for a new idea to be announced, cherished by one generation, turned upside down by the next, and only in a third to be validated in architectural designs. Something of the sort happened with the eighteenth-century idea of rational architecture, to which I shall refer later on. On the other hand it is possible for architectural style to be revolutionized without so much as one corollary gesture on the plane of theory. Who has ever had a more powerful effect on architecture than Michelangelo? Yet his effect on the theory of architecture was nil. So we must bear in mind about theory that it is a historical process with a life of its own in its own medium or words and that there is no question either of principles being abstracted wholly from practice or of practice being necessarily a reflection of theory. This makes a pretty big hole in the proposition called "a theory of modern architecture." But it brings us nearer to a realistic view of what we are discussing.

In the present century a fairly large number of books—I make it about 120—have been written about the nature and principles of architecture. Up to 1925 there was a modest issue of one book a year but in 1926 at least seven books (English, American, and French) appeared, though oddly enough not one of these recognized that any fundamental changes were taking place in architectural thought. The general tendency before 1927 was to rewrite the principles then stagnating in the Beaux-Arts tradition and to comment on them in essay style, but I do not know of a single book which investigated those principles historically or attempted to evaluate them philosophically (there is one outstanding exception which I will mention in a moment). After 1927 books stating the modern point of view began to appear. Between that year and the present there have been statements from Behrendt, Lurçat, Taut, Cheney, Platz, Hitchcock, Duncan, Gropius, Moholy-Nagy, Teague, Giedion, Fry, Saarinen, and Zevi, to mention only some of those who have produced books; to collect the statements appearing in the form of papers, articles, and catalogue introductions would be a mighty exercise in bibliography. The general character of all this writing is enthusiastic and propagandist. The authors tend to start with a belief in the new architecture and to write around their beliefs supporting them by picturesque and forceful analogies. Only rarely does one detect a realization that architectural thought is a continuing activity *sui generis* in which what is new must be distinguished by criticism of the past. But there are a few books of great penetration and to some of these we must now pay attention.

I suppose nobody will doubt that Le Corbusier's *Vers une architecture*[3] has been the most consequential book on architecture written in this century. Published thirty-four years ago, it is still widely quoted and quite frequently read. It is not and does not claim to be a theory of architecture. It is a series of critical essays, reprinted in the order in which they first appeared in *L'Esprit Nouveau,* starting in October 1920. In the whole course of these essays nothing absolutely new is proposed in the way of architectural principle, but a great deal that had been forgotten is brought into the light of the present and exhibited with a quite uncommon flair for paradox. I think it would not be an unfair generalization to describe *Vers une architecture* as a critique of the French rational tradition—a critique marking a new phase in that always vigorous and controversial zigzag of thought. This French rational tradition is not, of course, the Beaux-Arts tradition personified in Guadet, for which Le Corbusier expresses a good deal of contempt. It is, on the contrary, the tradition first of Jesuit intellectuals in the early eighteenth century, later of rebels and academy haters, and indeed "tradition," which suggests a handing down of embalmed principle, is not at all the right word. It is a historical process advancing by a series of contradictions and reassessments, of which latter *Vers une architecture* is the most recent. As I am going to suggest that this rational process is still a vital element in the contemporary theoretical situation perhaps I may briefly explain what I understand it to be.

It all hinges on the ancient body of Mediterranean beliefs, restated by Alberti;[4] and the hinge occurs in the age of Descartes. One could date its origin rather pedantically from Perrault's critique of Vitruvius.[5] It is picked up in the eighteenth century by the Abbé Laugier[6] whose two essays were the standard statements for half a century. But in 1802 Laugier was attacked as a muddler by Durand[7] who presented his students at the Polytechnique with an altogether tougher and more materialistic case. So far, the argument had proceeded against a background of belief in classical antiquity, but then, fifty years later, Viollet-le-Duc[8] took up a new position, still rationalist but transposing the background from classical to medieval antiquity and purporting to show that the thirteenth century was the sole repository of rationalist principle. Viollet-le-Duc was, directly or indirectly, the inspiration of many of the pioneers of the modern movement: Berlage, Horta, and Perret among them.

This is, of course, a grotesque simplification indicating only some of the more obvious peaks in a great range of argument. Many more names should go in, not all of them French: there is Cordemoy;[9] there is the mysterious Venetian rigorist Lodoli[10] whose influence is hard to estimate because he never wrote anything down; there is Frézier,[11] the engineer; there is half-French Pugin.[12] Again in rough caricature, one could sketch the process like this. Perrault said antiquity is the thing and look how rational; Lodoli seems to have said rationalism is the thing, down with antiquity; Laugier said up with *primitive* antiquity, only source of the rational; Durand said down with Laugier, rationalization means economics; Pugin said down with antiquity, up with Gothic and look how rational; Viollet-le-Duc said up with Gothic, prototype of the rational. Eventually a voice is heard saying down with all the styles and if it's rationalism you want, up with grain elevators and look, how beautiful!

Well, now, in this process, which I take to be the main heritage of the modern theorist, there are certain essentials which hold their own throughout. At the bottom of it all is the axiom that architecture is an affair of simple geometric form—regular solids[13] and their elementary divisions. This is inherited from Italian tradition and has a peculiar history of its own, passing from the quasimedieval numerology of Alberti to the visual objectivity of the Cartesian world and on to the empathetic apprehensions of the revolutionary school of Boullée and Ledoux. In some form or another it is always there.

Then there is the rational issue whose course through the eighteenth and nineteenth centuries I have already sketched.

But there is also the question of antiquity and the measure of its authority and one very important thing about the whole rational process is that it tends to exclude antiquity as an *absolute* authority. However, antiquity was obstinately there all the time. Only the theorists who never designed anything, like Lodoli and Laugier, could be really tough about antiquity. Those who designed had, in one way or another, to admit it for the important reason that the forms of classical antiquity or (in the nineteenth century) medieval antiquity, provided something which is essential to the creative designer— a bulwark of certainty, of unarguable authority on which his understanding leans while his conception of the building as a whole, as a *unity,* takes shape. The most interesting, indeed the dominating question, in a search for the modern *principia* is: where, if not in antique forms, or some equivalent substitute, is the source of unity?

Le Corbusier provides no answer to this in *Vers une architecture.* There is no reason why he should. The book is really nothing but a lightly etched reminder ("Trois rappels" is the title of the first chapter) of the main content of the rational process and it contains few ideas which could not be traced back into the line from Perrault to Viollet-le-Duc.

Le Corbusier's designs, let me say in parenthesis, are a different thing altogether. I have already said that architectural theory and architectural style are things apart— each with its autonomous life, and this is nowhere more obvious than in the case of the author of *Vers une architecture.* His conception of theory is simply the solid intellectual platform, with foundations deep in the past, on which he stands to do something which has nothing to do with the past whatever. Le Corbusier has not reasoned himself into those architectural conceptions which have so profoundly influenced the expression of modern building. Nor is there any mystery about how they have come about, for it is by now an accepted fact of contemporary art history that Le Corbusier's vision in the early days was that of the modern painters—the school of Picasso, Braque, and Léger; that after they had discovered the power of converting the commonplace into pure conceptual painting, Le Corbusier discovered the power of composing the commonplaces and crude ingenuities of industrial building into equivalent architectural realities. But there is nothing in *Vers une architecture* about that; and if the pictures of the author's own works were eliminated from the book it might easily be construed as foreshadowing some frozen neoclassicism not far removed from that of Auguste Perret.

Obviously, the only thing about *Vers une architecture* which helps us to envisage a case for a specifically new theory of architecture is the reillumination of principles already established. If we were to argue from the example of Le Corbusier alone we might well conclude that the theoretical process stemming from antiquity and the age of reason was, in one form or another, the theory appropriate to the modern movement in architecture. That *may* indeed be the case. But we cannot leave the matter there for in another quarter altogether there have been theoretical inquiries of considerable importance and entirely different character. I am thinking of the sphere of thought represented by the Bauhaus.

Bauhaus thought has been pretty copiously manifested: in Gropius's own writings about Gropius and the Bauhaus and in the *Bauhausbücher* of the twenties. But for anything like a systematic exposition of the Bauhaus theory the most significant book is Moholy-Nagy's *The New Vision: From Material to Architecture,* based on lectures given at the Bauhaus in 1923–28. These lectures were given after *Vers une architecture* had been published but they owe nothing to it, nor to the Esprit Nouveau circle from which it emerged. Moholy, of course, was a totally different kind of person from Le Corbusier—he represents in a fundamental sense that phenomenon of our time, the displaced person. Le Corbusier's Swiss background was happy and stable. Moholy's Hungarian background was far otherwise and when Le Corbusier was building a luxury villa on Lake Geneva, Moholy was pitched into a hideous and incomprehensible war without even the consolation of being on the winning side.[14] It is not surprising that whereas Le Corbusier turns naturally to a reassessment of the past, Moholy turns back on it altogether. I do not know how conscious he was of turning his back on Le Corbusier but his book is in some respects a negation of *Vers une architecture*. Admittedly he states what he calls the "basic law" of design as the obligation "to build up each piece of work solely from the elements which are required for its function,"[15] a statement which is the genuine old-style rationalist article (it could well be a quotation from Laugier), but he then instantly declares that the basic law has limitations and he proceeds to search for an ultimate authority.

This ultimate authority is of course likely to be the source of unity of which I have already spoken. It is the *something* occupying the place which used to be filled by "antiquity." What is it? Moholy says it is "biological." The artist's freedom, he says, is "in the last analysis determined biologically." The words "biological," "biologically" crop up again and again throughout the book. "Architecture," he says, "will be understood . . . as a governable creation for mastery of life, as an organic component in living." "The standard for architects . . . will revolve around the general basis, that of the biologically evolved manner of living which man requires." And, finally, "architecture will be brought to its fullest realization only when the deepest knowledge of human 'life as a total phenomenon in the biological whole is available."[16]

This preoccupation with biology and with the organic is obviously a very important issue in our investigation. The word "organic" especially has had an almost magical significance for architectural writers ever since Louis Sullivan wrote of it fifty odd years ago as "a word I love because I love the sense of life it stands for, the ten-fingered grasp of things it implies."[17] That is not a very scientific statement but I have not yet found, among the many writings about organic architecture, any statement that is. Yet it is constantly used as an ultimate, as if organic values (whatever they may be) were absolute values.

Moholy's treatment of the biological idea is more interesting than most since he presses it harder and, in doing so, shows, in one direction, its perilous inefficiency. When he declares that the artist's freedom is "in the last analysis determined biologically" he leads us surely to a determinism which begs the whole question. Moholy would like to construct a theory which is a perfect description of practice—which coincides with practice. He cuts himself off from inherited theory and postulates a new theory which would fit the biological (let us say pyschophysical) needs of man like a glove. I suppose, if the most far-reaching implications of cybernetics were realized, if the artist's functions were at last to be explicable in mechanistic terms, some such theory might be arrived at. But that is such an awfully long way off that it is hardly worth considering in relation to the modern movement now in course of evolution; and in any case I doubt if anybody yet sees the determination of the artistic needs of society as even a remotely possible point on the scientific horizon. Notwithstanding the fine perceptions and immensely valuable practical suggestions contained in Moholy's book, it seems to me that his insistence on the biological is a premature and purely verbal closure of the subject of modern architectural theory. It gives nothing to hold onto but this elusive myth of "biological" finality.

Those who have written about "organic" architecture have usually gone in a rather different direction from Moholy's. Frank Lloyd Wright's use of the expression "organic architecture" is generally considered to be his own emotional tag for all fine, free, and humane architecture, but especially for that of Frank Lloyd Wright. Behrendt, Steinmetz, Saarinen, and others have speculated on the "organic" in desultory philosophizings. Bruno Zevi has investigated various recent uses of the word and in his book, *Towards an Organic Architecture,* devotes a whole chapter to "the meaning and scope of the term organic in reference to architecture." He does not discover any evidence of strikingly profound thought on the subject nor does he commit himself to any precise meaning. But he does write off various spurious or outmoded interpretations and, at the end of his study, he does, in a single, rather casual remark, hit what I conceive to be the nail exactly on the head. He says that the organic conception of architecture is based "on a social idea and not on a figurative (I take it he means formal) idea."[18] That rather wide interpretation would, I suspect, command almost universal agreement.

Zevi throws out his comment as if its truth was pretty obvious and I suppose it is, but I want to underline the proposition and see how it relates to the picture of the developing theoretical process which I have outlined. I suggested a few moments ago that although the rationalist writers of the eighteenth and nineteenth centuries tended to exclude antiquity as the ultimate authority, antiquity remained insistently there as the *source of unity,* the focus at which the architectural design was realized. Where, I asked, if not in antique forms, can the source of unity lie? Zevi's remark points to the answer. The source of unity in modern architecture is in the social sphere, in other words in the architect's program.

From the antique (a world of form) to the program (a local fragment of social pattern): this suggests a swing in the architect's psychological orientation almost too violent to be credible. Yet, in theory at least, it has come about; and how it has come about could very well be demonstrated historically. First the rationalist attack on the authority of the antique; then the displacement of the classical antique by the medieval; then the introduction into medievalist authority of purely social factors (Ruskin); then the evaluation of purely vernacular architectures because of their social realism (Morris); and finally the concentration of interest on the social factors themselves and the conception of the architect's program as the source of unity—the source not precisely of forms but of adumbrations of forms of undeniable validity. The program as the source of unity is, so far as I can see, the one new principle involved in modern architecture. It seems to be the principle which can be discerned through the cloud of half-truths, aperçus, and analogies which is the theoretical effluent—not a very nice word, I'm afraid—of the modern movement.

Whether you accept this statement as a basic principle and a specifically modern principle depends upon a number of things. Mainly, there is the question, what a "program" is. A program is a description of the spatial dimensions, spatial relationships, and other physical conditions required for the convenient performance of specific functions. It is probably impossible to write out a satisfactory program without a certain number of architectural relationships being suggested on the way and the character of these relationships may well be something different from the relationships in a predetermined stylistic discipline. The chief difference is that they involve a process in time. It is difficult to imagine any program in which there is not some rhythmically repetitive pattern—whether it is a manufacturing process, the curriculum of a school, the domestic routine of a house, or simply the sense of repeated movement in a circulation system. Of course, this pattern does not dictate a corresponding pattern in the architect's plan or anything crude like that , but it does sanction relationships which are different from those sanctioned by the static, axially grouped dominants and subordinates of the classical tradition—different, but carrying an equivalent authority. The resultant unity can, I think, quite reasonably be described as a biological or organic unity, because it is the unity of a process. Moholy-Nagy[19] and after him Giedion[20] would see it as a space-time unity, and you will recall Giedion's brilliant analogies between modern architecture and the concepts of modern physics on the one hand and the Picasso revolution in modern painting (involving the concept of simultaneity) on the other. Not that such analogies prove anything; and there is always the danger that they may seem to prove far too much; they are phantasms of the Zeitgeist. The actual reason why the principle embodied here is new is this. It is only in the past half-century or so that the program has ceased to be evaluated merely quantitatively and has come to be evaluated qualitatively. This has to do with the fact that programs have become more complex, more challenging, and therefore more susceptible to qualitative generalization and evaluation. It has also to do with very much wider issues involved in the social revolutions and reorientations of our time.

If we accept this principle—unity deriving from the program—as truly a basic principle of modern architecture, how does it look when lined up with the inherited principles which we found that Le Corbusier had reilluminated in Vers une architecture? Here comes the crux of the whole matter. The conceptions which arise from a preoccupation with program have got, at some point, to crystallize into a final form and by the time the architect reaches that point he has to bring to his conception a weight of judgment, a sense of authority and conviction which clinches the whole design, causes the impending relationships to close into a visually comprehensible whole. He may have extracted from the program a set of interdependent relationships adding up to a unity of the biological kind, but he still has to face up to the ordering of a vast number of variables, and how he does this is a question. There is no common theoretical agreement as to what happens or should happen at that point. There is a hiatus. One may even be justified in speaking of a "missing architectural language." Gropius[21] has stated the difficulty as the lack of an "optical 'key' . . . as an objective common denominator of design"—something which would provide "the impersonal basis as a prerequisite for general understanding," which would serve "as the controlling agent within the creative act." That is a precise description of the functions served by antiquity in the classical centuries! The dilemma is really an enlargement of the flaw already apparent in mid-eighteenth-century theory—the flaw that while antiquity was eliminated as an absolute, nothing was introduced which took its place as a universally accredited language of architectural form.

The flaw seems now to have widened into a veritable dilemma. Can it be resolved? Well, I can think of two possible approaches to its resolution. The first involves an extension of the rationalist principle into the sphere of engineering, and the second involves a reconsideration of the geometrical basis and limitations of architecture.

Let us take the engineering question. The engineer is the heir to the basic tenet of the old rationalism—economy of means in construction. So long as traditional methods prevailed the architect could keep his eye on the ball, or at least persuade himself that he was doing so; but with the development of the science of the strength of materials and the application of mathematics to design he was rapidly overpassed by the engineer. The engineer ran away with the rationalist ball. It is no use pretending that we can lop off this issue as a stray limb of the rationalist process which has got outside the scope of architecture, because if we let the rationalist principle go modern theory collapses in a heap. No. It is necessary to declare that no theory of modern architecture can be logically complete which does not postulate the collaboration, immediate or remote, of architect and engineer; and here collaboration must stand for the design of components in factories as well as the personal achievements of a Nervi or a Candela.

But let us be clear about what the engineer's role really is and how different it is from that of the architect. For the architect, the source of unity for his design is, I have suggested, the program. The engineer seeks unity in another way and another direction altogether. He seeks it within one component—even if it is a very complex component comprising the whole sectional trace of a large building. And it is a unity of interdependent calculable issues adding up to a total whose criterion is performance. His search for finality and the architect's are as wide apart as they can be. It would be altogether too facile to suggest that they are even complementary. Nevertheless, a whole view of architecture must necessarily extend to this latest metamorphosis of the rationalist process in the hands of the engineer.

The idea can be and sometimes is upheld that the engineer, as a result of his enforcement of the rationalist principle, invents forms and formal arrangements which the architect then absorbs into his vocabulary of expression and uses, sometimes in a strictly engineering way—and sometimes not.[22] This certainly happens. But the engineer is concerned strictly with components and although he may contribute significant inventions he cannot contribute a continuously related system of inventions —i.e., a language.

Thus the engineering issue does not wholly resolve the dilemma of modern architectural theory, and so we turn to the ancient axiom that architecture is fundamentally concerned with the regular solids and simple ratios. It is getting to have an old-fashioned look, this axiom, especially in an age which has discovered geometries other than Euclidean. Moholy-Nagy was eager to go behind the axiom to "biological assumptions." Mr. Banham, in a recent article,[23] has offered us the attractive red herring (I think it's a herring) of topology. In the field of practice, unfamiliar and complex forms are cropping up. Candela has built a concrete church in which all the surfaces are hyperbolic paraboloids. But surely the axiom stands as an overall absolute necessity. Even if plans wriggle in the wildest of "free" curves, even if engineering science introduces forms of great precision but visually unreadable complexity, we shall always seek to read through the complex to the simple, to seek the assurance of those simplicities which must be implied even when they are not stated. Very well. On this principle of geometrical absolutes it is possible to erect systems or disciplines to guide the architect toward that final ordering of form which he must achieve. Of these systems the most celebrated is Le Corbusier's Modulor. But the Modulor, like any other apparatus of the kind, is a system of control, not of expression (Le Corbusier says this as clearly as it could be said). It is not a language. And if I say that in my opinion the erection of proportional disciplines—purely intellectual contrivances—does bring the *principia* of modern theory into satisfactory relationship to each other and to actuality, it may well be objected that this theory excludes almost everything that has been most valued in the art of architecture as a means of expression in the past three thousand years. In answer to that, I have two things to say. The first is that if you accept the principle that the program is the source of unity, the crucible of the architect's creative endeavor, you cannot postulate another principle, another crucible, at the other end of the designing process to satisfy the architect's craving for conspicuous self-expression. You cannot have it both ways. You certainly cannot have two sources of unity. Either the program is or it is not the source. It is part of my case for a theory of modern architecture that it is the source. If you do not accept this case, I think you must consider whether, after all, architectural theory does not stand very much where it stood in 1920, or 1800, or even 1750, and whether the position of an architect who is concerned about expression or style is not that of a man feeling his way back to classicism or neoclassicism, or, to put the finest possible point on it, crypto-neoclassicism.

The second thing that I would say is that it is quite possible that the missing language will remain missing, and that in fact the slightly uncomfortable feeling which some of us have that it ought to exist is nothing but the scar left in the mind by the violent swing which has taken place in the lifetime of one generation from an old order of principles to a new.

I have tried to demonstrate that in the light of all that has been written on architecture in the past thirty years a specifically modern theory of architecture does exist, and that it exists not as an arbitrary invention of our time but as a new stage in the long evolution of theory since those forgotten men whom even Vitruvius knew as the Ancients. Modern theory is part of the history of ideas. It is, I believe, only as the history of ideas that it can be taught. The main thing is to get that history right and to get it clear. It would be an outrageous assumption on my part that I have done either this evening, and I have certainly been more speculative than historical. I have presented what I feel may prove to be an exceedingly vulnerable thesis. I thank you for listening to me with such patience.

Notes

1. J. Guadet, *Eléments et théorie de l'architecture* (5th ed., 1909).

2. J. Belcher, *Essentials in Architecture* (1907).

3. Le Corbusier, *Vers une architecture* (1st ed., 1923). Trans. as *Towards a New Architecture* (1927 and 1946).

4. The *De Re Aedificatoria* was written about 1450. The standard English translation is that of G. Leoni (1726 and 1739); it is available in a reprint (ed. J. Rykwert, 1955).

5. C. Perrault, *Les Dix Livres d'architecture de Vitruve* (1673), bk. V, chap. i (note 1) and bk. VI, chap. v (note 8). These references are quoted by F. Algarotti, *Saggio sopre l'architettura* (vol. 3 in the *Opere,* 1791) as predictions of the rationalist attitude.

6. M. A. Laugier, *Essai sur l'architecture* (1753) and *Observations sur l'architecture* (1765).

7. J. N. L. Durand, *Précis des leçons données à l'Ecole Polytechnique* (1802).

8. E. Viollet-le-Duc, *Entretiens sur l'architecture* (1863–72).

9. De Cordemoy, *Nouveau traité de toute l'architecture* (1714).

10. For Lodoli see E. Kaufmann, *Architecture in the Age of Reason* (1955), pp. 95–99.

11. Frézier, *Dissertation sur les ordres d'architecture* (1738).

12. *The True Principles of Pointed or Christian Architecture* (1841) is a plea for Gothic as a rational style.

13. Dr. J. Bronowski warns me that "regular solids" in a strict sense includes figures never regarded as basic to architecture and excludes others which are. Time forbids reconsideration but, with this warning, my meaning will not, I think, be misunderstood.

14. For biographies of Le Corbusier and Moholy-Nagy, see M. Gauthier, *Le Corbusier, ou l'architecture au service de l'homme* (1944), and S. Moholy-Nagy, *Moholy-Nagy: Experiment in Totality* (1950).

15. *The New Vision,* p. 54.

16. Ibid., pp. 159–60.

17. *Kindergarten Chats* (1947). Elsewhere (p. 47) Sullivan uses "organic" to mean "the part must have the same quality as the whole," an idea which goes back to Alberti.

18. B. Zevi, *Towards an Organic Architecture* (1950), p. 76.

19. *The New Vision,* p. 163.

20. *Space, Time and Architecture* (3rd ed., 1954), p. 432.

21. *Scope of Total Architecture* (1956), p. 49.

22. For a discussion of this point by an engineer, see Ove Arup, "Modern Architecture: The Structural Fallacy," in *The Listener,* 7 July 1955.

23. "The New Brutalism," in *Architectural Review,* December 1955.

1957

The Arcimboldo-like head that appeared on the cover of *Architectural Review* in May 1957 was a collage made by the artist **John McHale** for a special issue entitled "Machine Made America." Seven years earlier (December 1950) the *Review* had published an issue of similar title, "Man Made America," that was "a record of sprawl and visual squalor." The later publication, as the editors noted, told a different story: "a success story—the story of how America is adding sheer quantity to the preexisting qualities of modern architecture. In terms of quantity, the U.S. is now the homeland of the modern movement, and quantity, backed by wealth, industry, and technical skill, is the prerequisite of architectural quality today. The volume of American building has quadrupled in a decade, and in its wake two generations of architects have experienced a surge of creative ability, while industry has responded, in barely half a decade, with the industrialization of the curtain wall. Beyond the sheer bulk of building now in hand, other causes for these radically new developments include the presence of some of the great European masters and the increasing influence of brilliant structural engineers. U.S. architecture has shown remarkable humility in learning lessons and accepting masters from wherever they come, and it has benefited enormously from both."

The British enthusiasm for America in these years was significantly stimulated by the activities of a group of artists, architects, and critics who gathered in 1952 as a critical voice within the new Institute of Contemporary Arts in London. Calling themselves the Independent Group (IG), the members shared an antagonism to the English high art establishment and an optimistic attitude toward popular culture, contemporary technology, mass media, and all things American. Meeting informally and under the Institute's auspices over the next five years, they debated the issues of the day—from Buckminster Fuller and Ronchamp to advertising, product design, fashion, Hollywood films, Detroit cars, jazz, and science fiction— and played a major role, either individually or together, in a series of notable exhibitions. Reyner Banham, who became an editor of the *Architectural Review* in the mid-1950s, was initially the group's prime mover. This role was subsequently assumed by the art critic Lawrence Alloway together with McHale. Among the architects frequenting IG circles were Peter and Alison Smithson, Colin St. John Wilson, Geoffrey Holroyd, James Stirling, Sam Stevens, and Peter Carter. Theo Crosby, an architect and the editor of *Architectural Design,* though not a member, was closely allied. The artist contingent comprised, besides McHale, Richard Hamilton, Eduardo Paolozzi, Nigel Henderson, Magda Cordell, and William Turnbull, the designer and critic Toni del Renzio, and the musician Frank Cordell.

The most sensational exhibition in which IG members had a hand was a show called "This Is Tomorrow" held at the Whitechapel Art Gallery in August 1956. It consisted of the work of twelve autonomous groups composed of IG members and others, each allotted a separate space. The resulting installation, seen by nearly 1,000 people a day, was, in Alloway's words, "a jumble of the present environment." Among the offerings of archaic utopias, semiological research, organic sculpture, space-frame structures, and other prognostications of future environments, the *tour de force* was a collaboration by McHale, Hamilton, and the architect John Voelker. It combined a fun house with an environment of sensory stimuli, optical illusions, and popular culture imagery. A central figure was a fourteen-foot-high cutout of Robby the Robot from the recently released American film *Forbidden Planet.* "Robots, mutants, and mechanomorphs furnish an image in the likeness of man which carries the strongest sense of wonder with a hint of dread," McHale was to write in an essay of 1959 called "The Expendable Ikon." McHale supplied many of the collage materials used for the installation, having made a collection of American glossy magazines during a sojourn in the United States in 1955. Hamilton, drawing on similar imagery, produced his famous collage of fetishized domesticity and bad taste, *What Is It That Makes Today's Homes So Different, So Appealing?* Printed in the catalogue and as a poster, it quickly became a pop-culture emblem.

The occasion for McHale's trip to America in 1955 had been, ironically, a fellowship to study color theory with former Bauhaus master Josef Albers at Yale. Instead, the trip confirmed his fascination with mass culture and industrial technology.

86–92 In the 1960s he moved permanently to the United States, having become a major proponent of the ideas of Buckminster Fuller, on whom he published a book in 1962. Among his later writings is a book of 1969 on world resources and space-age technology, *The Future of the Future.*

Meanwhile, the IG's legacy to the evolving architectural debate of the 1950s— *240–41, 370–78* closely bound up with contemporary polemics by the Smithsons and Banham *365–69, 389–91* over the New Brutalism, and anticipating the impact of Pop in the 1960s from Archigram to the Venturis—amounted to a vivid creative engagement with the products of industry and everyday life. While the group's preoccupations reflected the whetted appetites of an incipient consumer culture eager to leave behind the privations of wartime austerity, its activities also helped to demystify a puritanical and obsolescent modernism. For recent documentation on the IG milieu, see the catalogue edited by David Robbins, *The Independent Group: Postwar Britain and* *80–85* *the Aesthetics of Plenty* (1990). The European romance with the United States that had been rekindled in the aftermath of America's victory in the Second World War continued, during the period of the Cold War, to be based on an identification of technology with freedom.

From Architectural Review, *May 1957, cover. Courtesy of Magda Cordell McHale.*

Machine Made America
John McHale

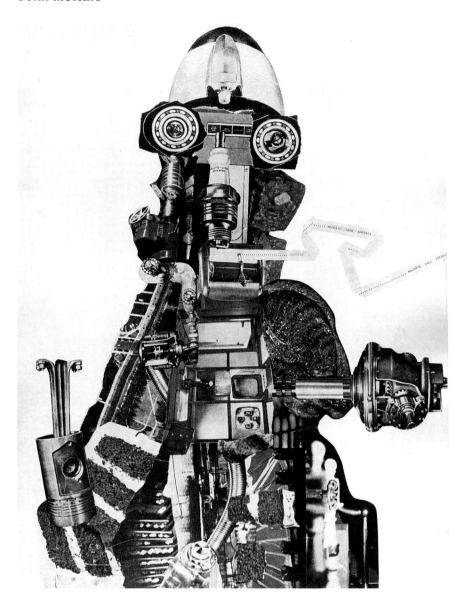

The cover personage, by John McHale, with the tetragram of power—Neutral, Drive, Low, Reverse—graven on its heart, was assembled from typical fragments of the cultural complex that he also symbolizes, Machine Made America. The source of material was one of America's favorite flattering mirrors, colored magazine illustrations, and reflects a world of infragrilled steak, premixed cake, dream kitchens, dream cars, machine tools, power mixers, parkways, harbors, tickertape, sparkplugs, and electronics.

1957

The term "New Brutalism" was first used in print in the December 1953 issue of *Architectural Design* in a statement accompanying **Alison and Peter Smithson**'s Soho House project. Drafted by Alison Smithson, it read, "It was decided to have no finishes at all internally, the building being a combination of shelter and environment. Bare brick, concrete, and wood . . . had this been built, it would have been the first exponent of the New Brutalism in England." According to their account, the Smithsons coined the term as an allusion—partly tongue in cheek—to the *béton brut* of Le Corbusier's Unité d'Habitation in Marseilles, attacked by a French official when under construction (and translated in an English newspaper) as "brutal," and also as a parody of the *Architectural Review's* penchant for baptizing neophyte tendencies (New Empiricism, New Humanism). But the idea was also bound up with the Smithsons' other major

181–83, 347–60
237–39

involvements of the 1950s: among them, the social-anthropological interests of Team 10, the Independent Group's preoccupations with spontaneous, nonformal sources of design, and the vitalist aesthetics of *art brut* as reinterpreted by artists like Jean Dubuffet and fellow Independent Group member Eduardo Paolozzi.

Like other architects of their generation—those who, as Reyner Banham put it, "interrupted their architectural training to fight a war to make the world safe for the modern movement"—the Smithsons fiercely rejected the sentimentalism of the welfare-state culture promoted in Britain in the late 1940s and early 1950s. Their first major realization, the Hunstanton school in Norfolk of 1949–54, flirted with another "ism," the New Palladianism that followed Rudolf Wittkower's *Architectural Principles in the Age of Humanism* (the building was in fact more Miesian than Palladian). Afterward they adverted, at least rhetorically, to a less academic, more "direct" approach. The powerful image of the Marseilles block, which dominated the architectural imagination during this period, elicited the Smithsons' admiration but also their criticism for its isolation from "patterns of human association" and incapacity for "growth and change." This critique was mounted at CIAM's congress in Aix-en-Provence in 1953 in a study grille entitled "Urban Reidentification." Displaying their Golden Lane housing project of 1952 with its street-decks in the air and Nigel Henderson's photographs of East London's slums, it helped to define the New Brutalism's iconographic repertory. An exhibition in London the same year, "Parallel of Art and Life," staged with Henderson and Paolozzi, further explored the as-found approach to materials and artifacts and stressed an "ethical" rather than aesthetic basis. Over the course of the 1950s the Smithsons sought to synthesize the brutalist idea out of sources ranging from Le Corbusier's Jaoul houses and Alvar Aalto's Baker dormitory at M.I.T. to Antonin Raymond's *Readers' Digest* building in Japan and

270–72

work by Louis Kahn. But the paucity of their own realized buildings made it difficult to test. The nitty-gritty of urban life abstracted in projects like Golden Lane and the "topologically" turned slab skewered by an elongated circulation tube in the Sheffield University competition of 1953 did not lack polemical force, but failed to substantiate their claims for the invention of a new way of life.

For a history of the polemics and influences surrounding this tendency by one of its original protagonists, Banham's essay in *Architectural Review*, December 1955, and his later book, *The New Brutalism: Ethic or Aesthetic* (1966), are indispensable. Banham himself would pursue an approach to

370–78

technology rooted less in anthropology than futurism after the mid-1950s. The following statement by the Smithsons, a reply to an "anonymous" panel discussion on the New Brutalism published in the same issue of *Architectural Design*, is a concise summary of their position at this date.

From Architectural Design, *April 1957, p. 113. Courtesy of the authors*

The New Brutalism
Alison and Peter Smithson

If Academicism can be defined as yesterday's answers to today's problems, then obviously the objectives and aesthetic techniques of a real architecture (or a real art) must be in constant change. In the immediate postwar period it seemed important to show that architecture was still possible, and we determined to set against loose planning and form—abdication, a compact disciplined, architecture.

Simple objectives once achieved change the situation, and the techniques used to achieve them become useless.

So new objectives are established.

From individual buildings, disciplined on the whole by classical aesthetic techniques, we moved on to an examination of the whole problem of human associations and the relationship that building and community has to them. From this study has grown a completely new attitude and a nonclassical aesthetic.

Any discussion of Brutalism will miss the point if it does not take into account Brutalism's attempt to be objective about "reality"—the cultural objectives of society, its urges, its techniques, and so on. Brutalism tries to face up to a mass-produced society, and drag a rough poetry out of the confused and powerful forces which are at work.

Up to now Brutalism has been discussed stylistically, whereas its essence is ethical.

1957

In the mid-1950s the English architect **James Stirling** published two influential essays in the *Architectural Review* on Le Corbusier's postwar work. The first was titled "From Garches to Jaoul: Le Corbusier's Domestic Architecture in 1927 and 1953" (November 1955). Here Stirling defined what he felt was a complete break between Le Corbusier's pre- and postwar architecture, expressing guarded admiration for the "sheer plastic virtuosity" of the two Jaoul houses recently built outside Paris. However, he objected to their technical regressiveness ("with the exception of glass no synthetic materials are being used; technologically they make no advance on medieval building") and concluded—in an echo of John

226–36 Summerson—by faulting their lack of a programmatic theory: "It is disturbing to find little reference to the rational principles which are the basis of the modern movement." In the second essay, "Ronchamp: Le Corbusier's Chapel and the Crisis of Rationalism" (March 1956), Stirling took the same tack, pointing out that although the church simulated the plasticity of poured concrete it was in fact constructed out of weight-bearing masonry. He also noted the references to vernacular sources. He ended by comparing Le Corbusier's late work to Mannerist architecture—a parallel indebted to a seminal essay by his mentor Colin Rowe, "Mannerism and Modern Architecture," published in 1950.

Stirling's reservations about the direction Le Corbusier's work was taking are revealing in terms of his own development. As he would write years later, "My own ambivalence was evident in the articles I published at the time. Since I had been drawing on Le Corbusier's work of the 1920s and 1930s . . . I was disoriented by his new direction, though it soon became important in my work. To most of us Le Corbusier seemed richer and more interesting than Mies, who had been the key figure slightly earlier. Le Corbusier could be tied in with popular culture more easily, and even his modular system, which was widely discussed after his book was translated, seemed to have an integrative potential that was lacking in Miesian grids."

An inheritor of the "functional tradition" brought to England by the MARS Group, Stirling had graduated from Liverpool School of Architecture, where he

205–25 had been Rowe's student, and was at the time of the writing that follows teaching at the Architectural Association in London. In 1954 a first commission for a low-cost housing project, Ham Common, enabled him to open his own practice in partnership with James Gowan. Also part of the Independent Group in these

237–39 years, he joined the architecture contingent there in discussions registering the impact of Le Corbusier's new work and shared their appreciation for American technology and culture. In the 1956 exhibition *This Is Tomorrow* he collaborated on an installation that turned photographs of soap bubbles into environmental sculpture. Stirling's struggle to come to terms with the new architectural climate under the combined pressures of Le Corbusier's "brutalist" poetics, the impact of popular culture, and the relative backwardness of British technology (compared to American) would come to fruition in 1959 with his highly original synthesis for Leicester Engineering Building, completed with Gowan in 1964.

In the following essay Stirling declares, "Today Stonehenge is more significant than the architecture of Sir Christopher Wren." A survey of the dominant British tendencies of the day, it continues the running debate on

107–9 regionalism rekindled in the 1940s. Stirling's conflicted response—a sense of betrayal of the modern movement's original program but openmindedness to the new developments—is the preparation for not only the breakthrough of Leicester, but his embrace in the 1970s of (as Rowe would say of Stirling's Staatsgalerie addition in Stuttgart) "an opportune and intelligent eclecticism."

From Architects' Year Book *7 (1957), pp. 62–68. Courtesy of the author.*

Regionalism and Modern Architecture
James Stirling

In postwar Britain, two styles or minor movements have emerged from the schools of architecture in addition to the eclecticism that is normal to them. The first style, which probably reached its peak about 1950–54, has been termed "neo-Palladian" in deference to Professor Wittkower's *Architectural Principles in the Age of Humanism,* published in 1949. The usual asymmetry of modern architecture was reconsidered and axially conceived schemes became more common. Various proportional systems were applied, in part due to the influence of Le Corbusier's publication, *Le Modulor.* The expression of this style is closely related to the "use of materials," and designs in steel or brick are frequently derivative of Mies van der Rohe, those in concrete or stone of Le Corbusier. It would appear that this style is in decline in some of the schools, although it is to be expected that the students of these postwar years may eventually build in this manner. This trend finds a parallel in the U.S.A. where the interval between qualifying and building is apparently shorter. The work of Johnson, Rudolph, and others might loosely be considered neo-Palladian.

The more recent trend in many ways is a reaction from the former and could be considered approximately a reassessment of indigenous and usually anonymous building and a revaluation of the experience embodied in the use of traditional methods and materials.[1] Le Corbusier's assimilation of Mediterranean domestic and native Indian architecture into his most recent buildings is symptomatic of this new manner. The most visually stimulating chapters of Kidder Smith's recent book *Italy Builds* were not those on Italian Modern and Italian Renaissance but that on the anonymous architecture of Italy.

Today Stonehenge is more significant than the architecture of Sir Christopher Wren.

Whereas the former movement was primarily an aesthetic one, the latter can advance considerable arguments with respect to economy, practicability, and policy, not least of which is the assumption that authorities will be more inclined to grant aesthetic approval to such design rather than to "modern." The MARS Group's contribution to CIAM X[2] was a most consistent example of this indigenous trend, but it is significant that this group was entirely concerned with low-cost housing.

Immediately after the war, much of the thinking about and some of the attempts at solving the problems of housing were in terms of prefabrication and mass production. This rational approach no longer appears acceptable either at an aesthetic or at a practical level, and creative thinking is now mainly directed toward the utilization of existing building methods and labor forces. This exploitation of local materials and methods is perhaps the only alternative to the conventional or the "contemporary" which is left open to the European architect when he is confronted with a minimum budget. The building industry of this country cannot subscribe to "modernism" in the design of a "one-off" house. It is significant that the new traditionalism is mainly confined to Europe, except Germany, and finds little response in America where technology and aesthetics have kept more evenly apace, and the schism between designer and constructor is less apparent. An American middle-income family can afford a house built by new methods and materials. the vital aspect of progressive architecture. In this country, the decline of technology, particularly in building and civil engineering, is forcing architects away from the radical or science

Martello tower on the south coast.

Farmhouse in Kent.

Tile kiln in Staffordshire.

Oast house in Kent.

"Mediterranean plastique." Traditional houses, Ibiza.

Storehouse in Liverpool.

fiction outlook. One only has to compare the Crystal Palace to the Festival of Britain, or the Victorian railway stations to recent airport terminals to appreciate the desperate situation of our technical inventiveness in comparison to the supreme position which we held in the last century. Whereas the Hertfordshire schools might be considered our best postwar effort, they do not set a standard either in conception or style, though at least they were initially motivated by a will to modernity.

The appearance of regionalism amongst our younger architects is but a reflection of the spread of this style in postwar Europe where, significantly, the only major architects who are not now resident in the U.S.A.—Le Corbusier and Alvar Aalto—are, of course, the innovators. Swedish architecture has surprisingly little influence on this new movement whose prime manifestations appear to be:

a. The plastique of folk and anonymous architecture: Initially stimulated by Mediterranean building, recently this interest has moved nearer home, with the examination of such anonymous buildings as Martello towers, oast houses, brick kilns, etc.; in fact, anything of any period which is unselfconscious and usually anonymous. It should be noted that the outside appearance of these buildings is an efficient expression of their specific functions whereas today they may be appreciated picturesquely and possibly utilized arbitrarily.

"The method of design to a modern mind can only be understood in the scientific, or in the engineer's sense, as a definite analysis of possibilities—not as a vague poetic dealing with poetic matters, with derivative ideas of what looks domestic, or looks farmlike, or looks ecclesiastical—the dealing with a multitude of flavors—that is what architects have been doing in the last hundred years. They have been trying to deal with a set of flavors—things that look like things but that were not the things themselves. Old farmhouses and cottages are things themselves—cottages and farmhouses."[3]

b. The application of orthogonal proportion and the obvious use of basic geometrical elements appears to be diminishing, and instead something of the variability found in nature is attempted. "Dynamic cellularism" is an architecture comprising several elements, repetitive or varied. The assemblage of units is more in terms of growth and change than of mere addition, more akin to patterns of crystal formations or biological divisions than to the static rigidity of a structural grid. This form of assemblage is in contrast to the definitive architecture and the containing periphery of, for example, a building such as Unité. It is significant that in large single-cell and usually symmetrical structures, e.g., a stadium and auditorium, that an aspect of neo-Palladianism is most relevant, particularly in the work of Catalano, Candela, and the North Carolina school.

c. A return to the last significant period of English architecture: a revaluation of Voysey, Mackintosh, and the turn of the century when we last held the initiative in Europe. It is obvious that the architecture of this period is still the most modern that we possess but in returning to the point of departure we may be implying that the Continental innovations of the twenties and thirties are incapable of development, presumably because they were foreign to our own experience and today they are academic and no longer valid in our present situation.

"The New Movement is anti-intellectual, anti-posh, and anti-official minded . . .,"[4] so commences a description of "The Movement" in postwar English literature to which the new architectural trends have some obvious affinities. At both the Third Programme and the Elvis Presley levels there is a revival of interest in folk art. The metropolitanism of Sartre and Moravia is being replaced on one hand by *Lucky Jim* provincialism and, on the other, the "mythissmus" of Dylan Thomas and Bert Brecht. It appears that the

James Stirling, [Woolton] house near Liverpool [1954]. Above: Photo of model. Below: Plan and section.

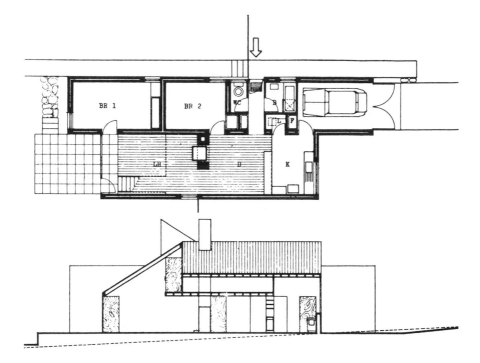

Above: Bird observatory, Scilly Isles. Fifth year design subject by Janet Kaye, Architectural Association School. Plan and photo of model. Below: Alvar Aalto, Säynätsalo, 1954.

recent trends are nationalistic and more the reflection of a "cottage" culture than the expression of supposedly undesirable ad-mass society.

The number of book references in this article is considerable, and indeed one of our vices is an overliterary approach to architecture. It would appear that theories of building are more important than realization. The influence of the camera must also have affected our observation. The range of the camera lens is a small angle focusing attention on the particular and distorting the overall. These media of communication have been useful in the last fifty years when programmatic architecture has almost entirely been built outside this country but their effectiveness is limited, and the transference from picture to reality—picturesque. A good aspect of the recent trend is the ability to be stimulated by actual contact with a local object even though its author may be unknown, and theories appertaining to its appearance unwritten.

By the end of the twenties, the strength of modern architecture lay in the closeness of its extremes. At about the time of the Bauhaus, a common synthesis of the recent past and a definite attitude toward the future was, in fact, if not international, at least universal in Europe. The works of Gropius and Aalto at this period, for instance, had a more or less common appearance. From the public's viewpoint this was an asset, and the new architecture convinced by its logic and style a small but influential part of that public. By the late thirties, modern architecture had percolated into remote corners of the world, encountering the infinite idiosyncrasies of locality, and, at the same time, architects, feeling the limitations of their style and becoming intent upon extending their vocabulary, embarked upon a process of diffusion, assimilation, and personalization. This process is still going on with the result that today it can in no way be said that there is any similarity in the recent work of Gropius and Aalto. If this period of dispersal is coming to an end, attempts may again be made to achieve a synthesis, with the possible revelation that modern architecture has divided into two, approximately one for either side of the Atlantic. The Old World exploiting, and contorting, traditional ways and means, and the New World inventing techniques and developing the appropriate expression of the modern attitude.

As a nation we will probably get the architecture we deserve and, at this stage, we might reconsider these new trends which may ultimately be recognized as standing apart from the mainstream of modern architecture.

"Thirty years ago there was something called 'modern' poetry. Go back to *The Waste Land,* and, if it is any length of time since you read it, I guarantee that one of the things you will notice is how much more *modern* it is than anything being written now; I mean 'modern' in the sense that Bauhaus architecture, Cubist painting, etc., are modern. This quality, this modernity, which was supposed to represent the twentieth century and set it apart from the nineteenth, had many absurd features, and the reaction away from it was quite justifiable; but it is becoming obvious by this time that the baby has been emptied away with the bathwater."[5]

Notes

1.   See "The Functional Tradition," special issue of *Architectural Review,* July 1957, pp. 5–73.

2.   See Theo Crosby, "Contributions to CIAM 10," *Architects' Year Book 7,* pp. 32–39.

3.   See W. R. Lethaby, *Form in Civilization: Collected Papers on Art and Labor* (London: Oxford Univ. Press, 1922).

4.   George Melly, *Intimate Review,* 1956.

5.   John Wain, "A Writer's Progress—IV," *The London Magazine,* November 1956, p. 61.

1957

The myth of **Alvar Aalto** as the "quiet man of the modern movement" more accurately describes the final two decades of his career, beginning in the late 1950s after Aalto had turned sixty, than the preceding period. During the earlier years Aalto often commented, frequently in an informal way, on current issues and on theoretical ideas. Foremost among his concerns from the mid-1930s on were the creation of an experiential architecture more responsive to human senses and emotions and the need to place limits on mechanization and technology through a less scientific, more intuitive approach to design. This point of view, while consistently expounded over the course of his career, found its most receptive audience in the second half of the century, when he was first accorded wide international recognition.

The following lecture, typifying Aalto's concern for the individual in a collective society, was presented at a symposium in Munich entitled "More Beautiful Housing" sponsored by the United German Carpet and Furniture Industries in which he was the featured speaker. As Aalto states, he had recently completed an apartment block for Interbau 1957, a demonstration housing project and exhibition sponsored by the West German government. Constructed in the Hansa district of West Berlin, an area between the Spree and Tiergarten almost totally destroyed by the war, this was a widely publicized initiative to reinvigorate the city and give it a progressive and international face. The catalogue bore the slogan "Wir wohnen gern modern"—we like to live modern.

125–28 Planning began in 1953, soon after the building of Stalinallee had been initiated in the East. The master plan, under the coordination of Otto Bartning, organized forty-eight widely spaced freestanding towers and lower-rise blocks in open parkland. Besides Aalto, an impressive international roster of invitees included Walter Gropius, Oscar Niemeyer, Eugène Beaudoin, Jacob Bakema, Arne Jacobsen, Otto Senn, F. R. S. Yorke, and the German architects Alexander Klein, Wassily Luckhardt, Egon Eiermann, Max Taut, and Hans Scharoun. Le Corbusier contributed a *unité* built (not very well) outside the district. Modeled in part on the Weissenhofsiedlung constructed thirty years earlier in Stuttgart to the master plan of Mies van der Rohe, the Interbau imposition was far more polyglot and disjunctive, too faithfully reflecting the divergence of current formal tendencies. Isolated in broad expanses of green, the buildings stood unrelated urbanistically. (A quarter century later, under the auspices of the Internationale Bauausstellung, another set of housing solutions would be offered to West Berlin by international architects, this time polemically returning to the traditional urban morphology of the perimeter block, though displaying a no less eclectic formal range.)

Despite the overall failure of the 1957 project, however, there were several notable individual efforts, in particular Aalto's scheme. The eight-story apartment block was his first permanent building realized in Europe outside of Finland, and as he states in the following, an attempt to invest the high-rise with some of the intimacy and privacy of the detached house. Recalling the plan for his own summer house in Muuratsalo of 1953 on a very different scale, the scheme expanded the conventional apartment balcony into a generous patio area around which the interior rooms were organized very effectively. Wolfgang Pehnt remarked on the building's "humane monumentality," calling it "an important corrective to the architecture of the right angle, the sharply cut cubic volume, and the thin wall plane" universal at this date in Germany ("Aalto in Deutschland," *Zodiac* 7, 1960).

Lecture given in Munich, 15 November 1957. Published in Karl Fleig, ed., Alvar Aalto: 1963–1970 *(New York: Praeger, 1971), pp. 6–8. Courtesy of Elissa Aalto for the Alvar Aalto Foundation.*

The Architect's Conscience
Alvar Aalto

Good housing does not necessarily have any formal cause; it is not merely a question of direct design or of color scheme. Good housing begins with the building of a given city, in fact even earlier.

Living quarters are dependent on the already constructed or planned city around them so that it is impossible to separate the two. Town planning, again, cannot be restricted to the mere designing of a city; it has to be looked at within the larger context of regional planning that links together a given urban area and its hinterland. Otherwise it is quite impossible to arrive at any solution that adequately meets human needs and furthers harmonious living within a community.

In the north, in the "semibarbaric" country where I was born, this town planning problem, to a certain extent, is naturally easier to resolve than in the densely populated countries of Central Europe. Finland, for instance, is as large in area as Germany, but it has a population of only four million. There is enough space available there to experiment, to play with the natural environment, and to bring external nature into close contact with the home. Unfortunately, this possibility is insufficiently exploited. Countries like Finland tend to be a little provincial. They want very much to copy the marvels of the outside world. Even today it remains the fashion to copy, let us say, Hollywood, the most badly constructed city that I know. And this is the case despite the fact that the situation of the Finns in their natural environment would yield excellent possibilities of developing a better type of housing on the basis of intelligent planning.

It is certainly not at all easy simply to build a new city in the midst of primeval nature. It is easy enough to say to an architect: Here you have a forest and here a lake; now please build a town here for twenty thousand people. Twenty thousand people do not amount to much by German standards, but up in the north this is a respectable population. I have just recently been asked whether the old European cities are not outmoded—they are indeed outmoded, so the argument ran, and nothing further can be done with them, and nowadays only brand new cities ought to be built. But I believe that we should not and must not go as far as this.

Human life consists, in equal degrees, of tradition and new creation. Traditions cannot be wholly cast off and regarded as used objects which have to be replaced by something new. In human life continuity is a vital necessity. It is perfectly possible to combine the old cities by means of good town planning methods with new natural reserves so that happy living conditions emerge. Of course, this is a very difficult achievement, but it is possible.

I have been asked whether in Finland every small town has its city planning official, by which is probably meant an architect who is concerned solely with town planning and public works. This is true of most Finnish towns. However, I think that for Finland this is still no solution. Towns and cities as physical phenomena contain problems too serious to be resolved merely by an official or an architect; architecture on a solid town planning basis poses problems that are too grave and too difficult.

Once a city is built, it is not possible to change it. I am standing here in a part of Europe in which the Roman legions once camped. Is it not clear that to this day the ground plans of cities are indirectly determined by the lines laid down by the Romans? Although these cities have been repeatedly destroyed and rebuilt, reminders still exist of the period of Roman occupation. This is a measure of the difficulty, even now, of altering the ground plan of a city or the mode of living of a residential district. It can only be hoped that the public at large will take an interest in such questions and that all possible endeavors are made to create the optimum town planning basis for our housing projects.

What, then, actually makes for happy living in a given area? Residing in a place is, *per se,* one of the great mysteries of human life. Why is the poor human creature fated to work, eat, and live in a dwelling? Not all animals, for instance, live in fixed abodes, but animals without exception feed. The housing problem is without doubt one of the most important we have to resolve. Our entire culture rests on the nature of our dwellings. Is happy living really guaranteed by the small house in a large park or by the undisturbed privacy of a family or by the densely packed great city? This question has yet to be and will in fact never be answered!

I recall that the Soviet Union once commissioned a German architect to draw up town planning projects for the regime then in power. It postulated a maximum size for the cities. No city was to have more than one hundred and fifty thousand inhabitants, and if at all possible, fewer, about sixty thousand. European cities have slipped out of the control of their planners or officials; they have become and are still in the process of becoming cities of millions which are psychologically and, what is more, physically impossible to live in. What then was the outcome of the above-mentioned Russian project? After years of discussion, the result was that the Russian government was of the opinion that intellectual contact, which alone makes living together worthwhile, can take place only in a great metropolis. New agrarian centers for a maximum of only one hundred and fifty thousand inhabitants also appeared old-fashioned in the eyes of the government.

Where then are the limits? Ought we to live isolated in open country or ought we to live in compact groups solely for reasons of intellectual contact? I believe that both approaches are necessary and possible.

Ought we to build detached houses or high-rise apartment houses? The ideal would be to be able to build a high-rise apartment house in which every apartment had the same physical qualities as a detached house. In Berlin I tried with my Interbau house to resolve this question, but naturally I was not able to come to any optimum solution. One simply cannot build a high-rise building having the same features as a single-family house. However, since we after all need both, we have to develop a high-rise culture, as it were, in which living approximates to that in a small private home as closely as possible.

Houses with open glass walls and balconies, where one can see every detail of what goes on inside, do not offer sufficient privacy. We have to build houses in which every single family really feels like a private family and is secluded as much as possible from neighbors. No matter what types of design lie ahead of us, no matter what life externally appears to be like, when hundreds of artificial satellites are flitting about, the family will always remain a primordial unit. We cannot proceed simply on the assumption that man is to live two lives, a collective life and a private one. The two complexes are as incompatible as sleep and work. We have to build houses which guarantee every human being a private life, somehow or other.

The problem can be solved in a thousand different ways, but this basic approach should be preserved. Architecture is not mere decoration; it is a deeply biological, if not a predominantly moral matter. Having touched upon the moral dimension, I now come to the formal side of the housing problem.

Interior decorating and external embellishments are attempts to compensate for the lack of contact between house and natural environment. I believe that every thinking person would support me here: the fact is proclaimed even in the very designs.

One could even facetiously maintain that the fabrics employed in the home are symbols of natural elements. Fabrics with their textures, colors, and designs represent the green fields and flowers, that is to say, a world which man in the great metropolis no longer possesses. Originally, in fact, fabrics were the raw material out of which the first furniture and the first interior appointments in the world were fashioned. There are entire cultures whose way of life is determined by woven fabrics; we need only think of the tents of nomads.

I have said that I evaluate the formal aspect from a moral point of view. It is impossible for me to say that one should do this and not that, prefer this and avoid something else. I believe that harmonious living in a house is the necessary physical principle that we need. This matter is more moral in nature than formal. Forms, designs, can be manifold and various, but it should be borne in mind that the best designs should comply with the classical norms, and there is good reason for this. They should be natural and vital, not coquettish.

Human life is a combination of tragedy and comedy. The shapes and designs which surround us are the music accompanying this tragedy and this comedy. The furniture, the fabrics, the color schemes, and the structures can be earnestly and happily made so that they produce no contrast to the tragedy and comedy of human life. In this they correspond to decent dress and to decent living.

All exaggerated designs make a mockery of us and even worse. I believe that if more moral aspects are taken into account, industry, with its vast range of potentialities, can avoid comic exaggerations and help man in many ways to live more harmoniously. If in these ways town planning, the home, the apartment, and interior fittings can be improved, we shall have the satisfaction that we too are able to let a little sunshine into the soul of unhappy mankind.

1957

In no country was the crisis of rationalism more strenuously debated than Italy. This was a function of both the polemical nature of the Italian intellectual milieu and the dispiriting products of postwar Italian reconstruction. The efforts to *77–79* provide a "house for everyone" had resulted in cheap but ugly housing and ill-considered solutions to larger urban problems. In this context, Bruno Zevi's *68–69* organicism momentarily seemed an answer to a too easily degraded functionalism. But the postwar questioning of "rationalism," as modernist architecture had come to be known in Italy, also grew out of the specific experience of the interwar years, when internal tensions began to engender a "postrationalist" critique. By the 1940s and 1950s avant-gardism, historicism, and the populist-existentialist strains of neorealism were inflecting functionalist doctrine in such a heterodox way that the question was unavoidable: did the present tendencies represent a break with rationalist architecture or a continuation, albeit in a modified form? These were the terms in which Ernesto *200–4* Rogers, editorial director of *Casabella-Continuità* after 1953, put the question in an editorial of April–May 1957 entitled "Continuity or Crisis?"

The same year, in the first issue of the journal *Zodiac,* a different answer to the question through a crucial redefinition of its terms—and a reply to both Zevi and a recent book by the theoretician Cesare Brande—came from the art historian **Giulio Carlo Argan**. Why, asked Argan, was "rationalism" perceived as the antagonist? In his view, the term had little to do with abstractness or the pursuit of objective knowledge. Rationalism was instead an *ideology,* he argued, a cultural response to a social crisis caused by the ascendancy of technology and its agencies over middle-class life. Modernist architects had been led to believe that society could survive only by transforming itself, and by their own mediating role in this transformation. What was called rationalism, in fact, was really political *radicalism,* a program aimed "at acting on a given social situation and at profoundly changing it." In their radical vocation, and in their conception of architecture as a form of *critique*, the architects of the modern movement ultimately had origins in the revolutionary thought of the Enlightenment. But it was their inability to carry out this vocation—less through error than being forced to make an impossible choice between humanism and technocracy—that now produced the sense of crisis. This negative experience explained, in Argan's view, why postwar architecture had become so evasive with respect to politics.

Le Corbusier's church of Ronchamp particularly exemplified the aporia of rationalism for Argan. In an engaged polemic of 1956 with Rogers, who had published it in *Casabella* in adulatory terms, he criticized the church as being "decisively, polemically antihistorical," accusing Le Corbusier of masking ersatz religiosity with baroque scenography. To the Marxist historian the Marseilles Unité d'Habitation represented a more correct course for a critical modernism; *176–80* so did the example of Walter Gropius. In an earlier book on Gropius and the Bauhaus (1951), Argan had dramatized the Bauhaus founder as an upholder of humane reason and constructive values in the face of an authoritarian regime and a brutal new technical civilization. Argan's "beautiful myth" of Gropius was influential for many years in Italian architecture culture. Faithful to his Crocean background, Argan explicitly refused to extend the judgment of rationalism's failure in ideological terms to its aesthetic and technical achievements—"the great heritage"—anticipating an argument that Jürgen Habermas would make twenty-three years later in an essay entitled "Modernity—An Incomplete Project."

Published as "Architettura e ideologia," Zodiac 1 (1957), pp. 47–52; Eng. trans. pp. 261–65. Republished in Giulio Carlo Argan, Progetto e destino: Saggi di arte e di letteratura (Milan: Il Saggiatore, 1965), pp. 82–90. Courtesy of the author.

Architecture and Ideology
Giulio Carlo Argan

Why has there been so much talk about "setting aside rationalism"; why have some even felt a need to uproot it, as if it were some kind of peril hanging over our culture; why have even its earliest and only approximate premises been challenged, as they have been in Cesare Brandi's recent book *Eliante?* True, those premises were already outdated, not only in the formal concreteness of factual works, but even in the statements made by the leading figures of the movement: Brandi himself, after having pointed out how programs conceived from a predominantly practical and technical point of view preclude any artistic merit, is later obliged to restate his condemnation by pointing out the abstractness and utopianism of the selfsame utilitarianism. It is a fact, then, that an extremely penetrating and sensitive critic like Brandi felt a need to dig up those old and much more than outdated premises; and that contemporary architects cannot help adopting "rationalism" as a point of reference, of departure, or term of comparison, or dialectical position, as if the artistic movement which arose at the beginning of this century and matured in Europe between the two wars implied the appeal to a principle or was to be regarded as a law or condition to any kind of architecture. This was a new classicism, then, or rather a total anticlassicism; but for this very reason absolute and apodictic: in fact, what is now happening to rationalism happened to classicism, which hardly ever constituted a precise formal system but for a long time influenced the work of artists as a particular way of approaching the problems of art.

The "rational" architectural approach may be the opposite of the classical, but "rationalism" certainly has something in common with classicism: how else can we explain that quality of "rationalism" the incongruence of which would be easily noticed if we only realized that periods of philosophical rationalism were marked by a fundamentally classical architecture, contriving to reflect in their structure the rationalistic qualities of a nature obeying constant and therefore objectively knowable laws. It is quite true that classicism and rationalism equally admit the geometrical basis of constructive form; but while classicist theoreticians consider geometry as a natural form *par excellence,* or rather as the very principle of every natural form, "rationalist" theoreticians consider it a constitutionally unnatural form, and, if anything, representative of the logical structure of the mind, or the mind itself separated, as it were, from its own quality of consciousness.

It is not enough to claim that "rationalist" architects are interested not in nature, but in society; this undoubtedly correct position must be followed by an examination of the attitude assumed toward society, beginning with the statement that such an attitude cannot in any case be considered analogous to that adopted by "classicists" toward nature. Carrying to the extreme the criticism of "rationalism," we might say that the limit (or the *felix culpa* of the Illuminists) of that approach lay in its not having carried to their extreme consequences the antinomy between nature and society, or having attributed to society a logical structure, and observance of constant laws, not unlike those which classical theoreticians recognized and exalted in nature. In an age in which the triumphs of scientific and technological research offered apparently unlimited opportunities for man's control of nature, many men (and not only architects) evidently believed that society could be transformed by processes analogous to those by which matter and natural form were being transformed. The mistake would have been unpardonable if "rationalism" had aimed, like classicism, at a gnostic end, the merely objective knowledge of certain constant laws of reality—the laws of society, in this case—rather than those of nature. Aiming, as they did, at acting on a given social situation and at profoundly changing it, we can no longer speak of objective error, nor even of abstractness and utopianism. It would be much nearer the truth to speak of "ideology"; and this is also shown in the fact that very soon theoreticians sought to replace the clearly improper term "rational" with the more technically exact term "functional," or "international," which is more in keeping with its ideological, or even "democratic" (it was Wright himself who suggested it), assumptions, which clearly allude to political thought and content.

Rationalism and radicalism

As for the leading figures of the "rationalist" movement, none of them ever displayed the speculative balance and the sure grasp of reality which are the typical qualities of the truly great rationalist; but neither did they pose as social reformers, prophets of a perfectly arranged, perfectly orchestrated social future moving to an eternally unvaried rhythm. This ideal of what society ought to be conceals an uneasiness at the thought of what really is; it is more a psychological compensation than a positive program; it can only be deplored that for so long society has been living on these psychological compensations, has been obliged to imagine its own well-being as something which belongs to the beyond, to paradise. Gropius is a tortured man living with vivid pain the crisis which World War I (not to mention World War II) did not resolve but rather created; Le Corbusier reacts to the situation with the paradoxical eruptiveness and capricious excitement of a Picasso—he is the first to discover that as soon as they are found the terse forms of "rationalism" change at sight into myths, idols, fetishes; Mies van der Rohe soars at great and rarefied intellectual heights, but he has experienced the dizziness of looking at the abyss below. What about the Italians? Persico finds "rationalism" a pretext for an indirect criticism, the breaking forth of suppressed political sentiments; for Pagano it is the lever with which he absurdly seeks to reverse a situation; for Terragni it is the basis of a will to poetry which the viciousness of our crude times threatened to suffocate. I believe these examples should be sufficient to show that the architectural movement dominant between the two wars was not in any way connected to a rationalist system (of which, moreover, there are no traces in other fields of culture) but to a glaring problem of human behavior, to a bitter political struggle; and in this sense it has such an advanced position, such an active role that one wonders whether this architecture had not been better defined "radical" rather than "rational." Seen in the historical perspective of the twenties and thirties it becomes, in fact, a rather important aspect of that kind of middle-class reformism which, as eighteenth-century liberalism became more radical, came into contact with the ideological themes and political action of socialism, accepting many of its claims, but also offering itself as an alternative to the growing revolutionary thrust of the working class.

The ideological crisis

This political tendency was, moreover, so thinly disguised that totalitarian regimes, usually quite insensitive to the ideological restlessness of culture, lost no time in discovering it; and not only did they proscribe and persecute such architecture as antinational and subversive, but also elected as their legitimate minister and representatives the last and most trivial (here the term "degenerate" really applies) configurations of academic classicism. The failure of "rational" architecture on the plane of aesthetic values is still to be proven; its failure on the political plane may sadden us, but it cannot be questioned. Perhaps then, notwithstanding the great problems of reconstruction it has been obliged to face and still faces, contemporary architecture, in dealing with ideological problems, has been very timid, not to say fearful.

One cannot objectively deny that the architecture of the last fifty years constitutes a considerable heritage; it has done away with many prejudices, has defined new concepts of space, form, function; it has perfected new working methods both in designing and in execution; it has established new relationships, with town planning on the one hand and with industrial production on the other. Can we accept this great heritage for all it is worth, separate these formal and technical achievements from the ideological tendencies and interests which produced them? It is obvious that the answer to this lies not in an analysis of the theses but of the ideological crises of "rational" architecture; or, to be more precise, of its political radicalism.

The political line of Le Corbusier or Gropius (to mention only two of the greatest exponents of the movement) can hardly be deduced from the great current of political ideas of our times; it is defined rather by the definition of their artistic program. But the more clearly they proclaim the "technical" character of their personality and their program, the more perfectly they fit into a cultural situation which tends to put forward the figure of the "technician" as a typically political figure and a figure of the greatest importance. And not only is it admitted that technical qualification implies, in itself, the right to the exercise of a directive and consequently political role, it also explicitly recognizes that inasmuch as technology is tantamount to development and progress, it cannot help bringing profound transformations into the structure of society and state. To the holders of great quantities of capital who counted on technicians to increase their wealth and power, the technicians reply by pointing out that the middle class can survive only if it succeeds in transforming itself; nor will it be enough to limit or reduce their own class privilege; they will have to reconstitute themselves as a nonclass or interclass, and act as mediating factors in the inevitable evolution from a hierarchical society to a functional classless society. Thus, at the very moment that architects declared themselves to be apolitical they assumed a clearly political position; certainly not out of hypocrisy or opportunism, but out of the persuasion (which is not only theirs) that true politics should develop by means of constructive dialectics rather than brutal and destructive conflicts of forces. Utopianism? I should rather say an erroneous evaluation of the actual condition of the European middle class, the illusion that its progressive impulse had not been completely exhausted, that middle-class elements which accepted democratic ideals were definitely stronger than those others who were firmly determined to turn back to impose violently the most obtuse and barbaric form of political "realism." Mere comparison with this "realism" made democracy seem utopia. Nor do I see how we can reprove these "rationalist" architects for having miscalculated the situation, if correctly evaluating it would have meant cleverly estimating each side's possibilities for success and then aligning themselves with the probable victors. Let us not forget what "architectural rationalism" meant in Italy and Germany, as a moral argument against the arrogance of the dictators; let us not underrate the gravity of the dilemma, which left no alternative between the rigor of Gropius and Le Corbusier and the artistic and moral baseness of the official architects.

Since history is not written with "ifs," there is no sense in wondering what might have been the fate of architecture if it had not been violently resisted and persecuted; if certain architects had not accepted political compromise in the naive hope of saving the integrity of form; if the war had not once again uprooted every hope of reasonably settling clashes of interests, classes, and states. Such reasoning could only lead to a rationalistic revival which no one (not even Gropius and Le Corbusier, to judge from their latest works) can reasonably desire; and it would repeat, but without any historical justification, the error of those who, in those critical years, confused faith in reason with the rationality then in force, and Kantian critique with criticism.

The value of a tradition

The responsibility which "rationalist" architects assumed before history was quite another thing; by committing art, architecture, to a position and to the political struggle, they spontaneously renounced all right to that immunity which had seemed so natural to art and which the proponents of "art for art's sake," as if perceiving the risks of the inevitable compromise, had tried to reassert as a last resort. But how could it be reasserted if its right rested on the ancient religious character and function of art and had to be immediately relinquished when that aesthetic end shifted, as it had, from the sphere of the transcendent to that of the contingent? It is easy today to comment ironically on the commitments of art and tell the old story of the *trahison des clercs;* by committing themselves on the political plane, endangering the very existence of art, modern artists have not made an unpardonable ideological mistake, but have obeyed a historical necessity, have developed premises which had been maturing for centuries in the European tradition of art. Let it be clearly understood that from the moment that art renounced its right to being representative of a religious confession or the formal configuration of a dogma, political compromise became much more than a probability; and perhaps rational architecture was only the last attempt to bring to society, by elevating it to a myth, a religiosity which could no longer be satisfied by the contemplation of nature. The first attempt to create art in an entirely human setting, to counterbalance religious art with layman's art, goes back much further, to the beginning of the eighteenth century, to the very premises of that illuministic thought on which is based even that idealistic aesthetic in the name of which today they would condemn every form of art found to be inspired by social or political interests. Nor was even this a pure statement of principles if the motive was the awareness that with the Baroque mode religious assumptions became intermixed with political assumptions, and the rather insistent call to the transcendent often betrayed powerful temporal interests. Time and again attention has been drawn to the bifurcation of seventeenth-century French art into two streams aimed respectively at the exaltation of the new principle of authority of the monarchical state and at resistance to it, with an explicit content of middle-class resistance. The dilemma to be faced, then, is not even that of religious art and lay art, but of conservative art on the one hand, which assumes the great values achieved as its own ideological basis and the eternal content of its own eternal formal beauty; and on the other hand, progressive art, which fits into the process of continual transformation, determination, and renovation of values. Nor is this lively and not uncommonly dramatic contrast between institutions and a criticism which tends to destroy them in order to renew them, or between dogmatic transcendence and transcendentalism itself, a problem only for art; it is the way of all thought, of all modern civilization from Leibniz and Kant until today, so that this same "rational" architecture and Mondrian's painting mark the point of arrival of the conception of art as transcendental critique. Or rather, only this remote Kantian ancestry in any way justifies the otherwise improper term "rational," and explains the much deprecated formal "*a priori* concepts" not as the mere application of geometric forms, but as the anxious aspiration and approach to geometric form understood as *a priori* forms of the mind. Nor is it necessary to point out how and as a result of what historical forces the first term of that dilemma has been gradually weakening and fading away while the dogmatic power of institutions has been giving way to critical reasoning; so that it can be said that the extreme stylistic degradation found in the official architecture of fascism and Nazism derives directly from ideological (and thus moral and political) degradation of the institutions which that architecture, rather than represent, basely agreed to serve.

The present situation

After the experience of World War II the criticism dealing with the cultural climate in which the so-called "rational" architecture was produced and developed appears all too easy; the limits of that culture are certainly not to be found in its greater political consciousness, but in its inability to pursue its political vocation with sufficient clarity and resolution. Similarly, the fact that democracy has been overcome in many countries and is everywhere passing through a crisis, does not mean that democracy is a mistaken or absurd political solution, but only that it has not resolved all its internal contradictions and lacks sufficient power to counter every attack from without. It is unquestionably true that abstractness and utopianism are not found merely in architectural social programs, but throughout the entire culture; just as it is true that abstractness and utopianism are responsible for the failure or limited effectiveness of the generous contribution made by European intellectuals to the political struggles of the twenties and thirties. Well, what then, if anything, could contemporary architects deduce from this bitter experience except the proof that the technical qualifications raised to such lofty height by the "rationalist" architects are in themselves hardly sufficient for political qualification?

The attempt, still going on, to depoliticize art and particularly architecture betrays the effects of the recent shock and is therefore quite humanly comprehensible; but it ceases to be such when through an excess of enthusiasm, proponents claim that "rational" architecture must be considered *sub specie aeternitatis* and not in the light of its political implications; or, worse, that it is to be compared with technical and industrial progress and not with the dramatic historical situation to which it tried to react. Even counterbalancing the formula "rational" with the formula "organic" is humanly comprehensible as a dialectic attempt to break through a suffocating atmosphere; but we must not forget that "organic" architecture is parallel and not subsequent to "rational" architecture, and operates in a not very dissimilar historical situation. The long-sought return to a "natural" society is no less utopian than the ideal of a "rational" society, nor is the theory of "intuition" less abstract than that of "logic"; and they are the sure signs of reactions to a social crisis, even though less serious and imminent than that to which "rational" architecture reacted. It is only right that this crisis now be put in world terms; that the experience of Wright and Aalto be included as essential terms of the problem; but a term cannot be assumed to be a solution, nor is there any reason for exempting Wright's and Aalto's work from a historical determinism to which we must add a political evaluation. It can easily be seen that in the fullness of plastic invention, perhaps even in the happy recovery of a long forgotten nature, these two masters sought the imaginative freedom of pure poetry; but neither can it be denied that the "rationality" of a Gropius, a Le Corbusier, or a Mies van der Rohe arose from the desire for a condition of liberty, if not from the last illusion of immunity in the thick of the battle. From the moment that liberty no longer meant boundless effusion in the immense kingdom of nature, but rather moral choice to make against each and every internal and external obstacle, the world has known no liberty which was not a painful and sometimes tragic liberation. Every freedom is always freedom from something; and the definition of that "from" is one of the most difficult steps on the road to freedom. Very probably the architects of the first half of the century, in Europe and America, have defined that "from" imperfectly; it is to be hoped that today's architects, committing themselves to going beyond the experience of that architecture, will be able to overcome the limits and the inhibitions which prevented that architecture from realizing all its plans, and at the same time will not forget what were the most genuine and vital elements of its moral force.

1957

Once portrayed by Luigi Moretti as "a serene man with an extraordinary force and faith in life," the Milanese architect **Gio Ponti** managed to be both at the center of Italian developments and unembattled by its polemics. A highly successful practitioner and gifted designer, a prolific editor and organizer, a teacher at Milan's Politecnic for twenty-five years, and a devout Catholic, he founded the journal *Domus* in 1928 and as its editorial director for almost forty years ecumenically promoted a range of progressive positions. His architecture and his many designs for industrial objects and furniture brought a refined sensibility to problems of mass production, making him an international figure in the design world. Initially immersed in the aestheticism of European turn-of-the-century bourgeois culture, he was converted to rationalism in the 1930s through his contacts with Giuseppe Terragni, Giuseppe Pagano, and the theoretician Edoardo Persico. In the mid-1950s a *tour de force* was his Pirelli building in Milan, engineered by Pier Luigi Nervi. The thirty-three-story reinforced concrete skyscraper, aerodynamically fared in plan, went up on the Milan skyline at the same date as the Velasca tower by the firm of Belgiojoso, Peressuti, and Rogers. The difference between the two monuments, the one elegantly articulated in the language of International Style modernism, the other resisting the dominant style

300–7
77–79, 200–4
in a dialect that would be called Neoliberty, mirrors the respective editorial policies of Ponti's stylish *Domus* and Ernesto Rogers's more tendentious *Casabella-Continuità* during these years.

Yet in a sense Ponti's impeccable taste belies his originality of thought. A combination of the traditional humanist steeped in "noble" Italian culture and the progressive thinker for whom architecture was an ethical and idealistic pursuit, Ponti represented, as Persico noted in the 1930s, "an isolated inventor for whom the history of art is not a progression but a succession of diversities." The following text comes from a unique book written in 1957 (revised from a version of 1940), *Amate l'architettura*, the title an injunction to "love architecture." In a prefatory note Ponti writes, "This book is for the lovers of architecture, for those who are enchanted by the civilization of architecture, for those who dream about an architecture that is itself a civilization (is it a dream?). It is not a book *on* architecture but a book *for* architecture." Aphoristic and anecdotal, the book is a freely organized collection of intuitive insights and more reasoned reflections, simultaneously speculative and topical. Ponti refers to it as an "autobiography," and perhaps one of the few books in the literature to which it compares is Aldo

392–98
Rossi's *A Scientific Autobiography* of 1981. Whereas the tone of Rossi's book is melancholy, however, Ponti's is joyous and rhapsodic. Art and architecture are viewed, as in the chapter following, as "human documents":

"Art does not consist in 'formality' (any form is good, so much so, in fact, that form is continuously changing). Art is a document, a witness of man . . . That is why works and monuments outside the realm of formally pure values, works like the pyramids and Milan's cathedral, belong to art. Because they are documents of grandeur, unrepeatable heroisms of history, of faith, of man. They speak."

Published in Gio Ponti, Amate l'architettura (Genoa: Società Editrice Vitali e Ghianda, 1957), pp. 109–20. English edition: In Praise of Architecture, trans. Giuseppina and Mario Salvadori (New York: F. W. Dodge Corporation, 1960), pp. 94–103. Courtesy of Lisa Licitra Ponti, Giovanna Ponti, Letizia Ponti, Giulio Ponti, Matteo Licitra, and Salvatore Licitra.

The Architect, the Artist
Gio Ponti

(I am evoking "the artist." Presumptuous word, obnoxious word when used professionally, as if one were always an artist, as if one could succeed in always being an artist! No, the artist is a man who has a disposition toward art, who has a vocation and sometimes succeeds.)

(We must always start by considering a work of architecture as a work of art and the architect as the artist. Buildings and builders are something else, something very respectable, but something else.)

(The real artists are not dreamers, as so many believe; they are terrible realists. They do not transpose reality into a dream but a dream into reality—written, drawn, musical, architectural reality. Do you realize that?)

When building in the country, the architect (the artist) must imagine his walls, his spaces, and the sky (and the changing light, the fog, and the multitudinous nights); he must imagine his walls, his spaces, and the waters; his walls, his spaces, and the trees; his walls, his spaces, and the people. The architect, when building in the green world, must proportion walls to trees (trees are proportioned to man).

(This is the "naturalistic genesis" of architecture. But I add that the architect reveals himself only through his imagination, an imagination independent of everything else.)

—The architect (the artist) must imagine for each window a person at the sill; for each door, a person passing through; for each stair, a person going up or down; for each portico, a person loitering; for each foyer, two people meeting; for each terrace, somebody resting; for each room, somebody living within. (The Italian word for room is *stanza,* a beautiful word; it means "to stay"; somebody staying there; a life.)

(This is the "animated genesis" of architecture. Yet architecture must reveal itself—and we must judge it—by itself, uninhabited, isolated in its own laws.)

—When imagining his interiors, the architect (the artist) must hear voices among the walls—women's voices, children's voices, men's voices. He must hear a song lilting from the windows. He must hear shouted names. He must hear whistles. He must hear the noises of human work.

(This is the "sonorous genesis" of architecture. Yet architecture reveals itself by its silences; its eloquence lies in its silence.)

—Blessed the ancient architect, who was originally a *muratore* or mason (a beautiful word derived from the Latin *mura,* wall). We architects of today have difficulties in understanding many things and have no feeling for them because we started out as students (what a mistake!). Things live in our intelligence before they do in our senses. For us, *nihil in sensu quod non fuerit in intellectu,* and not as for the ancients, *nihil in intellectu quod non fuerit in sensu.* Our upside-down Latin is our misfortune, a diminution of our resources, an impoverishment we have in common with engineers. Only the artists among us are saved, because poetry comes to their aid and makes them understand everything.

(What originated from the *muratore* was the "physical genesis" of architecture. Yet architecture goes beyond the senses; it is captured by the eyes but for the sake of the spirit.)

—The architect of today, the college architect, must learn from all the artisans—from the marble cutter (his polished and smooth surfaces, hammered surfaces, sealed surfaces), from the carpenter, the plasterer, the blacksmith, from all workers and craftsmen. He must learn things made by hand. Nothing, if not first in our hands.

(This is the "manual genesis" of architecture, its living creation. Yet architecture becomes a pure, abstract form.)

—The architect must also learn from the artisan how to love his trade; how beautiful it is to do something for the sake of doing. Art for art's sake is just that. It does not consist in a form of art without content but in the happiness of doing, doing without minding whether one succeeds or not. One is happy to sing just to be able to sing, and never mind how one sings; what matters is to sing; once in a while one of us will sing well.

(This is the "incantatory genesis" of architecture.)

—In order to understand everything about his wonderful trade, the architect (the artist) must have his buildings in his senses, that is, foresee them (see them first); he must have a tactile presentiment of them through their materials (smooth, rough, cold, and warm). He must test them beforehand with his own prescient eyes under every possible light of the sky (calm, stormy, summer, winter, bright, dull) and under every incidence of the sun (morning, afternoon, and twilight suns).

(This is the "sensuous genesis" of architecture.)

—The architect (the artist) must paint. For after all, he must compose landscapes even with his walls. Be it natural or urban, the architect is always constructing a landscape. He should paint for the sake of the appearance (the prospect) and the dimensions of his walls or surfaces; for the sake of their color; and for the sake of their relief (which he must be able to measure and have at his fingertips because of the play of the sun and light, a tactile thing).

(This is the "landscape genesis" of architecture.)

—The good work of an architect may inspire a landscape to a painter. Such architecture is not scenography (no painter would make a painting of a set, for as the set is itself painted, his picture would be but a painting painted twice) but a scene of its own and a landscape grounded in life and in nature. A painting is a "test" of the architect's work.

(This is the "scenic genesis" of architecture.)

—The architect (the artist) building a house should not look for praise of aesthetic, formal, or stylistic values, or of values grounded in taste. These values are soon dated. The highest praise he must aspire to is to be told by the owners of the house, "Sir, in the house you built for us we live (or lived) happily. It is dear to us. It is a happy episode in our life." But for such a compliment the architect must pay more attention to the owners than to aesthetics (and only thus will he reach permanent aesthetic values, expressed by means of right forms, of forms aesthetically beyond discussion, true forms, human forms).

(This is the "human genesis" of architecture.)

—The architect (the artist) must interpret the character of the man who lives in the house, of each man in each house; he must build houses to be lived in by men who are alive. *L'architecture est l'homme,* they say. They say. But not measured man. The man of Neufert's handbook is the measured man, and Neufert's handbook is not a technical book on architecture. Man is not to be measured; man is a character to be understood.

(This is the "psychological genesis" of architecture.)

(The architect who fails to interpret the life of the inhabitants, transforming it into an expression of civilization and culture, the architect who imposes on them his aesthetic feelings only—apart from his presumptuousness—does not build a house but a showcase, an exhibition, and reduces its inhabitants from living human beings to mannequins. They, of course, rebel, and thus come about all those supposed infractions of the presumptuous order of the aesthete-architect and his feelings of lèse-majesté.)

—The architect (the artist) must be curious about men and women so that he may divine their characters; the true architect should fall in love with the owners, men and women, of the house he is going to build or decorate.

(This is the "loving genesis" of architecture. Yet architecture reveals itself without sin.)

—The architect (the artist) is not afraid of limited means. The more limited he is, the less free to operate, the better his architecture. Then he works in desperation and performs miracles. He makes up for material difficulties with spiritual values. *Il faut décourager les arts.*

(This is the *nascita povera,* the impoverished birth of the arts. But later on everything is mysteriously rich.)

—The architect must despise what is "passing" (stylistic and formal aesthetics) and must look for what "remains" in life. Then he will find form (which will be what remains as life passes; a lovely contradiction).

—The architect must realize that the permanent values are those of his soul, of his greatness, of his singularity as a man. Art does not consist in "formality" (any form is good, so much so, in fact, that form is continuously changing). Art is a document, a witness of man, of *one* man, through *one* form, *one* expression of him. That is why art cannot be repeated, why a copy is not art, why a restoration is not art. That is why a drawing by Andrea del Sarto even if beautiful and perfectly finished has *less value* than an imperfect or unfinished design by Raphael. Because it is the document of a man who is *less great.* That is why works and monuments outside the realm of formally pure values, works like the pyramids and Milan's cathedral, belong to art. Because they are documents of grandeur, unrepeatable heroisms of history, of faith, of man. They speak.

Art, I repeat, does not lie in the form; it lies in the document of the man. Form is a thing perfect and complete. (Can we imagine an incomplete form?) Nevertheless form is not indispensable to art, because a mutilated statue (the Victory of Samothrace), an altered painting (the Cimabue in Assisi), a ruin (the "test of ruin" is the great test of architecture because architecture must be able to resist all injuries and express itself even through its remains) inspire us, notwithstanding their mutilation, alteration, or ruin, with an artistic emotion, because they are nevertheless *art.*

These works are documents of an artist because they emanate the spirit of the artist who created them, his magnanimity, his thought. A Man speaks.

This is the measure of art—the measure of Man. (Here the statement "Man is the measure of everything" assumes a different meaning. It becomes the measure of his heroism, of his life, of his own drama, that is, of his genuineness, of his autobiographical authenticity. Academicians are not authentic; technicians are not autobiographical; artists always are and only so. The value of Van Gogh's paintings does not consist only of their formal value, which has been copied by every imitator of Van Gogh with desolate and desolating reverence; their value lies also in his drama and in his autobiography; his paintings are its document. I say to the VanGoghists: "Go and cut your ears!" But we know that even this gesture cannot be repeated.)

Every man, I have said, shouts a cry before he dies (I do not mean the moment he dies, but before, during his life). History gathers it, if it is genuine.

—The architect (the artist) should doubt aesthetic and formal values. He should commit himself to the values of obligation and work. By these means he establishes his own true and valid document, the human document. The architect Muzio once said something very moving. "We have worked for a long time on this project; therefore it is beautiful." (A suggestive way of affirming those values of human obligation that adhere to a work and afterward radiate beauty.)

This is why medieval cathedrals are beautiful, with their innumerable statues, their infinite sense of obligation and work, their infinite faith, their infinite prayer, and their infinite love (an excess of love; art is something loved excessively; but there are still rejected lovers). In the Gothic cathedrals this is true even of *the work that cannot be seen,* ornamentation and sculpture (some undercuts, some decorations in the back that nobody can see but that still exist, bestowing supreme artistic worth; an issue of love).

I realize that if an ass of an architect worked even a hundred years we could never say of his work, "Therefore it is beautiful." But I still believe in this conviction about Beauty; it is the one I like best. What is beautiful must be somehow deserved. It is something God asks of us. The architects who become infatuated with schemes, who believe in predetermined theses and rules, in proportional tracings, graphs, and other miserable tomfooleries move me to laughter and to pity (among them are some real artists, but even these seem unaware of the fact that they are artists only when they disregard their schemes). They subscribe to such theories to get out of hard work, to avoid having to aspire to inspiration, to invoke it, provoke it, and to deliver themselves painfully of it (it is not easy). If their assumptions were correct, everybody would always accomplish perfection, even they. It never happens.

On the contrary, it so happens that all of us (and they too, notwithstanding their procedures) sometimes create something fine but more often something not so fine. Art cannot be made certain or constant. This would be too wonderful! Nobody is more naive about or further removed from art than a calculating man. (It is true—I have found it to be so myself—that works of art can be schematized afterward, *a posteriori;* we can then have fun rediscovering proportions, curves, inscriptions in circles, spirals, and the like. What cannot be done is to "produce" art by means of *a priori* rules. This would be too easy! Schemes as well as "tradition" and repetition do not exist in art; only history exists, and it does not repeat. And art is history.) Referring to schemes, Corbu says that his Modulor is only for those who know nothing about proportion (*Le modulor sert seulement à ceux qui ne comprennent rien à la proportion*).

I prefer the architect to "provoke" art by means of something else besides rules. I mean to express this by two paintings I have never painted but that would resemble a votive diptych. One would represent the architect kneeling near his bed, praying like a child, asking for architectural grace, for inspiration. The other would represent the architect asleep, with "ideas" coming to him, through a window open to the sky, along a wire or ray. Along that wire would travel house plans, solutions of volumes, shapes of furniture. This vision is valid, after all. We have our voices, but ideas visit us at night. They are received graces.

—The architect (the artist) must take time into consideration, for architecture must age well. New architecture is not yet perfect. Le Corbusier revealed to us the magic of "when the cathedrals were white." This whiteness was the beauty of those prestigious times. But the same cathedrals are now beautiful even if black. Their beauty is that they are *still* beautiful (and maybe even more beautiful).

Every beautiful piece of architecture has survived its original appearance, purpose, and function, and many have served many functions successively. The right of an architectural work to last—and finally, its right to be—lies only in its beauty and not in its function. For it assumes a new function—beauty. Beauty is the most resistant structure and the most resistant material. It opposes the destruction of man, himself the most ferocious ally of time.

—The architect (the artist) must not participate in the cult of beautiful materials; nothing is less spiritual and more material than a beautiful material. The fact that the Seagram building of Mies was made of bronze gave me some doubts about it. Palladio worked with modest materials. A beautiful material is the same for all. Only a few are able to create beauty out of a modest material. Beautiful materials do not exist, anyway. Only the right material exists.

So-called refined people are amateurs. They are not really refined because they always want beautiful, refined materials everywhere. Rough plaster in the right place is the beautiful material for that place. This is real refinement. To replace it with a "noble" material would be vulgar.

—The architect (the artist) must consider the functionality of architecture as an implicit fact, never as a goal. Functionality is the goal (and the limitation) of the engineer. A machine functions and is beautiful. Architecture that does nothing but function is not yet beautiful and is not even thoroughly functional. It functions entirely only if it is beautiful. Then it functions forever ("perpetuity," says Palladio). It must function at the artistic level, at the level of enchantment (*Qu'elle chante,* says Corbu). It functions even when it no longer functions poetically. It functions in history, in culture, in magic. This is the ultimate function of architecture—to surpass the function that originated it, to function at the level of art.

(The functionality of a machine consists of *its* motion; the functionality of a house, of a room, of a building consists of directing *our* motion.)

1957

Konrad Wachsmann, who began his career as a journeyman cabinetmaker and then studied architecture under Heinrich Tessenow and Hans Poelzig, worked in Berlin in the second half of the 1920s as chief architect of the largest factory in Europe making prefabricated wood elements. In 1941 he emigrated to America and began collaborating with Walter Gropius on a "Packaged House System." Commissioned by the newly established General Panel Corporation, this was a prefabricated building system designed to allow easy assembly on site, by unskilled labor, of a two-story structure. He and Gropius chose to work with wood as it was the only material then available that combined the advantages of quality, quantity, and economy. In the architects' view, the cheap modular building system afforded an efficient and rational solution to postwar housing manufacture.

176–80

It also represented, for Wachsmann, an idealized system of relations between building elements. Wachsmann's intellectual approach to problems of industrial technology led him to invent, from the 1940s on, a series of conceptually pure building systems in wood, metal, and tubular steel. Especially focused on the joint or point of structural coupling and the reduction of the constructional repertory to the fewest possible elements, Wachsmann's designs gave primacy to universal connectors and flexible components capable of being recombined in a maximum number of ways. His structures included spectacular space frames like the one commissioned by the United States Air Force in 1959, developed as a hangar spanning 120 feet between supports.

Throughout his career Wachsmann maintained a balance between applied work and theoretical research. Many of his pioneering experiments were carried out in educational settings like the Institute of Design in Chicago, where he served as professor from 1950 to 1956, and in various schools in Europe, where he conducted seminars based on his team approach to problem solving—a pedagogical method related to that proposed by Gropius for professional use. In 1956 the U.S. Department of State sponsored a several-year traveling exhibition of Wachsmann's work, the preparation of which was undertaken at the newly opened Hochschule für Gestaltung in Ulm. For this occasion Wachsmann wrote the text excerpted here, synthesizing his major ideas. Three years later he published an important book, *Wendepunkt im Bauen* (translated as *The Turning Point of Building*, 1961). Here Wachsmann traced the impact of the Industrial Revolution on construction and elaborated the theoretical bases of his own work.

86–92, 288–99

Taking a position akin to that of both Buckminster Fuller and Tomás Maldonado but always insisting on the essential contribution of aesthetics in the implementation of technical knowledge, Wachsmann concluded in his book, "The purposes of the age will be served by the universal designer who, like the industrial designer, will use industry as a complicated tool. The boundary lines between product, building element, and structure will become more and more blurred until they vanish altogether."

Published as "Vom Bauen in unserer Zeit" in Baukunst und Werkform *(January 1957), pp. 26–31. Translated by Lynnette Widder. Courtesy of Judith Wachsmann.*

On Building in Our Time
Konrad Wachsmann

Science and technology bring forward problems whose solution requires exacting studies before final results can be formulated.

The machine is the tool of our time. It is the cause of every effect manifested in the social order.

New materials, methods, processes, knowledge of statics and dynamics, planning techniques, and new social conditions must be accepted.

Buildings should develop indirectly, as a result of the multiplication of cells and elements, in accordance with the laws of industrialization.

Modular systems of coordination, scientific methods of experimentation, laws of automation, and precision influence creative thinking.

Highly complex problems of statics and mechanics demand the closest cooperation between industry and specialists organized in ideal master teams.

Humane and aesthetic ideas will gain new impetus through the uncompromising application of contemporary knowledge and resources.

These seven maxims serve as a fundamental explanation of my work. [. . .]

In order to clarify my thesis I will describe my own vision of the development of building in the future.

The preparations will be more complex, but the designer's constructional ideas will become much simpler. I cannot recall ever having seen a building that was *too* simple. I have mainly seen buildings that were not simple enough. But when I saw a truly simple building, I always found it very beautiful. I decline to make a distinction between simple and naive. Naiveté is a virtue. And I believe that truly modern building in the future will be less refined, and for this reason more naive.

The use of beams will disappear more and more. They will be replaced by horizontal slabs. Columns will also be thought of differently in the future than they now are. They will disappear almost entirely, until we no longer notice them even when they are there. Likewise, what we conceive of as walls, windows, and doors will change. I can imagine that only planes will exist: opaque, transparent, and movable. There will be openings and dynamic space. The mechanical installations of our structures will extend into unbelievably complicated systems, primarily in horizontal planes. But these slabs will also take very substantial loads. We will probably repress that which is often emphasized in the vertical.

In terms of structure, the tendency to follow the loads transmitted will probably govern. This may also lead to the systemized concentration of stresses in points. More and more, masses will dissolve into the smallest members which distribute space. These will meet at joints and thus create the impression of points in space bound by

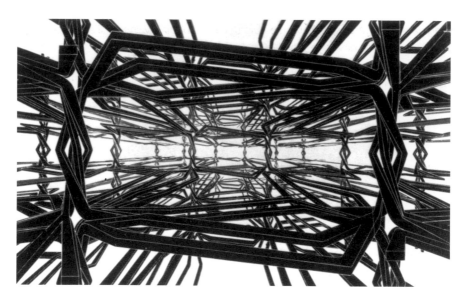

Perspectival representation of stresses in a multistory building. It is predicated on the development of only one structural element. This element is much more complex in detail than the simple three-legged member that appears in the drawing. The drawing is meant to demonstrate that the application of the machine, of new methods and processes, of new materials and the laws of multiplication, of the strong ordering device of modular coordinate systems and complicated static conditions, need not necessarily lead to monotony. On the contrary, they can produce completely new visual conceptions, as indeed occurred in the present case after the details were developed in an objective manner, without prior knowledge of the result. The unexpected and fantastical nature of this system arises not from a preconceived idea, but from rational reflection.

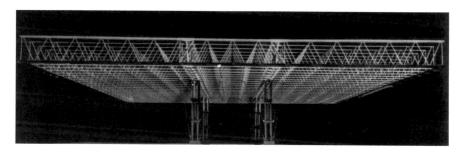

Hangar resting on four supports and cantilevering on all sides approximately twenty meters. The construction is of standardized tubes with uniform, electrically welded end plates.

imaginary lines. Materials distributed along these imaginary lines will again produce stresses through their own inflection and deformation. Curved and combined elements and projections will replace the columns and horizontal beams still acceptable today. We are generally persuaded already that the classical language of architecture is no longer precise enough to satisfy today's creative challenges. It is likewise difficult to imagine that any conception of a truly modern building could be realized by means of conventional or classical construction methods. This persuasion may be the reason that we tend today to accept large and pure technical constructions and dynamic mechanical machines as truly appropriate and modern.

Surface articulation will as good as disappear shortly; smooth surfaces will dominate. We are approaching a period in which people will again be able to recognize the play of lines created by joints and surface areas. Such weightless, massless planes will govern structures. More that ever before, lightness will be characteristic. Forces and weights will be suspended. One of the central ideas of future architecture will be the differentiation and separation of each object and each function, in detail and as a whole.

I will not go into how people will live together, nor into a discussion of urban and rural planning, nor of traffic problems. But I know that someday an order will prevail based on the repetition of a nucleus, a structural core of connections. It will be an order which informs the surfaces, structures, rooms, buildings, streets, plazas, parks, and cities and ultimately the whole panorama of the civilized world.

And here one hopes that the artist will come forward to translate facts and functions into the abstract language of art by exercising his genius and vision: then the history of art will begin anew.

Living as we do under such circumstances, and in preparation for this future condition, we must be satisfied with following functions and remaining impersonally objective and modest in our actions.

The effect follows the cause, "form follows function." As long as human beings have to adapt to new insights and scientific discoveries and to devote themselves to the study and analysis of practical experience, the dynamic condition celebrated in Sullivan's maxim will exist. And when they recognize their limitations, based on their own ability to understand, and thus become able to master all the surrounding factors not only technically but also socially and emotionally, then an ideal situation will become foreseeable. Then function will follow form, and causes will be subordinate to effects.

I can imagine no higher goal toward which mankind should strive.

1957

It is instructive to compare the following writing by **Louis Kahn** to his essay on

47–54 monumentality of thirteen years earlier. The theme of structural expressiveness remains his central preoccupation, but it is now transformed from a generalized enthusiasm for the aesthetic potential of contemporary engineering to a more personal and poetic statement drawn from his own experience and sensibility.

By the late 1950s Kahn had arrived at a mature design philosophy. Along with numerous smaller commissions, he had completed the Yale University Art Gallery and the Trenton Bathhouse and undertaken several major urban design projects for downtown Philadelphia. In 1957 he began work on the Richards Medical Building at the University of Pennsylvania, a first major statement of his seminal thesis of servant and served space. His early sketches already show the defining presence of "hollow stones"—a system of brick-clad volumetric shafts. Initially intended to provide the building's structural support, they ultimately served to separate stairs, elevators, animal quarters, air ducts, and other mechanical equipment from the major space of the work areas. "I do not like ducts. I do not like pipes. I hate them really thoroughly, but because I hate them so thoroughly I feel they have to be given their place," he explained. Kahn's concept of the functional utilization of the inner space of structural members seems to have been inspired by the lightweight technology of the tubular space

86–92 frame—in line with the ideas of Buckminster Fuller and his engineer colleague Robert Le Recolais, and explored in his own Philadelphia City Tower project of 1954 (with Anne Tyng)—but now, significantly, returned to a more archaic idiom. He thus embodied the modern "space order concept" of hollowness in terms of load-bearing solidity. In search of a new architecture of massiveness, monumentality, and closure, he reinterpreted formed concrete, rolled steel, and prefabricated joints in the context of Greco-Gothic construction.

In a more fully articulated statement of his philosophy, ultimately entitled "Form and Design" (first presented at CIAM's Otterlo meeting in 1959, later rewritten and widely circulated), Kahn defined his notion of the "form" or "preform" as a conceptual idea ordering all human institutions —"what a thing wants to be." Mediating this was "design"—the "how" of the building, its contingent circumstances. At Richards, despite the powerful symbolism of the volumetric assembly, the servant-served concept overrode its own functionality; inadequate control of light and ad hoc utilization of the laboratoriescast doubt on which was really the major and which the minor element of the *parti*. Form, in Kahn's own terms, had overpowered design. Kahn was to achieve a much fuller integration of his dialectical theses of servant-served and form-design in the Salk Institute Laboratories, a masterwork in La Jolla, California, of 1965.

Kahn's hierarchical distinction between functional and honorific spaces and his concept of revealed process had immediate impact in the early 1960s on

181–83, 319–24 architects like Team 10 and the Japanese Metabolists. Slightly later, in the developing climate of postmodernism, especially in Italy, it was his recourse to

392–98 history, to the mythos of collective memory and a typological interpretation of institutions, that guided his reception and "rediscovery." New scholarship on his career is contained in the recent exhibition catalogue by David Brownlee and David De Long, *Louis Kahn: In the Realm of Architecture* (1991). His insightful (and often awkward) verbalizations on architecture are collected in full in Alessandra Latour, ed., *Louis I. Kahn: Writings, Lectures, Interviews* (1991).

From Perspecta *4 (1957), pp. 2–3. Also published in discontinuous form in* Royal Architectural Institute of Canada Journal, *October 1957, pp. 375, 377. Courtesy of* Perspecta: The Yale Architectural Journal *and the* Royal Architectural Institute of Canada Journal.

Architecture Is the Thoughtful Making of Spaces
Louis Kahn

Reflect on the great event in architecture when the walls parted and columns became.

It was an event so delightful and so thought wonderful that from it almost all our life in architecture stems.

The arch, the vault and the dome mark equally evocative times when they knew what to do from how to do it and how to do it from what to do.

Today these form and space phenomena are as good as they were yesterday and will always be good because they proved to be true to order and in time revealed their inherent beauty.

In the architecture of stone the single stone became greater than the quarry. Stone and architectural order were one.

A column when it is used should be still regarded as a great event in the making of space. Too often it appears as but a post or prop.

What a column is in steel or concrete is not yet felt as a part of us.

It must be different from stone.

Stone we know and feel its beauty.

Material we now use in architecture we know only for its superior strength but not for its meaningful form. Concrete and steel must become greater than the engineer.

The expected wonders in concrete and steel confront us. We know from the spirit of architecture that their characteristics must be in harmony with the spaces that want to be and evoke what spaces can be.

Forms and spaces today have not found their position in order though the ways of making things are new and resourceful.

A space in architecture shows how it is made.

The column or wall defines its length and breadth; the beam or vault its height.

Nothing must intrude to blur the statement of how a space is made.

The forms characterizing the great eras of architecture present themselves and tempt us to adapt them to concrete and steel. The solid stones become thinner and eye deceiving devices are found to hide the unwanted but inevitable services. Columns and beams homogenized with the partitions and ceiling tile concealing hangers, conduits, pipes and ducts deform the image of how space is made or served and therefore presents no reflection of order and meaningful form.

We are still imitating the architecture of solid stones.

Building elements of solids and voids are inherent in steel and concrete. These voids are in time with the service needs of spaces. This characteristic combined with space needs suggest new forms.

One quality of a space is measured by its temperature by its light and by its ring.

The intrusion of mechanical space needs can push forward and obscure form in structure.

Integration is the way of nature. We can learn from nature.

How a space is served with light air and quiet must be embodied in the space order concept which provides for the harboring of these services.

The nature of spaces is further characterized by the minor spaces that serve it. Storage-rooms, service-rooms and cubicals must not be partitioned areas of a single space structure, they must be given their own structure.

The space order concept must extend beyond the harboring of the mechanical services and include the "servant spaces" adjoining the spaces served.

This will give meaningful form to the hierarchy of spaces.

Long ago they built with solid stones.

Today we must build with "hollow stones."

1957

"The fundamental characteristics of Futurist architecture will be obsolescence and transience," wrote Filippo Tommaso Marinetti in 1914 in the "Manifesto of Futurist Architecture." "Houses will last less long than we. Each generation will have to build its own city." More than forty years later the Hungarian-born architect and engineer **Yona Friedman**, likewise predicting that demographic facts and new habits of life would increasingly mitigate against a sedentary existence, proposed something even more radical: that all institutions founded on eternal norms be subject to periodic renewal—marriage, for example, every five years, property rights every ten years. The greatest obstacle to such a "general theory of mobility," as Friedman saw it, was the rigidity of the built environment. Housing, work places, and services tended to outlive their designers as well as their own usefulness because of the way they were constructed.

Friedman thus proposed a "mobile architecture," by which he intended not an architecture of moving parts but of flexibility, a system that offered built-in adaptability to new uses and was easily demountable. The latter took the form of a multideck inhabitable space-frame structure of indeterminate size, leaving the ground plane free for circulation and services. Dwelling units would fill in the above-ground voids between the structural members of the frame and could be reclustered at will. An infinitely extendable matrix of such open structures, multiplying surface area through their elevated levels, could give rise, in Friedman's view, to a new form of urbanism: the *spatial city*. Though inspired by Corbusian schemes, Friedman's vision of the future—illustrated in a series of diagrammatic sketches depicting the new urban system lofting over the old— was explicitly antiformal. Emphasizing scientific planning methods, the mobile utopia reduced the role of the architect and urban planner (professions that he saw as increasingly merged) to that of a specialist in infrastructures.

Friedman's critique had emerged out of CIAM's penultimate meeting in Dubrovnik in 1956, which he attended. He felt that the discussions on "mobility," "development," and "growth and change"—themes strongly promoted by the Smithsons and Team 10 at this date—were too vague. In late 1957, having relocated from Israel to Paris and earning his livelihood by making animated films, he founded the Groupe d'Etudes d'Architecture Mobile (GEAM), which included architects from France, Holland, Poland, and Israel. He also drafted a manuscript setting out his ideas. Among the readers to whom he sent it for comment, besides the members of GEAM, were Le Corbusier, Jacob Bakema, and the sociologist Roger Caillois, whose theories of play and leisure had been influential on him. Friedman consolidated his manuscript two years later and privately published a small edition. It attracted considerable interest in the technical-utopian wing of the profession; a copy sent to Buckminster Fuller initiated a friendship between the two. GEAM had its first working conference in Rotterdam in 1958 and issued a set of proposals in 1960 (for this document see Ulrich Conrads's *Programs and Manifestoes on 20th-Century Architecture*).

Friedman continued to develop a set of original ideas on "coherent planning" over the next decade. His analysis of leisure time and of the city as a place of collective encounter is not unrelated to the more anarchic aesthetics of Constant's New Babylon. Accused of being a technocrat, he defended his concept of mobile planning as flexible and conducive to individual management of private space: "Planning becomes bearable," he claimed, "because it is not definitive and the possibility of correction or experimentation is still there."

Written in 1957. Published in "L'Architecture Mobile" (privately printed, 1959), pp. 18, 19. Republished in Yona Friedman, L'Architecture mobile: vers une cité conçue par ses habitants *(Paris: Casterman, 1970), pp. 62–64. Courtesy of the author.*

181–83

86–92

314–18

Program of Mobile Urbanism
Yona Friedman

Summary of the program of mobile urbanism

The concepts determining life in society are in perpetual transformation (organized time and leisure time).

The concepts of familial cohabitation as well as the concepts of urban cohabitation (ownership of urban lands in their present sense) are obsolete.

New demands lead us to study the "mobility" of the city:

a.   New constructions serving for individual shelters must:
1.   touch a minimum surface of the ground;
2.   be demountable and movable;
3.   be transformable at will by the individual inhabitant.

b.   The foundation points containing the junctions with sewage systems, canalizations, supply of water and electricity, etc., must be at maximum distance, following present technical possibilities.

c.   The means of interior circulation in the city must be communal; automobiles and other individual means of circulation will remain out of the city and will only be used for interurban circulation. The city belongs to the pedestrians. Their movements must be protected from the weather.

d.   As to public shelters, the centers of concourse must be, according to their usage, "static" or "ambulatory" (basilicas or promenades). The constructions serving as their roofs (the public shelters) must be interchangeable and movable, like the dwellings.

Techniques

The techniques that correspond to this program have two principal characteristics:

1.   the structures rest on very elongated *pilotis* (long-legged structures);

2.   the structures are composed of a continuous three-dimensional framework whose voids are utilized as dwelling cells [habitats]; these structures are called containing structures, in relation to other structures that carry the dwelling cells, etc., composing a sort of *platform*. These last are called carrying structures.

Conclusion

To aid urban technicians to get out of their present difficulty the following are required:

1.   techniques which permit construction of temporary urban clusters conceived in terms of their periodic regrouping, according to necessity, and which do not entail the material loss represented by current demolitions;

2.   techniques which permit movement of networks of water and energy supply, sewers and circulation routes (networks that can follow the clusters) without degrading the terrain by being evident and without causing the losses represented by demolition;

3.   these techniques must lead to utilization of cheaper elements, simple to assemble and to demount, easy to transport (in terms of weight and bulk), and ready to be reutilized.

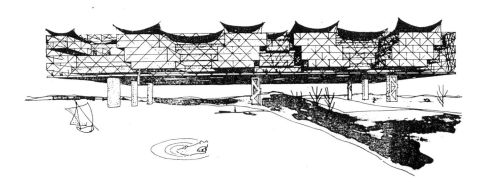

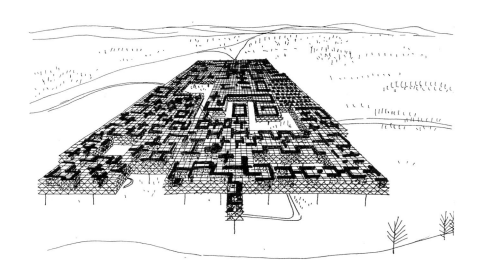

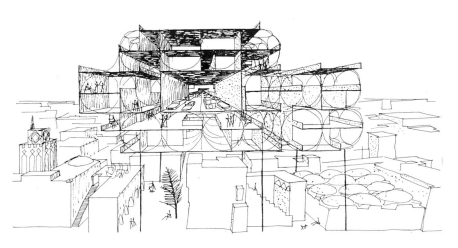

[From L'Architecture Mobile, *1959.]*

1958

Viennese emigré **Richard Neutra** was one of the chief early proselytizers of the European modern movement in America. From the refined athletic utopia of the Health House built for Philip Lovell in Los Angeles in 1929 to the mature and tempered position reflected in his essay "Human Setting in an Industrial Civilization" written thirty years later, Neutra served as mirror and lamp for the ascendancy of the new aesthetic in his adopted land.

31–41

Neutra had sought out Louis Sullivan upon his arrival in America in 1923, and a year later, when Sullivan died, met Frank Lloyd Wright at his funeral. This encounter led to an apprenticeship at Taliesin, where Neutra was lastingly affected by Wright's attitude to site, though interpreting it in a less romantic, more scientific vein. In his early enthusiasm for everything American, embodied in his book *Wie baut Amerika?* (1927), he expressed only slightly skeptical optimism about the Fordist ethos, playfully celebrating it by embellishing the Lovell house with Model-T headlights. But by 1954, in his book *Survival through Design*, he warned that the "overadvertised industrial technology" that had become the instrument of advanced design was "flooding us off our physiological bearings." In his attempt to salvage the human and biological values threatened by mechanization, he emphasized that "man is always in the middle of this ineluctable presence called the environment."

While the prewar Lovell house was to remain his definitive work, Neutra strove in the postwar years to elaborate his psychophysiological philosophy. His practice extended over a large and diverse range of projects, including (in a not entirely unsuccessful partnership with Robert Alexander) communal centers, schools, offices, and government buildings, and (on his own) a suite of single-family houses for clients of moderate and more substantial income in which he was able to implement more fully, and on occasion with much sensitivity, a "clinical" approach to individual environmental needs. In an article that appeared in 1951 in the *AIA Journal*, the architect Ralph Walker had claimed that modernism and its emigré exponents were engaged in "stripping down culture to unattractive minima or in twisting neurosis into nihilism." This accusation, crudely aimed at Gropius along with Neutra, Mies van der Rohe, Serge Chermayeff, Marcel Breuer. and others, unwittingly evokes a book like Theodor Adorno's *Minima Moralia*, published the same year. Adorno, another Viennese expatriate who settled in Los Angeles during this period, had become so disillusioned with Western reason as to express doubts that the world was still habitable. Neutra's diagnosis of a technological civilization's insensitive depletion of nature was only slightly less sobering than the Frankfurt School philosopher's indictment of modern culture; nonetheless he posited a philosophy of "biorealism" aimed at "survival through design." Walker's comments evoke the McCarthyite climate of these years, responsible for the cancellation, in 1951, of Neutra's controversial contract for large-scale public housing on Elysian Park Heights, considered "creeping socialism" by the *Los Angeles Times* and others. Yet despite such disappointments and other crises of a personal nature that undermined Neutra's later career, the architect never deviated from his vivid crusade for a better future.

In the following essay Neutra elaborates his biorealistic creed. An opening image recalls the visionary traffic schema he had advanced in a project of 1926 called "Rush City Reformed," but now in an ironic vein. The architect's postwar critique of a society that has realized its appetite for progress in an avaricious consumer culture is summed up in the apocalypse of one man emerging from the commuting masses, accidentally empowered when his stalled car jams the approach to the Golden Gate Bridge.

From Zodiac *2 (1958), pp. 69–75. Courtesy of Dion Neutra.*

Human Setting in an Industrial Civilization
Richard J. Neutra

Social cohesion and technical spread

The species *humana* has long had a wide global range out of which it now begins to burst by rockets into outer space. Its physical setting, once easily tended by local habituation, has turned into a design problem of so formidable a complexity that my humbleness before it deepens, the longer I attempt a contribution.

The United States may well have overextended herself, on the order of a business concern, internally and externally over long distance. Not only its political missions, its embassies, but its cinema films depicting American life, and misunderstandings of it, our commercial manners, our automobiles, have diffused their contemporary flavor and at least on the surface proselytized the world somewhat like the Roman imperium in antiquity and the still farther flung Hispano-Hapsburg empire of the post-Renaissance. We have converted the Pakistanis, not to Christianity, but to the right-hand-drive, and to endless rows of army trucks imported annually as appropriated by Congress. Our Quonset huts dot the jungle clearings of the "Paradise of the Pacific" and the South Seas, way beyond our legitimate trust territory.

But now all this is no longer just "Americanism," whatever the initial stages of the fantastic industrialized civilization of superhuman scale may originally owe to one or the other national focus. The steel sections from which Japanese elevated railway structures are built to carry thundering electric trains, and to corrode over neatly preserved and tended rural rice paddies, or in the midst of the sprawl of a Tokyo of eight million population—are rolled in Kiushu, not in Pittsburgh. The swarms of double-deck buses piling up at the Kowloon Star Ferry are of Hong Kong assembly and fabrication, like the Coca Cola locally bottled; the twelve new, miraculously mechanized beet sugar factories in the fields of ancient Anatolia are imports of French manufacturing talent to Turkey, even if their ingenuity of agrarian economy may be supported by U.S. "Economic Cooperation" dollars. From Manila to Caracas the Douglas and Lockheed airliners, laden with commercial "agents provocateurs" and tourists, the upholstery of the big cars from Detroit and the Hilton International hotels have brightly colored the mental and the physical scene, both conditioning minds and producing antagonism. These contemporary inserts abroad often are erratic islands strangely and offensively elevated in the midst of a wide sea of soft currency and direly low purchasing power.

Power, mammoth magnitude, mass transaction in material, energy, and megalopolitan turmoil are our American pride as well as our patient suffering.

An episode again and again tends to come to my mind. One of my clients lives in Orinda, east of the beautiful San Francisco Bay and, like a quarter million others, drives every morning to town over the world's proudly longest bridge.

Recently, he told me, he had a wonderful inspiring experience—a revelation of power. On the bridge approach his car broke down. For twenty minutes he was holding up behind him thirty-five thousand two-tone cars in shiny Duco. It was a magnificent picture. He could see their chromium-plated bumpers glittering in the morning sun, sparkling like the lovely waters of the Golden Gate beneath, as he looked in the other back mirror of his windshield. He could hear from far and near harmoniously whooping horns, as every driver longed to reach his parking place and busy office desk over there in downtown San Francisco. He said it was a moment to feel one's power, the thrilling power of the unprecedented progress of our wondrous age.

Not every enthusiast of progress and power has so lyrical a view when looking backward, in our early morning that now perhaps begins to approach a hot noonday.

Love for the New World of "liberty or death" was instilled in me about 1910 by indeed unequal bards of America, Adolf Loos, Louis Sullivan, and Frank Lloyd Wright. Yet I found myself also pitifully lonesome under the spell of fanciful superscale statistics and giantism in a hemisphere more and more reverberating of it from Vancouver to Buenos Aires.

In English the word "figure" stands for both number and shape—what Plato would have called *eidos* or what perhaps a school of German psychology terms *Gestalt*. American Jamesian Pragmatism has in its popularization veered toward utilitarian numerology, a cult of big numbers and of winning statistics, no matter how splendid writers and thinkers since Henry David Thoreau have in this country tried to uphold the humanities. They have bravely postulated a culture of cities, and found its continuity through all the only supposedly unmitigated dark ages, even that of Victorianism.

When much later, about 1930, returning from Zen Buddhist Japan and lecturing before students and colleagues in Asia, I was given the privilege to address also many countrymen in the then brand new "School of Social Research," lower Manhattan, or the gilded Blackstone Hotel on the central waterfront of Chicago, where an institute of industrial arts was to be born, I spoke of the ritual of perfectionism, intimately bound to human nature, of the Bauhaus where I had just been invited as a guest, the International Congresses for Modern Architecture, of history as Giedion sees it, the problems of mathematical rationalism long intertwined with timeless abstract classicism—and of my own ideas to make architecture a warm-tempered, nonabstract, most intimately enveloping environmental art, intensely close to nature—human nature as well as nature outside our skin.

In those days I urged to follow an old American tradition and bring vital Europeans, Gropius and Mies to the New World, while the old seemed to crumble; and they came and taught, so that I felt less lonesome.

But first, and long after, I had no clients at all. In the early twenties my solitude remained arctic in the midst of this scene of humming wheels. Anyone can see why, who glances through the trade journals of that period. I made drawings of tall office buildings somewhat like Lever Brothers, but instead the Woolworth Building went up with a fanfare.

But the Woolworth had such a ridiculous position in the city plan, such a misrelation to New York City Hall, the adjacent traffic arteries and East River bridge, that in my mind and on patient paper I began to "Reform Rush City" in dozens of studies all related to each other, like Balzac's stories in the *Comédie Humaine*. An *urbs* of wholesomeness with healthy pedestrian neighborhoods in the orbit, with rail-and-air transfers at the ends of a precalculated ribbon city along a spine of central industries and distributing facilities of goods, was one of the more comprehensive schemes which I analyzed and described in all detail. I was indeed deeply happy when Lewis Mumford, decades later, saw something exemplary in these lonely forgotten studies, included entire school and recreation systems, gravity centers of community life, and kept on laboring hard against the sprawling blight that befouls and outdistances nature around our cities.

Physis and physics
Apart from any sentimental attachment, I saw nature phylogenetically and ontogenetically

as our matrix, ever since I had as an adolescent boy started to study experimental physiological psychology in the ponderous tomes of the great Wilhelm Wundt. His observational curiosity readily fused with all that stirred in me as a future planner of communities and a designer of living spaces. Modern architecture, explained by the progress of engineering and technique, was the creed of us avant-gardists, and I passionately experimented with a wide array of constructional novelties, such as bolted and welded steel, sheet metal shaped and engineered into stress-taking stiffness, shot and vibrated concrete. Prefabrication and radiant heating I explored, and such efforts of mine were graciously reported as of interest and merit in scientific and trade journals, which in a technological civilization have a predominant readership. The romantic rhetoric of an age of glorious engineering possessed also me—so much so that all my Beaux-Arts colleagues of yesterday's vogue disparaged me as "just an engineer," a bad word, indeed intended as a mortifying insult at that time.

But this blame was not justly fixed on me, as in 1926 and 1927 I began the plans of the "Health House." It could have easily been called the first light residential steel structure—largely composed of most slender suspension members in tension, or it could well have been named the "glass" or the "gunite house." Although it was bristling with exciting technology from stem to stem and from frame to finish it was called Health House, and built it was with the patient, even passionate connivance of a physician preoccupied with the health-sustaining and therapeutic stimuli an architect has the chance to arrange for a lifetime around man, woman, and child—especially the child, in its so plastic and impressionable infancy.

When I used to my client the word "psychosomatic," it was then startlingly new, and I believe I never had heard it myself. But having had six years of Greek in school, it seemed to have a fused meaning most significant to me, most telling and serviceable.

Psychosomatically and in every other way an architect is not in the "quick turnover" but in the "long-range investment" business, if one can call his sacrificial profession any business at all. "Conservative," to use now a time-honored Latin word, meant to me preserving function and value, and I decided at this early age that frills and fashions were splendid for the ladies' apparel branch but bewildering to the person scraping together his savings, straining all his credit to build and to expose his life to a building for decades to come. An architect with fast-changing formal predilections, as a matter of course, scares him by equally fast obsolescence and decay of value. Entire neighborhoods get dated painfully and damagingly without a chance of improvement before physical depreciation and downright dilapidation relieves the surface of the earth of this dead weight, one time after another superseded by new stylishness. No cohesive community, placidly and slowly aging in unison and with a harmonious patina as of yore, is thinkable under such circumstances, and while architecture once used to be related to eternity, now it is subject to the latest copy of the fashion journal.

As Giulio Carlo Argan has expressed, it is an ominous step "from the sphere of the transcendent to that of the contingent" which architecture, the housing of man's activities, has taken. Some 40,000 architects and students of architecture around the globe can be a great help or harm to mankind. I was in recent years impressed to meet very many of them while on journeys of professional consultation, and found them with the same questions in mind and fairly uniformly bewildered because what they learn or have mastered today will, even in major aspects, not be good a few years hence. Yet man and his natural endowment is unchanged, and still poorly served.

Eagle Rock Park Playhouse, 1955. City recreation building opening wide into public hillside park. Suspension members of steel construction help omit obstructions of play area. Roll-up fronts on both sides permit expansion of interior play-space. [Photograph by Julius Shulman.]

It was not profound if modern architecture had been explained to the reluctant Philistine as timely "because this is a new day in engineering, in installations, in plate glass, plastics, and stainless steel . . ." A new day passes every twenty-four hours and the earth keeps spinning on to make us dizzy. Our gadgety property of yesterday becomes listlessly obsolete, overtaken by the Joneses who bought theirs this morning. We are restless, unsteady, impatient. The home is a place where one part of the family waits until the other brings back the car.

Yet mooring, anchorage, rooting are organic necessities, not even the freest bird can miss. He is even identified with the territory of his nesting and the "biochore," as zoologists call his specific habitat. I have on occasions thought of statistics from the mental health clinic of the Menninger Research group Topeka. Annually, somewhere between nine and twelve million know-how Americans cool their too hot heels in psychiatric waiting rooms, and one wonders where they could all park their cars.

Some seventy percent of the goods which reach the Brooklyn docks F.O.B. factory do so with only an eighteen miles speed per day. That this is what all our power and commotion have bought for us moderns makes one think of the sixteen miles a day mail coaches traveled over an almost roadless continent a hundred years ago. It is not merely a techno-economic disappointment. That eighty percent of overall costs of many goods, including manufacture, carrying charges, and plant overhead, go into the expense of distributing this merchandise over densely truck-clogged Manhattan, where thousands of taxis idle in a perpetual jam, brings to mind the biting of fingernails, the anxieties and neuroses which brain dynamicists have laboratory-produced by arrhythmic stop-go-stop innervations.

Modernity must not clash with the tradition of the so long fairly available calm nerves, natural protectors against stomach ulcers and hardened coronaries. True modernity will have to recognize readily the beneficial balance of cultural engrams and it will strive to "conserve" values and the steadiness derived from peaceful spatial-temporal integration. It will attentively salvage the most precious material that daily is under the urban designers' and the architects' hands: the human individual, although it is the one material least nationally advertised, and, in fact, not for sale.

Wear and tear on organic systems, physiological maintenance costs are overlooked by the "practical man." His supposedly pragmatic politics may have muddled through in ages of lesser velocities and mass transactions. I began to feel doubt that this experience of the past applies in our period of supercolossal stakes in the energy game. Our fireworks have become too bright, too noisy, and too rapid to adjust to. Automation may triumphantly turn ubiquitous, but it does not work at all for an automatic survival in the midst of wild artificialities, to which adaptation cannot be found even in eons while hourly progress goes on. No, not "progress"! We have—an awful plural of it—millions of progresses which take off each other's fenders, clash, crash into each other and never have been conceived in any sort of coordination. They have been conceived in terms of the technologically feasible and the commercially exploitable, hardly in terms of the biologically bearable.

I decided to look at architecture under the angle of Biological Realism, which if not *sub specie aeternitatis,* reckons at least with the long past of organic establishment that realistically deserves all respect from the designer of the human setting. The hardest facts, even economics, enter man's affairs via resilient neurocerebral tissue; no human fact is harder than that. The architect must keep it in mind and feel responsible for the subtle but vital preservation and satisfaction of human nerves and of life itself.

Beginning of our world

Survival starts before birth. There, in the womb, it is best insured. After the "birth trauma" the shock to get into our outer unassorted scene—a shock usually so much more grave than in animals—we all slip right into the hands of the architect. The architect surrounds the obstetrician and his surgical table, the infant nursery, and the nurse.

But before his physical arrangements enter our life there was the peace of paradise in the uterus. A very even, a wholesome and formative stimulation, and "even" thermal offering to the skin by the tepid liquid in which we float and almost perpetually with the same vestibular appeal of a steady suspended body position. We carry through all life a lovely sort of memory, an engram of this floating in warmth: rhythmic dynamics in the mother body, muffled acoustics in the pitch dark; as yet, no smells, no tastes, no vision.

Then comes that shock of birth: pains of stretched and squeezed tissue, sudden outer acoustical impacts. The eye is opened and fast changing brightnesses and shadows storm in on us, whirl about us like a tornado, the smells, the commotion of surroundings still amorphous, but terrifically powerful by contrast to the calm just gone. Things happen by the hour, by the second in the fast progressing maturation of the young organism, which has so much more neurocerebral endowment than any other "young animal" in the world. And it is born, issued and exposed to outer stimuli earlier, after a gestation period much more abbreviated than any. Comparative embryologists assume that human birth has through biological ages been more and more precipitated in order to confront this wonderfully receptive system with its needed abundance of neural food of stimulation.

No animal, and surely not man, is born in a litter of thirty or forty, but a tiny wide-open absorptive creature, he finds himself thrown into the infant nursery of the maternity ward with many bassinets filled with whining creatures. There are sharp smells of medications and antiseptics, and moving-about and talking-aloud nurses. There are appalling intensity—differentials from injudicious light—and thermal sources, the stark evaporation coolness of being "taken up" and out of wet diapers, or being made to stare at a luminaire overhead, startling sensations which never could have happened thirty minutes earlier in the womb. Yes, we now are in the hands of the architect, in this case the designer of the hospital. Is it a "patient-centered facility," or a dollar-and-cents-per-square-foot affair?

Aseptic hospitals have, to many, been the prototype of modern architecture. Americans have financed and built hospitals galore, but their principles do not include sufficiently the harmoniousness wrought into his sanatorium by the physician Kallinos of Pergamon, two hundred years before Christ. Its impressive ruins still give the idea of a drugless therapy of harmonious dance, choral singing, and soothing suggestions and stimulations to patients on a rhythmically arranged architectural promenade under vaultings of lovely repetitive shape.

In the stupendously formative weeks after birth, "stereognosis" begins to fuse the ever better synchronized passive sensorial input of millions of receptors, many muscles being innervated to explore and also help support inner and outer sensations.

Tactile shapes emerge, the nipple of a resilient breast is grasped by tiny lips, and a properly tempered and sweetened liquid enters over taste buds of the tongue and its thermal points. The suckling response is elicited and it continues until again other visceral, "enteroceptive" sensations of hunger are abated, or else the baby bursts out into auditive self-expression.

The inner and outer world, a combined cluster of excitations, is only slowly "differentiated" by counteractive inhibitory nervous phenomena which take their lifelong role to dam back and to narrow down toward specificity brute generalized excitatory processes. All of it plays into the cortical region, and *selectivity* starts and proves the most intricate and momentous capability of our brain.

The infant, often painfully, begins to distinguish this, that, and the third thing. All of it, though, is still very much less than "a thing." Only very slowly it acquires a degree of thingishness. Even before that, shapes, *Gestalten,* color tint-and-hue combinations, emerge as recognizable signals. They emerge out of the general chaotic din and a mass of unabsorbable, unordered litter of the outer scene. Shapes may be auditive like a bird call, a screeching door. But that door swinging open also changes the illuminative and thermal pattern, as well. The again and again sounded word "baby" seems to have a red mouth as its source. Shapes to the infant become multisensorial and later "cortically embroidered," but from the start they are tactile and thermal and visual, rolled in one, like that nippled breast.

Also space itself, and spaces, with tactile, later visual and auditory demarcations and distances, with intervals, and "directions" become impressive and retainable to "memory." For ever after the designer will depend on these early formed memories and consider them as basic to responses he may expect for his own work and offerings.

The young human begins to rise out of amorphousness, out of indeterminacy and ambiguity, into acuity, clarity, articulation, with less crude, confused energy patterns of excitation. Excitations are becoming better linked to inhibitory innervations, more firmly related to subcortical inductive effects in the thalamus where the basic emotions are brewed and have their seat. Here evolve fundamentals of what the psychologists used to call "motivations," emotive values to act upon. How long has the architect wondered in vain about the origin of likes and dislikes in his clients?

Endocrine discharges go with all these plus and minus "values." Anxiety, irritation, fatigues lead to "escape," all to the resolving of a bundled mass of impression, and further to ever refined differentiation. All of these are true survival devices.

But in life, and especially in the artificial surroundings designed by the architect of our setting, there are millions of occasions to make us sink back into vague and fuzzy indeterminacy, into unbalance, noncoordination of stimuli, and painful, ensuing ambiguity. These are the psychological "dissatisfactions" of design, often tiny but cumulative, which we who are responsible for it must learn to avoid. They are offenses against survival, infringements on a vigorous, wholesomely stabilized vitality.

Man has been endowed to emerge from the awful chaos, as the old mythos tells us, into the ordered "cosmos." It is one of perceptibility, and of a nervously assimilable time-space world. This space is no Euclidean-Newtonian abstraction, it is, so to speak, exuded by ourselves, by our organic equipment, almost like a snail's house by a snail and as concrete. It's profoundly related to our receptive and creative endowment of the "observer." And for what we are not endowed, that simply does not exist for us. There is mutual accommodation between our inner and the outer nature. The term "adaptation" seems too one-sided and simple.

Homo artifex, man the designer and architect, perilously tampers with all that wonderfully timed-together biological entity, unless he gets passionately interested in it and lets curiosity and its findings aid his intuition.

If Leonardo was systematically curious and yet an artist, we, in our famous age of science, are not better artists by being apathetic to the most fascinating contemporary observations. Mechanistic departmentalization is nineteenth-century stuff and loses sight of "total man," measure of things. The entity of the entire organism, the "stereognosis" of millions of receptors, fused in their interaction, should be our current view to guide the design of our artificial setting so that it becomes not too cumbersomely artificial.

Architecture—merely visual?

Yet architecture and vision, especially singled out, have been with preference related long before both of these concepts emerged into consciousness. Let us then, as architects, try to deal with the eye as now known.

We can look at it as one of "the five senses" as little as a chemist of today can operate with the "four elements," fire, water, air, and earth! The eye is in itself a multiple clustered endowment of specific receptions intimately interlocked, a fusion of amazingly varied functions on which the designer will have to act, if he hopes to be effective.

The ability to take in the breadth of an architectural interior or an urban scene is perhaps the first natural premise of such a design. Are humans equipped for taking in such breadth? They are, but in a most peculiar way does this intake differ from a wide-angle photograph, sharp throughout from rim to rim. The acuity of our vision is restricted to a tiny area of the vision field that coincides with the foveal area. It is a small spot on the retina characterized by great density of receptor spacing. This spacing widens progressively toward the periphery and thus the outer parts of our picture become more and more blurred and vague. Still, without peripheral vision we would altogether have only keyhole views of the world. For survival, animal eyes, long before ours, have very much depended on noticing fast movement, or intense brightness differentials, or color splashes on the periphery of the scene.

Whenever these occurrences were detected in the "vague-field," far from center, promptly attention could shift, the muscles would roll the eyeballs and turn the head. The "sharp vision" spot could be brought to bear on the item of suspicion or scrutiny.

There is then always vivid action and dynamic drama in our vision field and by no means ever static passivity on our part. The architect of broad space places, arranges, and spreads out for us his "vision lures" in the peripheral field and by their pattern elicits a corresponding pattern of active participation of muscular innervations. "Intellectual" and "emotional" events alike share in the design, while the eyes roll, the head turns.

But the head may also be brought to tilt, may be raised to gauge the height of a spire, of the Red Tower of Delhi, the vaultings of the Milan cathedral. They all look different when seen on an illustrated airline folder here in our hands. Why is the "real" impression so overwhelming? There on the spot the vestibular sense has been engaged in our inner ear to fuse the excitatory process of its own brain center with that of vision. Our body position and the balancing act in which we are engaged every minute of our wake-life bears deeply on our perception when, in awe, we stand before towering architecture, or following the designer's silent invitation, have our muscles drastically share the experience and we begin to walk through one of the many naves of the mosque of Cordova.

While we walk, our eyes partake in the parallactic shifts, which make the arches nearby move much faster than those of more and more distant naves, and acoustical reverberations echoing our steps on the stone paving supplement and strengthen our spatial awareness. The cool air currents and our own heat losses in this specifically widened space orient us by further, most emotive sensorials, but all of these are continuously merged, however we may shift conscious attention from one to the other.

Of course, not only breadth of visual space is always linked with muscular innervation. For depth we are dynamically urged to accommodate our elastic lens and also in minutely different degrees converge our two eyes for the miracle of stereoscopic finesse which most animals lack. Compared with this, the demarcation of adjacent shade and color areas is a much earlier and primitive acquisition. Our eyes do not only wander over it, but, even when seemingly fixed, their involuntary oscillation with some thirty tiny phase changes a second alternately exposes adjacent receptors to different contiguous shades on both sides of a sharp demarcation line, or to such in gradual transition. Without it the picture could not be articulated, no piers, arches or other architectural features could be distinguished from their background or in their shade-light modulation. As Ettore Sottsass feels, it is all to us a part of the structure in its inevitable unity of the dynamic and the static. Our experience of the architectural phenomenon to reach and move a human soul is, to begin with, one of very dynamic optics. We could dive here into the mysteries of color vision and the marvels of biological individuality, even individual deficiencies. They are so vastly different in both sexes, that a marked degree of color deficiency can indeed pass as a secondary sex characteristic of the common human male, like shaving in the morning.

The palette of art through its history, especially when conventionalism and its common conditioning was weakened, has been greatly increased by the boundless range of permutations in sensorial determinants of individuality. Beyond this lies the almost infinite billion-celled central system of the human brain which climaxes our potential for deviation from norm.

But to stay a moment longer at the threshold of this vast challenge to wonder: Color vision is another sense realm with separate receptors from those of scotoscopy, the vision of grays and shadows, to which the Greeks relegated the souls in dim Hades.

When the sun has sunk beyond the horizon, most of the world becomes scotoscopic to us except some colored clouds floating in the glow of the evening sky. Here the two act in a proportion changing from minute to minute, which seems particularly to move our being. Related to it is the strange realm of illuminative art, which extends some brightened and thus still color-warmed features into the colorless night. I have for many years indulged in the art-potential of this mingling of two sense experiences, which, in nature, stems from the soul-stirring moments of dawn and dusk.

Design for the individual

If architecture is soul-stirring, and indeed it can deeply be so, an uneasy question arises. "How" can it be so if we increasingly lose the immediate contact with the individual in an architectural mass treatment of people?

Intimate and fertile communication with its consumership is perhaps the most vital part of any professional practice, the physician and his patient, the legislator and the constituent, the lawyer and the man whose case he pleads. The minister, the artist, the architect are worth observing and can be kinescoped in their communicative tasks, to advise the student of these professions about their perhaps most significant phase.

Messages produced, given, and received have their physiological base, their anthropological background and social history. Recently they have stupendously rising technological instrumentation and extension. Our office had occasion to engage in the design of a Center of Communicating Arts attached to a "Living Library," an assorted auditoria group and theater, television studios, etc. The dramatic—as well as the fine—and linguistic arts, speech, as dance, all generate shaped messages. If these messages are well done, they are emotive and retainable in the memory. Architecture

The house of Neutra's secretary is a product of industry, as its outlying site and moderate economies depend on American motorization with a huge individual car ownership in Los Angeles, where one half million cars converge every morning to enter the "downtown" of a vastly decentralized city of only a few thousand inhabitants on each of its thousand square miles of metropolitan area. [Dorothy Serulic House, Tujunga, California, 1955. Photograph by Julius Shulman.]

is by no means an exception. It conveys carefully formed impacts and evokes running responses; be it the featured setting of a house of worship, a school or college campus, a housing project, an entire community.

But there appears a great difference for all these projects in the specifically feasible human interplay between the interrogating architect, who examines and clarifies the "syndrome," diagnoses the case in relation to the nature of the living occupants, and finally as a therapeut[ics] of human need prescribes the solution in his graphic design. There are rules set by others and by him in the procedure through the stages through which the advice seeker and the architect travel together. A dialogue with impersonal governmental agencies Adriano Olivetti has not found fertile.

Engaged in such dialogues with a school board, the public works office of a naval base, the manager of a commercial company, "a building and grounds committee" of a huge university, I have often met only intermediaries and thus felt largely frustrated to work on projects of impressive budgets, but a minimum of human contact. I yearn to see the flesh and blood inhabitant as client, to comprehend him physiognomically, face to face and in warm direct conversation. The clinical inspiration and "grass roots" experience may always be necessary, even if we had a multitude of laboratories and mountains of generalized statistics to inform us what the human requirements are. It seems to me a major problem in the mass activity of American architecture today not to lose concrete human contact. In abstract practice we may so easily indulge in our own individuality instead of feeling humbly but securely that it will always shine through our enthusiasm and devotion to service other living creatures in theirs. It is by no means interference with our creativity, if like a great actor or a great writer we excel in empathy and grasp the plastic richness of individuals, of real people. In our case as architects they are especially those who have trusted us to design their setting.

Many an architect professes to hate individual domestic projects, not only for their economic difficulty, but because he is tired of the long conversing, or because he "gets mad about it, how unreasonable the owner's wife is" and interferes with his inspiration. But who then is more "unreasonable"? And is pure reason really that exalted leverage the eighteenth century saw in it, free of emotional adulteration? A doctor or psychiatrist who keeps away from contact with patients and deals with them *in abstracto* because they annoy him would be a strange doctor, and a questionable servant or guide of society and mankind. It is the large control group of individual case experiences which give life inspiration and secure decisiveness to medical art, since Hippocrates.

Even an industrialized civilization and its architectural expression cannot dispense with the sacrificially minded service to the individual and the sympathy which specific small groups like a family need, where each member can speak up or be observed for himself in its needs. The clinical approach yields happy relationship and human successes, and an architecture beyond the powers of the photographic lens.

And so I have, in the thicket of many other possible approaches, in spite of all temptation of the monumental mass treatment and mass problems of our time, and in spite of all the economic soundness of mass fabrication which early and always interested me, never abandoned the direct "bedside contact." A clinician needs to know man not only theoretically, but in the flesh, not in captivity as a laboratory subject, but in the natural state, so to speak. Beneath all surface artificialities of progress, nature in its most minute manifestations and essential needs can never be discounted, after all. It is responsible for our very existence and has been our formative setting and mold for hundreds of thousand of years. To heed it is "Biological Realism."

1958

In 1957 Max Bill resigned from the Hochschule für Gestaltung at Ulm over differences with the chairman of the school's new triumvirate board, **Tomás Maldonado**. Maldonado, an Argentine painter and editor of *Nueva Vision* (a journal of art, architecture, and design widely read in Latin America, and the first journal in that part of the world to give coverage to industrial design), joined the founding faculty of the Ulm school in 1954 on Bill's invitation and published a book on Bill in 1955. His educational ideas, however, turned out to diverge substantially from Bill's. The latter's intention had been to continue the original Bauhaus "idea," updating the original curriculum for the needs of postwar society. Maldonado, on the other hand, believed the older school's philosophy of education through art to be obsolete and unable to respond to current conditions. In the following paper tracing the history of design education in relation to industrial development, Maldonado presented a radical manifesto for the Ulm school's new direction and his theory of "scientific operationalism"—a praxis based on "operational, manipulable, real knowledge."

157–62

Maldonado's argument was that aesthetic considerations, whether humanist (as in the Beaux-Arts tradition) or empiricist (as in the Bauhaus and other progressive schools), could no longer be paramount in a field determined by economics, technology, and social needs; on the contrary, the latter should determine design. As such, the designer's role was no longer to be an artist (serving Bill's elite of "good form" or catering to presumed popular taste through styling), nor was it even to be a constructor-inventor-planner on the Henry Ford model. Instead the designer should to be trained as a *coordinator* of all the diverse requirements of product fabrication and use. The coordinator was to operate "at the nerve centers of our industrial civilization, precisely where industry makes the most important decisions affecting our daily lives."

This argument encompassed architecture, henceforth understood at Ulm basically as industrialized building. Under Bill the program had been divided into five departments: product design, architecture, city planning, information, and visual communication. Maldonado reconstituted it in 1957 into two: industrial design (including product design and industrialized building) and visual and verbal communication. He also revamped the Bauhaus-derived introductory course, downplaying visual and manual training and stressing research methods and mathematics. In the 1960s, through internal debate as well as the influence of visiting faculty, the school's orientation underwent further revisions. The stress on methodology yielded to greater emphasis on praxis, and the technocratic approach to a critical theory of design, communication, and ergonomics.

In 1968 the school at Ulm suffered something of its predecessor's fate in being forced to close when funding was withdrawn by the conservative local government. More fatal to it in a large sense, though, was the paradox of being both ahead of and behind its time: ahead in that the profession of industrial design was still in its infancy during the 1950s; behind in its pursuit of an austere functionalism at a time when Germany had its sights set on new prosperity. For a history of the school's internal developments, see Kenneth Frampton, "Apropos Ulm: Curriculum and Critical Theory," in *Oppositions* 3 (May 1974). For the reception of the following document, see the discussion that followed its republication in *Stile Industria* (no. 21, 1959), including contributions by Reyner Banham, Gillo Dorfles, Ettore Sottsass, Jr., and others. A response by Max Bill to the changes implemented by Maldonado is "Der Modelfall Ulm: Zur Problematik einer Hochschule für Gestaltung," *form* 6 (Cologne, 1959).

Speech delivered at the International Exhibition in Brussels, 18 September 1958. Published in Ulm *2 (October 1958), pp. 25–40. Courtesy of the author.*

New Developments in Industry and the Training of the Designer
Tomás Maldonado

The ideas which supply the basis for what might be called the Bauhaus ideology are today, a quarter of a century after that institution closed, difficult to translate into the language of our present-day preoccupations. Furthermore, as we shall see, some of these ideas must now be refuted with the greatest vehemence as well as with the greatest objectivity.

It is, however, an undeniable historical fact that the closing of the Bauhaus ended a particularly fertile period in the history of the training of the designer, perhaps even its most brilliant period to date. From then until recently, design training, cut off from its original context, has passed into that category of subjects whose importance is always recognized but which are rarely favored with discussion and dissemination. This last period has undoubtedly been its least productive.

Nevertheless, during this same period there were a few isolated attempts to modify this state of affairs. It would be more than unjust not to remember them. Above all, I think of the efforts made by Walter Gropius, Josef Albers, and Laszlo Moholy-Nagy: efforts to introduce into America, under the most adverse historical circumstances, the theme of the training of the designer. It is clear that the goal which they set themselves was, at that time, not easy to reach. During those years, powerful external causes—directly or indirectly associated with Nazism or the war—hindered the free international exchange of ideas and experiences. Under such conditions the theme could not prosper; and in fact it did not.

The situation now may be said to have changed considerably. Today, not only has the true importance of design training been recognized, but the dissemination as well as the discussion of the theme has been fully fostered. The specialized magazines are full of articles in which the training of the designer is treated in the most minute detail and in its most subtle implications. The theme is publicly discussed. It is analyzed. One is asked to consider its importance to our technical civilization. Apart from this, there is no lack of purely informative contributions. Thus, these same magazines often publish complete issues documenting the institutions which today, in almost all industrially developed countries, are partially or wholly dedicated to the training of the designer. Each curriculum is minutely described, from the subjects taught up to the number of hours of attendance necessary; notes on the composition of the faculty are also given. This profusion of copious and carefully presented information would lead one to imagine that the schools of industrial design have already reached their maturity in every country, and all in the same way; in other words, that the question is one of institutions whose goals and methods are finally established. On the other hand, the pedagogic question has taken a leading role at the international congresses on industrial design, in the United States just as much as lately in Germany. The debate has sometimes been lively, but basically the differences have always been those of form rather than of content. In general, apart from a few fine shades of meaning, everyone has agreed on the correctness of the educational philosophy which flourishes today.

However, if the above-mentioned publications and international congresses present a very optimistic panorama of the present state of design training—a panorama which displays very few problems and many solutions—then these very same publications and congresses, as well as the best qualified theorists and specialists, show on the other hand a symptomatic state of disorientation regarding what industrial design is and ought to be.

In other words, while the training of the designer continues to vegetate in the shadow of an already legendary Bauhaus, industrial design itself seems to be in a particularly critical situation.

In the process of cultural assimilation of the most recent conquests of science and technics—a process which to a certain extent depends upon the effectiveness of the designer—it is clear that this contradiction could play a delaying role of prime importance. It will in fact play such a role, if we do not very quickly try to modify the status quo.

Let us now examine the possible ways of modifying it. In my view, this task should not start with general reflections on education, but with an extremely concrete analysis of the present situation of industrial design. Of course, such an analysis presents certain difficulties; above all because its limits must be restricted. However, without wishing to pretend to exhaust the subject, I should like to recount a few isolated aspects whose significance is particularly important in relation to the present situation of industrial design.

The first aspect on which I should like to touch is the so-called aesthetic factor in industrial design. The way in which this factor must be embodied in the product constitutes the preferred subject of all the industrial design theorists. This theme invariably seems tied up with the no less important one of industrial design as a form of art. In the field of industrial design, aesthetic-artistic speculations have particularly complex historical antecedents; their origin is not to be found in one given tendency and in one alone. That is to say that their origins are not unitary but complex. They are the result of a huge developmental process, to which diametrically opposed tendencies have contributed. The historical antecedents of aesthetic-artistic speculations in the field of industrial design are quite inseparable from the antecedents of industrial design itself. In this sense, it is interesting to note that one of the main components, the current of craft revival set in motion by John Ruskin and William Morris in the environment of the nineteenth century, is at the same time one of those which contributed most to the idea of industrial design as art. For Ruskin and Morris, art was the only possible way to restore dignity to man's everyday life. The artist, for his part, was the only one capable of deciding—incontrovertibly—where and where not beauty lay. The artist would recover his paradise lost, find once again his vocation of guide, of judge — above all of judge; the objects which constitute man's world—those which, from the noblest to the humblest, surround man and are at his service—all objects would be inspired by art and by the work of the artist.

But, if one could trace a path from the arts and crafts movement to industrial design, it would be no straight path. The relation between the two is indirect; it is often established through byways. There has been no lack of sharp diversions and crossroads; no less, indeed, than reconciliations of opposing tendencies. It is clear that the artistic romanticism of the arts and crafts movement had little future in its original form.

Its declarations against the machine, its decorative flamboyance made it unadaptable to the new requirements of the industrial world then in formation. Similar causes would later bring Art Nouveau to a dead end.

To understand how, in the course of its development, industrial design could overcome the influence of the arts and crafts ideology, it is necessary to take into account its other precursors: the current of the great nineteenth century bridge-builders and constructors of utilitarian structures, the current termed—the description is open to discussion—rationalist. Indifferent, even hostile to the aesthetic factor, the representatives of this movement built up a new concept of design. For them, design was to be identified with ideas of productivity in fabrication and assembly, with economy in materials, and with utilitarian function.

At the end of the last century and at the beginning of ours, a few architects thought—still in a confused and vacillating way—of the need for a compromise between the arts and crafts movement and the rationalism of the constructors. In America, Frank Lloyd Wright; in Europe, Hendrik Berlage, Peter Behrens, Otto Wagner, and Hermann Muthesius. Only Adolf Loos took up a brave and argumentative attitude toward the danger of such a compromise. Remember, for instance, his critical and sarcastic attitude in regard to the foundation of the Werkbund. But his theoretical position contained one very grave deficiency: industry was foreign to him.

Van de Velde, originally an orthodox follower of Morris, developed during these years toward a standpoint very similar to that of those who defended compromise. The part played by van de Velde at that time is complex and contradictory.

The inaugural manifesto of the Bauhaus in 1919, at Weimar, announced—not without declamatory *élan*—the union of the arts and the crafts and their future integration in a higher entity: architecture. It is a typical "arts and crafts" manifesto, which Ruskin and Morris could have signed without contradicting themselves.

All the same, very few years later, the Bauhaus took up certain positions which were correct in regard to the rationalist current. To some extent, neoplasticism and Russian constructivism came to replace the arts and crafts and expressionist attitudes. The aesthetic factor became more adaptable to the new requirements; compromise was now possible. The Bauhaus performed the miracle: the rationalist aesthetic of industrial production was transformed into reality. The industrial product posed a problem of form, of creating form artistically. One artistic repertoire was supplanted, but its place was taken by another repertoire, equally artistic. Among new aesthetic values to be taken into account were the so-called "truth" of materials. At the same time, the idea of function, inherited from the great engineers of the nineteenth century, was considered an essential factor. But it now had lost some of its original clarity; it was not quite clear to what it related. In France, Le Corbusier advanced similar views.

In 1928, Hannes Meyer took over the direction of the Bauhaus. Although today his personality and his activities may be very debatable, let us remember that at that time he was the only one who saw the danger of the artistic formalism of the Bauhaus, the only one to denounce it publicly and courageously. "Today," wrote Hannes Meyer, "the inventive capacity loses its way in empty schemes; the Bauhaus style has turned the head of the formalists." He added: "How many mysterious things one tries to explain through art, when in fact they are things which have to do with science."

The American economic crisis of 1930 gave the day to styling—a new variation of industrial design whose influence has in fact extended up to the present day. The Bauhaus, its followers and its sympathizers, denounced from the start the commercial opportunism of styling, its indifference to artistic and cultural values. But the problem was no easy one: from time to time the stylists created products which could not but have been approved by the partisans of the Bauhaus. Stylists such as Henry Dreyfuss or Walter Dorwin Teague were sometimes damned, at other times deified. One verdict seems to have been irrecoverable: the condemnation of Raymond Loewy.

Lately, the problem of styling has been much debated. One of the most lucid critics of industrial design, the Englishman Reyner Banham, asked us a little while ago to consider styling as a form of popular art. Styling of cars would thus belong to the same category of expression as the cinema, illustrated magazines, science fiction, comic strips, radio, television, dance music, and sport. According to Banham, cars should be considered as something more than useful objects; they should be objects with symbolic content. In opposition to the neoacademic slogan of the partisans of "good design," "a few rare flowers," he proposes a new slogan, "many wild flowers." The four principal points of his theory are as follows:

1. employment of the neoacademic aesthetic is not justified in the evaluation of products of mass demand;

2. the aesthetic of a product should be transitory;

3. the aesthetic should not depend on an abstract and eternal idea of quality, but rather on an iconography of socially accepted symbols;

4. these symbols should be immediate, and tied to the use and nature of the product.

In the deserts of boredom of the theories about industrial design, where commonplaces rather than original ideas abound, Banham's thesis seems at first approach very seductive. However, a deeper analysis reveals the fragility of some of his formulations and, above all, underlines much contradiction and inconsequence.

For example, Banham agrees that it is madness to judge industrial design as an art, while proposing to consider it as a popular art. The thesis that the products of styling may be the expression of the folklore of our century certainly has some truth in it; I could perhaps eventually agree with Banham on this point—always on condition that the huge circulating dinosaurs of Detroit are an authentic popular art, the art of the people. I am sure it is a question of art for the people. I am not convinced that the aerodynamic fantasies of vice-president Virgil Exner, responsible for the design of Chrysler automobiles, coincide with the artistic needs of the man in the street.

Today, everyone is aware that, in order to survive, the economic system of free competition demands constant change in consumer goods, but it is not established that this change must always be made in the same way; for example, always through mutations in the aesthetic form of the product. The "transitory aesthetic" is not, as Banham assumes, the only thing capable of responding to the need for change. This aesthetic today favors facade modifications, but hinders fundamental ones. When Banham speaks of a transitory aesthetic, he thinks of the problem of annual change in car models; but in my opinion the criticism that we could make of the automobile industry does not touch on its excess of change, but much more on its lack of change. The stylist sees his task as one of renovation, always renovation; but, with Richard S. Latham, we can recognize that his palette is very limited. Multiple variations in the aggressiveness of bumpers, the ferocity of headlights, or the generosity of tailfins do not in fact constitute a basic change. The automobile industry is in stagnation, for it does not get to the point of passing from artificial changes to essential and revolutionary changes; changes such as those accomplished by Henry Ford in proceeding from Model T to Model A have not recurred in the history of his firm. Many people complain of the disheartening diversity of the products of our economics of free competition, when basically it is more a question of deploring its depressing uniformity.

Finally, this English critic has not seen that the responsibility for the present-day crisis in industrial design should not fall exclusively on those whom he calls "neoacademic formalists," but also on the stylists. He does not wish to admit that formalism and styling are merely two sides of the same coin: the idea that the aesthetic factor is basic to the creation of the product, i.e. industrial design as art.

Neoacademicism is a right-wing aestheticism, an aesthetic for but few people, "rare flowers"; styling is a left-wing aestheticism, an aesthetic for many people, "wild flowers." The metaphor is doubtless pleasing, but I hold that the new tasks of the designer will have nothing to do with artistic horticulture, be it from the left or from the right.

The aesthetic factor merely constitutes one factor among others with which the designer can operate, but it is neither the principal nor the predominant one. The productive, constructive, economic factors—perhaps, too, the symbolic factors—also exist. Industrial design is not an art nor is the designer necessarily an artist. The majority of the objects exhibited in the museums, and in the exhibitions of "good design," are anonymous and often executed in technical offices by subordinate employees who never imagined that they were producing art. In return, the greatest horrors of contemporary industry have been executed in the name of beauty and of art. General Motors, which has distinguished itself in this direction, published three years ago a sort of catechism of styling for the automobile industry. This is an abundantly illustrated prospectus, in which the words "beauty" and "art" recur every two lines, until the definition is finally reached: "For the stylists, creation is the capacity of materializing beauty."

This example comes from the domain of styling, but the field which Banham calls neoacademic formalism is not poor in similar examples. Here too, in the name of beauty, of "good form," horrors were created which have no need to envy those of styling.

Of course, the question of determining what is a horror, and what is not, could be asked and debated forever. The point is that there is no longer any doubt that aesthetic considerations have ceased to be a solid conceptual basis for industrial design.

The second aspect of importance is the economic factor, i.e. the dependence of industrial design on the world of production and consumption. There are very great difficulties in throwing light on this subject, because up to the present time we lack a scientific study of the true economic role of industrial design. The reports of the market or motivation research organizations do not always deserve our confidence; it is clear that the interviewing methods (above all the style of the questionnaires, the particular sector of the population chosen for interview, and the desire to verify a preestablished thesis) very often efface the scientific rigor necessary to the observation and interpretation of the facts. The books, articles, and conferences on industrial design are generally sensationalistic, anecdotic, or ingenuous.

Let me quote one exception. In a paper read ten years ago at a meeting of the Swiss Werkbund, Gregor Paulsson touched on the subject in quite a different manner. As far as I know, this was the first attempt to analyze the economic implications of industrial design in the light of an economic theory of value. Paulsson tried to determine the place occupied by industrial design in the relations between producer and consumer. According to him, the producer is only interested in the exchange value of the product; the consumer, in the use value alone. For this reason, the "aesthetic void" is born of the indifference of the producer to the aesthetic factor. But very often the producer may see the sales value of the aesthetic factor. This is the moment of "aesthetic prostitution." Thus, styling would be a typical example of aesthetic prostitution, because the aesthetic factor merely serves the interests of the producer and his sales policy. Paulsson suggests that in order to fight against this opportunism it would be necessary to try to incorporate the aesthetic factor in the use value—to place it at the service of the consumer.

Paulsson's thesis, in spite of its novelty and its possibilities of development, is open to objection on many counts. For example, it does not avoid the error of continuing to consider the aesthetic factor as the only *raison d'être* of industrial design. On another count, from the viewpoint of the economic theory of value, Paulsson exaggerates the simplicity of the problem, most of all when he ensures that use value and exchange value are not interrelated. David Ricardo, commenting on Adam Smith, states: "Utility is not the measure of exchange value, even though it is absolutely essential to it." On the same question, Karl Marx wrote: "I do not separate use value and exchange value as though they were opposites . . . use value materially carries exchange value." We find similar statements in John Maynard Keynes and many other modern economists. Paulsson's thesis, that industrial design should operate with use value and not with exchange value, that it should stimulate the consumer's market and not that of the producer, is indefensible. It is impossible to verify it amid the competitive economic structure in which we live. As we shall see below, the situation is not very different in a socialist economy, where competition either does not exist or adopts more subtle force. The passage from producer to consumer, from exchange value to use value, is very complex. It is a process in which the connections of cause and effect are not easy to establish. It is senseless to design in a process of this kind, for the simple reason that the producer and consumer are also not entities which one can place once and for all in a fixed scheme.

There was a time, for example, when the competitive capacity of a firm was measured by the degree of rationalization of its production and not by the seductive power of its products over the consumer. This was the industrial philosophy of Henry Ford. Around 1930 arose the industrial philosophy of styling; competitive capacity came to depend upon the form of the product. Today, that which we have come to call the "Detroit crisis" could put an end to this period. It is quite possible that automation (to which we shall return below) entails a return, naturally on a different basis, to the industrial philosophy of Henry Ford.

In each of these periods, the producer-consumer relationship differs, for in each one the product functions in a different way. As a result, the designer cannot always have the same function or the same significance. In the first of the periods I have just recalled, the designer was the constructor, the inventor, the planner: Henry Ford himself was the great designer of this period. In the second period, the designer was the artist; it matters little whether his aesthetic was popular or purist. In the third period, he will be the coordinator. His responsibility will be to coordinate, in close collaboration with a large number of specialists, the most varied requirements of product fabrication and usage; his will be the final responsibility for maximum productivity in fabrication, and for maximum material and cultural consumer-satisfaction.

In order to simplify the analysis of Banham's thesis on the aesthetic factor, and Paulsson's on the economic factor, I have been obliged to leave many questions to one side.

One of these questions, and not the least important, concerns the difficulty of knowing objectively what a consumer is, without making abstract generalizations. Although each one of us may be a consumer, or perhaps precisely because of this, the information at our disposal is insufficient. I repeat that today we have many reasons to

[Hochschule für Gestaltung, Ulm. View into studios.]

mistrust our market and motivation research organizations. But we would like to be able to hope that empiric sociology, cultural anthropology, descriptive semiotics, hereditary psychology, the psychology of individual and social behavior, perception theory, etc., could at some time join together in a systematic study of the most subtle aspects of consumption.

Doubtless we know a certain amount about consumption, but it is clear that our knowledge is not at the level of our needs. We know, for example, that the freedom of the consumer is an illusion; or better, we could say (using the distinction made by Anatole Rapoport) that the consumer has the possibility of consuming what he likes, but not the probability of so doing. Here, I am not thinking merely of the material probability, but mainly of the psychological probability of purchase. Our competitive society is constructed on precisely this misunderstanding. Our possibilities are ours and ours alone, but of our probabilities we are not masters. True, we are free to consume; but only to consume what someone or other in some invisible place has previously decided is in our interest—and sometimes against it.

Again, we know that we often consume for projective or compensatory reasons. Through a process of symbolic transference, certain objects bring us real or illusory prestige, reputation, or security; others help us for a moment to temper our feelings of hostility or isolation.

These are the things we know. But many other aspects of consumption are not so easily labeled. Neither the psychoanalysts nor the professional critics of our civilization can give us a comprehensive explanation of all the phenomena of the world of consumption. The Marxists themselves do not succeed. One of them, the French philosopher Henri Lefebvre, recently wrote: "By the side of the scientific study of the productive relations which affect political economy, there is . . . room for a concrete study of appropriation: for a theory of needs." According to Lefebvre, this theory should answer the following questions: "where and in what field do living men make contact with objects of consumption? and how do they find what they look for? do needs form a whole? is there a 'needs system' or a needs structure? what is this structure?"

In the period which is now beginning, a scientific reply to each of these questions will be required by the designer. It will be the only way for him to replace, in his work, abstract generalizations about the consumer with objectively usable material.

The third and last aspect with which I should like to deal is the relation between productivity and industrial design. Productivity displays three attributes:

1. increase in production;
2. decrease in the unit cost price of the product;
3. improvement in the quality of the product.

In present-day large-scale industry, productivity has two complementary methods of attaining its ends:

1. operational research;
2. automation.

("Operational research," according to G. Kimbal and P. M. Morse, "is a scientific method whose purpose is to give management a quantitative basis for decisions relating to operations placed under its control." "Automation," according to Frank G. Woollard, "is the system and method of making processes automatic by the use of self-controlling, self-acting means for performing necessary operations in industrial or commercial undertakings.")

We have already mentioned a possible return by present-day industry to the productive philosophy of Henry Ford: the idea of productivity as the dominant factor. Little by little, vast sectors of industry realize that frenzied competition in ornamentation of products can seriously compromise their real interests. The first symptom and warning is the Detroit crisis: the surprising and unpleasant discovery of the slump in the sales of General Motors, Ford, and Chrysler cars. To replace a popular "look" with a purist "look" would be no solution to this problem. Large-scale industry seems to have already dimly seen that ornamentation, popular or purist, is an absurdity from the point of view of productivity.

Naturally, many people assert that the problem is incorrectly stated; that even an industry in full automation could produce the most absurd products. I do not doubt that the subtle stone lacework of the Hindu temple of Rajarani could be the subject of a fully automatic mass-production run, if a maharajah had a chance caprice. It is only in the light of productivity criteria that we could establish the justice or falsity of such an action. And I can assure you that the cost price would not be convincing.

There is also the argument that the designer is not faced with a new situation, since he has always been obliged to take into account materials, fabrication, and productivity, too. We agree. But the existence of a different level of acuteness is forgotten. Today, the requirements of productivity are much greater than before. Let me quote an example. At the Builders' Conference held in 1954 in Moscow, the popular ornamentation of Soviet architecture—the neoclassicism of the pastry cook—was condemned by Khrushchev, not because of revisions in the official Soviet aesthetic, but because of the productivity requirements of industrialized building, and because of the need to reduce the cost price per cubic meter.

We may be certain that, in the years to follow, productivity and industrial design go hand in hand; the demands of automation will to a great extent contribute to this. The new phase of industrial development is characterized by a new theory of the relationships between machine and product. The machine designed for the resultant product will be replaced by the machine designed to carry out fundamental operation. This is the thesis of Eric Laever and John J. Brown; its importance to industrial design is of the first order. If, in the past, the product to a certain extent determined the operative behavior of the machine, then in the future, it will be the operative behavior of the machine which will to a certain extent determine the product. This implies that the designer will, more than ever, have to obey factors foreign to his own individual field. One of the most typical activities of the new period will be what John Diebold terms redesign. "Fully automatic production," writes Diebold, "often begets the need to redesign the product as much as the process of production. . . . In the majority of cases, it will seem easier to renovate the consumer goods than the industrial equipment, which will have to carry out a predetermined function.'" The full automation of the English radio factory at Shepperton, for example, was only possible through redesign, according to the engineer John Sargrove.

Redesign can nevertheless have other reasons. A product may undergo essential modification in its shape and in its function because of the development of its various organs. In this direction it is most interesting to observe the phenomenon conventionally termed "miniaturization." The engineer J. W. Dalgleish gives the following definition: "The development of techniques that make possible electronic assemblies whose size is reduced to a limit primarily imposed by the smallest valves which are economically available." The radical reduction in the scale of tubes, and the introduction of transistors, has stimulated revolutionary modifications in huge areas of industrial production. Such modifications will be of profound significance to industrial design. It is clear that the change in scale of the product—considering the scale of use, the human scale, as fixed—poses exceptionally interesting and difficult problems for the designer. On the other hand, the peaceful use of atomic energy will open an absolutely new field of activity to the designer, where tasks await him which are completely different from those it is his habit to imagine.

Having considered the present-day problems of industrial design, we may now draw some conclusions about the training of the designer.

For some time, it was thought that the theme of education for industrial design could be isolated from the general context of higher education. This false conviction was fostered by the habit, inherited from the time of the Bauhaus, of considering training for industrial design as a primarily artistic phenomenon, only marginally pedagogic. But education for industrial design is only a special case of higher education. Many—I do not say all—of its problems should be visualized and solved in relation to other greater problems of education.

In this direction, it is most important to examine the example of the relationship between education for industrial design and the present crisis in scientific and technical education. Every day, it is stated that more scientists, more engineers, more technicians must be trained. Certainly this is a most important question; but in fact it is entered upon with extreme frivolity. Statesmen, educational administrators, and journalists believe that the problem is purely quantitative, that it can be solved by increasing the number of teachers and the construction of new school buildings, and by an ever larger number of students. True, these are indispensable measures, for without them it would be impossible to put the matter on a real basis; but they are not enough. We educators want to know on what educational philosophy to base our teaching. The two fundamental currents of contemporary pedagogy, neohumanist and progressive, are no longer of any help to us today.

This insufficiency is not only a fact of scientific and technical education, but also of education in industrial design. The didactic philosophy, from which the industrial design schools are still nourished, is in fact completely out of date. It is identified today with a tradition which is principally artistic: the Bauhaus tradition. (Thus, although Marianne Brandt's geometric tea-set "Bauhaus 1924" is now considered a museum curiosity, it is asserted that we must regard "Bauhaus 1924" pedagogical ideas as important today.)

But what significance has the Bauhaus tradition, from the viewpoint of the history of educational ideas? How does it express itself? What are its characteristics? It would seem that in practice, as an educational reality, the Bauhaus tradition is almost entirely reduced to its preparatory course. For many, this course constitutes the principal component of the Bauhaus didactical tradition; more, it is considered the indisputable basis for the education of the designer. Thus, I think it important that we examine that which was and is the basis of the teaching of this preparatory course.

To begin with, it must be said that the best qualified historians of the Bauhaus doubt the existence of a unified didactic principle in the preparatory course—as much at Weimar as at Dessau. But let us suppose for a moment that such a principle did exist, and that it had a unified character. We could imagine it as the result of a synthesis of the contributions of Itten, Kandinsky, Klee, Albers, and Moholy-Nagy. For a moment, let us forget their profound differences and look for their common factors. We shall thus discover a didactic principle whose general line could be described as follows: the student in the preparatory course should, through artistic and manual practice, free his expressive and creative powers and develop an active, spontaneous, and free personality; he should reeducate his senses, regain his lost psychobiological unity— that is to say, the idyllic state in which to see, to hear, and to touch are true adventures; finally, he should acquire knowledge not only intellectually but emotionally, not only through oral explanations but through action, not only through books but through work. Education through art. Education through doing. Such are the constants that we can separate out from the didactic thought of the master of the Bauhaus.

This characterization shows well enough that the Bauhaus was not a miracle. From a didactic viewpoint, it is easy to reveal its origins. For example, we can clearly distinguish the influence of the "movement for artistic education," founded at the end of the last century by Hans v. Marées and Adolf Hildebrandt; the influence of the "work schools" movement of Kerschensteiner; the influence of the "activism" of Maria Montessori; and the influence of the American "progressive education."

We cannot criticize the Bauhaus on this score. These movements were the most advanced manifestations of educational thought at the time. It was a matter of opposition to philological and verbalist "neohumanism," to philosophical idealism, to the academic crystallization of education. It was a question of argumentative exaltation of expression, intuition, and action, above all of "learning by doing." But this educational philosophy is in crisis. It is incapable of assimilating the new types of relations between theory and practice, engendered by the most recent scientific developments. We know now that theory must be impregnated with practice, practices with theory. It is impossible today to act without knowledge, or to know without doing. Operational scientific thought has bypassed the ingenuous dualisms, the pseudoproblems which so worried the first pragmatists.

Naturally, this crisis in "progressive" educational philosophy is interpreted by some as the great moment of revenge, as if the day of conservative education, of "neohumanism," had returned. "Learning by doing" is in crisis, they think; let us then go back to "learning by speaking." And let us speak only of Plato, of Aristotle, and of Thomas Aquinas. From existentialism to rigor. Such people make a great mistake. If today we must refute "progressive" education, we must also, even more energetically and decisively, refute "neohumanism."

A new educational philosophy is already in preparation; its foundation is scientific operationalism. It is no longer a question of the names of things, nor of things alone: it is a question of knowledge, but of operational, manipulable, real knowledge.

The designer is destined to integrate himself into that reality whose complexity and nuances I hope to have shown. He will have to operate at the nerve centers of our industrial civilization; precisely there, where the most important decisions for our daily life are made, and where, as a result, those interests meet which are most opposed and often most difficult to reconcile. Under these conditions, on what will the success of his task depend? On his inventive capacity, certainly, but also on the finesse and precision of his methods of thought and work, on the breadth of his scientific and technical knowledge, as well as on his capacity of interpreting the most secret and most subtle processes of our culture.

For the moment, one school alone is devoted to the formation of this new type of designer: the Hochschule für Gestaltung at Ulm. This school is the first example of the new philosophy of education. Sooner or later, I am sure, other schools will be able to profit from its experience and begin to follow the same path.

1959

In an article published in *Architectural Review* where he had recently become assistant editor, Reyner Banham launched an attack on the historicism that had come to the fore in Italy. Entitled "Neoliberty—the Italian Retreat from Modern Architecture," the article condemned the new tendency as a betrayal of modernism and an "infantile" regression. Significantly, the origins of Italian modernism for Banham lay not in the rationalism of the 1930s but in futurism. Banham's widely publicized comments were directed in large part at **Ernesto Rogers**, who had played a major role in the new tendency's formation, both as editor of *Casabella-Continuità* and as a principal of the BBPR, which had recently completed the Torre Velasca in the historic center of Milan. Banham's article elicited a strongly worded response from the Italian architect-editor two months later. Although Rogers's position as expressed here differs little from that expounded in earlier articles, his tone captures a sense of the stakes involved and of the role of the journals in foddering an international debate.

370–78

The term "Neoliberty" had been coined the previous year by Paolo Portoghesi in an article entitled "Dal Neorealismo al Neoliberty" published in *Comunità* (December 1958). Portoghesi noted the pervasiveness of the new tendency, describing it as "that vast impulse to reevaluate the first period of the modern movement (beginning with the neomedieval revivals and ending with rationalism) which has exerted a direct influence on the most recent production of certain Italian architects of both the *younger* generation and that of the *masters*." In his view, the first phase of "postrationalist" architecture, which he labeled "neorealist" by analogy to films like Roberto Rossellini's *Rome, Open City* (1944), had been animated by an empathetic identification with the plight of an Italian populace left homeless and impoverished by the war. Epitomized in the epic populism of Mario Ridolfi's INA housing on Viale Etiopia in Rome (1950–54), it emulated the ambience of working-class life, romanticizing its spontaneity and naturalism, and opposing formalist preoccupations as academic. The successor Neoliberty, in contrast, coincided with the "economic miracles" appearing throughout Europe by the late 1950s. Looking back to turn-of-the-century bourgeois building tradition, it cultivated eclecticism and fantasy while at the same time acting as a critique of rationalism's lack of expressiveness and of material richness. Portoghesi reserved judgment on the new tendency (later to be a background for his own work), relating it to Italy's Art Nouveau style, the brick expressionist school of Amsterdam, and early Frank Lloyd Wright. Wright himself had recently revived the manner in his Morris store in San Francisco (1949) and Masieri Foundation project in Venice (1952). It thus also had links to Bruno Zevi's organicism and to the work of Carlo Scarpa and Ignazio Gardella.

68–69

But the prime manifesto of Neoliberty was Roberto Gabetti and Aimaro Isola's Bottega d'Erasmo in Turin (1954), polemically published in 1957 in *Casabella*. It was followed (in notoriety) by the Velasca tower. The latter, which extended the stylistic connotations beyond the eponymous Liberty, evoked a medieval fortified tower at skyscraper scale. A few months after his argument with Banham, Rogers presented the building to his international colleagues at CIAM's meeting in Otterlo, justifying its silhouette as the product of functional and technical requirements as well as of a historical analysis of the preexisting urban context. He was attacked again, this time by Team 10 members Peter Smithson and Jacob Bakema. To Smithson's comments that the building was a formalistic exercise and dangerous model for imitation, Rogers replied, "There is one main difficulty that I see and that is that you think in English."

200–4
181–83

From Casabella-Continuità *228 (June 1959), pp. 2–4. Translated by Rebecca Williamson. Courtesy of Studio BBPR and Julia Banfi.*

The Evolution of Architecture: Reply to the Custodian of Frigidaires
Ernesto Nathan Rogers

There are sensations that one can never get rid of: as in Proust, where certain odors are connected with certain thoughts. Similarly, reading Mr. Banham's article in the *Architectural Review,* I cannot avoid remembering the amusing but decadent Victorian "pub" with its display cases of "stuffed fishes" and all the other customary trifles reconstructed in the cellar of the English review's offices. It is a way of recovering history through a particular society's representations, of painstakingly indulging in the most abstruse, dusty, and also most condemnable examples, to the point of absorbing that society's flavor.

It is probable that this "pub" shows only the negative pole of a cultural attitude to which the review has assumed a commitment with incomparable intelligence and seriousness. But it is clear that every battle conducted with such insistence ultimately has to involve some critical valuation before it may be entirely clarified.

It would be ungenerous to believe, because of possible errors or those that have already been noted, that the whole business ought to be condemned, or that one should go ahead and say that those responsible are oblivious to other problems that are much more significant in the formation of contemporary architectural consciousness.

Architectural Review and *Casabella* are, from the cultural point of view, the most engaged reviews in the world: the most audacious and, as a consequence, the most open to criticism. One may accept or refute their positions, but no one who examines them openmindedly will want to deny that both make valid contributions through their critical discoveries, thorough research, and proposals leading to a more valid framing of the problem of current architecture, thus breaking up the schemas of modernist formalism.

I would like those who speak about us and about Italian architecture to use equally respectful language, and not mistake fireflies for lanterns, nor mix up the cards on the table, nor content themselves with statements that are improvised and, in any case, superficial and hasty.

For this reason it displeases me that the same review for which we have demonstrated so much respect, having even dedicated an essay to it (Matilde Baffa, "L'Architettura al vaglio di una rivista inglese," *Casabella* no. 220), would give space to an editorial like Mr. Banham's "Neoliberty—the Italian Retreat from Modern Architecture."

An editorial cannot be judged by the same standards as just any article, inasmuch as it customarily expresses the opinion of those in charge; it is where the convictions of the journal acquire an official character.

Mr. Banham, oblivious to the environment in which he works, evidently believes he is directing his accusation at those who have considered "the remaining monuments of Art Nouveau in a degree of detail that bespeaks more than historical interest. Works of Gaudí, Sullivan, d'Aronco, Horta, and the Viennese school, in particular [he writes], have been described and illustrated even to the extent of the original drawings and colour-blocks of their exteriors, supported by texts that were far less expository or explanatory than they were eulogistic and rhetorical." If the articles have been rhetorical, we are at fault, as we would be at fault if, for example, we had written what appears in an editorial in *L'Architettura* (no. 37, November 1958, page 439): "Rationalism, consumed in the prodigious metamorphosis of Ronchamp, committed here its subtle,

NEOLIBERTY

The extent to which the famous names of Milanese architecture have retreated can be judged by these two blocks by Figini and Pollini, one of 1949 in the via Broleto, 1, and the other in the via Circo, completed last year, 2.

3 and 4, the relationship of the retreat to historical precedents can be measured by comparing two illustrations, 5 and 6, of a late villa by Otto Wagner (as they appeared in Bruno Zevi's magazine l'Architettura) with two recent works in which Ernesto Rogers was involved, the Aquila offices in Zaule, with their dummy pitched eaves concealing a flat roof behind, and the interior of the Italian Pavilion in Brussels, with its Wagnerian stained glass (and its *stupendous outburst of Milanese Chandelierism).

[From Reyner Banham, "Neoliberty—the Italian Retreat from Modern Architecture," Architectural Review, April 1959, p. 233.]

virtuous, extenuated suicide; at seventy-two, Mies van der Rohe has ended the game. This fact must be the point of departure for judging the various problems of contemporary language: the tending toward Liberty, the formalism of the Milanese school, the complicated research of Scarpa and the brutalism of D'Olivo, the clever empiricism of Gardella in Venice. These are beginnings, attempts, experiments, all of which are open to discussion but vital, real, indicative of the possibility of relaunching modern architecture. Having rendered homage to Mies in the gleaming mausoleum of rationalism, we go out drinking with these friends who are less perfect and respectable, who are at times hedonistic and dissolute, but who at least have the courage to continue a tradition which was, until yesterday, that of Mies, the tradition of anticonformism."

For us, on the other hand, the modern movement is not dead at all: our modernity is really in carrying forward the tradition of the Masters (including Wright). But to be sensitive to the beautiful (and not only to the value of documenting it) in some manifestations that are no longer sufficiently appreciated is certainly a respectable position. And likewise, it is respectable to historicize and update certain values left hanging because of the need for other struggles.

Mr. Banham believes he has found (probably in the dusty drawers of that Victorian furniture) the magic key with which to open the sluice gates of history at any point, enabling the flow to deviate in the direction of his own private breeding farms of blood-thirsty moray eels.

It might be said that, for him, using an old Ford is more justifiable than using a horse because the Ford comes after the Industrial Revolution while the horse is obviously before. This comparison might be deduced from the conventional layout of the whole article, where it is maintained that, as far as imitations go, the architects who today follows De Stijl is better than the one who adopts Liberty since the former "at least revives forms created since the watershed" between our time and a past that is now over. In other words, it is better to steal five lire than ten. Many times I have repeated that "formalism is any use of unassimilated forms: ancient or contemporary, cultivated or spontaneous" (*Casabella* no. 202). Conversely, critical and considered review of historical tradition is useful for an artist who refuses to accept certain themes in a mechanical manner. For Mr. Banham, however, determinism of forms according to an abstract line of development seems to take the place of a concept of history.

From this derives his aptitude for bestowing absolutions and excommunications, which can only mummify reality.

No less objectionable is his system of elevating some poor person so high as to make him totter, only then to throw him so far down as to render him unrecognizable.

And even someone like me who, in line with his principles of freedom of opinion, is ready to consider any criticism, is not disposed to endure that which—like this—is contradictory not only in its evaluation of the facts, but even in its exposition of these facts, which require far more precise information and above all more correct citation.

Personally, it does not flatter me to be called the "hero-figure of European architecture in the late forties and early fifties" if I am then considered one of those responsible (together with Belgiojoso and Peressutti) for having curated the Italian section of the 1958 Industrial Design exhibition in London (with works by Albini and other first-rate colleagues) "which seemed to be little more than a hymn of praise to Milanese *borghese* taste at its queasiest and most cowardly."

I am responding because, in spite of everything (and certainly because of the authority of the journal that sponsors it), the article treating Italian matters with such presumption has been much talked about here; I am responding because I am the main person condemned and because along with me are cited my two associates; because it is necessary to disentangle the discussion from a prejudice concerning a name, that of Neoliberty, with which, according to the extemporaneous classifications typical of Banham, architects of various ages, responsibilities, and tendencies are associated; and finally because, if this extended meaning of the name is granted, there ought to be included in it all those who attempt to avoid what I want to call by its true name, and that is conformism and formalism. The silence, for example, concerning a Gardella, a Ridolfi, a Michelucci, an Albini, a Samonà, engenders further confusion in the already great confusion of what has been said. I respond because I do not want to be accused of positions that we have not taken. Finally, I respond because, in refuting other people's affirmations, I hope to make it understood that I do not indulge in the attitude of "tout va très bien, madame la marquise," but rather that I worry, at least as much as Mr. Banham, about a certain dangerous trend of Italian architecture, the analysis of which I do not intend to evade insofar as it concerns my own responsibility as artist, critic, and teacher.

Mr. Banham declares himself to be disillusioned because, in the aftermath of the war, he had placed many hopes in us (in us Milanese above all), having even created a myth in order to locate us.

But who substantiates these "illusions" for him? Some Roman architects: Moretti and Vagnetti. The first in particular. He himself, anticipating our reaction, declares that we will, for our part, reject this interpretation of his. In fact, it is obvious that an adroit but willful formalism is not only not indicative of the supposed goals not reached by us, but it also denies the theoretical and above all moral presuppositions of our struggle, which shuns aestheticism and intellectual games.

As far as the work of the young architects goes: of Aulenti; the Novara group of Gregotti, Meneghetti, and Stoppino; as well as of Gabetti and Isola, it is not true that *Casabella* has published them "with evident editorial approval," because if it is obvious that nothing appears in this journal without my consent to its publication, I have openly shown my criticism precisely of the tendentious and conclusory value of these products, limiting myself to considering them significant examples of some young people intelligent enough to react to modernist formalism.

If, then, one wants to accuse them of being led, after an initially correct impulse, by a negative polemic, over and beyond an equally necessary action of positive reelaboration, that corresponds exactly to thoughts I expressed in *Casabella* no. 215 ("Continuity or Crisis?").

But this is not what Mr. Banham maintains, taking an extract as imprecise as it is unfaithful from an article by Aldo Rossi, "Il passato e il presente nella nuova architettura," where, with clearness and honesty, the latter criticizes his own friends on precisely those points concerning which Mr. Banham makes him look like a kind of demagogue of the bourgeois spirit.

On the other hand, in the very same issue of *Casabella*, no. 219, Aldo Rossi, making a critique of Hans Sedlmayr's book against modern art ("Una critica che rispingiamo"), and voicing a position widespread among young people in Italy, underscores the difference between a reactionary critique and a progressive critique of the modern movement: "The rejection of the values of the modern world necessarily implies a new barbarism, since *in any case* today it is not possible to ignore how much the modern world has characterized the Europe of these last years. . . . In essence the motive of decisive dissent is still this: that this type of criticism does not point to a prospect of development, an alternative *within* modern culture, but poses itself as negation *of* modern culture."

Every alternative or development that we have supported has always been *within modern culture,* and it is for this reason that our task is laborious and difficult. Why has Banham, who wants to be the expert on things Italian, not sought to read better and more, rather than insist on his definitions of "Milanese" and "Torinese," which smack of banality?

Nor are Gabetti and Isola and the others in the same category because, if the definition of Neoliberty can be applied to the Bottega d'Erasmo (and to other works by other young architects sprouting up here and there in Italy), it can also be applied only if uselessly distorted to the different groups whose nostalgias, more than to Liberty, hark back perhaps to Dutch expressionism (for Aulenti) or to the eclecticism of Boito and Berlage (for Gregotti and Associates). As for the works of the "Cooperative of Architects and Engineers of Reggio Emilia," they are not at all Neoliberty and could almost be taken for examples of what Banham calls "current architecture."

Nor are Figini and Pollini Ncoliberty; this is obvious even when they indulge in naturalistic thinking. If I were not driven to polemic by Banham's tone, I would find some usefulness in the alarm he has sounded, but that little bit of sanity that can be found in his observations and that might readily be agreed with—at least as indication of motives to investigate—finishes by corrupting itself in the tortuousness of his discussion, so much that his generalized accusation against the most recent manifestations not only goes beyond the modern movement in Italy, but displays such a rigid incomprehension of many fundamental events that it ends up indicting the wider developmental possibility of all international history. To listen to him, in modern Italian architecture, "the backstage influence of Marinetti (whom Sartoris once acknowledged in print as a patron of the movement) . . . was most likely to be felt."

What does it matter to us that Sartoris says this? One who has dull vision deforms everything he sees: "'modern' was practiced as a *style,* since it could not be practiced as a total *discipline*—as the literally hollow formalism of Terragni's Casa del Fascio at Como brilliantly demonstrates." Does Banham not see the relationship between form and content and does he not know of Terragni's struggles to give a moral content and form to fascism through his work? (He was unfortunately deceived.) And why did Pagano, Banfi, Labò die, if not because their artistic discipline could not do other than oppose itself to the rules of the dictatorship?

Banham ought to have recognized in a subtler manner that which has repeatedly been observed by our own writers: namely, the continuous dramatic struggle of culture in general against the contingencies of Italian society (before, during, and after fascism); from this he would have had to infer the difficulty of identifying art with life: the dialectical relationship, the persistent lovers' quarrel, the conquests, the misunderstandings, the rejections, the redemptions. Then he would have intuited one of the most interesting aspects of our history: precisely that Italian architecture, in its authentic examples, is a moral act and, at least implicitly, an instrument of political struggle, alternating successes with failures, as in the entire political history of Italian progressive tendencies, but certainly not for this reason worthless or condemnable.

After the war of liberation and the stupendous period of partisan struggle, it seemed that the world, Europe, and Italy were resurrected to a definitely better life, and we fed ourselves on hopes, imagining that they represented reality, even though we were forced to see that everywhere these were new utopias. Since then all of Italian society—that which is progressive and aware—clamors for breath so as not to be caught on the shoals of officialism. And the fact that there exists an architecture more loaded with feelings than with reason is not owed to a retreat by architects. Quite the contrary! It is a struggle against the current. What happens in the communal offices, in the administrative offices, must be noted. As ever, the small company of those who believe in art must grit their teeth to break a path beyond the barricades.

Is it not the case that Ridolfi, Gardella, B.B.P.R., Albini, Samonà, Michelucci, and Piccinato, among the most strenuous defenders of modernity, no longer do what they did before, and precisely for this reason are consistent; has Banham ever asked himself this? It cannot be believed that these people and many others would all at once have become irresponsible to the point of abdicating the conquests so laboriously achieved.

Their strength has really been that of having understood the modern movement as a "continuous revolution," that is to say, as a continuous development of the principle of adherence to the changeable contents of life.

Little by little the thematic became richer, and as a consequence the exigencies became subtler. Formal issues, therefore, became more difficult, because they tried to encompass an ever greater number of propositions—the widening of the architectural problematic and the immediate effect of critical thought; the historicist revision of all historical periods and especially those closest in time, which had been distorted through the normal opposition caused by the dialectical traffic between generations.

And Liberty too was better understood (and why not?) when there were still energies to collect and channel.

Liberty cannot be considered only in terms of its historical definition, as progenitor of modernity, but must also be considered in terms of its own values, which correspond, moreover, to a recognition so necessary that as a young student I already wrote about it in a thesis project.

What is there to be afraid of?

There is no doubt that it is necessary to look at the experiences of the past (at all of them), though naturally without letting oneself become entangled in them, as unfortunately—and I am the first to recognize it—happens to some.

This complex process of revision, however slow and elaborate, has been misinterpreted by those less prepared, who have been shocked by it. But it must be recognized in any case that such revision could make even the best ignore some cultural component (like the technological) to which more attention was paid in other moments. But progress is the result of choices and of suspensions of judgment, which at every moment can err by incompleteness; progress is paid for also with some mistakes. Yet I am persuaded that along with the dangers that Italian architecture is running, awareness does surface, despite the arrogant goading of Mr. Banham, who plays the part of *custodian of Frigidaires* and who furthermore believes that "the revolution . . . began with electric cookers, vacuum cleaners, the telephone, the gramophone, and all those other mechanized aids to gracious living that are still invading the home, and have permanently altered the nature of domestic life and the meaning of domestic architecture." Now that we are here, I would also add the blender, which would serve to make a nice cocktail together with the other revolutions which, according to him, have their "milestones" in the "Foundation Manifesto of Futurism, the European discovery of Frank Lloyd Wright, Adolf Loos's 'Ornament and Crime,'

Hermann Muthesius's lecture to the Werkbund Congress of 1911, the achievement of fully Cubist painting, and so forth." All that is lacking is a bit of salt.

I am persuaded that the whole experience has been useful. It has been so useful that Italian architectural criticism and production have taken, despite everything, some steps that in many countries are yet to be attempted.

The latter will certainly take these steps, and perhaps in a different direction, in accordance with what the particular cultural and economic conditions suggest, but I do not believe our experience, that of a proven historical consciousness, of the necessary usefulness of culture in the order of space and time—of the relation between new work and those preexisting factors—to be of little import, nor do I believe that these ought to be discarded with such superficiality.

Anyway, we do not presume to be the only ones who are moving forward: much more luminous examples come to us from the Masters: Le Corbusier has created Chandigarh with the echo of all India; Gropius the Embassy of Athens, steeped in Greek history; Mies a "monument" with the Park Avenue skyscraper in New York; and Wright, before he died, works which, while highly consistent in spirit, cannot be confined within the letter of many of his preceding declarations.

No one has stopped; concerning the Masters themselves one could paradoxically paraphrase an aphorism of Nietzsche: "He who remains a disciple rewards his own master badly."

This is so in our case, all the more for those of us who do not like to get frozen in slavish dogmatics.

If all that departs from the configurations of academic modernism or does not succumb, out of ill-advised escapism, to the bravado of formalism is Neoliberty, then we shall be in large and good company.

But if Neoliberty is really that tendency which retraces the steps of Liberty itself, then what we are talking about is giving the right frame to a little picture whose figures are represented, in Italy, by certain young architects who—I hope—are sufficiently aware as not to believe they sum up all of Italian architecture in themselves. And it is also to be hoped that they will soon notice some useless misunderstandings into which they have fallen. To conclude, I would like to invite Mr. Banham, who I believe knows English better than Italian, to read directly from *The Poetry of Architecture* by John Ruskin, a great Englishman, without repeating the outdated interpretation of Marinetti, a "revolutionary" Fascist who died wearing the cap of the Academy: "We shall consider the architecture of nations as it is influenced by their feelings and manners, as it is connected with the scenery in which it is found, and with the skies under which it was erected."

He will find there some starting points for the evolution of architecture.

1959

A landmark event of the late 1950s was the building of Brasilia. Only Le Corbusier's design for India's capital of Chandigarh (begun in 1951) constituted a comparable model for the total imposition of a new city based on modernist principles. Relocated from the coast to an empty desert plateau in the country's interior, Brazil's new capital was shaped to the master plan of Lúcio Costa, whose freehand diagram of a city axially organized in the form of an airplane won a competition held by the new government of Juscelino Kubitschek in 1956. Built in a record three and a half years, it represented a vivid testament of the national will to impose an absolute and modern image on the *tabula rasa*. The scheme's structural extravagance and monumentality were above all due to the genius of **Oscar Niemeyer**, who served as head of architecture and planning for the project. His "Plaza of the Three Powers" at the honorific apex of Costa's plan, juxtaposing the volumes of the presidential palace, supreme court, and congress, distilled the rhetoric of administrative power to the point of surreality.

Brazil's interest in modern architecture went back to the mid-1920s, when Costa in partnership with the Russian emigré Gregori Warchavchik had introduced the new movement into the country. With the revolution of Getúlio Vargas of 1930 and with Costa's appointment as director of the national school of fine arts in Rio de Janeiro, modernism increasingly became a matter of progressive policy in a nation ambitiously aspiring to industrialization on the European model. In this climate the tutelage of Le Corbusier proved decisive in 1936 when the latter was invited to consult with Costa and other leading Brazilian architects—including Affonso Eduardo Reidy, landscape architect Roberto Burle Marx, and the then twenty-nine-year-old Niemeyer—on the design of the Ministry of Education and Public Health. The building, erected from 1937 to 1943 in Rio, was the first full-fledged realization of the skyscraper projected for the Ville Radieuse.

In the years following, Niemeyer garnered international attention as he rapidly moved from the more rationally constrained style of the master toward a virtuoso manner that Le Corbusier himself was to characterize as "baroque with reinforced concrete," not without a certain admiration (this despite the fact that he would reproach critics for using this same term with respect to Ronchamp). Niemeyer affirmed his belief in "an almost unlimited plastic freedom" in the following article for *Módulo*, a journal that he directed and that served as a record of the building of Brasilia starting in the mid-1950s. Seeking to rebut charges of gratuitous form-making leveled against his work, he argued that the force-fitting of functions into the rigid schemes prescribed by modern rationalism was a far more troubling instance of formalism. Published in 1960, the article was written a year earlier according to Niemeyer. In an elaboration, "Contradiction in Architecture" (*Módulo* 31, December 1962), he complained of the lack of imagination in recent work as a "basic contradiction" between modernism "and the beautiful romantic architecture of the past . . . a contradiction that cannot merely be summed up in different plastic characteristics imposed and justified by a new technique and new programmes, but that strikes deep into the creative act itself, into the attitude that the architect adopts toward the work to be designed, formerly lyrical and imaginative, now timid and vacillating, tethered to the theories that the professional critics—often quite ineptly—strive to maintain and that, by lack of sensibility or conviction, [the architect] still respects."

For contemporary reaction to Niemeyer's work, see "Report on Brazil" (*Architectural Review*, October 1954), especially the criticisms by Max Bill.

From Módulo *21 (December 1960), pp. 2–7. In revised English translation as* "Thoughts on Brasilia" *in Willi Stäubli, ed.,* Brasilia *(London: Leonard Hill Books, 1966), pp. 21–23. Courtesy of the author.*

Form and Function in Architecture
Oscar Niemeyer

I can understand the criticism of art, fair and honest often enough, but it is my opinion that the architect should pursue his work in accordance with his own tendencies and possibilities, accepting such criticism with neither revolt nor submission, realizing it is frequently sound and constructive, but ever subject to the confirmation that time alone can bring.

Countless are the examples that justify this point of view, and works that were once not understood later win universal respect and admiration.

This article that I am submitting tackles the subject and speculates upon the problems of form in architecture. It is the testimony of an architect, with no theoretical or erudite pretensions, based merely on his work and his professional experience.

I am in favor of an almost unlimited plastic freedom, a freedom that is not slavishly subordinate to the reasons of any given technique or of functionalism, but which makes an appeal to the imagination, to things that are new and beautiful, capable of arousing surprise and emotion by their very newness and creativeness; a freedom that provides scope—when desirable—for moods of ecstasy, reverie, and poetry. Of course, this freedom cannot be used freely. In urban localities, for instance, I am, on the contrary, all for restricting it or, rather, for preserving the unity and harmony of the overall plan by avoiding solutions that do not wholly fit into it, however inspired they may be and however high their architectural level. And with this end in view, in Brasilia, in the urban sections to which I am alluding, regulations are set up to cover volumes, free spaces, heights, facing materials, etc., in order to prevent the city from proliferating, like other modern cities, in a regime of disharmony and confusion. But in private houses, in remote buildings, surrounded by free spaces, total freedom of conception is allowed, naturally within the rules of proportion that have always been required of architecture.

However, this criterion of plastic freedom is bitterly opposed in certain sectors of contemporary architecture. This opposition comes from the timid, from those who feel that they are better off and more comfortable encompassed by rules and restrictions, restrictions that permit of no fantasy, no compromise, no contradiction of the functionalist principles they adopt. Which lead them unprotestingly to solutions so often repeated as to become vulgar at times. And in the field of discussion, they are unshakable in their defense of functionalism, constructive reasons, the convenience of standardization, etc., tenets that are unsound when it is a question of special jobs where the problem of outlay is secondary. Thereupon they adduce social reasons which they deem to require simple, economic projects, as if this argument were not long outdated, at any rate for whoever is really interested in the social problem and knows that its solution evades the attributions of architects and architecture, and demands, outside of professional activities, a coherent attitude in support of progressive movements. And they react defensively against plastic speculation in the elements of structure, which they want strictly functional, considering such speculation to be formalistic and contrary to technical reasoning, forgetting the while that they also are involved in compromises of this order, undoubtedly more serious and more difficult for them to explain.

They insist, for instance, on solutions based on simple, compact plans, aiming at pure geometrical volumes—a solution that I sometimes adopt, without, however, accepting it as dogmatic—and to this end, they cram into preestablished forms

[Oscar Niemeyer, roof plaza of the National Congress, Brasilia, with the cupolas of the Senate and Chamber of Deputies (1957–60).]

complex programs (*figure 1*) which, if they are to meet precisely those functional requirements so zealously defended, stand in need of a different, more complex treatment (*figure 2*). And so, in order to maintain the desired purism, apparent purism, they create true formalism, the gravest and most incontestable formalism, for it does not consist in plastic speculation in the structural elements of architecture, but in a distortion of architecture itself and what it has to offer that is essentially basic and functional. And, unfeelingly, they fix architectonic details that are repeated and imposed as the characteristics of a new school, a school that tends toward formalism and monotony, stripping buildings of the indispensable character that should be suggested by what they are to be used for and by the suitability of the design. Thus public buildings, schools, theaters, museums, residences, etc. all come to have an identical appearance (*figure 3*), despite their widely varying programs, programs that should lead to solutions of the utmost interest in which full use is made of the possibilities of modern technique.

In making these comments, I do not mean to take up an aggressive attitude toward this current of thought, but simply to show the weakness of the arguments with which adepts and the critics who support them seek to belittle architecture of a freer and more creative type, which I personally prefer and which in reality only scares and intimidates a mere handful of architects.

Within this architecture, I endeavor to shape my projects, characterizing them whenever possible by the structure itself, which is never based on the radical impositions of functionalism, but—and always—on a search for new and varied solutions, logical if possible within the static system. Therein, I fear no contradiction of form with technique and function, in the certitude that they alone remain the solutions that are beautiful, unexpected, and harmonious. To this end, I accept any device, any compromise, convinced that architecture is not just a matter of engineering, but an exteriorization of mind, imagination, and poetry.

In the Palace of Congress, for instance, the composition was worked out according to this principle, taking into account the demands of architecture and urbanism, volumes, free spaces, visual depth and perspective, and especially the intention of endowing it with a character of great monumentality by means of the simplification of its elements and the adoption of pure, simple forms. Thence was derived the whole project of the Palace and advantage was taken of the local topography to create a monumental esplanade on a level with the avenues flanking it, and therein to locate the domes that were to distinguish it hierarchically (*figure 4*). Had the Palace been designed in the academic spirit, or with an eye to adverse criticism, instead of this esplanade which has surprised many a visitor with its dignity, we should have had a tall structure (*figure 5*), blocking the view (*figure 6*) that now stretches out in depth, away and beyond the building, over the esplanade, between the domes, embracing the Place of the Three Powers and the other architectonic elements that go to compose it, enhancing them plastically and thus making the overall perspective richer and more varied (*figure 7*).

Now in the three Palaces of the Uplands, Justice, and the Dawn, I have restricted my speculations to the form of the supports or columns strictly so called. I did not want to adopt the usual sections—cylindrical or rectangular columns—which would have been simpler and cheaper, but sought other forms that, even though they might run counter to certain functionalist precepts, would give the buildings character, lightening them and creating an appearance of unattachment, as though they were merely

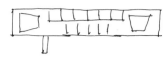

1

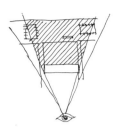

6

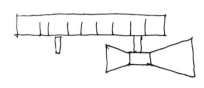

2

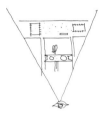

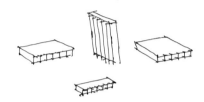

3

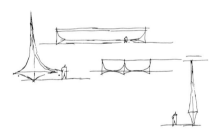

7

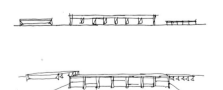

4

8

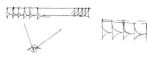

5

9

resting on the ground (*figure 8*). This justifies the forms adopted, with the ends tapering to a point, forms that greet the visitor with new and unexpected aspects; spreading out in a series of harmonious curves or, when he stands in the middle of the Place of the Three Powers, surrounding him—as Jean-Paul Sartre puts it—in the fan, as it were, of their plastic interplay; or again changing and acquiring new and different aspects, as though they were not just things, inert and static (*figure 9*). And it pleased me to feel that these forms imbued the Palaces with features, however modest, that were original and their own, and—which is still more important for me—forge a link with the old architecture of colonial Brazil, not by the obvious use of the elements common to those days, but by expressing the same plastic intention, the same love of curves and richly refined forms that is so telling a characteristic of the colonial style.

But in designing those Palaces, I was also concerned with the atmosphere they would give the Place of the Three Powers. I had no intention of making it cold and technical with the hard classic purity of straight lines already expected of it. On the contrary, I wanted it to abound in forms, a thing of dreams and poetry like the mysterious paintings of Garzou. New forms, to amaze by their lightness and freedom of creation. Forms that were not anchored to earth rigidly and statically, but uplifted the Palaces as though to suspend them, white and ethereal, in the endless nights of the uplands. Forms of surprise and emotion, designed above all to withdraw the visitor—be it for a few brief instants—from the difficult problems, at times overwhelming, that life poses for all of us.

1959

Trained as a painter, the Dutch artist **Constant** Nieuwenhuys became involved with surrealist circles in Paris after the war. His encounter with the Danish artist *172–75* Asger Jorn led them in 1948 to found the Cobra group together with the Belgian poet Christian Dotremont. Cobra was dedicated to the vitalism of *art brut* and opposed to all rationalistic forms of expression. After Cobra's dissolution in 1951 Constant moved to London for two years. There he became convinced that traditional painting was irrelevant to contemporary problems stemming from a "mechanized, technoid environment" and began to study the relation between urban space and human behavior. In 1953 he collaborated with the Dutch *347–60* architect Aldo van Eyck on a "color-space" installation in the Stedelijk Museum in Amsterdam. In the accompanying manifesto, entitled "For a Spatial Colorism," the authors rejected the use of color for decorative or functional ends, calling for the development of a chromatic "plastic reality" in architecture analogous to that in painting. Three years later, after attending the First World Conference of Free Artists staged by Jorn and the Italian painter Giuseppe Pinot-Gallizio in Alba, Italy, Constant joined their International Movement for an Imaginist Bauhaus. As a member of its "experimental laboratory," he explored the idea of unitary *167–71* urbanism (a concept originated by a related group, the International Lettrists, headed by Guy Debord in Paris), designing a pavilion for the laboratory, a plan of Alba based on "psychogeographic" routes, and an encampment for the gypsies who had been passing through this town in Italy for centuries. The last project became the first realization of unitary urbanist theory. Based on the notion of a mobile and nomadic architecture, it also served as the starting point of a scheme for a utopian city which Constant would call the "New Babylon."

In 1957, after a founding meeting in Alba, Jorn's Imaginist Bauhaus and Debord's International Lettrist merged with several other radical groups to form the International Situationist. As a protagonist of the new movement during its initial stage of development, Constant continued to elaborate the idea of unitary urbanism in projects and writings. The statement that follows was published in the first of the new series of *Potlatch,* formerly the Lettrist organ—its name derived from a ritual exchange of goods practiced by the Northwest Coast Indians, reinterpreted by Marcel Mauss in his *Essay on the Gift* and later by Georges Bataille as an expression of humanity's desire for "unconditional expenditure." In his article Constant criticizes functionalist urbanism, epitomized by the French *grands ensembles* of the 1950s, for its sterility. Drawing on the *427–36* ideas of the Dutch historian Johann Huizinga and Henri Lefebvre's philosophy of everyday life, he calls for a city conducive to psychic needs for play and creative use of leisure, proposing psychogeographic study techniques and models as a testing ground: "the science fiction of architecture."

Constant resigned from the Situationist group in 1960 when its program shifted from unitary urbanism to more directly political activities. A poetic fantasist of great plastic sensibility, he continued to develop the New Babylon on his own, envisioning a global system of megastructural "sectors," their labyrinthine circuits separated by green spaces. Commenting freely on the *266–69* space frames of Konrad Wachsmann and the suspended mast structures of *86–92* Buckminster Fuller, Constant imagined the citizens of a postrevolutionary future living in perpetual circulation and indeterminacy, liberated from fixed modes of production by cybernetic technology and able to reinvent their own environment on a purely creative basis. "The *homo ludens* of the future society will not have to make art, for he can be creative in the practice of his daily life."

Published as *"Le Grand Jeu à Venir"* in Potlatch: Informations intérieures de l'Internationale situationniste 1 (30), 15 July 1959. Courtesy of the author.

The Great Game to Come
Constant

1. The necessity to construct whole cities rapidly and in large number, a necessity that involves the industrialization of underdeveloped countries and the prolonged crisis of housing since the war, has propelled urbanism to a central position among the problems of the present day. We in fact consider that all development is impossible in this culture without new conditions for our everyday surroundings. Urbanism must take stock of such conditions. First of all, it is necessary to state that the initial experiments undertaken by teams of architects and sociologists have faltered from lack of collective imagination, a fact we hold responsible for their limited and arbitrary approach. Urbanism as it is conceived by professional urbanists today is reduced to the practical study of housing and of circulation as isolated problems. The total lack of ludic solutions in the organization of social life prevents urbanism from rising to the level of creation, and the sad and sterile aspect of the majority of new housing districts testifies to this hideously.

2. The Situationists, explorers who specialize in play and leisure pastimes, understand that the visual aspect of cities counts only in relation to the psychological effects which it will be able to produce and which must be calculated as part of the sum of functions to be anticipated. Our conception of urbanism is not limited to buildings and their functions, but extends to the entire usage one will be able to make of them, or at least to imagine for them. It goes without saying that this usage will have to change as social conditions demand, and that our conception of urbanism is therefore above all dynamic. We also reject the establishment of buildings in a fixed landscape that now passes for the new urbanism. On the contrary, we think that all static and unalterable aspect must be avoided, and that the variable or furniturelike character of architectural elements is the condition of a supple relation with the events that they will live through.

3. Consciousness of future leisure time and the new situations that we are beginning to construct must profoundly change the prevailing idea that is the point of departure for urbanistic study; we can already enlarge our knowledge of the problem by experimentation with certain phenomena linked to the urban ambience: the animation of different streets, the psychological effects of diverse surfaces and constructions, the rapid change of the look of a space by ephemeral elements, the rapidity with which the ambience of places changes, and the variations possible in the general ambience of different neighborhoods. The *dérive*, as practiced by the Situationists, is an efficacious means for studying these phenomena in existing cities and drawing some provisory conclusions. The psychogeographic notion thus obtained has already led to the creation of plans and models of an imaginist type, which one can call the science fiction of architecture.

4. The technical inventions that are today at the service of humanity will play a great role in the construction of future city-ambiences. It is notable and significant that these inventions have up to the present added nothing to existing cultural activities, and that artist-creators have not known how to employ them. The possibilities of the cinema, of television, of radio, of rapid travel and communications have not been utilized, and their effect on cultural life has been the most miserable. The exploration of technology and its utilization for higher ends of a ludic nature is one of the most urgent tasks for bringing about the creation of a unitary urbanism at the scale that future society demands.

Pre-Situationist model, with circulation for contemporary automobiles.

1960–1968

1960 Kenzo Tange, plan for Tokyo Bay (–1961; project)
Giovanni Michelucci, church on the Autostrada del Sole, near Florence
Riccardo Morandi, underground automobile exhibition pavilion, Turin
Skidmore, Owings & Merrill (Natalie de Blois), Pepsi-Cola Company headquarters,
New York City
Gino Valle, Zanussi factory offices, Pordenone, Italy (–1961)

1961 Noriaki Kurokawa, Helix City (project)
Kenzo Tange, olympic arenas, Tokyo (–1964)
Carlo Scarpa, refurbishing of Querini Stampaglia Foundation, Venice (–1963)
Le Corbusier, Carpenter Center, Harvard University, Cambridge,
Massachusetts (–1965)
Alvaro Siza, swimming pool, Leça da Palmeira, Matosinhos, Portugal (–1966)
Georges Candilis, Alexis Josic, Shadrach Woods, housing, Toulouse-le-Mirail,
France (–1968)
Herbert Greene, House on the Prairie, Norman, Oklahoma (–1962)

1962 Louis Kahn, National Assembly, Dacca, Bangladesh (–1983)
Max Urbahn, Vertical Assembly Building for N.A.S.A., Cape Kennedy, Florida (–1966)
Arata Isozaki, Prefectural Library, Oita, Japan (–1966)
Denys Lasdun, University of East Anglia, Norwich, England (–1968)
Bertrand Goldberg Associates, Marina City, Chicago
Michael Webb, Sin Center (project)
Ricardo Bofill and Taller de Arquitectura, Xanadú housing, near Alicante, Spain (–1967)
José Luis Sert, married students housing, Harvard University, Cambridge,
Massachusetts (–1964)
Robert Venturi and John Rauch, Vanna Venturi House, Chestnut Hill, Philadelphia

1963 Kevin Roche and John Dinkeloo, Ford Foundation, New York City (–1968)
Claude Parent and Paul Virilio, church of Sainte-Bernadette, Nevers, France (–1966)
Georges Candilis, Alexis Josic, Shadrach Woods, with Manfred Schiedhelm and Jean
Prouvé, Free University, Berlin (–1973)
Giancarlo de Carlo, student housing, Urbino, Italy (–1966)
Charles Moore, Donlyn Lyndon, William Turnbull, Richard Whitaker (MLTW), Sea Ranch
Gualala, California

1964 Peter Cook and Archigram, Plug-in City (–1966; project)
Louis Kahn, First Unitarian Church, Rochester, New York
James Stirling, History Faculty Building, Cambridge University, Cambridge, England
O. M. Ungers, Twente polytechnic, Enschede, Holland (project)
Peter and Alison Smithson, Economist building, London
F. J. Saenz de Oiza, Torres Blancas, Madrid (–1966)

1965 Kenzo Tange, plan for Skopje, Yugoslavia
Le Corbusier, Venice hospital (project)
Fritz Wotruba with Fritz Mayr, church of the Holy Trinity, Georgenberg, Austria
Aldo Rossi, Monument to the Partisans, Segrate, Italy
Skidmore, Owings & Merrill (Walter Netsch), University of Illinois campus, Chicago
Aldo van Eyck, Sonsbeek sculpture pavilion, Arnhem, Holland
Cedric Price, Potteries Thinkbelt (–1966; project)
Hans Hollein, Retti candle shop, Vienna
Richard Meier, Smith house, Darien, Connecticut (–1967)

1966   Marcel Breuer, Whitney Museum of American Art, New York City
Balkrishna Doshi, School of Architecture and Planning, Gujarat University,
Ahmedabad, India (–1968)
Ludwig Leo, Institute for Waterways and Shipbuilding, Berlin (–1974)
Ralph Erskine, housing, Tibro, Sweden
Aldo Rossi and Giorgio Grassi, San Rocco housing, Monza, Italy (project)
Charles Gwathmey, Robert Gwathmey house and studio, Amagansett, New York
John Hejduk, One-Half House (project)

1967   NER Group, proposal for Moscow (project)
Gottfried Böhm, town hall, Bensberg, Germany
Aurelio Galfetti, Flora Ruchat-Roncati, Ivo Trümpy, public swimming facility,
Bellinzona, Switzerland
Frei Otto, German pavilion, Expo '67, Montreal
Buckminster Fuller, geodesic dome, U.S. pavilion, Expo '67, Montreal
Moshe Safdie, Habitat, Expo '67, Montreal
Gunnar Birkerts, Federal Reserve Bank, Minneapolis, Minnesota
Carlo Aymonino, Monte Amiata residential complex, Gallaratese, Milan (–1973)
Peter Eisenman, Barenholtz pavilion (House 1), Princeton, New Jersey (–1968)
Michael Graves, Hanselman House, Fort Wayne, Indiana (–1970)

1968   Archigram, Instant City (–1971; project)
Reima Pietilä and Raili Paatelainen, Dipoli student club, Otaniemi, Finland
Coop Himmelblau, Villa Rosa installation, Vienna
Haus-Rucker-Co, Pulsating Yellow Heart construction, Vienna
John Lautner, Elrod house, Palm Springs, California

1960

Preparations for the World Design Conference held in May 1960 in Tokyo—the first such international event to be staged in Japan—served to consolidate the position of a new generation of postwar Japanese architects emerging from the wing of their mentors Kunio Maekawa and Kenzo Tange. Both Maekawa and Tange had been strongly influenced by the work of Le Corbusier and CIAM, seeking in the late 1940s and 1950s to amalgamate a monumental and expressionistic modernism with Japanese tradition. Works like Tange's Peace Center in Hiroshima (1949–56) marked the devastation of the first atomic bomb with an evocative freestanding monument. For the younger architects, however, formed out of the "charred ruins" of the war and now riding the tide of very rapid economic development, it seemed imperative to move beyond a historicist and hybrid modernism toward an architecture for a mass-oriented society.

Prior to the conference, architects Kiyonori Kikutake, **Masato Ohtaka**, **Fumihiko Maki**, and Noriaki Kurokawa and critic Noboru Kawazoe put forward a series of urban proposals in a bilingual pamphlet entitled "Metabolism." "'Metabolism' is the name of the group in which each member proposes future designs of our coming world through his concrete designs and illustrations," they wrote in the introductory statement. "We regard human society as a vital process—a continuous development from atom to nebula. The reason why we use such a biological word, the metabolism, is that we believe design and technology should be a denotation of human vitality."

181–83   In Europe Team 10 had been rethinking the organic analogy in architecture since the early 1950s. Most broadly conceived, it had to do with "growth and change." Now translated into specifically Japanese terms it was a response to the spatial needs of a national population that—as Kurokawa would note—was ten times as dense as that of the United States, concentrated on a usable surface area comprising twenty per cent of the country's land mass, and commuting to work daily in numbers that formerly might have constituted a national migration. To accommodate the accelerating flows of population, materials, and information, the Metabolists advanced a transformable technology based on prefabricated components and replacement or addition of obsolescent parts according to a "metabolic cycle." The latter was understood less in scientific terms than as a metaphor or microcosm of the cycles found in nature at large. If this symbolic conception of dynamic growth remained foreign to Western paradigms, it was coupled with a sophisticated approach to technology
266–69   at least partly inspired by the ideas of Konrad Wachsmann, whose lectures in Japan in 1955 had been attended by Kurokawa, Kawazoe, Kikutake, and Arata
402–7   Isozaki. Wachsmann's theory of flexible structure, emphasis on team problem-solving, and background in prefabricated wood construction systems seemed to have a natural affinity with Japanese building tradition. The Metabolists were also influenced by the concept of servant and served space developed by Louis
270–72   Kahn at the Richards Research Laboratories in Philadelphia, begun in 1957, and by Kahn's plan for center city Philadelphia of 1959, where an "architecture of movement" was created by elevated viaduct streets. Kahn's architectural reinterpretation of what traditionally were infrastructural spaces was productively translated by the Metabolists by way of the traditional Japanese notion of the "in-between" or relational space.

Maki, who had been educated at Cranbrook and Harvard and had worked in the offices of S.O.M. and José Luis Sert, was at this time teaching at Washington University in St. Louis. He was instrumental in conveying Kahn's and
273–75   Team 10's ideas to Japan, as well as those of Yona Friedman's Paris-based Groupe d'Etudes d'Architecture Mobile (GEAM). In the 1960 pamphlet, Ohtaka and Maki proposed a concept of "group form" as one type of Metabolist

planning. The two architects were engaged at this time in a project for the redevelopment of the Shinjuku area of Tokyo, one of the city's largest business centers and a transportation hub through which one million people passed daily. Their idea of group form involved a "master system" of dynamic open structuring, intended as a critique of the traditional compositional plan. In the Shinjuku project petal-shaped plan forms became the functional and symbolic lineaments of a multicentered assemblage of services and recreational facilities that could be modified and added onto as needed. Maki would further elaborate the concept of group form in his book *Investigations in Collective Form*, published in St. Louis (1964).

The proposals of Kikutake and Kurokawa in the 1960 Metabolist publication were even more daring. Kikutake projected an industrial city for a population of 500,000 floating in Sagami Bay off of Tokyo and making use of a system of 100- to 300-meter-high masts arranged in a hexagonal geometry from which were hung "sails" of residential "mova-blocks." Kurokawa offered several utopian schemes including a "plant type community" consisting of a tower-stem with cantilevering branches containing housing and communal facilities, a central communications and service core, and underground production spaces.

Among the foreign notables to attend the World Design Conference were Kahn, the Smithsons, Jean Prouvé, and Paul Rudolph. Tange presented his megaform plan for Tokyo Bay, signaling a shift from his earlier monumentalism to the new growth and change school. Over the next few years Metabolist concepts generated interest among Japanese building firms involved in mass production of housing, and members of the group were employed in practical research on steel and concrete prefabrication systems. Although the Metabolists' activity failed to result in further joint pronouncements or a major body of realized work, their synthesis of high technology and symbolic expression, in buildable rather than purely utopian terms, made their contribution central in the debates of the first half of the 1960s on open form and systems approaches to design and planning. It also presented significant affinities with the work of Team 10 members Georges Candilis, Alexis Josic, and Shadrach Woods, whose schemes for Toulouse-le-Mirail, France (1961) and for the Free University of Berlin (1963–73, with Prouvé collaborating on the structural detailing) interpreted the idea of organic urban growth in terms of open-ended "stem" and "web" infrastructures.

Metabolism thus served to concentrate international attention on a country that Western architecture culture had up to this point considered outside the mainstream. Although the movement gave way to more eclectic tendencies in Japan by the mid-1960s, the Osaka Exposition of 1970 was the occasion for a vivid swan song. This event, coordinated by Kawazoe, had major participation by Japanese industries. Among the virtuoso pavilions of the Japanese architects was Kurokawa's "Beautilion" for the Takara metals company, a structural lattice of bent steel tubes carrying suspended capsules and services and offering plug-in flanges for expansion in any direction. The Metabolists were joined by an international roster of architects who had pursued related conceptions during the previous decade: among them, the Archigram group, Christopher Alexander, Yona Friedman, Hans Hollein, Giancarlo de Carlo, and Moshe Safdie; Safdie's Habitat housing at the Montreal Exposition of 1967 had given a late impetus to the idea of the expandable cellular megastructure. For a history of the Metabolist movement, see Kurokawa's *Metabolism in Architecture* (1977)

From Kiyonori Kikutake, Noboru Kawazoe, Masato Ohtaka, Fumihiko Maki, and Noriaki Kurokawa, Metabolism: The Proposals for New Urbanism *(Japan: Yasuko Kawazoe, 1960), pp. 58–59. Courtesy of Fumihiko Maki.*

325–34

365–69, 379–88
459–62

Toward Group Form
Fumihiko Maki and Masato Ohtaka

What kind of living space shall there be for men who have shaken off the dust of the Middle Ages? This was a fundamental question which started a new movement in modern architecture. "Less is more," or "From God's scale to human scale." These phrases well illustrate a basic principle of the modern spirit. In a sense, the new movement was the development of the modern spirit itself, while it was taking the form of visual expression.

In parallel with this movement, the development of modern painting took a similar course. For instance, the freedom in form and color, uninhibited expression of individual feelings, the acceptance of fantasy, or experimentation to expose even the inner world of man on canvas, all these are attempts to visualize the modern spirit.

There is, however, one great difference between these two pioneering movements in the course of development, although both are closely related to the development of the modern spirit. Whereas architecture has been more conscious of logic and principles, painting has been more individualistic. In architecture, our society has been always either much generalized or idealized; in painting, on the contrary, society has been always expressed through the inner eyes of individual painters. (There are some exceptions, of course, like Gaudì who was an extremely individualistic architect or Mondrian who was a painter with a more scientific approach.)

Through this development, modern painting has become so diverse and personal that in certain instances any identity or common ground with the rest of society is difficult to detect. On the other hand, architecture has gradually lost its individuality and manifold expressions, and as a result, the architect's concept of our society is becoming more stereotyped.

We thus now face a turning point in architecture and painting. Lately, however, the criticism of functional architecture, the rise of regionalism, and intense discussion of the relationship between tradition and modern architecture all indicate that architects are again becoming interested in individuality and regional expression in building. Our architecture is moving forward. Yet so far there has been no strong attempt to create a new total image to express the vitality of our society, at the same time embracing individuality and retaining the identity of individual elements.

The biggest issue in contemporary politics and economics is the organization of an orderly society without sacrificing the fundamental freedom of the individuals who make up the society. In the pursuit of this idea men of the coming age must meet this challenge in politics and economics.

In architecture and urbanism, as in politics and economics, we must build up new concepts and methods that will not only strengthen the individuality of our visual environment but also endow the physical forms of our world with qualities that truly mirror our rapidly changing society.

We believe that the concept of group form we are now proposing will be one of the most vital methods in this respect. For although we are conscious of the architectural development of the individual buildings that are elements of the group, we try also to create a total image through the group, that is again a reflection of growth and decay in our life process. This is an effort to conceive a form in relationship to an ever-changing whole and its parts.

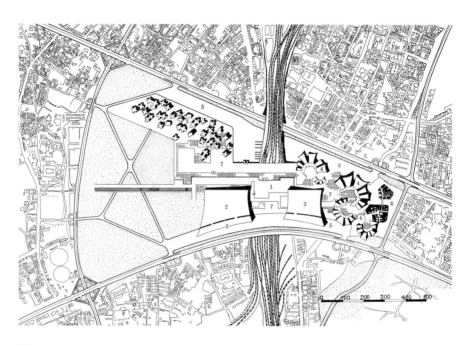

[Shinjuku district restoration, ground plan.] Master form: **1.** Shinjuku terminal—trains + subway + buses + taxis; **2.** shopping town—550,000 square feet, twice present shopping space; **3.** office town— working place for 70,000 people; **4.** amusement square—twice present amusement space; **5.** garage way—slow traffic + parking space for 20,000 cars; **6.** old town; **7.** esplanade—sun, shade, and water.

Toward group form

In the past, man has tried to discover the secret of natural phenomena and the substance of the universe. In the latter half of the twentieth century, however, in the fields of both science and the humanities, we are more concerned with grasping the total picture and the underlying relations among phenomena rather the study of individual phenomena.

We now limit our discussion to the problem of structure in our urban society. Compared with ancient and medieval cities, modern cities are characterized by:

1. The coexistence and conflict of amazingly heterogeneous institutions and individuals.

2. Unpredictably rapid and extensive transformations in society.

It is questionable, however, whether in urban design we have the visual language with which we can create the space that responds to and comprehends such characteristics of our urban society. Most of our cities fall either into utter confusion or monotonous patterns built by a few dogmatic architects. Such cities lack individuality not only in the elements that perform their complex functions, but also an overall unifying character. They also lack elasticity and flexibility in adjusting to social and economic change. We again lack an adequate visual language to cope with the superhuman scale of modern highway systems and with views from airplanes.

The idea of *group form* which we suggest here begins with solving such problems. Our idea of group form stands firmly against the image we have had in architecture for thousands of years; that is, the image of a single structure, complete in itself — for example, the Pyramids, the Parthenon, a Gothic church—or the Seagram building by Mies van der Rohe. Our idea stands also against the other image of making an exquisite static composition, using several buildings as its elements, for instance, the Horyu-ji, the Piazza San Marco, Chandigarh, or Brasilia. In short, we are trying to surpass these approaches.

In this "group architecture" just mentioned, the relationship between the elements and the totality may be represented as TOTALITY = Σ ELEMENTS, and the balance thus obtained is destroyed at the moment a single element is taken out of the group.

In the group form, on the other hand, the relationship is represented as TOTALITY $\supset \Sigma$ ELEMENTS, where $\supset$ = inclusion.

Here the totality embraces the elements; in other words, the total image of the group is not basically altered, even though some elements are taken out, or different elements added.

Now comes the question of conceiving and grasping such a total image and also investigating the systems of these elements out of which the whole is built up.

In our proposed Shinjuku redevelopment project, this idea is applied as follows:

The amusement squares, for instance, are conceived as images of flowers. The plaza forms a center about which opera houses, theaters, concert halls, movie theaters, variety theaters, etc., radiate like petals. The total image will be well maintained even if certain petals are missing. In the shopping town, the spaces for various shopping activities for retailing, wholesaling, window shopping, drinking, eating, and chatting, all are conceived as a group. Then in the office town, the group of towers extends densely in a tight space like the Milky Way. While in single structures columns, beams, arches, and other devices are used to create space freely, in the group form, walls, shafts, floors, and units[1] are basic components for building the visual environment. Space within and without is developed simultaneously. Accepting certain accidental design results, we shall be able to express the feeling of concentrated urban energy in the group form.

In city planning the concept of "master planning" has been often criticized for the following shortcomings: First, the whole plan cannot be comprehended until it is completed. Second, when completed, it may well become socially obsolete. Then, at the worst, the plan is never completed. A master plan is basically a static concept, whereas the concept of master form we are proposing here is dynamic. Master form is an entity that is elastic and enduring through any change in a society. Therefore, master form is one of the principles of a more dynamic approach in urban design, and the concept of group form is basic to the conception of the master form. Group form by no means denies the validity of single structure architecture or of architectural groups. Rather it includes them. We consider a "static composition" one possibility in the group form. The group form after all is the pursuit of a total image. Therefore, it is not necessary to limit composition to inorganic, geometrical, structural, or mechanical patterns. Rather group form is an intuitive, visual expression of the energy and sweat of millions of people in our cities, of the breath of life and the poetry of living.

Note

1.   *Wall:* Any medium which separates space horizontally. *Floor:* Any medium which separates space vertically. *Shaft:* Element which transfers objects from one level to another. *Unit:* A cell or block which performs a specific function.

1961

Kenzo Tange rose to preeminence in Japan in 1949 when he won first prize in a competition to design the Hiroshima Peace Center on the site where the first atomic bomb had fallen four years earlier. A student of Kunio Maekawa, who had in turn been trained by Le Corbusier and Antonin Raymond, Tange was strongly affected by European modernism. He presented his Hiroshima project at CIAM's eighth congress in Hoddesdon in 1951, and in 1959 traveled to Otterlo to attend CIAM's final gathering. There he was among the few to express regret about CIAM's disintegration at a moment when he felt it more useful "to lay emphasis on the links that unite us all." At the same time he was strongly receptive to the new ideas on mobility being advanced by the Smithsons and Team 10. Taking exception to Ernesto Rogers's attempt to identify his work with a return to Japanese tradition, he stated that he did not wish to be so conservative as "Rogers himself in the case of the Torre Velasca," adding that "Creative work is expressed in our times in a union of technology and humanity. . . .Tradition can, to be sure, participate in a piece of creation, but it can no longer be creative itself." Two projects done at this time—for a terraced residential complex standing on an island in Boston's Back Bay (1959) and, above all, a plan for restructuring Tokyo (1960)—clearly marked a departure from the more object-oriented monumentality of Hiroshima (completed in 1956) and the *béton brut* expressionism of his Kurashiki Town Hall (1958–60).

Tange's plan for Tokyo, designed in collaboration with Sadao Watanabe, Koji Kamiya, Noriaki Kurokawa, Arata Isozaki, and Heiki Koh, was first presented at the World Design Conference held in Tokyo in 1960. Comparable in visionary scope to Le Corbusier's 1922 Ville Contemporaine for Paris, a city for three million inhabitants, Tange's plan provided for ten million, a density on which Tokyo's population was verging at this date. The scheme was predicated on mass movement, speed, and automated communication. Rejecting the traditional fixed master plan, Tange approached the city as a living organism subject to a continuous cycle of growth and change—an idea derived from Team 10 and being developed at this time by the Metabolist group (among them Kurokawa)—seeking a form of organization responsive to dynamic patterns of urban flow and changing function. Believing that "the only way to save Tokyo is to change its basic structure," he rejected the model of the centripetal core expanding according to a radial-concentric pattern with outlying satellites, a schema he considered obsolete and dysfunctional for a city of this magnitude (and which had been proposed for Tokyo in 1956 on the model of Abercrombie and Forshaw's plan for Greater London), taking his cue instead from the linear city proposals that had been developed by various architects since the beginning of the century. To solve the problem of the city's exhaustion of buildable surface area, he boldly located a new civic axis running from the modern business center of Tokyo into the middle of Tokyo Bay, where a chain of megastructural space frames interlinked a cyclical system of superhighways and mass transit flanked by floating residential development.

The audacious proposal was worked out and even defended by Tange in pragmatic terms. Yet it entailed nothing less than a total redefinition of the city itself. The late-twentieth-century city was, in his view, "not merely a collection of people and functions," but "an open complex linked together by a communication network." Its function was no longer "to produce objects," but to "act as a brain center performing countless invisible tasks." If the period from 1920 to 1960 had been one of functionalism, Tange noted in a subsequent writing, the new period would be one of "structurism": "the process of formalizing the communicational activities and flows within spaces."

Despite Tange's emphasis on his scheme's flexibility and openness,

181–83, 240–41

300–7

319–24

though, it was widely criticized for both its technological determinism and axial monumentality. Fumihiko Maki, a member of the Metabolist group, suggested that even though the megastructure allowed for changeable infill, it could itself become obsolete and thus prove "a great weight about the neck of urban society." Maki proposed instead "the system that permits the greatest efficiency and flexibility with the smallest organizational structure." The critique of "major structures" versus "minor objects" and the "overestimation of technology and productive progress for their own sake" was echoed by Aldo van Eyck, among others, while another Team 10 representative, Peter Smithson, objecting to the regimentation and overscaling of the components, raised the specter of Big Brother, charging that the vision of a megalopolis the majority of whose population was engaged in "tertiary" activities—communications—was not only unrealistic economically but failed to reckon with the political consequences of such a "centralized nation-city."

347–60
181–83

The debate opened by Tange's project had important repercussions on related tendencies around the world. The issue was approached in France as a debate over the "spatial city," while in Italy it was reframed in terms of the "new urban dimension" and the question of "total form." The critic Manfredo Tafuri, in an early essay entitled "The New Urban Dimension and the Function of Utopia" (*Architettura, cronache e storia,* February 1966), cautioned against "concepts of a global and all-resolving urban form, alternative in the sense of dissolving existing structures; of the identification of a utopia of scale with a social utopia .; of the cathartic value attributed to technological prophecy; of the reintegration of city and nature; and finally, of formal exaggeration introduced as an urban value in itself."

273–75
399–401
449–55

Published in Japanese in Shinkenchiku, *March 1961. In English in* Japan Architect, *April 1961, pp. 10, 12, 16, 18, 28, 32. Republished in slightly revised form in Udo Kultermann, ed.,* Kenzo Tange: Architecture and Urban Design *(Zurich: Verlag für Architektur Artemis, 1970), pp. 114 ff. Courtesy of the author.*

A Plan for Tokyo, 1960: Toward a Structural Reorganization
Kenzo Tange

1. The nature of a city of 10,000,000: the importance of its existence and the necessity of its growth

Tokyo, New York, London, Paris, Moscow—all masses of population that have passed or will soon pass the 10,000,000 mark. People call them "overgrown cities," but before deciding whether they are really overgrown or not, we must first consider the conditions that necessitate their development, the importance of their existence, and the true nature of their functions.

The technological revolution of the twentieth century, and particularly of its latter half, is causing drastic changes in economic structure, in social system, and in living environment. Technical systems involving huge energy, such as that produced from the atom, and electronic controls are rapidly improving the industrial structure and furthering its organization. As a result, the circulation that occurs before and after production, as opposed to production itself, is becoming a more and more important part of the economic process. In order to control economic cycles in our capitalistic society and to encourage uninterrupted growth, it is becoming increasingly necessary to plan and organize this circulation. In the capitalistic societies the ties between government and business are becoming stronger, and in socialist countries they are already stronger than that.

Furthermore, it is now impossible to plan an industrial undertaking without reference to technological research or to the prospects for demand. The stimulation of demand, which we refer to in Japanese as the "revolution in consumption," has become an unavoidable part of economic circulation; without the mass communication that produces this stimulation there can be no mass production. This phase of the economy is beginning to control people's modes of living and their concept of life.

The process of economic circulation within a given country is determined by a complicated system of relationships in which government, politics, finance, control of production and consumption, technology, and communications are all intimately and mutually linked. The portion of the population which has charge of this system—we might call this the tertiary industrial population—has been greatly increased during the second industrial revolution. The growth in this sector of the population, the increase in its productivity, and the rise in its income are indices of economic expansion.

The functions that are gathering together in cities of the ten-million class are the pivotal functions of this tertiary phase of industrial production, and the people in the cities are the people who perform these functions. They are the organization men. In response to their high level of consumption, it is only natural that the tertiary functions of consumption, such as sales and services, should concentrate in the cities. Again, in Japan, which depends upon imports for raw materials, the factories concentrate in the coastal areas around the cities, in pursuit of the capital and the consumptive demand centered there. The factories, however, do not constitute the source of energy for the cities of 10,000,000. The source of energy is, after all is said and done, the tertiary production functions.

What I speak of as organization is not a single enterprise. It is neither fixed nor closed. It is a type of organization that results from the invisible network of communication produced by the technological revolution, an open organization in which any combination of function and function, of function and man, of man and man is possible. By virtue of this organization, the individual functions go together to form the comprehensive function of a city of 10,000,000.

At any class level and in any field, organizations—they might be called conferences—are formed and dissolved. This organizational activity, while entailing many expenses, decides everything, creating wisdom, producing values, and connecting them with the world. Tokyo, a city of 10,000,000, is the organization of the pivotal functions of Japan, and as such it is so important that it controls the fate of the entire country. At the same time, world conditions are reflected in this organization with gradually increasing sensitivity.

People say that the organization man is alone, but even more alone is the man who is separated from this network. It is in order to connect themselves with this network that people gather in the cities. The telephone, the radio, television, the portable telephone, the video-telephone—all these indirect means of communication give rise to a greater demand and need for direct communication. When men carry messages, when they attempt to preserve the links between the various functions, there is a flow of movement, and it is this movement that makes the urban organization an organization. The city of 10,000,000 is an aggregation of a moving, flowing population.

Tokyo, then, is not merely a collection of people and functions. It is also an open organization in which the various functions communicate with each other and create the total function. What gives this organization its organic life is the flowing movement of the 10,000,000 people who are engaged in the communication of functions.

2. The physical structure of Tokyo: limitations and inconsistencies of the centripetal radial structure

Communication is the factor that gives organic life to the organization that is Tokyo. This city of 10,000,000 is, in effect, an open complex linked together by a communication network. As the technical means for communication improve, men instinctively feel the need for direct communication, and since transportation is necessary for direct communication, the transportation system is the basic physical foundation for the functional operation of the city.

The functions which are gathered in Tokyo seek closer mutual communication, and as a result they are drawn toward the center of the city. This civic center, once formed, grows larger and larger. At the same time, the people who perform the functions spread out into the suburbs in an effort to find cheap land. The city therefore assumes a form that is centripetal and radial. This has been the typical urban pattern since the Middle Ages, and the natural pattern that a city will follow if left to grow freely.

As the central urban district grows, there are more and more commuters, and as the suburbs grow, they travel farther. Hence the murderous confusion in the train stations of Tokyo today. The movement of the commuters is repeated daily at definite intervals. It constitutes a regular, permanent flow, which is sustained by the mass transportation organs. Though private railways and subways carry a certain percentage of the people, the main burden is shouldered by the national railway system.

With the growth of social organization and the division of functions, there is more and more free, individually motivated movement. In opposition to the steady flow of the commuters, this is a variable flow—one might say a flowing mobility. It is this mobility that gives the open organization of the city its organic life. And as leisure time increases, this flow grows larger, sustained largely by automobiles, which grow more and more numerous with the expansion of the economy.

Automobiles carry the flowing movement of traffic in the heart of the city and to a lesser degree in and between the urban subcenters. Though the number of automobiles per capita is less in Tokyo than in Western countries, it is growing fast, and with it the steady flow of commuters who drive their own cars is swelling.

In the center of the city, where the pivotal functions are concentrated, the variable flow is increasing at an accelerating rate. The result is that traffic in this area has almost reached a state of paralysis, but this does not alter the fact that the flow is both necessary and inevitable. Such mobility is needed to maintain the life of a city of 10,000,000. And it should be kept in mind that the increase in the flow is not what causes traffic confusion. Confusion results from the fact that the structure of the city cannot sustain the necessary mobility of the times. This is the failure of the radial city in which traffic moves toward the center.

The traditional radial plan can perhaps provide the mobility required by a city of 1,000,000, but that of 10,000,000 is beyond its limitations. In Tokyo, where movement is increasing by the day, it is urgent that a new system of transportation be constructed. And one which will bring city, buildings, and transportation into a single organic entity.

In addition, since the speed and scale of movement in the city is destroying the spatial order of the city, it is necessary to find a new order.

3. A plan for Tokyo, 1960: a proposal for a change in structure

As a reflection of Japan's economic expansion, Tokyo is developing and spreading at a rapid pace, and the flow of movement within the city is increasing in scale and speed. The human drive behind this growth is tremendous.

And yet this tremendous human drive is having the adverse effect of exposing Tokyo's incongruities, of throwing the city's functions into confusion, and of slowing down movement to the point of paralysis.

Many people consider that growth itself has produced confusion in the city, and that if growth is contained, the situation will improve. It is impossible, however, to curtail this growth, for that would be attempting to reverse a necessary historical trend.

We do not oppose such measures as the redistribution of factories throughout the country, the construction of satellite cities, or the removal of governmental and educational institutions to other locations. Such measures might in some respects be advantageous. In our opinion, however, the Tokyo that remained after these measures had been taken would still writhe in urban confusion. Furthermore, the causes that lead to the city's expansion would still remain in operation.

Tokyo will not be saved unless we keep our vision firmly fixed on Tokyo itself. Nothing is accomplished by escapism; there may be open spaces to which existing urban installations could be moved, but the problem of Tokyo's growth would continue.

People say that the city's expansion has been too rapid, but the real difficulty has been that our plans have been too small and our policies too old-fashioned. People are forever saying "we must be practical," but the type of "practicality" that has been exercised in Tokyo is impractical in the extreme. It is unrealistic and backward-looking.

We, for our part, recognize the necessity of Tokyo's growth, the importance of its existence, and the validity of the functions that it performs. Furthermore, we believe it possible to direct the human drive that has created the confusion of today into new channels, and for this reason we place forward a plan which we regard as both constructive and practical.

The city of 10,000,000 is an organism which has appeared only in the latter half of the twentieth century. It is a historical novelty. In order to remain alive and to grow, it must have a structure befitting the twentieth century. Instead, however, the radial pattern of the Middle Ages, with its centripetal traffic system and its rows of buildings along the sides of streets, has been allowed to grow and grow without basic alteration.

The result is that the permanent structure of the modern metropolis is incompatible with the movement that is necessary to the life of the metropolis. The old body can no longer contain the new life. The radial pattern is incapable of the mobility that the city of 10,000,000 requires. Furthermore, the population of Tokyo twenty years from now will be about 15,000,000.

This is the inconsistency that lies at the root of Tokyo's confusion. There is only one way to save Tokyo, and that is to create a new urban structure which will make it possible for the city to perform its true basic functions.

We are not trying to reject the Tokyo that exists and build an entirely new city. We wish instead to provide the city with a revised structure which will lead to its rejuvenation. We are talking not merely of "redevelopment," but of determining a direction along which redevelopment should proceed. Redevelopment that is not orientated in a definite direction cannot solve the problems that face Tokyo.

In our proposal, the basic aims of redevelopment should be as follows:
1.   To shift from a radial centripetal system to a system of linear development;
2.   To find a means of bringing the city structure, the transportation system, and urban architecture into organic unity;
3.   To find a new urban spatial order which will reflect the open organization and the spontaneous mobility of contemporary society.

4.   From a radial structure to a linear structure: a proposal for cycle transportation

In the age when cities developed around central squares or plazas and when people lived within limits prescribed by regional societies, the central square was the nucleus of communication, and the cathedral, the castle, and the city hall were the spiritual supports, as well as the symbols, of urban life. Horses and carriages moving along radial streets past rows of buildings must have formed a very harmonious ensemble.

Now, however, mass communication has released the city from the bonds of a closed organization and is changing the structure of society itself. In the society with an open organization and in the pivotal city of this organization the mobility involved in free, individual communication is assuming a larger and larger scale. This movement, added to the fixed movement of regular commuters, has led to extreme confusion in the larger cities.

The urban system developed in the Middle Ages cannot withstand this movement, and the centripetal pattern is seeking to reform itself from within.

We reject the concept of the metropolitan civic center in favor of a new concept which we call the civic axis. This is tantamount to rejecting the closed organization of the centripetal pattern in favor of an open organization which makes possible a development along a linear pattern. In effect, we are proposing that the radial structure of Tokyo be replaced by an axis which develops linearly.

The evolution of radial cellular bodies into vertebrates and the changing of eggs into bodies are instances of the sort of development we have in mind, and they illustrate its necessity.

The manufacturing processes in modern factories will gradually be divided, and

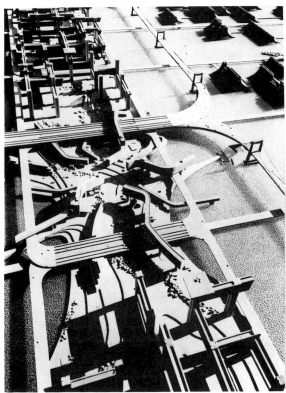

the all-purpose machines which make for centralization will be broken down into component parts. At the same time, however, the work performed by these smaller machines will be unified by the linear movement of a conveyor system.

If the various functions of a great city were distributed along a line, communication linking them could be carried out in a minimum of time by movement along that line. Nothing could be simpler or quicker. The entire movement of a city of 10,000,000 would be sustained by this communication.

The cathedral, which sat quietly at the center of the closed organization, was the symbol of the city of the Middle Ages. For the open organization of the contemporary city of 10,000,000 the civic axis, along which the arterial movement that sustains urban life takes place, is a fitting symbol.

We propose for this civic axis a system of cyclical transportation. It is estimated that the Tokyo of twenty years hence will have a population of 15,000,000. This will probably mean that 2,000,000 or 2,500,000 people will have to gather along the civic axis in order to perform necessary urban functions. In addition it may be expected that five or six million people will flow into the axis each day. While many of these people will rely on mass transportation, there will also be flowing mobility of individual traffic. The present system of street and ordinary highways could never withstand the strain of such a volume.

With the existing system of highways, at the points of interchange it is unfeasible to have more than three lanes in one direction. The three-level cyclical system that we propose, however, overcomes this limitation with a series of overlapping links. In each link all traffic is one-way, but in any two neighboring links the direction of circulation is opposite, so that at the points where the links overlap, movement in both links is in the same direction. The overlapping links serve as points of interchange, the connection between upper and lower links being accomplished by means of ramps. The number of ramps is equal to the number of lanes, and the ramps alternate with continuing lanes. This type of highway could be made to handle ten times, or even thirty times, as much traffic as the present freeways, and a civic axis with a system of cycles of this design could serve as a rapid and effective means of communication for a city of any size.

The three levels of traffic would be divided in accordance with the speed of vehicles moving along them, and the lowest level would be divided in accordance with the speed of vehicles moving along them, and the lowest level would be a unit of a man-made "ground" which would contain several levels of parking space.

The cyclical transportation system is composed of a series of unending links, each link of which serves as a steady cycle of flow. Any number of links could be employed, so that the civic axis could develop unit by unit. A system of this sort would make it possible for any number of people to move freely and quickly among the functions lined up along the axis.

5. Organic unification of the city, the transportation system, and architecture: a proposal for unifying the core system and the *pilotis*

Transportation today is changing the relationship that links the city structure with traffic and architecture. Indeed, the automobile is completely overturning this relationship. In the past, people walked along a street until they arrived at their destination and then walked directly into a door. This fact has since ancient times determined the system of traffic and architecture in cities. The appearance of the horse and carriage created no need for a new system, and even when railways and trolleys were invented, people felt no serious doubts about the old one. The problems and these new modes of transportation created were solved by means of stations.

In our age the automobile has altered the relationship between streets and buildings, but the old system remains in existence. The confusion that prevails in our cities today results largely from the fact that the automobile and the street system are incompatible.

The basic difference between the automobile and mass transportation facilities like the train and streetcar is that the automobile theoretically makes it possible for individuals to move freely from door to door. In other words, the automobile provides not mass, but individual transportation.

The appearance of the automobile has led to the division of vehicles and pedestrians, with the result that the relationship between street and buildings has come to resemble the relationship between railways and buildings. Even though buildings open on a street, it is usually impossible to park cars in front of them. There is need for a new sequence in which the automobile moves from high-speed highways to low-speed highways and then to parking spaces from which the passengers in the automobile can approach buildings. In other words, there is need for a new organization in which the urban system, the traffic system, and the architectural system are organically unified.

In response to this problem, the architectural pioneers of the early twentieth century developed the *pilotis* as a means for releasing ground space. Their idea was to create a public space on the ground where the movement necessary to modern society could take place and a quiet private space above ground where men could live and work. The *pilotis* area would serve as a link between the two types of space, and automobiles would move about on the ground without disturbing life within the private space above.

We have been using *pilotis* arrangements since we drew up the plans for the Hiroshima Peace Memorial. In the Tokyo City Hall, the *pilotis* area was divided into two levels, a lower one for automobiles and an upper one for pedestrians, and in our plan for a comprehensive metropolitan center for Tokyo, we carried this system through another stage of development. In general, this sort of solution appears to be one of the most promising means of redeveloping urban areas.

We are also proposing to make use of the core system, in which the vertical traffic in buildings as well as the service arteries—water ducts and electric wiring—are gathered together in single shafts forming the nuclei of buildings. The cores of buildings would become branches of the urban transportation and service arteries, so that architecture would be integrated with the urban system.

In our plan for Tokyo, we have devised means of unifying the core system and the *pilotis*. As we envision them, the cores of buildings take the place of columns, creating "columnless" *pilotis* areas under the buildings. This system is unified with the cyclical transportation system we propose.

Each link of the transportation system contains a unit of area with multilevel parking space. People would enter the parking space in their cars, get out of the vehicles, and then ride up into buildings in elevators situated in vertical cores. In this way the unit urban area and the highway system would intermesh, and there would be spatial order as well as a speed hierarchy linking, first, streets, interchanges, parking spaces, and buildings, and second, high speed, low speed, human speed, and immobility. Urban space would be restored to life.

6. The restoration of spatial order in the city: a new urban spatial order reflecting the open society and flowing organization of the city

In contemporary civilization and in the cities of 10,000,000 which form the nuclei of contemporary civilization, the speed and scale that have been made possible by modern technology are destroying spatial order.

The plazas, cathedrals, and city halls of the Middle Ages had a mass human scale which was united to the masses of people gathered in the urban centers, and which harmonized with the human scale of the roads radiating from them. Today, however, huge highways carrying high-speed traffic have intruded themselves into the old system. They represent a superhuman scale, which in no way harmonizes with the architecture of the late nineteenth century and the first half of the twentieth century.

The accumulation of capital in our time will doubtless work to increase the scale of construction still further, causing the order of urban space to be shaken to its very foundations. The new large-scale structures, which have long life cycles, will form the major framework of the cities, and they will be one of the decisive elements in the new urban spatial systems. When we consider that traffic can move at 100 kilometers per hour or more, however, the vastness of the new structures ceases to seem vast. The flow and speed of the present will doubtless lead to even larger-scale construction.

Nevertheless, man himself continues to walk in steps of a meter or so, and we are still surrounded by the unchanging human scale. Furthermore, whereas the life cycle of large-scale construction is growing longer, the life cycle of our houses and the articles we use in daily activities is gradually growing shorter. This fact results from our ever-increasing reliance upon manufactured goods and from our tendency to take up new things and discard them more and more rapidly.

Individuality, freedom, and spontaneity form an ever-strengthening antithesis to the control of technology. Man desires more and more to exercise his own individual choice in matters that concern houses, gardens, streets, and plazas.

There are, then, two conflicting extremes—the major structures which have long life cycles and which, while restricting individual choice, determine the system of the age, and the minor objects that we use in daily living, which have a short life cycle and which permit the expression of free individual choice. The gap between the two is gradually growing deeper.

The important task facing us is that of creating an organic link between these two extremes and, by doing so, to create a new spatial order in our cities. The centripetal hierarchy of the cities of the Middle Ages will no longer serve, for it represents an order determined by the fact that man walked on his own two feet. In the moving, flowing cities of our time, pedestrian traffic and automobile traffic intersect, and the direction of both is variable. Movement is not closed and centripetal, but open and fluctuating.

The spatial order in cities will doubtless become richer in content as time goes on. It will come to include not only spaces of an orderly nature, but free, nonordered spaces as well.

We have put forth several plans dealing with the spatial relation of the two extremes. In the Kurashiki City Hall, the M.I.T. plans, the W.H.O. plans, and in the present plan for Tokyo, we have tried to provide freedom within a more systematic spatial structure, and in the Kagawa Housing project as well as the plans for housing on the filled-in land in this project, we have tried to find order within free disorder in groups of buildings.

We must seek order in freedom and freedom in order. It is by relating these two extremes that we will create a new spatial organization for contemporary cities.

1961

The economic prosperity that arrived in Europe in the 1950s did not reach Spain until the early 1960s when mass tourism made major inroads into the country and when Franco responded to the crisis in the economy by instituting a new program for stabilization and replacing a number of political appointees with specialized technicians. These changes, opening Spain to industrial development, were coupled with the relaxation of censorship in the cultural arena, encouraging democratization and effectively neutralizing the long-standing leftist opposition to the dictatorship. For architects, a profession whose ranks were still small, this meant major new opportunities to work. By the mid-1960s, especially in Madrid, architects only a few years out of school were building whole sectors of the city, and the favorable conditions were transforming both the profession and the schools into thriving and increasingly outward-looking institutions.

These developments contrasted with the situation of the preceding decades, when fascism in a more virile moment had arrested the development of the *Movimiento Moderno* flourishing under the Second Republic and largely insulated Spain from European critical debates. Though never as coherent as fascist architecture in Italy, the state architecture of the 1940s, when not merely occupied with the pragmatics of reconstruction, pursued an expression that was grandiose, "profoundly Spanish," and meant to belie the country's technical and economic poverty. The few architects who sought in the 1950s to combat this climate and continue in the tradition of GATEPAC (the Spanish affiliate of CIAM and primary exponent of rationalism from 1930 to 1936, when it was outlawed) did so under inauspicious conditions and, in resisting the official route of monumentality and folklorism, acquired a pioneer status for the succeeding generation. Foremost among them was **José Antonio Coderch de Sentmenat**, whose work was singled out by Alberto Sartoris and Gio Ponti at a meeting in Barcelona in 1949 as the sole achievement of note in an otherwise uncertain architectural scene. Two years later he helped to wrest Spain from its provincialism by winning the country's first grand prize at the Milan Triennale. Coderch was to exert a major influence on Spanish architects and students over his career. A founding member of Grupo R—a group formed in Barcelona in 1950 committed to the "reintegration of architecture and culture"—he gave an early impetus to its program with his housing on Paseo Nacional in Barcelona (1952–54), elegantly translating traditional elements like movable blinds into a modernist language. As Ricardo Bofill would write in *Zodiac* 15 (1965), an issue devoted to Spanish architecture, Coderch "was the architect of greatest national significance in the [1950s], and perhaps the only one who found a personal form of expression that was really rooted in the vital tradition of the country."

Coderch would attend CIAM's Otterlo meeting, and afterward become a member of Team 10. The following essay was originally written to Team 10 on the solicitation of Jacob Bakema as a kind of self-introduction. Bakema's response to Coderch's rather jesuitical message was to send the Spanish architect a copy of Antoine de Saint Exupéry's *The Little Prince*. The essay was later widely published, and revised and amplified by Coderch as late as 1977.

First published as "No son genios lo que necesitamos ahora/Non é di genii che abbiamo bisogno," in Domus, *November 1961, n.p. Republished in Spanish in* Cuadernos de Arquitectura de Barcelona *46 (1961), p. 44. Published in English in Alison Smithson, ed., "Team 10 Primer," Architectural Design, December 1962, pp. 566–68. Revised as "Speech on Admission to the Royal Fine Arts Academy of San Jorge," in J. A. Coderch de Sentmenat, Conversaciones/ Conversations, ed. Enric Soria Badía (Barcelona: Editorial Blume, 1979), pp. 178–81. Courtesy of Anna Maria Giménez de Coderch.*

181–83

It's Not Geniuses We Need Now
J. A. Coderch de Sentmenat

It is neither my intention nor desire to join the ranks of those who delight in talking and theorizing about architecture. But I have had to state my views and have, therefore, felt obliged to submit, in all humility, the following.

An old and famous American architect (if my memory serves me well) said to another who was much younger and was asking for his advice: "Open your eyes wide and look; it is much easier than you think." He also said to him: "Behind every building that you see there is a man that you don't see." A man, he said. He did not mention whether he was an architect or not.

No, I do not think that it is a genius that we need at this time. Genius is an occurrence that is an Act of God. Nor do we need High Priests or dubious Prophets of Architecture, or great doctrinaires. There is something of a living tradition that is still within our reach, and also many ancient moral doctrines concerning our trade or profession (and I use these terms in their best traditional sense) of architect and ourselves. We need to take advantage of what little there is left of the constructive tradition, and, above all, the moral tradition in this epoch when the most beautiful of our words have lost their real meaning.

We need thousands and thousands of architects to think less about "Architecture," money, or the cities of the year 2000, and more about their trade as architects. Let them work tied by a leg so that they cannot stray too far from the earth in which they have their roots or from the men they know best; let them always clutch a firm foundation based on dedication, goodwill, and honor.

To bring this about I believe that we must first rid ourselves of many ideas which appear clear but are false, of many hollow words, and work with that goodwill that is translated into one's own work and teaching rather than with a mere concentration on doctrinairism. I think that the best teaching is that which teaches our trade, teaches us to work with great faith, or, in short, that which teaches us to be architects, knowing, at the same time, as we must, that we can all make mistakes. It is also the example of working, continuously watching in order not to confuse human frailty, the right to be mistaken (a cloak which if wrongly used can cover a multitude of sins), with inconstancy of will, immorality, or the cold calculation of the climber or "getter-on." In Spain, my parents used to tell me, a gentleman, an aristocrat, is the person who finds himself unable to do certain things which even the law, the Church, and the majority approve of or permit.

We must all, every one of us, individually constitute a new "aristocracy." This is an urgent problem, so urgent that it must be tackled at once. The main thing is to begin to work and then, and only then, can we talk about it.

We must pit ourselves against money, against the vanity of success, against excess of property or earnings, against inconstancy and haste, and against the lack of spiritual life or conscience; we must put instead dedication, craftsmanship, goodwill, time, the bread we need for every day, and above all, love, which is acceptance and giving, not possession and domination—all these must be taken hold of and clung to, for these are the true values.

Seeing and knowing more or less profoundly the works or forms (the exterior signs of spiritual richness) of the great masters is considered to be culture, or architectural formation.

The same means of classification are applied to our craft or profession as are used (exterior signs or economic richness) in our materialistic society. And then we lament or complain because there are no great architects under sixty, because the majority of architects are bad, because the new urbanization is antihuman, because our ancient cities, towns, and villages are destroyed, and houses and towns are built like film sets along the length of our beautiful Mediterranean coasts. It is strange that so much is said and published about the exterior signs of the Great Masters (truly very valuable signs) and that their moral value is hardly mentioned.

May it not also be considered curious that people write and talk of their weakness and frailty as an attractive oddity or a tidbit for gossip, or just as being mistaken, and at the same time conceal as a forbidden subject or as an anecdote their attitude to life or to their work?

Is it also not curious that here we have Gaudí, very near to us (I myself know persons who have worked with him) and so much is said of his work and so little of his moral position or of his dedication? It is still more curious to contrast between the great value placed on Gaudí's work and the silence or ignorance that exists on the moral position or attitude presented by Gaudí to the problem of architecture. The former, that is, Gaudí's work, is beyond our reach to do, and the latter, which is Gaudí's approach to his work, is something which we can all do, or at least attempt. We cannot reach his genius, but we must emulate his devotion and work. And every architect can do it easily if he wishes. We must concentrate on the things we can do, and not on what we cannot.

The real spiritual culture of our profession has always belonged to a few. The circumstance that enables nearly anyone to have the possibility of access to this culture is the heritage of all, and is one that is not generally taken. Neither unfortunately do we accept cultural behavior which should be obligatory and in the consciousness of us all.

But the conditions on which we have to base our work vary continuously. There are religious, moral, social, and economic problems, together with those of teaching, and, in this modern world, possibly the most important sources of energy, which can all play a part in changing, unsuspectingly, the face and structure of our society (some brutal changes whose meanings are lost to us are also possible). All these different problems can impede honorable long-range planning.

It is ingenuous to think that the ideal and the practice of our profession may be condensed into slogans, such as the sun, light, air, greenness, social architecture, and so many others. A formalistic base, dogmatic, above all if it is only partial, is in itself bad, save on exceptional and catastrophic occasions. From all this it may be deduced that, in my opinion, among the many different paths that each thinking architect will choose to follow there must be something in common, something which must be in all of us; and here I return to the beginning of what I have written; this I have done without wishing to give anybody a lesson, but only with a profound and sincere conviction.

1961

In 1949 the Title I slum clearance provision of the Federal Housing Act had empowered urban administrators and public housing bureaucrats—epitomized

55–63 by Robert Moses, Public Works Commissioner of New York City—to meet postwar housing needs by building superscale high-rise apartment blocks. By the early 1960s, the degraded incarnations of the Radiant City, first idealistically proposed by Le Corbusier in the 1920s, were being so ruthlessly implemented under the pragmatic imperatives of "urban renewal" that architecture journalist **Jane Jacobs** was driven to direct political action in order to defeat a Housing and Redevelopment Board plan that threatened to bulldoze her neighborhood in downtown Manhattan. In *The Death and Life of Great American Cities,* written earlier the same year, she had lovingly portrayed the same West Village streets as a counter to the "blight of dullness" of present-day planning. Incorporating sociological insights, economic analysis, and persuasive prose to challenge the orthodoxies of professional planners, Jacobs optimistically endorsed the pluralist city, spelled out in phrases like "exuberant diversity" and "planning for vitality." Her "realistic" prescriptions for civic-minded behavior and safe street life—"eyes on the street"—were directed against the single-use zoning that was then normative practice in urban planning, a legacy of CIAM's functionally compartmentalized urbanism. Yet the problem with functionalism was more than a matter of good intentions gone awry for Jacobs. Her book unequivocally indicted the entire modernist tradition of the designed urban utopia as "statistical."

The response to Jacobs's passionate book was enormous and none of it neutral. Touching a receptive chord among those in both the profession and the lay public seeking amelioration for urban decay, rampant inner-city crime, and the middle-class's flight to the suburbs, the book was widely reviewed in both the popular and architectural press. The professional readership, stung by her idolatrous assault on modernism's "sacred cows" (as *Progressive Architecture* put it in a feature of April 1962), faulted the uncredentialed author for amateurism and adherence to a single model as a panacea—low-rise high-density housing on mixed-used streets—even while acknowledging the thrust of her argument.

107–9 Lewis Mumford, whose book *The City in History* was published the same year, was provoked by Jacobs's attack on the Garden City ideal, of which he had been a career-long proponent. In Jacobs's view, the planned suburbs of Ebenezer Howard, Patrick Geddes, and others were simply the horizontal and antiurban correlates of Le Corbusier's towers-in-the-park. Mumford responded with a twenty-page review in the *New Yorker* (December 1, 1962) entitled, with some sexism, "Mother Jacobs' Home Remedies." "If people are housed in sufficiently congested quarters—provided only that the buildings are not set within superblocks—and if there is a sufficient mishmash of functions and activities," he wrote sarcastically, "all her social and aesthetic demands are satisfied."

442–45 Yet Jacobs's book helped unleash the community activism of the 1960s. It is often credited with more. A decade later, when the authorities in St. Louis dynamited the notorious Pruitt-Igoe public housing block—an award-winning design by Minoru Yamasaki of the mid-1950s later plagued by a high incidence of crime ascribed to its anonymous corridors and unsafe open spaces—many saw it as the auto-da-fé of modern architecture and a symbolic confirmation of Jacobs's diagnosis. The impact of design on urban crime would be studied in greater depth by Oscar Newman in his widely read *Defensible Spaces* (1972).

The following excerpt comes from the introduction to Jacobs's book. She would return to the economics of housing in *The Economy of Cities* (1969).

From Jane Jacobs, The Death and Life of Great American Cities *(Random House, 1961), pp. 4–6. Copyright © 1961 Jane Jacobs. Courtesy Random House, Inc.*

from *The Death and Life of Great American Cities*
Jane Jacobs

[. . .] There is a wistful myth that if only we had enough money to spend—the figure is usually put at a hundred billion dollars—we could wipe out all our slums in ten years, reverse decay in the great, dull, gray belts that were yesterday's and day-before-yesterday's suburbs, anchor the wandering middle class and its wandering tax money, and perhaps even solve the traffic problem.

But look what we have built with the first several billions: Low-income projects that become worse centers of delinquency, vandalism, and general social hopelessness than the slums they were supposed to replace. Middle-income housing projects which are truly marvels of dullness and regimentation, sealed against any buoyancy or vitality of city life. Luxury housing projects that mitigate their inanity, or try to, with a vapid vulgarity. Cultural centers that are unable to support a good bookstore. Civic centers that are avoided by everyone but bums, who have fewer choices of loitering place than others. Commercial centers that are lackluster imitations of standardized suburban chain-store shopping. Promenades that go from no place to nowhere and have no promenaders. Expressways that eviscerate great cities. This is not the rebuilding of cities. This is the sacking of cities.

Under the surface, these accomplishments prove even poorer than their poor pretenses. They seldom aid the city areas around them, as in theory they are supposed to. These amputated areas typically develop galloping gangrene. To house people in this planned fashion, price tags are fastened on the population, and each sorted-out chunk of price-tagged populace lives in growing suspicion and tension against the surrounding city. When two or more such hostile islands are juxtaposed the result is called "a balanced neighborhood." Monopolistic shopping centers and monumental cultural centers cloak, under the public relations hoohaw, the subtraction of commerce, and of culture too, from the intimate and casual life of cities.

That such wonders may be accomplished, people who get marked with the planners' hex signs are pushed about, expropriated, and uprooted much as if they were the subjects of a conquering power. Thousands upon thousands of small businesses are destroyed, and their proprietors ruined, with hardly a gesture at compensation. Whole communities are torn apart and sown to the winds, with a reaping of cynicism, resentment, and despair that must be heard and seen to be believed. A group of clergymen in Chicago, appalled at the fruits of planned city rebuilding there, asked,

Could Job have been thinking of Chicago when he wrote:

Here are men that alter their neighbor's landmark . . . shoulder the poor aside, conspire to oppress the friendless.

Reap they the field that is none of theirs, strip they the vineyard wrongfully seized from its owner . . .

A cry goes up from the city streets, where wounded men lie groaning . . .

If so, he was also thinking of New York, Philadelphia, Boston, Washington, St. Louis, San Francisco, and a number of other places. The economic rationale of current city rebuilding is a hoax. The economics of city rebuilding do not rest soundly on reasoned investment of public tax subsidies, as urban renewal theory proclaims, but also on vast, involuntary subsidies wrung out of helpless site victims. And the increased tax returns from such sites, accruing to the cities as a result of this "investment," are a mirage, a pitiful gesture against the ever increasing sums of public money needed to combat disintegration and instability that flow from the cruelly shaken-up city. The means to planned city rebuilding are as deplorable as the ends.

Meantime, all the art and science of city planning are helpless to stem decay—and the spiritlessness that precedes decay—in ever more massive swatches of cities. Nor can this decay be laid, reassuringly, to lack of opportunity to apply the arts of planning. It seems to matter little whether they are applied or not. Consider the Morningside Heights area in New York City. According to planning theory it should not be in trouble at all, for it enjoys a great abundance of parkland, campus, playground, and other open spaces. It has plenty of grass. It occupies high and pleasant ground with magnificent river views. It is a famous educational center with splendid institutions—Columbia University, Union Theological Seminary, the Julliard School of Music, and half a dozen others of eminent respectability. It is the beneficiary of good hospitals and churches. It has no industries. Its streets are zoned in the main against "incompatible uses" intruding into the preserves for solidly constructed, roomy, middle- and upper-class apartments. Yet by the early 1950s Morningside Heights was becoming a slum so swiftly, the surly kind of slum in which people fear to walk the street, that the situation posed a crisis for the institutions. They and the planning arms of the city government got together, applied more planning theory, wiped out the most run-down part of the area and built in its stead a middle-income cooperative project complete with shopping center, and a public housing project, all interspersed with air, light, sunshine, and landscaping. This was hailed as a great demonstration in city saving.

After that, Morningside Heights went downhill even faster.

Nor is this an unfair or irrelevant example. In city after city, precisely the wrong areas, in the light of planning theory, are decaying. Less noticed, but equally significant, in city after city the wrong areas, in the light of planning theory, are refusing to decay.

Cities are an immense laboratory of trial and error, failure and success, in city building and city design. This is the laboratory in which city planning should have been learning and forming and testing its theories. Instead the practitioners and teachers of this discipline (if such it can be called) have ignored the study of success and failure in real life, have been incurious about the reasons for unexpected success, and are guided instead by principles derived from the behavior and appearance of towns, suburbs, tuberculosis sanatoria, fairs, and imaginary dream cities—from anything but cities themselves. [. . .]

1961

Educated at the Architectural Association in London in the late 1940s, **Alan Colquhoun** began practice in the socially progressive milieu of the postwar London County Council Architects Office. There, along with William Howell, Colin St. John Wilson, John Killick, Peter Carter, and other talented younger architects, he worked on a series of "Corbusian" housing schemes like the Bentham Road Estate, designed in the 1950s. An occasional participant in the discussions that took place at the Institute of Contemporary Arts together with Independent Group

237–39   members Reyner Banham, James Stirling, Peter Smithson, and others, he figured among a generation of English architects who were highly critical of the watered-down modernism of the welfare state while at the same time seeking to move beyond the prewar MARS Group's doctrinaire functionalism. Colquhoun was affected by Rudolf Wittkower's *Architectural Principles in the Age of Humanism*, which appeared in book form in 1949; taken with Le Corbusier's *Modulor*, published in 1950, Wittkower's studies reintroduced ideas of classical proportion into modernism. The "New Palladianism," so called, gained credence for Colquhoun especially through several important essays by Wittkower's pupil

205–25   Colin Rowe. Le Corbusier was then (and would remain for Colquhoun) the prime example and model: like Rowe and many of his generation, Colquhoun saw him as the link—even more than Mies van der Rohe—between the European classical tradition and the modern movement. In 1954, when the *Architectural Review* was still proselytizing its empiricist philosophy of Townscape, he wrote a

114–20   pointed letter to the editors protesting Nikolaus Pevsner's attempt to draw a parallel between Corbusian free planning and eighteenth-century English Picturesque theory, stating, with the succinct reasoning that was to become characteristic of his criticism, that "no purely visual 'theory' basing itself on the universal validity of forms independent of structure and function appears to be adequate. It is because this fact has been lost sight of that so much of postwar British architecture is effete and superficial."

A quiet but constant intellectual presence on the English scene, Colquhoun was engaged in practice and part-time teaching at the Architectural Association in these years (except for six months in the Paris office of Candilis and Woods). His emergence as an essayist came in the 1960s. Among his first important writings was the following review of Banham's *Theory and Design in the First Machine Age*. The book, published in 1960, represented a decisive break with Banham's Pevsnerian background, giving an aesthetic rather than determinist reading to the machine. Banham included a dedication to Colquhoun, citing as "a lodestone for these studies" the latter's insight that "what distinguishes modern architecture is surely a new sense of space and the machine aesthetic."

In his review, Colquhoun reconsiders the modern movement in light of Banham's thesis that "between Futurist dynamism and . . . Academic caution the theory and design of the First Machine Age were evolved." Though appreciative of Banham's breadth and originality, Colquhoun criticizes his friend for failing to apply his aesthetic interpretation of technology consistently, as exemplified by

370–78   Banham's tendentious view of Buckminster Fuller as *deus ex machina* of an effectively realized futurism—a conclusion that not only forms the book's

86–92   dénouement but colors its entire argument. Colquhoun argues that Fuller's approach to technology was no less idealist than Le Corbusier's, advising "an acceptance of the symbolic role of architecture and of other than purely technical values"—a theme to which he would return repeatedly in future essays.

From British Journal of Aesthetics *(January 1962), pp. 59–65. Republished in Alan Colquhoun,* Essays in Architectural Criticism: Modern Architecture and Historical Change *(Cambridge, Mass.: MIT Press, 1981), pp. 21–25. Courtesy of the author.*

The Modern Movement in Architecture
Alan Colquhoun

A reevaluation of the significance of artistic expression in a world revolutionized by the machine has been, consciously or unconsciously, at the root of all the avant-garde movements of the last fifty years. But whereas in literature, music, and painting, the machine, as a direct protagonist, has played an intermittent and often purely picturesque role, in architecture it has been fundamental to the development of new forms and the evolution of aesthetic theory. This fact has tended to obscure the equally important subjective factors which lie behind man's need to give expression to symbolic forms and which are as relevant to architecture as they are to the other arts. Critical histories of the modern movement in architecture (e.g., Nikolaus Pevsner's *Pioneers of Modern Design*) have tended to concentrate on its social and technical influences or on those movements immediately preceding it, such as Art Nouveau and the English Free Style. In stressing its active and craftsmanlike aspects at the expense of its theoretical background, they have given the impression that the forms of modern architecture were a spontaneous outgrowth from an immediate and radical past.

In *Theory and Design in the First Machine Age* Reyner Banham has shifted this emphasis and has investigated precisely those sources which were taboo to an earlier generation of writers on the modern movement. In his opening chapter he gives the following summary of the causes of the architectural revolution which occurred during the first decade of the century: "These predisposing causes were . . . firstly, the sense of an architect's responsibility to the society in which he finds himself . . .; secondly, the Rationalist, or structural, approach to architecture . . . codified in Auguste Choisy's magisterial *Histoire* . . . ; and, thirdly, the tradition of academic instruction . . . owing most of its energy and authority to the Ecole des Beaux-Arts in Paris." It is clear that in giving this entirely new weight to the influence of the Beaux-Arts, Dr. Banham intends to establish some thesis on the modern movement, though what this is to be is not immediately apparent.

The Beaux-Arts, which came in for the most virulent attacks from the first modern architects, taught certain principles of plan organization and form composition whose foundations went back to eighteenth-century theories of psychological response and to that recurrence of Neoplatonic doctrine which had been enshrined in the academies. The idea that art contained certain principles independent of its craft or technical aspect was as strong at the end of the nineteenth century as it was at the time of Etienne-Louis Boullée; it was the mental atmosphere which produced at once an academic like Charles Blanc and a revolutionary like Paul Cézanne. It needed very little to strip these ideas of stylistic clothing and to conceive of an architecture or an art based on principles of abstract form, owing allegiance to universal values. Modern architecture crystallized when this movement collided and partly merged with those rationalist and moral theories which embraced the new structural techniques and the new social consciousness emerging toward the end of the last century.

Dr. Banham shows how the academic tradition, especially as summed up in the writings of Julien Guadet at the end of the century, continued to have an influence even on those modern architects who were loudest in their vituperations against the Beaux-Arts. This is, in fact, one of the main themes of his book, and it is the conclusions that he draws from the effect of this influence that would seem to make Dr. Banham vulnerable to criticism. Although he postpones the disclosure of his critical position until the end of the book, his general attitude begins to make itself clear at a fairly early stage. That he evidently does not look upon the facts that he has uncovered with detachment shows itself in his constantly pejorative use of the term "academic" as if the presence of academic features constituted a self-evident condemnation of works which otherwise might pass the test of modernity. His final thesis is that by their persistence in believing in certain "constant" architectural values modern architects like Le Corbusier were led to a misunderstanding of the Machine Age with which they were trying to come to terms. It is undeniable that Le Corbusier made simultaneous claims for his architecture which were incompatible, but Dr. Banham is concerned not only with the theories by which the architects rationalized their work but with this work itself. He accepts the general theory that modern architecture is a branch of technics and condemns the buildings of the 1920s because they failed to live up to this theory. According to him, in seeking to arrive at perfected and final forms, especially those based on Phileban solids which they took to result logically from machine technology, they closed the door to the natural evolution of mechanical forms and arrived at a premature academicism.

This argument seems to rest on the assumption that the evolution of architectonic forms is a constant flow and that the technical processes out of which it emerges are capable of only a single and literal interpretation at any one moment. It may be true that in evaluating history a certain interpretation seems to have been inevitable; but this would presumably be the interpretation that actually did take place, not one that *should* have taken place. This seems to be a very different thing from claiming that the interpretation should have been determined solely by the objective facts of the technical process.

Whatever the contradictions in the rationale of the avant-garde movement, it would appear that Dr. Banham has oversimplified, and so falsified, the essential ideas behind those theories which led to functionalism. In their pure form they seem to represent a position at the opposite extreme from the traditional notions of the nature of art and the role of the artist. In the latter the architect, as artist, is seen as the manipulator of tangible and visual form according to laws belonging to architecture itself, and deriving its ultimate justification from psychological facts which govern man's apprehension of the world. In the former, architectural form is seen to derive from causes which lie within the matrix of the world and which are outside the architect, whose own thought is a part of that matrix. According to this view the architect acts as midwife, as it were, to the forces of nature and bears witness to its hidden laws. He performs no specifically "artistic" acts, since he is merely the medium through which the technique becomes substantiated. The object which results is a "created" thing only insofar as it partakes of the creative forces latent in the universe and has absorbed just so many of those forces as are appropriate to the problem to be solved. It is not an artifact apart from other artifacts and emits no special kind of effulgence.

This would seem to be fundamentally an idealist view, and it is to this view that functionalism adheres. Far from being utilitarian and pragmatic, functionalism sought to spiritualize the mechanical process and to destroy the dichotomy of the mechanical and the spiritual, of determinism and free will. Le Corbusier's constant use of biomorphic parallels to mechanical forms is indicative of this and reveals a type of thought analogous to that of Théodule Armand Ribot in his discovery of the role of motor forces in the creation of emotional states. At this generalized level of thinking, one can see a curious inversion if one compares Piet Mondrian's philosophy with that of functionalism. Superficially they would seem to be at opposite poles of thought, yet in both there is a rejection of mediate steps between man and the absolute. The rejection of natural forms as a subject for painting is equivalent to the rejection of derivative and subjective forms in architecture. Art for art's sake and the architecture of complete engagement are one and the same thing.

It would seem that this attitude differs from the "traditional" one rather in its perfectionism than in its adherence to a more demonstrable truth. If, as Dr. Banham shows, academic systems of thought persisted even in those works which laid claim to the most extreme functionalism, it would seem to indicate that they were a necessary ingredient of practice which could not be assimilated into the rationale. In the writings of Le Corbusier we see the two attitudes lying side by side—on the one hand, the unitary view in which form and function are presented as identical; on the other, the idealist view that function is preceded by form. But Le Corbusier made no claims to be writing a systematic treatise, and it could be that the contradictions in the argument represent a necessary conflict of ideas which can only be resolved in the works themselves—a dialectical sequence the third term of which can only be introduced at the level of symbolic representation. It would seem just as reasonable to assume that we come into the world with certain paraphernalia with which to fashion the world in our likeness as it is to assume that we make our debut naked except for our techniques—that we are historical animals, in the sense that we carry history in our mental attitudes as well as in our accomplishments.

Although Dr. Banham is too scrupulous a historian to commit himself to certain movements or personalities, it is to the Futurists and to Buckminster Fuller that he evidently feels most strongly drawn. The Futurists were undoubtedly an important germinating influence on the modern movement, even if in the excitement of discovering new and hitherto neglected material he probably exaggerates this influence. Yet the precise degree of influence is unimportant, since the Futurists represent only one aspect of the complex cross-fertilization of ideas which took place at the time. Dr. Banham deplores the absence, in Le Corbusier's plans, of those Futurist qualities which he detects in his sectional organization. Yet the same "impure" qualities exist in the Futurists themselves, and it can hardly be denied that a reconstruction of Antonio Sant'Elia's Central Station in the *Città Nuova* would reveal a thoroughly Beaux-Arts *parti*. If the Futurists are to be taken as the fountainhead of an architecture of revolution, then the presence of academic features would seem to be a necessary component of this revolution. To extract from Le Corbusier the academic and from a Futurist the dynamic aspects in order to show that the former is *retardataire* and the latter progressive would appear to be a procedure of dubious historical validity.

The case of Buckminster Fuller is rather different, and in introducing him as the *deus ex machina* of his argument, Dr. Banham is raising the fundamental question of the validity of architecture itself in any sense that we understand that term. Fuller represents an extreme form of the functionalist dogma. He criticized the European moderns just at the time when all avant-garde opinion was on their side and at the same time produced a series of projects which owed nothing to any preconceived notion of formal organization. Yet if Fuller's philosophy rests on the idea of an "unhaltable trend to constantly accelerating change," he nonetheless, in the Dymaxion House project as in the domes, presents a final form—the image of a technique which has reached an optimum of undifferentiation. Nor could it be denied that Fuller's attitude toward mathematics conceals a certain mysticism; and if this differs considerably from the Platonism of Le Corbusier, it is no more rational and should therefore equally be condemned by Banham on the grounds of its not representing a truly positive and pragmatic attitude toward technology. The difference between Fuller and Le Corbusier lies not in the ideal importance which they attach to mathematics but in the symbolic role it plays. In Fuller's domes the forms are identified by their lines of force, resembling those High Gothic structures where a framework alone defines the volumes which it encloses and seeming to exemplify Fuller's philosophy of the forms of art being absorbed back into the technical process. In Le Corbusier, the plastic act is hypostatized. His forms are, as it were, congealed in space, as in a solid graph. In both, the Phileban solids play an essential part; in both, the aesthetic and the discipline are identified. But whereas in the case of Fuller the formulation and the identification take place on a supersensuous level and the aesthetic is transmuted into the act, in the case of Le Corbusier the act becomes solidified in the sensuous object. With Fuller the idea explains the form; with Le Corbusier the form explains the idea. To argue, as Dr. Banham does, that mathematics is a discipline of a negative kind which is totally absorbed in the end product would reduce the constructive principle to a purely empirical level. Yet Fuller's domes, which are pure structure, are conceived and presented as objects of aesthetic value and are charged with a meaning surpassing that of particular occasion or use. In fact, Fuller's domes are "ideal" structures every bit as much as is a building by Mies van der Rohe or Le Corbusier. Their difference is that they constitute an idea on such a general level that no articulation of activity is expressed.

It seems, indeed, that man has an ineradicable urge to extract from the flow of events a token of stasis, a fixed point against which to measure himself. And indeed, although a state of constant flux may be the nature of the world as it is presented to us, the concept of continuous change, considered as an object of factual experience such as technical development, is itself an abstraction. We must set it against the palpable tendency of the senses and intellect to see the world in the form of recognizable and nameable wholes.

But in spite of the weight he gives to the opinions of Fuller in the last chapter of the book, Dr. Banham's final view of the modern movement remains ambivalent. If Fuller were right, the whole *oeuvre* of the European architects of the 1920s would be invalid, since its impact clearly lies in formal patterns which are not solely dictated by techniques. If it is true, on the other hand, that these architects were concerned not with the literal but with the symbolic interpretation of the machine, then Fuller's criticisms fall to the ground, and the meaning attributed to the role of the machine in architecture is more important than the degree to which structures reflect the course of machine technology as such. And Dr. Banham seems to confirm this view when he analyzes the works themselves and allows his sensibility free play. He discusses at length Walter Gropius's Werkbund Pavilion from a purely aesthetic point of view and devotes several pages of analysis to the two buildings which he has chosen to represent the movement at its point of climax, Mies van der Rohe's Barcelona Pavilion and Le Corbusier's Villa Savoye at Poissy-sur-Seine. Of these he says: "Their status as masterpieces rests, as it does with most other masterpieces of architecture, upon the authority and felicity with which they give expression to a view of men in relation to their environment." This sentence clearly implies an acceptance of the symbolic role of architecture and of other than purely technical values.

It is curious that, having admitted that certain buildings of the period are masterpieces, Dr. Banham should reject those mystiques without which they could not have come into existence. One wonders by what criterion he judges a masterpiece and by what casuistry he would be able to demonstrate that a building was simultaneously a masterpiece and a failure. The ambiguity that existed in the Modern Movement, and which Dr. Banham wants to tidy away from the face of history, lies in the fact that the functionalist theory was, in a profound sense, the outcome of attitudes prevalent in the nineteenth century, although in conflict with them on a superficial level. The breaking apart of the ancient and medieval traditions, in which idealism and pragmatism, the creative act and the craft discipline, were inseparable, did not finally occur until the mid-eighteenth century, and it ushered in a period of history in which the conscious search for the unity of the architectural act became the main preoccupation. What is known as the academic tradition was, in fact, the beginning of a revolution rather than the end of a period of decline, and the final distinction which it drew between the crafts and the liberal arts was prophetic of the rise of an architecture produced on the drawing board and in the workshop, owing nothing to manual sensibility and habit. It is this fractured condition of architecture that the whole Modern Movement reflects.

Dr. Banham's book commands our admiration in its method of analysis and its presentation of a comprehensive picture of the Modern Movement. But it would have been more objective if the author had drawn his conclusions more exclusively from the historical evidence which he himself has adduced. He has demonstrated that many of the overt aims of the movement were not achieved; but it may well be that these aims themselves were often of doubtful value, and that the true meaning of the movement lies in the unconscious substratum of the theory and is to be recognized in the works themselves. That a personal point of view should enter into a historical judgement is inevitable and even desirable; yet one is left with the feeling that the last word on the Modern Movement has not been said—and will not be said for a very long time to come.

1962

In 1947 at Bridgwater the young Dutch architect **Aldo van Eyck** attended his
100–2 first CIAM meeting. There he voiced a critique of the abstract functionalism that
CIAM had pursued since 1928. Deploring the fact that "the struggle between
imagination and common sense ended tragically in favor of the latter," Van Eyck
asked whether "CIAM intend[s] to 'guide' a rational and mechanistic conception
of progress toward an improvement of human environment, or . . . to change this
conception." Over the next decade this question remained at the heart of CIAM's
ultimately unsuccessful attempt to reorient itself, and Van Eyck, as a member of
Team 10, helped to bring about its demise. For its Otterlo meeting in 1959, he
prepared a special issue of *Forum,* the Dutch journal he would edit from 1959 to
1963, which was in effect CIAM's obituary and a manifesto of his own concerns.

The 1950s had been a significant period of contacts and activities for Van
Eyck. Trips to central Africa, first inspired by his reading of Marcel Griaule's
ethnological account of Dogon culture in the Surrealist journal *Minotaure,*
spurred his interest in anthropology and primitive dwelling forms. This interest
found its way into CIAM's discussions at Aix-en-Provence in 1953 by way of his
friendship with Sigfried Giedion, chairman of the aesthetics commission.
107–9 Recasting the debate on regionalism, the commission report acknowledged, "a
primitive Cameroon hut has more aesthetic dignity than most prefabricated
houses." But despite such accommodations, the stand taken by the old CIAM
176–80 guard—Gropius's "dear industry happy future teamwork no art no primadonnas
kind of gruel" (as Van Eyck later put it)—proved unpalatable to the young
architects gathering around Van Eyck, Jacob Bakema, and Peter and Alison
181–83 Smithson. Team 10 was born at a meeting in Doorn, Holland, the following spring.
314–18 Van Eyck was also close in the early 1950s to the Dutch artists Constant
and Karel Appel, who belonged to the avant-garde group Cobra and espoused
an art of spontaneity and *art brut* directness. Their aesthetic, which influenced
240–41 the Smithsons as well, represented a kind of dialectical other or "counterform" to
the legacy of De Stijl. But the latter would remain a vital inspiration for Van Eyck.
It became the crux of an argument with the older Rotterdam architect W. van
Tijen, whose technical-social rationalism Van Eyck attacked as lacking in
Rietveld's imagination. Van Eyck's architecture also had affinities with the work of
270–72 Louis Kahn at this time, as evident in the resemblances (perhaps unconscious)
between Kahn's Trenton Bathhouse (1954–59) and his seminal Children's Home
in Amsterdam of 1955–60. Less concerned with what the building "wanted to be"
than with its inhabitants' experience of it, though, Van Eyck diverged from Kahn
in his more anthropological conception of space.

Many of Van Eyck's key ideas recur in the following essay, which he wrote
as an introduction to a special issue of *Forum* on Pueblo architecture. Among
these are the notion of "twinphenomena"—the both/and nature of things—and of
"identifying devices," elements that make a space humanly comprehensible. The
"configurative discipline," an idea Van Eyck developed from 1954 on, is a design
method in which part and whole reinforce each other's identity in a relationship of
reciprocity, summarized in the paraphrase of Alberti, "a city is a huge house and
a house a tiny city." The city becomes "a hierarchy of superimposed configurative
systems multilaterally conceived" —a metonymic rather than additive solution to
325–34 the "aesthetics of the great number" (and thus a critique of Tange's megaform).
The method was later applied by Van Eyck's followers Piet Blom and Herman
Hertzberger, though in a more didactic spirit. It also led to an altercation with
Christopher Alexander over the city-as-tree analogy: in Van Eyck's view, the city,
379–88 like the tree, was too poetic a figure to be quantified, even as a semilattice.

From Forum 3 (August 1962), pp. 81–93. Courtesy of the author.

Steps toward a Configurative Discipline
Aldo van Eyck

Open up that window and let the foul air out.—Jelly Roll Morton

Architecture—planning in general—breathes with great difficulty today. Not because of the erroneous obstacles society casts in its way, but because architects and planners refuse to extend the truth that man breathes both in and out into built form. The breathing image epitomizes my conception of twinphenomena—we cannot breathe one way, either in or out. As to what Jelly Roll cried: which window and what foul air? The "window" is relativity and the "foul air" . . . well, it is what exudes from the aggressive halves into which twinphenomena are brutally split by some disease of the mind which, in our particular part of the world, has been devoutly cultivated for 1962 years!

Right-size
I am again concerned with twinphenomena; with unity and diversity, part and whole, small and large, many and few, simplicity and complexity, change and constancy, order and chaos, individual and collective; with why they are ignobly halved and the halves hollowed out; why too they are withheld from opening the windows of the mind!

As abstract antonyms the halves are rendered meaningless. As soon, however, as they are permitted to materialize into house or city their emptiness materializes into cruelty, for in such places everything is always too large and too small, too few and too many, too far and too near, too much and too little the same, too much and too little different. There is no question of right-size (by right-size I mean the right effect of size) and hence no question of human scale.

What has right-size is at the same time both large *and* small, few *and* many, near *and* far, simple *and* complex, open *and* closed; will furthermore always be both part *and* whole and embrace both unity *and* diversity.

No, as conflicting polarities or false alternatives these abstract antonyms all carry the same luggage: loss of identity and its attribute—monotony. Monotony not merely in the sense of uniform because, as I have already said:

If a thing is too much and too little the same, it will also be too much and too little different. Right-size will flower as soon as the mild gears of reciprocity start working— in the climate of relativity; in the landscape of all twinphenomena.

The amorphous and additive character of all new towns—their heterogeneous monotony—is the immediate result of the complete absence of right-size. Those urban functions which were not forgotten were compartmentalized. The actual building elements were subsequently arranged academically according to a trivial infill habit, and the open space between them is so casually articulated and emptied of every civic meaning that they loom up like oversized objects, pitilessly hard and angular, in a void (what Candilis justly calls *espace corridor*).

Within the tyrannical periphery of such objects there is no room for emotion; nor is there any in the resulting emptiness between these objects. Emptiness has no room for anything but more emptiness.

All urban ingredients curdle, all urban colors clash. Just planned wasteland.

The devaluation of various abstract antonyms
Now the object of the reciprocal images contained in the statement *make a bunch of*

places of each house and every city; make of each house a small city and of each city a large house is to unmask the falsity which adheres to many abstract antonyms: adheres not merely to small versus large, many versus few, near versus far, but also to part versus whole, unity versus diversity, simplicity versus complexity, outside versus inside, individual versus collective, etc., etc.

It seems to me that these reciprocal images furthermore upset the existing architect-urbanist hierarchy. It is what I wanted them to do—gladly.

To proceed from the idea of dwelling, in the sense of "living" in a house, in order to arrive at the idea of living, in the sense of "dwelling" in a city, implies proceeding simultaneously from the idea of living, in the sense of "dwelling" in a city, in order to arrive at the idea of dwelling, in the sense of "living" in a house. That is as simple and involved as it actually is!

When I say, therefore, make a welcome of each door and a countenance of each window: make of each a place, because man's home-realm is the inbetween realm—the realm architecture sets out to articulate—the intention is again to unmask false meaning and to load the meaning of size with what right-size implies! As soon as the equilibrating impact of the inbetween realm—extended so that it coincides with the bunch of places both house and city should be—manifests itself in a comprehensibly articulated configuration, the chances that the terrifying polarities that hitherto harass man's right composure may still be reconciled will certainly be greater.

It is still a question of twinphenomenon, a question of making the inbetween places where they can be encountered, readily mitigating psychic strain. What is direly needed is a dimensional change in both our way of thinking and working which will allow the quantitative nature of each separate polarity to be encompassed and mitigated by the qualitative nature of all twinphenomenon combined: the medicine of reciprocity.

First approach to a configurative discipline

Commenting on some housing projects by Piet Blom (published in *Forum* 7, 1959, and 5, 1960–61) I stressed the fact that these projects did not depend on current types of housing, since the latter have amply proved their own obsolescence, especially in a larger context. Nor do these projects depend on the current narrow views of what inside and outside, individual and public space mean; nor for that matter on the frozen quartet of functions and the foolish severing of urbanism from architecture into two conflicting disciplines.

They successfully demonstrate the validity of a way of thinking and corresponding design process which I have advocated for many years.

By liberating oneself of the abject burdens mentioned above, by crossing the frontier of established practice—though not of what is plausible—and making constructive use of the kind of capacity rejection of the obsolete precludes if new valid forms are to replace it, it is now possible to invent dwelling types which do not lose their specific identity when multiplied, but, on the contrary, actually acquire extended identity and varied meaning once they are configurated into a significant group.

What is essentially similar becomes essentially different through repetition instead of what is but arbitrarily "different" becoming arbitrarily "similar" through addition (a universal city-molesting sickness).

Each individual dwelling possesses the potential to develop, by means of configurative multiplication, into a group (subcluster) in which the identity of each dwelling is not only maintained but extended in a qualitative dimension that is specifically relevant to the particular multiplicative stage to which it belongs. Whilst the resulting group is, in turn, fortified in the next multiplicative stage by a new identity which will again enrich that which precedes it.

As it is, all hitherto adopted methods impoverish whatever limited identity a preceding numerical stage may possess as such. In fact the absurd truth of it is that the identity of a dwelling, if it has any at all, is at present almost invariably such that it is incapable of surviving the very first repetitive stage, i.e., that of the single block! This demonstrates that the established design mechanism is unable to cope with plurality; that it deals with the wrong singular in a basically wrong—additive—way.

It is of course true that the plural must first acquire meaning in human terms if it is to be guided by the still unexplored aesthetics of number.

But the reverse is equally true. We simply cannot embark on one without the other—they are both part and parcel of the same problem.

The identity of a smaller cluster—its intrinsic "gestalt" in human terms, i.e., its real "dwelling" potential—is embraced and intensified in that of the larger one which grows out of it through further repetition, whilst the identity of the larger cluster is latently present in the smaller one. This, of course, points toward the meaning of unity through plurality and diversity; diversity through unity and configurative similarity, but also toward the need to articulate both interior and exterior space as clearly and consistently, since only their complete ambivalent accordance can ultimately constitute the sequences of places that must accommodate the occasions which real urban existence calls for.

This is why I propose so emphatically not only a far greater comprehensibility at all stages of multiplication but also a radical enlargement of scale in the sense of far greater configurative compactness. Furthermore, a greater audacity of form and articulated place-clarity within a closely knit compound rather than an amorphous texture of inevitably oversized items (oversized, however measurably insignificant) additively arranged in space-emptiness.

But it is also why I propose a greater urbanity since this implies a far closer meshing of all urban functions, aspects, and kinds of human association. A far greater affinity toward their interdependent multimeaning on the part of the architect is a first condition. Hence the citylike nature of a house and the houselike nature of a city.

All configurative stages of multiplication—simultaneously rather than consecutively conceived—cannot acquire real significance until they coincide to some extent at least with the illusive configuration of the individual and the collective. Fuel for the entire process as well as recipient of the engendered warmth.

To achieve this end, more is required than a fugal configuration of dwellings. We must indeed proceed from this but we must also proceed from more than this. Why is apparent enough, since it is those functions that every plurality of people required in order to exist within an urban cluster in a fashion and degree of urbanity pertinent to it which must further identify each configurative stage.

We must do all that can be done in our field to make each citizen know why it is good to live citizenlike in a city built for citizens, for a city is not a city if it is just an agglomeration for a very large "population"—a meaningless accretion of quantities with no real room for anything beyond mere survival.

Coincidence of urban identity and dwelling configuration

It is a question of multiplying dwellings in such a way that each multiplicative stage acquires identity through the significance of the configuration at that stage.

I say, through the "significance" of the configuration in order to make it clear that it is not merely a matter of visual form, since this alone would be purely academic, but of significant content transposed through structural and configurative invention into architecture. Each multiplicative stage should therefore achieve its appropriate identity by assimilating spontaneously within its structural pattern those public facilities this stage requires and which inseparably belong to it.

The·important question here is, therefore, how to identify the part in terms of the whole, i.e., what can identify it beyond the multiplicative stage reached. How is one to comprehend whether the cluster one resides in is self-contained and independent, or a dependent configurative part of a larger cluster?

To put it in general terms: by what means can the degree of "urbanity" (literally used as derived from *urban*) that belongs to the particular complexity and scale of a given urban entity be identified throughout—i.e., become significantly comprehensible in terms of what it actually is?

It seems to me that at each multiplicative stage large elements with a wide specifically civic meaning or city-forming potential, beyond that of the immediate public requirements the stage calls for locally, should be included within its configuration.

On a city level these elements are so manifold that if meaningfully localized in a framework of urban reference they could help to impart a specific urban identity to each subarea—a different one, moreover, in each case. Such decentralization of the civic possibilities that belong to a large city would impart citylike identity evenly instead of concentrating it in one or a few centers. It would, at any rate, counteract the kind of urban congestion through overpressure, which of course goes hand in hand with suburban anemia as its equally nefarious counterpart, and impute fuller urban context to the subareas beyond their specifically local context.

Each citizen would thus "inhabit" the entire city in time and space. (See John Voelker's scheme, *Forum* 1, 1960.)

It may sound paradoxical but decentralization of important city-scale elements will lead to a greater appreciated overall homogeneity. Each subarea will acquire urban relevance for citizens that do not reside there. The urban image—awareness of the total urban cluster—is then no longer represented by strictly personal place-reference, different for each citizen, and a center common to all, but, apart from such personal place-reference, by a gamut of truly civic elements more or less equally distributed and relevant to all citizens. As I have already suggested, such elements will bring varied specific identity to each subarea. They will, moreover, induce citizens to go to parts of the city otherwise meaningless to them.

How obsolete the accepted ingredients with which most city plans and housing projects are additively concocted really are, certainly in Holland, is demonstrated by the schemes which have tentatively succeeded in reestimating the meaning of many, if not yet all, urban ingredients and inventing new forms and ideas for them by means of one single simultaneous configurative discipline. Those housing projects which are real sources of inspiration today demonstrate new dwelling types; new methods of access; communication and integrating public facilities through a single complex, constructive, and sequential discipline.

All these matters coincide in that they constitute part of each other's immediate counterform and are contained in each other's embracing periphery.

The house, for instance, is thus also part of the street, whilst the street, reinterpreted, is included in the house in that it is not necessarily exterior to it in the limited sense—nor, for that matter, are external living spaces. All ingredients are redefined and closely meshed.

The vehemence of vast plurality

Provided the dimension of a given cluster is fairly small, whether independent or part of a larger urban complex, the suggested configurative process could no doubt bring about the required overall comprehensibility. In city scale clusters or entire cities, however, the forces and movements which result from these forces—the vehemence of vast plurality—are so great that functional and emotional conflicts ensue with which even the sequential configurative process I have referred to cannot fully cope. This is due to the heaping up of quanta which, even if they may one day be so interadjusted as to become compatible, confront us today in their apparent discrepancy as irreconcilables which the citizen can no longer respond to positively, but which together, nonetheless, belong to the essence of the citizen's environment.

The accumulative nature of cities today is such that the forces which cause it, and the movements which ensue, cannot be canalized adequately in time and space by any of the ideas and methods hitherto accepted by urbanists whether in the CIAM tradition or not.

Amorphous texture versus comprehensible structure

Nor will the configurative process manifested in the outstanding schemes already referred to, which deal with the grouping of a large though still limited number of dwellings and the public facilities this number requires, suffice, unless the "infrastructures" are so conceived that identity is maintained locally as well as throughout the entire city-compound. If this fails, what we shall end up with will, in spite of the desired opposite, again become an amorphous additive texture instead of a comprehensible configurative structure; a mere arrangement, still, of *some* urban components instead of a meaningful configuration of *all* urban components in the right association.

Locally the configurated subareas will, no doubt, be richer and more habitable by virtue of the same fugal process of thinking that brought about the housing schemes mentioned. A great advance indeed—but the vastness of the urban areas covered and the numerical problems that go with it can well cause the successful establishment of identity during the initial stages of multiplicative configuration to be discontinued during the further ones so that textural incomprehensibility instead of structural comprehensibility will again result. It is not my intention to devaluate what has been gained so far by reciprocal thinking and the configurative design process that goes with it. The process is certainly the right one; it must only be extended because, as yet, it has the numerical limits I have just dealt with. But they can be resolved if new structural devices are invented that have urban validity for all citizens and impose a clear, large, and comprehensible overall framework on the whole urban entity within which the smaller numerically limited configurations are integrated and acquire overall specifically urban identity. These large structural devices may be the "infrastructures" about which the Smithsons have thought a great deal; they may be the "megastructures" which have also occupied the minds of Tange, Maki, Ohtaka, and Kurokawa.

(An inspiring scheme for a total and very compact habitat on which Piet Blom is at the moment working—it will be published in a forthcoming number—attempts to integrate the smaller and larger urban components by means of a single configurative discipline, proving tentatively that this is certainly possible.)

Without such large identifying structures the vehemence of the forces and movements that belong to a city—and make it a city—cannot but assault the identity meaningful configuration may have acquired within it. Whilst it is certainly possible to guide repetition through the initial stages of multiplication—the schemes already published demonstrate this effectively—it is not possible to maintain, extend, or augment identity through any number of stages by continuing the fugal process beyond the stages it can cope with.

Whether it will be necessary to subordinate it from the start to a large structural service framework (Tokyo Bay plan), or whether the configurative process can become so rich that it incorporates all components, including the most intimate, as Blom's new plan (albeit for a much smaller cluster) attempts, is a question of crucial importance. I, for my part, do not believe that these two concepts are incompatible. On a vast metropolitan scale, at any rate, their integration seems inevitable. The configurative discipline already discussed should at all costs be extended and enriched as far as possible.

Already in Forum *7, 1959, the necessity to uncover the still hidden laws of numerical aesthetics—what I call harmony in motion—was brought forward. Failure to govern multiplicity creatively, to humanize number by means of articulation and configuration has already led to the curse of the new towns!*

They demonstrate how the identity of the initial element—the dwelling—has hardly proved able to survive even the very first multiplicative stage—those in Holland are terrifying examples of organized wasteland. The fact is that in most cases the initial elements had no identity to lose anyway!

The aesthetics of number

In order that we may overcome the menace of quantity now that we are faced with *l'habitat pour le plus grand nombre,* the aesthetics of number, the laws of what I should like to call "harmony in motion" must be discovered. Projects should attempt to solve the aesthetic problems that result through the standardization of constructional elements; through the repetition of similar and dissimilar dwellings within a larger housing unit; through the repetition or grouping of such housing units, similar or dissimilar; through the repetition of such housing groups, similar or dissimilar (theme and its mutation and variation), as I put it in Aix-en-Provence. We must continue the search for the basic principles of a new aesthetic and discover the aesthetic and human meaning of number. We must impart rhythm to repetitive similar and dissimilar form, thereby disclosing the conditions that may lead to the equilibration of the plural, and thus overcome the menace of monotony.

The formal vocabulary with which man has hitherto successfully imparted harmony to the singular and particular cannot help him to equilibrate the plural and the general. Man shudders because he believes that he must forfeit the one in favor of the other; the particular for the general; the individual for the collective; the singular for the plural; rest for movement. But rest can mean fixation—stagnation—and multiplicity does not necessarily imply monotony. The individual (the singular) less circumscribed within him (it) self will again appear in another dimension as soon as the general—the repetitive—is subordinated to the laws of dynamic equilibrium, i.e., harmony in motion.

Having suggested that it is due both to the great area covered and the quantitative aggression of the forces vast plurality entails which tend to invalidate the configurative articulation of repetitive elements beyond the first stages of multiplication, it is obvious and reasonable to suggest that identity beyond these first stages—real city identity—can only be established by the very quanta which tend to obstruct the sequential process halfway. With this in view, it is clear that large city-forming attributes—other than circulation—must be introduced stage by stage in the whole configurative process to impart localized full-city identity, whilst bold infrastructures must generate a framework within which all configurative stages of multiplication—i.e., not merely the initial ones—become meaningfully comprehensible. Failure to govern mobile quanta through infrastructures will make it impossible for cities to become more than vast disorganized accretions that frustrate the very needs they are meant to provide for.

It is too often claimed that the great metropolis defeats its own ends in principle! This, of course, is the kind of sentimental loose thinking that stands in the way of any solution that proves the opposite.

Urban transmutability

If it were possible to comprehend a city as a complex with a certain finality, or as a determined mechanism geared to a kind of urban existence which is fairly constant in time and space—subject only to either slow gradual change or sudden mutations at very long intervals—it would perhaps also be possible to rely on the extended configurative discipline. But a city is no such thing—no longer at any rate. I am prone to speak instead of a city as an organism, since this suggests quite predictable "natural" change and growth according to fixed inherent impulses and external forces.

The "organic" image of a city is therefore as false and misleading as the mechanical one. Without wanting to be nasty, both sprout from the same sentimental and rational type of mind; a type, moreover, that is invariably addicted to technological advance for its own sake, and all too common among architects and urbanists. A city, however, is a very complex artifact and, like all artifacts, fits no pseudobiological analogy. It is a man-made aggregate subject to continual metamorphosis to which it either manages or fails to respond. Accordingly, it is either transfigured or disfigured. Our experience is founded on the latter, our hopes on the former—that is the plight we are in now. But we know this much, *that transfigurative potential implied enduring and dynamic identity; lack of it: disfigurement, loss of identity, and paralysis.*

A city is only transmutable as a whole if its components are also transmutable. One change can effect, delay, or check another change, but this does not alter the fact that each component is subject to change of some kind. Transmutations seldom coincide in time and degree nor are they effected at the same tempo. Such incongruity is simply the spontaneous outcome of urban life. It is a reality that must be accepted and understood.

A city is chaotic and necessarily so. One can no more rule this truth out than one can rule out the eternally incongruous desires of man. The manifold functions of a city must be adequately organized in the light of all aspects of mobility, not for the sake of subduing the chaotic element they incur, for this is happily as impossible as it is undesirable, but in order to avoid their reciprocal elimination (functional paralysis), mechanical stagnation, and the human distress implied.

Are we such fools as not to realize this? All these nefarious properties do not exude from either order or chaos as such but from the mismanagement of both. Order and chaos form yet another twinphenomenon which, if split into incompatible polarities, turns both halves into a twin-negative. Now architects and urbanists today are addicted to this splitting mania. Their particular nature seems to make them as wary of chaos as they are willing to bestow order.

One cannot eliminate chaos through order, because they are not alternatives. Sooner or later it will dawn upon the mind that what it mistook for order is not really order, but the very thing that causes the stagnation, paralysis, and distress falsely attributed to chaos.

It will also dawn upon the mind that what such "order" is supposed to dispel—chaos—is quite a different thing from the negative effects brought about in trying to do anything so foolish.

Chaos is as positive as its twinsister order.

It is clear that the time has come to reconsider the entire configurative process in the light of the many aspects mobility embraces in order to discover new spatial, structural, and constructive possibilities for our cities.

Kenzo Tange, referring to his Tokyo Bay plan, says: "The spatial order in cities will doubtless become richer in content as time goes on. It will come to include not only spaces of an order of nature but free, nonordered spaces as well." "We must seek order in freedom and freedom in order." "It is by relating these two extremes that we will create a new spatial organization for contemporary cities."

As fully as the order-freedom reciprocity appeals to me, as little can I cope with order and freedom as extremes which they only are as long as they are negatives (insofar as the chaotic element is here rightly implied in the word *freedom*). Since there must always be some kind of space between the alleged extremes, a distinguishable borderline between ordered and nonordered space is unthinkable. They are not separate categories that can be locally provided for.

The fulfillment of a great desire—the metropolis

A lot has been written about circulation—its mechanical and numerical connotations. It is still too often handled in the abstract, as one of many urban functions. But circulation cannot be fully understood in terms of function—that is why we have hitherto failed to come to terms with it. Transportation is a particular aspect of communication, communication a particular aspect of mobility in general. Now mobility is not merely an aspect of city life, it is of the very essence of human association, whilst cities in principle are meant to provide the framework for human association in its most complex and varied form.

Cities tend to become more magnetic, and consequently larger and larger, as the web of association is intensified and its range extended. I say it this way and not the other way around because it is important to comprehend the expanding city in the light of man's basic desire to communicate, i.e., from a positive human need, and not from statistical, economical, and technological inevitability in an impersonal hence negative sense.

I believe it is because this quantitative attitude still prevails that the project of urban expansion seems terrifying instead of gratifying, and the solutions ubiquitously proposed so functionally inadequate and contrary to the growing communicative need of the citizen.

There is one more question Tange's excellent exposé of the Tokyo plan poses. I should like to deal with it here briefly because it immediately concerns the argument of the present essay. He says:

"The speed and scale of contemporary life call for a new spatial order in cities.

Nevertheless man himself continues to walk in steps of a meter or so and we are still surrounded by the unchanging human scale.

"Furthermore, whereas the life cycle of large-scale constructions is growing longer, the life cycle of our houses and the articles we use in daily activities is gradually growing shorter. This fact results from our ever-increasing reliance upon manufactured goods and from our tendency to take up new things and discard them more and more rapidly. Individuality, freedom, and spontaneity form an ever-strengthening antithesis to the control of technology. Man desires more and more to exercise his own individual choice in matters that concern houses, gardens, streets, and plazas.

"There are then two conflicting extremes—the *major structures* which have a long life cycle and which, while restricting individual choice, determine the system of the age, and the *minor objects* that we use in daily living which have a short life cycle and which permit the expression of free individual choice. The gap between the two is gradually growing deeper. The important task facing us is that of creating an organic link between these two extremes and, by doing so, to create a new spatial order in our cities!"

Some basic objections to this concept, which I underline fully, have been thus formulated by Fumihiko Maki and Masato Ohtaka in an essay on Group Form (St. Louis: Washington University, 1961):

"Tange's megaform concept depends largely on the idea that change will occur less rapidly in some realms than it will in others, and that the designer will be able to ascertain which of the functions he is dealing with fall in the long cycle of change, and which in the shorter. The question is, can the designer successfully base his concept on the idea that, to give an example, transportation methods will change less rapidly than the idea of a desirable residence or retail outlet?

"Sometimes the impact and momentum of technology become so great that a change occurs in the basic skeleton of social and physical structure. It is difficult to predict to which part of a pond a stone will be thrown and which way ripples will spread. If the megaform becomes rapidly obsolete, as well it might, especially in those schemes which do not allow for two kinds of change cycle, it will be a great weight about the neck of urban society.

"The ideal is not a system, on the other hand, in which the physical structure of the city is at the mercy of unpredictable change. The ideal is a kind of master form which can move into ever new states of equilibrium and yet maintain visual consistency and a sense of continuing order in the long run.

"Inherent in the megastructure concept, along with a certain static nature, is the suggestion that many and diverse functions may beneficially be concentrated in one place. A large frame implies some utility in combination and concentration of function. That utility is sometimes only apparent. We frequently confuse the potential that technology offers with a kind of compulsion to 'use it fully.' Technological possibility can be sanguinely useful only when it is a tool of civilized persons. Inhuman use of technological advance is all too frequently our curse. Optimum productivity does not ever depend on mere concentration of activities and workers.

"Paul Goodman says in *Communitas*: 'We could centralize or decentralize, concentrate population or scatter it. . . . If we want to continue the trend away from the country, we can do it; but if we want to combine town and country values in an agri-industrial way of life, we can do that. . . . It is just this relaxing of necessity, this extraordinary flexibility and freedom of choice of our techniques, that is baffling and frightening to people. . . . Technology is a sacred cow left strictly to (unknown) experts, as if the form of the industrial machine did not profoundly affect every person.' . . .

Technology must not dictate choices to us in our cities. We must learn to select modes of action from among the possibilities technology presents in physical planning. If the megastructure concept presents the problems outlined above, it also has great promise."

Motive, means, and end in confusion

I have nothing against the megaform concept; on the contrary, this essay is a plea for a configurated megaform, i.e., for the city as a single complex megaform in which the conflicting extremes, about which Tange speaks, are not resolved, however, by "creating an organic link," but are simply not accepted as conflicting categories.

Were it not for the fact that Tange seeks order in freedom and freedom in order, what are now but doubts as to some albeit vital implications with regard to motive, means, and end would have become real objections.

I would contend that it is primordially man's nature as a social being to seek immediate intercourse with his fellow men and participate as an individual in the doings of society at large.

This is in fact as much a consequence of consciousness as man's specific ability to evolve the means, technological and economical, with which he manages not merely to survive physically but, beyond that, to frame more effectively all the shades of human intercourse he seeks. As soon as his physical survival is secured—a stage as yet only reached in a small part of the world—what lies beyond survival as such becomes paramount—and, one would imagine, well within reach. This is my point of view:

Once this stage is reached I think one can say, without looking for reservations which can easily be construed, that ultimately man tends to move toward large cities simply because he wants to, and that he does so because it is his nature to gather and communicate in as varied a way as possible. It is not merely because he must, in that impersonal economical factors or systems of production necessitate him to do so.

We cannot solve the problem of the expanding metropolis if we continue to approach it negatively. That the metropolis "explodes" instead of expanding naturally—I am thinking among other things of the suburban disease—is based on an existing negative status quo.

Even if the vicious circle qualities are evident, we must start from the simple positive truth that cities expand because man today is drawn toward them for intrinsically human reasons—because the desire to communicate and participate is a primordial attribute of consciousness. In order to accomplish this end he has developed technological and economical means with which—quite apart from whether or not these succeed or fail—to accomplish the terrific human clustering his desire for complex association demands. That there is an emotional chasm between the way the increased speed and scale this desire causes manifests itself and the desire itself is evident. But this is no reason to disparage either the ultimate human validity of the great metropolis or the increase in speed and scale of contemporary life which has, of course, in many ways unfortunately developed in a way both arbitrary, impersonal, and hence inhuman.

Of this I am convinced, one is certainly putting the cart before the horse when one suggests that man must adapt himself mentally and emotionally in order to accommodate himself to his own artifacts because he fails to build them as a means toward an end he fundamentally desires.

Technology and economics are servants of man's desire toward achieving kinds of human association beyond those which survival necessitates (in the light of his hobby for making bombs and rockets I cannot help adding: so I would like to think!). If instead they have become the very tyrants that frustrate this great desire, so much for that; this should never be allowed to alter the right relation between motive, means, and end.

Herein lies the danger of labeling the two conflicting extremes *major structures* and *minor objects,* as Tange does, since the minor objects are always the *end,* in that they appertain to daily living, whilst the major structures (must they determine the system of the age?) are the *means* (the servant), in that they are conceived to help the end accord with the desire. It seems strange, therefore, that Tange calls minor what I would call the major end.

As long as architects desire to create a new spatial order for our cities, because they not only desire to bridge the great "gap," but because they think that it is these "major structures which, while restricting individual choice, determine the system of the age," they will not fully succeed, because this concept is founded on false premises—on a technological slant—albeit a different one from that which infected CIAM for so long.

This is also why the whole concept of "open" versus "closed" form, cherished by astute architects today, is, in my opinion, untenable and erroneous. I detect in Tange's intellectual excursions into the realm of social, economical, aesthetic, and historical criticism, with which he attempts to fortify the open-versus-closed-form concept, a continuation of the same overestimation of technology and productive progress for their own sake which also infected the minds of so many architects and urbanists of the former generation. A "closed" concept, to use Tange's word just once!

In view of Japan's incredible technological development and its formidable impact on an enormous impoverished population, Tange's attitude is very understandable. His audacious Tokyo Bay plan could only have been conceived in a country confronted with such terrific plurality. The Smithsons also attribute major importance to the structures that must be invented to identify a city as a city, but they very wisely use the term "infrastructure"! It must be remembered that their Berlin and London circulation schemes came after many years of thinking about association in the sphere of the intimate "minor structures" that concern the spaces, houses, and articles we use in our "daily activities." The danger that the Smithsons will put the cart before the plodding horse is therefore so small that there is still hope for Team X. Their concept, it seems to me, of motive, means, and end is sound, simple, and safe—"open," if I may use that word as well, just once!

To return to the problem of mobility and how it affects the configurative discipline for which this essay makes a plea. A city's effective transmutability depends on whether the various aspects of urban mobility have been structurally recognized.

I mean by the various aspects of mobility everything which appertains to urban movement, growth, and change. This includes so many things that they cannot be listed (as long as they are appreciated!). Yet it is important here to point to a few primary aspects:

- the sensorial and emotional impact of urban environment on the citizen as he moves through it in general—the nature of this impact in light of the different ways and speeds the citizen moves from one place to another and what he experiences en route;
- mutations of use, aspect, and functional potential due to the natural cycles, small and

large—the seasons (including weather), night and day, age-phases of the human being;

• the relation between the nature and tempo of the different phases of human life and the overall nature and tempo of urban life—and the way the latter changes;

• change of dwelling, neighborhood, or city with regard to the individual or a particular group of citizens (the right and the desire for such change is increasing, whereas the possibilities are decreasing!);

• furthermore all mutations in size, quantity, place, kind, form, and function of all urban components—the incongruity as to speed, time, extent, and place of one mutation in relation to others.

(See also *Forum* 7, 1959, p. 236, Dubrovnik report on Mobility.)

I am prone to suggest that our cities will not be able to exist in time and space unless all these aspects are supported by the configurative discipline which is being evolved to reestablish and perpetuate their identity for the sake of the purpose cities stand for . . . because it is so blatantly obvious.

And yet, when Willem van Bodegraven read an essay he had written on urbanism and the time factor to the Dutch CIAM group in 1952, the reaction of the older generation was such that it is perhaps best forgotten. "We are faced with the necessity of evolving structure and forms which can develop in time; which can remain a unity and maintain the coherence of the components at all stages of their growth. The absence of this must lead to self-destruction."

This means that the identity of the whole should be latent in the components whilst the identity of the components should remain present in the whole.

It does not imply, however, that these identities need or should remain constant in the face of mutations. On the contrary, it is exactly this potential to change face without losing it which cities must acquire in order to fulfill their purpose in space and time: the provision of places where vast numbers of people can live, benefiting liberally from all the varied forms of human association and activity large cities can best furnish.

A city should embrace a hierarchy of superimposed configurative systems multilaterally conceived (a quantitative not a qualitative hierarchy). The finer grained systems—those which embrace the multiplied dwelling and its extension—should reflect the qualities of ascending repetitive configurative stages as has already been put forward. All systems should be familiarized one with the other in such a way that their combined impact and interaction can be appreciated as a single complex system—polyphonal, multirhythmic, kaleidoscopic, and yet perpetually and everywhere comprehensible. A single homogeneous configuration composed of many subsystems, each covering the same overall area and equally valid, but each with a different grain, scale of movement, and association potential. These systems are to be so configurated that one evolves out of the other—is part of it. The specific meaning of each system must sustain the meaning of the other. Structural qualities must contain textural qualities and vice versa—in terms of consecutive place-experience structure and texture must be ambivalent. For only then can wrong emphasis of the structural and amorphousness of the textural be avoided, i.e., the reciprocal meaning of small and large; many and few; part and whole; unity and diversity; simplicity and complexity be established and right-size guaranteed.

The large structures (infrastructures) must not only be comprehensible in their own right, they must above all—this is the crucial point—assist the overall comprehensibility of the minutely configured intimate fabric which constitutes the immediate counterform of each and every citizen's everyday life. They must not only be able to absorb reasonable mutation within themselves but also permit them within the intimate smaller fabric they serve.

Reasonable mutations should be possible without loss of the identity of that which changes; of that which is immediately affected by it, or of the whole; without one reasonable change hindering or invalidating another reasonable change.

Flexibility and false neutrality

Flexibility as such should not be overemphasized or turned into yet another absolute, a new abstract whim. The prevailing tendency to desire great neutrality for the sake of extreme transmutability is as dangerous as the existing urban rigidity from which this tendency springs as a reaction. Significant archetypal structures should have enough scope for multimeaning without having to be continually altered.

We must beware of the glove that fits all hands and therefore becomes no hand.

Identifying devices

In *Forum* 7, 1959, we referred to the need for new "identifying devices" brought forward by Team X at Dubrovnik in 1956. Without these a house will not become a house, a street not a street, a village not a village, and a city not a city. They should be structurally bolder and far more meaningful than those which satisfy architects and urbanists today. They must, above all, be of a higher order of invention, so that the congeniality and human immediacy of the small, intimate configuration can become of a higher order through them.

Make a bunch of places of each house and each city, for a city is a huge house and a house a tiny city. Both must serve the same person in different ways and different persons in the same way.

At a city level many closely related identifying devices will be necessary to establish a rich scale of comprehensibility. Identifying devices can be artifacts—new or historical—or given by nature and more or less intensely exploited. In the past it was often a church, a palace, a great wall, a harbor, a canal, an important street or square—often, too, a river, valley, hill, or seafront. Many of these are still valid beyond their visual impact.

We know this well enough, but I am not so sure if we are sufficiently aware of the fact that it is those identifying devices—call them images—which not only articulate visually but also frame civic association between people, i.e., which still possess direct physical meaning and still bear witness to this day by day, which remain in our memory most persistently. They articulate places for simple occasions in which we are able to participate directly. I need not name them since everybody has found his own—and more than can ever be listed. They make continents your own. Yet although the human validity of such places is recognized again and again, as soon as they are reencountered, the wonderful effect they have is sorrowfully forgotten the moment architects and urbanists grab a pencil. But we cannot continue to exploit old identifying images— those we have inherited—passively with impunity. They cannot possibly survive continual molestation nor can their identity be maintained unconditionally.

The time has come to invent new significant identifying devices that perpetuate in a new way the essential human experiences the old ones provided for so well. At the same time these new ones must provide for equally essential experiences the older ones no longer provide for or never did.

[. . .]

1963

Twenty-seven-year-old **Oswald Mathias Ungers** took part in his first CIAM
conference in Aix-en-Provence in 1953, joining the discussions with future Team
10 members that would lead to CIAM's breakup. One of the small number of

181–83

German architects to attend CIAM's postwar meetings, Ungers found himself in
agreement with the critique of the functionalist city leveled by the Smithsons,
Aldo van Eyck, Jacob Bakema, and other young architects. Their "brutalist," "as
found" approach to building seemed to coincide with his own rejection of the
abstract and materialistic modernism dominant in Germany in the 1950s and with
his developing concept of *genius loci*. Ungers would continue to associate with
the group into the 1970s, organizing a Team 10 meeting in Berlin in 1965, when
Shadrach Woods's design for the Free University was beginning construction.
Yet his position increasingly diverged from theirs. In a clash between Ernesto
Rogers and Peter Smithson over the Velasca tower at CIAM's Otterlo conference

200–4, 300–7

in 1959, Ungers already gravitated to the Italian architect's contextual approach
rather than to Smithson's condemnation of the tower for its neohistoricism. The
split would be confirmed in the late 1970s, when postmodernism was in full
bloom with Ungers as one of its protagonists. In an open letter entitled "A

347–60

Message to Mathias Ungers from a Different World," Van Eyck admonished that
history "is not a warehouse for memories but a gathering body of experience."

This schism was less clear at the earlier date. Buildings like Ungers's brick
housing at Cologne-Nippes (1957) could be compared to the Dutch school or,
closer to home, some architecture built in Hamburg and Berlin in the 1920s.
Nikolaus Pevsner, in an article entitled "Modern Architecture and the Historian:
The Return of Historicism" (1961), related Ungers's work to German expressionism
—specifically Mies van der Rohe's monument to Karl Liebknecht and Rosa
Luxemburg of 1926. But these proved to be tangential readings. Ungers's work
was more directed against the school of Hans Scharoun, whose influence was
"virtually tyrannical" (in Ungers's description) in the early 1960s in Berlin. As a
student of Egon Eiermann, he rejected Scharoun (who once spoke of the spaces
in his Philharmonic Hall as vineyards rather than rooms) for his expressionistic
language and his antiurbanism. To Ungers the tradition of Schinkel was decisive:
architecture was a matter of rationally determined form-making, the city a
sequence of rigorously ordered spaces. With projects like the student housing at
the Twente Polytechnic in Enschede, Holland (1964), and the Museums of
Prussian Culture in the Berlin Tiergarten (1965), Ungers arrived at first articulations
of a historicist geometry he was later to call his "infinite catalogue of urban forms."

In 1960 Ungers wrote a polemic together with Reinhard Gieselmann in
which he stated, "[Architecture's] creative function is to manifest the task by
which it is confronted, to integrate itself into that which already exists, to
introduce points of emphasis and rise above its surroundings." In the more
radical statement of three years later that follows—for his prize-winning "Neue
Stadt" project for a residential district in Cologne—he posits a purely formal and
analogical approach to urban design based on "intrinsic" morphologies and
"independent of all functional determination." A rhythmical combination of low-
and high-rise housing, the project was an "attempt to create an integrated spatial
image of the city." Here his thinking converges with the emerging neorationalism

392–98
205–25

of Aldo Rossi—who had introduced Ungers's work to Italy in *Casabella* in 1960—
and also looks forward to the figure-ground aesthetics of the Cornell school,
where Ungers was to teach for more than a decade starting in 1965.

From Werk, *July 1963, p. 281. Republished in revised form as "Stadt als Kunstwerk"
in Ulrich Conrads et al., eds.,* Hommage à Werner Hebebrand *(Berlin: Akademie der
Künste, 1965), pp. 19–20. Translated by Lynnette Widder. Courtesy of the author.*

The City as a Work of Art
O. M. Ungers

The city is governed by the same formal laws as the individual houses that comprise it. The house's structure is simultaneously the basis for the structure of the city. Only the dimensions are different. The role of the walls, columns, piers, and volumes that constitute the house is assumed in the city by closed rows of houses, freestanding buildings, and interrelated blocks. The single difference in the translation from house to city is scale. The fundamental composition is in both cases the same.

The ancient atrium house, which arose from a building volume closed to the outside, reveals with absolute consistency the composition of the ancient city, for example Priene. Just as the house comprised many similar cells organized around the atrium, individual buildings stood in relation to the city's open space, the agora. With the passage of time, the ancient courtyard house evolved into the modern urban perimeter block. What formerly was atrium became courtyard. The constitutive element was no longer the single space but the single building; the city's structure was no longer determined by single buildings but by entire blocks. Thus understood, the composition of New York does not differ from that of Priene.

Similar analyses can be applied to a medieval city structure, which is determined by buildings of various heights and breadths lining the streets and by the maintenance of the street wall, a common practice in the last century.

A Renaissance palace complex made up of rows of similar rooms, a city like Freudenstadt in which buildings are organized in rows, and modern slab buildings unmistakably reflect the same structure. Circulation through spaces by means of a central double-loaded corridor relates, by analogy, to the addition of housing units to slab buildings along an access street.

An immediate connection exists between the unifying structure of a Japanese house and the consequent urban complex in which the same spatial composition is recognizable.

The ordering of a group of autonomous buildings such as Ledoux proposed, the English turn-of-the-century Garden City comprising freestanding single-family houses, and Le Corbusier's 1920s skyscraper project for Paris are without question structurally related.

Comparisons between building and city are possible not only within domestic architecture—independent of place and historical epoch—but also in terms of the structural composition of larger buildings such as office buildings, castle complexes, churches, schools, etc. It should suffice to say that the structure of a city is fundamentally determined by the sum of individual buildings, and that the apartment plan and the city plan are dependent upon each other as they determine each other.

When the appearance of various urban compositions is said to be the result of sociological, cultural, technical, or historical causality, it is an explanation rooted in functional determination and causality. The exigencies that stem from this viewpoint, however, can be modified only through the ordering of structural connections. They do not themselves offer a compositional direction or impulse: Architecture and the directly related discipline of city building contain their own formal laws, which are grounded in the essence of form. This essence is independent of all functional determination and exists on the strength of its own compositional force as a permanent principle in all epochs and cultures. Neither the building nor the city is a cultural product that is based

Model of apartment blocks. Only the "positive" spaces are executed plastically, while the "negative" spaces are left free. [O. M. Ungers, "Neue Stadt," Cologne, 1963.]

upon many external considerations. Each has its own structure and grows according to internal, not external, formal laws. Today we address this question: how can the most structurally varied forms, which have appeared over the passage of time and only in some cases stand immediately next to each other, be brought together in a unified whole? This question cannot be answered by sociology, traffic planning, or technology—these are just tools—but only by the insights won from the morphological study of form. From this study arises the demand for the *city as a work of art*.

The project shown here stems from the intention to place single buildings in relation to each other so that new spatial connections result. Positive volumetric form and negative interstitial space are brought into correlation. In the interplay between volumes and space is expressed the complex's character, which arises from its ability to organize two realms—internal and external—to a specific purpose.

The phenomenon of double intentionality, which Sörgel calls the Janus face of architecture, is the essential formative factor of an urban ensemble. It is apparent in the street spaces, places, and relations between building volumes. The combination of bodies with connective elements, as it is realized here, offers the possibility of allowing spatial movement to advance further and further, and of extending communal space uninterruptedly in all directions. The single volume becomes a building element that maintains its position in an overall composition based upon spatial extension in all directions. The volume achieves this status because of its ability to continue this extension and to enlarge it at will until it becomes an omnipresent spatial totality, the true goal of architecture. [. . .]

1964

The future members of Archigram—Warren Chalk, **Peter Cook**, Dennis Crompton, David Greene, Ron Herron, Michael Webb—were students in the

237–39

1950s when the Independent Group was staging its confrontation between high art and popular culture at the Institute of Contemporary Arts in London. Inspired

240–41, 370–78

by the polemical energies of the Smithsons, Reyner Banham's enthusiasm for technology, and Theo Crosby's revitalizing role on the English editorial scene, they began their collaboration casually, unlike the more politicized architectural radicals soon to emerge elsewhere in Europe. Peter Cook later recounted, "In late 1960, in various flats in Hampstead, a loose group of people started to meet: to criticize projects, to concoct letters to the press, to combine to make competition projects, and generally prop one another up against the boredom of working in London architectural offices. . . . The main British magazines did not at that time publish student work, so that Archigram was reacting to this as well as the general sterility of the scene. The title came from the notion of a more urgent and simple item than a journal, like a 'telegram' or 'aerogramme,' hence 'archi(tecture)-gram.'"

Archigram 1 appeared in May 1961. It consisted of a page of kaleidoscopic imagery and words lithographed on cheap paper with a separate foldout. Greene, the poet of the group, wrote, "The poetry in bricks is lost. We want to drag into building some of the poetry of countdown, orbital helmets, discord of mechanical body transportation methods and leg walking." That program roughly defined the iconoclastic and visionary series of urban proposals that the group would realize in the ephemeral medium of the broadsheet, assembled with memorable graphic, fold-out, and pop-up ingenuity in the course of nine issues. If the first two numbers were provocational in a general sense, with *Archigram* 3, devoted to expendability and consumerism, the group presented a more focused manifesto. Living City, the first full-group project, staged at the I.C.A. in 1963, was an effort to express the urban vitality in a "throwaway environment." *Archigram* 4, a space comic issue, zoomed in on "the context of the near future." In the opening editorial, reprinted here, Cook posed the question of "the fast-moving object as part of the total aesthetic." With number 5, of the same year,

273–75, 325–34

the focus shifted to megastructures—clusters and molehills—while Cook's Plug-in City of 1964–66 combined with Chalk's Capsule Homes to bring the group's ideas on stacking, servicing, and technical transformability to a point of intensity. After 1965 the aggressive sci-fi monumentality relaxed into more domestic

86–92

notions of "survival kits" and Fulleresque standard-of-living packages, also inspired by the antiarchitectural stance of Cedric Price. This trend began with Webb's Auto-Environment of 1966 and culminated in the inflatables of Instant City (1968–71). *Archigram* 8 (1968) summed up the group's "preoccupations": metamorphosis, nomad, comfort, hard-soft, emancipation, exchange, response. Seemingly a predictable allegory of mid-1960s psychedelic space-age British counterculture, the effect was nonetheless arresting by virtue of the group's inventiveness in translating its generation's concerns into architectural images.

27–30

It was also an ultimate riposte to the postwar humanism of the "masters." In the 1967 edition of *Space, Time and Architecture* Sigfried Giedion denounced Archigram's machinism in the name of Le Corbusier, who had just died. The

181–83

group had also gone too far for the Smithsons (ribbed below for the use of the cut corner in their Economist buildings); the Smithsons responded in 1973 with

459–62, 437–41
456–58, 319–24

their book *Without Rhetoric*. But for more radical architects—in Austria, Italy, and France; in Japan, where the plug-in dreams became buildable; and in schools everywhere—Archigram offered a vivid critique of current practice, liberating speculations about urban design in an advanced industrial society.

From Amazing Archigram *4 (1964). Courtesy of Peter Cook.*

Zoom and "Real" Architecture
Peter Cook (Archigram)

We return to the preoccupation of the first *Archigram*—a search for ways out from the stagnation of the architectural scene, where the continuing malaise is not just with the mediocrity of the object, but, more seriously, with the self-satisfaction of the profession backing up such architecture. The line that "modern architecture has arrived" seems more than ever inappropriate.

Certainly it has never been more possible to produce buildings that are at once well mannered . . . and quite gutless. Great British architecture now has more to do, organically, with the "line-of-least resistance" tradition—from Queen Anne's Mansions to the Hilton through Dolphin Square—than with the New Architecture of the twenties and thirties. Though it would be ridiculous to force a "heroic" phase in the present decade, the cycle has too quickly reached the "tragic."

Mainstream-fanciers can currently report further unashamed use by everybody of the 45° corner, stepped section, 3-D precast panel, and the rest—a cosmetic borrowed from the originals' beauty-box to tart up the latest least-line (tradition) scheme.

It would have been too easy to look over one's shoulder and fill Archigram with three dozen of the respected goodies of the last fifty years (interesting that so many would be pre-1930), and the comment, "What have we lost? What are we missing?" Yet set against such a feeling of loss is the continuance of something that has not yet disappeared into historical perspective—a tradition that is still developing, and is still original to many of the basic gestures of modern architecture. It shares much of its expression with those dim, neurotic, enthusiastic days of the Ring, *Der Sturm,* and the Futurist *Manifesto*—the architectural weirdies of the time feeding the infant modern movement. Our document is the *space-comic;* its reality is in the gesture, design, and a natural styling of hardware new to our decade—the capsule, the rocket, the bathyscope, the Zidpark, the handy-pak.

Is it possible for the space-comic's future to relate once again with buildings-as-built? Can the near-reality of the rocket-object and hovercraft-object, which are virtually ceasing to be cartoons, carry the dynamic (but also noncartoon) building with them into life as it is? Or shall we be riding in these craft amongst an environment made of CLASP? The ridiculousness of such a situation can be compared with the world of Schinkel seen by the Futurists.

There is the same consistency in an "Adventure-Comic" city of the 1962–63 period and in Bruno Taut's projects for Alpine Architecture of 1917, the same force of prediction and style. The cross-fertilization can come from the "design" world, but only—and this is the point—when the idea is big enough—so we frequently find conditioned environments of domes over cities and representations of tensegrity nets in cartoons. The point made in *Edilizia Moderna* 80, where the movement-tube emerged as an essential aspect of the more sophisticated skyscraper city (as opposed to a city which is a collection of skyscrapers—and relative to only one level of horizontal circulation), has long been realized by the comics' skyscraper cities.

One of the greatest weaknesses of our immediate urban architecture is the inability to contain the fast-moving object as part of the total aesthetic—but the comic imagery has always been strongest here. The representation of movement-objects and movement-containers is consistent with the rest, and not only because "speed"

[Archigram 4. cover. By Warren Chalk.]

[Archigram 4, page 1. Cartoon strip assembled by Warren Chalk.]

is the main gesture.

The positive quality that the rocket (both actual and represented), the Futurist scribble, and the space-city share is their ultimateness—which has most significance as a counterweight to so-called "real" architecture. We connect this material with serious projects for making living space, entertainment space—and the city, in the context of the near future.

Cedric Price's work has particular relevance to this "connection" with reality. Price is almost the only architect in England actually building tensegrity structures, pop-up domes, and disposable buildings—and therefore coming to grips with the near future. The towers (page 26) are also relevant to this situation in the never-land between gesture and architectural laboratory work.

It is significant that with this material there exists an inspirational bridge, stretching both forty years into the past and perhaps forty years into the future, and perhaps the answer lies neither in heroics nor tragedy, but in a reemergence of the courage of convictions in architecture.

1965

Historian, critic, and sharp-witted essayist **Reyner Banham** trained as an aeronautical engineer during the Second World War before coming under the tutelage of art historian Nikolaus Pevsner at the Courtauld Institute in London in the late 1940s. There he completed a dissertation that would be rewritten and published in 1960 as *Theory and Design in the First Machine Age,* revising the *sachlich* narrative of modern architecture rendered by Pevsner in his classic *Pioneers of the Modern Movement* of 1936. In the postwar period Pevsner would himself retrench from the Gropius line of his earlier book, rediscovering the

114–20 perennial virtues of English empiricism and Townscape picturesque, which he promoted as an editor of *Architectural Review,* and later acknowledging the importance of "antirationalist" currents, especially Art Nouveau and German expressionism. Meanwhile, Banham, who began contributing regularly to *Architectural Review* in 1952 and would become assistant editor in 1959, was increasingly concerned with the relationship between architecture and

341–46 technology, in particular the symbolic or aesthetic interpretation of technology by modern architects. This would lead him to an "other" genealogy of modernism

300–7 giving primacy to Italian futurism—*une architecture autre,* as he put it in 1955.

Banham was also involved during these years in the activities of the
237–39 Independent Group and the inception of the New Brutalism, a tendency
240–41 propounded by Peter and Alison Smithson which Banham did much to explicate and promote through an article in *Architectural Review* in 1955 (reworked as a book in 1966). Banham's exuberant endorsement of popular culture, industrial design, the American way of life, and new technologies, and his dislike for traditionalism and aestheticism of any kind, subsequently led him away from the Smithsons—whose work, he felt, took a regressive and formalistic turn with their "archaeological" Patio and Pavilion installation at the *This Is Tomorrow* exhibition

86–92 of 1956—and to embrace the work of Buckminster Fuller as a radical populist response to social needs and prophetic embodiment of a Marinettian future.

The following essay, accompanied on its original publication by a vivid set of drawings by François Dallegret and published the same year as the Plug-in

365–69 City of Archigram (a group with whom Banham preserved strongly paternalistic relations), reflects the Banham polemic at its most visionary and at the same time most satirical. It proposes an architecture of ultimate antimonumentality: the house as a minimal membrane of enclosure, dematerialized of all but its essential mechanical services. Inspired by Fuller's Dymaxion with its central service core and later geodesic designs where all space-defining elements were coterminous with the structure's skin, Banham's "unhouse" was "an extension of the Jeffersonian dream beyond the agrarian sentimentality of Frank Lloyd Wright's Usonian Broadacre vision . . . ," as he put it, "power-point homesteading in a paradise garden of appliances." Banham was to return to this "gas-powered pastorale" and the advantages of the portable life-style in "The Great Gizmo," published in *Industrial Design* in September 1965.

After a stay in Chicago in 1964–66, Banham eventually moved permanently to the United States, teaching at New York State University in Buffalo and then the University of California at Santa Cruz. His prolific writings and books—including *The Architecture of the Well-Tempered Environment* (1969), *Los Angeles: The Architecture of Four Ecologies* (1971), and *A Concrete Atlantis* (1986)—reflect his passionate commitment to advancing a pragmatic technology for the controlled environment.

From Art in America, *April 1965, pp. 109–18. Republished with commentary in* Charles Jencks and George Baird, eds., Meaning in Architecture *(New York: George Braziller, 1969), pp. 109–18. Courtesy of Mary Banham.*

A Home Is Not a House
Reyner Banham

When your house contains such a complex of piping, flues, ducts, wires, lights, inlets, outlets, ovens, sinks, refuse disposers, hi-fi reverberators, antennae, conduits, freezers, heaters—when it contains so many services that the hardware could stand up by itself without any assistance from the house, why have a house to hold it up? When the cost of all this tackle is half of the total outlay (or more, as it often is) what is the house doing except concealing your mechanical pudenda from the stares of folks on the sidewalk? Once or twice recently there have been buildings where the public was genuinely confused about what was mechanical services, what was structure—many visitors to Philadelphia take quite a time to work out that the floors of Louis Kahn's laboratory towers are not supported by the flanking brick duct boxes, and when they have worked it out, they are inclined to wonder if it was worth all the trouble of giving them an independent supporting structure.

No doubt about it, a great deal of the attention captured by those labs derives from Kahn's attempt to put the drama of mechanical services on show—and if, in the end, it fails to do that convincingly, the psychological importance of the gesture remains, at least in the eyes of his fellow architects. Services are a topic on which architectural practice has alternated capriciously between the brazen and the coy—there was the grand old let-it–dangle period, when every ceiling was a mess of gaily painted entrails, as in the council chambers of the U.N. building, and there have been fits of pudicity when even the most innocent anatomical details have been hurriedly veiled with a suspended ceiling.

Basically, there are two reasons for all this blowing hot and cold (if you will excuse the air conditioning industry's oldest-working pun). The first is that mechanical services are too new to have been absorbed into the proverbial wisdom of the profession; none of the great slogans—form follows function, *accusez la structure*, firmness commodity and delight, truth to materials, *wenig ist mehr*—is much use in coping with the mechanical invasion. The nearest thing, in a significantly negative way, is Le Corbusier's *pour Ledoux, c'était facile—pas de tubes*, which seems to be gaining proverbial-type currency as the expression of profound nostalgia for the golden age before piping set in.

The second reason is that the mechanical invasion is a fact, and architects— especially American architects—sense that it is a cultural threat to their position in the world. American architects are certainly right to feel this, because their professional specialty, the art of creating monumental spaces, has never been securely established on this continent. It remains a transplant from an older culture and architects in America are constantly harking back to that culture. The generation of Stanford White and Louis Sullivan were prone to behave like *émigrés* from France, Frank Lloyd Wright was apt to take cover behind sentimental Teutonicisms like *lieber Meister,* the big boys of the thirties and forties came from Aachen and Berlin anyhow, the pacemakers of the fifties and sixties are men of international culture like Charles Eames and Philip Johnson, and so too, in many ways, are the coming men of today, like Myron Goldsmith.

Left to their own devices, Americans do not monumentalize or make architecture. From the Cape Cod cottage through the balloon frame to the perfection of permanently pleated aluminum siding with embossed wood-graining, they have tended to build a brick chimney and lean a collection of shacks against it. When Groff Conklin wrote (in "The Weather-Conditioned House") that "a house is nothing but a hollow shell . . . a shell is all a house or any structure in which human beings live and work really is. And most shells in nature are extraordinarily inefficient barriers to cold and heat . . .," he was expressing an extremely American view, backed by a long-established grass-roots tradition.

And since that tradition agrees with him that the American hollow shell is such an inefficient heat barrier, Americans have always been prepared to pump more heat, light, and power into their shelters than have other peoples. America's monumental space is, I suppose, the great outdoors—the porch, the terrace, Whitman's rail-traced plains, Kerouac's infinite road, and now, the Great Up There. Even within the house, Americans rapidly learned to dispense with the partitions that Europeans need to keep space architectural and within bounds, and long before Wright began blundering through the walls that subdivided polite architecture into living room, games room, card room, gun room, etc., humbler Americans had been slipping into a way of life adapted to informally planned interiors that were, effectively, large single spaces.

Now, large single volumes wrapped in flimsy shells have to be lighted and heated in a manner quite different and more generous than the cubicular interiors of the European tradition around which the concept of domestic architecture first crystallized. Right from the start, from the Franklin stove and the kerosene lamp, the American interior has had to be better serviced if it was to support a civilized culture, and this is one of the reasons that the U.S. has been the forcing ground of mechanical services in buildings —so if services are to be felt anywhere as a threat to architecture, it should be in America.

"The plumber is the quartermaster of American culture," wrote Adolf Loos, father of all European platitudes about the superiority of U.S. plumbing. He knew what he was talking about; his brief visit to the States in the nineties convinced him that the outstanding virtues of the American way of life were its informality (no need to wear a top hat to call on local officials) and its cleanliness—which was bound to be noticed by a Viennese with as highly developed a set of Freudian compulsions as he had. That obsession with clean (which can become one of the higher absurdities of America's lysol-breathing Kleenex-culture) was another psychological motive that drove the nation toward mechanical services. The early justification of air-conditioning was not just that people had to breathe: Konrad Meier ("Reflections on Heating and Ventilating," 1904) wrote fastidiously of " . . . excessive amounts of water vapour, sickly odours from respiratory organs, unclean teeth, perspiration, untidy clothing, the presence of microbes due to various conditions, stuffy air from dusty carpets and draperies . . . cause greater discomfort and greater ill health."

(Have a wash, and come back for the next paragraph.)

Most pioneer air-conditioning men seem to have been nose-obsessed in this way; best friends could just about force themselves to tell America of her national B.O.— then, compulsive salesmen to a man, promptly prescribed their own patent improved panacea for ventilating the hell out of her. Somewhere among these clustering concepts—cleanliness, the lightweight shell, the mechanical services, the informality and indifference to monumental architectural values, the passion for the outdoors— there always seemed to me to lurk some elusive master concept that would never quite come into focus. It finally became clear and legible to me in June 1964, in the most highly appropriate and symptomatic circumstances.

I was standing up to my chest hair in water, making home movies (I get that NASA kick from taking expensive hardware into hostile environments) at the campus beach

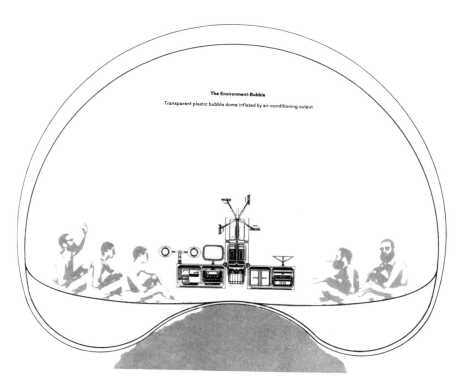

The Environment-Bubble

Transparent plastic bubble dome inflated by air-conditioning output

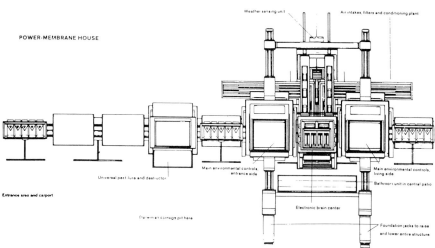

POWER-MEMBRANE HOUSE

Weather sensing unit

Air intakes, filters and conditioning plant

Main environmental controls, entrance side

Main environmental controls, living side

Bathroom unit in central patio

Universal port-lure and destructor

Electronic brain center

Entrance area and carport

Darwinian carnage pit here

Foundation jacks to raise and lower entire structure

at Southern Illinois. This beach combines the outdoor and the clean in a highly American manner—scenically it is the old swimmin' hole of Huckleberry Finn tradition, but it is properly policed (by sophomore lifeguards sitting on Eames chairs on poles in the water) and it's *chlorinated* too. From where I stood, I could see not only immensely elaborate family barbecues and picnics in progress on the sterilized sand, but also, through and above the trees, the basketry interlaces of one of Buckminster Fuller's experimental domes. And it hit me then, that if dirty old Nature could be kept under the proper degree of control (sex left in, streptococci taken out) by other means, the United States would be happy to dispense with architecture and buildings altogether.

Bucky Fuller, of course, is very big on this proposition: his famous nonrhetorical question, "Madam, do you know what your house weighs?" articulates a subversive suspicion of the monumental. This suspicion is inarticulately shared by the untold thousands of Americans who have already shed the deadweight of domestic architecture and live in mobile homes which, though they may never actually be moved, still deliver rather better performance as shelter than do ground-anchored structures costing at least three times as much and weighing ten times more. If someone could devise a package that would effectively disconnect the mobile home from the dangling wires of the town electricity supply, the bottled gas containers insecurely perched on a packing case, and the semi-unspeakable sanitary arrangements that stem from not being connected to the main sewer—then we should really see some changes. It may not be so far away either; defense cutbacks may send aerospace spin-off spinning in some new directions quite soon, and that kind of miniaturization talent applied to a genuinely self-contained and regenerative standard-of-living package that could be towed behind a trailer home or clipped to it could produce a sort of U-haul unit that might be picked up or dropped off at depots across the face of the nation. Avis might still become the first in U-Tility, even if they have to go on being a trying second in car hire.

Out of this might come a domestic revolution beside which modern architecture would look like Kiddibrix, because you might be able to dispense with the trailer home as well. A standard-of-living package (the phrase and the concept are both Bucky Fuller's) that really worked might, like so many sophisticated inventions, return Man nearer to a natural state in spite of his complex culture (much as the supersession of the Morse telegraph by the Bell Telephone restored his power of speech nationwide). Man started with two basic ways of controlling environment: one by avoiding the issue and hiding under a rock, tree, tent, or roof (this led ultimately to architecture as we know it) and the other by actually interfering with the local meteorology, usually by means of a campfire, which, in a more polished form, might lead to the kind of situation now under discussion. Unlike the living space trapped with our forebears under a rock or roof, the space around a campfire has many unique qualities which architecture cannot hope to equal, above all, its freedom and variability.

The direction and strength of the wind will decide the main shape and dimensions of that space, stretching the area of tolerable warmth into a long oval, but the output of light will now be affected by the wind, and the area of tolerable illumination will be a circle overlapping the oval of warmth. There will thus be a variety of environmental choices balancing light against warmth according to need and interest. If you want to do close work, like shrinking a human head, you sit in one place, but if you want to sleep you curl up somewhere different; the floating knucklebones game would come to rest somewhere quite different from the environment that suited the meeting of the initiation rites steering committee . . . and all this would be jim dandy if campfires were not so perishing inefficient, unreliable, smoky, and the rest of it.

But a properly set-up standard-of-living package, breathing out warm air along the ground (instead of sucking in cold along the ground like a campfire), radiating soft light and Dionne Warwick in heartwarming stereo, with well-aged protein turning in an infrared glow in the rotisserie, and the icemaker discreetly coughing cubes into glasses on the swing-out bar—this could do something for a woodland glade or creekside rock that *Playboy* could never do for its penthouse. But how are you going to manhandle this hunk of technology down to the creek? It doesn't have to be that massive; aerospace needs, for instance, have done wild things to solid-state technology, producing even tiny refrigerating transistors. They don't as yet mop up any great quantity of heat, but what are you going to do in this glade anyhow; put a whole steer in deep freeze? Nor do you have to manhandle it—it could ride on a cushion of air (its own air-conditioning output, for instance) like a hovercraft or domestic vacuum cleaner.

All this will eat up quite a lot of power, transistors notwithstanding. But one should remember that few Americans are ever far from a source of between 100 and 400 horsepower—the automobile. Beefed-up car batteries and a self-reeling cable drum could probably get this package breathing warm bourbon fumes o'er Eden long before microwave power transmission or miniaturized atomic power plants come in. The car is already one of the strongest arms in America's environmental weaponry, and an essential component in one nonarchitectural antibuilding that is already familiar to most of the nation—the drive-in movie house. Only, the word *house* is a manifest misnomer— just a flat piece of ground where the operating company provides visual images and piped sound, and the rest of the situation comes on wheels. You bring your own seat, heat, and shelter as part of the car. You also bring Coke, cookies, Kleenex, Chesterfields, spare clothes, shoes, the Pill, and god-wot else they don't provide at Radio City.

The car, in short, is already doing quite a lot of the standard-of-living package's job—the smoochy couple dancing to the music of the radio in their parked convertible have created a ballroom in the wilderness (dance floor by courtesy of the Highway Dept., of course) and all this is paradisal till it starts to rain. Even then, you're not licked— it takes very little boosting, and the dome itself, folded into a parachute pack, might be part of the package. From within your thirty-foot hemisphere of warm dry *Lebensraum* you could have spectacular ringside views of the wind felling trees, snow swirling through the glade, the forest fire coming over the hill, or Constance Chatterley running swiftly to you know who through the downpour.

But . . . surely, this is not a home, you can't bring up a family in a polythene bag? This can never replace the time-honored ranch-style trilevel with four small boys and a private dust bowl. If the countless Americans who are successfully raising nice children in trailers will excuse me for a moment, I have a few suggestions to make to the even more countless Americans who are so insecure that they have to hide inside fake monuments of Permastone and instant roofing. There are, admittedly, very sound day-to-day advantages to having warm broadloom on a firm floor underfoot, rather than pine needles and poison ivy. America's pioneer house builders recognized this by commonly building their brick chimneys on a brick floor slab. A transparent airdome could be anchored to such a slab just as easily as could a balloon frame, and the standard-of-living package could hover busily in a sort of glorified barbecue pit in the middle of the slab. But an airdome is not the sort of thing that the kids, or a distracted Pumpkin Eater, could run in and out of when the fit took them—believe me, fighting your way out of an airdome can be worse than trying to get out of a collapsed rain-soaked tent if you make the wrong first move.

But the relationship of the services kit to the floor slab could be rearranged to get over this difficulty; all the standard-of-living tackle (or most of it) could be redeployed on the upper side of a sheltering membrane floating above the floor, radiating heat, light, and whatnot downward and leaving the whole perimeter wide open for random egress—and equally casual ingress, too, I guess. That crazy modern movement dream of the interpenetration of indoors and outdoors could become real at last by abolishing the doors. Technically, of course, it would be just about possible to make the power membrane literally float, hovercraft style. Anyone who has had to stand in the ground-effect of a helicopter will know that this solution has little to recommend it apart from the instant disposal of waste paper. The noise, power consumption, and physical discomfort would be really something wild. But if the power membrane could be carried on a column or two, here and there, or even on a brick-built bathroom unit, then we are almost in sight of what might be technically possible before the Great Society is much older.

The basic proposition is simply that the power membrane should blow down a curtain of warmed/cooled/conditioned air around the perimeter of the windward side of the un-house, and leave the surrounding weather to waft it through the living space, whose relationship in plan to the membrane above need not be a one-to-one relationship. The membrane would probably have to go beyond the limits of the floor slab, anyhow, in order to prevent rain blow-in, though the air curtain will be active on precisely the side on which the rain is blowing and, being conditioned, will tend to mop up the moisture as it falls. The distribution of the air curtain will be governed by various electronic light and weather sensors, and by that radical new invention, the weathervane. For really foul weather automatic storm shutters would be required, but in all but the most wildly inconstant climates, it should be possible to design the conditioning kit to deal with most of the weather most of the time, without the power consumption becoming ridiculously greater than for an ordinary inefficient monumental type house.

Obviously, it would still be appreciably greater, but this whole argument hinges on the observation that it is the American Way to spend money on services and upkeep rather than on permanent structure as do the peasant cultures of the Old World. In any case, we don't know where we shall be with things like solar power in the next decade, and to anyone who wants to entertain an almost-possible version of air-conditioning for absolutely free, let me recommend "Shortstack" (another smart trick with a polythene tube) in the December 1964 issue of Analog. In fact, quite a number of the obvious common-sense objections to the un-house may prove to be self-evaporating: for instance, noise may be no problem because there would be no surrounding wall to reflect it back into the living space, and, in any case, the constant whisper of the air-curtain would provide a fair threshold of loudness that sounds would have to beat before they began to be comprehensible and therefore disturbing. Bugs? Wild life? In summer they should be no worse than with the doors and windows of an ordinary house open; in winter all right-thinking creatures either migrate or hibernate; but, in any case, why not encourage the normal process of Darwinian competition to tidy up the situation for you? All that is needed is to trigger the process by means of a general purpose lure; this would radiate mating calls and sexy scents and thus attract all sorts of mutually incompatible predators and prey into a compact pool of unspeakable carnage. A closed-circuit television camera could relay the state of play to a screen inside the dwelling and provide a twenty-four-hour program that would make the ratings for *Bonanza* look like chicken feed.

And privacy? This seems to be such a nominal concept in American life as factually lived that it is difficult to believe that anyone is seriously worried. The answer, under the suburban conditions that this whole argument implies, is the same as for the glass houses architects were designing so busily a decade ago—more sophisticated landscaping. This, after all, is the homeland of the bulldozer and the transplantation of grown trees—why let the Parks Commissioner have all the fun?

As was said above, this argument implies suburbia which, for better or worse, is where America wants to live. It has nothing to say about the city, which, like architecture, is an insecure foreign growth on the continent. What is under discussion here is an extension of the Jeffersonian dream beyond the agrarian sentimentality of Frank Lloyd Wright's Usonian Broadacre version—the dream of the good life in the clean countryside, power-point homesteading in a paradise garden of appliances. This dream of the unhouse may sound very antiarchitectural but it is so only in degree, and architecture deprived of its European roots but trying to strike new ones in an alien soil has come close to the anti-house once or twice already. Wright was not joking when he talked of the "destruction of the box," even though the spatial promise of the phrase is rarely realized to the full in the all-too-solid fact. Grass-roots architects of the Plains like Bruce Goff and Herb Greene have produced houses whose supposed monumental form is clearly of little consequence to the functional business of living in and around them.

But it is in one building that seems at first sight nothing but monumental form that the threat or promise of the unhouse has been most clearly demonstrated—the Johnson House at New Canaan. So much has been misleadingly said (by Philip Johnson himself, as well as others) to prove this a work of architecture in the European tradition, that its many intensely American aspects are usually missed. Yet when you have dug through all the erudition about Ledoux and Malevich and Palladio and stuff that has been published, one very suggestive source or prototype remains less easily explained away—the admitted persistence in Johnson's mind of the visual image of a burned-out New England township, the insubstantial shells of the houses consumed by the fire, leaving the brick floor slabs and standing chimneys. The New Canaan glass house consists essentially of just these two elements, a heated brick floor slab, and a standing unit which is a chimney/fireplace on one side and a bathroom on the other.

Around this has been draped precisely the kind of insubstantial shell that Conklin was discussing, only even less substantial than that. The roof, certainly, is solid, but psychologically it is dominated by the absence of visual enclosure all around. As many pilgrims on this site have noticed, the house does not stop at the glass, and the terrace, and even the trees beyond, are visually part of the living space in winter, physically and operationally so in summer when the four doors are open. The "house" is little more than a service core set in infinite space, or alternatively, a detached porch looking out in all directions at the Great Out There. In summer, indeed, the glass would be a bit of a nonsense if the trees did not shade it, and in the recent scorching fall, the sun reaching in through the bare trees created such a greenhouse effect that parts of the interior were acutely uncomfortable—the house would have been better off without its glass walls.

When Philip Johnson says that the place is not a controlled environment, however, it is not these aspects of undisciplined glazing he has in mind, but that "when it gets cold I have to move toward the fire, and when it gets too hot I just move away." In fact, he is simply exploiting the campfire phenomenon (he is also pretending that the floor heating does not make the whole area habitable, which it does) and in any case, what does he mean by controlled environment? It is not the same thing as a uniform environment, it is simply an environment suited to what you are going to do next, and whether you guild a stone monument, move away from the fire, or turn on the air conditioning, it is the same basic human gesture you are making.

Only, the monument is such a ponderous solution that it astounds me that Americans are still prepared to employ it, except out of some profound sense of insecurity, a persistent inability to rid themselves of those habits of mind they left Europe to escape. In the open-fronted society, with its social and personal mobility, its interchangeability of components and personnel, its gadgetry and almost universal expendability, the persistence of architecture-as-monumental-space must appear as evidence of the sentimentality of the tough.

1965

Critical of the intuitive and unrigorous approaches to design prevalent in the 1950s, **Christopher Alexander** sought a rational methodology that could be used as a generating system in the built environment. Applying set and problem-solving theory and computer diagrams to architectural analysis, he pursued his thesis that "there is a deep and important underlying structural correspondence between the pattern of a problem and the process of designing physical form which answers that problem."

Alexander was born in Vienna and studied architecture, mathematics, and physics at Cambridge University. In 1958 he began doctoral studies in architecture at Harvard, also doing research at Harvard's Center for Cognitive Studies. With Serge Chermayeff he authored *Community and Privacy* (1963), an effort to define and map the functional criteria of public and private space in relation to the clustering of residential form. His dissertation, published in 1964 as *Notes on the Synthesis of Form,* used empirical observation and survey data to analyze social patterns in villages in India. He presented his conclusions in the form of a set of hierarchical "stem" diagrams. These, aiming to give an objective and unified description of formal phenomena, received widespread attention.

Alexander's first opportunity to put his theories into action came in 1964 when the San Francisco Bay Area Rapid Transit system invited him to program its new subway stations (this was also the inception of his tenure at the University of California at Berkeley). After identifying 390 different functional requirements for the stations, Alexander realized that his stem and tree diagrams contained the same flaw as traditional organizational methodologies in that they could not account for accident, overlap, or continuity. Moreover, as critics had already pointed out with respect to his *Notes,* no matter how specific and multiple the parameters, such diagrams were ultimately arbitrary. This realization led him to the following essay, a self-critique of his earlier analyses, in which he postulated the "semilattice," a concept adapted from set theory, as a more complex model. "A City Is Not a Tree" was widely republished and had major influence in Europe and Japan as well as the United States.

The problem remained for Alexander's later work of transforming an analytical into a generative design tool. Design methods derived from systems theory and influenced by structural linguistics and semiology had gained a significant following in architecture by the mid-1960s. Alexander's innovation was in coupling these models with an anthropological approach to the environment. His book *A Pattern Language Which Generates Multi-Service Centers* (1968) proposed a method for combining environmental patterns according to rules similar to those established by Noam Chomsky in linguistics. "A pattern," wrote Alexander, "defines an arrangement of parts in the environment which is needed to solve a recurrent social, psychological, or technical problem." Later, participating in community-based building projects in underdeveloped areas of Latin America, he used the concept of the kit of parts to correlate design process and functional requirements with traditional building craft. Among the results was a set of generic plans for *barriada* houses in Peru. His interest in preindustrial construction, spontaneous urban formations, and archetypal patterns of settlement eventually led him from Chomsky's generative grammar to a semantic model. Paradoxically, the search for "egoless" design through an objective-empirical method derived from modern systems theory brought him to the mythic perspective of "the timeless way of building."

From Architectural Forum, *May 1965, pp. 58–61. Part 1 published in* Architectural Forum, *April 1965, pp. 58–62. Both parts revised and republished in full in* Design, *February 1966, pp. 46–55. Courtesy of the author.*

A City Is Not a Tree (Part 2)
Christopher Alexander

In the first part of this article, we saw that the units of which an artificial city is made up are organized to form a tree. So that we get a really clear understanding of what this means, and shall better see its implications, let us define a tree once again:

Whenever we have a tree structure, it means that within this structure, no piece of any unit is ever connected to other units, except through the medium of that unit as a whole.

The enormity of this restriction is difficult to grasp. It is a little as though the members of a family were not free to make friends outside the family, except when the family as a whole made a friendship.

In simplicity of structure the tree is comparable to the compulsive desire for neatness and order that insists the candlesticks on a mantlepiece be perfectly straight and perfectly symmetrical about the center. The semilattice, by comparison, is the structure of a complex fabric; it is the structure of living things; of great paintings and symphonies.

It must be emphasized, lest the orderly mind shrink in horror from anything that is not clearly articulated and categorized in tree form, that the idea of overlap, ambiguity, multiplicity of aspect, and the semilattice, are not less orderly than the rigid tree, but more so. They represent a thicker, tougher, more subtle and more complex view of structure.

Let us now look at the ways in which the natural, when unconstrained by artificial conceptions, shows itself to be a semilattice.

A major aspect of the city's social structure which a tree can never mirror properly is illustrated by Ruth Glass's redevelopment plan for Middlesborough, a city of 200,000 which she recommends be broken down into twenty-nine separate neighborhoods. After picking her twenty-nine neighborhoods by determining where the sharpest discontinuities of building type, income, and job type occur, she asks herself the question: "If we examine some of the social systems which actually exist for the people in such a neighborhood, do the physical units defined by these various social systems all define the same spatial neighborhood?" Her own answer to this question is, *no.*

Each of the social systems she examines is a nodal system. It is made of some sort of central node, plus the people who use this center. Specifically she takes elementary schools, secondary schools, youth clubs, adult clubs, post offices, greengrocers, and grocers selling sugar. Each of these centers draws its users from a certain spatial area or spatial unit. This spatial unit is the physical residue of the social system as a whole, and is therefore a unit in the terms of this paper. The units corresponding to different kinds of centers for the single neighborhood of Waterloo Road are shown in *figure 1.*

The hard outline is the boundary of the so-called neighborhood itself. The white circle stands for the youth club, and the small solid rings stand for areas where its members live. The ringed spot is the adult club, and the homes of its members form the unit marked by dashed boundaries. The white square is the post office and the dotted line marks the unit which contains its users. The secondary school is marked by the spot with a white triangle in it. Together with its pupils, it forms the system marked by the dot-dashed line.

As you can see at once, the different units do not coincide. Yet neither are they disjoint. They overlap.

We cannot get an adequate picture of what Middlesborough is, or of what it ought to be, in terms of twenty-nine large and conveniently integral chunks called neighborhoods. When we describe the city in terms of neighborhoods, we implicitly assume that the smaller elements within any one of these neighborhoods belong together so tightly that they only interact with elements in other neighborhoods through the medium of the neighborhood to which they themselves belong. Ruth Glass herself shows clearly that this is not the case.

Below are two pictures of the Waterloo neighborhood. For the sake of argument I have broken it into a number of small areas. *Figure 2* shows how these pieces stick together in fact, and *figure 3* shows how the redevelopment plan pretends they stick together.

There is nothing in the nature of the various centers which says that their catchment areas should be the same. Their natures are different. Therefore the units they define are different. The natural city of Middlesborough was faithful to the semilattice structure they have. Only in the artificial tree conception of the city are their natural, proper, and necessary overlaps destroyed.

Take the separation of pedestrians from moving vehicles, a tree concept proposed by Le Corbusier, Louis Kahn, and many others. At a very crude level of thought this is obviously a good idea. It is dangerous to have sixty-mile-an-hour cars in contact with little children toddling. But it is not *always* a good idea. There are times when the ecology of a situation actually demands the opposite. Imagine yourself coming out of a Fifth Avenue store; you have been shopping all afternoon; your arms are full of parcels; you need a drink; your wife is limping. Thank God for taxis.

Yet the urban taxi can function only because pedestrians and vehicles are not strictly separated. The prowling taxi needs a fast stream of traffic so that it can cover a large area to be sure of finding a passenger. The pedestrian needs to be able to hail the taxi from any point in the pedestrian world, and to be able to get out to any part of the pedestrian world to which he wants to go. The system which contains the taxicabs needs to overlap both the fast vehicular traffic system and the system of pedestrian circulation. In Manhattan pedestrians and vehicles do share certain parts of the city, and the necessary overlap is guaranteed (*figure 4*).

Another favorite concept of the CIAM theorists and others is the separation of recreation from everything else. This has crystallized in our real cities in the form of playgrounds. The playground, asphalted and fenced in, is nothing but a pictorial acknowledgment of the fact that "play" exists in an isolated concept in our minds. It has nothing to do with the life of play itself. Few self-respecting children will even play in a playground.

Play itself, the play that children practice, goes on somewhere different everyday. One day it may be indoors, another day in a friendly gas station, another day down by the river, another day in a derelict building, another day on a construction site which has been abandoned for the weekend. Each of these play activities, and the objects it requires, forms a system. It is not true that these systems exist in isolation, cut off from the other systems in the city. The different systems overlap one another, and they overlap many other systems besides. The units, the physical places recognized as play places, must do the same.

In a natural city this is what happens. Play takes place in a thousand places—it fills the interstices of adult life. As they play, children become full of their surroundings. How can a child become filled with his surroundings in a fenced enclosure? He cannot.

1965

1

2

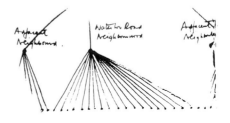

3

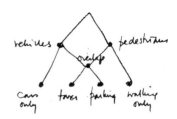

4

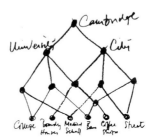

5

6

The isolated campus

A similar kind of mistake occurs in trees like that of Goodman's Communitas, or Soleri's Mesa City, which separate the university from the rest of the city. Again, this has actually been realized in common American form of the isolated campus.

What is the reason for drawing a line in the city so that everything within the boundary is university, and everything outside is nonuniversity? It is conceptually clear. But does it correspond to the realities of university life? Certainly it is not the structure which occurs in nonartificial university cities.

Take Cambridge University, for instance. At certain points Trinity Street is physically almost indistinguishable from Trinity College. One pedestrian crossover in the street is literally part of the college. The buildings on the street, though they contain stores and coffee shops and banks at ground level, contain undergraduates' rooms in their upper stories. In many cases the actual fabric of the street buildings melts into the fabric of the old college buildings so that one cannot be altered without the other.

There will always be many systems of activity where university life and city life overlap: pub-crawling, coffee drinking, the movies, walking from place to place. In some cases whole departments may be actively involved in the life of the city's inhabitants (the hospital-*cum*-medical school is an example). In Cambridge, a natural city where university and city have grown together gradually, the physical units overlap because they are the physical residues of city systems and university systems which overlap (*figure 5*).

Let us look next at the hierarchy of urban cores, realized in Brasilia, Chandigarh, the MARS plan for London, and, most recently, in the Manhattan Lincoln Center, where various performing arts serving the population of greater New York have been gathered together to form just one core.

Does a concert hall ask to be next to an opera house? Can the two feed on one another? Will anybody ever visit them both, gluttonously, in a single evening, or even buy tickets from one after going to a concert in the other? In Vienna, London, Paris, each of the performing arts has found its own place, because all are not mixed randomly. Each has created its own familiar section of the city. In Manhattan itself, Carnegie Hall and the Metropolitan Opera House were not built side by side. Each found its own place, and now creates its own atmosphere. The influence of each overlaps the parts of the city which have been made unique to it.

The only reason that these functions have all been brought together in the Lincoln Center is that the concept of performing art links them to one another.

But this tree, and the idea of a single hierarchy of urban cores which is its parent, do not illuminate the relations between art and city life. They are merely born of the mania every simpleminded person has for putting things with the same name into the same basket.

The total separation of work from housing, started by Tony Garnier in his industrial city, then incorporated in the 1929 [*sic*] Athens Charter, is now found in every artificial city and accepted everywhere zoning is enforced. Is this a sound principle? It is easy to see how bad conditions at the beginning of the century prompted planners to try to get the dirty factories out of residential areas. But the separation misses a variety of systems which require, for their sustenance, little parts of both.

Jane Jacobs describes the growth of backyard industries in Brooklyn. A man who wants to start a small business needs space, which he is very likely to have in his own backyard. He also needs to establish connections with larger going enterprises and with their customers. This means that the system of backyard industry needs to belong both to the residential zone and to the industrial zone—these zones need to overlap. In Brooklyn they do (*figure 6*). In a city which is a tree, they can't.

Finally, let us examine the subdivision of the city into isolated communities. As we have seen in the Abercrombie plan for London, this is itself a tree structure. The individual community in a greater city has no reality as a functioning unit. In London, as in any great city, almost no one manages to find work which suits him near his home. People in one community work in a factory which is very likely to be in another community.

There are, therefore, many hundreds of thousands of worker-workplace systems, each consisting of a man plus the factory he works in, which cut across the boundaries defined by Abercrombie's tree. The existence of these units, and their overlapping nature, indicates that the living systems of London form a semilattice. Only in the planner's mind has it become a tree.

The fact that we have so far failed to give this any physical expression has a vital consequence. As things are, whenever the worker and his workplace belong to separately administered municipalities, the community which contains the workplace collects huge taxes and has relatively little on which to spend the tax revenue. The community where the worker lives, if it is mainly residential, collects only little in the way of taxes, and yet has great additional burdens on its purse in the shape of schools, hospitals, etc. Clearly, to resolve this inequity, the worker-workplace systems must be anchored in physically recognizable units of the city which can then be taxed.

It might be argued that, even though the individual communities of a great city have no functional significance in the lives of their inhabitants, they are still the most convenient administrative units, and should, therefore, be left in their present tree organization.

However, in the political complexity of a modern city, even this is suspect.

Edward Banfield, in a recent book called *Political Influence*, gives a detailed account of the patterns of influence and control that have actually led to decisions in Chicago. He shows that although the lines of administrative and executive control have a formal structure which is a tree, these formal chains of influence and authority are entirely overshadowed by the ad hoc lines of control which arise naturally as each new city problem presents itself. These ad hoc lines depend on who is interested in the matter, who has what at stake, who has what favors to trade with whom.

This second structure, which is informal, working within the framework of the first, is what really controls public action. It varies from week to week, even from hour to hour, as one problem replaces another. Nobody's sphere of influence is entirely under the control of any one superior; each person is under different influences as the problems change. Although the organization chart in the mayor's office is a tree, the actual control and exercise of authority is semilatticelike.

Trapped in a tree

Now, why is it that so many designers have conceived cities as trees when the natural structure is in every case a semilattice? Have they done so deliberately, in the belief that a tree structure will serve the people of the city better? Or have they done it because they cannot help it, because they are trapped by a mental habit, perhaps even trapped by the way the mind works; because they cannot encompass the complexity of a semilattice in any convenient mental form; because the mind has an overwhelming predisposition to see trees wherever it looks and cannot escape the tree conception?

I shall try to convince you that it is for this second reason that trees are being proposed and built as cities—that it is because designers, limited as they must be by the capacity of the mind to form intuitively accessible structures, cannot achieve the complexity of the semilattice in a single mental act.

Let me begin with an example.

Suppose I ask you to remember the following four objects: an orange, a watermelon, a football, and a tennis ball. How will you keep them in your mind, in your mind's eyes? However you do it, you will do it by grouping them. Some of you will take the two fruits together, the orange and the watermelon, and the two sports balls together, the football and the tennis ball. Those of you who tend to think in terms of physical shape may group them differently, taking the two small spheres together—the orange and the tennis ball and the two larger and more egg-shaped objects—the watermelon and the football. Some of you will be aware of both.

Let us make a diagram of these groupings (*figure 7*).

Either grouping taken by itself is a tree structure. The two together are a semilattice. Now let us try and visualize these groupings in the mind's eye. I think you will find that you cannot visualize all four sets simultaneously—because they overlap. You can visualize one pair of sets and then the other, and you can alternate between the two pairs extremely fast, so fast that you may deceive yourself into thinking you can visualize them all together, but in truth, you cannot conceive all four sets at once in a single mental act. You cannot bring the semilattice structure into a visualizable form for a single mental act. In a single mental act you can only visualize a tree.

This is a problem we face as designers. While we are not, perhaps, necessarily occupied with the problem of total visualization in a single mental act, the principle is still the same. The tree is accessible mentally, and easy to deal with. The semilattice is hard to keep before the mind's eye, and therefore hard to deal with.

It is known today that grouping and categorization are among the most primitive psychological processes. Modern psychology treats thought as a process of fitting new situations into existing slots and pigeonholes in the mind. Just as you cannot put a physical thing into more than one physical pigeonhole at once, so, by analogy, the processes of thought prevent you from putting a mental construct into more than one mental category at once. Study of the origin of these processes suggests that they stem essentially from the organism's need to reduce the complexity of its environment by establishing barriers between the different events which it encounters.

It is for this reason—because the mind's first function is to reduce the ambiguity and overlap in a confusing situation, and because, to this end, it is endowed with a basic intolerance for ambiguity—that structures like the city, which do require overlapping sets within them, are nevertheless persistently conceived as trees.

The same rigidity dogs even the perception of physical patterns. In experiments by Huggins and myself at Harvard, we showed people patterns whose internal units overlapped, and found that they almost always invented a way of seeing the patterns as a tree—even when the semilattice view of the patterns would have helped them perform the task of experimentation which was before them.

The most startling proof that people tend to conceive even physical patterns as trees is found in some experiments of Sir Frederick Bartlett. He showed people a pattern for about one quarter of a second and then asked them to draw what they had seen. Many people, unable to grasp the full complexity of the pattern they had seen, simplified the patterns by cutting out the overlap. In *figure 8,* the original is shown at the top, with two fairly typical redrawn versions below it. In the redrawn versions, the circles are separated from the rest: the overlap between triangles and circles disappear.

These experiments suggest strongly that people have an underlying tendency, when faced by a complex organization, to reorganize it mentally in terms of nonoverlapping units. The complexity of the semilattice is replaced by the simpler and more easily grasped tree form.

You are no doubt wondering by now what a city looks like which is a semilattice, but not a tree. I must confess that I cannot yet show you plans or sketches. It is not enough merely to make a demonstration of overlap—the overlap must be the right overlap. This is doubly important, because it is so tempting to make plans in which overlap occurs for its own sake. This is essentially what the high-density "life-filled" city plans of recent years do. But overlap alone does not give structure.

It can also give chaos. A garbage can is full of overlap. To have structure, you must have the right overlap, and this is for us almost certainly different from the old overlap which we observe in historic cities. As the relationships between functions change, so the systems which need to overlap in order to receive these relationships must also change. The recreation of old kinds of overlap will be inappropriate, chaotic instead of structured.

The work of trying to understand just what overlap the modern city requires, and trying to put this required overlap into physical and plastic terms, is still going on. Until the work is complete, there is no point in presenting facile sketches of ill-thought-out structure.

Overlapping triangles

However, I can perhaps make the physical consequences of overlap more comprehensible by means of an image. The painting illustrated is recent work by Simon Nicholson (*figure 9*). The fascination of this painting lies in the fact that although constructed of rather few simple triangular elements, these elements unite in many different ways to form the larger units of the painting—in such a way, indeed, that if we make a complete inventory of the perceived units in the painting, we find that each triangle enters into four or five completely different kinds of unit, none contained in the others, yet all overlapping in that triangle.

Thus, if we number the triangles and pick out the sets of triangles which appear as strong visual units, we get the semilattice shown in *figure 10*.

Three and 5 form a unit because they work together as a rectangle; 2 and 4 because they form a parallelogram; 5 and 6 because they are both dark and pointing the same way; 6 and 7 because one is the ghost of the other shifted sideways; 4 and 7 because they are symmetrical with one another; 4 and 6 because they form another rectangle; 4 and 5 because they form a sort of Z; 2 and 3 because they form a rather thinner kind of A; 1 and 7 because they are at opposite corners; 1 and 2 because they are a rectangle; 3 and 1 because they point the same way as 5 and 6, and form a sort of off-center reflection; 3 and 6 because they enclose 4 and 5 ; 1 and 5 because they enclose 2, 3, and 4 . . . I have only listed the units of two triangles. The larger units are even more complex. The white is more complex still, and is not even included in the diagram because it is harder to be sure of its elementary pieces.

The painting is significant, not so much because it has overlap in it (many paintings have overlap in them), but rather because this painting has nothing else in it except overlap. It is only the fact of the overlap, and the resulting multiplicity of aspects which

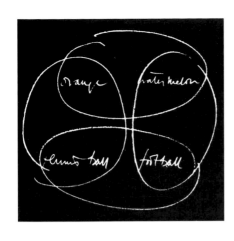

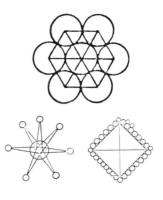

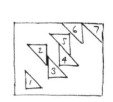

8

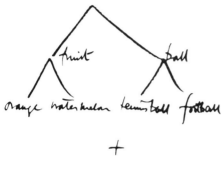

9

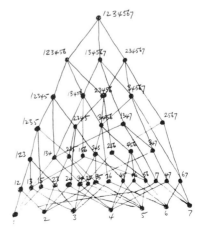

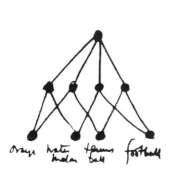

7

10

1966

One of the group of young collaborators hand-picked by Ernesto Rogers shortly after he took over the editorship of *Casabella-continuità*, **Aldo Rossi** began contributing to the journal in 1955 while still a student at the Milan Politecnic (from which he would graduate in 1959). These were years when the most polemically engaged Italian architects of the earlier generation—Rogers, Ludovico Quaroni, Giuseppe Samonà, and others—were overturning the modernist myth of a *tabula rasa* architecture abstracted from the historical development of the city, in search of a new relationship between architecture and urbanism. As Rossi's early writings attest, he was much engaged in these debates. At the same time, an article of 1959 on Adolf Loos already hints at the more detached poetics of his later work.

200–4, 300–7

In the early 1960s Rossi became involved in teaching—first in Arezzo as assistant to Quaroni, then in Venice alongside Carlo Aymonino, eventually returning to Milan in 1965. Here and in new writings, he began to elaborate his ideas on architectural morphology and urban typology. These would fully emerge in *The Architecture of the City* in 1966. A project of 1962 for a Monument to the Resistance in Cuneo announced his preoccupation with primary forms simplified to the extreme and suffused with dramatic tensions. He also began collaborating with Giorgio Grassi, whose work coincided with his not only in its rationalism but in its radical view of architecture's disciplinary autonomy.

In 1966 the publication of *The Architecture of the City* proved a major event. With Robert Venturi's *Complexity and Contradiction in Architecture*, it effectively broke the stranglehold of functionalist thought. Though marred stylistically by repetitiousness, the book was hugely influential, going through four Italian editions in a dozen years and quickly being translated into several languages. What was seminal in Rossi's modern-day search for "the fixed laws of a timeless typology" was his assertion of the architecture of the city as the fundamental artifact of human culture and the repository of collective memory. Citing the work of the French school of urban geography founded by Marcel Poète in the 1920s, Rossi evoked the role of the singular place—the *locus*, whether a natural element or man-made monument—within the formal repertory and historical transformation of the urban fabric. He stressed the complexity of the city's evolution, condemning "naive functionalism" while insisting on the value of typological study as a rational basis for design.

389–91

In the years following, Rossi's work became increasingly autobiographical. Veering from the urban science aspired to in his book and from Grassi's rigorist concept of architecture as *mestiere*, he embraced the poetics of the "analogous city," an oneiric self-referentiality drawing on the fragmented unconscious of collective form. This leap into the postmodern imagination would be marked with a second book, *A Scientific Autobiography*, given its initial publication by the Institute for Urban Studies in New York in 1981. At the same time, the potency of Rossi's forms—popularized through his evocative drawings—and of the thesis of the earlier book coalesced the neorationalist movement that became known around the world as the Tendenza. *The Architecture of the City* would appear in English in 1982 also under the imprint of the Institute for Architecture and Urban Studies. The latter was instrumental in introducing the Italian school to the United States in the 1970s through the efforts of its director, Peter Eisenman, whose own work had been influenced by the prewar rationalism of Giuseppe Terragni.

From Aldo Rossi, L'architettura della città (Padua: Marsilio, 1966), pp. 25–30; footnotes omitted. English edition: The Architecture of the City *(Cambridge, Mass.: MIT Press, 1982), trans. Diane Ghirardo and Joan Ockman, pp. 32–41. Courtesy of the author. Translation courtesy of MIT Press.*

from *The Architecture of the City*
Aldo Rossi

The urban artifact as a work of art

[...] As soon as we address questions about the individuality and structure of a specific urban artifact, a series of issues is raised which, in its totality, seems to constitute a system that enables us to analyze a work of art. As the present investigation is intended to establish and identify the nature of urban artifacts, we should initially state that there is *something in the nature of urban artifacts that renders them very similar—and not only metaphorically—to a work of art.* They are material constructions, but notwithstanding the material, something different: although they are conditioned, they also condition.

This aspect of "art" in urban artifacts is closely linked to their quality, their uniqueness, and thus also to their analysis and definition. This is an extremely complex subject, for even beyond their psychological aspects, urban artifacts are complex in themselves, and while it may be possible to analyze them, it is difficult to define them. The nature of this problem has always been of particular interest to me, and I am convinced that it directly concerns the architecture of the city.

If one takes any urban artifact—a building, a street, a district—and attempts to describe it, the same difficulties arise which we encountered earlier with respect to the Palazzo della Ragione in Padua. Some of these difficulties derive from the ambiguity of language, and in part these difficulties can be overcome, but there will always be a type of experience recognizable only to those who have walked through the particular building, street, or district.

Thus, the concept that one person has of an urban artifact will always differ from that of someone who "lives" that same artifact. These considerations, however, can delimit our task; it is possible that our task consists principally in defining an urban artifact from the standpoint of its manufacture: in other words, to define and classify a street, a city, a street in a city; then the location of this street, its function, its architecture; then the street systems possible in the city and many other things.

We must therefore concern ourselves with urban geography, urban topography, architecture, and several other disciplines. The problem is far from easy, but not impossible, and in the following paragraphs we will attempt an analysis along these lines. This means that, in a very general way, we can establish a logical geography of any city; this logical geography will be applied essentially to the problems of language, description, and classification. Thus, we can address such fundamental questions as those of typology, which have not yet been the object of serious systematic work in the domain of the urban sciences. At the base of the existing classifications there are too many unverified hypotheses, which necessarily lead to meaningless generalizations.

By using those disciplines to which I have just referred, we are working toward a broader, more concrete, and more complete analysis of urban artifacts. The city is seen as the human achievement *par excellence;* perhaps, too, it has to do with those things that can only be grasped by actually experiencing a given urban artifact. This conception of the city, or better, urban artifacts, as a work of art has, in fact, always appeared in studies of the city; we can also discover it in the form of greatly varying intuitions and descriptions in artists of all eras and in many manifestations of social and religious life. In the latter case it has always been tied to a specific place, event, and form in the city.

The question of the city as a work of art, however, represents itself explicitly and scientifically above all in relation to the conception of the nature of collective artifacts, and I maintain that no urban research can ignore this aspect of the problem. How are collective urban artifacts related to the works of art? All great manifestations of social life have in common with the work of art the fact that they are born in unconscious life. This life is collective in the former, individual in the latter; but this is only a secondary difference because one is a product of the public and the other is for the public: the public provides the common denominator.

Setting forth the problem in this manner, Claude Lévi-Strauss brought the study of the city into a realm rich with unexpected developments. He noted how, more than other works of art, the city achieves a balance between natural and artificial elements; it is an object of nature and a subject of culture. Maurice Halbwachs advanced this analysis further when he postulated that imagination and collective memory are the typical characteristics of urban artifacts.

These studies of the city which embrace its structural complexity have an unexpected and little-known precedent in the work of Carlo Cattaneo. Cattaneo never explicitly considered the question of the artistic nature of urban artifacts, but the close connection in his thinking between art and science as two concrete aspects of the development of the human mind anticipates this approach. Later I will discuss how his concept of the city as the ideal principle of history, the connection between country and city, and other issues that he raised relate to urban artifacts. While at this point I am mostly interested in how he approaches the city, in fact Cattaneo never makes any distinction between city and country since he considers that all inhabited places are the work of man: ". . . every region is distinguished from the wilderness in this respect: that it is an immense repository of labor. . . . This land is thus not a work of nature; it is the work of our hands, our artificial homeland."

City and region, agricultural land and forest become human works because they are an immense repository of the labor of our hands. But to the extent that they are our "artificial homeland" and objects that have been constructed, they also testify to values; they constitute memory and permanence. The city is in its history. Hence, the relationship between place and man and the work of art—which is the ultimate, decisive fact shaping and directing urban evolution according to an aesthetic finality—affords us a complex mode of studying the city.

Naturally we must also take into account how people orient themselves within the city, the evolution and formation of their sense of space. This aspect constitutes, in my opinion, the most important feature of some recent American work, notably that of Kevin Lynch. It relates to the conceptualization of space, and can be based in large measure on anthropological studies and urban characteristics. Observations of this type were also made by Maximilien Sorre using such material, particularly the work of Marcel Mauss on the correspondence between group names and place names among Eskimos. For now, this argument will merely serve as an introduction to our study; it will be more useful to return to it after we have considered several other aspects of the urban artifact—of the city, that is, as a great, comprehensive representation of the human condition.

I will interpret this representation against the background of its most fixed and significant stage: architecture. Sometimes I ask myself why architecture is not analyzed in these terms, that is, in terms of its profound value as a human thing that shapes reality and adapts material according to an aesthetic conception. It is in this sense not only the place of the human condition, but itself a part of that condition, and is represented in the city and its monuments, in districts, dwellings, and all urban artifacts that emerge from inhabited space. It is from this point of view that a few theorists have tried to analyze the urban structure, to sense the fixed points, the true structural junctions of the city, those points from which the activity of reason proceeds.

I will now take up the *hypothesis of the city as a man-made object,* as a work of architecture or engineering that grows over time; this is one of the most substantial hypotheses from which to work.

It seems that useful answers to many ambiguities are still provided by the work of Camillo Sitte, who in his search for laws of the construction of the city that were not limited to purely technical considerations took full account of the "beauty" of the urban scheme, of its form: "We have at our disposal three major methods of city planning, and several subsidiary types. The major ones are the gridiron system, the radial system, and the triangular system. The subtypes are mostly hybrids of these three. Artistically speaking, not one of them is of any interest, for in their veins pulses not a single drop of artistic blood. All three are concerned exclusively with the arrangement of street patterns, and hence their intention is from the start a purely technical one. A network of streets always serves only the purposes of communication, never of art, since it can never be comprehended sensorily, can never be grasped as a whole except in a plan of it. In our discussions so far street networks have not been mentioned for just that reason; neither those of ancient Athens, of Rome, of Nuremberg, or of Venice. They are of no concern artistically, because they are inapprehensible in their entirety. Only that which a spectator can hold in view, what can be seen, is of artistic importance: for instance, the single street or the individual plaza."

Sitte's admonition is important for its empiricism, and it seems to me that this takes us back to certain American experiences which we mentioned above, where artistic quality can be seen as a function of the ability to give concrete form to a symbol. Sitte's lesson beyond question helps to prevent many confusions. It refers us to the technique of urban construction, where there is still the actual moment of designing a square and then a principle which provides for its logical transmission, for the teaching of its design. But the models are always, somehow, the single street, the specific square.

On the other hand, Sitte's lesson also contains a gross misperception in that it reduces the city as a work of art to one artistic episode having more or less legibility rather than to a concrete, overall experience. We believe the reverse to be true, that the whole is more important than the single parts, and that only the urban artifact in its totality, from street system and urban topography down to the things that can be perceived in strolling up and down a street, constitutes this totality. Naturally we must examine this total architecture in terms of its parts.

We must begin with a question that opens the way to the problem of classification—that of the typology of buildings and their relationship to the city. This relationship constitutes a basic hypothesis of this work, and one that I will analyze from various viewpoints, always considering buildings as moments and parts of the whole that is the city. This position was clear to the architectural theorists of the Enlightenment. In his lessons at the Ecole Polytechnique, Durand wrote, "Just as the walls, the columns, &c., are the elements which compose buildings, so buildings are the elements which compose cities."

Typological questions

The city as above all else a human thing is constituted of its architecture and of all those

Palazzo della Ragione, Padua.

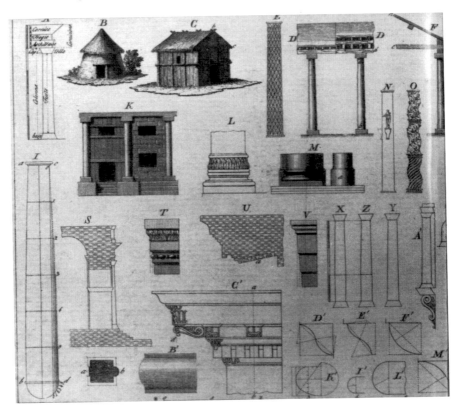

From Francesco Milizia, Principj di Architettura Civile, *1832.*

works that constitute the true means of transforming nature. Bronze Age men adapted the landscape to social needs by constructing artificial islands of brick, by digging wells, drainage canals, and watercourses. The first houses sheltered their inhabitants from the external environment and furnished a climate that man could begin to control; the development of an urban nucleus expanded this type of control to the creation and extension of a microclimate. Neolithic villages already offered the first transformations of the world according to man's needs. The "artificial homeland" is as old as man.

In precisely this sense of transformation the first forms and types of habitation, as well as temples and more complex buildings, were constituted. The *type* developed according to both needs and aspirations to beauty; a particular type was associated with a form and a way of life, although its specific shape varied widely from society to society. The concept of type thus became the basis of architecture, a fact attested to both by practice and by the treatises.

It therefore seems clear that typological questions are important. They have always entered into the history of architecture, and arise naturally whenever urban problems are confronted. Theoreticians such as Francesco Milizia never defined type as such, but statements like the following seem to be anticipatory: "The comfort of any building consists of three principal items: its site, its form, and the organization of its parts." I would define the concept of type as something that is permanent and complex, a logical principle that is prior to form and that constitutes it.

One of the major theoreticians of architecture, Quatremère de Quincy, understood the importance of these problems and gave a masterly definition of type and model:

"The word 'type' represents not so much the image of a thing to be copied or perfectly imitated as the idea of an element that must itself serve as a rule for the model. . . . The model, understood in terms of the practical execution of art, is an object that must be repeated such as it is; type, on the contrary, is an object according to which one can conceive works that do not resemble one another at all. Everything is precise and given in the model; everything is more or less vague in the type. Thus we see that the imitation of type involves nothing that feelings or spirit cannot recognize. . . .

"We also see that all inventions, notwithstanding subsequent changes, always retain their elementary principle in a way that is clear and manifest to the senses and to reason. It is similar to a nucleus around which the developments and variations of forms to which the object was susceptible gather and mesh. Therefore a thousand things of every kind have come down to us, and one of the principal tasks of science and philosophy is to seek their origins and primary causes so as to grasp their purposes. Here is what must be called 'type' in architecture, as in every other branch of human inventions and institutions. . . . We have engaged in this discussion in order to render the value of the word *type*—taken metaphorically in a great number of works— clearly comprehensible, and to show the error of those who either disregard it because it is not a model, or misrepresent it by imposing on it the rigor of a model that would imply the conditions of an identical copy."

In the first part of this passage, the author rejects the possibility of type as something to be imitated or copied because in this case there would be, as he asserts in the second part, no "creation of the model"—that is, there would be no making of architecture. The second part states that in architecture (whether model or form) there is an element that plays its own role, not something to which the architectonic object conforms but something that is nevertheless present in the model. This is the *rule,* the structuring principle of architecture.

In fact, it can be said that this principle is a constant. Such an argument presupposes that the architectural artifact is conceived as a structure and that this structure is revealed and can be recognized in the artifact itself. As a constant, this principle, which we can call the typical element, or simply the type, is to be found in all architectural artifacts. It is also then a cultural element and as such can be investigated in different architectural artifacts; typology becomes in this way the analytical moment of architecture, and it becomes readily identifiable at the level of urban artifacts.

Thus typology presents itself as the study of types that cannot be further reduced, elements of a city as well as of an architecture. The question of monocentric cities or of buildings that are or are not centralized, for example, is specifically typological; no type can be identified with only one form, even if all architectural forms are reducible to types. The process of reduction is a necessary, logical operation, and it is impossible to talk about problems of form without this presupposition. In this sense all architectural theories are also theories of typology, and in an actual design it is difficult to distinguish the two moments.

Type is thus a constant and manifests itself with a character of necessity; but even though it is predetermined, it reacts dialectically with technique, function, and style, as well as with both the collective character and the individual moment of the architectural artifact. It is clear, for example, that the central plan is a fixed and constant type in religious architecture; but even so, each time a central plan is chosen, dialectical themes are put into play with the architecture of the church, with its functions, with its constructional technique, and with the collective that participates in the life of that church. I tend to believe that housing types have not changed from antiquity up to today, but this is not to say that the actual way of living has not changed, nor that new ways of living are not always possible. The house with a loggia is an old scheme; a corridor that gives access to rooms is necessary in plan and present in any number of urban houses. But there are a great many variations on this theme among individual houses at different times.

Ultimately, we can say that type is the very idea of architecture, that which is closest to its essence. In spite of changes, it has always imposed itself on the "feelings and reason" as the principle of architecture and of the city. [. . .]

1966

273–75, 325–74
The theme of the "great number"—how to accommodate a continuously increasing population—and of large-scale urban form tended to be elaborated during the late 1950s and early 1960s within the technical-utopian framework of the megastructure and the debates on dynamic process, mobility, and mass communications. While this discussion had an Italian counterpart, notably in Umberto Eco's semiological theory and his book on the "open work" (1962), the discussion of what came to be known in Italy as the new urban dimension underwent a rather different development. Here, concern centered on the formulation of concrete design strategies linking historic urban centers to developments in the countryside. Responding to the dramatic changes that had taken place in the Italian landscape during the previous decade—especially in the northern industrial zone triangulating Milan, Turin, and Genoa—architects acknowledged the destructive effect of uncoordinated local initiatives. Giuseppe Samonà was among the first to address the problem, calling, in an essay entitled "La nuova dimensione della città" (1959), for an integrated and realistic planning approach to urban and territorial expansion.

Over the next several years the *città-territorio* became a major subject of discussion, bound up not only with quantitative and technical considerations but also cultural and formal ones. It was **Vittorio Gregotti** who most articulately framed the latter with the publication in 1966 of a special issue of *Edilizia Moderna*, of which he was then editor, entitled "La forma del territorio." He also published a book, *Il territorio dell'architettura,* the same year, from which the following extract is taken. Milanese and of the same generation as Aldo Rossi, Gregotti had come to maturity during the transforming years of the postwar economic miracle. He was old enough to have attended CIAM's "heart of the

135–36
300–7
city" conference in Hoddesdon and to have worked on the design of the Velasca tower in the office of the BBPR, and was also among the circle of young collaborators—with Rossi, Gae Aulenti, Guido Canella, and a handful of others—to come under the wing of Ernesto Rogers during the years when *Casabella-*

392–98
continuità played its major role. While Rossi would stress the cultural and geographical specificity of urban places in *The Architecture of the City*, Gregotti

200–4
undertook to extend Rogers's *preesistenze ambientali* to the territorial scale, positing a fluid new relationship between the built organism and the rules of formal typology. This "anthropogeographic" approach was based not on metaphorical but material considerations: the topography and ecology of a region, its history and culture. Drawing on research into the visual perception of urban form by the American Kevin Lynch as well as on insights offered by communications theory, structural linguistics, and anthropology, Gregotti sought to synthesize this diverse material within the architect's domain of competence.

The scale of several of Gregotti's subsequent projects, notably a winning competition design for the new University of Calabria campus at Cosenza (1974), permitted him to test his ideas. Rejecting the monolithic megastructure for the spatial limits of fixed, finite volumes, he sought to infuse his forms with a sense of their own artificiality in the landscape and of the geographic "modification" they performed. In an essay of 1982, "L'architettura dell'ambiente," written shortly after succeeding Tomás Maldonado as editor of *Casabella*, Gregotti returned to his abiding theme, describing the relation of the building to the site as the "essence of architectural work."

Published as "Architettura, ambiente, natura," in Vittorio Gregotti, Il territorio dell' architettura *(Milan: Feltrinelli, 1966), pp. 92–94. Revised from the introduction to "La forma del territorio," special issue of* Edilizia moderna, *no. 87–88 (1966), pp. 1–11. Courtesy of the author and Giangiacomo Feltrinelli Editore.*

Architecture, Environment, Nature
Vittorio Gregotti

[…] it appears clear that the problem of the formal structuring of the anthropogeographic environment compels a revision of the concept of nature as a value as it has been constituted in the tradition of modern architecture: that is, both as social wealth to be redistributed, and as a value by which to calibrate the very meaning of constructive activity as growth and process. These two extreme positions can be characterized on the one hand by Le Corbusier's idea of a nature that enters into the city by means of architecture, admirably represented not only in the Plan Voisin but above all in some extraordinary "geographic" sketches like those for Rio de Janeiro and São Paulo; and on the other hand by Frank Lloyd Wright in the theoretical argument of *Living City* and the project for Broadacre City, where city and countryside are two inseparable factors subject to laws of creativity that are organic in nature.[1]

Nature has successively been for man an indomitable force from which to defend himself, mother and irrational enemy, unknown fury; and alternatively unknown benefactress from which it has been necessary to obtain favors. Above all it has coincided with the earth, with the ground, as producer of direct sustenance in confrontation with the community that has occupied that ground, thus becoming a measure of fertility, a stable bond between inhabitant and place; in this sense, agriculture has been the fundamental means of regulating and assigning a rational form to nature. Finally, in the industrial age, as man proceeded to excavate the land in order to extract resources, production and consumption have been distanced from the place; technological exploitation constructs and erects according to its own rationality and relations, according to aims whose outcome is always other than the circumstance in which they arise.

To combat nature or to "enter into" it to the point of penetration; to grasp its dialectical aspects with respect to concentration; to order it geometrically, or to make of it, in cultivating one's garden, ideal nature, a chosen cosmological precinct, earthly paradise, nature propitious to human living as against wild nature; or pedagogically to invoke it as mirror of truth and goodness of man—these are attitudes to which have corresponded, each in turn, precise and differentiated architectural responses.

This idea of the landscape as total environmental aggregation which we have sought to offer to architecture in this book should impel us, rather than toward conservation or reconstruction of separate natural values, toward a recognition of the materiality of the integral anthropogeographical environment as operable and continuously able to be subjected to intentional actions, and should refer us to its total usability as an indispensable value, recognizable as an environmental structure transcending that of a cultural model. It is a matter, in part, of questioning technological values as fundamental to the image of one's surroundings, in order to repropose, on the other hand, their integral physicality, the living body of nature in which we take part, as communication and recognition of new possibilities. It is not a matter of seeking the construction of a physical environment from which to influence or direct human behavior; we wish simply to render the physical environment more available.

The means for defining the modes of this usability can in the most general way perhaps be provided by anthropology as the general science of man, capable of bringing together sociological, ethnological, and psychological elements in their various meanings and of founding a thematics of human behavior, of strategizing man's desire of expansion beyond the surface of things.[2] The task that this discipline of ours will have to face in this perspective remains largely to be investigated: above all it will have to be a task of clarification and reduction, aiming at the simplification, schematization, and unification of terminology, of symbologies of representation, of design procedures.[3] It will have to proceed from extensive experimental research, concretely based in design, to found on experience communicable schemes of behavior. And at the same time it will have to search to contradict those same results by confronting them continuously with the dialectic of history: as always the construction of the scheme must arise together with the hope of its future contestation.

Notes

1.   Le Corbusier, *Manière de penser l'urbanisme* (Paris: Denoël, 1946); Frank Lloyd Wright, *Living City* (New York: Horizon Press, 1958).

2.   Beyond the appendixes of Kevin Lynch's *The Image of the City* (Cambridge, Mass.: MIT Press, 1960) cited earlier, not very many theoretical or historical works on architecture approach the problem from this point of view: several chapters (in other respects very debatable) of E. A. Gutkind's book *Revolution of Environment* (London: K. Paul, Trench, Trubner and Company, 1946); the essay "L'Analisi anthropologica del paesaggio" by Paolo Caruso in *Edilizia Moderna* 87–88 (1966); and a few other things. Extremely rich and of enormous interest, however, is the material offered by anthropology. Here we have consulted Marcel Mauss, *Esquisse d'une théorie générale de la magie* (Paris: Presses Universitaires de France, 1950), in particular the essay on the gift; Claude Lévi-Strauss, *Anthropologie structurale* (Paris: Plon, 1958), *La Pensée sauvage* (Paris: Plon, 1962), and *Tristes tropiques* (Paris: Plon, 1955); and Lucien Lévy-Bruhl, *La Mentalité primitive*, 15th ed. (Paris: Presses Universitaires de France, 1960).

3.   An interesting system of notation is, for example, the one proposed by Lawrence Halprin in his book *Cities* (New York: Reinhold Publishing Corporation, 1963) and elaborated in a recent article in the July 1965 issue of *Progressive Architecture,* where he proposes a system (much inspired by modern dance and music) that he calls "Motation" to notate movement in urban structures—a type of symbolic scenography of the visible in its elements of sequence (horizontal signs, vertical signs, times, and distances being the four parameters). See also in this regard the report of an attempt at an "urbanography" in the April 1966 issue of *Progressive Architecture;* and finally Paul Spreiregen, "Guide Lines for the Visual Survey," *AIA Journal,* April 1963.

object in motion. Even something fixed, like a work of architecture, when set down in the constantly metamorphosing city, is part of growth, change, and metabolism. All design methods posit understanding of the section revealed by the severance (decision) at a certain point in time. They are all, therefore, related to concrete acts. The designer must attempt to foresee from the present moment the ultimate form of the object he is designing. The ultimate condition is the point of origin to which all things return.

The city as virtual structure

In terms of urban design, my image of ruins, while related to various elements of the actual city, ultimately is separate from them. It is a product of the imagination, a created, virtual structure that I have cast into the process of transformation occurring in the actual city.

Certain approaches are necessary in order to give this virtual structure actual form. One of them is abstraction; that is, the creation of a new urban concept born solely of the imagination. In my virtual city, residential spaces can be established in the air, over the sea, or under the ground. They are all mutually balanced and movable. Distance is lost. Labor is transformed to play. Production and consumption are synonymous. For the sake of maintaining this kind of utopia, destruction must be rationalized. This city is a vision by a visionary designer who fills it entirely with his own vocabulary items. This work is lonely, like the work of Buckminster Fuller, who forty years ago introduced his Dymaxion to the world for the sake of giving technological expression to ultimates of universal compositional principles. His geodesic dome settled on earth suddenly like an immense unidentified flying object. The thought behind it was discontinuous with traditional continuity.

There is no point in discussing here Kafka's interpretation of the castle in his novel of the same name. I interpret it to mean the city of today. It is a virtual image, a space of the imagination. The land surveyor is never able to return to the castle. Even if he managed to get inside, he would be unable to survey it. Only uncertain, unreliable signals reach him by telephone, the sole medium of communication with the lord of the castle. The total pattern producing these vague, random signals seems analogous with a human brain and is an organic entity. In other words, it is something like the modern urban structure covered as it is with various communications networks.

Since it is an imaginary mechanism, the castle has an imaginary spatial system that is easy to theorize. If it can be analyzed as an analogue, it might be possible to actualize it by means of systems analysis.

But for us, the virtual city ruled by codes is not something to view from afar, as the villagers view Kafka's castle. In a confused way it fits down on the expanding actual city. We experience it in daily-life spaces. Sometimes we are perplexed by it and require not the old laws of perspective, but a new surveying technique in order to decode its double structure (in different terms, to actualize it). Though distance is lost, though material objects have lost their meaning, we must nonetheless search for a new surveying method to come to grips with the invisible objects confronting us. And this will enable us to extract another approach. In other words, by means of systems analysis, which we are beginning to be able to command, we will create a set system from urban spaces in which groups of code elements float in suspension.

The various spatial compositional elements are reduced to codes, and attention is paid solely to their relations. The computer is transformed into a range-finder. But absolute distance disappears as the systems themselves become units of measurement. Instead of being represented in terms of perspective, space becomes a code-sprinkled schema. The observer's eye is not turned on external positions accepted as absolute but is swept inside the object and pluralized. As long as they are systematized, operations can be tied in with computers. At this stage, the city begins to be reorganized as a system model. Probably cybernetics will be the basis for this reorganization.

Before going on with my main theme—the pursuit of urban space supported by cybernetics—I should like to compare the condition today with the one prevailing in the 1920s, the honeymoon period of modern urban planning. During the fifty years that have passed since then, an absolute change in appearance has taken place before us. Rapid technological developments have fundamentally altered the urban situation and our ways of conforming to it.

From coordination to simulation

At the initial stage of urban mechanization, many visionaries produced city plans. By 1920, all of the elements and machines composing the city today were already available, if only in imperfect form: the railway, the automobile, the elevator, and—still experimentally—horizontal pedestrian conveyor belts. All kinds of proposals from fantasy to practical innovation were advanced, and all of them shared one profound inspiration: mechanical technology, just then starting to evolve. Some of the most important visionary plans of the time include Antonia Sant' Elia's Città Nuova; Bruno Taut's Alpine Architecture, gleaming like crystal on the tops of the Alps; Frederick Kiesler's Space City, with its infinite development possibilities; the immense horizontal and vertical structures of the constructivist city by Iakov Chernikhov and others; and Theo van Doesburg's multilevel Transportation City. Though none of them was intended for actualization, all of these plans were translations of space made possible by technical advances into mechanical city terms. With at least some elements of practical possibility, they all offered actual images of a new set of circumstances. Theoretical abstraction took place parallel with this visionary planning, as Le Corbusier's metaphorical definition of a house as a machine for living reveals.

The metaphor of the machine involves analyzing the whole into component parts, assigning each part a function, and then reassembling all functions. It was assumed that the same kind of compositional principle could be applied to the city. The *Athens Charter,* the result of years of research conducted by CIAM (formed in 1928), is filled with functionalist urban planning images. Cities were thought to be composed of four functions: daily life, work, relaxation, and circulation. And urban design too was controlled by these functions. An organic image was posited from the outset, and all efforts were directed toward it. Design process was concentrated entirely on the organization and coordination of elements or on the discovery of a structure to serve as an assembly theory. Many vocabulary items were worked out to conform with such efforts.

Theories of composition and integration dominated the mechanical period. The practical condition making their dominating influence possible was industrialization, the nucleus of this was mass production. Ford Motors's assembly line became the accepted standard. The Taylor system was introduced completely into architecture. The use of production models was investigated, and coordination was a major topic of discussion. Innovations and increases in production rapidly filled cities with machine-made products.

The course of urban design, according to my system, can be classified into four stages:

1. The substantial stage, in which direct connections are made between architectural forms and urban planning;

2. The functional stage, based on abstract principles developed by CIAM;

3. The structural stage, which we first began to notice in the 1950s;

4. The semiotic, or symbolic, stage, which we are only beginning to develop now.

Technological developments over the past fifty years have been the necessary conditions for a shift like the above. As the functionalist and structuralist stages were directly linked with mechanical production theories, so the semiotic stage has evolved from electronics theories. Mass production was made possible by the assembly line; and computers have made possible feedback channels. Coordination of disorganized, fragmentary products will be replaced by simulation, establishing various different kinds of models. The results of this transition are certain to alter the major themes of urban design. In this connection Marshall McLuhan made the following interesting suggestion about electronic music in relation to traditional music:

"With the electronic musical instrument, any tone can be made available in any intensity for any length of time. Note that the older symphony orchestra was, by comparison, a machine of separate instruments that *gave the effect of organic unity*. With the electronic instrument, one starts with organic unity as an immediate effect of perfect synchronization. This makes the attempt to create the effect of organic unity quite pointless. Electronic music must seek other goals."[1]

Through the medium of the musical instrument, according to McLuhan, electronic speed-up transforms the goals of art. A rupture similar to the one between traditional and electronic music can be seen preceding what I call the semiotic, or symbolic, stage of thought on urban design.

This is no doubt connected with the controlling power of simulation through the medium of the computer. The elements of urban composition are no longer judged in terms solely of external form but are understood on the basis of the combinations of totally invisible systems. Simulation, then, is first setting up a model of a city containing innumerable abstract systems and then proceeding to work out hypothetical conditions on the basis of a comparison of this model with reality. Today's construction of virtual cities through simulation is entirely different from the fantasy and utopian plans of the twenties. Now impractical, fantastic city models can be produced only through the systems process. And, even if such a model is totally disparate and incompatible with urban reality, once it has been expressed as a model, simulation becomes possible. This means that, through computers, its possibilities become linked with the possibility of flow into the actual city. Under such conditions, considerations of totality, creation of visual order, and formal unity lose significance. But all kinds of cities can be planned: City on the Sea, City in the Air, Labyrinth City, City for the Dead, and so on. In the process of expressing these ideas in models and manipulating them so that they overlap with the real city, the designer acts as a pilot and must not be swayed by his own fixed, preconceived concepts, since he is dealing with constant mutual response between reality and hypothesis. His city designing resembles push-button warfare.

Cybernetic environment

Though I may be jumping to conclusions, I suspect that urban spaces—including, of course, architectural spaces—will be of the following nature. The conditions below must be developed as future design themes, but they can be found existing in the city right now.

1. The environment will be enveloped in a protective membrane for the sake of preserving definite, balanced conditions;

2. Spaces will be extensively interchangeable;

3. The environment will include a wide variety of movable equipment;

4. A man-machine system will be developed;

5. This system will possess a self-instructing feedback channel.

Although, in the invisible city, the value of human sight will diminish, the five senses will be more greatly stimulated than they are in the city of today. Now that the age of generating city forms has passed out of its range of responsibility, urban design must expand its field by concentrating on invisible systems, in which technology and planning overlap. From this standpoint, it is clear that the conditions outlined above become proper objects of design work.

In more concise terms, urban space—an extremely abstract term—is a place where human beings can support an environment for city-style living through the full application of modern electronic technology. The five conditions above are the necessary characteristics of such an environment, defined in urban-design terms.

This environment is, as Edward Hall says, a space for the transmission of the various communications and information processes supporting modern culture; as Marshall McLuhan says, something that instantaneously involves human beings; from the systems-engineering viewpoint, the assembly of all events embodying changing systems; in terms of art, a work that, as Alan Kaprow says, all people, willy-nilly, must be part of; and, finally, the place of active relations arising among human beings and their surroundings. These approaches—from practically all fields—to the concept of environment reveal the kinds of work and thought now being devoted to general experiments on the invisible parts of the city.

For me, the modern city is a nest of invisibilities, a place, like the labyrinth in *Through the Looking Glass,* where it is impossible to grasp the things that fly out toward one. It is still impossible to know its true form or to make forecasts about the future behind the looking glass. Cybernetics lies at the foundation of the predicted spaces accompanying the five conditions. The space itself can be called a cybernetics environment. Adopting this attitude may provide an Ariadne's thread to lead us out of the maze of the city interior.

Note

1.   Marshall McLuhan, *Understanding Media: The Extensions of Man* (New York: McGraw Hill, 1964).

1966

Claude Parent, an architect closely associated with sculptors and artists in France during the 1950s and 1960s, and **Paul Virilio**, a young painter and self-described "architect-urbanist," began their collaboration in 1963 with a design for a bunker-shaped *béton brut* church at Nevers. Two different tendencies converged in their work at this date.

One was the idea of architecture as sculpture. This brought Le Corbusier's

64–67 postwar call for an urban-monumental synthesis of the major arts together with some recent manifestations of a more individualistic or expressionist nature— among them, Frederick Kiesler's Endless House, Frank Lloyd Wright's scheme

308–13 for the Guggenheim Museum, Oscar Niemeyer's buildings in Brazil, and Mathias Goeritz's work with Luis Barragan in Mexico, not to mention Le Corbusier's own designs for Ronchamp and the Philips pavilion at the 1958 Brussels World's Fair. Seen as a poetic approach to form and a critique of the functionalist planning

314–18 typifying the *grands ensembles* being built by the French government, the tendency acquired a strongly utopistic strain in the work of a number of French architects working outside the professional mainstream in the early 1960s. A major influence on Parent during these years was André Bloc, originator of Groupe Espace (an organization founded in 1951 on the premise of an integration of the arts), author of the book *De la sculpture à l'architecture* (1964), and editor of *L'Architecture d'Aujourd'hui*. Parent also collaborated with the artists Nicolas Schöffer, with whom he elaborated a theory of the "spatial-dynamic" city in the 1950s, Yves Klein, and Jean Tinguely. Virilio, for his part, fascinated by military planning and the spatio-temporal implications of geopolitical organization, began in 1958 to study abandoned World War II bunkers along the Atlantic coast. Observing children playing inside the massive, cryptlike forms that were stranded on the beaches at inclined angles because of the erosion of the dunes, he noted how their tilted geometry produced a vertiginous sense of disequilibrium. This gave him an intuition of the power of sculptural space not predicated on the right angle.

The second tendency affecting Parent and Virilio's work, which emerged from the then widespread discourse on mobility, open form, and flexibility

181–83 initiated by Team 10 as a critique of CIAM urbanism. It centered around the multilevel urban megastructure, an idea that reached its peak around 1960 in

325–34, 319–24 Japan in the projects of Kenzo Tange and the Metabolists, and in France with

273–75 schemes by Yona Friedman, Paul Maymont, and others for "spatial cities." A project by Parent of this date, *Villes cônes éclatées* (1960), was no less total an urban vision, but it challenged the technoscientific bent of the other proposals by predicating movement not on transformable equipment but on perceptual shifts in the inhabitant's position and orientation along the sloping sides of its monumental conic forms.

After their collaboration at Nevers, Virilio's and Parent's respective research on perceptual psychology and the experience of unstable spaces led them jointly to elaborate a "theory of of the oblique." In 1966, as its "permanent manifesto," they launched a journal called *Architecture Principe*, from which the following statement by Virilio is taken. The publication ran for nine issues in 1966. The title was intended to convey the idea that architecture involved a disciplined application of theoretical principles rather than gratuitous acts of creative expression. The concept of oblique architecture derived from a critique of the way horizontal and vertical organization separated architecture from urbanism, canalizing movement around built obstacles. Utilization of the oblique plane, they argued, could permit "habitable circulation," with movement and housing sectionally integrated in a unitary artificial landscape. The result, radicalizing the classic Corbusian elements of ramps, architectural promenade, and roof terrace into a vast sculptural ensemble, was explicitly monumental.

As such, their work elicited criticism at a conference on experimental architecture held in 1966 in Folkestone, England, to which they were invited along with Archigram and other radical groups. This caused them to be satirized as "Prix de Romists of cosmic thought" by left-wing students at the Ecole des Beaux-Arts. Parent and Virilio defended themselves, claiming that the "total communication" afforded by their collective urban form and the psychophysical "potentialism" of occupying an inclined plane overcame the fixed architectural and social relationships inherent in traditional static structures.

365–69
456–58

Temperamentally and politically different, Parent and Virilio's collaboration soon parted company. In 1968 a conflict resulted from Parent's "aristocratic" attitude toward the student uprisings. Virilio took an active role, affixing a famous poster to the door of the Sorbonne chapel carrying a slogan borrowed from *Architecture Principe* 8: "Imagination seizes power." In 1970 the collaboration ended when Virilio chose not to participate with Parent in an exposition on the oblique at the Venice Biennale, citing his desire to avoid "official manifestations." However, he continued to advance the thesis. Appointed director of the Ecole Spéciale d'Architecture in the academic reforms following 1968, he lectured on the oblique for a number of years and in 1975 staged an exhibition on "bunker archaeology" (the subject of *Architecture Principe* 7) at the Museum of Decorative Arts in Paris. Parent, though largely giving up theoretical activity for built practice after the 1960s, published a book in 1970 entitled *Vivre à l'oblique* and another in 1981, *Entrelacs de l'oblique*.

"Architecture is a form of consciousness," Virilio and Parent wrote in September 1968 in *L'Architecture d'Aujourd'hui*, explaining their concept. "The submission to the idea of stability and vertical equilibrium is still an absolute in architecture, while in fields like philosophy or economic theory this vocabulary has long been left behind in favor of ideas of transference, displacement, and thus successive instability . . . stability is nothing more than the image of man mentally subjected to the magnetism of the earth. From now on this representation is anachronistic. It can only hinder our imagination." This rhetoric would have an echo in the 1980s in another radical movement. Amalgamating ideas from the literary-philosophical thought of Deconstruction and the dynamic imagery of Russian constructivism, "Deconstructivist" architects would posit forms intended to subvert architecture's conventional relation to the ground plane. Virilio himself, whom Parent once described affectionately as a "new Cassandra," would go on to become an important theorist of postmodern culture and urbanism. For more on Parent and Virilio's work in the 1960s, see Michel Ragon's *Claude Parent: Monographie critique d'un architecte* (1982) and the chapter entitled "Entre architecture-sculpture et pluridisciplinarité" in Jacques Lucan's *France: Architecture 1965–1988* (1989).

From Architecture Principe *1 (February 1966), unpaged [1–2]. Courtesy of the author* .

The Oblique Function
Paul Virilio

If physical nature is characterized by periodicity, the historical world is defined by polarity.

Moreover different types of human groupings have been of major importance in the successive modes of urbanization and thus in the origin of architectural forms.

This process of polarization (whose development need not be complicated here by more specific analysis) has, up to this point, accommodated the addition of individual dwellings in the town, then the addition of dwelling units in the apartment block, this then multiplied in all the apartment blocks of the city—each of these successive entities undergoing a change in volume, followed by universalization.

But these different modifications have above all resulted from an element that for a long time has wrongly been considered the effect of the others: orientation in space.

If the village was characterized by horizontality—a conquest of the soil broken only by the vertical aspiration of the church or chateau—the city has been but a succession of verticalities aimed at social conquest, New York being a culmination of this spatial direction.

If all the attempts to arrive at a new type of urban entity have failed, the garden city of the nineteenth century as well as the satellite city, it is because those who have been responsible for them have disregarded the predominance of an original axis of elevation as motive force for the other components of the whole.

They have been fascinated by the additive aspect of human groupings, which is conditioned by the barbarism of industrial civilization in the process of coming into being.

Thus an urbanism of subjugation has succeeded an urbanism of reaction.

Important as are elements of number and type, it is now proven that they are powerless to realize a new mode of urbanization by themselves.

And we are now confronted by the overriding necessity to accept as a historical fact the end of the vertical as axis of elevation, the end of the horizontal as permanent plan, in order to defer to the oblique axis and the inclined plan, which realize all the necessary conditions for the creation of a new urban order and permit as well a total reinvention of the architectural vocabulary.

This tipping of the plane must be understood for what it is: the third spatial possibility of architecture.

Above: Interior detail. Below: Habitat on inclined plane.

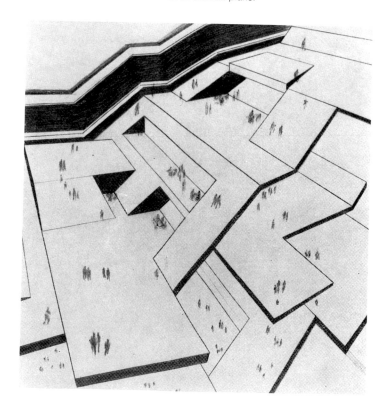

1967

"Eiffel saw his tower in the form of a serious object, rational, useful; men return it to him in the form of a great baroque dream which quite naturally touches on the borders of the irrational . . . architecture is always dream and function, expression of a utopia and instrument of a convenience." **Roland Barthes**'s essay of 1964, "The Eiffel Tower," was an object lesson for architects in reading urban form. In an application of post-Saussurean linguistics to the city, Barthes interpreted the great modern monument of Paris as the iconic center of a reciprocal optical system, at once receptacle of all gazes in the city and universal point of view. As such, it functioned as a signifier free of any fixed referent, a pure and empty sign, "ineluctable because it *means everything.*"

It was the tower's very functionlessness that made it so powerful as a symbol, in Barthes's view, an insight he would later transpose to an interpretation of Japanese culture as an "empire of signs," indecipherable (to the Western eye), and therefore triggering a similar exorbitance of metaphor. Tokyo, for Barthes, occupied by the lacuna of the royal palace, was a case like the Eiffel Tower of an empty center—an absent presence, seductively waiting to be filled.

402–7

Barthes's theory of the "infinitely metaphorical nature of urban discourse," a function of the city's complex multiplicity and therefore inherent resistance to fixed relations of meaning, made the city a privileged semiological context, "a poem," as he puts it in the essay that follows. But the "language of the city" went beyond a mere analogy to speech or writing, Barthes argued. In the broader sense of semiology as a general discourse concerning signification, the city represented a concrete inscription of the collective unconscious in space, a structure of signs and their relationships susceptible to precise linguistic analysis.

With functionalism's displacement, the intense interest in semiology on the part of architects in the 1960s—stimulated by the writings of Barthes, Umberto Eco in Italy, Noam Chomsky in the United States, and others—suggested a renewed search for a codifiable system of architectural meaning. It also accorded with an intellectual shift in culture generally: signification now was seen as conventional rather than natural. The efforts to interpret architecture as a linguistic structure led in various directions, running the gamut from perceptual and semantic studies like those of Kevin Lynch on the "readability" of urban form (closer to communications theory than semiology) and Christian Norberg-Schulz's *Intentions in Architecture* (1965); to more design-oriented approaches concerned with typology, morphology, and generative structures; to directly Barthesian readings like that by the Argentine architects Mario Gandelsonas and Diana Agrest theorizing architecture as a field of knowledge production.

379–88, 399–401

Yet Barthes himself had already made the move beyond structuralism to poststructuralism in his textual reading of the city. Like Jacques Derrida, his discovery of the empty center and the absence of fixed signification led him to a celebration of the free play of the signifier and its endless deferrals of meaning. The city, in its role as quintessential site of social interchange, of encounters with the other, became suffused with an "erotic dimension." For the Barthesian interpreter—no more a social scientist but a *flâneur,* an "avant-garde reader"— the city was an experience much like that which Barthes was later to describe in *The Pleasure of the Text* (1973) as a "text of bliss."

From a colloquium at the University of Naples Institute of Architectural History in 1967. Originally published in Op. cit. *10 (1967) in Italian. First published in French in* L'Architecture d'Aujourd'hui *153 (December 1970). Published in English in Roland Barthes,* The Semiotic Challenge, *trans. Richard Howard (New York: Hill and Wang, 1988), pp. 191–201. Courtesy of Hill and Wang.*

Semiology and Urbanism
Roland Barthes

The subject of this discussion concerns a certain number of the problems of urban semiology.

But I must add that anyone who wants to sketch a semiotics of the city must be at once a semiologist (a specialist in signs), a geographer, a historian, an urbanist, an architect, and probably a psychoanalyst. Since it is obvious that this is not my case— as a matter of fact, I am none of all this except, barely, a semiologist—the reflections I shall present to you are those of an amateur, in the etymological sense of the word: an amateur of signs, one who love signs, an amateur of cities, one who loves the city. For I love both the city and signs. And this double love (which is probably, as a matter of fact, only one love) impels me to believe, perhaps with a certain presumption, in the possibility of a semiotics of the city. On what conditions or rather with what precautions and what preliminaries will an urban semiotics be possible?

This is the theme of the reflections I shall present. I should like first of all to remind you of a very familiar thing which will serve as a point of departure: human space in general (and not only urban space) has always been a signifying space. Scientific geography and especially modern cartography can be considered as a kind of obliteration, a censorship objectivity has imposed upon signification (an objectivity which is a form like any other of the image-repertoire). And, before speaking of the city, I should like to recall several phenomena of the cultural history of the West, more specifically of Greek antiquity: the human habitat, the "oekoumène," as we can glimpse it through the first maps of the Greek geographers: Anaximander, Hecataeus, or through the mental cartography of a man like Herodotus, constitutes a veritable discourse, with its symmetries, its oppositions of sites, with its syntax and its paradigms. A map of the world by Herodotus, graphically realized, is constructed like a language, like a sentence, like a poem, on oppositions: hot countries and cold countries; then on the opposition between men on the one hand, and monsters and chimeras on the other, etc.

If we turn from geographical space to urban space, strictly speaking, I shall remind you that the notion of *Isonomy*, created for sixth-century Athens by a man like Cleisthenes, is a truly structural conception by which the center alone is privileged, since all the citizens have relations with it which are at the same time symmetrical and reversible.[1] At this period, the conception of the city was exclusively a signifying one, for the utilitarian conception of an urban distribution based on functions and usages, which incontestably prevails in our day, will appear much later on. I wanted to point out this historical relativism in the conception of signifying spaces.

Finally, it is in a recent past that a structuralist like Lévi-Strauss has produced, in *Tristes Tropiques*, a form of urban semiology, even if on a reduced scale, apropos of a Bororo village whose space he has studied according to an essentially semantic approach.

It is strange that, parallel to these strongly signifying conceptions of inhabited space, the theoretical elaborations of the urbanists have not hitherto granted, if I am not mistaken, anything but a very reduced status to problems of signification.[2] Of course, there are exceptions; several writers have discussed the city in terms of signification. One of the authors who has best expressed this essentially signifying nature of urban space is, I believe, Victor Hugo. In *Notre-Dame de Paris,* Hugo has written a very fine chapter, of an extremely subtle intelligence, "This will kill that"; *this,* which is to say the book, *that,* which is to say the monument. By expressing himself thus, Hugo gives evidence of a rather modern way of conceiving the monument and the city, actually as a writing, as an inscription of man in space. This chapter of Hugo's is devoted to the rivalry between two modes of writing, writing in stone and writing on paper. Moreover, this theme can find its current version in the remarks on writing by a philosopher like Jacques Derrida. Among present-day urbanists, signification is virtually unmentioned: one name stands out, therefore, that of the American Kevin Lynch, who seems to be closest to these problems of urban semantics insofar as he is concerned with conceiving the city in the very terms of the perceiving consciousness, i.e., of identifying the image of the city in the readers of that city. But in reality, Lynch's researches, from the semantic point of view, remain quite ambiguous: on the one hand, there is a whole vocabulary of signification in his work (for example, he grants a good deal of attention to the *readability* of the city, and this is a very important notion for us) and, as a good semanticist, he has the sense of *discrete units:* he has tried to rediscover in urban space the discontinuous units which, within limits, somewhat resemble phonemes and semantemes. He calls these units paths, enclosures, districts, intersections, points of reference. These are categories of units which might readily become semantic categories. But on the other hand, despite this vocabulary, Lynch has a conception of the city which remains more gestaltist than structural.

Aside from those authors who explicitly entertain the notion of a semantics of the city, we note a growing consciousness of the functions of symbols in urban space. In several studies of urbanism based on quantitative estimations and on motivation-research, we see appearing—in spite of everything, even if this is only for memory's sake—the purely qualitative motif of symbolization frequently used even today to explain other phenomena. We find for example in urbanism a relatively common technique: simulation; now, the technique of simulation leads, even if it is used in a rather narrow and empirical spirit, to a more thorough investigation of the concept of *model,* which is a structural or at the very least a prestructuralist concept.

At another stage of these studies in urbanism, the demand for signification appears. We gradually discover that there exists a kind of contradiction between signification and another order of phenomena, and that consequently signification possesses an irreducible specificity. For instance, certain urbanists, or certain of those investigators who are studying urban planning, are obliged to note that, in certain cases, there exists a conflict between the functionalism of a part of the city, let us say of a neighborhood or a district, and what I should call its semantic content (its semantic power). Hence they have noted with a certain ingenuousness (but perhaps we must begin with ingenuousness) that Rome presents a permanent conflict between the functional necessities of modern life and the semantic burden communicated to the city by its history. And this conflict between signification and function constitutes the despair of the urbanists. There also exists a conflict between signification and reason, or at least between signification and that calculating reason which wants all the elements of a city to be uniformly recuperated by planning, whereas it is increasingly obvious that a city is a fabric formed not of equal elements whose functions can be inventoried, but of strong elements and nonmarked elements (we know that the opposition between the sign and the absence of sign, between the measurable degree and zero degree, constitutes one of the major processes in the elaboration of signification). From all evidence, each city possesses this kind of rhythm; Kevin Lynch has noted as much: there exists in every city, from the moment when it is truly inhabited by man, and made by him, that basic rhythm of signification which is opposition, alternation and juxtaposition of marked and nonmarked elements. Lastly, there exists an ultimate conflict between signification and reality itself, at least between signification and that reality of objective geography, the reality of maps. Investigations made by psychosociologists have shown that, for example, two neighborhoods are contiguous if we rely on the map, i.e., on "reality," on objectivity, whereas, from the moment they receive two different significations, they are radically split in the image of the city: signification is experienced in complete opposition to objective data.

The city is a discourse, and this discourse is actually a language: the city speaks to its inhabitants, we speak to our city, the city where we are, simply by inhabiting it, by traversing it, by looking at it. Yet, the problem is to extract an expression like "language of the city" from the purely metaphorical stage. It is metaphorically very easy to speak of *the language of the city* as we speak of the language of the cinema or of the language of flowers. The real scientific leap will be achieved when we can speak of the language of the city without metaphor. And we can say that this is precisely what happened to Freud when he first spoke of the language of dreams, emptying this expression of its metaphorical meaning in order to give it real meaning. We too, we must confront this problem: how to shift from metaphor to analysis when we speak of the language of the city? Once again, it is to the specialists in the urban phenomenon that I am referring, for even if they are quite remote from these problems of urban semantics, they have nonetheless already noted (I am quoting the results of one investigation) that "the usable data in the social sciences offer a form poorly adapted to an integration into models." Indeed, if we have difficulty inserting into a model the urban data supplied us by psychology, sociology, geography, demography, this is precisely because we lack a final technique, that of symbols. Consequently, we need a new scientific energy in order to transform such data, to shift from metaphor to the description of signification, and it is here that semiology (in the broadest sense of the word) may by a still unpredictable development afford us some assistance. It is not my intention to evoke here the procedures for discovering an urban semiology. It is likely that such procedures would consist in dissociating the urban text into units, then in distributing these units into formal classes, and, thirdly, in finding the rules of combination and of transformation for these units and for these models. I shall confine myself to three observations which have no direct relation with the city but which might usefully orient us toward an urban semiology, insofar as they draw up a balance sheet for current semiology and take account of the fact that, in recent years, the semiological "landscape" is no longer the same.

The first observation is that "symbolism" (which must be understood as a general discourse concerning signification) is no longer conceived nowadays, at least as a general rule, as a regular correspondence between signifiers and signifieds. In other words, one notion of semantics which was fundamental some years ago has become outdated; this is the lexicon notion, i.e., that of a set of lists of corresponding signifieds and signifiers. This erosion of the notion of lexicon is to be found in many sectors of research. First of all, there is the distributive semantics of Chomsky's disciples, such as Katz and Fodor, who have launched an attack in force against the lexicon. If we turn from the realm of linguistics to that of literary criticism, we see that the thematic criticism which has prevailed for some fifteen or twenty years, at least in France, and which has formed the essential part of the studies which we know as the new criticism, is nowadays limited, remodeled to the detriment of the signifieds which that criticism proposed to decipher. In the realm of psychoanalysis, finally, we can no longer speak of a term-to-term symbolism; this is obviously the dead part of Freud's work: a psychoanalytic lexicon is no longer conceivable. All this has cast a certain credit on the word "symbol," for this term has always (till today) suggested that the signifying relation was based on the signified, on the presence of the signified. Personally, I use the word "symbol" as referring to a syntagmatic and/or paradigmatic but no longer semantic signifying organization: we must make a very clear distinction between the semantic bearing of the symbol and the syntagmatic or paradigmatic nature of this same symbol.

Similarly it would be an absurd undertaking to attempt to elaborate a lexicon of the significations of the city by putting sites, neighborhoods, functions on one side, and significations on the other, or rather by putting on one side the sites articulated as signifiers and on the other the functions articulated as signifieds. The list of the functions that a city's neighborhoods can assume has been known for a long time; there are by and large some thirty functions for a neighborhood (at least for a neighborhood of the center-city: a zone which has been closely studied from the sociological point of view). This list can of course be completed, enriched, refined, but it will constitute only an extremely elementary level for semiological analysis, a level which will probably have to be revised subsequently: not only because of the weight and pressure exerted by history, but because, precisely, the signifieds are like mythical beings, of an extreme imprecision, and because at a certain moment they always become the signifiers of something else: the signifieds pass, the signifiers remain. The hunt for the signified can therefore constitute only a provisional undertaking. The role of the signified, when we manage to isolate it, is only to afford us a sort of testimony as to a specific state of the signifying distribution. Further, we must note that we attribute an ever-growing importance to the *empty signified,* to the empty site of the signified. In other words, the elements are understood as signifiers more by their own correlative position than by their content. Thus Tokyo, which is one of the most intricate urban complexes imaginable from the semantic point of view, nonetheless possesses a sort of center. But this center, occupied by the imperial palace which is surrounded by a deep moat and hidden by verdure, is experienced as an empty center. As a more general rule, the studies made of the urban core of different cities have shown that the central point of the center of the city (every city possesses a center), which we call the "solid core," does not constitute the culminating point of any particular activity, but a kind of empty "heart" of the community's image of the center. Here too we have a somehow empty place which is necessary to the organization of the rest of the city.

The second remark is that symbolism must be defined essentially as the world of signifiers, of correlations, and above all of correlations which can never be imprisoned in a full signification, in a final signification. Henceforth, from the point of view of descriptive technique, the distribution of elements, i.e., of signifiers, "exhausts" semantic discovery. This is true for the Chomskian semantics of Katz and Fodor and even for the analyses of Lévi-Strauss which are based on the clarification of a relation which is no longer analogical but homological (this is a demonstration made in his book on totemism, one rarely cited). Hence we discover that, if we want to produce the semiology of the city, we must intensify, more meticulously, the signifying division. For this, I appeal to my experience as an amateur of cities. We know that, in certain cities, there exist certain spaces which present a very extended specialization of functions; this is true, for example, of the Oriental *souk* where one street is reserved for the tanners and another exclusively for the silversmiths; in Tokyo, certain parts of the same neighborhood are quite homogeneous from the functional point of view: we find there only bars or snack bars or places of entertainment. Yet we must go beyond this first aspect and not limit the semantic description of the city to this unit; we must try to dissociate microstructures in the same way we can isolate tiny sentence fragments within a long period; hence we must get into the habit of making a very extended analysis which will lead to these microstructures, and conversely we must accustom ourselves to a broader analysis, which will lead to macrostructures. We all know that Tokyo is a polynuclear city; it possesses several cores around five or six centers; we must learn to differentiate semantically these centers, which moreover are indicated by railroad stations. In other terms, even in this domain, the best model for the semantic study of the city will be furnished, I believe, at least at the start, by the sentence of discourse. And here we rediscover Victory Hugo's old intuition: the city is a writing; the man who moves about in the city, i.e., the city's user (which is what we all are, users of the city), is a sort of reader who, according to his obligations and his movements, samples fragments of the utterance in order to actualize them in secret. When we move about in a city, we are all in the situation of the reader of Queneau's *100,000 Million Poems,* where we can find a different poem by changing a single verse; unknown to us, we are something like that avant-garde reader when we are in a city.

Lastly, the third observation is that nowadays semiology never posits the existence of a definitive signified. Which means that the signifieds are always signifiers for others, and reciprocally. In reality, in any cultural or even psychological complex, we find ourselves confronted with infinite chains of metaphors whose signified is always recessive or itself becoming a signifier. This structure is beginning to be explored, as you know, in Lacan's psychoanalysis, and also in the study of writing, where it is postulated if it is not actually explored. If we apply these notions to the city, we shall doubtless be led to emphasize a dimension which I must say I have never seen cited, at least never clearly, in the studies and investigations of urbanism. This dimension I should call the *erotic* dimension. The eroticism of the city is the teaching which we can derive from the infinitely metaphorical nature of urban discourse. I am using this word *eroticism* in its broadest sense: it would be absurd to identify the eroticism of a city merely with the neighborhood reserved for such pleasures, for the concept of the place of pleasure is one of the stubbornest mystifications of urban functionalism; it is a functional and not a semantic notion; I am using eroticism or *sociality* here without differentiation. The city, essentially and semantically, is the site of our encounter with the other, and it is for this reason that the center is the gathering point of any city; the center-city is instituted above all by the young, the adolescent. When the latter express their image of the city, they always tend to limit, to concentrate, to condense the center; the center-city is experienced as the exchange-site of social activities and I should almost say of erotic activities in the broad sense of the term. Still better, the center-city is always experienced as the space in which certain subversive forces act and are encountered, forces of rupture, ludic forces. Play is a theme which is very often underlined in the investigations of the center; in France there is a series of investigations concerning the attraction exerted by Paris upon its suburbs, and through these investigations it has been observed that for the periphery Paris as a center was always experienced semantically as the privileged site where the other is and where we ourselves are the other, and the site where one plays. On the contrary, everything which is not the center is precisely what is not ludic space, everything which is not alterity: family, residence, identity. Naturally, especially in terms of the city, we would have to investigate the metaphorical chain, the chain which substitutes for Eros. We must especially investigate, among the major categories, other great habits of humanity, for example food and shopping, which are actually erotic activities in a consumer society. I refer once again to the example of Tokyo: the great railway stations which are the points of reference of the main neighborhoods are also great department stores. And it is certain that the Japanese railroad station, the station-as-shop, has a unique signification and that this signification is erotic: purchase or encounter. Then we would have to explore the deep images of the urban elements. For example, many investigations have emphasized the imaginary function of the *watercourse* which, in any city, is experienced as a river, a canal, a body of water. There is a relation between the road and the watercourse, and we know that the cities which offer most resistance to signification, and which moreover often present difficulties of adaptation for their inhabitants, are precisely the cities lacking water, the cities without seaside, without a body of water, without a lake, without a river, without a watercourse; all these cities offer difficulties of life, of legibility.

To conclude, I should like to say merely this: in the observations I have just made, I have not approached the problem of methodology. Why? Because, if we seek to undertake a semiology of the city, the best approach, in my opinion, as indeed for any semantic enterprise, will be a certain ingenuity on the reader's part. It will require many of us to attempt to decipher the city where we are, beginning, if necessary, with a personal report. Mustering all these readings of various categories of readers (for we have a complete range of readers, from the sedentary to the foreigner), we would thereby elaborate the language of the city. This is why I shall say that the most important thing is not so much to multiply investigations or functional studies of the city as to multiply the readings of the city, of which, unfortunately, till now, only the writers have given us some examples.

Starting from these readings, from this reconstitution of a language or of a code of the city, we might orient ourselves toward means of a more scientific nature: investigation of units, syntax, etc., but always remembering that we must never try to fix and render rigid the signifieds of the units discovered, for historically these signifieds are extremely imprecise, challengeable, and unmanageable.

Every city is somewhat constructed, created by us in the image of the galley *Argo* of which each piece was no longer an original one, yet which still remained the ship *Argo,* i.e., a group of readily legible and identifiable significations. In this attempt at a semantic approach to the city, we must try to understand the interplay of signs, to understand that any city is a structure but that we must never attempt and never hope to fill that structure.

For the city is a poem, as has often been said and as Hugo put it better than anyone, but not a classical poem, not a poem centered on a subject. It is a poem which deploys the signifier, and it is this deployment which the semiology of the city must ultimately attempt to grasp and to make sing.

Notes
1.   On Cleisthenes and Isonomy, cf. P. Leveque and P. Vidal-Naquet, *Clisthène l'Athénien* (Paris: Macula, 1983).
2.   Cf. F. Choay, *L'Urbanisme: utopie et réalités* (Paris: Editions du Seuil, 1965).

1967

The implications for architecture theory and practice of the writings of French philosopher and historian **Michel Foucault** were profound. Beginning in the 1960s with *Madness and Civilization: A History of Insanity in the Age of Reason* (first published in French in 1961, translated 1965), *The Birth of the Clinic: An Archaeology of Medical Perception* (1963, translated 1973), and *The Order of Things, An Archaeology of the Human Sciences* (1966, translated 1970), Foucault's "archaeological" project of demythifying and reconstructing the origins of modern reason and its institutions necessarily encompassed architecture, understood in its broadest possible sense as a discipline—an order of discourse—having to do with "the spatialization of knowledge." Within this perspective, the study of space, which modern philosophy in its positivistic affiliation with science had subordinated to that of time, again became crucial to understanding the distribution, circulation, and regulation of the human subject.

Working his way out of the scientific Marxism of Louis Althusser, Foucault sought to reconstitute critical theory toward a conception of knowledge that was founded on a systematic description of the material relations between history and the formation of consciousness, but no longer beholden, like previous critiques of ideology, to unmasking "truth." He elected to study the evolution of modern social order in its most "problematized" or intensified moments and contexts: moments of rupture rather than continuity, and contexts exceptional rather than normative, those in which "all the real arrangements . . . that can be found within society are at one and the same time represented, challenged, and overturned." Thus beginning from the "epistemological break"—a concept derived from Gaston Bachelard—of the Enlightenment, he focused his inquiry on the formation of modern institutions like the insane asylum, the teaching hospital, and later the prison, places where deviant or noneveryday behavior was subjected to a regime and technology of normalization. In the following paper of 1967, Foucault terms such places *heterotopias*. Distinguished from utopias by their disparate and concrete existence within reality, they represent counterarrangements that are "other" with respect to society and as such potentially liberative in their "contestation of the space in which we live."

After the political upheavals of 1968 Foucault would more explicitly link his investigation of the production of knowledge with questions of power. He would now describe his method as "genealogical" rather than archaeological, working, as he put it in a seminal essay, "Nietzsche, Genealogy, History" (1971), to establish "not the anticipatory power of meaning, but the hazardous play of dominations." Rationalism, a historical phenomenon beyond good and evil, was to be seen as both capable of producing terror through its disciplinary regime and indispensable in the evolution of human knowledge. For historians of post-Enlightenment architecture—Manfredo Tafuri and Anthony Vidler, to mention just two—Foucault's approach would have the powerful influence of an "event of thought" in the philosopher's own sense. Foucault would return specifically to questions of built space on several occasions, notably in remarks on Jeremy Bentham's Panopticon entitled "The Eye of Power" (1977).

449–45

From a paper delivered at the Centre d'études architecturales, Paris, in March 1967. Published in part in L'Architettura *150 (April 1968), pp. 822–23. Published in present version as "Des Espaces Autres" in* Architecture Mouvement Continuité *5 (October 1984), pp. 46–49. Republished in English in* Lotus International *48/49 (1985/86), pp. 9–17; and* Diacritics, *vol. 16, no. 1 (spring 1986), pp. 22–27. Translated by Jay Miskowiec. Forthcoming in M. François Ewald, ed.,* Dits et Ecrits de Michel Foucault *(Paris: Editions Gallimard). Courtesy of Editions Gallimard.*

Of Other Spaces: Utopias and Heterotopias
Michel Foucault

As is well known, the great and obsessive dread of the nineteenth century was history, with its themes of development and stagnation, crisis and cycle, the accumulation of the past, the surplus of the dead and the world threatened by cooling. The nineteenth century found the quintessence of its mythological resources in the second law of thermodynamics. Our own era, on the other hand, seems to be that of space. We are in the age of the simultaneous, of juxtaposition, the near and the far, the side by side and the scattered. A period in which, in my view, the world is putting itself to the test, not so much as a great way of life destined to grow in time but as a net that links points together and creates its own muddle. It might be said that certain ideological conflicts which underlie the controversies of our day take place between pious descendants of time and tenacious inhabitants of space. Structuralism—or at least what is lumped together under this rather too vague label—is the attempt to establish between elements that may have been split over the course of time, a set of relationships that juxtapose them, set them in opposition or link them together, so as to create a sort of shape. Actually it is not so much a question of denying time as of a certain way of dealing with what we call time and which goes by the name of history.

For one thing the space which now looms on the horizon of our preoccupations, our theories and our systems, is not an innovation in Western history, having a history of its own. Nor is it possible to deny its fatal entanglement with time. To provide a very rough outline of its history, it could be said that there was a hierarchical system of places in the Middle Ages: places that were sacred and profane, protected and, on the contrary, open and undefended, urban places and rural places (for the real life of men anyhow). In cosmological theory, supercelestial places existed, in contrast to the celestial place, opposed in its turn to the terrestrial place; there were places where things could be found because they had been shifted there by violence and there were other places where, on the contrary, things found their natural position and rest. This hierarchy, contrast, and mingling of places made up that which might, very approximately, be called medieval space. That is to say, the space of localization.

This space of localization was opened up by Galileo, for the real scandal caused by Galileo's work was not the discovery, or rediscovery, of the earth's movement around the sun, but the assertion of an infinite and infinitely open space, in which the space of the Middle Ages was to some extent dissolved. The location of a thing, in fact, was no longer anything more than a point in its movement, its rest nothing but its movement slowed down infinitely. In other words, from Galileo onward, ever since the seventeenth century, localization was replaced by extension.

Nowadays arrangement has taken over from extension, which had once replaced localization. It is defined by relationships of neighborhood between points and elements, which can be described formally as series, trees, and networks.

On the other hand, we know very well the importance of the problems of arrangements in contemporary technology: storage of information or of the partial results of a calculation in the memory of a machine; circulation of discrete elements to random outlets (automobiles, for instance, or even sounds transmitted over telephone lines); location of labeled or coded elements within a randomly divided set, or one that is classified according to univocal or multiple systems, etc.

In a still more concrete manner, the problem of position is posed for men in demographic terms. The question of the arrangement of the earth's inhabitants is not just one of knowing whether there will be enough room for all of them—a problem that is in any case of the greatest importance—but also one of knowing what are the relations of vicinity, what kind of storage, circulation, reference, and classification of human elements should take preference in this or that situation, according to the objective that is being sought. In our era, space presents itself to us in the form of patterns of ordering.

In any case, I feel that current anxiety is fundamentally concerned with space, much more than with time: the latter, probably, merely appears to us as one of the many possible patterns of distribution between elements that are scattered over space.

Now, it may be that contemporary space has not yet lost those sacred characteristics (which time certainly lost in the nineteenth century), in spite of all the techniques that assail it and the web of knowledge that allows it to be defined and formalized. Of course, a theoretical desanctification of space, for which Galileo's work gave the signal, has already occurred: it remains to be seen whether we have achieved its desanctification in practice. It may be, in fact, that our lives are still ruled by a certain number of unrelenting opposites, which institution and practice have not dared to erode. I refer here to opposites that we take for granted, such as the contrast between public and private space, family and social space, cultural and utilitarian space, the space of pleasure and the space of work—all opposites that are still actuated by a veiled sacredness.

The (immense) work of Bachelard and the descriptions of the phenomenologists have taught us that we do not live in a homogeneous and empty space, but in a space that is saturated with qualities, and that may even be pervaded by a spectral aura. The space of our primary perception, of our dreams and of our passions, holds within itself almost intrinsic qualities: it is light, ethereal, transparent, or dark, uneven, cluttered. Again, it is a space of height, of peaks, or on the contrary, of the depths of mud; space that flows, like spring water, or fixed space, like stone or crystal.

In any case, these analyses, however fundamental for contemporary thought, are primarily concerned with inner space. But it is about external space that I would like to speak now. The space in which we live, from which we are drawn out of ourselves, just where the erosion of our lives, our time, our history takes place, this space that wears us down and consumes us, is in itself heterogeneous. In other words, we do not live in a sort of a vacuum, within which individuals and things can be located, or that may take on so many different fleeting colors, but in a set of relationships that define positions which cannot be equated or in any way superimposed.

Certainly, one could undertake the description of these different arrangements, looking for the set of relationships that defines them. For instance, by describing the set of relationships that defines arrangements of transition, roads, trains (and, with regard to the latter, think of the extraordinary bundle of relations represented by something through which one passes, by means of which we pass from one point to another, and which, in its turn, has the power of passing). Through the sets of relationships that define them, one could describe arrangements where one makes a temporary halt: cafes, cinemas, beaches. It would be equally possible to define, through its network of relations, the arrangements of rest, closed or partly open, that make up the house, the bedroom, the bed, etc. . . . However I am only interested in a few of these arrangements: to be precise, those which are endowed with the curious property of being in relation with all the others, but in such a way as to suspend, neutralize, or invert the set of relationships designed, reflected, or mirrored by themselves. These spaces, which are in rapport in some way with all the others, and yet contradict them, are of two general types.

First of all, the utopias. These are arrangements which have no real space. Arrangements which have a general relationship of direct or inverse analogy with the real space of society. They represent society itself brought to perfection, or its reverse, and in any case utopias are spaces that are by their very essence fundamentally unreal.

There also exist, and this is probably true for all cultures and all civilizations, real and effective spaces which are outlined in the very institution of society, but which constitute a sort of counterarrangement, of effectively realized utopia, in which all the real arrangements, all the other real arrangements that can be found within society, are at one and the same time represented, challenged, and overturned: a sort of place that lies outside all places and yet is actually localizable. In contrast to the utopias, these places which are absolutely *other* with respect to all the arrangements that they reflect and of which they speak might be described as heterotopias. Between these two, I would then set that sort of mixed experience which partakes of the qualities of both types of location, the mirror. It is, after all, a utopia, in that it is a place without a place. In it, I see myself where I am not, in an unreal space that opens up potentially beyond its surface; there I am down there where I am not, a sort of shadow that makes my appearance visible to myself, allowing me to look at myself where I do not exist: utopia of the mirror. At the same time, we are dealing with a heterotopia. The mirror really exists and has a kind of comeback effect on the place that I occupy: starting from it, in fact, I find myself absent from the place where I am, in that I see myself in there.

Starting from that gaze which to some extent is brought to bear on me, from the depths of that virtual space which is on the other side of the mirror, I turn back on myself, beginning to turn my eyes on myself and reconstitute myself where I am in reality. Hence the mirror functions as a heterotopia, since it makes the place that I occupy, whenever I look at myself in the glass, both absolutely real—it is in fact linked to all the surrounding space—and absolutely unreal, for in order to be perceived it has of necessity to pass that virtual point that is situated down there.

As for the heterotopias in the proper sense of the word, how can we describe them? What meaning do they have? We might postulate, not a science, a now overworked word, but a sort of systematic description. Given a particular society, this would have as its object the study, analysis, description, and "reading," as it is the fashion to call it nowadays, of those different spaces, those other places, in a kind of both mythical and real contestation of the space in which we live. Such a description might be called heterotopology. Its first principle is that there is probably not a single culture in the world that is not made up of heterotopias. It is a constant feature of all human groups. It is evident, though, that heterotopias assume a wide variety of forms, to the extent that a single, absolutely universal form may not exist. In any case, it is possible to classify them into two main types. In so-called primitive societies, there is a certain kind of heterotopia which I would describe as that of crisis; it comprises privileged or sacred or forbidden places that are reserved for the individual who finds himself in a state of crisis with respect to the society or the environment in which he lives: adolescents, women during the menstrual period or in labor, the old, etc.

In our own society, these heterotopias of crisis are steadily disappearing, even though some vestiges of them are bound to survive. For instance, the boarding school in its nineteenth-century form or military service for young men has played a role of this kind, so that the first manifestations of male sexuality could occur "elsewhere," away from the family. For girls there was, up until the middle of this century, the tradition of the honeymoon, or "voyage de noces" as it is called in French, an ancestral theme. The girl's defloration could not take place "anywhere" and at that time, the train or the honeymoon hotel represented that place which was not located anywhere, a heterotopia without geographical coordinates.

Yet these heterotopias of crisis are vanishing today, only to be replaced, I believe, by others which could be described as heterotopias of deviance, occupied by individuals whose behavior deviates from the current average or standard. They are the rest homes, psychiatric clinics, and, let us be clear, prisons, in a list which must undoubtedly be extended to cover old-people's homes, in a way on the border between the heterotopia of crisis and that of deviance. This is because in a society like our own, where pleasure is the rule, the inactivity of old age constitutes not only a crisis but a deviation.

The second element of my description: over the course of its history, a society may take an existing heterotopia, which has never vanished, and make it function in a very different way. Actually, each heterotopia has a precise and well-defined function within society and the same heterotopia can, in accordance with the synchroneity of the culture in which it is located, have a different function.

Let us take, for example, the curious heterotopia of the cemetery. This is certainly an "other" place with respect to ordinary cultural spaces, and yet it is connected with all the locations of the city, the society, the village, and so on, since every family has some relative there. In Western culture, one might say that it has always existed. And yet it has undergone important changes.

Up until the end of the eighteenth century, the cemetery was located in the very heart of the city, near the church.

Within it, there existed a hierarchy of every possible type of tomb. There was an ossuary where the corpses lost their last traces of individuality, there were some individual tombs, and there were the graves inside the church, which conformed to two models, either a simple slab of marble, or a mausoleum with statues, etc. The cemetery, situated in the sacred space of the church, has taken on quite another character in modern civilization. It is curious to note that in an age which has been very roughly defined as "atheist," Western culture has inaugurated the so-called cult of the dead.

After all, it was very natural that, as long as people actually believed in the resurrection of the body and the immortality of the soul, not a great deal of importance was given to the mortal remains. On the contrary, from the moment when people were no longer so certain of survival after death, it became logical to take much more care with the remains of the dead, the only trace, in the end, of our existence in the world and in words.

In any case, it is from the nineteenth century onward that each of us has had the right to his own little box for his little personal decomposition, but it is only from the nineteenth century on that the cemetery began to be shifted to the outskirts of the city. In parallel to this individualization of death and the bourgeois appropriation of the cemetery, an obsession with death as "sickness" has emerged. It is supposed that the dead transmit sickness to the living and that their presence and proximity to the houses and church, almost in the middle of the street, spreads death. This great concern with the spread of sickness by contagion from cemeteries began to appear with insistence toward the end of the eighteenth century, but the cemeteries only moved out to the suburbs during the course of the nineteenth. From then on, they no longer constituted the sacred and immortal wind of the city, but the "other city," where each family possessed its gloomy dwelling.

Third principle. The heterotopia has the power of juxtaposing in a single real place different spaces and locations that are incompatible with each other. Thus on the rectangle of its stage, the theater alternates as a series of places that are alien to each other; thus the cinema appears as a very curious rectangular hall, at the back of which a three-dimensional space is projected onto a two-dimensional screen. Perhaps the oldest example of these heterotopias in the form of contradictory locations is the garden. Let us not forget that this astounding and age-old creation had very profound meanings in the East, and that these seemed to be superimposed. The traditional garden of the Persians was a sacred space that was supposed to unite four separate parts within its rectangle, representing the four parts of the world, as well as one space still more sacred than the others, a space that was like the navel, the center of the world brought into the garden (it was here that the basin and jet of water were located). All the vegetation was concentrated in this zone, as if in a sort of microcosm. As for carpets, they originally set out to reproduce gardens, since the garden was a carpet where the world in its entirety achieved symbolic perfection, and the carpet a sort of movable garden in space. The garden is the smallest fragment of the world and, at the same time, represents its totality, forming right from the remotest times a sort of felicitous and universal heterotopia (from which are derived our own zoological gardens).

Fourth principle. Heterotopias are linked for the most part to bits and pieces of time, i.e., they open up through what we might define as a pure symmetry of heterochronisms. The heterotopia enters fully into function when men find themselves in a sort of total breach of their traditional time. Then it is easy to see how the cemetery is a highly heterotopian place, in that it begins with that strange heterochronism that is, for a human being, the loss of life and of that quasi-eternity in which, however, he does not cease to dissolve and be erased.

Generally speaking, in a society like ours, heterotopia and heterochronism are organized and arranged in a relatively complex fashion. In the first place there are the heterotopias of time which accumulate *ad infinitum,* such as museums and libraries. These are heterotopias in which time does not cease to accumulate, perching, so to speak, on its own summit. Yet up until the end of the seventeenth century, these had still been the expression of an individual choice. The idea of accumulating everything, on the contrary, of creating a sort of universal archive, the desire to enclose all times, all eras, forms, and styles within a single place, the concept of making all times into one place, and yet a place that is outside time, inaccessible to the wear and tear of the years, according to a plan of almost perpetual and unlimited accumulation within an irremovable place, all this belongs entirely to our modern outlook. Museums and libraries are heterotopias typical of nineteenth-century Western culture.

Along with this type, bound up with the accumulation of time, there are other heterotopias linked to time in its more futile, transitory and precarious aspects, a time viewed as celebration. These then are heterotopias without a bias toward the eternal. They are absolutely time-bound. To this class belong the fairs, those marvelous empty zones outside the city limits, that fill up twice a year with booths, showcases, miscellaneous objects, wrestlers, snake-women, optimistic fortune-tellers, etc. Very recently, a new form of chronic heterotopia has been invented, that of the holiday village: a sort of Polynesian village which offers three short weeks of primitive and eternal nudity to city dwellers. It is easy to see, on the other hand, how the two types of heterotopia, that of the festival and that of the eternity of accumulating time, come together: the huts on the island of Jerba are relatives in a way of the libraries and museums. And in fact, by rediscovering Polynesian life, is not time abolished at the very moment in which it is found again? It is the whole story of humanity that dates right back to the origins, like a kind of great and immediate knowledge.

Fifth principle. Heterotopias always presuppose a system of opening and closing that isolates them and makes them penetrable at one and the same time. Usually, one does not get into a heterotopian location by one's own will. Either one is forced, as in the case of the barracks or the prison, or one must submit to rites of purification. One can only enter by special permission and after one has completed a certain number of gestures. Heterotopias also exist that are entirely devoted to practices of purification that are half religious, half hygienic (the Muslim "hammams"), or apparently solely hygienic (Scandinavian saunas).

Other heterotopias, on the contrary, have the appearance of pure and simple openings, although they usually conceal curious exclusions. Anyone can enter one of these heterotopian locations, but, in reality, they are nothing more than an illusion: one thinks one has entered and, by the sole fact of entering, one is excluded. I am reminded, for instance, of those famous rooms to be found on big farms in Brazil and throughout South America in general. The front door did not give onto the main part of the house, where the family lived, so that any person who happened to pass by, any traveler, had the right to push open that door, enter the room, and spend the night there. Now, the rooms were arranged in such a way that anyone who went in there could never reach to the heart of the family: more than ever a passing visitor, never a true guest. This type of heterotopia, which has now almost entirely vanished from our civilization, might perhaps be recognized in the American "motel" room, which one enters with one's own vehicle and lover and where illicit sex is totally protected and totally concealed at one and the same time, set apart and yet not under an open sky.

Finally, the last characteristic of heterotopias is that they have, in relation to the rest of space, a function that takes place between two opposite poles. On the one hand they perform the task of creating a space of illusion that reveals how all of real space is more illusory, all the locations within which life is fragmented. On the other, they have the function of forming another space, another real space, as perfect, meticulous, and well-arranged as ours is disordered, ill-conceived, and in a sketchy state. This heterotopia is not one of illusion but of compensation, and I wonder if it is not somewhat in this manner that certain colonies have functioned.

In a number of cases they have played, at the level of the general organization of terrestrial space, the genuine role of a heterotopia. An example of this, from the first wave of colonization in the seventeenth century, might be some of the Puritan colonies founded by the English in America, which were absolutely perfect places.

Or those extraordinary Jesuit colonies, set up in South America: wonderful, totally regulated colonies, in which human perfection was actually reached. The Jesuits of Paraguay had established settlements in which existence was regulated point by point. The village was laid out according to a strict pattern around a rectangular square at one end of which stood the church; on one side, the college, on the other the cemetery, while, facing the church, there was a street which met another at a right angle. Each family's hut lay on one of these two axes, reproducing exactly the symbol of Christ. Thus Christianity made its fundamental mark on the space and geography of the American world.

The daily life of individuals was regulated not by the whistle, but by the bell: the same hour of awakening laid down for all, with meals at midday and five o'clock. Afterward people went to bed and, at midnight, came what was known as the conjugal awakening: at this sound of the monastery's bell, each of them did his and her duty.

Brothels and colonies, here are two extreme types of heterotopia. Think of the ship: it is a floating part of space, a placeless place, that lives by itself, closed in on itself and at the same time poised in the infinite ocean, and yet, from port to port, tack by tack, from brothel to brothel, it goes as far as the colonies, looking for the most precious things hidden in their gardens. Then you will understand why it has been not only and obviously the main means of economic growth (which I do not intend to go into here), but at the same time the greatest reserve of imagination for our civilization from the sixteenth century down to the present day. The ship is the heterotopia *par excellence*. In civilizations where it is lacking, dreams dry up, adventure is replaced by espionage, and privateers by the police.

1967

In the 1960s the recourse by many leftist architects to sociology and politics reflected a fundamental questioning of the architect's role in society. In France, in the increasingly turbulent atmosphere that would culminate in the student upheavals of 1968, critics inside and outside the profession were asking whether there was still a need for architects at all. The traditional figure of the architect as form-giver, "isolated in his 'liberal' profession like a demigod," as one writer put it, "an individual artisan enshrined in corporate egoism," was not only *passé* but a complicitous symbol of what was wrong with the existing system.

A central intellectual figure within this context was the Marxist philosopher and sociologist **Henri Lefebvre**, whose multivolume *Critique de la vie quotidienne,* begun in the late 1940s, focused on the relations between everyday life in modern society and urbanism. The evolution of many of Lefebvre's central themes—the need for play and spontaneity in daily life, the suppression of human vitality through bureaucratic planning, the eruptive role of "moments" of radical possibility in urban experience—paralleled the rise of the bleak and anonymous social housing developments built on the outskirts of French cities in the 1950s and 1960s, immemorialized by Jean-Luc Godard in his film *Alphaville* (1965) and decried by Lefebvre. In influential writings of the 1960s, notably *Le Droit à la ville* (1968), the title chapter of which appears here, he sought to bridge the gap between urban practice and theory—to outline a *praxis* of the city synthesizing objective analysis and "experimental utopia." The latter involved the deployment of the "imaginary" in the production of new concepts of urban life. Critical of what he saw as the three dominant architectural ideologies of the day—structuralism, formalism, and functionalism—in equal measure, Lefebvre assailed architects for their mechanistic application of these partial models. Through his own totalistic approach he aimed to counter the overspecialization of the various disciplines acting on the city, including architecture, while offering a perspective that, despite its globalism, remained open to future transformations.

167–71 Lefebvre's ideas were translated into urban agitprop by the International Situationists, an avant-garde group led in the 1960s by Guy Debord. Debord used Lefebvre's concept of the festival to attack the "society of the spectacle," depicted in his book of 1967. Another group of young Lefebvre protégés, also influenced by the Situationists, was Utopie, founded in 1967. Its interdisciplinary membership included urban historian Hubert Tonka, theorist Jean Baudrillard, feminist Isabelle Auricoste, and architects Jean Aubert, Jean-Paul Jungmann, *365–69, 459–62* and Antoine Stinco; like other radical architects at the time, Aubert, Jungmann, and Stinco were experimenting with pneumatic structures. The group published two issues of *Utopie: Revue de sociologie de l'urbain,* a journal dedicated to a revolutionary critique of the city, culture, and power, illustrated with comic strip satires and "detourned" images. Lefebvre's essay "De la science à la stratégie urbaine" appeared in the second issue along with critiques by Baudrillard of technology and of "a society not exactly of repression but of persuasion." In *456–58* spring 1968, when the student movement coalesced at the University of Nanterre where Lefebvre had been an outspoken faculty member since 1965, the explosive disruptions of daily life appeared to many to be the apotheosis of his philosophy, confirming the revolutionary potential of urban action.

Le Droit à la ville is dated "Paris, 1967 (Centenary of *Capital*)." In 1970 Lefebvre founded the journal *Espaces et Sociétés* with Anatole Kopp. In 1973 he published a sequel to *Le Droit à la ville* entitled *Espace et politique,* and in 1974 a *magnum opus, La Production de l'espace,* now translated into English.

From Henri Lefebvre, Le Droit à la ville *(Paris: Editions Athropos, 1968), pp. 115–33. Translated by Christian Hubert. Courtesy of Editions Economica, Paris.*

The Right to the City
Henri Lefebvre

Theoretical analysis must redefine the forms, functions, and structures of the city (economical, political, cultural, etc.) as well as the social needs inherent to urban society. Until now, only individual needs, their motivations marked by what is known as consumer society (the bureaucratic society of programmed consumption), have been considered and have in fact been more manipulated than effectively recognized and examined. Social needs have an anthropological basis; they have opposite and complementary aspects: they include the need for security and the need for openness, the need for certainty and the need for adventure, that of the organization of labor and that of play, needs for predictability and unpredictability, for unity and difference, for isolation and encounter, for exchanges and investments, for independence (even solitude) and communication, for immediacy and for long-term perspective. The human being also needs to accumulate energy as well as to expend it, even to waste it in play. He needs to see, to hear, to touch, and to taste, and he needs to unify these perceptions in a "world." In addition to these anthropological requirements which are socially developed (that is to say sometimes separated, sometimes combined, in one instance compressed and in another distended) one must add specific needs which are not satisfied by the commercial and cultural complexes that urbanists take rather meagerly into account. It is a matter of the need for creative activity, for work (not just products and material consumer goods); of the needs for information, for symbolism, for imagination, for play. A fundamental desire resides in these specific needs, which finds its specific embodiments, its *moments,* in play, in sexuality, in corporeal activities like sports, in creative activity, in art and in learning, which more or less overcome the specialized division of labor. In the end, the needs of the city and of urban life are only given free expression in the perspectives which emerge here and the horizons that they open up. Are not needs for designated places, places of simultaneity and encounter, places where exchange does not pass into exchange value, commerce, and profit— are these not specific urban needs? Is there not also the need for a time for such encounters, such exchanges?

Today the requisite *analytical science of the city* exists only in its barest outlines. Its concepts and theories, currently in their beginning stages, can only advance along with urban reality in formation, with the *praxis* (the social practice) of urban society. The current move beyond the ideologies and practices that blocked the horizon, those bottlenecks of knowledge and action that marked a threshold to be crossed is proceeding only with difficulty.

The *science of the city* has the city as its object. This science borrows its methods, procedures, and concepts from the specialized sciences. Synthesis eludes it on two fronts. First, inasmuch as a truly total synthesis, based on analysis, can only consist of a systematization and programming that are strategic. Second, because its object, the city as a developed reality, is itself decomposing. The inquiry which seeks to cut up and recompose the fragments of the city confronts a historical entity already modified. As a social text, this historical city no longer expresses a series of coherent prescriptions for spending time in relation to symbols, to a style. The text recedes. It takes on the quality of a document, of an exhibition, of a museum. It is no longer possible to inhabit the historically formed city in concrete practice. It has become a mere object of cultural consumption for tourists, for an aesthetic attitude avid for spectacle and the picturesque.

The city is dead even to those who seek to know it most sympathetically. And yet the *urban* still persists, in a state of dispersal and alienation, as a seed, as a virtuality. What the eye sees and analysis distinguishes in this landscape can at best be the passing shadow of a future object in the light of a rising sun. It is impossible to envisage the reconstituting of the old city, only the construction of a new city, on a new basis, at another scale, in other conditions, in another society. Neither return to the past (to the traditional city) nor headlong flight into the future, toward a colossal and unformed agglomeration—this is the prescription. In other words, as far as the city is concerned, the object of inquiry has not been given. The past, the present, and the future are not to be separated. Thought studies a *virtual object*. It calls for new procedures.

The career of the old classical humanism ended long ago, and badly. The old humanism is dead. Its embalmed and mummified corpse is heavy and doesn't smell good. It occupies many a public place, transforming each one into a cemetery with a human appearance: museums, universities, various publications. Then there are the new towns and periodicals devoted to urbanism. They serve as packaging for trivialities and platitudes. "Human scale," they say. When it is immoderation that we should take as our task, and create "something" on the measure of the universe.

This old humanism met its death in the two world wars, during the demographic surges that accompanied the great massacres, in the face of the brutal demands of economic competition and under the impetus of poorly mastered techniques. Humanism is not even an ideology anymore, barely a theme of official rhetoric.

As if the death of classical humanism implied that of man as well, we have recently heard cries of "God is dead, and man is too." There is nothing new in these slogans for best-sellers, taken up in turn by irresponsible advertising. The Nietzschean meditation on the theme started almost a century ago, during the Franco-Prussian war of 1870, an ill omen for the culture and civilization of Europe. When Nietzsche announced the death of God and that of man, he did not leave a gaping void; nor did he fill it in with whatever baggage was at hand: with language and linguistics. He announced the Superman as well, whom he thought was to come. He overcame the nihilism that he diagnosed. Those authors who coin theoretical and poetic currency a century too late plunge us back into nihilism. Since the time of Nietzsche, the dangers of the Superman have made themselves all too cruelly clear. In addition, the "new man" born of industrial production and rational planning as such has only been a disappointment. There is one more path available, that of urban society and of that which is human as creative work in a society which would be a work, not a product. Either the supersession of the old "social animal" and of the inhabitant of the old city, the urban animal, in favor of urban man, polyvalent, polysensory, and capable of complex and transparent relations to "the world" (his environment and himself); or nihilism. If man is dead, who should we build for? How should we build? It scarcely matters whether the city has disappeared for it to be necessary to think the city anew, to reconstruct it on a new set of principles, or to supersede it altogether. It scarcely matters whether terror reigns, whether the atomic bomb is dropped, whether the world explodes. What is important? Who thinks? Who acts? Who still speaks and for whom? If meaning and purpose disappear, if we can no longer consider them as part of a praxis, then nothing of importance or interest remains. And what is one to reply, what is one to do if the capacities of the "human being"—technique, science, imagination, art, or their absence—are set up as autonomous agents and if reflective thought simply accepts this observation?

The old humanism is receding in the distance and disappearing behind us. We are becoming less and less nostalgic and only occasionally turn back to gaze upon its outline stretched across the road. It was the ideology of the liberal bourgeoisie. It turned its attention to the people, to human suffering. It sustained the rhetoric of poetic souls, of grand sentiments and good consciences. It was concocted out of Greco-Latin citations sprinkled with Judeo-Christian elements. A ghastly cocktail, enough to make one vomit. Only a few "left" intellectuals (do any intellectuals still remain on the "right"?), neither revolutionary nor openly reactionary, neither dionysiac nor apollonian, still have a taste for this sorry potion.

We must direct ourselves toward a new humanism, toward a new praxis and an other being, that of urban society. We must get away from the myths that threaten our will by destroying the ideologies that turn us back from this project and the strategies that divert its course. Urban life has yet to begin. Today we are concluding the inventory of the debris of a millennium in which the country dominated the town, whose ideas, whose "values," whose taboos and prescriptions were for the most part of agrarian origin, whose dominants were rural and "natural." Only sporadically did cities manage to emerge from the vastness of the countryside. Rural society was (and remains) one of unabundance, of scarcity and deprivation accepted or rejected, of prohibitions that developed and normalized those deprivations. It was also a society of festivals, but this, its best aspect, has been lost and is what should be resurrected, not the myths and limitations! A crucial observation: the crisis of the traditional city goes with the worldwide crisis of agrarian society, which is equally traditional. They go together and indeed coincide. It is for "us" to resolve this double crisis, particularly in the creation of both the new city and the new form of life in the city. The revolutionary states (including the U.S.S.R. ten or fifteen years after the October revolution) have sensed the development of society based on industry, but only as a premonition.

In the preceding sentences, the term "we" is only a metaphor. It designates the interested parties. Neither the architect nor the urban planner, neither the sociologist nor the economist, neither the philosopher nor the politician, can pluck the new forms and new relations out of the air. To be more specific, the architect cannot work miracles any more than the sociologist. Neither one creates social relations. Under certain favorable conditions, they can help tendencies to find expression (to take on form). Only social life (praxis) in its global capacity has such power—or lacks this power. The people mentioned above, either separately or as a team, can clear the path. They can also propose, try out, prepare forms. They can also (and most importantly) make an inventory of their acquired experiences, draw lessons from failures, help give birth to the possible, through a maieutics nourished by science.

At this point we must indicate the urgent necessity of a transformation of intellectual procedures and instruments. Recalling some of the formulations we used elsewhere, we consider certain mental procedures that still remain unfamiliar to be indispensable.

a. *Transduction.* This is an intellectual operation which can be carried out methodically and which differs from induction, from classical deduction, and also from the construction of "models," from simulation, and from the simple expression of hypotheses. Transduction constructs and develops a theoretical object, a *possible* object on the basis of information that applies to reality as well as to a problematic raised by that reality. Transduction entails a constant feedback between the conceptual framework and empirical observation. Its theory (methodology) gives form to certain spontaneous mental operations of the urbanist, the architect, the sociologist, the political scientist, the philosopher. It brings rigor to invention and knowledge to utopianism.

b. *Experimental utopia.* Who is not a *utopian* today? Only narrowly specialized practitioners who work on demand without the least critical examination of the norms and constraints stipulated of them. Only these relatively uninteresting individuals escape utopianism. Everyone else is utopian, including futurologists, the planners projecting the Paris of the year 2000, the engineers who built Brasilia, and so on! But there are several utopianisms. Isn't the worst the unacknowledged one, which wears the mantle of positivism and imposes in its name the strictest constraints and the most derisory lack of technique?

Utopia should be considered experimentally, by studying its implications and consequences in the field. They may surprise. What are and what will be socially successful places? How can we detect them? According to what criteria? What modes of time, what rhythms of daily life inscribe themselves, write themselves, prescribe themselves in these "successful" places, that is to say, places which are conducive to happiness? This is what is interesting.

Other indispensable intellectual procedures: to discern, without dissociating them, three fundamental theoretical concepts—structure, function, and form. To know their range of influence, their areas of application, their limits, and their reciprocal relations; to understand that they form a whole, but that the elements of the whole have a certain independence and relative autonomy; not to privilege one of them, which gives rise to an ideology, that is to say a dogmatic and closed system of significations—structuralism, formalism, or functionalism. To use them one by one, on an equal footing, for the analysis of the real (an analysis which is never exhaustive, never without residue) as well as for the operation of "transduction." To firmly understand that the same function can be carried out by different structures, that there is no unique link between the terms. That function and structure take on different forms which both reveal and conceal them—that this triple aspect constitutes a "whole" which is more than these aspects, elements, and parts.

Among the intellectual tools we possess, there is one that merits neither disdain nor absolute privilege: the *system* (or rather *subsystem*) of significations.

Politicians have their own systems of signification—ideologies—which allow them to subordinate their actions and their social influence to their strategies.

At the ecological level, the humble inhabitant has his own system of significations (or rather his subsystem). The simple fact of living here or there entails the reception, the adoption, and the transmission of such a system, for example the one that goes with the habitat of the detached dwelling. The inhabitant's system of signification tells of his activities and passivities; it is received but also modified in practice. It is perceived.

Architects seem to have established and made dogma out of a complex of significations, poorly explained as such and expressed under diverse terms: "function," "form," "structure"; or rather functionalism, formalism, and structuralism. They develop these notions not on the basis of the meanings that are perceived and experienced by the inhabitants, but from facts of habitation, as they themselves interpret them. These facts are verbal and discursive, tending toward metalanguage. They involve writings and visualizations. Because of the fact that architects constitute a social body, that they are tied to institutions, their system tends to close up, to impose itself, and to escape all criticism. This allows for the system to be formulated and set up as *urbanism* by extrapolation, without any other procedure or precaution.

The theory which could legitimately be called *urbanism,* which would tie into the significations of the old practice of *inhabitation* (that is to say, the human) and which would add to these partial facts the general theory of urban *time-spaces* and which would lead to a new practice stemming from its development—this urbanism already exists virtually. It can only be thought of as the practical implication of a complete theory of the city and of the urban, superseding the currents schisms and separations. In particular the split between the philosophy of the city and the science (or sciences) of the city. Current urbanistic projects may find their place in this trajectory, but only when subjected to vigilant critical examination of their ideological and strategic implications.

Insofar as one can define it, our object—*the urban*—will never be fully present and realized in our thought of today. More than any other object, its nature as a whole is extremely complex in nature, both in action and in potential. As an object of research it reveals itself in piecemeal fashion and will perhaps never be known exhaustively. To take this "object" as real and truthful is an ideology, a mythifying operation. Our inquiry must consider a vast number of methods for seizing this object, without fixating on one procedure. Analytic divisions must adhere as closely as possible to the internal articulations of this "thing" which is not a thing; they will give rise to reconstructions that can never be complete. Descriptions, analyses, attempts at synthesis can never claim to be exhaustive or definitive. Every notion, every arsenal of concepts comes into play: form, structure, function, level, dimension, dependent and independent variables, correlations, totality, ensemble, systems, etc. Here as elsewhere, but here even more, the residue is the most precious. The construction of every "object" will itself be subjected to critical review. Insofar as possible, it will be carried out and subjected to experimental verification. The science of the city requires a historical time frame to establish itself and to direct its social practice.

While it is necessary, this science is not sufficient. We can see not only its necessity but also its limits. Urbanistic thought proposes the establishment or the reconstitution of highly original (and localized) social units, particularized and centralized, whose relations and tensions would reestablish an urban unity endowed with a complex internal order, not without structure but with a supple structure and hierarchy. More specifically, sociological reflection aims at the understanding and the reconstitution of the integrative capacities of the urban as well as the conditions for practical participation. Why not? On one condition: one should never exempt these specialized and thus partial attempts from criticism, from verification in practice, from an overall perspective.

Knowledge can thus construct and propose "models." Each "object" in this sense is none other than a model of urban reality. And yet such a "reality" will never become manageable like a material object, it will never become instrumentalized. This holds true even for the most operational forms of knowledge. Who would not wish the city to become what it once was: the act and creation of a complex thought? But one remains at the level of wish and aspiration if one does not determine an *urban strategy.* Such a strategy cannot but take into account both existing strategies and previously acquired knowledge: the science of the city, the knowledge directed at the planning of growth and control of development. To mention "strategy" is to refer to the hierarchy of "variables" to be taken into account, some of which have strategic capacities, while others remain at the tactical level—and is also to refer to the forces capable of realizing this strategy in the field. Only groups, classes, or segments of social classes capable of revolutionary initiatives can assume the burden and fully accomplish solutions to urban problems; the renovated city will become the creation of these social and political forces. The first task is to undo the strategies and dominant ideologies within contemporary society. The fact that there are several groups and several strategies with their own differences (between private interests and the state, for example) does not change the situation. From issues of land ownership to problems of segregation, each project of *urban reform* calls into question the structures of the existing society, of immediate (individual) and quotidian relations, as well as those that are intended to be imposed by constraint and institution on what remains of urban reality. While *reformist* in itself, the strategy of urban reform becomes "necessarily" revolutionary, not because of the force of events but because of its opposition to what is already in place. An urban strategy based on the science of the city needs a social basis and political force to be effective. It cannot act on its own. It cannot help but rely on the existence and actions of the working class, the only class capable of putting an end to a segregation aimed essentially against it. Only this class, as a class, can decisively contribute to the reconstitution of the center destroyed by segregation and redeployed in the menacing forms of "centers of decision-making." This is not to say that the working class alone will make urban society, but that nothing is possible without it. Integration without the working class is meaningless, and without it disintegration will continue, masked by a nostalgia for integration. This is not just an option, but a whole horizon of possibility that opens up or closes down. When the working class remains silent, when it does not act and cannot accomplish what theory defines as its "historic mission," then both the "subject" and the "object" are missing. And reflective thought ratifies this absence. As a result, one must develop two series of proposals:

a. *A political program of urban reform* defined neither by the managers nor by the possibilities of current society, not subjected to "realism" although based on the study of reality (in other words: reform not limited to reformism). This program will thus have a singular and even paradoxical character. It will be in the form of a proposal to the existing political forces, to the parties. One can even add that it will be submitted preferentially to the parties of the "left," the political entities that represent or seek to represent the working class. But this program will not be set forth as a function of these forces and formations. Its specific character will be in relation to knowledge. It will thus contain a scientific aspect. It will be *proposed* (even though this may entail modifications by those who take it on). The political forces should assume their responsibilities. In this domain which affects the future of modern society as well as its producers, we appeal to the responsibility to history which ignorance and indifference put at risk.

b. Intensively elaborated *urban projects* that include "models" and forms of urban space and time without concern for whether they can be realized today, for whether they are utopistic (which is to say, "utopian" projects). It would appear that these models cannot result from simple analysis of existing cities and urban types nor from the simple combination of elements. The possible forms of time and space, unless proven otherwise, are to be invented and proposed to praxis. Imagination must be deployed, not the imaginary which allows for escape and evasion, which is the conveyor of ideologies, but the imaginary which is engaged in *appropriation* (of space, of time, of physiological activity, of desire). Why not counter the idea of the eternal city with ephemeral cities, the fixed center with multiple moving centers? Every daring gesture is permitted. Why limit these proposals to the single morphology of time and space? Why not include in this plan proposals for life styles, for ways of living in the city, for development of the urban?

Short-term, medium-term, and long-term proposals will all enter these two series and will constitute the urban strategy proper.

The society we live in seems directed toward plenitude or at least satiation (of durable goods and objects, quantity, satisfaction, rationality), but in fact it opens up a colossal void. Ideologies dance about in this void. The fog of rhetoric spreads across it. One of the greatest ambitions for active thought, moving out of speculation and contemplation, and away from the fragmentary divisions of specialized knowledge, is to populate this lacuna, and not simply with words.

In a period in which ideologues carry on about structures, the destructuring of the city is an indication of the depths of disintegration (both social and cultural). This society, taken as a whole, reveals itself *lacking*. There are holes, sometimes gaping voids between the subsystems and the structures that are consolidated by various means (constraint, terror, ideological persuasion). These empty places are not the products of chance. They are also sites of possibility. They contain elements that float freely or are dispersed without the strength to assemble them. What is more: the structuring activity and the power of the social vacuum tend to prohibit the actions or the simple presence of such a force. The instances of the possible can only be realized in the course of a radical metamorphosis.

In this conjuncture, ideology claims to give an absoluteness to "scientificity," the science which applies to the real, dividing it up, recombining it, and on this basis dispelling the possible and blocking the path. In such a context science (that is to say the specialized sciences) has no more than a *programmatic* effect. It procures certain elements for a program. But if one takes these elements for an already constituted totality, if one tries to execute the program literally, then one comes to treat the virtual object as a technical object, already available. This is an uncritical project, without self-criticism, and when carried out, this project realizes an ideology, the ideology of technocrats. The programmatic is insufficient. It becomes transformed in the course of being carried out. Only the social force which is capable of investing itself in the urban, through the course of a long political experience, can take on the responsibility for realizing a program for urban society. In return, the science of the city brings a theoretical and critical foundation, a positive base, to that perspective. Utopia controlled by dialectical reason provides a safety barrier to fictions of scientificity, to imagination without direction. This foundation and basis keeps thought from losing itself in pure program as well. The dialectical movement presents itself here as a relation between science and political power, as a dialogue which actualizes the relations of "theory–practice" and "positivity–critical negativity."

Like science, *art* is necessary but not sufficient. It brings its own long meditation on life as drama and pleasure to the realization of urban society. Above all, it restores the sense of the creative work. It gives multiple figures of *appropriated* time and space: not passively endured, not accepted with resignation, but transformed into creation. Music reveals the appropriation of time, painting and sculpture the appropriation of space. If the sciences discover partial determinisms, art (as well as philosophy) shows how a totality is born out of partial determinisms. It is incumbent upon the only social force capable of realizing urban society to unite effectively and efficiently (in "synthesis") art, technique, and knowledge. Art and the history of art, as much as the science of the city, should enter into reflections on the urban in order to put its images into effect. This meditation geared toward realization in action will thus be both utopian and realistic and will overcome the distinction between the two. One can even assert that the greatest utopianism will become one with the optimum realism.

Among the contradictions that characterize our epoch we encounter those (particularly harsh) ones between the realities of society and the achievements of civilization inscribed there. On the one hand genocide, on the other the capacities (medical and others) that can save a child or prolong life. One of the last, but certainly not the least, of those contradictions comes to light precisely here: between the *socialization of society* and *general segregation.* There are many others, for example the contradiction between being called a *revolutionary* and being attached to an outdated productivist rationalism. The individual does not disappear in the midst of the social effects caused by the pressures of the masses, but is instead affirmed. Certain *rights* come to light. They enter into customs or prescriptions more or less followed by actions. We know how these concrete "rights" come to complete the abstract rights of man and citizen that were inscribed on the front of buildings by democracy in its revolutionary beginnings: the rights of age and sex (of women, children, and the elderly); rights of condition (the proletarian, the peasant); rights to education and instruction; rights to work, to culture, to leisure, to health, and to housing. Despite, and even through, the terrible destruction, the world wars, the threats, the nuclear terror. The pressure of the working class has remained necessary (but not sufficient) for the recognition of these rights, for them to become part of custom, for their inscription in law, even if incompletely.

Rather oddly, the *right to nature* (to the countryside and "pure nature") has come into social practice in the past few years in the form of *leisure activities.* It has advanced by way of the protests that have become commonplace against noise, against fatigue, against the "concentrationary" universe of the cities (as the city decays and explodes). A strange course of events, we would say. Nature gains exchange value and becomes merchandise. It is bought and sold. The various leisure activities that are commercialized, industrialized, institutionalized, destroy the "natural" which is now to be trafficked in. What one calls "nature" becomes the ghetto of leisure, a separate place of pleasure and a refuge for "creativity." But urban people bring the urban along with them, even if they do not bring urbanity! Once they colonize it, the countryside loses its own qualities, those properties and charms of rural life. The urban ravages the countryside; this urbanized countryside dispossesses and replaces the rural: an extreme case of the misery of the inhabitants, of the habitat, and of inhabitation. Are not the right to nature and the right to the countryside self-destroying?

In the face of this right, or pseudoright, the *right to the city* becomes a rallying cry, a demand. This right takes a slow and tortuous route through unexpected detours — through nostalgia, tourism, the return to the heart of historic cities, the requirements of existing centers or of newly created ones. The demand for nature, the desire to enjoy it, diverts attention from the right to the city. This last demand expresses itself only indirectly, as a tendency to flee the deteriorating and unrenovated city, to flee the alienated form of "urban life" rather than the forms which have yet to "really" exist. The need and "right" to nature frustrate the right to the city without altogether escaping it. (This does not mean that one should not preserve vast "natural" spaces in the face of the spread of the exploded city.)

The *right to the city* cannot be considered a simple visiting right or a return to the traditional city. It can only be formulated as the *right to urban life,* in a transformed and renewed form. It scarcely matters if the urban fabric encroaches upon the countryside and what remains of country life. No matter, as long as the "urban," the place of encounter, the prime value of exchange, inscribed in space and time as the highest value, finds its morphological basis and practical and sensual realization. This requires an integral theory of the city and of urban society, using all the resources of science and art. Only the working class can become its agent, the bearer or social support of this achievement. Here still, as it did a century ago, the very existence of the working class negates and contests the strategy of segregation directed against it. As it did a century ago, although under new conditions, it unifies the interests of society as a whole (going beyond the immediate and superficial), and especially the interests of those who *inhabit*. The superrich and the new bourgeois aristocracy (who can deny it?) no longer inhabit. They go from palace to palace, from chateau to chateau, they manage a fleet or a country from their yacht. They are everywhere and nowhere. This is one reason that they are so fascinating to people who are steeped in the everyday. They transcend the quotidian. They own nature and let their henchmen produce culture. Is it really necessary to describe at length the conditions of the young, of students and intellectuals, of the armies of workers with or without white collars, of provincials, of the colonized and semicolonized of every sort—all those who endure a well-organized existence? Is it necessary to spell out the pathetic misery without tragedy of the inhabitants of the working-class suburbs, of those who live in residential ghettos, in the decaying centers of the traditional cities and in the misguided proliferations far from these centers? One has merely to open one's eyes in order to understand the daily life of a person who runs from his housing to a near or distant station, to a crowded subway, to the office or factory, only to take the same route back in the evening in order to recover the strength to start all over in the morning. The portrait of this general misery would not be complete without the image of the "compensations" that conceal it and become means of its escape and evasion.

1967

In an exhibition at the Museum of Modern Art in New York in 1972 entitled "Italy: the New Domestic Landscape," curator Emilio Ambasz brought to international attention the achievements of Italian product design in the preceding decades, seeking to explain how such a small and belatedly industrialized country had come to play so large a role in design developments. The economic boom of the 1950s had vastly expanded the market for domestic goods. As elsewhere, the new class of design-conscious Italian consumers identified the goods afforded by an advancing democratic capitalism with an enlightened aesthetic of "good form" and a perennial process of *aggiornamento*—keeping up with new tendencies on the international scene. At the same time, materialistic aspirations to *la dolce vita* stirred a desire to recapture the bourgeois traditions of style and craftsmanship repressed by modernism. The result was a vigorous and ultimately fertile debate. In the 1950s and 1960s, out of the "land of good design," as Alessandro Mendini put it in the catalogue, came a succession of high-quality and varied commercial products combining functionality with stylishness. Associated with the progressive entrepreneurship of Adriano Olivetti and other firms, they bore the signatures of talented designers like Marcello Nizzoli, Franco Albini, Gio Ponti, Gae Aulenti, and Marco Zanuso, and extended from the antidesign experimentalism of Ettore Sottsass, Jr., to the ergonomic research of a designer like Enzo Mari.

pp. 157–62

pp. 300–7

pp. 260–67
pp. 172–75

By the mid-1960s, however, the fetishization of the designed object, its complicity with an elite taste, and the absence of broader social aims provoked a radical critique by designers and architects seeking not just to reform the profession but to challenge its very premises. In this context, in November 1966, some young architects in Florence organized an exhibition entitled "Superarchitecture": "Superarchitecture is the architecture of superproduction, of superconsumption, of superinduction of consumption, of the supermarket, of the superman, of the super gasoline. Superarchitecture accepts the logic of production and of consumption, operating upon it with an action of demystification." Out of this critique came the formation of two groups,

Superstudio and Archizoom, and a little later others like Group 9999 and the Turinese Gruppo Strum. Inspired by Archigram in England and by the Viennese avant-garde, the Italian radicals focused more on the consumer object and the domestic environment. In late 1967 Superstudio's founders, Adolfo Natalini and Cristiano Toraldo di Francia (subsequently joined by Alessandro Magris, Roberto Magris, and Gian Piero Frassinelli), wrote the manifesto that follows, calling for an "evasive"—subversive—design practice "assuming poetry and the irrational as its method, and trying to institutionalize continuous evasion of everyday dreariness created by the equivocations of rationalism and functionality."

365–69, 459–62

In the years after 1968, Superstudio relinquished product design entirely, acknowledging that, as Toraldo di Francia put it, "to continue designing furniture, objects, and similar household decorations was no solution to the problems of living, nor to those of life; even less was it serving to save the soul." The group graphically allegorized an abstract technological environment in collision with atavistic nature. Their Continuous Monument of 1969, an encroaching universal grid, portrayed "a form of architecture emerging all at once from a single continuous environment: the world rendered uniform by technology, culture, and all the other inevitable forms of imperialism." With this they pushed to dystopian limits the unified and rational design methodology idealistically envisaged after the Second World War in Ernesto Rogers's maxim "from a spoon to a city."

77–79

Written in 1967. Published as "Design d'invenzione e design d'evasione: Superstudio," in Domus 475 (6 June 1969), p. 28. Republished in "Superstudio & Radicals," Japan Interior Design (1982), pp. 228–30. Courtesy of Adolfo Natalini.

Invention Design and Evasion Design
Superstudio

It would appear that the fact that the world is round and rotates is now beyond discussion.

There is still room for discussion, however, about how we are to live on it. And particularly on whether everything should be invented all over again every day or whether on the other hand it is enough to cling tightly to the appropriate gravity straps against the centrifugal force and keep on breathing.

And this is possible, or obligatory rather, for those who live in the cubic boxes about which so much has already been said. In other words for the lucky inhabitants and owners of block apartments, small villas, and civilized housing in general, and then, by natural kinship, for all the owners and users of refrigerated portions of established truth and the commonplace . . .

If on the contrary we face the problem of making our reckonings with reality at every moment, if we face the problem of living creatively, living truly that is, regular breathing is no longer enough and we must invent on each occasion the utensils for "doing things" and find the answers to new queries.

Only in this way, by taking a creative attitude, can we avoid the prefabricated answers imposed by the big monopolies of truth.

But contestation of the system, rejection of the products imposed by the consumer industry as the only true answer at this particular moment of history, will not be achieved through a total rejection of the products and the activities connected with them. Salvation does not lie in a primitive Arcadia or even in Alice's Wonderland. Arcadia and Wonderland, or the self-sufficient civilization of craftsmanship (or even the nonacquisitive one of the Hippies) and the hyperconsumer society of Supermarkets and Carnaby Street: on one hand a magic world in which the utensil is the object of a rite, on the other a code of liturgical regulations governing nonexistent objects.

But seeing that "you cannot go backward," and that the process is irreversible (and revivals confirm this), and seeing that the system offers us transparent or nonexistent objects (the sales system sells only one product: itself), and seeing also that we need something in order to live (utensils, signs, totems . . .), we put the process of design back into motion. If, then, the problem is one of living creatively and finding the true answers to our problems, of avoiding the prefabricated answers imposed by the great monopolies of truth (the pitfalls of the affluent society), we then come to propose "invention design" as an alternative or variant to "product design" or "industrial design" as currently conceived. But any valid design is always invention design (and in this connection think back to the meaning of the terms "design" and "invention" in Renaissance tracts).

The term to use, then, may well be "evasion design."

Evasion design, punning and easy overtones of political disengagement apart, is the activity of planning and operating in the field of industrial production assuming poetry and the irrational as its method, and trying to institutionalize continuous evasion of everyday dreariness created by the equivocations of rationalism and functionality.

Every object has a practical function and a contemplative one: and it is the latter that evasion design is seeking to potentiate. Thus there is an end to the nineteenth-century myths of reason as the explanation of everything, the thousand variations on

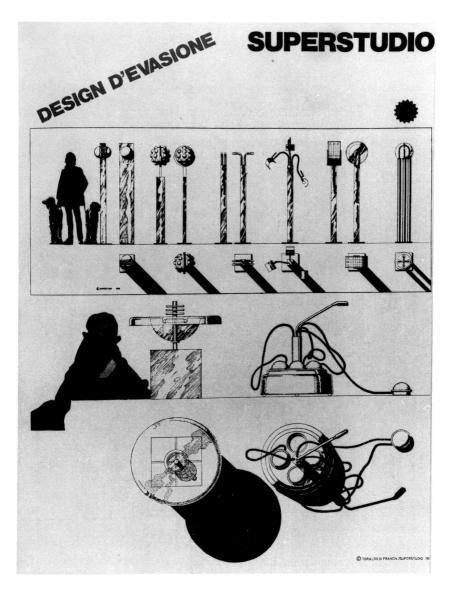

Adolfo Natalini, Cristiano Toraldo di Francia, Piero Frassinelli, and Roberto Magris, designs for high and low lamps ("Falling Star" and "Narghilé") [1968].

the theme of the four-legged chair, aerodynamic shapes, and the sterilization of dreams.

We need in fact to begin all over again: the data are those of experience and those of myth, those of technology and consumer demand, those of repressed desires.

The important thing is to keep on asserting ourselves, to go on making our mark on things. The important thing is to "be there." Perhaps one of the most disturbing manifestations of our time is the sit-in, the pacific protest meeting at which everyone sits on the ground.

What we want to do is lay the foundations for an existence this is one long protest: a "be-in."

This means involving all the users of our products and creating an operative area.

Such total involvement may be achieved in two ways: by supplying products that are poetically functional or by supplying patterns of behavior.

In the first case you supply multisignificant (ambiguous) products, objects of universal use, and each user puts them to the use he thinks fit.

In the second case you supply the rules of a game to be played with all kinds of objects, or containers that can be filled with all kinds of things.

To switch our attention to interior space, this may become a genuine space of involvement (a stage for a continuous performance or, in other words, a place for happenings, a place for the be-in) by the agency of the design products we place in it.

While on this subject we should clarify the fact that this operation belongs to the first of the modes of operation to which we referred earlier: we thus put on the market poetically functional objects in containers of any kind, even if they are indifferent or degraded like those supplied by the building trade today. It is obvious that we can see this only as a "rescue" operation: it is not the total operation to which we aspire (supplying and shaping the whole human environment).

It is only a way of taking action "here and now" in an existing situation. Evasion design, then, to evade everyday dreariness, or rather evasion design to make it possible to live with everyday dreariness.

All this is because: apart from those fortunate mortals who can afford to build their own "house" (ideally in their own image and likeness), and those lucky enough to find one in which it is possible to live even without putting paintings up on the walls, those who live in "residential blocks" usually live in a room, a cubic box without memories, with vague indications of top and bottom, entrance and exit, a Euclidean parallelepiped painted white or distempered in bright colors, washable or no, but always without surprises and without hope.

We should remember however that "it is poetry that makes you live," and that life is lived not only in hermetically sealed boxes made for small parallel lives, but also in the city and in cars, in the supermarkets, in the cinemas, on the motorways. . . . And an object may be an adventure in space, or an object of worship and veneration, and become a shining intersection point of relationships . . .

Thus evasion design aims at working on the theory of introducing foreign bodies into the system: objects with the greatest possible number of sensory properties (chromatic, tactile, etc.), charged with symbolism, and images with the aim of attracting attention, or arousing interest, of serving as a demonstration and inspiring action and behavior.

Objects in short that succeed in modifying the container-unit and involving it totally together with its occupier.

We shall build on the ruins of our own wars and those of others, on the smoking ruins of private and public guerilla warfare, on the clouds of numerous mushrooms, atomic ones and those of peyote.

We shall construct huge and indestructible objects thoroughly shockproof because as flexible and manageable as the willow branches in Japanese prints.

We shall have soft pyramids and looking-glass furniture and rooms for the contemplation of everyday poetry.

We shall have microscopes and kaleidoscopes to investigate the mysteries of stupidity and boredom.

We shall make journeys with airline itineraries around the world, tightening only the seat belts of the intelligence, but without fear, and we shall construct with a single everyday purpose: living with poetry.

With no time for analysis or denunciation, with little time for bitter ironies and cruel tricks of the intellect: we wish to rediscover the heart and raise it on high. *Sursum corda.*

We shall no longer do anything except for love and in hope and we shall surely die of ingenuity, happy.

Our problem is to go on producing objects big brightly colored cumbersome useful and full of surprises, to live with them and play with them together and always find ourselves tripping over them till we get to the point of kicking them and throwing them out, or else sitting down on them or putting our coffee cups on them, but it will not in any way be possible to ignore them.

They will exorcise our indifference.

Things that can modify time and space and serve as signposts for a life that is going ahead.

1967

During the 1960s American "grass-roots" political activism became a tool for social change in the hands of the urban underprivileged. The violent riots of 1965 and 1967 in the ghettos of Watts and Newark stood as *de facto* plebiscites on the persistence of harsh urban conditions. "Advocacy planning" was an effort at a more constructive response, coupling direct democratic initiative with planning know-how. As defined by **Paul Davidoff** in *The Journal of the American Institute of Planners* (November 1965), the term was an omnibus for diverse planning and policy strategies. It especially targeted Lyndon Johnson's "War on Poverty" and "Model Cities" programs for failing to deliver the broad reforms they had promised.

Davidoff, who was trained as a lawyer, first turned his attention to urban affairs as a result of handling eviction cases stemming from Title I. He took up planning studies at Yale and then, dissatisfied with the formalistic approach there, at the University of Pennsylvania, where he came under the tutelage of Lewis Mumford. City planning schemes that relied on fixed design and implementation criteria were everywhere under attack in the mid-1960s. As alternatives, the "probabilistic planning" of Melvin Webber, the sociological analyses by Herbert Gans in his book *The Urban Villagers* (1962), and Jane

338–40 Jacobs's assault on modernist housing all drew attention to the most characteristic aspect of the American city—its pluralistic makeup—and the consequent need of localized strategies for community-based decision making.

Describing advocacy as "professional support for competing claims about how the community should develop," Davidoff defined the advocate's role as to oppose projects that threatened the local neighborhood by educating the client about impending plans; to organize response through community awareness, group participation, and especially alternative schemes; and to represent the client group in front of city agencies. A preferred format for interaction was the community design workshop, which often occupied a neighborhood storefront. By giving substance and support to community and constituent interests, the advocate could make the planning process more sensitive to economic forces and replace "top-down" schemes with plans taking diverse needs into account.

The groups that emerged in many cities, with names like the Real Great Society and the Los Angeles Urban Workshop, reflected the plurality of political interests which was advocacy's prime tenet. At the same time, many activists remained skeptical of the strategy's ability to cure problems of poverty and racism. Richard Hatch, whose group ARCH (Architects' Renewal Committee in Harlem) was active as early as 1964, held that endemic social ills undercut the type of community organization on which advocacy relied. Others argued that despite the advocate's efforts the planning bureaucracy precluded a true public referendum. Nonetheless, in one of advocacy's major victories, Hatch's group succeeded in generating wide community opposition to a gymnasium planned by Columbia University to displace a neighboring public park used by Harlem residents. The project became emblematic during the student protests that took place on Columbia's campus in 1968 and it was ultimately abandoned.

The American advocacy movement also had counterparts in Europe and developing countries. In Italy, Giancarlo de Carlo had warned as early as 1948 that "the housing problem cannot be solved from above." In 1969–75, in a model collaboration with local steelworkers, he realized the ideal of "user participation" in the design and construction of the Mateotti complex in Terni outside Rome. A

379–89 participatory approach was also used in the *barriadas* of Latin America, where planners worked with the indigenous population for improved housing conditions.

From Perspecta *11 (1967), pp. 158–59. Courtesy of Linda Davidoff and* Perspecta: The Yale Architectural Journal.

Democratic Planning
Paul Davidoff

The city planning process is neutral. It may be used in support of a number of different values. It may be used for liberal or conservative or radical purposes. It may be used to support the status quo or it may be used to assist the development of social change along predetermined lines.

City planning in the United States has reflected the culture of which it is a part. It has been used to support economic growth and to maintain the present distribution of opportunities and of goods and services. Because the present distribution of such things as wealth, income, education, and health is unequal, city planning has supported the maintenance of such inequalities. Zoning and urban renewal have been used as a means of preserving the separation of income classes and racial groups. Planning has been employed for the purpose of maintaining segregated housing and segregated schools.

Historically, planners and those concerned with the planning process have not sought to make city planning a political device. Political is used here in the sense that the goals of public policy are open to debate through the political process. Rather than being open to public political debate, planning decisions have historically been made in the relative isolation afforded by the establishment of independent planning commissions. The commissions have been composed of the good men of the community, and have been expected to operate without exposure to the corrupting influence of electoral politics. City planners and city planning commissioners have not openly avowed a set of political, social, or economic goals. It has been assumed that the professional planner, an expert in the field, would conscientiously serve the public interest. It has not been assumed that the public interest consists of diverse interest groups with competing ideas of what public policy is best; instead, it has been assumed that the public interest is unitary, and self-evident, and that political bias would only distort its interpretation.

In most American cities only one agency, the planning commission, and its technical staff, the city planning department, have proposed plans for the community. As a result of this unitary planning communities are not in general offered a set of alternate plans representing different political, social, economic values; instead they are offered only one plan and then are limited in their choice to a yes or no vote.

I do not mean to suggest that we do not need recommendations from a central planning agency. Such direction is essential, but it should not constitute the only form of planning within a community. Plans representing the values of different interest groups in a community should also be made public. In a society in which political parties at the municipal level have differing concepts of appropriate public policy, the party platforms would themselves contain plans for the future development of the community.

Planning should be made a plural process, a process in which a number of competing plans are presented to the public. Rather than being isolated in a commission, the political forces that produce differing ideas about the form of a future community should be encouraged to work out differing plans, each supported by the technical expertise available to a skilled planning staff or consultant's office. This means that a new organization of planning practice has to come into existence, of a kind that has been called advocate planning.

Advocate planning implies the commitment of professional planners and designers to representing the interests of their client organizations. This commitment implies a willingness to take sides in political battles, rather than attempting to synthesize all interests into a public interest which is presumably served by a public plan. In many cases, this commitment is supplied by the convictions of the planners themselves, rather than by the fees which an organization is prepared to pay to a consultant. In recent years one group has begun to have its values represented by advocate planners. This is the group comprising the unrepresented in our society, the poor and the Negro. The advocates of the poor have in several cases been architects or architect-planners.

In New York City the Architects' Renewal Committee in Harlem, directed by Richard Hatch, has played a vital role in enabling community organizations in Harlem to participate more actively in the formulation of plans. In Boston the Urban Planning Aid under the direction of Robert Goodman and Dennis Blackett has played a similar role in proposing plans alternative to those prepared by the planning agencies in Cambridge and Boston. Another organization in San Francisco, PANR (Planners and Architects for Neighborhood Regeneration), played a similar role in that community.

One of the best known examples of advocate planning is the case of the alternative plan for Cooper Square in New York City, prepared by the widely known planning consultant Walter Thabit. Although at this time the alternative plan has not been accepted, it is quite apparent that the final plan for the Cooper Square area will either be the plan proposed by the residents of the community or at least a plan which recognizes the strong desires of that community not to have its present lower-class residents replaced by middle-class immigrants. It is true that these plans are in support of a particular part of our population. It need not, however, always be the case that only the poor are give the support of a professional planner working on a voluntary basis. Fee-paying organizations such as chambers of commerce, bank associations, supermarket chains, and taxpayers' groups are free to hire advocate planners who could plead their cause before central planning agencies.

While it is true that the unitary planning practice tends to diminish the political content of planning, a number of other factors tend to restrain city planning practice from dealing effectively with the nation's problems. The first of these factors has been planners' tendency to focus primarily upon the physical environment. This narrow perspective keeps the planner from seeing the city for which he plans as a system; instead he is limited to seeing only a part of the system, land uses and community facilities. Recently the American Institute of Planners has indicated that its concept of the range of planners' concern soon will be broadened to include consideration for economic and social as well as physical factors. If this change takes place it will be possible for planners to meet their aspirations for becoming comprehensive in their concerns. The Urban Planning Program at Hunter College sees city planning as concerned with all areas of public interest, including the social, the political, the economic, and the physical. While Hunter's is perhaps the first planning school to conceive of the role of the planner in such broad terms, it seems apparent that a number of other planning schools will follow Hunter in this view.

Perhaps the factor most limiting the ability of the city planner to deal effectively with problems in urban areas is the view that the basic problems confronting urban populations are such urban phenomena as congestion, pollution, and sprawl. These, while important, are secondary. The major problem confronting American cities today is the fact that such a large number of those denied political, social, and economic opportunities are residents of urban areas. The problem essentially is not an urban one; it is national and international.

Instead of seeking to create social equity, the present administration, like earlier liberal administrations, seems concerned only with assuaging the hurt of poverty. Rather than overcoming injustice, it seeks to mitigate pain. The War on Poverty is the classic example of the Great Society's inability to work for rapid large-scale social change. It might better be described as an alliance of the liberals with the oligarchs to minimize poverty sufficiently to allow the nation to pursue its course along accustomed paths. Instead of concentrating on its avowed goals of creating a Great Society, the Administration has chosen to focus its energies on destroying life and property in Asia.

Comprehensive planning in a democratic society would seek to redress the fundamental injustices of that society: inequality, prejudice, galling poverty. In our metropolitan regions, comprehensive planning would be aimed at carrying out federal requirements for equal participation by all communities in the solution of these social problems. As a precondition for receiving federal funds, a local community should be required to demonstrate that it is providing a fair share of the region's housing units and job opportunities for all classes of the region's population. Moreover, strong federal incentives should be offered to communities that participate in the establishment of educational, recreational, and other facilities serving the population of the whole region.

It is particularly important that each community demonstrate that it is contributing to solving problems of racial integration in its region.

At the federal level, it is necessary that provision be made for more equitable national distribution of income and opportunities. For example, it is necessary that instead of building only 20,000 public housing units a year, about half a million should be built. If the goal of providing a decent home in a suitable living environment for every American family is to be met in our generation, this is the kind of program magnitude that will be needed. At the recent Ribicoff hearings on city problems, estimates of upward of a trillion dollars over a ten- to twenty-year period were made to meet the needs of the decaying central cities. At a time when our GNP will average about a trillion dollars a year, a one trillion dollar allocation for solving our social problems is not absurd.

Democratic planning, then, requires both the active participation of differing groups in the preparation of plans that reflect their interest, and the synthesis of these interests in broad plans for the national and metropolitan regions that deal comprehensively with our social problems. The reconciliation of these two types of planning—advocate or plural planning and comprehensive social planning requires the existence of a healthy political process, one which elicits strong leadership and one which is capable of generating and sustaining powerful challenges to that leadership. Planners and designers may, within such a system, act either as political men or as technicians whose skills reflect others' political interests, or both.

1968

In an article entitled "A Significance for A&P Parking Lots, or Learning from Las Vegas" published in *Architectural Forum* in March 1968 and written by **Robert Venturi** and **Denise Scott Brown**, the incipient populism of Venturi's earlier

389–91   *Complexity and Contradiction in Architecture* came to fruition. The authors would test their ideas in a design studio and field study conducted with Steven Izenour at Yale School of Architecture that fall, publishing it in 1972 in book form as *Learning from Las Vegas,* along with two other chapters: one a more generalized argument derived from the first, entitled "Ugly and Ordinary Architecture, or the Decorated Shed," the other a catalogue of buildings designed by the Venturi firm —"Some Decorated Sheds"—from 1965 on. The following article by Scott Brown represents a first formulation of the decorated shed thesis.

In the transition from "complexity and contradiction" to "ugly and ordinary," the aesthetic criteria of Venturi's earlier book gave way to an empirical sociology and semiotics (still in a purely formal context) derived from current American social planning and communications theory. The reliance on ideas developed by

442–45   Herbert Gans, Melvin Webber, Paul Davidoff, and others reflected the inputs of Scott Brown, a South African educated at the Architectural Association in London in the early 1950s and then in urban planning at the University of Pennsylvania under Gans. Scott Brown brought to the husband-wife team (who began collaborating as early as 1960) not only the perspective of social science, but

240–41   also her firsthand experience of New Brutalist "socioplastics" and Independent
237–39   Group ideas, the latter having anticipated the American Pop movement by several years. The "almost all right" of Main Street, U.S.A., suggested in *Complexity and Contradiction*—"The main justification for honky-tonk elements in architecture is their very existence," Venturi had written—now became a didactic "judgment-deferred" analysis of the vernacular in places like Las Vegas and Levittown, and ultimately confirmed for its vitality and diversity. In an exchange with the Venturis published in 1971 in *Casabella,* Kenneth Frampton, one of the most vociferous critics of their position, argued that the would-be populism of the Strip was no more than the manipulation of the American consumer through advertising and other mythification: Las Vegas was created not *by* the people but, more cynically, *for* the people. Scott Brown retaliated by calling Frampton an "armchair revolutionary" with little understanding of American culture.

The second part of *Las Vegas* was focused on a semiotic distinction between the duck and the decorated shed—the building as a symbol in itself through its formal or spatial features as opposed to the building as a structure to which symbolism was applied. The authors felt the latter was more honest. Scott Brown later recalled how the concept evolved: "['On Ducks and Decoration'] was written while we were conducting the Las Vegas studio at Yale. Seeing modestly decorated Victorian warehouses through the train window on our weekly trip to New Haven; working in [Paul Rudolph's] Art and Architecture Building there; analyzing Las Vegas strip signs and reading *God's Own Junkyard* by Peter Blake, prescribed for the studio—one day all joined to form the now famous (or infamous) argument on the unadmitted symbolism of architectural form. I wrote the first draft . . . it was rewritten and extended in Part 2 of *Learning from Las Vegas.* In this early formulation, 'duck' is used metaphorically for the first time, but we refer to 'decoration' not 'decorated shed'; that idea came later."

The Venturis' validation of popular culture and its "forgotten symbolism" resulted in the advent of a Pop architecture in which high architecture emulated low. It also took inspiration from Andy Warhol's soup cans, Ed Ruscha's parking lots, and Tom Wolfe's *Kandy-Kolored Tangerine-Flake Streamline Baby.*

From Architecture Canada, *October 1968, pp. 48–49. Courtesy of the authors.*

On Ducks and Decoration
Denise Scott Brown and Robert Venturi

Loos equated decoration with sin; Perret believed it always hid a fault in construction. International stylists believed it was valid as the *joie d'esprit* of the individual craftsman as he worked by hand on the great cathedrals sculpting to the glory of God, but that in a machine age the I-thou relation with materials and construction is lost and so is the point of decoration; the same *joie d'esprit* should now, it was felt, be expressed through the beautiful and precise use of machine-made building elements and the eloquent spaces of the building itself. The whole building is the decoration.

This may have been literally and ironically more true than was intended. Contemporary painting and sculpture is now generally accepted as a formal source of early modern architecture—whole buildings from this period, in fact, resembled constructivist sculptures or cubist paintings. But this happened on an unconscious level. Architects such as Le Corbusier lived their connection to the arts intensely and it came through in their work.

A vocabulary of forms whether consciously possessed or not is probably as important in the synthesizing process which gets from functional requirements to a building as is a load of bricks. Whether you call it "composition" or "plastic organization" you have to have a philosophy about it. Your philosophy may be more or less useful depending on how well it helps you relate forms to requirements.

Later architects have taken too literally the functionalist dictum and allowed the formal vocabulary (still unadmitted) to stultify. We don't admit the importance of having a philosophy about forms, because a good building should arise like Venus purely from the functional requirements. But since this is impossible, a repertoire of old hand-me-downs, from Le Corbusier, Mies van der Rohe, or Lou Kahn slips in unnoticed while the pieties of each on antiformalism are mouthed.

Because applied decoration is still taboo the whole building is still the decoration. Only now, artists like Le Corbusier, sensitive to what they are denying, are not involved, so the formal vocabularies are dull, unsuited, and unrevised for today's needs. The more interesting the attempts of our best, most avant-garde architects at mannered complexity supposedly derived from structure and program, the more uninteresting their buildings become: they may heave themselves up on needless *pilotis,* corset themselves in rusted iron stays, zap out and up in plan and section ten stories, making twenty apartments with "bad space," or welcome in a heedless multitude to an unused piazza. They do these deeply distorting things for the sake of appearance, but they have no "decoration."

We believe a new interest in the architecture of communication involving symbolism and mixed media will lead us to reevaluate the eclectic and picturesque styles of the last century, to reappraise our own commercial architecture—pop architecture, if you wish—and finally to face the question of decoration. We have distinguished in a previous article[1] between two types of heraldry in the commercial environment: the sign which *is* the building (for example, the roadside duck, first brought to fame in Peter Blake's book) and the sign which *fronts* the building. The first distorts the less important inside function of drawing you in. The second, applied to the building or separated from it with the parking lot between, allows the modest eating function to take place without distortion in a modest building, right for it, and permits the symbolic function its own leeway as well—they need not coincide and it is probably cheaper and easier if they don't.

Our thesis is that most architects' buildings today are ducks: buildings where an expressive aim has distorted the whole beyond the limits of economy and convenience; and that this, although an unadmitted one, is a kind of decoration, and a wrong and costly one at that. We'd rather see the need admitted and the decoration applied where needed, not in the way the Victorians did it but to suit our time, as easily as the billboard is pasted on its superstructure; with the building it is applied to allow it to go its own conventional way, no more distorted than are the functional wind bracing and catwalks of the superstructure. This is an easier, cheaper, more direct, and basically more honest approach to the question of decoration; it permits us to get on with the task of making conventional buildings conventionally and to deal with their symbolic needs with a lighter, defter touch. It may lead us to reevaluate Ruskin's horrifying statement, "architecture is the decoration of structure." But add to it Pugin's warning: it is all right to decorate construction, but never construct decoration.[2]

Notes

1.   "Learning from Las Vegas, or a Significance for A & P Parking Lots," *Architectural Forum,* March 1968.

2.   We are grateful to Mr. Alan Lapidus, A.I. A., for this indirect quotation.

1968

From its inception in 1926, the Istituto Universitario di Architettura di Venezia (IAUV), had represented an alternative to the academic establishment in Rome and the polytechnics of Milan and Turin, Italy's chief centers of architecture education. But it was Giuseppe Samonà's appointment as director of the Venice institute in 1945 that decisively transformed it into a privileged enclave for independent architectural thought. Over the next quarter century Samonà brought the country's most creative and challenging architects and intellectuals

68–69 —Carlo Scarpa, Ignazio Gardella, Franco Albini, Bruno Zevi, Giancarlo de Carlo, Leonardo Benevolo, Carlo Aymonino—to teach there, while instigating a revision of modernism in terms of a lucidly conceived politics of culture and urbanism.

In 1968, at Samonà's invitation, the thirty-three-year-old **Manfredo Tafuri**, then teaching in Palermo, entered into this context. A graduate of the architecture school in Rome, where he had been affected by the Marxist phenomenology of the philosopher Galvano della Volpe (later rejected as

253–59 "sugary") and Giulio Carlo Argan's ideological criticism, Tafuri was very close to the architect Ludovico Quaroni, on whom he wrote a monograph published by Adriano Olivetti's publishing house Comunità in 1964. He also collaborated with a group of young architects interested in the "new urban dimension," a theme

399–401 introduced earlier by Samonà. Alongside this activity, which extended to a book on modern architecture in Japan, he undertook a major study of the Renaissance.

In Venice Tafuri continued to divide his attention between humanism— Palladio, Sansovino, Guarini—and modernism, devoting himself to an ideological critique of history in a broad sociocultural context. (He was later to say of his project of critical history, "I am not a historian of architecture, but *also* a historian of architecture.") With Benevolo's departure for Rome, he founded the Institute of Architectural History within the IAUV, gathering a brilliant group of colleagues: Giorgio Ciucci and Mario Manieri-Elia from Rome, Francesco Dal Co, Marco de Michelis, and the philosopher Massimo Cacciari. In 1968 he published a discourse on method, *Theories and History of Architecture,* the introduction of which follows. The book's title harbors a subtle Marxist distinction; later, in *The*

419–26 *Sphere and the Labyrinth* (1980), he would insist on the *plurality* of history, revealing the distance he had traveled under the intellectual impact of Venice, engaged in rereadings of the Frankfurt School (especially Walter Benjamin) and poststructuralism. Tafuri now revised *Theories and History* in the direction of Cacciari's negative thought, pushing his diagnosis of modernism's ideological crisis to a polemical extreme. In an essay entitled "Per una critica dell'ideologia architettonica," published in 1969 in *Contropiano* (a journal directed by Cacciari and the literary historian Alberto Asor Rosa), he argued that there could no longer be a class architecture, an architecture for a "liberated society," only a class criticism of architecture. This stance provoked accusations of nihilism from

288–99 Tomás Maldonado, for one, whose "hopes in design" Tafuri in turn scorned as reproducing the ideological illusions of modernism. Tafuri expanded his essay as *Project and Utopia: Design and Capitalist Development* in 1973. The English

392–97 edition (1976) included a drawing by Aldo Rossi on the jacket, inscribed to Tafuri and entitled, not unambiguously, "Architecture Assassinated."

For an illuminating study of the impact of Tafuri's thought and the "school of Venice" in Italy and France, see Jean-Louis Cohen, *La Coupure entre architectes et intellectuels, ou les enseignements de l'italophilie* (1984).

From Manfredo Tafuri, Teorie e storia dell'architettura *(Rome and Bari: Laterza, 1968), pp. 9–18. English edition:* Theories and History of Architecture *(London: Granada, 1980), trans. Giorgio Verrecchia, pp. 1–9. Courtesy of the author and Gius. Laterza & Figli .*

Introduction to *Theories and History of Architecture*
Manfredo Tafuri

That architectural criticism finds itself, today, in a rather difficult situation, is not a point that requires much underlining. To criticize, in fact, means to catch the historical scent of phenomena, put them through the sieve of strict evaluation, show their mystifications, values, contradictions, and internal dialectics, and explode their entire charge of meanings. But in the period we live in, mystifications and brilliant eversions, historical and antihistorical attitudes, bitter intellectualizations and mild mythologies mix themselves so inextricably in the production of art that the critic is bound to start an extremely problematic relationship with his accepted operative practice, particularly in considering the cultural tradition in which he moves. In fighting a cultural revolution there exists an intimate complicity between criticism and activity.

The critic who has embraced the revolutionary cause points all his weapons against the old order, digs out its contradictions and its hypocrisies, and builds a new ideological stack that may lead to the creation of myths: in every revolution myths are the force-ideas necessary to force the situation. But when the revolution—and there is no doubt that the artistic avant-gardes of the twentieth century have fought for a revolution—has reached its goals, criticism loses the support it had found in its total commitment to the revolutionary cause. Then, in order not to lose its purpose, criticism will have to turn to the history of the reforming movement, showing its shortcomings, contradictions, betrayed goals, failures, and, particularly, its complexity and fragmentation. Now the generous myths of the initial heroic period, having lost their role as powerful ideas, are reduced to subjects of debate.

In our case, facing so many explosions of intricate movements, agitations, new questions, and the resulting multiform and chaotic panorama of architectural international culture in the seventies, the main disturbing problem for those critics who do not wish to bury their heads in the sand, or live in an escapist peace with worn-out myths, is still the historical assessment of the present contradictions. This implies a courageous and honest scrutiny of the very foundations of the modern movement: in fact, a thorough investigation of whether it is still legitimate to speak of a modern movement as a monolithic corpus of ideas, poetics, and linguistic traditions. One must not, then, turn away from the vista of laborious, uncertain, and frustrated efforts that architects have accumulated. It may be one's duty to speak of escapism, renunciations, withdrawals, and the waste of usable assets. But this is not enough. The critic that stops at these considerations, which are so obvious as to be almost useless, has already betrayed his foremost task, which is to explain, to diagnose exactly, and to avoid moralizing in order to see, in the context of negative facts, what are the mistakes we are now paying for, and which are the new values nesting in the difficult and disconnected set of circumstances we live in, day by day. The main danger, in this case, is being caught in the very ambiguity from which one tries to extract a logical structure and a meaning, as preconditions to any future operation directed toward a new working hypothesis.

Today it is even more necessary for the critic to be open-minded, to accept, without the falsifying veil of prejudices, totally confused proposals. Today, as never before, there is a need for stricter attitudes, for a deep sense and knowledge of history, as well as for a watchful eye, in order to sort out, in the vast context of historical movements, broad research, or single projects, the influences dictated by fashion— and even cultural snobbism—from the forces of renewal.

The architect can always find some sort of coherence in the contradictions of the "job" of planning, but the critic content with such a situation would either be simply skeptical, or unforgivably superficial. By researching on a firm basis the possibilities contained in the poetics and codes of contemporary architecture, it is possible to salvage a cultural positivism and constructivism, even if often limited to marginal questions. But the critic conscious of the transient and *dangerous* situation of modern architecture cannot allow himself illusions or artificial enthusiasms in the same way as he cannot allow himself—and this is perhaps more important—apocalyptic or intimist attitudes. (The critic is like the person who has decided to walk on a tightrope while constantly changing winds do their best to blow him down.) The image is not at all rhetorical: since the modern movement discovered its own multiformity, with relative shock, the initial partnership between committed criticism and new architecture and, indeed, the identification of criticism with an activity that shares its premises and problems, has necessarily weakened. The merging of the character of architect and critic in the same person—almost the norm in architecture, unlike other techniques of visual communication—has not entirely covered up this rupture: the split personality of the architect who writes and theorizes and also practices is commonplace.

It is for this reason that the *pure critic* begins to be seen as a dangerous figure: and to be labeled with the stamp of a movement, a trend, or a poetic. As the kind of criticism that needs to keep its distance from the operative practice must constantly demystify that practice in order to go beyond its contradictions or, at least, render them with a certain precision, one sees the architects trying to *capture* that criticism; trying, in fact, to exorcise it. Trying to avoid capture may be interpreted as fear by the ignorant or dishonest. But the critic, in order to return to his proper task—objective and unprejudiced historical diagnosis and not the job of prompter or "proofreader"—needs, on the contrary, a great deal of courage, because in attempting to historicize the dramatic meanings of the present moment, he is walking on mined ground.

It is useless hiding from the fact that the threat hanging over the head of those wanting to "understand" by radically demolishing every contemporary myth is the same as that felt by Vasari in the second half of the sixteenth century: more and more one is invited to answer the tragic question of the historical permissibility of the modern movement's continuity with tradition.

Merely to pose the question of whether contemporary architecture finds itself, or not, at a radical turning point has value as a symptom. It means that one feels, at the same time, inside and outside the historical tradition, steeped in it yet beyond it, ambiguously involved in a figurative revolution that, entirely founded on the permanent opposition to every acquired truth, turns its weapons upon itself. As Rosenberg wrote, contesting the false radicalism of Sir Herbert Read:

Neither revolutionary art nor revolutionary criticism can get out of it: revolutionary art is a contradiction. It declares that art is art in being against art; and then tries to establish itself as the soundest kind of art. It demands of the critic that he take "explosiveness" as an aesthetic principle, and that he protects this principle against being blown to bits by the "conscious negation" of principles.

At war with themselves, revolutionary art and criticism cannot avoid the ridiculous. Yet upon the contradiction of revolution depends the life of art in this revolutionary epoch, and art and criticism must continue to embrace its absurdities.[1]

But, perhaps, it is not quite enough just to accept the ridiculousness of the situation. The task of criticism has, in fact, changed. If the problem is to operate a sort of changing selection without *a priori* leanings, in order to identify the structure of the problems that are confusedly faced and then left untackled by the new generations and by the few culturally alive masters of the "third generation" of the modern movement, one cannot give, once and for all, the terms of comparison for the foundation of a historical analysis. Criticism is bound, like architecture, continually to revolutionize itself in the search for adequate parameters.

It is no longer possible to trust what has been the traditional safety valve of criticism: the absolution or condemnation of the work in itself. The futility of such a dogmatic attitude on the part of the critic is even clearer. Having said this, let us avoid a possible misunderstanding: we do not at all mean to say that we should get rid of judgment and be content with a sort of relativistic limbo where *tout se tient*. What we would rather emphasize is the difficulty of anyone who is bound to be in daily touch not with badly or well-finished work, but rather with endless unfulfilled intentions, with new impulses bogged down in the most disheartening and traditional contexts, with reticent intuitions and with intentionally unrealizable projects. Is it possible to evaluate in a traditional way such a disconcerting vista, or is it not, rather, the specific task of the critic to understand its intrinsic meaning, and establish some order through a temporary suspension of judgment?

In an unprejudiced examination of the current situation of architectural culture, the inconsistency and elusiveness of so much current production makes it obvious that one is facing a tacit and perhaps unconscious effort to state, on the one hand, the ineffective nature of architecture, and on the other, to find, however confused, a new and unforeseen dimension for architectural activity. It is because of that we have spoken of the possible new availability of the critic: a rigorous and controlled availability, of course, but adequate to the tasks set by the historical moment.[2]

At this point there emerges the essential question of a rigorous formulation of the critic's basic tools. After all, the criticism of modern architecture has been obliged to proceed, almost until today, along rails laid on unprejudiced empiricism: perhaps this was the only viable route as, too often, the art of our century has jumped the fence of ideological conventions, of speculative foundations, of the very same aesthetics available to the critic. So much so that the only authentic criticism of modern art came, especially between 1920 and 1940, from those with enough courage not to derive their analytical methods from existing philosophical systems but from direct and empirical contact with the thoroughly new questions of the avant-gardes.

One must not judge this empirical criticism in a hurry. Through it Pevsner, Behne, Benjamin, Giedion, Persico, Giolli, Argan, Dorner, and Shand went, before World War II, beyond the limitations of the thinking of their time, deriving, from the poetics of modern art, the ability to read the new phenomena in the light of an open process, of perpetual mutability, of vindication of the casual, the nonrational, the gestural, and the absurd. Postwar criticism has been able to graft onto this empirical tradition the contributions of Lukacsian realism, existentialism, relativism, Husserlian phenomenology, some Bergsonian recouping of the past, a revitalized Fiedlerian pure-visibilism, Croce, and, more recently, Gestalt psychology, structural linguistics, semantics, semiology, information theory, and anthropological structuralism.

Critical eclecticism then? Perhaps; but at least not completely negative. This eclecticism has shown that, in part, the questions posed by modern architecture are more advanced than those successively faced by the traditional methods; and in part it has shown the operative independence of criticism, so much so that the philosophers themselves have admitted to receiving stimuli and new concepts from it.[3]

But once glimpsed, the crisis of critical operability (because it is no longer possible to take a single position in favor of one current in modern architecture), once discovered, the imminent dialectic of contemporary art, empiricism, and eclecticism begin to look like dangers, like instruments unable to provide a rigorous criticism. Lately architectural critics have shown a symptomatic interest in the researches that have introduced, in the social sciences and the analysis of linguistic and visual communications, methods analogous to those of the empirical and experimental sciences. Today semiology and structuralism are also on the agenda in architectural studies. And one can show immediately the positive contributions made by them to the analysis of planning: first of all they satisfy the need for a scientific basis, and the need for objectivity is particularly felt in times of deep uncertainty and restlessness. Secondly, they offer a systematic commitment to understanding the phenomena that justify the poetics of anguish and crisis, by now become evasive and imperative through wear and tear. Any criticism, to do more than whining, must, basically, make a diagnosis. And as diagnostic methods—once recognized as such and not as fashionable doctrines or as a single dogmatic corpus—structuralism and semiology have already shown their efficiency. But they have also shown the danger and the ideology hiding behind their apparent lack of ideology. Once more, then, criticism is called upon to give its contribution: to choose, and to place within a well-founded historicism the materials on offer.

If it is true, though, as François Furet[4] has written, that the fascination felt by the French leftist intelligentsia for the structuralism of Lévi-Strauss is due to the fact that "simply and progressively the structural description of a man-made object has taken the place, in history, of the advent of the man-god," it is true also that a large part of modern art had foreseen this substitution: from Dada and some aspects of De Stijl and from Russian constructivism to Le Corbusier, if one reads it correctly. And one cannot say that the acceptance of the end of the myth of humanist anthropocentrism has not led, so far as those artistic experiences are concerned, to a new and more authentic attitude in man toward the world structured by him.

Somehow we could consider Lévi-Strauss the Parmenides of this neo-Eleatic flavored *(malgré soi)* philosophy: structure and order against disorder in history, the permanence of Being against the phenomenology of Becoming, the stability of the common mechanisms to which man is reduced against Sartrian dialectical reason (but one is already beginning to see the first skirmishes of the neo-Zenoni demolishing paradoxes). For the moment we are interested in understanding the meaning of some considerable nodes between the structuralist vogue and certain phenomena at the center of artistic and architectural culture. To justify these nodes it is not necessary to rely on the hypothesis of direct influences, which are almost certainly nonexistent. The very fact that it is not possible to demonstrate such a direct exchange becomes, at this point, an independent point of interest, showing the existence of a common horizon created by a common attitude to the present historical condition.

It is of particular relevance to note, here, that ethnological structuralism in its original meaning, Foucault's "archaeology of human sciences," the antihumanist orgy of Pop art, the search for a *new* objectivity by Kahn and his followers, insist—all of them—on the same ideal area (and we would have said ideological, if this term would not take on here the tone of polemical paradox). To discover that this ideal area is all based on antihistorical knowledge and activity might frighten or disconcert. But we shall be far less disconcerting if we try to go further, to dig deeper into the phenomena and not to be led by inadequate ideological pulls.

Has modern art not presented itself, from the very beginning, in the European avant-garde movements, as a true challenge to history? Has it not tried to destroy not only history, but even itself as a historical object? Dada and De Stijl are not all that antithetical if seen from this very particular point of view. But this is not all. The gap between Louis Kahn's myth of Order, with his hermetic delving into the material offered by history so as to dehistorify, to the extreme, architectural planning; and the neoplastic mysticism tending to resolve oppositions and contrasts in a messianic appeasement is not as crucial as it may first appear when we compare works like the Salk laboratories and the Schroeder house.

The traditional antihistoricism of the avant-gardes finds, then, a kind of confirmation in the very experiences that are trying to overcome it. And there is a reason. "Myth is against history," Barthes tells us, and myths carry on their mystification by hiding the artificial (and the ideological artificiality) behind the mask of a fake "naturalism."[5] If we accept these premises, then the present moment, so totally bent on avoiding, through *new myths,* the commitment of understanding the present, cannot help turning even the researches that, with renewed vigor and rigor, try to plan a systematic and objective reading of the world, of things, of history, and of human conventions into *fashion* and *myth.*

In architectural culture, in particular (but the point applies to all techniques of visual communication), looking for a more advanced criticism seems to compromise the very basis of the critical spirit. In 1957 Argan wrote:

If we have a crisis on hand, it is not the crisis of criticism, and not just from yesterday, that has upset the great ideologies, conceptions, and systems. And this should not be, by itself, a cause for despair: criticism is built on crises, and one should only think of it as criticism that goes beyond its own results. The outcome of the crises is unforeseeable: criticism does not allow predestined salvations or condemnations. However salvation—salvation of the critical spirit inherited from the Enlightenment by modern art and culture—is likely, if criticism is to be criticism of experiences and not of hypotheses: if it will show itself to be, even in art, historical criticism.[6]

Well, twenty years after Argan stated his lucid diagnosis, we can say that, today more than ever, art and architecture have been dominated by the ineffability of hypothesis, and have been so little creators of experiences. Nor, we must add, has criticism perhaps ever assumed such a minimal historicist character as the one that goes hand in hand with the proliferation of architecture.

From this brief survey, it follows that the critic who wants to make historical the experiences of contemporary architecture and who tries to rescue historicity from the web of the past, finds himself against the current. To what degree then does this opposition involve the historicity of the modern movement? And to what degree is the separation from the flow of praxis symptomatic of a deep crisis of *operative criticism,* or is there an opening, in criticism, for a new operative *modus*? And again, what is the relationship that history and criticism can legitimately start with the new sciences and the theories of communication, and still preserve their specific prerogatives, their specific roles, and their specific methods?

These are, basically, the questions at the core of this book: in it, perhaps, one should look for guidelines and temporary solutions more than for definitive answers. We are convinced that methodologies of history should closely relate with the tasks that history itself, in the problem of its development, offers to those who refuse to be swallowed up by the daily mythologies, and by the mythologies—similar and opposed—of catharsis that many would like to conjure up from the gradual and silent annihilation of "historical reason."

Notes

1.   Harold Rosenberg, *The Tradition of the New* (Horizon Press, 1959). In the same essay ("Revolution and the Concept of Beauty"), Rosenberg denounces the ambiguous links between political revolutions and artistic revolutions, referring to the confusion—today considerably reduced—present in the American culture of the forties and fifties. But his diagnosis still contains a relevant truth when he states that "The result [of those ambiguities] is an atmosphere of bad conscience, of dupery and self-dupery. It is not too much to say that bad conscience about revolution is the specific malady of art today."

2.   This availability is made even more necessary by the artistic experience's continuous permutation of semantic areas, often one superimposed on the other. For this reason the crisis of every defined aesthetic, sanctioned by the semantic criticism historicized by Plebe and taken by Garroni to a "plural notion of art," needs an extremely complex critical attitude and an aesthetic "that suggests an open artistic field, open and unpredictable" (as later recognized by Anceschi). (Cf. Armando Plebe, *Processo all'estetica* [Florence: La Nuova Italia, 1952]; Emilio Garroni, *La crisi semantica delle arti* [Rome: Officina Ed., 1964], pp. 109 ff.; Luciano Anceschi, *Progetto di una sistematica dell'arte* [Milan: Mursia, 1962], and idem, "Critica, Filosofia, Fenomenologia," in *Il Verri* 18 [1967], pp. 13–24.) Within this sphere, criticism, having lost the hope of finding preexisting support in a rigorously philosophical aesthetic, finds new autonomy and new responsibilities.

3.   On this subject, the results of the round table at the INARCH, Rome, March 1961, are of considerable interest. (Discussions by G. Calogero, R. Assunto, R. Bonelli, A. Plebe.) They partially appeared in *L'Architettura cronache e storia,* vol. 7, no. 71 (1961), pp. 336–37.

4.   François Furet, "Gli intellettuali francesi e lo structuralismo," in *Tempo Presente,* no. 7 (1967), p. 14.

5.   We are obviously referring to Roland Barthes's *Mythologies.*

6.   Giulio Carlo Argan, "La crisi dei valori" (1957), now in *Salvezza e caduta dell'arte moderna* (Milan: Il Saggiatore, 1964), p. 38.

1968

By the mid-1960s students and faculty at the Ecole Nationale Supérieure des Beaux-Arts (E.N.S.B.A.) were becoming increasingly restive. In line with the vast expansion taking place throughout French higher education, the enrollment in architecture increased from 4,000 to 6,000 between 1960 and 1967. Yet in 1965 there were only nine *patrons* (studio masters) and twenty assistants on the state payroll for nearly 3,000 students in Paris in twenty-three studios. In the provinces the ratio was worse. Still more untenable was the school's antiquated pedagogy and qualification process. A 250-year-old bastion of the *vieille académie,* the school barely acknowledged the contribution of modern architecture until 1965, the year Le Corbusier died. It continued to perpetuate a system of *concours* instituted in the eighteenth century, a marathon of competitions and grades frequently described as a form of social Darwinism. In the later years the thirty-six-day-long Prix de Rome ordeals were plagued by rampant cheating and plagiarism. A diploma, which had traditionally ensured entree into an elite system of professional patronage, no longer guaranteed even this to the larger number of graduates of the 1960s. The curriculum was likewise indifferent to social realities. Not until 1962 was a specific urban site given as part of a Grand Prix program. It hardly seems surprising that students in 1967 would demand the "right" to design social housing. One of the system's few saving graces was a long-standing provision for "exterior" ateliers—studios run by architects outside the school who were solicited by the students themselves and appointed upon petition. The catch was that these *patrons* were unpaid by the Ecole and, to the disadvantage of their students, did not regularly participate on juries or in the awarding of prizes. Nonetheless the *ateliers libres* gave students a chance to work with architects far more progressive in orientation than the official faculty. Under this arrangement Georges Candilis took charge of an atelier in 1964. Later, with other exterior studios, it became a prime catalyst for student radicalism.

At the same time, the problems specific to the **Ecole des Beaux-Arts** *427–36* were part of a much larger set of grievances against French education and society. The protest against inequities in the academic system was reinforced by an increasingly militant assault on injustices outside it. The criticism mounted by the various factions that came to be known as the New Left was brought to a head by the Gaullist government's inability to respond to growing labor unrest in 1967, the American aggression in Vietnam, and hopes of a radical alliance between the working class and intellectuals (at least on the part of the latter). The hated housing developments built for blue-collar habitation in the French suburbs in the 1950s and 1960s—Sarcelles on the outskirts of Paris being the most notorious—came to epitomize the invidious results of an "architecture of technocracy." Likewise deplored, and implicating architects, were working conditions in the construction industry. "Three deaths a day on the construction site" became a rallying cry in the briefly realized student-worker coalition.

For a contemporary chronicle of the actions leading up to the incendiary "events of May" at the Ecole des Beaux-Arts, and of the school's dissolution and reorganization into eight *unités pédagogiques,* see the issue of *Architectural Design* edited by Martin Pawley and Bernard Tschumi in September 1971. The famous "Motion of May 15" that follows was adopted by the **Strike Committee** a week after the strike was declared in Paris and a day after occupation of the school's premises began. The students remained in the school for more than five weeks. With the building's "liberation" on June 27, the revolution was effectively over, leaving a generation of architects to come to grips with its legacy.

Published as "Motion de 15 Mai" in "Spéciale Mai 68," Architecture, Mouvement, Continuité, *July 1968, p. 11.*

Motion of May 15
Strike Committee, Ecole des Beaux-Arts

Wednesday, May 15, 12:00

Why are we prolonging the struggle? What are we fighting against? We are fighting against the class-based University; we want to organize the struggle against all its aspects:

1. We oppose the social discrimination that operates throughout the course of study, from the primary to the higher grades, to the disadvantage of working-class children and poor peasants.

We want to fight against the system of examinations and competitions, principal means of this discrimination.

2. We oppose the content of the teaching and the pedagogical forms in which it is disseminated. Everything is organized so as to ensure that the products of the system acquire neither critical consciousness nor knowledge of social and economic realities.

3. We oppose the role society expects intellectuals to play: to be watchdogs of the system of economic production, to be technocratic managers, to see to it that each person feels very happy with his lot, especially when he is being exploited.

What do these criticisms mean for the school of architecture? For the school of painting and sculpture? It is certainly up to the Commissions to define it precisely, but we can already do so as far as architecture is concerned:

• We want to contest the domination of the curriculum by the profession through the Conseil de l'Ordre and other corporate bodies. We are against the Masters system as a pedagogical method. We are against the conformist ideology disseminated by the system. The teaching of architecture must not solely consist of the repetition of what the master does, to the point where the student is finally a carbon copy.

• We want to fight against the conditions of architectural production, which in fact subordinate it to the interests of public or private developers. How many architects have agreed to carry out large or small Sarcelles? How many architects take into account in the notes they keep on their commissions the conditions of information, hygiene, and worker security on the construction site; and do it in such a way that any developer heeds their appeals? Everyone knows that there are three deaths a day in France in the construction industry.

• We want to contest the content of a curriculum that is particularly conservative, particularly irrational and unscientific, in which impressions and personal habits continue to prevail over objective knowledge.

The ideology of the prix de Rome is still alive.

In short we want to take stock of the real relations between the school and society; we want to fight against its class character.

We have to realize that we cannot fight this fight alone. We must not harbor illusions that the university will be able to establish within its faculties the seeds of real autonomy with respect to bourgeois society as a whole.

The university must fight side by side with the workers, who are the principal victims of the social discrimination carried out by the system of instruction. The fight against the class-based university must be linked organically to the fight of all workers against the capitalist system of exploitation.

It is necessary for us to engage: to call into question the relations that now govern the profession and the curriculum:

- To challenge the present separation of the E.N.S.B.A. from university studies;
- To refuse to allow any form of preselection in admissions to the school;
- To contest the present system of examinations and competitions;
- To prepare for the workers' struggle;
- To prepare for the struggle against the reform decrees;
- To establish real links with the workers' struggle.

On all these questions, we must have the freest possible debates.

All teachers must speak out.
Organized forms of struggle must be found.

1968

After two years of architecture study in the United States in 1958–60, **Hans Hollein** returned to his home city of Vienna where he began collaborating with his compatriot Walter Pichler. Within a short time the two had emerged as the leading figures in a group of radical architects working in that city. Hollein and Pichler jointly produced a manifesto in 1962 entitled "Absolute Architecture" in which they declared in separate statements that architecture was a ritualistic expression of pure, elemental will and sublime purposelessness. The following year a four-day exhibition of their work at the Galerie Sankt Stephan had a catalytic effect on the Viennese scene. Hollein's models and drawings conjuring up archetypal monuments, abstract urban complexes, and infrastructures of unspecified function and scale gave a potent image to an iconoclastic and visionary architecture. So did his surrealistic montage of 1964 depicting an aircraft carrier beached in the Austrian wheat fields. A first commission in 1965, for the Retti candle shop, allowed him to realize some of his ideas on a small scale. Detailed in an elegantly technical language, the shop exhibited a facade of symbolistic symmetries rendered paradoxical by an illusionist play of mirrors and metallic surfaces within.

After further collaborations with Pichler on sculptural architecture and then on pneumatic environments—a concept also pursued in the late 1960s by two younger Viennese groups, Coop Himmelblau and Haus-Rucker-Co—the paths of the two architects diverged. The following statement by Hollein appeared as an introduction to a thirty-page compendium of images which he assembled in a memorable issue of *Bau*. The pictorial selection—ranging from pneumatic and tent structures by Frei Otto and works by Claes Oldenburg, Christo, and Joseph Beuys to a portrait of revolutionary hero Che Guevara—is a vivid montage of 1960s aesthetic counterculture. Hollein's statement reveals his continuing expansion of the concept of architecture, not only to embrace other media, but to transcend its own physicality into a comprehensive and invisible technical

86–92   environment. Buckminster Fuller's message is explicit here, as is that of Marshall McLuhan. The latter had written (in *Understanding Media*, 1964), "During the mechanical ages we had extended our bodies in space. Today . . . we have extended our central nervous system itself in a global embrace, abolishing both space and time as far as our planet is concerned. Rapidly we approach the final phase of the extensions of man—the technological simulation of consciousness."

From the building to the book to the media environment: with his pronouncement of the end of the Gutenberg galaxy McLuhan gave one more turn of the screw to Victor Hugo's *ceci tuera cela*. Hollein's rituals of a "cultic architecture" looked back to the future via the technological tribalism of the global

402–7   village. Like Arata Isozaki's work in Japan and other neo-avant-garde
365–69 . manifestations around the world in these years—including Archigram in England
437–41   and Superstudio in Italy, with whom there were close contacts—the Viennese movement inspired by Hollein belongs to a current of technological prophecy directly responding to the cultural crisis of postindustrial society. For a rich compilation of the work of the Vienna architects, including poetic delineators like Friedrich St. Florian and Raimund Abraham and experimental groups like Coop Himmelblau, whose interventions at this date recall Frederick Kiesler's multimedia explorations and the "happenings" on the American art scene, see a recent book by one of the movement's progenitors: Günther Feuerstein, *Visionäre Architektur Wien 1958/1988* (1988).

As published under the title "Alles ist Architektur" in Bau *1/2 (1968), p. 2. Revised in English in the catalogue* Hollein *(Chicago: Richard Feigen Gallery, 1969). Courtesy of the author.*

Everything Is Architecture
Hans Hollein

Limited and traditional definitions of architecture and its means have lost their validity. Today the environment as a whole is the goal of our activities—and all the media of its determination: TV or artificial climate, transportation or clothing, telecommunication or shelter.

The extension of the human sphere and the means of its determination go far beyond a built statement. Today everything becomes architecture. "Architecture" is just one of many means, is just one possibility.

Man creates artificial conditions. This is Architecture. Physically and psychically man repeats, transforms, expands his physical and psychical sphere. He determines "environment" in its widest sense.

According to his needs and wishes he uses the means necessary to satisfy these needs and to fulfill these dreams. He expands his body and his mind. He communicates.

Architecture is a medium of communication.

Man is both—self-centered individual and part of a community. This determines his behavior. From a primitive being, he has continuously expanded himself by means of media which were thus themselves expanded.

Man has a brain. His senses are the basis for perception of the surrounding world. The means for the definition, for the establishment of a (still desired) world are based on the extension of these senses.

These are the media of architecture—architecture in the broadest sense.

To be more specific, one could formulate the following roles and definitions for the concept "Architecture":

Architecture is cultic; it is mark, symbol, sign, expression.

Architecture is control of bodily heat—protective shelter.

Architecture is determination—establishment—of space, environment.

Architecture is conditioning of a psychological state.

For thousands of years, artificial transformation and determination of man's world, as well as sheltering from weather and climate, was accomplished by means of *building*. The *building* was the essential manifestation and expression of man. Building was understood as the creation of a three-dimensional image of the necessary as spatial definition, protective shell, mechanism and instrument, psychic means and symbol. The development of science and technology, as well as changing society and its needs and demands, has confronted us with entirely different realities. Other and new media of environmental determination emerge.

Beyond technical improvements in the usual principles, and developments in physical "building materials" through new materials and methods, intangible means for spatial determination will also be developed. Numerous tasks and problems will continue to be solved traditionally, through building, through "architecture." Yet for many questions is the answer still "Architecture" as it has been understood, or are better media not available to us?

Architects have something to learn in this respect from the development of military strategy. Had this science been subject to the same inertness as architecture and its consumers, we would still be building fortification walls and towers. In contrast, military planning left behind its connection to building to avail itself of new possibilities for satisfying the demands placed upon it.

New York während des Streiks der Müllabfuhr

ALLES IST ARCHITEKTUR

Otto Mühl, 1965, Materialaktion

Obviously it no longer occurs to anyone to wall-in sewage canals or erect astronomical instruments of stone (Jaipur). New communications media like telephone, radio, TV, etc. are of far more import. Today a museum or a school can be replaced by a TV set. Architects must cease to think only in terms of *buildings*.

There is a change as to the importance of "meaning" and "effect." Architecture affects. The way I take possession of an object, how I use it, becomes important. A building can become entirely information—its message might be experienced through informational media (press, TV, etc.). In fact it is of almost no importance whether, for example, the Acropolis or the Pyramids exist in physical reality, as most people are aware of them through other media anyway and not through an experience of their own. Indeed, their importance—the role they play—is based on this effect of information.

Thus a building might be *simulated* only.

An early example of the extension of buildings through media of communication is the telephone booth—a building of minimal size extended into global dimensions. Environments of this kind more directly related to the human body and even more concentrated in form are, for example, the helmets of jet pilots who, through telecommunication, expand their senses and bring vast areas into direct relation with themselves. Toward a synthesis and to an extreme formulation of a contemporary architecture leads the development of space capsules and space suits. Here is a "house"—far more perfect than any building—with a complete control of bodily functions, provision of food and disposal of waste, coupled with a maximum of mobility.

These far-developed physical possibilities lead us to think about psychic possibilities of determinations of environments. After shedding the need of any necessity of a physical shelter at all, a new freedom can be sensed. Man will now finally be the center of the creation of an individual environment.

The extension of the media of architecture beyond pure tectonic building and its derivations first led to experiments with new structures and materials, especially in railroad construction. The demand to change and transport our "environment" as quickly and easily as possible forced a first consideration of a broad range of materials and possibilities—of means that have been used in other fields for ages. Thus we have today "sewn" architecture, as we have also "inflatable" architecture. All these, however, are still material means, still "building materials."

Little consequent experimentation has been undertaken to use nonmaterial means (like light, temperature, or smell) to determine an environment, to determine space. As the use of already existing methods has vast areas of application, so could the use of the laser (hologram) lead to totally new determinations and experiences. Finally, the purposeful use of chemicals and drugs to control body temperature and body functions as well as to create artificial environments has barely started. Architects have to stop thinking in terms of buildings only.

Built and physical architecture, freed from the technological limitations of the past, will more intensely work with spatial qualities as well as with psychological ones. The process of "erection" will get a new meaning, spaces will more consciously have haptic, optic, and acoustic properties, and contain informational effects while directly expressing emotional needs.

A true architecture of our time will have to redefine itself and expand its means. Many areas outside traditional building will enter the realm of architecture, as architecture and "architects" will have to enter new fields.

All are architects. Everything is architecture.

Selected Bibliography

General histories and reference works
Leonardo Benevolo. *History of Modern Architecture*. Vol. 2. Cambridge: MIT Press, 1971.
Ulrich Conrads. *Programs and Manifestoes on 20th-Century Architecture*. Cambridge: MIT Press, 1975.
Philip Drew. *The Third Generation: The Changing Meaning in Architecture*. New York: Praeger, 1972.
Kenneth Frampton. *Modern Architecture: A Critical History*. New York: Oxford Univ. Press, 1980.
John Jacobus. *Twentieth-Century Architecture: The Middle Years, 1940–1965*. New York: Praeger, 1966.
Charles Jencks. *Modern Movements in Architecture*. New York: Anchor Press, 1973.
Jürgen Joedicke. *Architecture since 1945: Sources and Directions*. New York: Praeger, 1969.
Manfredo Tafuri and Francesco Dal Co. *Modern Architecture*. Vol. 2. New York: Rizzoli, 1986.
A. M. Vogt, U. Jehle-Schulte Strathaus, B. Reichlin. *Architektur 1940–1980*. Frankfurt: Propylaeon, 1980.
Bruno Zevi. *Storia dell'architettura moderna*. 6th ed. rev. Turin: Giulio Einaudi, 1975.

Books on national architectures
Amadeo Belluzzi and Claudia Conforti, *Architettura italiana 1944–1984*. Rome–Bari: Laterza, 1985.
Carlos Flores. *Arquitectura española contemporanea*. Bilbao: Aquilar, 1961.
William H. Jordy. *The Impact of European Modernism in the Mid-Twentieth Century*. Vol. 4, *American Buildings and Their Architects*. Garden City, New York: Anchor Books, 1972.
G. E. Kidder-Smith. *Sweden Builds: Its Modern Architecture and Land Policy*. New York: Bonnier, 1956.
———. *Switzerland Builds. Its Native and Modern Architecture*. New York: Bonnier, 1958.
Jacques Lucan. *France: Architecture 1965–1988*. Paris: Electa Moniteur, 1989.
Gérard Monnier. *Histoire critique de l'architecture en France 1918–1950*. Paris: Philippe Sers, 1990.
Manfredo Tafuri. *History of Italian Architecture 1944–1985*. Cambridge: MIT Press, 1989.
See also the following series: Jul Bachmann and Stanislaus von Moos, *New Directions in Swiss Architecture;* Robin Boyd, *New Directions in Japanese Architecture;* Francisco Bullrich, *New Directions in Latin American Architecture;* Günther Feuerstein, *New Directions in German Architecture;* Vittorio Gregotti, *New Directions in Italian Architecture;* Anatole Kopp, *New Directions in Soviet Architecture;* Udo Kultermann, *New Directions in African Architecture;* Roylston Landau, *New Directions in English Architecture;* Robert A. M. Stern, *New Directions in American Architecture*. New York: Braziller, 1968–69.

Thematic works and works on related subjects
Archigram. "The Forties." *Archigram* 6 (1967).
Reyner Banham. *Megastructure: Urban Futures of the Recent Past*. London: Thames & Hudson, 1976.
———. *The New Brutalism: Ethic or Aesthetic?* New York: Reinhold, 1966.
Jean-Louis Cohen. *La Coupure entre architectes et intellectuels, ou les enseignements de l'italophilie*. Paris: Ecole d'Architecture Paris-Villemin, 1984.
Trevor Dannatt. *Modern Architecture in Britain*. London: Batsford, 1959.
Serge Guilbaut. *How New York Stole the Idea of Modern Art*. Chicago: Univ. of Chicago Press, 1983.
Günther Feuerstein. *Visionäre Architektur Wien. 1958/1988*. Berlin: Ernst & Sohn, 1988.
Peter Hall. *Cities of Tomorrow: An Intellectual History of City Planning in the 20th Century*. Oxford: Blackwell, 1988.
Klaus Herdeg. *The Decorated Diagram: Harvard Architecture and the Failure of the Bauhaus Legacy*. Cambridge: MIT Press, 1983.
Kathryn Hiesinger and George H. Marcus. *Design since 1945*. Philadelphia: Philadelphia Museum of Art, 1983.
Kisho Kurokawa. *Metabolism in Architecture*. London: Studio Vista, 1977.
H.-R. Hitchcock and A. Drexler, eds. *Built in USA: Post-war Architecture*. New York: Museum of Modern Art, 1952.
Frederic James Osborne and Arnold Whittick. *The New Towns: Answer to Megalopolis*. London: L. Hill, 1963.
Ernesto N. Rogers. *Editoriali di architettura*. Turin: Giulio Einaudi, 1968.
———. *Esperienza dell'architettura*. Turin: Giulio Einaudi, 1958.
David Robbins, ed. *The Independent Group: Postwar Britain and the Aesthetics of Plenty*. Cambridge: MIT, 1990.
Elizabeth A. T. Smith, ed. *Blueprints for Modern Living: History and Legacy of the Case Study Houses*. Cambridge: MIT Press, and Los Angeles: Museum of Contemporary Art, 1989.
Alison Smithson, ed. *The Emergence of Team 10 out of CIAM*. London: Architectural Association, 1982.
Elizabeth Sussman, ed. *On the Passage of a Few People through a Rather Brief Moment of Time: The Situationist International 1957–1972*. Cambridge: MIT Press, 1989.
Hans Maria Wingler. *The Bauhaus: Weimar, Dessau, Chicago*. Cambridge: MIT Press, 1979.

Index of Authors